LITERATURE
AND
GENDER

THINKING CRITICALLY THROUGH
FICTION, POETRY, AND DRAMA

Robyn Wiegman
University of California, Irvine

Elena Glasberg
California State University, Los Angeles

THE LONGMAN LITERATURE AND CULTURE SERIES

General Editor: Charles I. Schuster, University of Wisconsin—Milwaukee

LONGMAN

An imprint of Addison Wesley Longman, Inc.

New York · Reading, Massachusetts · Menlo Park, California · Harlow, England
Don Mills, Ontario · Sydney · Mexico City · Madrid · Amsterdam

Acquisitions Editor: Laura McKenna
Development Editor: Katharine Glynn
Supplements Editor: Donna Campion
Marketing Manager: John Holdcroft
Project Manager: Bob Ginsberg
Design Manager: John Callahan
Text Designer: David Munger/DTC
Cover Designer: Kay Petronio
Cover Photo: PhotoDisc, Inc.
Photo Researcher: David Munger/DTC
Prepress Services Supervisor: Valerie A. Vargas
Senior Print Buyer: Hugh Crawford
Electronic Page Makeup: Deanna Campbell/DTC
Printer and Binder: Courier Companies Inc.
Cover Printer: Coral Graphic Services, Inc.

For permission to use copyrighted material, grateful acknowledgment is made to the copyright holders on pp. 395–398, which are hereby made part of this copyright page.

Library of Congress Cataloging-in-Publication Data

Wiegman, Robyn.
     Literature and gender : thinking critically through fiction, poetry, and drama / Robyn Wiegman, Elena Glasberg.
          p.   cm. -- (The Longman literature and culture series)
     Includes bibliographical references and index.
     ISBN 0-321-01260-7
     1. College readers. 2. English language--Rhetoric--Problems, exercises, etc.
3. Critical thinking--Problems, exercises, etc. 4. Gender identity--Literary
collections. I. Glasberg, Elena. II. Title. III. Series.
PE1417.W457   1999
810.8--dc21   98-47249
                                                                                      CIP

Please visit our website at http://longman.awl.com

ISBN 0-321-01260-7

12345678910—CRS—01009998

CONTENTS

Part I
LEARNING   13

How are we taught to believe in and rely on gender to name ourselves? What kinds of social practices initiate us into gendered understandings of the world?

POETRY

FICTION

Drama

Part II
Living   117

How are our everyday lives shaped by gender? What social institutions—law, religion, education, marriage, family, work, the military, the media—produce and regulate gender? How is power gendered?

Poetry

FICTION

DRAMA

Part III

RESISTING   259

How do we resist gender norms and beliefs? What new genders and new gender relations do writers imagine in place of the old?

POETRY

FOREWORD

If an answer does not give rise
to a new question from itself,
it falls out of the dialogue.
—Mikhail Bakhtin

The *Longman Literature and Culture Series,* of which this volume is a part, presents thoughtful and diverse approaches to the teaching of literature. Each is devoted to a special topic and designed for classes ranging from composition courses with a literature emphasis to introductory courses in literature to literature courses that focus on special topics, American studies, and cultural studies courses. Although the selections in each volume can be considered in terms of their formal literary properties, the power of these works also derives from their ability to induce students to read, re-read, think, sort out ideas, and connect personal views to the explicit and implicit values expressed in the literary works. In this way, the *Longman Literature and Culture Series* teaches critical analysis and critical thinking, abilities that will serve all students well, regardless of their majors.

Popular Fiction focuses on prose fiction through the exploration of many types of fiction not ordinarily studied in the college classroom. *Literature and the Environment; Literature, Culture, and Class; Literature, Race, and Ethnicity;* and *Literature and Gender* are all multigenre, with thematic clusters of readings exploring the central topic of the individual anthologies. These thematic clusters create series of links, allusions, and inflections among a wide variety of texts, and in this way, invite students to read actively and think critically. Meaningful contexts for the readings are provided by an introduction to each volume as well as chapter introductions and headnotes for every selection. An Instructor's Manual is also available for each anthology. These anthologies can be used in combination with each other, individually, and with other texts to suit the focus of the course.

- *Popular Fiction: An Anthology,* by Gary Hoppenstand (Michigan State University), is a collection of historical and contemporary works of prose fiction, including such authors as Edgar Allan Poe, Janet Dailey, Tony Hillerman, Walter Mosely, Stephen King, and Octavia Butler, and representing five popular genres: detective, romance, adventure, horror, and science fiction.

- *Literature and the Environment: A Reader on Nature and Culture,* by Lorraine Anderson, Scott Slovic (University of Nevada, Reno), and John P. O'Grady (Boise State University), is a thematic multigenre anthology that explores our relationship to nature and the role literature can play in shaping a culture responsive to environmental realities. It includes early writers such as John Muir, Henry David Thoreau, and Mary Austin, alongside contemporary voices such as Gary Snyder and Terry Tempest Williams.

- *Literature, Culture, and Class: A Thematic Anthology,* by Paul Lauter (Trinity College) and Ann Fitzgerald (American Museum of Natural History), is a consideration of class in "classless" America, including such authors as Edith Wharton, F. Scott Fitzgerald, Woody Guthrie, Alice Childress, Jimmy Santiago Baca, and Dorothy Allison. The selections allow students to better understand their own economic, political, and psychological contexts through learning about the ways in which social class and "class consciousness" have been experienced and changed over time in America.

- *Literature, Race, and Ethnicity: Contested American Identities,* by Joseph Skerrett (University of Massachusetts, Amherst), invites students to examine the history, depth, and persistence of the complex cultural attitudes toward race and ethnicity in America. The selections span from the late 1700s to the present, including a variety of genres from poems and letters to fiction and autobiography, essays, speeches, advertisements, and historical documents, with works by such writers as Thomas Jefferson, Frederick Douglass, Jacob Riis, Henry James, Langston Hughes, Maxine Hong Kingston, Constantine Panunzio, Lorna Dee Cervantes, Lawson Inada, and Louise Erdrich.

- *Literature and Gender: Thinking Critically Through Fiction, Poetry, and Drama,* by Robyn Wiegman (University of California, Irvine) and Elena Glasberg (California State University, Los Angeles), assembles a provocative array of literary texts by such writers as Charlotte Perkins Gilman, Ernest Hemingway, Adrienne Rich, Tobias Wolff, Sherman Alexie, and Rita Dove, which explore the links between cultural beliefs, social institutions, sexual roles, and personal identity.

Although no single anthology, or series for that matter, can address the full complexity of literary expression, these anthologies do hope to engage students in the critical process of analysis by connecting literary texts to current social and cultural debates. In addition, these anthologies frame literature in pedagogically innovative ways, ways that will enable those students who find literature difficult to read, who think meaning is somehow locked inside a text, to critically engage with issues of interpretation, biography, and context. In this way, students begin to see that literature is a cultural expression that emerges from a complex consideration of and response to the world they share with the writers they read.

Very often, literary texts invite discussion in the classroom of explosive issues, provoking students to argue about the sexism of a short story or the racism expressed by a character. These anthologies, however, encourage students to take a step backward so that they can interrogate the cultural contexts of diverse works of literature. This shift away from the personal and toward the cultural should invite thoughtful and considered classroom discussion. Once students perceive this cultural frame, they will be better able to engage with texts, to see them as both profound expressions of the ordinary and eloquent achievements written by real people living in real time.

In addition, no set of anthologies can hope to resolve completely what is intended by the two central terms that anchor this discussion: "literature" and "culture." One of the most exciting contemporary discussions in English departments today centers on the very definition of literature: what it is, what it excludes, and what makes it work. If figuring out what we mean by "the literary" is difficult, determining the definition of "culture" is probably impossible. Like "nature," a term that John Stuart Mill analyzed over a hundred years ago, "culture" seems to designate everything or nothing at all. Is it something we make or does it make us? Is culture a neutral term designating human social activity, or something akin to class and status, a quality that marks you as either refined or vulgar, well-bred or common?

Not that we presume to have the correct answers or even all the appropriate questions. We realize that both the questions and the answers will be tentative and exploratory. Literature, it seems to all of us involved in this series, demands a willingness to maintain uncertainty, to probe multiple possibilities. It invites analysis and demands interpretation. It provokes conversations. This is the intention of the *Longman Literature and Culture Series*: to invite readings and rereadings of texts and contexts, of literature within the cultural and culture within the literary. Rather than answers, these anthologies pose questions and invitations.

Crafted to the vision of the individual editors, *Popular Fiction; Literature and the Environment; Literature, Culture, and Class; Literature, Race, and Ethnicity;* and *Literature and Gender* present an extraordinary range of material in such a way as to unsettle previous readings and provoke new ones. We hope the *Longman Literature and Culture Series* provides a welcoming invitation to all students to see that literature is deeply reflective of the fabric of everyday life.

CHARLES I. SCHUSTER
General Editor
University of Wisconsin, Milwaukee

ACKNOWLEDGMENTS

This textbook has benefited from the generous intellectual contributions of reviewers, editors, and members of the production team. We want to thank Carolyn Barros (University of Texas at Arlington), Jennifer Brody (University of California, Riverside), Bruce Burgett (University of Wisconsin—Madison), Anne Goldman (University of Colorado at Boulder), Nancy Gray (College of William and Mary), Mara Kirk Hars (University of Minnesota—Duluth), Elyce Rae Helford (Middle Tennessee State University), Margaret Himley (Syracuse University), Beth McCoy (SUNY—Geneseo), Teresa McKenna (University of Southern California), Sylvia O'Sullivan (University of Maryland), Paula Robison (Temple University), Warren Rosenberg (Wabash College), Anne Rowe (Florida State University), Julia Sawyer (University of Pittsburg), Nina Schwartz (Southern Methodist University), Stephanie Smith (University of Florida), Pamela Takayoshi (University of Louisville), Paula Treichlin (University of Illinois at Urbana). We are especially grateful for Kathy Smeilis's diligence in securing the many copyright permissions essential to a volume such as this. Lisa Moore, Katharine Glynn, and the series editor Charles Schuster provided critical guidance throughout the various stages of *Literature and Gender*'s development. This book was their idea and its final materialization demonstrates their commitment to offering undergraduates innovative and ever-demanding literary selections. Finally, we want to thank the many brilliant authors who allowed us to reprint their work.

ROBYN WIEGMAN
ELENA GLASBERG

INTRODUCTION

Literature and Gender is designed with a single goal in mind: to introduce students to current issues in literary and gender studies through wide-ranging, multicultural selections of the most powerful literature written in the United States in the past century. Organized around three key concepts—"Learning," "Living," and "Resisting"—this textbook offers outstanding examples of poetry, fiction, and drama that compellingly speak to the everyday pleasures, pains, and possibilities of women's and men's lives. At the end of the text, we provide both a glossary to define the terms highlighted throughout this introduction and an essay by Charles Schuster, "Writing About Literature and Culture." This essay, written by a specialist in composition, is a hands-on guide to aid students in their writing about literature. It provides an important linkage between the kinds of critical thinking skills we discuss below and the necessary role that writing plays in the study of literature.

Literature and Gender offers readers an opportunity to explore issues about the relationship between literary practices and gender as a primary category of human identity. The literary selections presented in this textbook have been assembled with broad questions in mind: How has twentieth-century U.S. literature grappled with the question of gender? What kinds of changes, if any, do we see in the depiction of gender across the course of the century? To what extent have writers challenged or reinforced ideas about the differences and similarities between men and women? Do male and female writers think differently about gender? Are representations of gender influenced by literary forms (poetry, fiction, drama)? How have race, class, sexuality, and nationality shaped literary representations of gender? In considering these questions, readers will engage in **critical thinking**, which is a term we use to define an approach to the study of literature that analyzes the interaction between literary expression and social life by rigorously challenging cultural biases, inherited assumptions, and accepted ways of viewing both literature and the everyday world.

In the broadest sense, critical thinking is a mode of intellectual engagement that finds no pleasure in the "obvious," but seeks instead to question the most fundamental aspect of a task, belief, or social practice. In the context of *Literature and Gender*, critical thinking begins by contemplating the central activity demanded by the text: reading literature. What, after all, does it mean to "read"? And why read "literature" as opposed to other kinds of cultural texts? These questions point toward the embedded assumptions that inform *Literature and Gender:* the co-authors have assumed that literature is an important object for critical scrutiny; that the study of its forms, language use, and social meanings is a necessary part of any humanistic education; and that the practice of reading carefully and well is a vital intellectual skill. These assumptions have governed the way the textbook has been assembled, influencing not only the kinds of texts we have chosen to include, but the way we present information in the introduction and glossary. Such assumptions do not need to be accepted without question. Indeed, the critical thinker will want to pause over the framing ideas that construct this textbook, questioning the privileged position given to both literature and gender.

At the same time, critical readers need to think carefully about their own histories and practices of reading and the differences between a simple reading of a text and a critical interpretation of it. To read carefully and well—to become a **critical reader**—requires attention to a wide range of issues, from the basic elements of a text (its word choice and organization) to its more complex symbolic and social meanings. In addition, critical readers consider how writers produce literary texts in the context of specific literary forms (**genres**) and traditions. All genres carry general rules or **conventions** about how a text will look on the page, how it will move from one idea or point in time to the next, and under what circumstances audiences will encounter it. Most importantly for our purposes, genre conventions often have distinct gender associations, with the western being the quintessential masculine form and the romance the feminine. These ways of thinking about the text demonstrate that gender meanings accrue not only to the identities of writers and characters, but to literary forms themselves. By linking language, form, and social context, critical readers produce a complex interpretation of a literary text.

In addition to these elements of reading literature, critical thinking requires an informed understanding of the relationship between readers and texts. Many of us have been trained to find value in literature by seeing ourselves in its situations and characters. A poem or play becomes "good" because it reflects lifestyles, scenarios, and characters that are familiar. The critical reader questions the basis of this identification. Does a story have to be "like me" to be critically interesting to me as a reader? Can I find pleasure in texts that depict lives radically different from my own? These questions point to the way that our expectations about a text may derive from the specificities of our social position—our gender, race, class, sexuality, and/or national identity. By relating their individual histories as readers to the larger coordinates of social identity, critical readers provide nuanced interpretations of the personal and social factors that shape their engagement with literary texts.

In forging a connection among self, society, gender, and literature, critical thinking expands the interpretive strategies we use to explore both what and how texts mean. It enables readers to understand their own power as interpretive agents and the ways that social forces condition interpretation. Critical reading thus explores the most far-reaching issues in society, pushing us toward considerations of the role that literature plays in the creation of individual and group identities, especially those contingent on gender. To guide you toward these goals, we offer a series of manageable questions to accompany your reading of *Literature and Gender*:

In what ways is this text familiar or unfamiliar to you?

What expectations and assumptions do you bring to the text that might affect your reading of it?

Does your race, gender, class, sexuality, and/or nationality affect how you respond to the text?

Does the text use a genre form that has a history of gender associations? Does that history affect the way you read the text or the way the text is assembled?

To what extent does the author's sex influence your interpretation of the text?

What gendered meanings are created by language use and/or imagery?

Does the text challenge or conform to either social or literary expectations about gender?

What Is Gender?

Gender, some people say, is the most natural of all phenomena. It is the "thing" that defines who we are, the roles we play in society, the way we look, and most of all, how we think of ourselves. And yet, for all the importance of gender to notions of the self and society, people also claim that gender is arbitrary and in no way predicts or limits individual capacity. For many of us, gender is paradoxically the most immediate factor in our lives and the least significant: it seems to tell both the whole story about us and nothing concrete at all.

We're not the first people to note the omnipresence of gender. Thinkers of all kinds—poets, dramatists, scientists, politicians, philosophers, feminists, and yes, students in introductory literature courses—rely on notions of gender to frame their arguments, to tell stories, and to delve into the workings of nature and society. Even the features of life that we take most for granted are gendered. Designations of family—father, mother, daughter, son—are gendered. Toys are gendered. Occupations are gendered. Colors are gendered. Clothes are gendered. And so is language.

Does it matter that our daily lives and the language we use (whether we are aware of it or not, whether we care or not) are gendered? To answer this question, we have to spend some time thinking about both the meaning of gender and the purposes to which gender has been put.

From Sex to Gender

Let's begin with the most commonplace notion of gender available in the United States today: gender states your biological **sex**. If you have male genitalia, you will be **masculine**, which means that you will be naturally inclined toward physical activity, math, political leadership, and power tools. If, on the other hand, you have female genitalia, you will be **feminine**, which means you will have natural instincts for nurturance, housecleaning, sentimentality, and the color pink. According to this most common way of thinking about gender, "normal" girls will always be feminine and "normal" boys will always be masculine. Feminine boys and masculine girls are abnormal.

Wait, some people might say, the above descriptions are obsolete gender stereotypes. Today, everyone knows that girls don't have to be housewives but can be corporate leaders or firefighters, while men can nurture babies without shame. Much of the strict binary thinking historically tied to gender has now given way, as people are more willing to concede the overlapping of gender identities. Some people even point to **feminism** to identify the social movement that has challenged the way people think about gender, opening up new possibilities for both men and women in terms of social roles, occupations, and familial responsibilities. At the end of the twentieth century, we might argue, gender binaries are less rigid than ever.

And yet, no matter how much the stereotypes we associate with women and men have changed, the single idea or **ideology** that gender equals sex remains widely accepted; human beings in our society continue to be organized into two and only two distinct types: male and female. For many people, these types are natural, based on biological differences related to reproduction. We've all heard this argument: because women give birth, people say, there is a natural, indisputable difference between men and women, and it is this difference that has natural consequences in the ordering and functioning of society.

The critical thinker may want to pause here and consider carefully this line of argument. Does it necessarily follow that because human bodies are capable of different things that social roles and responsibilities must also be different? This question has serious implications when we consider not just the idea that gender = sex, but the use to which that idea has been put in the organization of society.

Reproduction, Patriarchy, and Power

What has reproductive capacity meant for women? This question has a contradictory answer. On the one hand, we can say that women have been exalted as the mothers of all life, worshiped in various religions, imaged as the creative muse, and held in high esteem as the caretakers and nurturers of society. On the other hand, women's reproductive capacities have often been a liability. Motherhood has been honored only under certain circumstances. For instance, social scorn has long accompanied childbearing for the unmarried woman and for women from poor economic backgrounds. And a variety of employment opportunities have been denied women because of the idea that, given their reproductive capabilities, their natural place is in the home. While some beliefs concerning the relation of women's bodies to their social roles and abilities have changed in the late twentieth century, we still debate the incompatibility of military duty and women's monthly reproductive cycles, and some people continue to dismiss the idea that a woman could be president, citing her liability to "unstable" hormonal shifts.

The conflicting consequences of women's ability to bear children says a great deal about the relationship between gender ideology and power, chiefly that production and reproduction should be divided according to sex. Assigning the world of children and domestic work to women and the public realm of production and governance to men, this **sexual division of labor**, as scholars call it, is a characteristic of **patriarchal** societies. Patriarchy most literally refers to a social system in which property passes from father to son, but it is more widely used to describe any social organization in which men dominate in positions of familial and governmental leadership. In patriarchal societies, women often cannot own property, as was the case in the United States until late in the nineteenth century, and their labor in the home typically is unpaid. Instead, housework is free, part of the more general "natural" work of childbearing.

The historical origins of patriarchy are not well known, though scholars have spent a great deal of time forming a variety of hypotheses. For some scholars, patriarchy is a consequence of the fact that while maternity in reproduction has always been obvious (the mother gives birth), paternity, until DNA testing, was not. In this view, the patriarchal family provided a way for men to gain control of the reproductive process by quite literally owning their wives and offspring. Even in the United States, women were the legal property of men until well into the nineteenth century. For other scholars, patriarchal organization is historically tied to the idea of property and will be most prominent in societies in which goods and/or land are used to forge exchanges between groups, whether in pre-capitalist agrarian societies or contemporary industrial **capitalist** ones.

Still other scholars have been less concerned with patriarchy's origin than with its effects on relations between men and women in different societies and historical contexts. One element of patriarchal organization that seems to be consistent is women's subordination to men in families, government, and the economy. It is because of this subordination that people often speak of patriarchy as a social structure in which men and the masculine occupy the position of the norm or the "universal" while women and the feminine are always "different"—different, that is, from men. The universal status of the masculine can be evinced in a number of ways, but the English language's use of "he" as a generic to mean both male and female is perhaps our most powerful everyday example. In this usage, male and female are not just different, but unequally so, as "she" can refer only to women.

Does this mean that patriarchy is always a privilege for men? Not exactly. After all, patriarchy prescribes very stringent roles for both women and men, and its definitive codes for masculinity assume not only that men are naturally inclined to leadership, but that they relish the opportunity to become aggressive and domineering. Many of the stories and poems in this textbook, however, will explore the deep ambivalence that many men in U.S. society share about the requirements of patriarchal masculinity. To talk about patriarchy is not, therefore, to talk about men as a homogenous group, but to identify and interrogate a social system that defines and organizes relations among men and women (and masculinity and femininity) in particular and unequal ways.

Gender, Race, and Class

The critical reader might have a few questions about this sexual division of labor mentioned above. Her mother or grandmother or aunt—perhaps the woman next door—did not labor solely in the family home, and her father never had an easy time finding work in the so-called public sphere. What concepts, the critical reader may wonder, do we need in order to understand how the ideals of male as breadwinner and female as homemaker have not always matched the experiences of men and women in U.S. society?

Women, of course, have always worked outside the home. The idea that domesticity is natural has governed the kinds of work available to them, and the unpaid nature of housework has carried over into and justified its low pay. In the last century, according to census documents, the jobs employing the largest number of women have been primarily service-oriented: servants, cooks, garment makers, secretaries, teachers, office clerks, nurses, and nursing aides. What we see in this list is the extension of women's assumed role as mother, homemaker, and caretaker to the public realm.

The sexual division of labor is thus an economic class system based on an understanding of gender grounded in biological sex: through it we can begin to understand gender as class. However, gender is not the only factor that maintains class division. Racial and ethnic categorizations are also significant. Consider, for instance, the occupation of "servant" in the list of jobs for women above. From 1890 to 1940, more women in the United States worked as servants than in any other single occupation. Many of these were African-American and immigrant women from Asia and Eastern Europe—women whose range of choices for economic survival was far more narrow than for U.S.-born white women of the middle and upper classes. While the sexual division of labor takes shape according to notions of male and female difference, what constitutes women's work or men's work is additionally affected by the **hierarchies** of **race**, **ethnicity**, and **class** that have long been a structural component of U.S. society.

Significantly, much of the new scholarly work in gender studies concerns itself with the intersection between gender and other categories of difference. For instance, scholars have explored the way that the masculine ideals of strength and aggression have profoundly shaped the stereotypes of men of color, with African-American males and Latinos often being depicted as excessively and dangerously masculine (the gangster image). At the same time, Asian-American males are frequently associated with the feminine, depicted as delicate and beautiful (the loyal housekeeper). In these instances and the many others we might think of, notions of masculinity are shaped and differentiated according to race and ethnicity, so much so that for many scholars it is always necessary to interpret gender in relation to them.

This focus on multiple differences has arisen for a variety of reasons. First, it demonstrates a deepening critical awareness that patriarchy is not a uniform system of male privilege; in some social contexts, in fact, women of a privileged race or class may have power over men of another race or class. Second, it is a response to our growing cultural awareness that the United States is a diverse society. The **multiculturalism** of this nation necessitates an analysis of the various **identities** that shape our understanding of ourselves both as individuals and as collective participants in a wider culture. And third, the emphasis on gender's complex relationships to race, ethnicity, and sexuality is a product of a particular debate in gender studies concerning the origin and meaning of sex itself, a debate explored at length below.

Nature versus Culture

The debate over the origin and meaning of sex differences, often referred to as **essentialism** versus **social constructionism**, returns to the scene of gender's seemingly natural creation: sex. For essentialists, there is no question that men and women are inherently different because there is no escape from biology. This is not to say that essentialists believe that biology justifies wage discrimination based on sex, but they do emphasize that the differences registered in our society about men and women are natural, not socially produced. Essentialist understandings of gender will always rely on biological sex.

Social constructionists, on the other hand, argue that differences between men and women are not a product of nature, but of society. For the constructionist, even the idea of biological sex distinction is created in culture, since it is always from the position of culture and not nature that we "read" and interpret the human body. Social constructionists would not necessarily deny, however, that there are physical differences between women and men, but they would argue that such differences have meaning only through their social interpretation. In this view, biology is not the science of the human body in a state of nature but the study of the body permeated by the very ideologies of sex and gender found throughout U.S. society.

At the heart of the essentialist-social constructionist debate, then, is a struggle over the way we understand sex differences. Neither side wholly denies that there are differences; the argument concerns how we will explain them. And much of the disagreement occurs because of the social implications attending each explanation.

Take the issue of sexual violence. Essentialists explain why men are more sexually violent toward their heterosexual partners than women by referring to natural masculine aggression, testosterone surges, and innate sex drives. While no one thinks that it is acceptable for men to rape and abuse women, the essentialist argument relies on the idea that sexual violence is a consequence of male biology. The constructionist will contend instead that men are not inherently violent, but that in our culture certain patterns of violence emerge as structural elements of masculinity, of what it means to be a "man."

At stake in each of these explanations is a political vision for the future of relations between women and men. If the essentialists are correct, men and women are as they are, and little can be changed. We might be able to create laws and codes to contain male violence or to protect women from it, but the differences between the sexes will remain. The constructionist position, which counters essentialism's tacit approval of the status quo, carries the hope for transforming society and of modifying the way we come to think about being male or female. Since, in the constructionist view, gender identities and roles are not natural but socially created, they can and do change.

This emphasis on a social as opposed to a biological explanation of a range of perceived human differences has enabled scholars to discuss and analyze the ways in which notions of race and ethnicity too do not reflect a natural order but are created by human practices and assumptions and are thus subject to change. Such a perspective seeks to understand, for example, how people of Jewish descent in the United States were not considered white until after World War II, when their identity shifted from a racial designation to one framed by religious experience and culture. For a number of scholars, the Jews "became" white—in the same way that Irish and Italian immigrants also "became" white—through complex social and political factors. In this view, then, racial categories are historically created, and it is the job of the critical thinker to consider the various factors that contribute to the formation of any particular identity.

Critical Directions

It is the constructionist position that currently holds more sway in gender studies, partly because of its determined focus on prying apart the commonplace assumption that gender = sex. This focus offers a number of interpretive possibilities for the critical reader. First, it allows you to think about the relationship between the author and his/her text in more complicated ways. For instance, some of the texts in this anthology do not make clear the gender of the narrative voice. Will we assume a gender to match the sex of the author? To what extent will the author's sex guide our interpretation of her/his text? By refusing to assume that sex = gender, we will open ourselves to the possibility that the gender of texts and the sexes of authors are not necessarily the same.

Second, by differentiating sex and gender, the critical reader can look at characters and plots in terms of **identification** instead of biology. Some characters do not identify with the gender roles and characteristics traditionally accorded their sex. Thus we have men and boys who explore the emotional contexts of life in ways that defy the stereotypical ideas of masculinity by being more "feminine." Or we see female characters resisting the feminine characteristics of passivity and obedience to be more "masculine." In some cases, characters cross-identify with the gender roles assigned to the opposite sex; in other cases, they are more **transgender**, moving back and forth between the binary distinctions of masculine and feminine, creating new combinations of gender, perhaps creating new genders altogether.

The third critical advantage we gain by disengaging sex from gender is in analyzing sexuality. Our society assumes that **heterosexuality**, or sexual activity between women and men, is natural and, further, that the biological fact of sex difference necessitates the norm of heterosexuality. From this point of view, **homosexuality**—sexual attraction to one's own sex—is seen as a failure of normal gender identifications. Gay men are thus stereotyped as feminine and called "fairies" while lesbians are viewed as male-wannabes. So intertwined are the assumptions about biological sex, gender, and sexuality that homosexuality was first clinically defined as "gender inversion," and it is this idea that continues to hold sway today. At the heart of the sex/gender equation, then, is a biologically based assumption that masculine and feminine gender identities form a complementary heterosexual relation.

This blurring of gender and sexual identities makes it impossible to think about the diversity of human sexual expression and attraction. For instance, **bisexuality** has become a particularly fruitful area of research precisely because of the way that male and female bisexuals defy the dictates of the sex/gender equation. What this new work suggests is twofold: first, that gender identity and sexual practices are not mere extensions of one another, and second, that being female or male does not necessarily predict or limit sexual expression or practice. After all, there are a variety of gender identifications and characteristics within each category of sexual practice, homosexual or heterosexual, and the critical reader will want to be prepared to think broadly about both.

As the foregoing discussion indicates, the critical reader's approach to gender requires that we analyze some of our culture's most firmly held beliefs, not just the seeming naturalness of gender as biology, but the norm of heterosexuality as well.

As part of this analysis, we need to consider not only how these beliefs function, but what work they do in our society, what work we do in service to them, and how they relate to other categories of difference, including race, class, and ethnicity.

Why Literature?

Our conversation so far has stressed the elements of critical reading that will guide the critical reader's inquiry into the complexities of gender. But we haven't yet addressed an obvious question: Why is literature the framework for such an inquiry? To answer this question, we need to consider literature as the categorical name we give to that human activity through which individual and social meanings are crafted in written form. For instance, we distinguish between a poem and, say, a laundry list not so much on the basis of their subject matter (indeed a contemporary poet might well present a laundry list as a poem), but on the manner and mode of their engagement with words. This engagement is perhaps the single most important quality that differentiates literature from other kinds of writing since it is through the careful execution of language that authors create the emotional contexts necessary to make readers yearn to read more.

But literature is more than the careful use of language: it relies on conventions and formulas and is produced within specific histories of standards or modes of judgment. What constitutes literature, what is acceptable in literature, and what is considered "good" literature varies according to the values and assumptions of a culture. And it is precisely because literature is so tied to the culture in which it is created that it becomes an important site for our investigation into the meaning of gender.

Authors and Canons

What's the first thing that comes to mind at the word *literature*? Most likely you think of some version of written expression in fictional form packed with deep meaning. This written expression comes to us in a book, published by an author who has placed the meaning in the text for the reader to dig out. The better the reader, the closer she will come to the author's original intentions. Sound familiar? Such premises about literature have been common in literary study in the twentieth century. But like the other topics we have been discussing in this introduction, this too—the assumptions we have been taught about literature, **authorship**, and meaning—are in need of questioning. How, after all, can we ever be sure of the author's meaning? If the author is dead, what information will guarantee her/his intentions? Can a text only mean what the author intended?

These questions have become increasingly important as the standard features of literary study have begun to give way. In the past twenty years, in fact, literary study in the academy has undergone a rapid and radical reconstruction. Where an earlier generation of scholarship stressed a **canon** of great works as the central texts to be read and studied, the new literary scholarship rethinks the idea of canon and the conditions under which authors and texts were selected as "great" in the first place. Much of the impetus for this reconsideration has arisen from scholars who are themselves part of those social groups—women, African Americans, Chicanos and Latinos, Native Americans, Asian Americans—typically excluded from the canon of great literature.

In rethinking the canon as the basis of literary study, scholars have pointed to the way that the written word is not a universally privileged form of cultural expression, but the specific one adopted by certain cultures. They have pointed out how, even in those cultures in which literacy is most honored, the skills of reading and writing have not been available on an equal basis to everyone. Women, for instance, were typically denied formal education until a century ago. And throughout the nineteenth century, slaves in the United States were legally forbidden, on the threat of death, to learn how to read and write. While much of this has greatly changed in the twentieth century, the point is this: authorship as a category of cultural activity is inseparable from the ways race, class, and gender define people's roles in society, their opportunities, and the work they are enjoined to perform. The critique of the canon as a set of privileged texts is aimed not at discounting the achievement of those texts, but at expanding the texts and issues we consider valuable and worthy of study, including the very issue of what makes authorship possible.

In addition to literacy, authorship also importantly requires access both to the publication and distribution of one's writing as well as to the academic critical establishment through which canons are created. Some of the writers we now consider "great" were ushered into that greatness by literary critics who devoted their scholarly activity to the study of specific authors. Herman Melville, author of the now classic novel *Moby-Dick* (1852), for instance, did not achieve a wide readership until the 1930s; even American literature as a separate category within English departments was not standard until after World War II as a new generation of scholars emerged who made claims about the distinctiveness of writing in the United States. What this means is that the canon, while presented as the greatest works of literature ever produced, is itself an idea produced—or constructed—under specific historical conditions. Great literature may be great, then, not because of its intrinsic or essential qualities, but because of the views of persuasive literary critics.

What This Book Does

Literature and Gender assembles texts written by many different kinds of Americans, immigrants and native born, male and female, dead and living. The texts demonstrate the diversity of gender practices as they relate to differences of race, ethnicity, class, and sexuality. The cumulative effect of this textbook is to increase your ability to positively negotiate the changing demands of masculinity and femininity in a multicultural society. To that end, the selections are primarily drawn from twentieth-century U.S. culture.

The general organization of the book is simple. Three primary sections collect literary texts under a rubric that stresses a particular aspect of the social creation of gender: "Learning," "Living," and "Resisting." By foregrounding a verb, each section assumes a person's being affected by a process—and the various processes being described cover some of the most crucial critical conversations in the study of gender, from the fairy tales that teach us how to read to the science fiction fantasies that challenge us to think of the world anew.

We begin in "Learning" with texts that focus for the most part on family relations as they structure the way we learn—sometimes early in life, sometimes later—not only how to read gender, but how to think of ourselves as gendered. The second section, "Living," considers the institutional forms in which gender norms are constructed and imposed, looking especially at heterosexuality, marriage, law, the workplace, the military, and the mass media. In the process, issues such as sexual violence, romance, infidelity and reunion, and death are covered. "Resisting," the final section, traces both obvious rebellions against gender norms as well as less conscious resistance posed by individuals and, further, it does so by presenting a variety of genre formulas for thinking through and beyond sex and gender.

Each literary selection is preceded by a brief biographical note about the author. At the end of the selections we provide a glossary of the key terms used in this introduction and an essay by Charles Schuster that focuses on the relationship between critical thinking and effective writing. We hope that this anthology will challenge you to analyze carefully the ways you have been taught to think about both gender and literature. We especially hope that you will find the literary selections compelling representations of the diversity of human experience and that in studying them, you will be energized to turn a critical eye on, quite literally, everything in the world.

How are we taught to believe in and rely on gender to name ourselves? What kinds of social practices initiate us into gendered understandings of the world?

LEARNING

Can you remember the first time you knew you were a girl or a boy? If so, how did this knowledge come to you?

Such moments of clarity are often associated with biological functions. By the time we are old enough to go unaccompanied to the bathroom in public, we know that depending on our genitals, we go to only one door, either "ladies" or "gentlemen." Gradually, we learn to rely on sex for our own self-understanding. Now when someone asks us, "How do you know you are a man or a woman?" we "just know," and in this knowing we seem to be referencing something more than biological sex. The nearly unnoticed passage between being pointed in the direction of the right door and "just knowing" exemplifies the process by which sex is transformed into **gender**. In this transformation, male and female shifts to **masculinity** and **femininity**, and a host of psychological attributes and social behaviors become the unspoken basis of our gendered **identities**.

But how do we, as individuals, get from sex to gender? And how do so many of our daily behaviors come to have specifically gendered associations? Think here of the magazines we choose to read, the food we eat, the fingernails we groom, the deodorant we buy. So many of the nonbiological accessories of life—clothing, hairstyles, furniture, jewelry—are gendered. The world of **commodities** is itself a gendered world. How does society shape from a simple separation of doors an entire social system predicated on gender?

The answer to this last question is complex and varied, and certainly not the stuff of easy, one-line answers. One place to begin is with the individual who enters into the world that gender has already built and moves through its many institutions, such as education, the family, the law, and the military. In these institutions and in the language that gives us access to interpersonal communication, we learn that certain ways of dressing, holding our bodies, certain likes and dislikes are gender appropriate and that by adopting these mannerisms and beliefs we will gain social approval. For this reason, many of us find a certain comfort in gender. It offers explanations; it gives us seemingly solid identities. How many times have we heard the phrase: "That's just like a guy," or "What did you expect from a woman?" It doesn't matter if we approve or disapprove of the behavior being referred to; what matters is that gender makes the behavior seem natural and inevitable.

The selections in this section provide approaches to understanding the power of gender as social education and control. They present characters in a variety of engagements with the rules, spoken and unspoken, of gender. Whether we read Raymond Carver's story of a newborn baby, Anne Sexton's poetic revamping of the "Cinderella" tale, or Elizabeth Bishop's narrative poem "In the Waiting Room" about coming to self-awareness as a white six-year-old girl, the texts in this section demonstrate that gender is a process that shapes an individual, consciously and unconsciously, throughout life.

Lois Gould's "X" **parodies** the entire field of scientific childrearing that began with the popularity of Dr. Benjamin Spock's *Well Baby Book* in the 1950s. The "Xperiment" described in the story, in which the Jones couple rears an un-gendered child named X, draws out the many anxieties about the relation of sex to gender in our society. Because no one but the parents know X's sex, people can't figure out how to interact with X, what games to play with X, what emotions to share with X, or even how to address X. The story makes clear the child has a sex, but in keeping it unspoken, the equation of sex to gender is broken. Because Gould plays with the norms of white middle class childrearing practices and explores the way distinctions of gender are effects of social practices, "X" has attracted nationwide attention since it first appeared in the feminist magazine *MS.* in 1971.

Yet sex and gender remain stitched together by a number of forces, not the least of which is the ability of children and adults to police one another's gender development. Lonny Kaneko's "The Shoyu Kid" depicts the often brutal ways that boys enforce among themselves strict codes of masculinity, even in the face of nagging inconsistencies and fears. In Carson McCullers's short story "Like That," a southern white child imagines that she can avoid by an act of will the constricting codes of adult femininity that are so powerfully outlined in Jamaica Kincaid's "Girl," a **prose poem** organized as a list of commands to a female child concerning her coming role as a woman.

Kincaid's poem, whose edicts of proper femininity are clearly set within a Caribbean cultural milieu, reminds us that gender is always connected to **race, ethnicity**, and **class**. In Richard Wright's coming-of-age story, "The Man Who Was Almost A Man," for instance, the main character's awareness of the stakes of adult masculinity cannot be separated from the social circumstances of being an African American in the 1940s rural South. In a similar way, Li-Young Lee's "Persimmons" demonstrates how the Chinese-American narrator is shaped by the forces of contesting cultural codes, as his father and the American schoolteacher offer different lessons about language, observation, and authority. For the young characters in Toni Cade Bambara's "The Lesson," a trip to a toy store serves as the pretext for exploring how gender shapes the work roles of the women in their neighborhood, but also how economic differences among people are mapped onto the landscape of the entire city. This story achieves much of its power through its use of **symbolism**, as the children window-shop through a world of economic privilege they have never before imagined.

The centrality of family and of **heterosexuality** to the lessons of gender are explored in the dramatic text that ends this section. In Cherríe Moraga's *Giving Up the Ghost*, the playwright manipulates the conventional unity of time, **setting**, and action by presenting two characters who are the same woman at different ages. This strategy stages in provocative ways a struggle and reconciliation over the meaning of the character's womanhood.

Taken together, the texts in this section demonstrate the ways in which the transformation from sex to gender is part and parcel of the everyday work of living. Learning gender does not, however, end neatly, but is an ongoing process of negotiation. The rules change, as do the contexts in which we find ourselves.

POETRY

ELIZABETH BISHOP

1911-1979

Elizabeth Bishop was born in Worcester, Massachusetts. She attended Vassar College for women and spent many years living and writing in Key West, Florida and Brazil. In the 1950s, she began her teaching career, first at the University of Washington and later at Harvard University. Winner of the 1956 Pulitzer Prize, Bishop is known for the precision of her observation and for her consciousness of the complexities of national and gendered belongings. Her preoccupations with travel and the meaning of place are reflected throughout her major works, as the titles indicate: North & South *(1946),* Questions of Travel *(1965), and* Geography III *(1976).*

IN THE WAITING ROOM

In Worcester, Massachusetts,
I went with Aunt Consuelo
to keep her dentist's appointment

and sat and waited for her
in the dentist's waiting room.
It was winter. It got dark
early. The waiting room
was full of grown-up people,
arctics and overcoats,
lamps and magazines.
My aunt was inside
what seemed like a long time
and while I waited I read
the *National Geographic*
(I could read) and carefully
studied the photographs:
the inside of a volcano,
black, and full of ashes;
then it was spilling over
in rivulets of fire.
Osa and Martin Johnson
dressed in riding breeches,
laced boots, and pith helmets.
A dead man slung on a pole
—"Long Pig," the caption said.
Babies with pointed heads
wound round and round with string;
black, naked women with necks
wound round and round with wire
like the necks of light bulbs.
Their breasts were horrifying.
I read it right straight through.
I was too shy to stop.
And then I looked at the cover:
the yellow margins, the date.

Suddenly, from inside,
came an *oh!* of pain
—Aunt Consuelo's voice—
not very loud or long.
I wasn't at all surprised;
even then I knew she was
a foolish, timid woman.
I might have been embarrassed,
but wasn't. What took me
completely by surprise
was that it was *me:*
my voice, in my mouth.
Without thinking at all
I was my foolish aunt,

I—we—were falling, falling,
our eyes glued to the cover
of the *National Geographic,*
February, 1918.

I said to myself: three days
and you'll be seven years old.
I was saying it to stop
the sensation of falling off
the round, turning world
into cold, blue-black space.
But I felt: you are an *I,*
you are an *Elizabeth,*
you are one of *them.*
Why should you be one, too?
I scarcely dared to look
to see what it was I was.
I gave a sidelong glance
—I couldn't look any higher—
at shadowy gray knees,
trousers and skirts and boots
and different pairs of hands
lying under the lamps.
I knew that nothing stranger
had ever happened, that nothing
stranger could ever happen.
Why should I be my aunt,
or me, or anyone?
What similarities—
boots, hands, the family voice
I felt in my throat, or even
the *National Geographic*
and those awful hanging breasts—
held us all together
or made us all just one?
How—I didn't know any
word for it—how "unlikely" . . .
How had I come to be here,
like them, and overhear
a cry of pain that could have
got loud and worse but hadn't?

The waiting room was bright
and too hot. It was sliding
beneath a big black wave,
another, and another.

Then I was back in it.
The War was on. Outside,
in Worcester, Massachusetts,
were night and slush and cold,
and it was still the fifth
of February, 1918.

                                                    —1976

JAMAICA KINCAID

B. 1949

Jamaica Kincaid was born in Antigua and emigrated to the United States in 1965. Initially working as a baby-sitter and receptionist, Kincaid began publishing in The New Yorker, *where "Girl" first appeared before it was collected in* At the Bottom of the River *(1983). In 1985, Kincaid's novel* Annie John *garnered her national attention as a powerful emergent writer. Her other novels,* Annie Gwen Lilly Pam and Tulip *(1989),* Lucy *(1990), and* The Autobiography of My Mother *(1996) have solidified her reputation as a lyrical and emotionally complex writer. Her essay "A Small Place" (1988) indicts colonialism in the West Indies, while* My Brother *(1997) explores issues of AIDS and transnational identity and family bonds.*

GIRL

Wash the white clothes on Monday and put them on the stone heap; wash the color clothes on Tuesday and put them on the clothesline to dry; don't walk bare-head in the hot sun; cook pumpkin fritters in very hot sweet oil; soak your little cloths right after you take them off; when buying cotton to make yourself a nice blouse, be sure that it doesn't have gum on it, because that way it won't hold up well after a wash; soak salt fish overnight before you cook it; is it true that you sing benna in Sunday school?; always eat your food in such a way that it won't turn someone else's stomach; on Sundays try to walk like a lady and not like the slut you are so bent on becoming; don't sing benna in Sunday school; you mustn't speak to wharf-rat boys, not even to give directions; don't eat fruits on the street—flies will follow you; *but I don't sing benna on Sundays at all and never in Sunday school;* this is how to sew on a button; this is how to make a buttonhole for the button you have just sewed on; this is how to hem a dress when you see the hem coming down and so to prevent yourself from looking like the slut I know you are so bent on becoming; this is how you iron your father's khaki shirt so that it doesn't have a crease; this is how you iron your father's khaki pants so that they don't have a crease; this is how you grow okra—far from the house, because okra tree harbors red ants; when you are growing dasheen, make sure it gets plenty of water or else it makes your throat itch when you are eating it; this is how you sweep a corner; this is how you sweep a whole house; this is how you sweep a yard; this is how you smile to someone you don't like too much; this is how you smile to someone you don't like at all; this is how you smile to someone you like completely; this is how you set a table for tea; this is how you set a table for dinner; this is how you set a table for dinner with an important guest; this is how you set a table for lunch; this is how you set a table for breakfast; this is how to behave in the presence of men who don't know you very well, and this way they won't recognize immediately the slut I have warned you against becoming; be sure to wash every day, even if it is with your own spit; don't squat down to play marbles—you are not a boy, you know; don't pick people's flowers—you might catch something; don't throw stones at blackbirds, because it might not be a blackbird at all; this is how to make a bread pudding; this is how to make doukona; this is how to make pepper pot; this is how to make a good medicine for a cold; this is how to make a good medicine to throw away a child before it even becomes a child; this is how to catch a fish; this is how to throw back a fish you don't like, and that way something bad won't fall on you; this is how to bully a man; this is how a man bullies you; this is how to love a man, and if this doesn't work there are other ways, and if they don't work don't feel too bad about giving up; this is how to spit up in the air if you feel like it, and this is how to move quick so that it doesn't fall on you; this is how to make ends meet; always squeeze bread to make sure it's fresh; *but what if the baker won't let me feel the bread?;* you mean to say that after all you are really going to be the kind of woman who the baker won't let near the bread?

—1983

LI-YOUNG LEE

B. 1957

Li-Young Lee was born in Jakarta, Indonesia, where his father was a political prisoner and refugee. After immigrating to the United States and attending universities in Pennsylvania, Arizona, and New York, Lee published a book of poems, Rose *(1986), followed by* The City in Which I Love You *(1990). He is one of the best-known of a new generation of bilingual poets who explore the meeting of Asian and American cultures. This theme appears in the following selection in the context of the narrator's budding sexuality on the one hand, and his relationship to his father on the other. In 1995, Lee published* The Winged Seed: A Remembrance.

PERSIMMONS

In sixth grade Mrs. Walker
slapped the back of my head
and made me stand in the corner
for not knowing the difference
between *persimmon* and *precision*.
How to choose

persimmons. This is precision.
Ripe ones are soft and brown-spotted.
Sniff the bottoms. The sweet one
will be fragrant. How to eat:
put the knife away, lay down newspaper.
Peel the skin tenderly, not to tear the meat.
Chew the skin, suck it,
and swallow. Now, eat
the meat of the fruit,
so sweet,
all of it, to the heart.

Donna undresses, her stomach is white.
In the yard, dewy and shivering
with crickets, we lie naked,
face-up, face-down.
I teach her Chinese.
Crickets: *chiu chiu.* Dew: I've forgotten.
Naked: I've forgotten.
Ni, wo: you and me.
I part her legs,
remember to tell her
she is beautiful as the moon.

Other words
that got me into trouble were
fight and *fright, wren* and *yarn.*
Fight was what I did when I was frightened,
fright was what I felt when I was fighting.
Wrens are small, plain birds,
yarn is what one knits with.
Wrens are soft as yarn.
My mother made birds out of yarn.
I loved to watch her tie the stuff;
a bird, a rabbit, a wee man.

Mrs. Walker brought a persimmon to class
and cut it up

so everyone could taste
a *Chinese apple.* Knowing
it wasn't ripe or sweet, I didn't eat
but watched the other faces.

My mother said every persimmon has a sun
inside, something golden, glowing,
warm as my face.

Once, in the cellar, I found two wrapped in newspaper,
forgotten and not yet ripe.
I took them and set both on my bedroom windowsill,
where each morning a cardinal
sang, *The sun, the sun.*

Finally understanding
he was going blind,
my father sat up all one night
waiting for a song, a ghost.
I gave him the persimmons,
swelled, heavy as sadness,
and sweet as love.

This year, in the muddy lighting
of my parents' cellar, I rummage, looking
for something I lost.
My father sits on the tired, wooden stairs,
black cane between his knees,
hand over hand, gripping the handle.
He's so happy that I've come home.
I ask how his eyes are, a stupid question.
All gone, he answers.

Under some blankets, I find a box.
Inside the box I find three scrolls.
I sit beside him and untie
three paintings by my father:
Hibiscus leaf and a white flower.
Two cats preening.
Two persimmons, so full they want to drop from the cloth.

He raises both hands to touch the cloth,
asks, *Which is this?*

This is persimmons, Father.

Oh, the feel of the wolftail on the silk,

the strength, the tense
precision in the wrist.
I painted them hundreds of times
eyes closed. These I painted blind.
Some things never leave a person:
scent of the hair of one you love,
the texture of persimmons,
in your palm, the ripe weight.

—1986

MARGE PIERCY

B. 1936

Marge Piercy is a novelist, essayist, and poet whose political and artistic commitments stem from the antiwar movement of the 1960s and from feminism. Educated at the University of Michigan and Northwestern University, Piercy's writing career began with the publication of Breaking Camp *in 1968. Since then, she has been a prolific producer of fiction and poetry, publishing such noteworthy volumes as* Small Changes *(1973),* Woman On the Edge of Time *(1976),* The Moon Is Always Female *(1980),* Gone to Soldiers *(1987),* He, She, and It *(1991), and* City of Darkness, City of Light: A Novel *(1996). She currently lives in Massachusetts.*

BARBIE DOLL

This girlchild was born as usual
and presented dolls that did pee-pee
and miniature GE stoves and irons
and wee lipsticks the color of cherry candy.
Then in the magic of puberty, a classmate said:
You have a great big nose and fat legs.

She was healthy, tested intelligent,
possessed strong arms and back,
abundant sexual drive and manual dexterity.
She went to and fro apologizing.
Everyone saw a fat nose on thick legs.

She was advised to play coy,
exhorted to come on hearty,
exercise, diet, smile and wheedle.

Her good nature wore out
like a fan belt.
So she cut off her nose and her legs
and offered them up.

In the casket displayed on satin she lay
with the undertaker's cosmetics painted on,
a turned-up putty nose,
dressed in a pink and white nightie.
Doesn't she look pretty? everyone said.
Consummation at last.
To every woman a happy ending.

—1982

ALBERTO ALVARO RIOS

B. 1952

Alberto Alvaro Rios was born in Nogales, Arizona, to a Mexican father and a British mother. He is the author of short stories, poems, essays, and a novel. His first book of poetry, Whispering to Fool the Wind *(1981), received the prestigious Walt Whitman Award from the American Academy of Poets. His other works include* Iguana Killer: Twelve Stories of the Heart *(1984),* The Five Indiscretions *(1985),* The Lime Orchard Woman *(1988),* The Warrington Poems *(1989),* Teodoro Luna's Two Kisses *(1990), and* Pig Cookies and Other Stories *(1995). Rios has degrees in English, psychology, and creative writing and teaches at Arizona State University, where he has administrated programs in creative writing and Hispanic research and development. Rios's work meditates on cross-cultural identity and on the cultural legacies of Catholicism.*

THE PURPOSE OF ALTAR BOYS

Tonio told me at catechism
the big part of the eye
admits good, and the little
black part is for seeing
evil—his mother told him
who was a widow and so
an authority on such things.
That's why at night
the black part gets bigger.

That's why kids can't go out
at night, and at night
girls take off their clothes
and walk around their
bedrooms or jump on their
beds or wear only sandals
and stand in their windows.
I was the altar boy
who knew about these things,
whose mission on some Sundays
was to remind people of
the night before as they
knelt for Holy Communion.
To keep Christ from falling
I held the metal plate
under chins,
while on the thick
red carpet of the altar
I dragged my feet
and waited for the precise
moment: plate to chin
I delivered without expression
the Holy Electric Shock,
the kind that produces
a really large swallowing
and makes people think.
I thought of it as justice.
But on other Sundays the fire
in my eyes was different,
my mission somehow changed.
I would hold the metal plate
a little too hard
against those certain same
nervous chins, and I
I would look
with authority down
the tops of white dresses.

—1982

THEODORE ROETHKE

1908-1963

Theodore Roethke grew up in Saginaw, Michigan, and attended the University of Michigan. Part formal verse practitioner and part confessional poet, Roethke's mature poems are marked by the grace with which they control the messy emotions they depict. Roethke supported himself teaching, which he found alternately exhilarating and exhausting as its demands intersected with his manic-depressive disorder. His books include Open House *(1941),* The Lost Son and Other Poems *(1948), and* Sequence, Sometimes Metaphysical, Poems *(1963). He received the Pulitzer Prize in poetry in 1954 for his collection* The Waking.

MY PAPA'S WALTZ

The whiskey on your breath
Could make a small boy dizzy;
But I hung on like death:
Such waltzing was not easy.

We romped until the pans
Slid from the kitchen shelf;
My mother's countenance
Could not unfrown itself.

The hand that held my wrist
Was battered on one knuckle;
At every step you missed
My right ear scraped a buckle.

You beat time on my head
With a palm caked hard by dirt,
Then waltzed me off to bed
Still clinging to your shirt.

—1942

ANNE SEXTON

1928-1974

Anne Sexton began writing poetry later in her life as a form of therapy. She published her first book of poems, To Bedlam and Back, *in 1960. A classmate of Sylvia Plath at Smith College for women, Sexton wrote powerfully frank poems about the social position of women, as she seems to have struggled deeply with the demands of femininity. A onetime fashion model and the mother of two children, Sexton committed suicide in 1974. Her books include* All My Pretty Ones *(1962),* Live or Die *(1967), which won the Pulitzer Prize,* Love Poems *(1969),* Transformations *(1971),* The Book of Folly *(1972), and* The Death Notebooks *(1974). That Awful Rowing Toward God* appeared posthumously in 1975.

CINDERELLA

You always read about it:
the plumber with twelve children
who wins the Irish Sweepstakes.
From toilets to riches.
That story.

Or the nursemaid,
some luscious sweet from Denmark
who captures the oldest son's heart.
From diapers to Dior.
That story.

Or a milkman who serves the wealthy,
eggs, cream, butter, yogurt, milk,
the white truck like an ambulance
who goes into real estate
and makes a pile.
From homogenized to martinis at lunch.

Or the charwoman
who is on the bus when it cracks up
and collects enough from the insurance.
From mops to Bonwit Teller.
That story.

Once
the wife of a rich man was on her deathbed
and she said to her daughter Cinderella:
Be devout. Be good. Then I will smile

down from heaven in the seam of a cloud.
The man took another wife who had
two daughters, pretty enough
but with hearts like blackjacks.
Cinderella was their maid.
She slept on the sooty hearth each night
and walked around looking like Al Jolson.
Her father brought presents home from town,
jewels and gowns for the other women
but the twig of a tree for Cinderella.
She planted that twig on her mother's grave
and it grew to a tree where a white dove sat.
Whenever she wished for anything the dove
would drop it like an egg upon the ground.
The bird is important, my dears, so heed him.

Next came the ball, as you all know.
It was a marriage market.
The prince was looking for a wife.
All but Cinderella were preparing
and gussying up for the big event.
Cinderella begged to go too.
Her stepmother threw a dish of lentils
into the cinders and said: Pick them
up in an hour and you shall go.
The white dove brought all his friends;
all the warm wings of the fatherland came,
and picked up the lentils in a jiffy.
No, Cinderella, said the stepmother,
you have no clothes and cannot dance.
That's the way with stepmothers.

Cinderella went to the tree at the grave
and cried forth like a gospel singer:
Mama! Mama! My turtledove,
send me to the prince's ball!
The bird dropped down a golden dress
and delicate little gold slippers.
Rather a large package for a simple bird.
So she went. Which is no surprise.
Her stepmother and sisters didn't
recognize her without her cinder face
and the prince took her hand on the spot
and danced with no other the whole day.

As nightfall came she thought she'd better
get home. The prince walked her home

and she disappeared into the pigeon house
and although the prince took an axe and broke
it open she was gone. Back to her cinders.
These events repeated themselves for three days.
However on the third day the prince
covered the palace steps with cobbler's wax
And Cinderella's gold shoe stuck upon it.
Now he would find whom the shoe fit
and find his strange dancing girl for keeps.
He went to their house and the two sisters
were delighted because they had lovely feet.
The eldest went into a room to try the slipper on
but her big toe got in the way so she simply
sliced it off and put on the slipper.
The prince rode away with her until the white dove
told him to look at the blood pouring forth.
That is the way with amputations.
They don't just heal up like a wish.
The other sister cut off her heel
but the blood told as blood will.
The prince was getting tired.
He began to feel like a shoe salesman.
But he gave it one last try.
This time Cinderella fit into the shoe
like a love letter into its envelope.

At the wedding ceremony
the two sisters came to curry favor
and the white dove pecked their eyes out.
Two hollow spots were left
like soup spoons.

Cinderella and the prince
lived, they say, happily ever after,
like two dolls in a museum case
never bothered by diapers or dust,
never arguing over the timing of an egg,
never telling the same story twice,
never getting a middle-aged spread,
their darling smiles pasted on for eternity.
Regular Bobbsey Twins.
That story.

—1971

CATHY SONG

B. 1955

Cathy Song was born in Oahu, Hawaii, and received a BA from Wellesley College and an MFA from Boston University. Her first collection of poems, Picture Bride, *won the Yale Younger Poets Award in 1983 and propelled her to national prominence. Two subsequent volumes have appeared:* Frameless Windows, Squares of Light *in 1988 and* School Figures *in 1994. In 1991, she cooperated with Juliet Kono on a literary collection entitled* Sister Stew: Fiction and Poetry by Women. *Her poetry appears regularly in literary journals, including* Asian-Pacific Literature, Hawaii Review, Poetry, *and* Seneca Review. *She lives and teaches in Honolulu.*

THE YOUNGEST DAUGHTER

The sky has been dark
for many years.
My skin has become as damp
and pale as rice paper
and feels the way
mother's used to before the drying sun
parched it out there in the fields.

Lately, when I touch my eyelids,
my hands react as if
I had just touched something
hot enough to burn.
My skin, aspirin colored,
tingles with migraine. Mother
has been massaging the left side of my face
especially in the evenings
when the pain flares up.

This morning
her breathing was graveled,
her voice gruff with affection
when I wheeled her into the bath.
She was in a good humor,
making jokes about her great breasts,
floating in the milky water
like two walruses,
flaccid and whiskered around the nipples.
I scrubbed them with a sour taste
in my mouth, thinking:

six children and an old man
have sucked from these brown nipples.

I was almost tender
when I came to the blue bruises
that freckle her body,
places where she has been injecting insulin
for thirty years. I soaped her slowly,
she sighed deeply, her eyes closed.
It seems it has always
been like this: the two of us
in this sunless room,
the splashing of the bathwater.

In the afternoons
when she has rested,
she prepares our ritual of tea and rice,
garnished with a shred of gingered fish,
a slice of pickled turnip,
a token for my white body.
We eat in the familiar silence.
She knows I am not to be trusted,
even now planning my escape.
As I toast to her health
with the tea she has poured,
a thousand cranes curtain the window,
fly up in a sudden breeze.

                                        −1983

FICTION

TONI CADE BAMBARA
1939-1995

Toni Cade Bambara was born in New York City and educated in Italy, France, and the United States. Her work experience was varied, taking her from the New York State Department of Welfare to the Metropolitan Hospital in New York City before she joined the faculty at Stephens College and later Emory University (in Atlanta). Before publishing her well-known novel, The Salt Eaters (1980), Bambara produced two volumes of short stories,

Gorilla, My Love (1972) and The Sea Birds Are Still Alive: Collected Stories *(1977). She also edited the highly influential* The Black Woman Anthology *(1970), which was a standard text in Women's Studies courses for two decades. Throughout her career, she was committed to teaching, studying, and providing creative outlets for African-American women writers, particularly those working within the storytelling tradition.*

THE LESSON

Back in the days when everyone was old and stupid or young and foolish and me and Sugar were the only ones just right, this lady moved on our block with nappy hair and proper speech and no makeup. And quite naturally we laughed at her, laughed the way we did at the junk man who went about his business like he was some big-time president and his sorry-ass horse his secretary. And we kinda hated her too, hated the way we did the winos who cluttered up our parks and pissed on our handball walls and stank up our hallways and stairs so you couldn't halfway play hide-and-seek without a goddamn gas mask. Miss Moore was her name. The only woman on the block with no first name. And she was black as hell, cept for her feet, which were fish-white and spooky. And she was always planning these boring-ass things for us to do, us being my cousin, mostly, who lived on the block cause we all moved North the same time and to the same apartment then spread out gradual to breathe. And our parents would yank our heads into some kinda shape and crisp up our clothes so we'd be presentable for travel with Miss Moore, who always looked like she was going to church, though she never did. Which is just one of the things the grown-ups talked about when they talked behind her back like a dog. But when she came calling with some sachet she'd sewed up or some gingerbread she'd made or some book, why then they'd all be too embarrassed to turn her down and we'd get handed over all spruced up. She'd been to college and said it was only right that she should take responsibility for the young ones' education, and she not even related by marriage or blood. So they'd go for it. Specially Aunt Gretchen. She was the main gofer in the family. You got some ole dumb shit foolishness you want somebody to go for, you send for Aunt Gretchen. She been screwed into the go-along for so long, it's a blood-deep natural thing with her. Which is how she got saddled with me and Sugar and Junior in the first place while our mothers were in a la-de-da apartment up the block having a good ole time.

So this one day Miss Moore rounds us all up at the mailbox and it's puredee hot and she's knockin herself out about arithmetic. And school suppose to let up in summer I heard, but she don't never let up. And the starch in my pinafore scratching the shit outta me and I'm really hating this nappy-head bitch and her goddamn college degree. I'd much rather go to the pool or to the show where it's cool. So me and Sugar leaning on the mailbox being surly, which is a Miss Moore word. And Flyboy checking out what everybody brought for lunch. And Fat Butt already wasting his peanut-butter-and-jelly sandwich like the pig he is. And Junebug punchin on Q.T.'s arm for potato chips. And Rosie Giraffe shifting from one hip to the other waiting for somebody to step on her foot or ask her if she from Georgia so she can kick ass, preferably Mercedes'. And Miss Moore asking us do we know what money is, like we a bunch of retards. I mean real money, she say, like it's only poker chips or monopoly papers we lay on the grocer. So right away I'm tired of this and say so. And would much rather snatch Sugar and go to the Sunset and terrorize the West Indian kids and take their hair ribbons and their money too. And Miss Moore files that remark away for next week's lesson on brotherhood, I can tell. And finally I say we oughta get to the subway cause it's cooler and besides we might meet some cute boys. Sugar done swiped her mama's lipstick, so we ready.

So we heading down the street and she's boring us silly about what things cost and what our parents make and how much goes for rent and how money ain't divided up right in this country. And then she gets to the part about we all poor and live in the slums, which I don't feature. And I'm ready to speak on that, but she steps out in the street and hails two cabs just like that. Then she hustles half the crew in with her and hands me a five-dollar bill and tells me to calculate 10 percent tip for the driver. And we're off. Me and Sugar and Junebug and Flyboy hangin out the window and hollering to everybody, putting lipstick on each other cause Flyboy a faggot anyway, and making farts with our sweaty armpits. But I'm mostly trying to figure how to spend this money. But they all fascinated with the meter ticking and Junebug starts laying bets as to how much it'll read when Flyboy can't hold his breath no more. Then Sugar lays bets as to how much it'll be when we get there. So I'm stuck. Don't nobody want to go for my plan, which is to jump out at the next light and run off to the first bar-b-que we can find. Then the driver tells us to get the hell out cause we there already. And the meter reads eighty-five cents. And I'm stalling to figure out the tip and Sugar say give him a dime. And I decide he don't need it bad as I do, so later for him. But then he tries to take off with Junebug foot still in the door so we talk about his mama something ferocious. Then we check out that we on Fifth Avenue and everybody dressed up in stockings. One lady in a fur coat, hot as it is. White folks crazy.

"This is the place," Miss Moore say, presenting it to us in the voice she uses at the museum. "Let's look in the windows before we go in."

"Can we steal?" Sugar asks very serious like she's getting the ground rules squared away before she plays. "I beg your pardon," say Miss Moore, and we fall out. So she leads us around the windows of the toy store and me and Sugar screamin, "This is mine, that's mine, I gotta have that, that was made for me, I was born for that," till Big Butt drowns us out.

"Hey, I'm goin to buy that there."

"That there? You don't even know what it is, stupid."

"I do so," he say punchin on Rosie Giraffe. "It's a microscope."

"Whatcha gonna do with a microscope, fool?"

"Look at things."

"Like what, Ronald?" ask Miss Moore. And Big Butt ain't got the first notion. So here go Miss Moore gabbing about the thousands of bacteria in a drop of water and the somethinorother in a speck of blood and the million and one living things in the air around us is invisible to the naked eye. And what she say that for? Junebug go to town on that "naked" and we rolling. Then Miss Moore ask what it cost. So we all jam into the window smudgin it up and the price tag say $300. So then she ask how long'd take for Big Butt and Junebug to save up their allowances. "Too long," I say. "Yeh," adds Sugar, "outgrown it by that time." And Miss Moore say no, you never outgrow learning instruments. "Why, even medical students and interns and," blah, blah, blah. And we ready to choke Big Butt for bringing it up in the first damn place.

"This here costs four hundred eighty dollars," says Rosie Giraffe. So we pile up all over her to see what she pointin out. My eyes tell me it's a chunk of glass cracked with something heavy, and different-color inks dripped into the splits, then the whole thing put into a oven or something. But for $480 it don't make sense.

"That's a paperweight made of semi-precious stones fused together under tremendous pressure," she explains slowly, with her hands doing the mining and all the factory work.

"So what's a paperweight?" asks Rosie Giraffe.

"To weigh paper with, dumbbell," say Flyboy, the wise man from the East.

"Not exactly," say Miss Moore, which is what she say when you warm or way off too. "It's to weigh paper down so it won't scatter and make your desk untidy." So right away me and Sugar curtsy to each other and then to Mercedes who is more the tidy type.

"We don't keep paper on top of the desk in my class," say Junebug, figuring Miss Moore crazy or lyin one.

"At home, then," she say. "Don't you have a calendar and pencil case and a blotter and a letter-opener on your desk at home where you do your homework?" And she know damn well what our homes look like cause she nosys around in them every chance she gets.

"I don't even have a desk," say Junebug. "Do we?"

"No. And I don't get no homework neither," say Big Butt.

"And I don't even have a home," say Flyboy like he do at school to keep the white folks off his back and sorry for him. Send this poor kid to camp posters, is his specialty.

"I do," says Mercedes. "I have a box of stationery on my desk and a picture of my cat. My godmother bought the stationery and the desk. There's a big rose on each sheet and the envelopes smell like roses."

"Who wants to know about your smelly-ass stationery," say Rosie Giraffe fore I can get my two cents in.

"It's important to have a work area all your own so that . . ."

"Will you look at this sailboat, please," say Flyboy, cuttin her off and pointin to the thing like it was his. So once again we tumble all over each other to gaze at this magnificent thing in the toy store which is just big enough to maybe sail two kittens across the pond if you strap them to the posts tight. We all start reciting the price tag like we in assembly. "Handcrafted sailboat of fiberglass at one thousand one hundred ninety-five dollars."

"Unbelievable," I hear myself say and am really stunned. I read it again for myself just in case the group recitation put me in a trance. Same thing. For some reason this pisses me off. We look at Miss Moore and she lookin at us, waiting for I dunno what.

"Who'd pay all that when you can buy a sailboat set for a quarter at Pop's, a tube of glue for a dime, and a ball of string for eight cents? It must have a motor and a whole lot else besides," I say. "My sailboat cost me about fifty cents."

"But will it take water?" say Mercedes with her smart ass.

"Took mine to Alley Pond Park once," say Flyboy. "String broke. Lost it. Pity."

"Sailed mine in Central Park and it keeled over and sank. Had to ask my father for another dollar."

"And you got the strap," laugh Big Butt. "The jerk didn't even have a string on it. My old man wailed on his behind."

Little Q.T. was staring hard at the sailboat and you could see he wanted it bad. But he too little and somebody'd just take it from him. So what the hell. "This boat for kids, Miss Moore?"

"Parents silly to buy something like that just to get all broke up," say Rosie Giraffe.

"That much money it should last forever," I figure.

"My father'd buy it for me if I wanted it."

"Your father, my ass," say Rosie Giraffe getting a chance to finally push Mercedes.

"Must be rich people shop here," say Q.T.

"You are a very bright boy," say Flyboy. "What was your first clue?" And he rap him on the head with the back of his knuckles, since Q.T. the only one he could get away with. Though Q.T. liable to come up behind you years later and get his licks in when you half expect it.

"What I want to know is," I says to Miss Moore though I never talk to her, I wouldn't give the bitch that satisfaction, "is how much a real boat costs? I figure a thousand'd get you a yacht any day."

"Why don't you check that out," she says, "and report back to the group?" Which really pains my ass. If you gonna mess up a perfectly good swim day least you could do is have some answers. "Let's go in," she say like she got something up her sleeve. Only she don't lead the way. So me and Sugar turn the corner to where the entrance is, but when we get there I kinda hang back. Not that I'm scared, what's there to be afraid of, just a toy store. But I feel funny, shame. But what I got to be shamed about? Got as much right to go in as anybody. But somehow I can't seem to get hold of the door, so I step away from Sugar to lead. But she hangs back too. And I look at her and she looks at me and this is ridiculous. I mean, damn, I have never ever been shy about doing nothing or going nowhere. But then Mercedes steps up and then Rosie Giraffe and Big Butt crowd in behind and shove, and next thing we all stuffed into the doorway with only Mercedes squeezing past us, smoothing out her jumper and walking right down the aisle. Then the rest of us tumble in like a glued-together jigsaw done all wrong. And people lookin at us. And it's like the time me and Sugar crashed into the Catholic church on a dare. But once we got in there and everything so hushed and holy and the candles and the bowin and the handker-chiefs on all the drooping heads, I just couldn't go through with the plan. Which was for me to run up to the altar and do a tap dance while Sugar played the nose flute and messed around in the holy water. And Sugar kept givin me the elbow. Then later teased me so bad I tied her up in the shower and turned it on and locked her in. And she'd be there till this day if Aunt Gretchen hadn't finally figured I was lyin about the boarder takin a shower.

Same thing in the store. We all walkin on tiptoe and hardly touchin the games and puzzles and things. And I watched Miss Moore who is steady watchin us like she waitin for a sign. Like Mama Drewery watches the sky and sniffs the air and takes note of just how much slant is in the bird formation. Then me and Sugar bump smack into each other, so busy gazing at the toys, 'specially the sailboat. But we don't laugh and go into our fat-lady bump-stomach routine. We just stare at that price tag. Then Sugar run a finger over the whole boat. And I'm jealous and want to hit her. Maybe not her, but I sure want to punch somebody in the mouth.

"Watcha bring us here for, Miss Moore?"

"You sound angry, Sylvia. Are you mad about something?" Givin me one of them grins like she tellin a grown-up joke that never turns out to be funny. And she's lookin very closely at me like maybe she plannin to do my portrait from memory. I'm mad, but I won't give her that satisfaction. So I slouch around the store bein very bored and say, "Let's go."

Me and Sugar at the back of the train watchin the tracks whizzin by large then small then gettin gobbled up in the dark. I'm thinkin about this tricky toy I saw in the store. A clown that somersaults on a bar then does chin-ups just cause you yank lightly at his leg. Cost $35. I could see me askin my mother for a $35 birthday clown. "You wanna who that costs what?" she'd say, cocking her head to the side to get a better view of the hole in my head. Thirty-five dollars could buy new bunk beds for Junior and Gretchen's boy. Thirty-five dollars and the whole household could go visit Granddaddy Nelson in the country. Thirty-five dollars would pay for the rent and the piano bill too. Who are these people that spend that much for performing clowns and $1,000 for toy sailboats? What kinda work they do and how they live and how come we ain't in on it? Where we are is who we are, Miss Moore always pointin out. But it don't necessarily have to be that way, she always adds then waits for somebody to say that poor people have to wake up and demand their share of the pie and don't none of us know what kind of pie she talkin about in the first damn place. But she ain't so smart cause I still got her four dollars from the taxi and she sure ain't gettin it. Messin up my day with this shit. Sugar nudges me in my pocket and winks.

Miss Moore lines us up in front of the mailbox where we started from, seem like years ago, and I got a headache for thinkin so hard. And we lean all over each other so we can hold up under the draggy-ass lecture she always finishes us off with at the end before we thank her for borin us to tears. But she just looks at us like she readin tea leaves. Finally she say, "Well, what did you think of F.A.O. Schwartz?"

Rosie Giraffe mumbles, "White folks crazy."

"I'd like to go there again when I get my birthday money," says Mercedes, and we shove her out the pack so she has to lean on the mailbox by herself.

"I'd like a shower. Tiring day," say Flyboy.

Then Sugar surprises me by sayin, "You know, Miss Moore, I don't think all of us here put together eat in a year what that sailboat costs." And Miss Moore lights up like somebody goosed her. "And?" she say, urging Sugar on. Only I'm standin on her foot so she don't continue.

"Imagine for a minute what kind of society it is in which some people can spend on a toy what it would cost to feed a family of six or seven. What do you think?"

"I think," say Sugar pushing me off her feet like she never done before, cause I whip her ass in a minute, "that this is not much of a democracy if you ask me. Equal chance to pursue happiness means an equal crack at the dough, don't it?" Miss Moore is beside herself and I am disgusted with Sugar's treachery. So I stand on her foot one more time to see if she'll shove me. She shuts up, and Miss Moore looks at me, sorrowfully I'm thinkin. And somethin weird is goin on, I can feel it in my chest.

"Anybody else learn anything today?" lookin dead at me. I walk away and Sugar has to run to catch up and don't even seem to notice when I shrug her arm off my shoulder.

"Well, we got four dollars anyway," she says.

"Uh hunh."

"We could go to Hascombs and get half a chocolate layer and then go to the Sunset and still have plenty money for potato chips and ice cream sodas."

"Un hunh."

"Race you to Hascombs," she say.

We start down the block and she gets ahead which is O.K. by me cause I'm going to the West End and then over to the Drive to think this day through. She can run if she want to and even run faster. But ain't nobody gonna beat me at nuthin.

—1972

RAYMOND CARVER
1939-1988

Raymond Carver was born in Clatskanie, Oregon. He received his BA from Humboldt State College and attended the University of Iowa Writers' Workshop. Expert in writing both fiction and poetry, Carver's list of awards is long. His stories are collected in several books, including Will You Please Be Quiet, Please? *(1976) and* Cathedral *(1983), while his poetry appears in* Winter Insomnia *(1970) and* At Night the Salmon Move *(1976). Carver was at various times a lecturer in creative writing at universities in Iowa, Texas, and California. He was a professor at Syracuse University at the time of his death. Carver's influence on contemporary short fiction cannot be underestimated. His exceptional ear for vernacular language and use of dialogue highlight the absurd quality of everyday incidents. His short stories provide the basis for Robert Altman's 1991 film* Short Cuts.

THE FATHER

The baby lay in a basket beside the bed, dressed in a white bonnet and sleeper. The basket had been newly painted and tied with ice blue ribbons and padded with blue quilts. The three little sisters and the mother, who had just gotten out of bed and was still not herself, and the grandmother all stood around the baby, watching it stare and sometimes raise its fist to its mouth. He did not smile or laugh, but now and then he blinked his eyes and flicked his tongue back and forth through his lips when one of the girls rubbed his chin.

The father was in the kitchen and could hear them playing with the baby.

"Who do you love, baby?" Phyllis said and tickled his chin.

"He loves us all," Phyllis said, "but he really loves Daddy because Daddy's a boy too!"

The grandmother sat down on the edge of the bed and said, "Look at its little arm! So fat. And those little fingers! Just like its mother."

"Isn't he sweet?" the mother said. "So healthy, my little baby." And bending over, she kissed the baby on its forehead and touched the cover over its arm. "We love him too."

"But who does he look like, who does he look like?" Alice cried, and they all moved up closer around the basket to see who the baby looked like.

"He has pretty eyes," Carol said.

"*All* babies have pretty eyes," Phyllis said.

"He has his grandfather's lips," the grandmother said. "Look at those lips."

"I don't know . . ." the mother said. "I wouldn't say."

"The nose! The nose!" Alice cried.

"What about his nose?" the mother asked.

"It looks like somebody's nose," the girl answered.

"No, I don't know," the mother said. "I don't think so.

"Those lips . . ." the grandmother murmured. "Those little fingers . . ." she said, uncovering the baby's hand and spreading out its fingers.

"Who does the baby look like?"

"He doesn't look like anybody," Phyllis said. And they moved even closer.

"*I* know! *I* know!" Carol said. "He looks like *Daddy!* Then they looked closer at the baby.

"But who does Daddy *look* like?" Phyllis asked.

"Who does Daddy *look* like?" Alice repeated, and they all at once looked through to the kitchen where the father was sitting at the table with his back to them.

"Why, nobody!" Phyllis said and began to cry a little.

"Hush," the grandmother said and looked away and then back at the baby.

"Daddy doesn't look like *anybody!*" Alice said.

"But he has to look like *somebody,*" Phyllis said, wiping her eyes with one of the ribbons. And all of them except the grandmother looked at the father, sitting at the table.

He had turned around in his chair and his face was white and without expression.

—1945

LOIS GOULD

B. 1938

Lois Gould was educated at Wellesley College. She has worked as a journalist and police reporter as well as a director of Ladies Home Journal. *Gould gained her reputation in the 1970s for a series of popular novels including* Such Good Friends *(1970),* Necessary Objects *(1972),* Final Analysis *(1972), and* Sea Change *(1976). Her collected essays are titled* Not Responsible for Personal Objects *(1978) and her most recent novel is* No Brakes: A Novel *(1997). Her short story "X" first appeared in* MS. *magazine in 1972 and received instant fame. Since that time, "gender neutral" childrearing has become an ever greater topic of debate, leading* MS. *in 1981 to reprint "X" in the version that appears in this volume.*

X

Once upon a time, a Baby named X was born. It was named X so that nobody could tell whether it was a boy or a girl.

Its parents could tell, of course, but they couldn't tell anybody else. They couldn't even tell Baby X—at least not until much, much later.

You see, it was all part of a very important Secret Scientific Xperiment, known officially as Project Baby X.

This Xperiment was going to cost Xactly 23 billion dollars and 72 cents. Which might seem like a lot for one Baby, even if it was an important Secret Scientific Xperimental Baby.

But when you remember the cost of strained carrots, stuffed bunnies, booster shots, 28 shiny quarters from the tooth fairy . . . you begin to see how it adds up.

Long before Baby X was born, the smartest scientists had to work out the secret details of the Xperiment, and to write the *Official Instruction Manual,* in secret code, for Baby X's parents, whoever they were.

These parents had to be selected very carefully. Thousands of people volunteered to take thousands of tests, with thousands of tricky questions.

Almost everybody failed because, it turned out, almost everybody wanted a boy or a girl, and not a Baby X at all.

Also, almost everybody thought a Baby X would be more trouble than a boy or a girl. (They were right, too.)

There were families with grandparents named Milton and Agatha, who wanted the baby named Milton or Agatha instead of X, even if it *was* an X.

There were aunts who wanted to knit tiny dresses and uncles who wanted to send tiny baseball mitts.

Worst of all, there were families with other children who couldn't be trusted to keep a Secret. Not if they knew the Secret was worth 23 billion dollars and 72 cents—and all you had to do was take one little peek at Baby X in the bathtub to know what it was.

Finally, the scientists found the Joneses, who really wanted to raise an X more than any other kind of baby—no matter how much trouble it was.

The Joneses promised to take turns holding X, feeding X, and singing X to sleep.

And they promised never to hire any baby-sitters. The scientists knew that a baby-sitter would probably peek at X in the bathtub, too.

The day the Joneses brought their baby home, lots of friends and relatives came to see it. And the first thing they asked was what kind of a baby X was.

When the Joneses said, "It's an X!" nobody knew what to say.

They couldn't say, "Look at her cute little dimples!"

On the other hand, they couldn't say, "Look at his husky little biceps!"

And they didn't feel right about saying just plain "kitchy-coo."

The relatives all felt embarrassed about having an X in the family.

"People will think there's something wrong with it!" they whispered.

"Nonsense!" the Joneses said cheerfully. "What could possibly be wrong with this perfectly adorable X?"

Clearly, nothing at all was wrong. Nevertheless, the cousins who had sent a tiny football helmet would not come and visit any more. And the neighbors who sent a pink-flowered romper suit pulled their shades down when the Joneses passed their house.

The *Official Instruction Manual* had warned the new parents that this would happen; so they didn't fret about it. Besides, they were too busy learning how to bring up Baby X.

Ms. and Mr. Jones had to be Xtra careful. If they kept bouncing it up in the air and saying how *strong* and *active* it was, they'd be treating it more like a boy than an X. But if all they did was cuddle it and kiss it and tell it how sweet and dainty it was, they'd be treating it more like a girl than an X.

On page 1654 of the *Official Instruction Manual,* the scientists prescribed: "plenty of bouncing and plenty of cuddling, *both.* X ought to be strong and sweet and active. Forget about *dainty* altogether."

There were other problems, too. Toys, for instance. And clothes. On his first shopping trip, Mr. Jones told the store clerk. "I need some things for a new baby." The clerk smiled and said, "Well, now, is it a boy or a girl?" "It's an X," Mr. Jones said, smiling back. But the clerk got all red in the face and said huffily, "In *that* case, I'm afraid I can't help you, sir."

Mr. Jones wandered the aisles tryng to find what X needed. But everything was in sections marked BOYS or GIRLS: "Boys' Pajamas" and "Girls' Underwear" and "Boys' Fire Engines" and "Girls' Housekeeping Sets." Mr. Jones went home without buying anything for X.

That night he and Ms. Jones consulted page 2326 of the *Official Instruction Manual.* It said firmly: "Buy plenty of everything!"

So they bought all kinds of toys. A boy doll that made pee-pee and cried "Pa-Pa." And a girl doll that talked in three languages and said, "I am the Pres-i-dent of Gen-er-al Mo-tors."

They bought a storybook about a brave princess who rescued a handsome prince from his tower, and another one about a sister and brother who grew up to be a baseball star and a ballet star, and you had to guess which.

The head scientists of Project Baby X checked all their purchases and told them to keep up the good work. They also reminded the Joneses to see page 4629 of the *Manual*, where it said, "Never make Baby X feel *embarrassed* or *ashamed* about what it wants to play with. And if X gets dirty climbing rocks, never say, 'Nice little Xes don't get dirty climbing rocks.'"

Likewise, it said, "If X falls down and cries, never say, 'Brave little Xes don't cry.' Because, of course, nice little Xes *do* get dirty, and brave little Xes *do* cry. No matter how dirty X gets, or how hard it cries, don't worry. It's all part of the Xperiment."

Whenever the Joneses pushed Baby X's stroller in the park, smiling strangers would come over and coo: "Is that a boy or a girl?" The Joneses would smile back and say, "It's an X." The strangers would stop smiling then and often snarl something nasty—as if the Joneses had said something nasty to *them.*

Once a little girl grabbed X's shovel in the sandbox, and zonked X on the head with it. "Now, now, Tracy," the mother began to scold, "little girls mustn't hit little—" and she turned to ask X, "Are you a little boy or a little girl, dear?"

Mr. Jones, who was sitting near the sandbox, held his breath and crossed his fingers.

X smiled politely, even though X's head had never been zonked so hard in its life. "I'm a little X," said X.

"You're a *what?*" the lady exclaimed angrily. "You're a little b-r-a-t, you mean!"

"But little girls mustn't hit little Xes, either!" said X, retrieving the shovel with another polite smile. "What good's hitting, anyway?"

X's father finally X-haled, uncrossed his fingers, and grinned.

And at their next secret Project Baby X meeting, the scientists grinned, too. Baby X was doing fine.

But then it was time for X to start school. The Joneses were really worried about this, because school was even more full of rules for boys and girls, and there were no rules for Xes.

Teachers would tell boys to form a line, and girls to form another line.

There would be boys' games and girls' games, and boys' secrets and girls' secrets.

The school library would have a list of recommended books for girls, and a different list for boys.

There would even be a bathroom marked BOYS and another one marked GIRLS.

Pretty soon boys and girls would hardly talk to each other. What would happen to poor little X?

The Joneses spent weeks consulting their *Instruction Manual.*

There were 249 and one-half pages of advice under "First Day of School." Then they were all summoned to an Urgent Xtra Special Conference with the smart scientists of Project Baby X.

The scientists had to make sure that X's mother had taught X how to throw and catch a ball properly, and that X's father had been sure to teach X what to serve at a doll's tea party.

X had to know how to shoot marbles and jump rope and, most of all, what to say when the Other Children asked whether X was a Boy or a Girl.

Finally, X was ready.

X's teacher had promised that the class could line up alphabetically, instead of forming separate lines for boys and girls. And X had permission to use the principal's bathroom, because it wasn't marked anything except BATHROOM. But nobody could help X with the biggest problem of all—Other Children.

Nobody in X's class had ever known an X. Nobody had even heard grown-ups say, "Some of my best friends are Xes."

What would other children think? Would they make Xist jokes? Or would they make friends?

You couldn't tell what X was by its clothes. Overalls don't even button right to left, like girls' clothes, or left to right, like boys' clothes.

And did X have a girl's short haircut or a boy's long haircut?

As for the games X liked, either X played ball very well for a girl, or else played house very well for a boy.

The children tried to find out by asking X tricky questions, like, "Who's your favorite sports star?" X had two favorite sports stars: a girl jockey named Robyn Smith and a boy archery champion named Robin Hood.

Then they asked, "What's your favorite TV show?" And X said: "Lassie," which stars a girl dog played by a boy dog.

When X said its favorite toy was a doll, everyone decided that X must be a girl. But then X said the doll was really a robot, and that X had computerized it, and that it was programmed to bake fudge and then clean up the kitchen.

After X told them that, they gave up guessing what X was. All they knew was they'd sure like to see X's doll.

After school, X wanted to play with the other children. "How about shooting baskets in the gym?" X asked the girls. But all they did was make faces and giggle behind X's back.

"Boy, is *he* weird," whispered Jim to Joe.

"How about weaving some baskets in the arts and crafts room?" X asked the boys. But they all made faces and giggled behind X's back, too.

"Boy, is *she* weird," whispered Susie to Peggy.

That night, Ms. and Mr. Jones asked X how things had gone at school. X tried to smile, but there were two big tears in its eyes. "The lessons are okay," X began, "but . . ."

"But?" said Ms. Jones.

"The Other Children hate me," X whispered.

"Hate you?" said Mr. Jones.

X nodded, which made the two big tears roll down and splash on its overalls.

Once more, the Joneses reached for their *Instruction Manual.* Under "Other Children," it said:

"What did you Xpect? Other Children have to obey silly boy-girl rules, because their parents taught them to. Lucky X—you don't have rules at all! All you have to do is be yourself.

"P.S. We're not saying it'll be easy."

X liked being itself. But X cried a lot that night. So X's father held X tight and cried a little, too. X's mother cheered them up with an Xciting story about an enchanted prince called Sleeping Handsome, who woke up when Princess Charming kissed him.

The next morning, they all felt much better, and little X went back to school with a brave smile and a clean pair of red and white checked overalls.

There was a seven-letter-word spelling bee in class that day. And a seven-lap boys' relay race in the gym. And a seven-layer-cake baking contest in the girls' kitchen corner.

X won the spelling bee. X also won the relay race.

And X almost won the baking contest, Xcept it forgot to light the oven. (Remember, nobody's perfect.)

One of the Other Children noticed something else, too. He said, "X doesn't care about winning. X just thinks it's fun playing boys' stuff *and* girls' stuff."

"Come to think of it," said another one of the Other Children, "X is having twice as much fun as we are!"

After school that day, the girl who beat X in the baking contest gave X a big slice of her winning cake.

And the boy X beat in the relay race asked X to race him home.

From then on, some really funny things began to happen.

Susie, who sat next to X, refused to wear pink dresses to school any more. She wanted red and white checked overalls—just like X's.

Overalls, she told her parents, were better for climbing monkey bars.

Then Jim, the class football nut, started wheeling his little sister's doll carriage around the football field.

He'd put on his entire football uniform, except for the helmet.

Then he'd put the helmet *in* the carriage, lovingly tucked under an old set of shoulder pads.

Then he'd jog around the field, pushing the carriage and singing "Rockabye Baby" to his helmet.

He said X did the same thing, so it must be okay. After all, X was now the team's star quarterback.

Susie's parents were horrified by her behavior, and Jim's parents were worried sick about his.

But the worst came when the twins, Joe and Peggy, decided to share everything with each other.

Peggy used Joe's hockey skates, and his microscope, and took half his newspaper route.

Joe used Peggy's needlepoint kit, and her cookbooks, and took two of her three baby-sitting jobs.

Peggy ran the lawn mower, and Joe ran the vacuum cleaner.

Their parents weren't one bit pleased with Peggy's science experiments, or with Joe's terrific needlepoint pillows.

They didn't care that Peggy mowed the lawn better, and that Joe vacuumed the carpet better.

In fact, they were furious. It's all that little X's fault, they agreed. X doesn't know what it is, or what it's supposed to be! So X wants to mix everybody *else* up, too!

Peggy and Joe were forbidden to play with X any more. So was Susie, and then Jim, and then *all* the Other Children.

But it was too late: the Other Children stayed mixed-up and happy and free, and refused to go back to the way they'd been before X.

Finally, the parents held an emergency meeting to discuss "The X Problem."

They sent a report to the principal stating that X was a "bad influence," and demanding immediate action.

The Joneses, they said, should be *forced* to tell whether X was a boy or a girl. And X should be *forced* to behave like whichever it was.

If the Joneses refused to tell, the parents said, then X must take an Xamination. An Impartial Team of Xperts would Xtract the secret. Then X would start obeying all the old rules. Or else.

And if X turned out to be some kind of mixed-up misfit, then X must be Xpelled from school. Immediately! So that no little Xes would ever come to school again.

The principal was very upset. X, a bad influence? A mixed-up misfit? But X was a Xcellent student! X set a fine Xample! X was Xtraordinary!

X was president of the student council. X had won first prize in the art show, honorable mention in the science fair, and six events on field day, including the potato race.

Nevertheless, insisted the parents, X is a Problem Child. X is the Biggest Problem Child we have ever seen!

So the principal reluctantly notified X's parents and the Joneses reported this to the Project X scientists, who referred them to page 85769 of the *Instruction Manual.* "Sooner or later," it said, "X will have to be Xamined by an Impartial Team of Xperts.

"This may be the only way any of us will know for sure whether X is mixed up— or everyone else is."

At Xactly 9 o'clock the next day, X reported to the school health office. The principal, along with a committee from the Parents' Association, X's teacher, X's classmates, and Ms. and Mr. Jones, waited in the hall outside.

Inside, the Xperts had set up their famous testing machine: the Superpsychiamedicosocioculturometer.

Nobody knew Xactly how the machine worked, but everybody knew that this examination would reveal Xactly what everyone wanted to know about X, but were afraid to ask.

It was terribly quiet in the hall. Almost spooky. They could hear very strange noises from the room.

There were buzzes.

And a beep or two.

And several bells.

An occasional light flashed under the door. Was it an X ray?

Through it all, you could hear the Xperts' voices, asking questions, and X's voice, answering answers.

I wouldn't like to be in X's overalls right now, the children thought.

At last, the door opened. Everyone crowded around to hear the results. X didn't look any different; in fact, X was smiling. But the Impartial Team of Xperts looked terrible. They looked as if they were crying!

"What happened?" everyone began shouting.

"*Sssh,*" ssshed the principal. "The Xperts are trying to speak."

Wiping his eyes and clearing his throat, one Xpert began: "In our opinion," he whispered—you could tell he must be very upset—"in our opinion, young X here—"

"'Yes? Yes?" shouted a parent.

"Young X," said the other Xpert, frowning, "is just about the *least* mixed-up child we've ever Xamined!" Xclaimed the two Xperts, together. Behind the closed door, the Superpsychiamedicosocioculturometer made a noise like a contented hum.

"Yay for X!" yelled one of the children. And then the others began yelling, too. Clapping and cheering and jumping up and down.

"*SSSH!*" SSShed the principal, but nobody did.

The Parents' Committee was angry and bewildered. How *could* X have passed the whole Xamination?

Didn't X have an *identity* problem? Wasn't X mixed up at *all?* Wasn't X *any* kind of a misfit?

How could it *not* be, when it didn't even *know* what it was?

"Don't you see?" asked the Xperts. "X isn't one bit mixed up! As for being a misfit—ridiculous! X knows perfectly well what it is! Don't you, X?" The Xperts winked. X winked back.

"But what *is* X?" shrieked Peggy and Joe's parents. "*We* still want to know what it is!"

"Ah, yes," said the Xperts, winking again. "Well, don't worry. You'll all know one of these days. And you won't need us to tell you."

"What? What do they mean?" Jim's parents grumbled suspiciously.

Susie and Peggy and Joe all answered at once. "They mean that by the time it matters which sex X is, it won't be a secret any more!"

With that, the Xperts reached out to hug Ms. and Mr. Jones. "If we ever have an X of our own," they whispered, "we sure hope you'll lend us your instruction manual."

Needless to say, the Joneses were very happy. The Project Baby X scientists were rather pleased, too. So were Susie, Jim, Peggy, Joe, and all the Other Children. Even the parents promised not to make any trouble.

Later that day, all X's friends put on their red and white checked overalls and went over to see X.

They found X in the backyard, playing with a very tiny baby that none of them had ever seen before.

The baby was wearing very tiny red and white checked overalls.

"How do you like our new baby?" X asked the Other Children proudly.

"It's got cute dimples," said Jim. "It's got husky biceps, too," said Susie.

"What kind of baby is it?" asked Joe and Peggy.

X frowned at them. "Can't you tell?" Then X broke into a big, mischievous grin. "It's a Y!"

—1972, 1981

Gish Jen

B. 1955

Gish Jen was born to Chinese immigrant parents in New York City. After attending Harvard University (initially as a premed student), Jen tried business school and eventually began writing full-time at the University of Iowa

Writers' Workshop. Jen's stories and novel, Typical American *(1991), mine the often hilarious and uneven process of Americanization for a Chinese-American family in which the American-born children's initiation into, in Jen's phrase, "the American society," puts them out-of-sync with the language and cultural beliefs of their less assimilated parents. Her books of stories include* Making Language *(1993) and* Mona In the Promised Land *(1996).*

In the American Society

I. His Own Society

When my father took over the pancake house, it was to send my little sister Mona and me to college. We were only in junior high at the time, but my father believed in getting a jump on things. "Those Americans always saying it," he told us. "Smart guys thinking in advance." My mother elaborated, explaining that businesses took bringing up, like children. They could take years to get going, she said, years.

In this case, though, we got rich right away. At two months we were breaking even, and at four, those same hotcakes that could barely withstand the weight of butter and syrup were supporting our family with ease. My mother bought a station wagon with air conditioning, my father an oversized, red vinyl recliner for the back room; and as time went on and the business continued to thrive, my father started to talk about his grandfather and the village he had reigned over in China—things my father had never talked about when he worked for other people. He told us about the bags of rice his family would give out to the poor at New Year's, and about the people who came to beg, on their hands and knees, for his grandfather to intercede for the more wayward of their relatives. "Like that Godfather in the movie," he would tell us as, his feet up, he distributed paychecks. Sometimes an employee would get two green envelopes instead of one, which meant that Jimmy needed a tooth pulled, say, or that Tiffany's husband was in the clinker again.

"It's nothing, nothing," he would insist, sinking back into his chair. "Who else is going to take care of you people?"

My mother would mostly just sigh about it. "Your father thinks this is China," she would say, and then she would go back to her mending. Once in a while, though, when my father had given away a particularly large sum, she would exclaim, outraged, "But this here is the U—S—of—A!"—this apparently having been what she used to tell immigrant stock boys when they came in late.

She didn't work at the supermarket anymore; but she had made it to the rank of manager before she left, and this had given her not only new words and phrases, but new ideas about herself, and about America, and about what was what in general. She had opinions, now, on how downtown should be zoned; she could pump her own gas and check her own oil; and for all she used to chide Mona and me for being "copycats," she herself was now interested in espadrilles, and wallpaper, and most recently, the town country club.

"So join already," said Mona, flicking a fly off her knee.

My mother enumerated the problems as she sliced up a quarter round of water-melon: There was the cost. There was the waiting list. There was the fact that no one in our family played either tennis or golf.

"So what?" said Mona.

"It would be waste," said my mother.

"Me and Callie can swim in the pool."

"Plus you need that recommendation letter from a member."

"Come on," said Mona. "Annie's mom'd write you a letter in a sec."

My mother's knife glinted in the early summer sun. I spread some more news-paper on the picnic table.

"*Plus* you have to eat there twice a month. You know what that means." My mother cut another, enormous slice of fruit.

"No, I *don't* know what that means," said Mona.

"It means Dad would have to wear a jacket, dummy," I said.

"Oh! Oh! Oh!" said Mona, clasping her hand to her breast. "Oh! Oh! Oh! Oh! Oh!"

We all laughed: my father had no use for nice clothes, and would wear only ten-year-old shirts, with grease-spotted pants, to show how little he cared what any-one thought.

"Your father doesn't believe in joining the American society," said my mother. "He wants to have his own society."

"So go to dinner without him." Mona shot her seeds out in long arcs over the lawn. "Who cares what he thinks?"

But of course we all did care, and knew my mother could not simply up and do as she pleased. For in my father's mind, a family owed its head a degree of loyalty that left no room for dissent. To embrace what he embraced was to love; and to embrace something else was to betray him.

He demanded a similar sort of loyalty of his workers, whom he treated more like servants than employees. Not in the beginning, of course. In the beginning all he wanted was for them to keep on doing what they used to do, and to that end he con-centrated mostly on leaving them alone. As the months passed, though, he expected more and more of them, with the result that for all his largesse, he began to have trouble keeping help. The cooks and busboys complained that he asked them to fix radiators and trim hedges, not only at the restaurant, but at our house; the wait-resses that he sent them on errands and made them chauffeur him around. Our head waitress, Gertrude, claimed that he once even asked her to scratch his back.

"It's not just the blacks don't believe in slavery," she said when she quit.

My father never quite registered her complaint, though, nor those of the others who left. Even after Eleanor quit, then Tiffany, then Gerald, and Jimmy, and even his best cook, Eureka Andy, for whom he had bought new glasses, he remained mostly convinced that the fault lay with them.

"All they understand is that assembly line," he lamented. "Robots, they are. They want to be robots."

There *were* occasions when the clear running truth seemed to eddy, when he would pinch the vinyl of his chair up into little peaks and wonder if he were doing things right. But with time he would always smooth the peaks back down; and when business started to slide in the spring, he kept on like a horse in his ways.

By the summer our dishboy was overwhelmed with scraping. It was no longer just the hashbrowns that people were leaving for trash, and the service was as bad as the food. The waitresses served up French pancakes instead of German, apple juice instead of orange, spilt things on laps, on coats. On the Fourth of July some greenhorn sent an entire side of fries slaloming down a lady's *massif centrale*. Meanwhile in the back room, my father labored through articles on the economy.

"What is housing starts?" he puzzled. "What is GNP?"

Mona and I did what we could, filling in as busgirls and bookkeepers and, one afternoon, stuffing the comments box that hung by the cashier's desk. That was Mona's idea. We rustled up a variety of pens and pencils, checked boxes for an hour, smeared the cards up with coffee and grease, and waited. It took a few days for my father to notice that the box was full, and he didn't say anything about it for a few days more. Finally, though, he started to complain of fatigue; and then he began to complain that the staff was not what it could be. We encouraged him in this—pointing out, for instance, how many dishes got chipped—but in the end all that happened was that, for the first time since we took over the restaurant, my father got it into his head to fire someone. Skip, a skinny busboy who was saving up for a sportscar, said nothing as my father mumbled on about the price of dishes. My father's hands shook as he wrote out the severance check; and he spent the rest of the day napping in his chair once it was over.

As it was going on midsummer, Skip wasn't easy to replace. We hung a sign in the window and advertised in the paper, but no one called the first week, and the person who called the second didn't show up for his interview. The third week, my father phoned Skip to see if he would come back, but a friend of his had already sold him a Corvette for cheap.

Finally a Chinese guy named Booker turned up. He couldn't have been more than thirty, and was wearing a lighthearted seersucker suit, but he looked as though life had him pinned: his eyes were bloodshot and his chest sunken, and the muscles of his neck seemed to strain with the effort of holding his head up. In a single dry breath he told us that he had never bussed tables but was willing to learn, and that he was on the lam from the deportation authorities.

"I do not want to lie to you," he kept saying. He had come to the United States on a student visa, had run out of money, and was now in a bind. He was loath to go back to Taiwan, as it happened—he looked up at this point, to be sure my father wasn't pro-KMT—but all he had was a phony social security card and a willingness to absorb all blame, should anything untoward come to pass.

"I do not think, anyway, that it is against law to hire me, only to be me," he said, smiling faintly.

Anyone else would have examined him on this, but my father conceived of laws as speed bumps rather than curbs. He wiped the counter with his sleeve, and told Booker to report the next morning.

"I will be good worker," said Booker.

"Good," said my father.

"Anything you want me to do, I will do."

My father nodded.

Booker seemed to sink into himself for a moment. "Thank you," he said finally. "I am appreciate your help. I am very, very appreciate for everything." He reached out to shake my father's hand.

My father looked at him. "Did you eat today?" he asked in Mandarin.

Booker pulled at the hem of his jacket.

"Sit down," said my father. "Please, have a seat."

My father didn't tell my mother about Booker, and my mother didn't tell my father about the country club. She would never have applied, except that Mona, while over at Annie's, had let it drop that our mother wanted to join. Mrs. Lardner came by the very next day.

"Why, I'd be honored and delighted to write you people a letter," she said. Her skirt billowed around her.

"Thank you so much," said my mother. "But it's too much trouble for you, and also my husband is . . ."

"Oh, it's no trouble at all, no trouble at all. I tell you." She leaned forward so that her chest freckles showed. "I know just how it is. It's a secret of course, but you know, my natural father was Jewish. Can you see it? Just look at my skin."

"My husband," said my mother.

"I'd be honored and delighted," said Mrs. Lardner with a little wave of her hands. "Just honored and delighted."

Mona was triumphant. "See, Mom," she said, waltzing around the kitchen when Mrs. Lardner left. "What did I tell you? I'm just honored and delighted, just honored and delighted." She waved her hands in the air.

"You know, the Chinese have a saying," said my mother. "To do nothing is better than to overdo. You mean well, but you tell me now what will happen."

"I'll talk Dad into it," said Mona, still waltzing. "Or I bet Callie can. He'll do anything Callie says."

"I can try, anyway," I said.

"Did you hear what I said?" said my mother. Mona bumped into the broom closet door. "You're not going to talk anything; you've already made enough trouble." She started on the dishes with a clatter.

Mona poked diffidently at a mop.

I sponged off the counter. "Anyway," I ventured, "I bet our name'll never even come up."

"That's if we're lucky," said my mother.

"There's all these people waiting," I said.

"Good," she said. She started on a pot.

I looked over at Mona, who was still cowering in the broom closet. "In fact, there's some black family's been waiting so long, they're going to sue," I said.

My mother turned off the water. "Where'd you hear that?"

"Patty told me."

She turned the water back on, started to wash a dish, then put it back down and shut the faucet.

"I'm sorry," said Mona.

"Forget it," said my mother. "Just forget it."

Booker turned out to be a model worker, whose boundless gratitude translated into a willingness to do anything. As he also learned quickly, he soon knew not only how to bus, but how to cook, and how to wait table, and how to keep the books. He fixed the walk-in door so that it stayed shut, reupholstered the torn seats in the dining room, and devised a system for tracking inventory. The only stone in the rice was that he tended to be sickly; but, reliable even in illness, he would always send a friend to take his place. In this way we got to know Ronald, Lynn, Dirk, and Cedric, all of whom, like Booker, had problems with their legal status and were anxious to please. They weren't all as capable as Booker, though, with the exception of Cedric, whom my father often hired even when Booker was well. A round wag of a man who called Mona and me *shou hou*—skinny monkeys—he was a professed nonsmoker who was nevertheless always begging drags off of other people's cigarettes. This last habit drove our head cook, Fernando, crazy, especially since, when refused a hit, Cedric would occasionally snitch one. Winking impishly at Mona and me, he would steal up to an ashtray, take a quick puff, and then break out laughing so that the smoke came rolling out of his mouth in a great incriminatory cloud. Fernando accused him of stealing fresh cigarettes too, even whole packs.

"Why else do you think he's weaseling around in the back of the store all the time," he said. His face was blotchy with anger. "The man is a frigging thief."

Other members of the staff supported him in this contention and joined in on an "Operation Identification," which involved numbering and initialing their cigarettes—even though what they seemed to fear for wasn't so much their cigarettes as their jobs. Then one of the cooks quit; and rather than promote someone, my father hired Cedric for the position. Rumors flew that he was taking only half the normal salary, that Alex had been pressured to resign, and that my father was looking for a position with which to placate Booker, who had been bypassed because of his health.

The result was that Fernando categorically refused to work with Cedric.

"The only way I'll cook with that piece of slime," he said, shaking his huge tattooed fist, "is if it's his ass frying on the grill."

My father cajoled and cajoled, to no avail, and in the end was simply forced to put them on different schedules.

The next week Fernando got caught stealing a carton of minute steaks. My father would not tell even Mona and me how he knew to be standing by the back door when Fernando was on his way out, but everyone suspected Booker. Everyone but Fernando, that is, who was sure Cedric had been the tip-off. My father held a staff meeting in which he tried to reassure everyone that Alex had left on his own, and that he had no intention of firing anyone. But though he was careful not to mention Fernando, everyone was so amazed that he was being allowed to stay that Fernando was incensed nonetheless.

"Don't you all be putting your bug eyes on me," he said. *"He's* the frigging crook." He grabbed Cedric by the collar.

Cedric raised an eyebrow. "Cook, you mean," he said.

At this Fernando punched Cedric in the mouth; and the words he had just uttered notwithstanding, my father fired him on the spot.

With everything that was happening, Mona and I were ready to be getting out of the restaurant. It was almost time: the days were still stuffy with summer, but our window shade had started flapping in the evening as if gearing up to go out. That year the breezes were full of salt, as they sometimes were when they came in from the East, and they blew anchors and docks through my mind like so many tumbleweeds, filling my dreams with wherries and lobsters and grainy-faced men who squinted, day in and day out, at the sky.

It was time for a change, you could feel it; and yet the pancake house was the same as ever. The day before school started my father came home with bad news.

"Fernando called police," he said, wiping his hand on his pant leg.

My mother naturally wanted to know what police; and so with much coughing and hawing, the long story began, the latest installment of which had the police calling immigration, and immigration sending an investigator. My mother sat stiff as whalebone as my father described how the man summarily refused lunch on the house and how my father had admitted, under pressure, that he knew there were "things" about his workers.

"So now what happens?"

My father didn't know. "Booker and Cedric went with him to the jail," he said. "But me, here I am." He laughed uncomfortably.

The next day my father posted bail for "his boys" and waited apprehensively for something to happen. The day after that he waited again, and the day after that he called our neighbor's law student son, who suggested my father call the immigration department under an alias. My father took his advice; and it was thus that he discovered that Booker was right: it was illegal for aliens to work, but it wasn't to hire them.

In the happy interval that ensued, my father apologized to my mother, who in turn confessed about the country club, for which my father had no choice but to forgive her. Then he turned his attention back to "his boys."

My mother didn't see that there was anything to do.

"I like to talking to the judge," said my father.

"This is not China," said my mother.

"I'm only talking to him. I'm not give him money unless he wants it."

"You're going to land up in jail."

"So what else I should do?" My father threw up his hands. "Those are my boys."

"Your boys!" exploded my mother. "What about your family? What about your wife?"

My father took a long sip of tea. "You know," he said finally. "In the war my father sent our cook to the soldiers to use. He always said it—"the province comes before the town, the town comes before the family."

"A restaurant is not a town," said my mother.

My father sipped at his tea again. "You know, when I first come to the United States, I also had to hide-and-seek with those deportation guys. If people did not helping me, I'm not here today."

My mother scrutinized her hem.

After a minute I volunteered that before seeing a judge, he might try a lawyer.

He turned. "Since when did you become so afraid like your mother?"

I started to say that it wasn't a matter of fear, but he cut me off.

"What I need today," he said, "is a son."

My father and I spent the better part of the next day standing in lines at the immigration office. He did not get to speak to a judge, but with much persistence he managed to speak to a judge's clerk, who tried to persuade him that it was not her place to extend him advice. My father, though, shamelessly plied her with compliments and offers of free pancakes until she finally conceded that she personally doubted anything would happen to either Cedric or Booker.

"Especially if they're 'needed workers,'" she said, rubbing at the red marks her glasses left on her nose. She yawned. "Have you thought about sponsoring them to become permanent residents?"

Could he do that? My father was overjoyed. And what if he saw to it right away? Would she perhaps put in a good word with the judge?

She yawned again, her nostrils flaring. "Don't worry," she said. "They'll get a fair hearing."

My father returned jubilant. Booker and Cedric hailed him as their savior, their Buddha incarnate. He was like a father to them, they said; and laughing and clapping, they made him tell the story over and over, sorting over the details like jewels. And how old was the assistant judge? And what did she say?

That evening my father tipped the paperboy a dollar and bought a pot of mums for my mother, who suffered them to be placed on the dining room table. The next night he took us all out to dinner. Then on Saturday, Mona found a letter on my father's chair at the restaurant.

> Dear Mr. Chang,
>
> You are the grat boss. But, we do not like to trial, so will runing away now. Plese to excus us. People saying the law in America is fears like dragon. Here is only $140. We hope some day we can pay back the rest bale. You will getting intrest, as you diserving, so grat a boss you are. Thank you for every thing. In next life you will be burn in rich family, with no more pancaks.
>
> > Yours truley,
> > Booker + Cedric

In the weeks that followed my father went to the pancake house for crises, but otherwise hung around our house, fiddling idly with the sump pump and boiler in an effort, he said, to get ready for winter. It was as though he had gone into retirement, except that instead of moving South, he had moved to the basement. He even took to showering my mother with little attentions, and to calling her "old girl," and when we finally heard that the club had entertained all the applications it could for the year, he was so sympathetic that he seemed more disappointed than my mother.

II. In the American Society

Mrs. Lardner tempered the bad news with an invitation to a bon voyage "bash" she was throwing for a friend of hers who was going to Greece for six months.

"Do come," she urged. "You'll meet everyone, and then, you know, if things open up in the spring . . ." She waved her hands.

My mother wondered if it would be appropriate to show up at a party for someone they didn't know, but "the honest truth" was that this was an annual affair. "If it's not Greece, it's Antibes," sighed Mrs. Lardner. "We really just do it because his wife left him and his daughter doesn't speak to him, and poor Jeremy just feels so *unloved*."

She also invited Mona and me to the goings on, as "*demi*-guests" to keep Annie out of the champagne. I wasn't too keen on the idea, but before I could say anything, she had already thanked us for so generously agreeing to honor her with our presence.

"A pair of little princesses, you are!" she told us. "A pair of princesses!"

The party was that Sunday. On Saturday, my mother took my father out shopping for a suit. As it was the end of September, she insisted that he buy a worsted rather than a seersucker, even though it was only ten, rather than fifty percent off. My father protested that it was as hot out as ever, which was true—a thick Indian summer had cozied murderously up to us—but to no avail. Summer clothes, said my mother, were not properly worn after Labor Day.

The suit was unfortunately as extravagant in length as it was in price, which posed an additional quandary, since the tailor wouldn't be in until Monday. The salesgirl, though, found a way of tacking it up temporarily.

"Maybe this suit not fit me," fretted my father.

"Just don't take your jacket off," said the salesgirl.

He gave her a tip before they left, but when he got home refused to remove the price tag.

"I like to asking the tailor about the size," he insisted.

"You mean you're going to *wear* it and then return it?" Mona rolled her eyes.

"I didn't say I'm return it," said my father stiffly. "I like to asking the tailor, that's all."

The party started off swimmingly, except that most people were wearing bermudas or wrap skirts. Still, my parents carried on, sharing with great feeling the complaints about the heat. Of course my father tried to eat a cracker full of shallots and burnt himself in an attempt to help Mr. Lardner turn the coals of the barbeque; but on the whole he seemed to be doing all right. Not nearly so well as my mother, though, who had accepted an entire cupful of Mrs. Lardner's magic punch, and seemed indeed to be under some spell. As Mona and Annie skirmished over whether some boy in their class inhaled when he smoked, I watched my mother take off her shoes, laughing and laughing as a man with a beard regaled her with navy stories by the pool. Apparently he had been stationed in the Orient and remembered a few words of Chinese, which made my mother laugh still more. My father excused himself to go to the men's room then drifted back and weighed anchor at the hors d'oeuvres table, while my mother sailed on to a group of women, who tinkled at length over the clarity of her complexion. I dug out a book I had brought.

Just when I'd cracked the spine, though, Mrs. Lardner came by to bewail her shortage of servers. Her caterers were criminals, I agreed; and the next thing I knew I was handing out bits of marine life, making the rounds as amicably as I could.

"Here you go, Dad," I said when I got to the hors d'oeuvres table.

"Everything is fine," he said.

I hesitated to leave him alone; but then the man with the beard zeroed in on him, and though he talked of nothing but my mother, I thought it would be okay to get back to work. Just that moment, though, Jeremy Brothers lurched our way, an empty, albeit corked, wine bottle in hand. He was a slim, well-proportioned man, with a Roman nose and small eyes and a nice manly jaw that he allowed to hang agape.

"Hello," he said drunkenly. "Pleased to meet you."

"Pleased to meeting you," said my father.

"Right," said Jeremy. "Right. Listen. I have this bottle here, this most recalcitrant bottle. You see that it refuses to do my bidding. I bid it open sesame, please, and it does nothing." He pulled the cork out with his teeth, then turned the bottle upside down.

My father nodded.

"Would you have a word with it please?" said Jeremy. The man with the beard excused himself. "Would you please have a goddamned word with it?"

My father laughed uncomfortably.

"Ah!" Jeremy bowed a little. "Excuse me, excuse me, excuse me. You are not my man, not my man at all." He bowed again and started to leave, but then circled back. "Viticulture is not your forte, yes I can see that, see that plainly. But may I trouble you on another matter? Forget the damned bottle." He threw it into the pool, and winked at the people he splashed. "I have another matter. Do you speak Chinese?" My father said he did not, but Jeremy pulled out a handkerchief with some characters on it anyway, saying that his daughter had sent it from Hong Kong and that he thought the characters might be some secret message.

"Long life," said my father.

"But you haven't looked at it yet."

"I know what it says without looking." My father winked at me.

"You do?"

"Yes, I do."

"You're making fun of me, aren't you?"

"No, no, no," said my father, winking again.

"Who are you anyway?" said Jeremy.

His smile fading, my father shrugged.

"Who are you?"

My father shrugged again.

Jeremy began to roar. "This is my party, *my party,* and I've never seen you before in my life." My father backed up as Jeremy came toward him. *"Who are you? WHO ARE YOU?"*

Just as my father was going to step back into the pool, Mrs. Lardner came running up. Jeremy informed her that there was a man crashing his party.

"Nonsense," said Mrs. Lardner. "This is Ralph Chang, who I invited extra especially so he could meet you." She straightened the collar of Jeremy's peach-colored polo shirt for him.

"Yes, well we've had a chance to chat," said Jeremy.

She whispered in his ear; he mumbled something; she whispered something more.

"I do apologize," he said finally.

My father didn't say anything.

"I do." Jeremy seemed genuinely contrite. "Doubtless you've seen drunks before, haven't you? You must have them in China."

"Okay," said my father.

As Mrs. Lardner glided off, Jeremy clapped his arm over my father's shoulders. "You know, I really am quite sorry, quite sorry."

My father nodded.

"What can I do, how can I make it up to you?"

"No thank you."

"No, tell me, tell me," wheedled Jeremy. "Tickets to casino night?" My father shook his head. "You don't gamble. Dinner at Bartholomew's?" My father shook his head again. "You don't eat." Jeremy scratched his chin. "You know, my wife was like you. Old Annabelle could never let me make things up—never, never, never, never, never."

My father wriggled out from under his arm.

"How about sport clothes? You are rather overdressed, you know, excuse me for saying so. But here." He took off his polo shirt and folded it up. "You can have this with my most profound apologies." He ruffled his chest hairs with his free hand.

"No thank you," said my father.

"No, take it, take it. Accept my apologies." He thrust the shirt into my father's arms. "I'm so very sorry, so very sorry. Please, try it on."

Helplessly holding the shirt, my father searched the crowd for my mother.

"Here, I'll help you off with your coat."

My father froze.

Jeremy reached over and took his jacket off. "Milton's, one hundred twenty-five dollars reduced to one hundred twelve-fifty," he read. "What a bargain, what a bargain!"

"Please give it back," pleaded my father. "Please."

"Now for your shirt," ordered Jeremy.

Heads began to turn.

"Take off your shirt."

"I do not take orders like a servant," announced my father.

"Take off your shirt, or I'm going to throw this jacket right into the pool, just right into this little pool here." Jeremy held it over the water.

"Go ahead."

"One hundred twelve-fifty," taunted Jeremy. "One hundred twelve . . ."

My father flung the polo shirt into the water with such force that part of it bounced back up into the air like a fluorescent fountain. Then it settled into a soft heap on top of the water. My mother hurried up.

"You're a sport!" said Jeremy, suddenly breaking into a smile and slapping my father on the back. "You're a sport! I like that. A man with spirit, that's what you are. A man with panache. Allow me to return to you your jacket." He handed it back to my father. "Good value you got on that, good value."

My father hurled the coat into the pool too. "We're leaving," he said grimly. "Leaving!"

"Now, Ralphie," said Mrs. Lardner, bustling up; but my father was already stomping off.

"Get your sister," he told me. To my mother: "Get your shoes."

"That was *great*, Dad," said Mona as we walked down to the car. "You were *stupendous*."

"Way to show 'em," I said.

"What?" said my father offhandedly.

Although it was only just dusk, we were in a gulch, which made it hard to see anything except the gleam of his white shirt moving up the hill ahead of us.

"It was all my fault," began my mother.

"Forget it," said my father grandly. Then he said, "The only trouble is I left those keys in my jacket pocket."

"Oh *no*," said Mona.

"Oh no is right," said my mother.

"So we'll walk home," I said.

"But how're we going to get into the *house*," said Mona.

The noise of the party churned through the silence.

"Someone has to going back," said my father.

"Let's go to the pancake house first," suggested my mother. "We can wait there until the party is finished, and then call Mrs. Lardner."

Having all agreed that that was a good plan, we started walking again.

"God, just think," said Mona. "We're going to have to *dive* for them."

My father stopped a moment. We waited.

"You girls are good swimmers," he said finally. "Not like me."

Then his shirt started moving again, and we trooped up the hill after it, into the dark.

—1996

LONNY KANEKO

B. 1939

Lonny Kaneko, born in Seattle, Washington, writes short fiction, drama, and poetry. During World War II he and his family were interned at Minidoka, a detention camp for Japanese Americans in Idaho. The camp serves as the setting for "The Shoyu Kid," which contrasts typical children's play with the severity of life governed by military force. Kaneko's fiction and poetry, including Coming Home From Camp *(1986), has appeared in* Playboy *and various literary magazines. He has received a National Endowment for the Arts Fellowship in poetry. "The Shoyu Kid" was first published in* Amerasia Journal *and reprinted in the important collection of Chinese-American and Japanese-American writers* The Big Aiiieeeee! *(1991) edited by Jeffery Paul Chan, Frank Chin, Lawson Fusao Inada, and Shawn Wong.*

THE SHOYU KID

We were ready for him. The three of us were crouched in the vines expecting the Kid to come stumbling into the garden. Itchy was to my right trying to tell me about what he'd seen earlier in the morning. Something about the sun rising from the wrong direction. I was too busy looking for the Kid to pay much attention. Jackson was in front of Itchy, ready to close off the Kid's escape in case he should see us before we could jump him. He came this way every day. Usually when there was nothing else to do he would wander into the patch and sit down in the heat of the late morning sun and pull out a chocolate bar and eat it slowly so that by the time he finished his face and hands were streaked gooey brown. There was a dark lingering haze on the western horizon, and I wondered if it would rain.

"Here he comes."

"Shhh."

"Get your butt down. Shit, I think he heard us."

The Kid had stopped at the edge of the walk and was looking around. His dirty cotton bib coveralls billowed loosely over bare, unwashed feet. I couldn't see his eyes, but I knew they were watery. They always were. The Kid was always on the verge of crying. And he usually had his arms full of dog, his skinny weiner dog that Jackson nicknamed Kraut.

"Shutup."

The Kid stopped about six feet in front of Jackson, still too far away for Jackson to nab him. I heard him drawing the snot back into his nose. It was his trademark, that sniffing. He sounded like the old men who snuff tobacco. Itchy flattened his face in the dirt, and I did the same, holding my breath, trying not to inhale the dust that rose over the ground. It was already coating my tongue. The vines coiled around my right wrist and reached inside the back of my shirt.

We waited a long time. When I looked up, the Kid was gone.

"Hey, where'd he go?"

"I donno."

"That way. Around the building." Jackson was up and flying down the edge of the garden with Itchy and me not far behind. At the corner of the building, he pulled up, flattened himself against the wall and like a soldier in a war movie, peered around the corner. We pulled up behind him, puffing, and he turned and put a finger to his lips and inched an eye like a periscope around the corner. His body relaxed, and he turned back to us. "He's gone."

"Which way'd he go?"

"Maybe he turned up one of the rows."

So we ran half the length of the block, checking the walkways between the barracks to see if the Kid had turned up one of them. Nothing but a couple of girls the Kid's age trying to skip rope and Glenn Miller music from the window of one of the barracks. We skirted three old women, who, like old women, stood in the shade of the barracks talking. It was already too hot for them to be out weeding the gardens. Jackson always greeted the women smoothly.

"Good morning, obasan," and they in return flashed smiles, and as if on cue made some comment in Japanese about Ichiro and Hiroshi and Masao growing up to be fine lads. Jackson hated to be called Hiroshi and would make a face or thumb his nose as soon as they turned their backs, but today he was too puzzled about the Kid's disappearing to remember his ritual.

"Hey, let's try over there." Itchy was pointing to the large garage and storage area that stood at right angles to the rows of barracks. We ran across the road to the garage—I guess that's what it was because Furuta, the cop, used to leave his car there. Beyond the garage was a road that was part of the system that connected all of the blocks of barracks and beyond that was the fence that surrounded our whole camp. When we first arrived, soldiers used to march around the fence. In the distance were hills that stretched as far as we could see. The past few days the hills had been covered with sheep so white that the hills had blended with the clouds. But this morning the sheep were gone, leaving us alone in the middle of a wide saucer of gray, overgrazed rangeland.

"C'mon. The Kid must be behind the building." Itchy pulled at my arm.

"But we aren't supposed to go over there."

"You're chicken. There aren't any more soldiers patrolling that fence."

"Geez, I know that."

"Well, I'm going to look." Itchy took off and pressed up against the side of the garage as Jackson had done before. Jackson followed, crouching like a cat stalking prey. And I went too.

Itchy was already peering around the corner like an Indian from behind a tree, when his body went stiff. He motioned us back, but he stayed fixed at the corner for another minute; then he took off past us running as hard as he could. Jackson and I turned and ran too. Itchy turned the corner of the garage, cut across the street, zagged past the second row of barracks and cut into the walkway in front of the third, almost hitting the old women and stumbling over one of the girls with the rope. We followed as fast as we could. I heard a shout and a dog barking behind us and urged my palomino to even greater speeds, following Itchy's dust. At the end of the third barrack we cut down the middle of the block and slipped into the side door of the laundry room where Jackson slowed so suddenly I almost galloped over him.

Mrs. Furuta had her little girl in a cast iron laundry tub, giving her a bath, and Jackson as he always did, stopped to take a look at the girl's naked body. Not obviously. He just strolled past Mrs. Furuta, said "Good morning, is Joyce having a bath?" just as if he couldn't tell what was happening in front of his eyes, and Mrs. Furuta said in Japanese "Go. Get out of here. You aren't supposed to play here," and we turned and ran on through and out the back door. At the door Jackson stopped and gave Mrs. Furuta's bent back the finger.

Jackson circled the laundry building, peered in through the window to get another look, then went into a cowboy pose, his thumbs hooked into his pockets.

Itchy, who had run straight through the building, was waiting for us. "Is anybody following us?"

"Nyaa."

"Hey, Itchy, what were we running for?"

"Nothing."

"Nothing?"

"C'mon, what happened?"

"Did you see Joyce?" Itchy was changing the subject. "Little girls are sure funny to look at, aren't they?"

"Itchy, you act like you ain't never seen a naked girl before."

"Well, have you? I mean really seen one, Jackson? Seen what kind of prick they have?"

"They don't have one,"

"That's what I mean. Do you know what to do with it?"

"Everyone knows. You get this hard on, see, and . . ."

"Jackson, you got a hard on?" Itchy's face was tight.

"Yeah, don't you? You're supposed to."

"N-no."

"What are you, Itchy, some kind of queer or something. Don't you know you're supposed to have a hard on when you see a naked girl?" Jackson was getting wound up on his favorite subject. I sneaked a look at Jackson, and I think he was lying.

"Hey, Itchy, what'd you see?" I was still curious what we were running from. "Was the Kid back of the garage?"

"Kinda."

"What do you mean, kinda?"

"There was a soldier back there."

"A soldier? And the Kid?"

"He was there, too."

"Yeah?"

"And he had a chocolate bar."

"So that's where he gets them."

"Yeah."

"Maybe we can get some, too." Jackson was coming to life again. "Who was the soldier?"

"That red-headed one."

"What the hell was he doing way over here?" Jackson took great pains to sound like his older brother sometimes. "They don't patrol here any more. They're supposed to stay by the gate. Let's check it out tomorrow. Maybe he'll give us some too."

"Uh, no thanks."

"Why not, Itchy? Chicken?"

"Kinda."

"Whaddayou mean, Itchy? Shit, talk plain will you?" Jackson was leaning into Itchy.

"There's something strange about that guy. I mean that's the same red-headed soldier who used to stand there at the fence and point his gun at me like he was going to shoot."

I remembered that, too. So did Jackson. It was enough to make us nervous. "Well, how does the Kid do it? Maybe the guy's changed. Let's ask the Kid."

"Are you kidding? That snot-nosed brat. Makes me nervous to look at him, too."

I knew what Itchy meant. The Kid always had that heavy snot dripping from his nose. Like a perpetual cold. Except that the snot was the color of soy sauce. Jackson's older brother told him the reason the Kid had brown snot was because he used too much soy sauce, and it just dripped out of his nose. We all stopped using shoyu when we heard that.

The Kid used to follow us around all the time as if he were a pet. And Jackson would get him to bring food from the lunch line or steal pies. Then the Kid quit hanging around like he used to and he started showing up with the chocolate candy every now and then. His mother used to make him wear white shirts and polished shoes, but I guess the dust must have gotten to her, and she gave up. Later, I thought it was the chocolate that made the Kid's snot brown because it didn't used to be when he trailed after us.

"Ichirooo! Ichirooo!" It was Itchy's mother calling him for lunch so we decided to meet later at the clubhouse. Actually there was no house, just a place by the bridge over the irrigation ditch, on the far edge of the garden that we had marked with a couple of stolen signs. I was sure Itchy hadn't told us everything; so after he left, Jackson and I made a pact to be sure to get Itchy to spill what he had seen.

The sky was noticeably cloudier after lunch. A gray haze had drifted in front of the sun, but the heat had gotten physical, like a weight around my chest. I heard the shouting while I was eating lunch, and when I came out there was a crowd gathered behind our barrack. The kids were jumping up and down and cheering. The women were shouting and laughing. I looked for Itchy and Jackson but didn't see them, so I squeezed through to see what was going on. My cousin Aya's grandfather was scurrying between the hollyhocks, leaping awkwardly every now and then as if he were stepping on nails. He was a skinny old man whose feet seemed to be moving in two directions at once while his body was heading in a third. His arms, weighted by a heavy, blunt spade seemed to be confused about moving in a fourth direction. His khaki shirt was open and his ribbed cotton undershirt was stained by sweat and the flying dust. Suddenly a group of women and children along the sidewalk leaped almost in unison. "There he is!" "He's there!" "Get him!" "Kill him!" They were screaming and laughing at the same time and I saw something brown dart past them and head directly toward me. It stopped still for a moment, its eyes wide and staring blankly. It darted sharply to the left and headed straight for the Shoyu Kid, who was standing at the corner of the first barrack. He kicked out with his foot and jumped back at the same time, blinking wildly to keep back his tears, and almost falling over backward. Meantime, Oisan had figured out which direction the animal had gone and took a shortcut across a patch of hollyhocks and sunflowers, leaving them bent and broken. The spade arced over his head and clanged dully as it struck at the furry blur and banged against the base of the barrack instead.

"He's gone underneath!" someone next to me shouted.

"Did you see the size of that rat?"

"Is that what it is?" Jackson shouldered up beside me as everyone spread out and surrounded the barrack.

I tried peering into the hole through which the animal had entered and saw only the faint glow of daylight haloing the inky dark. I wondered how dark and frightening it must be to be trapped underneath a barrack with no way out.

"What are we going to do?"

"Hey, kid, get away from there." Someone was pulling me back.

"We can't just stand around here all day. It's too hot. Besides, at night it'd slip away."

"We've got to kill it."

The voices were insistent. "Kill it. Kill it." The old man looked bewildered. Somehow he had gotten started in the chase that now had ended with a colony of people laughing and rattling the base boards that both penned and protected the victim. We were a tribe readied for a primitive hunt.

Jackson came up with a solution, "Plug all the holes to the crawl space, Oisan, and then send the weiner dog in."

The old man's face lit up. "And then we can wait for it here at the hole where it entered, eh? Smart boy."

"But Oisan, it's not a rat." It was the Shoyu Kid. "I saw it, Oisan, and it was really scared."

The old man patted the Kid on the head, then wiped his hand unconsciously on his trouser leg. We took the Kid's dog and shoved him under the barrack anyway and waited for some sound or sign of movement. The Kid might have been right. It had been big as a rabbit when it stopped in front of me. After a while, the old man went up and put his eye to the hole, then he went to the crawl space door and unhooked it. We hung back as if the beast would come charging out. No sign. Not even the dog. A few people started drifting back to their homes, but a sizeable group still crowded around the old man, who hunched there on his heels, holding his spade ready like an executioner's ax. After a while he said, "Maybe it is a jack rabbit and it has a burrow under the barrack." Maybe calling it a jack rabbit was better than believing it was a rat that had just shimmied up into your bedroom.

Jackson tugged at my elbow and motioned to the Shoyu Kid. He was still standing at the corner where the rat had entered the building.

"Let's get him now."

And we casually worked our way over to the Kid.

"Was it a rat, Kid?"

"If it wasn't, what was it, Kid?"

He started to back away from us, but he knew it would be useless to run.

"You got any chocolate, Kid?"

"Hope your dog didn't get lost under there, Kid."

Then Jackson was close enough and was on him and swung him around the corner of the barrack before the Kid could yell and half carried him across the road and to the west side of the garage.

"Jeez, it's hot today." Itchy had seen us and came around the corner complaining.

Jackson smiled his John Wayne smile and took the Kid by the overall straps where the lapels should be and shoved the kid up against the side of the garage. "You'd better shape up and talk, Kid."

The Kid's face was twisted open and the tears were already rolling down his face. He seemed to have stopped breathing.

"Where'd you get your chocolate bars, Kid?"

No answer.

Again. This time I grabbed his other arm and twisted it up behind his back.

"C'mon, Kid, you better talk if you know what's good for you." Jackson's face was dead serious, his eyes narrowed into black flickering jets of hate. "We'll tear you limb from limb if you don't talk, Kid. We know you got them from the soldier, so you may as well speak up." He was the cavalry colonel threatening a turncoat Indian scout; he was a police interrogator breaking a burglar; he was an army intelligence officer ripping into a prisoner of war. His face was impassive. Perfect.

The Kid looked up, then bent his head moaning and sniffling snot, which now was a brown ribbon between his nose and lips.

Jackson took the Kid's other arm and started to give him an Indian burn, rubbing his palms tightly over the Kid's wrists until they turned pink. The Kid started to scream and his body slumped to the dirt so suddenly the arm I held slipped free. But still he hadn't admitted to anything. He was moaning for us to stop. The pain was getting to him. Jackson's face was suddenly animated. He lost his John Wayne pose and was beginning to enjoy his job.

"Listen, Kid," he continued, "we know the soldier gives you candy. We seen you with it every day. Why does he give it to you? C'mon. Speak up. Or we'll take it away from you next time. Every time." Then suddenly he changed his tactic. "You. You're a spy, aren't you Kid. Admit it. You give the soldier our military secrets."

The Kid started to say something about Mommy, but just then Jackson twisted the wrist again and it was bright red, shining brightly, a blood red band burning the surrounding grayish flesh of his arm. "We just," the Kid blurted, "we just play games."

The Kid slumped and sobbed great breaths.

"Let's pants him." Jackson reached for the Kid's grimy pants and I flipped open the flaps of the coverall suspenders. Jackson grabbed the cuffs and tugged.

"No." The Kid tried to cover up.

When Jackson tugged again the pants gave way around the Kid's hipless waist and bagged at his knees, the bib still covering him decently. "No," the Kid was saying, "I didn't do anything. I just played with his chimpo like he asked."

Jackson stopped, his mouth dropped open. "You what? You whore! Queer!" He was shouting "Queer! Queer!" and yanking at the pants at the same time and there staring at us with its single eye squinting in Jackson's face was a little white prick like a broken pencil between equally white but shapeless thighs. Jackson was immobilized, his face slack in surprise and Itchy moved away.

And then Jackson was at him again. "You played with the sonofabitch soldier? Goddam queer!" and Jackson's hands were fumbling for the Kid's prick and he was pulling as if he were going to pull it off and the Kid was convulsing on the ground, trying to roll away, his face smeared brown. Jackson's face was set, his eyes were distant, as if he were remembering the Kid standing there in front of him in white shirt and short pants, pie in hand, waiting for Jackson to pat him on the head for a job well done, or Jackson remembering how he would give the soldiers the finger as they marched around the fence, how he had made Itchy and me accompany him down to the gate one night to steal the hastily painted government signs. The Kid was a traitor to a lost cause and though he couldn't really blame the Kid, he didn't have to let him do it, either.

"I didn't do nothing, honest. I didn't." But I couldn't tell whether in his convulsions the Kid was crying or laughing.

Jackson stood up abruptly and looked at his hands. He wiped them on his pants. Then we heard it, "Geooooogie. Geooooogie." It was the Kid's mother.

When Jackson looked up, Itchy was already heading down the length of the garage, planning to come out onto the main street from the other end of the building. "You better not say nothing about this or we'll cut it off, Kid." It was pure Bogey. Just then Kraut came barking around the corner and Jackson grabbed my arm and pushed me stumbling after Itchy.

I stopped at the corner of the garage to catch my breath and kicked at the dog. The Kid was pulling up his pants, a lone figure almost as gray as the desert. Far to the west, the land met with a sky that now was even darker, more ominous than nightfall.

We met again after dinner. The sun had gone down, but there was still a strange glow in the horizon that had never before been there. The air had a definite odor to it. Jackson was sitting at the edge of the clubhouse, next to the irrigation ditch, looking out at the strange, lingering sunset. Itchy was off to one side, sitting by himself.

"What do you think it is? The end of the world?"

"Nyaa," said Jackson. "My brother says there's a fire out there."

"I saw it this morning, too. It looked like a sunrise when I got up to pee. But I knew the sun never comes up from over there."

"It's a fire, Itchy." Jackson's voice was soft, tired. "And they're fighting it out there. My brother went out this afternoon with a group of fathers to help. It'll be out pretty soon."

We sat there in silence and watched it glowing red, an ember that seemed to burn without flickering, without warmth.

Jackson was rubbing his palms into the dirt.

"Jeez," Itchy was talking more to himself than to Jackson or me, "I thought the guy was just taking a leak behind the garage. Goddam queers. Jeezus, everyone's queer." He stood up and threw a rock at the Off Limits sign we had taken. And missed. He picked up another and missed again. "Do you think the Kid will squeal?"

"Nyaa. Who cares." Jackson's voice was quiet, almost a curse. He threw a stone at the other sign. It hit the wood above the words MINIDOKA RELOCATION CENTER. Jackson continued to stare at the red glow, his face pale in the spotlight from the fence a hundred yards off. He was sitting very still, and his eyes were soft and wide like a rabbit's.

—1976

BOBBIE ANN MASON

B. 1940

Bobbie Ann Mason was born in Kentucky and attended Harpur College, the University of Kentucky, and the University of Connecticut, concentrating on journalism and English. Many of the works in her two collections, Shiloh and Other Stories *(1982) and* Love Life: Stories *(1988), explore the eccentricities of daily life in rural Kentucky. Her novel* In Country *(1985) was made into a film of the same name in 1989 and is widely appreciated for representing the Vietnam War from the perspective of a noncombatant U.S. woman. Three other novels round out her oeuvre,* Spence and Lila *(1988),*

Feather Crowns (1993), and The Girl Sleuth *(1995). Mason taught at Mansfield State College in Mansfield, Pennsylvania, before devoting herself full-time to writing. She currently lives in Kentucky.*

STATE CHAMPIONS

In 1952, when I was in the seventh grade, the Cuba Cubs were the state champions in high-school basketball. When the Cubs returned from the tournament in Lexington, a crowd greeted them at Eggner's Ferry bridge over Kentucky Lake, and a convoy fourteen miles long escorted them to the county seat. It was a cold day in March as twelve thousand people watched the Cubs ride around the courthouse square in convertibles. The mayor and other dignitaries made speeches. Willie Foster, the president of the Merit Clothing Company, gave the players and Coach Jack Story free suits from his factory. The coach, a chunky guy in a trench coat like a character in a forties movie, told the crowd, "I'm mighty glad we could bring back the big trophy." And All-Stater Howie Crittenden, the razzle-dazzle dribbler, said, "There are two things I'm proud of today. First, we won the tournament, and second, Mr. Story said we made him feel like a young mule."

The cheerleaders then climbed up onto the concrete seat sections of the Confederate monument and led a final fight yell.

Chick-a-lacka, chick-a-lacka chow, chow, chow
Boom-a-lacka, boom-a-lacka bow, wow, wow
Chick-a-lacka, boom-a-lacka, who are we?
Cuba High School, can't you see?

The next day the Cubs took off in the convertibles again, leading a motorcade around western Kentucky, visiting the schools in Sedalia, Mayfield, Farmington, Murray, Hardin, Benton, Sharpe, Reidland, Paducah, Kevil, La Center, Barlow, Wickliffe, Bardwell, Arlington, Clinton, Fulton, and Pilot Oak.

I remember the hoopla at the square that day, but at the time I felt a strange sort of distance, knowing that in another year another community would have its champions. I was twelve years old and going through a crisis, so I thought I had a wise understanding of the evanescence of victory.

But years later, in the seventies, in upstate New York, I met a man who surprised me by actually remembering the Cuba Cubs' championship. He was a Kentuckian, and although he was from the other side of the state, he had lasting memories of Howie Crittenden and Doodle Floyd. Howie was a great dribbler, he said. And Doodle had a windmill hook shot that had to be seen to be believed. The Cubs were inspired by the Harlem Globetrotters—Marques Haynes's ball-handling influenced Howie and Goose Tatum was Doodle's model. The Cuba Cubs, I was told, were, in fact, the most incredible success story in the history of Kentucky high-school basketball, and the reason was that they were such unlikely champions.

"Why, they were just a handful of country boys who could barely afford basketball shoes," the man told me in upstate New York.

"They were?" This was news to me.

"Yes. They were known as the Cinderella Cubs. One afternoon during the tournament, they were at Memorial Coliseum watching the Kentucky Wildcats practice. The Cubs weren't in uniform, but one of them called for a ball and dribbled it a few times and then canned a two-hand set shot from midcourt. Adolph Rupp happened to be watching. He's another Kentucky basketball legend—don't you know anything about Kentucky basketball? He rushed to the player at midcourt and demanded, 'How did you do that?' The boy just smiled. 'It was easy, Mr. Rupp,' he said. 'Ain't no wind in here.'"

Of course, that was not my image of the Cuba Cubs at all. I hadn't realized they were just a bunch of farm boys who got together behind the barn after school and shot baskets in the dirt, while the farmers around complained that the boys would never amount to anything. I hadn't known how Coach Jack Story had started them off in the seventh grade, coaching the daylights out of those kids until he made them believe they could be champions. To me, just entering junior high the year they won the tournament, the Cuba Cubs were the essence of glamour. Seeing them in the gym—standing tall in those glossy green satin uniforms, or racing down the court, leaping like deer—took my breath away. They had crew cuts and wore real basketball shoes. And the cheerleaders dressed smartly in Crayola-green corduroy circle skirts, saddle oxfords, and rolled-down socks. They had green corduroy jackets as well as green sweaters, with a *C* cutting through the symbol of a megaphone. They clapped their hands in rhythm and orchestrated their elbows in a little dance that in some way mimicked the Cubs as they herded the ball down the court. "Go, Cubs, Go!" "Fight, Cubs, Fight!" They did "Locomotive, locomotive, steam, steam, steam," and "Strawberry shortcake, huckleberry pie." We had pep rallies that were like revival services in tone and intent. The cheerleaders pirouetted and zoomed skyward in unison, their leaps straight and clean like jump shots. They whirled in their circle skirts, showing off their green tights underneath.

I never questioned the words of the yells, any more than I questioned the name Cuba Cubs. I didn't know what kind of cubs they were supposed to be—bear cubs or wildcats or foxes—but I never thought about it. I doubt if anyone did. It was the sound of the words that mattered, not the meaning. They were the Cubs. And that was it. Cuba was a tiny community with a couple of general stores, and its name is of doubtful origin, but local historians say that when the Cuba post office opened, in the late 1850s, the Ostend Manifesto had been in the news. This was a plan the United States had for getting control of the island of Cuba in order to expand the slave trade. The United States demanded that Spain either sell us Cuba at a fair price or surrender it outright. Perhaps the founding fathers of Cuba, Kentucky (old-time pronunciation: Cubie), were swayed by the fuss with Spain. Or maybe they just had romantic imaginations. In the Jackson Purchase, the western region of Kentucky and Tennessee that Andrew Jackson purchased from the Chickasaw Indians in 1818, there are other towns with faraway names: Moscow, Dublin, Kansas, Cadiz, Beulah, Paris, and Dresden.

The gymnasium where the Cuba Cubs practiced was the hub of the school. Their trophies gleamed in a glass display case near the entrance, between the principal's office and the gymnasium, and the enormous coal furnace that heated the gym hunched in a corner next to the bleachers. Several classrooms opened onto the gym floor, with the study hall at one end. The lower grades occupied a separate building, and in those grades we used an outhouse. But in junior high we had the privilege of using the indoor rest rooms, which also opened onto the gym. (The boys' room included a locker room for the team, but like the outhouses, the girls' room didn't even have private compartments.) The route from the study hall to the girls' room was dangerous. We had to walk through the gym, along the sidelines, under some basketball hoops. There were several baskets, so many players could practice their shots simultaneously. At recess and lunch, in addition to the Cuba Cubs, all the junior high boys used the gym, too, in frantic emulation of their heroes. On the way to the rest room you had to calculate quickly and carefully when you could run beneath a basket. The players pretended that they were oblivious of you, but just when you thought you were safe and could dash under the basket, they would hurl a ball out of nowhere, and the ball would fall on your head as you streaked by. Even though I was sort of a tomboy and liked to run—back in the fifth grade I could run as fast as most of the boys—I had no desire to play basketball. It was too violent.

Doodle Floyd himself bopped me on the head once, but I doubt if he remembers it.

The year of the championship was the year I got in trouble for running in the study hall. At lunch hour one day, Judy Howell and I decided to run the length of the gym as fast as we could, daring ourselves to run through the hailstorm of basketballs flying at us. We raced through the gym and kept on running, unable to slow down, finally skidding to a stop in the study hall. We were giggling because we had caught a glimpse of what one of the senior players was wearing under his green practice shorts (different from the satin show shorts they wore at the games), when Mr. Gilhorn, the history teacher, big as a buffalo, appeared before us and growled, "What do you young ladies think you're doing?"

I had on the tightest Levi's I owned. When they were newly washed and ironed, they fit snug. My mother had ironed a crease in them. I had on a cowboy shirt and a bandanna.

Mr. Gilhorn went on, "Now, girls, do we run in our own living rooms? Peggy, does your mama let you run in the house?"

"Yes," I said, staring at him confidently. "My mama always lets me run in the house." It was a lie, of course, but it was my habit to contradict whatever anybody assumed. If I was supposed to be a lady, then I would be a cowboy. The truth in this instance was that it had never occurred to me to run in our house. It was too small, and the floorboards were shaky. Therefore, I reasoned, my mother had never laid down the law about not running in the house.

Judy said, "We won't do it again." But I wouldn't promise.

"I know what would be good for you girls," said Mr. Gilhorn in a kindly, thoughtful tone, as if he had just had a great idea.

That meant the duckwalk. As punishment, Judy and I had to squat, grabbing our ankles, and duckwalk around the gym. We waddled, humiliated, with the basketballs beating on our heads and the players following our progress with loud quacks of derision.

"This was your fault," Judy claimed. She stopped speaking to me, which disappointed me because we had been playmates since the second grade. I admired her short blond curls and color-coordinated outfits. She had been to Detroit one summer.

During study-hall periods, we could hear the basketballs pounding the floor. We could tell when a player made a basket—that pause after the ball hit the backboard and sank luxuriously into the net before hitting the floor. I visited the library more often than necessary just to get a glimpse of the Cubs practicing as I passed the door to the gym. The library was a shelf at one end of the study hall, and it had a couple of hundred old books—mostly hand-me-downs from the Graves County Library, including outdated textbooks and even annuals from Kentucky colleges. That year I read some old American histories, and a biography of Benjamin Franklin, and the "Junior Miss" books. On the wainscoted walls of the study hall were gigantic framed pictures, four feet high, each composed of inset portraits of all the faculty members and the seniors of a specific year. They gazed down at us like kings and queens on playing cards. There was a year for each frame, and they dated all the way back to the early forties.

In junior high, we shared the study hall with the high-school students. The big room was drafty, and in the winter it was very cold. The boys were responsible for keeping the potbelly stove filled with coal from the coal pile outside, near where the school buses were parked. In grade school during the winter, I had worn long pants under my dresses—little starched print dresses with gathered skirts and puffed sleeves. But in junior high, the girls wore blue jeans, like the boys, except that we rolled them up almost to our knees. The Cuba Cubs wore Levi's and green basketball jackets, and the other high-school boys—the Future Farmers of America—wore bright-blue FFA jackets. Although the FFA jackets didn't have the status of the basketball jackets, they were beautiful. They were royal-blue corduroy, and on the back was an enormous gold eagle.

I had a crush on a freshman named Glenn in an FFA jacket. He helped manage the coal bucket in the study hall. Glenn didn't ride my bus. He lived in Dukedom, down across the Tennessee line. Glenn was one of the Cuba Cubs, but he wasn't one of the major Cubs—he was on the B team and didn't yet have a green jacket. But I admired his dribble, and his long legs could travel that floor like a bicycle. When I waited at the edge of the gym for my chance to bolt to the girls' room, I sometimes stood and watched him dribble. Then one day as I ran pell-mell to the rest room, his basketball hit me on the head and he called to me flirtatiously. "I got a claim on her," he yelled out to the world. If a boy had a claim on a girl, it meant she was his girlfriend. The next day in study hall he showed me an "eight-page novel." It was a Li'l Abner comic strip. In the eight-page novel, Li'l Abner peed on Daisy Mae. It was disgusting, but I was thrilled that he showed me the booklet.

"Hey, let me show you these hand signals," Glenn said a couple of days later, out on the playground. "In case you ever need them." He stuck his middle finger straight up and folded the others down. "That's single F," he said. Then he turned down his two middle fingers, leaving the forefinger and the little finger upright, like horns. "That's double F," he said confidently.

"Oh," I said. At first I thought he meant hand signals used in driving. Cars didn't have automatic turn signals then.

There were other hand signals. In basketball, the coach and the players exchanged finger gestures. The cheerleaders clapped us on to victory. And with lovers, lightly scraping the index finger on the other's palm meant "Do you want to?" and responding the same way meant "Yes." If you didn't know this and you held hands with a boy, you might inadvertently agree to do something that you had no intention of doing.

Seventh grade was the year we had a different teacher for each subject. Arithmetic became mathematics. The English teacher paddled Frances High and me for stealing Jack Reed's Milky Way from his desk. Jack Reed had even told us he didn't mind that we stole it, that he wanted us to have it. "The paddling didn't hurt," I said to him proudly. He was cute, but not as cute as Glenn, who had a crooked grin I thought was fascinating and later found reincarnated in Elvis. In the study hall I stood in front of the stove until my backside was soaked with heat. I slid my hands down the back of my legs and felt the sharp crease of my Levi's. I was in a perpetual state of excitement. It was 1952 and the Cuba Cubs were on their way to the championship.

Judy was still mad at me, but Glenn's sister Willowdean was in my class, and I contrived to go home with her one evening, riding her unfamiliar school bus along gravel roads far back into the country. Country kids didn't socialize much. To go home with someone and spend the night was a big event, strange and unpredictable. Glenn and Willowdean lived with three brothers and sisters in a small house surrounded by bare, stubbled tobacco fields. It was a wintry day, but Willowdean and I played outdoors, and I watched for Glenn to arrive.

He had stayed late at school, practicing ball, and the coach brought him home. Then he had his chores to do. At suppertime, when he came in with his father from milking, his mother handed him a tray of food. "Come on and go with me," he said to me. His Levi's were smudged with cow manure.

His mother said, "Make sure she's got her teeth."

"Have you got your teeth, Peggy?" Glenn asked me with a grin.

His mother swatted at him crossly. "I meant Bluma. You know who I meant."

Glenn motioned with a nod of his head for me to follow him, and we went to a tiny back room, where Glenn's grandmother sat in a wheelchair in a corner with a heater at her feet. She had dark hair and lips painted bright orange and a growth on her neck.

"She don't talk," Glenn said. "But she can hear."

The strange woman jerked her body in a spasm of acknowledgment as Glenn set the supper tray in her lap. He fished her teeth out of a glass of water and poked them in her mouth. She squeaked like a mouse.

"Are you hungry?" Glenn asked me as we left the room. "We've got chicken and dumplings tonight. That's my favorite."

That night I slept with Willowdean on a fold-out couch in the living room, with newspaper-wrapped hot bricks at our feet. We huddled under four quilts and whispered. I worked the conversation around to Glenn.

"He told me he liked you," Willowdean said.

I could feel myself blush. At supper, Glenn had tickled me under the table.

"I'll tell you a secret if you promise not to tell," she said.

"What?" I loved secrets and usually didn't tell them.

"Betty Jean's going to have a baby."

Willowdean's sister Betty Jean was a sophomore. On the school bus her boy-friend, Roy Matthews, had kept his arm around her during the whole journey, while she cracked gum and looked pleased with herself. That evening at the supper table, Glenn and his brothers had teased her about Roy's big feet.

Willowdean whispered now, "Did you see the way she ate supper? Like a pig. That's because she has to eat for two. She's got a baby in her stomach."

"What will she do?" I asked, scared. The warmth of the bricks was fading, and I knew it would be a freezing night.

"Her and Roy will live with us," said Willowdean. "That's what my sister Mary Lou did at first. But then she got mad and took the baby off and went to live with her husband's folks. She said they treated her better."

The high-school classes were small because kids dropped out, to have babies and farm. They seemed to disappear, like our calves going off to the slaughterhouse in the fall, and it was creepy.

"I don't want to have a baby and have to quit school," I said.

"You don't?" Willowdean was surprised. "What do you want to go to school for?"

I didn't answer. I didn't have the words handy. But she didn't seem to notice. She turned over and pulled the quilts with her. In the darkness, I could hear a mouse squeaking. But it wasn't a mouse. It was Willowdean's grandmother, in her cold room at the back of the house.

That winter, while basketball fever raged, a student teacher from Murray State College taught Kentucky history. She was very pretty and resembled a picture of Pocahontas in one of the library books. One time when she sat down, flipping her large gathered skirt up, I saw her panties. They were pink. She was so soft-spoken she didn't know how to make us behave well enough to accomplish any classwork. Daniel Boone's exploits were nothing, compared to Doodle Floyd's. During the week the Cubs were at the tournament, Pocahontas couldn't keep us quiet. The school was raising money for next year's basketball uniforms, and each class sold candy and cookies our mothers had made. Frequently there was a knock at the door, and some kids from another grade would be there selling Rice Krispies squares wrapped in waxed paper, or brownies, or sometimes divinity fudge. One day, while Pocahontas was reading to us about Daniel Boone and the Indians, and we were throwing paper wads, there was a sudden pounding on the door. I was hoping for divinity, and I had a nickel with me, but the door burst open and Judy Howell's sister Georgia was there, crying, "Judy Bee! Mama's had a wreck and Linda Faye's killed."

Judy flew out of the room. For one moment the class was quiet, and then it went into an uproar. Pocahontas didn't know what to do, so she gave us a pop quiz. The next day we learned that Judy's little sister Linda Faye, who was three years old, had been thrown into a ditch when her mother slammed into a truck that had pulled out in front of her. The seventh-grade class took up a collection for flowers. I was stunned by the news of death, for I had never known a child to die. I couldn't sleep, and my mind went over and over the accident, imagining the truck plowing into the car and Linda Faye pitching out the door or through the window. I created various scenes, ways it might have happened. I kept seeing her stretched out stiff on her side, like the dead animals I had seen on our farm. At school I was sleepy, and I escaped into daydreams about Glenn, imagining that I had gone to Lexington, too, to watch him in triumph as he was called in from the sidelines to replace Doodle Floyd, who had turned his ankle.

It was a sober, long walk from the study hall to the rest room. The gymnasium seemed desolate, without the Cubs practicing. I walked safely down the gym, remembering the time in the fourth grade when I was a flower girl in the court of the basketball queen. I had carried an Easter basket filled with flower petals down the center of the gym, scattering rose petals so the queen could step on them as she minced slowly toward her throne.

I was too scared to go to the funeral, and my parents didn't want me to go. My father had been traumatized by funerals in his childhood, and he didn't think they were a good idea. "The Howells live so far away," Mama said. "And it looks like snow."

That weekend, the tournament was on the radio, and I listened carefully, hoping to hear Glenn's name. The final game was crazy. In the background, the cheerleaders chanted:

Warren, Warren, he's our man
If he can't do it
Floyd can—
Floyd, Floyd, he's our man
If he can't do it
Crittenden can—

The announcer was saying, "Crittenden's dribbling has the crowd on its feet. It's a thrilling game! The Cubs were beaten twice by this same Louisville Manual squad during the season, but now they've just inched ahead. The Cubs pulled even at 39–39 when Floyd converted a charity flip, and then Warren sent them ahead for the first time with a short one-hander on Crittenden's pass. The crowd is going wild!"

Toward the end of the game, the whole Coliseum—except for a small Manual cheering section—was yelling, "Hey, hey, what do you say? It looks like Cuba all the way!"

As I listened to the excited announcer chatter about huddles and time-outs and driving jumps and hook shots, I forgot about Judy, but then on Sunday, when I went to the courthouse square to welcome the Cubs home, her sister's death struck me again like fresh news. Seeing so many people celebrating made me feel uncomfortable, as if the death of a child always went unnoticed, like a dead dog by the side of the road. It was a cold day, and I had to wear a dress because it was Sunday. I wanted to see Glenn. I had an audacious plan. I had been thinking about it all night. I wanted to give him a hug of congratulations. I would plant a big wet kiss on his cheek. I had seen a cheerleader do this to one of the players once after he made an unusual number of free throws. It was at a home game, one of the few I attended. I wanted to hug Glenn because it would be my answer to his announcement that he had a claim on me. It would be silent, without explanation, but he would know what it meant.

I managed to lose my parents in the throng and I headed for the east side of the square, where the dime store was. Suddenly I saw Judy, with her mother, in front of a shoe store. I knew the funeral had been the day before, but here they were at the square, in the middle of a celebration. Judy and her mother were still in their Sunday church clothes. Judy saw me. She looked straight at me, then turned away. I pretended I hadn't seen her, and I hurried to the center of the square, looking for Glenn.

But when I finally saw him up ahead, I stopped. He looked different. The Cubs, I learned later, had all gone to an Army surplus store and bought themselves pairs of Army fatigue pants and porkpie hats. Glenn looked unfamiliar in his basketball jacket—now he had one—and the baggy Army fatigues instead of his Levi's. The hat looked silly. I thought about Judy, and how her sister's death had occurred while Glenn was away playing basketball and buying new clothes. I wanted to tell him what it was like to be at home when such a terrible thing happened, but I couldn't, even though I saw him not thirty feet from me. As I hesitated, I saw his parents and Willowdean and one of his brothers crowd around him. Playfully, Willowdean knocked his hat off.

The tournament was over, but we were still wild with our victory. Senior play practice started then, and we never had classes in the afternoon because all the teachers were busy coaching the seniors on their lines in the play. Maybe they had dreams of Broadway. If the Cubs could go to the tournament, anything was possible. Judy returned to school, but everyone was afraid to speak to her. They whispered behind her back. And Judy began acting aloof, as though she had some secret knowledge that lifted her above us.

On one last cool day in early spring we had cleanup day, and there were no classes all day. Everyone was supposed to help clean the school grounds, picking up all the discarded candy wrappers and drink bottles. There was a bonfire, and instead of a plate lunch in the lunchroom—too much like the plain farm food we had to eat at home—we had hot dogs, boiled outside in a kettle over the fire. The fat hot dogs in the cold air tasted heavenly. They steamed like breath. Just as I finished my hot dog and drank the last of my RC (we had a choice between RC Cola and Orange Crush, and I liked to notice which people chose which—it seemed to divide people into categories), Judy came up behind me and whispered, "Come out there with me." She pointed toward the graveyard across the road.

I followed her, and as we walked between solemn rows of Wilcoxes and Ingrahams and Morrisons and Crittendens, the noise of the playground receded. Judy located a spot of earth, a little brown heap that was not grassed over, even though the dandelions had already come up and turned to fluff. She knelt beside the dirt pile, like a child in a sandbox, and fussed with a pot of artificial flowers. She straightened them and poked them down into the pot, as if they were real. As she worked tenderly but firmly with the flowers, she said, "Mama says Linda Faye will be waiting for us in heaven. That's her true home. The preacher said we should feel special, to think we have a member of our family all the way up in heaven."

That was sort of how I had felt about Glenn, going to Lexington to the basketball tournament, and I didn't know what to say. I couldn't say anything, for we weren't raised to say things that were heartfelt and gracious. Country kids didn't learn manners. Manners were too embarrassing. Learning not to run in the house was about the extent of what we knew about how to act. We didn't learn to congratulate people; we didn't wish people happy birthday. We didn't even address each other by name. And we didn't jump up and spontaneously hug someone for joy. Only cheerleaders claimed that talent. We didn't say we were sorry. We hid from view, in case we might be called on to make appropriate remarks, the way certain old folks in church were sometimes called on to pray. At Cuba School, there was one teacher who, for punishment, made her students write "I love you" five hundred times on the blackboard. "Love" was a dirty word, and I had seen it on the walls of the girls' rest room—blazing there in ugly red lipstick. In the eight-page novel Glenn had showed me, Li'l Abner said "I love you" to Daisy Mae.

—1990

CARSON McCULLERS

1917-1967

Carson McCullers was born in Columbus, Georgia, and went to New York City to study music and writing. Her first novel, The Heart Is a Lonely Hunter *(1940), was published when she was 23 to wide critical acclaim. Several of her subsequent novels—*Reflections in a Golden Eye *(1941),* A Member of the Wedding *(1946), and* The Ballad of the Sad Cafe *(1951)—have been made into successful films, in 1967, 1968, and 1991, respectively. Her* Collected Works *appeared in 1987. She has one volume of poetry,* Sweet as a Pickle and Clean as a Pig: Poems *(1964). Ill much of her life and bedridden from the age of 31, McCullers continued to write, dictating her stories and plays, many of which revolved around young female characters.*

LIKE THAT

Even if Sis is five years older than me and eighteen we used always to be closer and have more fun together than most sisters. It was about the same with us and our brother Dan, too. In the summer we'd all go swimming together. At nights in the wintertime maybe we'd sit around the fire in the living room and play three-handed bridge or Michigan, with everybody putting up a nickel or a dime to the winner. The three of us could have more fun by ourselves than any family I know. That's the way it always was before this.

Not that Sis was playing down to me, either. She's smart as she can be and has read more books than anybody I ever knew—even school teachers. But in High School she never did like to priss up flirty and ride around in cars with girls and pick up the boys and park at the drug store and all that sort of thing. When she wasn't reading she'd just like to play around with me and Dan. She wasn't too grown up to fuss over a chocolate bar in the refrigerator or to stay awake most of Christmas Eve night either, say, with excitement. In some ways it was like I was heaps older than her. Even when Tuck started coming around last summer I'd sometimes have to tell her she shouldn't wear ankle socks because they might go down town or she ought to pluck out her eyebrows above her nose like the other girls do.

In one more year, next June, Tuck'll be graduated from college. He's a lanky boy with an eager look to his face. At college he's so smart he has a free scholarship. He started coming to see Sis the last summer before this one, riding in his family's car when he could get it, wearing crispy white linen suits. He came a lot last year but this summer he came even more often—before he left he was coming around for Sis every night. Tuck's O.K.

It began getting different between Sis and me a while back, I guess, although I didn't notice it at the time. It was only after a certain night this summer that I had the idea that things maybe were bound to end like they are now.

It was late when I woke up that night. When I opened my eyes I thought for a minute it must be about dawn and I was scared when I saw Sis wasn't on her side of the bed. But it was only the moonlight that shone cool looking and white outside the window and made the oak leaves hanging down over the front yard pitch black and separate seeming. It was around the first of September, but I didn't feel hot looking at the moonlight. I pulled the sheet over me and let my eyes roam around the black shapes of the furniture in our room.

I'd waked up lots of times in the night this summer. You see Sis and I have always had this room together and when she would come in and turn on the light to find her nightgown or something it woke me. I liked it. In the summer when school was out I didn't have to get up early in the morning. We would lie and talk sometimes for a good while. I'd like to hear about the places she and Tuck had been or to laugh over different things. Lots of times before that night she had talked to me privately about Tuck just like I was her age—asking me if I thought she should have said this or that when he called and giving me a hug, maybe, after. Sis was really crazy about Tuck. Once she said to me: "He's so lovely—I never in the world thought I'd know anyone like him—"

We would talk about our brother too. Dan's seventeen years old and was planning to take the co-op course at Tech in the fall. Dan had gotten older by this summer. One night he came in at four o'clock and he'd been drinking. Dad sure had it in for him the next week. So he hiked out to the country and camped with some boys for a few days. He used to talk to me and Sis about Diesel motors and going away to South America and all that, but by this summer he was quiet and not saying much to anybody in the family. Dan's real tall and thin as a rail. He has bumps on his face now and is clumsy and not very good looking. At nights sometimes I know he wanders all around by himself, maybe going out beyond the city limits sign into the pine woods.

Thinking about such things I lay in bed wondering what time it was and when Sis would be in. That night after Sis and Dan had left I had gone down to the corner with some of the kids in the neighborhood to chunk rocks at the street light and try to kill a bat up there. At first I had the shivers and imagined it was a smallish bat like the kind in Dracula. When I saw it looked just like a moth I didn't care if they killed it or not. I was just sitting there on the curb drawing with a stick on the dusty street when Sis and Tuck rode by slowly in his car. She was sitting over very close to him. They weren't talking or smiling—just riding slowly down the street, sitting close, looking ahead. When they passed and I saw who it was I hollered to them. "Hey, Sis!" I yelled.

The car just went on slowly and nobody hollered back. I just stood there in the middle of the street feeling sort of silly with all the other kids standing around.

That hateful little old Bubber from down on the other block came up to me. "That your sister?" he asked.

I said yes.

"She sure was sitting up close to her beau," he said.

I was mad all over like I get sometimes. I hauled off and chunked all the rocks in my hand right at him. He's three years younger than me and it wasn't nice, but I couldn't stand him in the first place and he thought he was being so cute about Sis. He started holding his neck and bellering and I walked off and left them and went home and got ready to go to bed.

When I woke up I finally began to think of that too and old Bubber Davis was still in my mind when I heard the sound of a car coming up the block. Our room faces the street with only a short front yard between. You can see and hear everything from the sidewalk and the street. The car was creeping down in front of our walk and the light went slow and white along the walls of the room. It stopped on Sis's writing desk, showed up the books there plainly and half a pack of chewing gum. Then the room was dark and there was only the moonlight outside.

The door of the car didn't open but I could hear them talking. Him, that is. His voice was low and I couldn't catch any words but it was like he was explaining something over and over again. I never heard Sis say a word.

I was still awake when I heard the car door open. I heard her say, "Don't come out." And then the door slammed and there was the sound of her heels clopping up the walk, fast and light like she was running.

Mama met Sis in the hall outside our room. She had heard the front door close. She always listens out for Sis and Dan and never goes to sleep when they're still out. I sometimes wonder how she can just lie there in the dark for hours without going to sleep.

"It's one-thirty, Marian," she said. "You ought to get in before this."

Sis didn't say anything.

"Did you have a nice time?"

That's the way Mama is. I could imagine her standing there with her nightgown blowing out fat around her and her dead white legs and the blue veins showing, looking all messed up. Mama's nicer when she's dressed to go out.

"Yes, we had a grand time," Sis said. Her voice was funny—sort of like the piano in the gym at school, high and sharp on your ear. Funny.

Mama was asking more questions. Where did they go? Did they see anybody they knew? All that sort of stuff. That's the way she is.

"Goodnight," said Sis in that out of tune voice.

She opened the door of our room real quick and closed it. I started to let her know I was awake but changed my mind. Her breathing was quick and loud in the dark and she did not move at all. After a few minutes she felt in the closet for her nightgown and got in the bed. I could hear her crying.

"Did you and Tuck have a fuss?" I asked.

"No," she answered. Then she seemed to change her mind. "Yeah, it was a fuss."

There's one thing that gives me the creeps sure enough—and that's to hear somebody cry. "I wouldn't let it bother me. You'll be making up tomorrow."

The moon was coming in the window and I could see her moving her jaw from one side to the other and staring up at the ceiling. I watched her for a long time. The moonlight was cool looking and there was a wettish wind coming cool from the window. I moved over like I sometimes do to snug up with her, thinking maybe that would stop her from moving her jaw like that and crying.

She was trembling all over. When I got close to her she jumped like I'd pinched her and pushed me over quick and kicked my legs over. "Don't," she said. "Don't."

Maybe Sis had suddenly gone batty, I was thinking. She was crying in a slower and sharper way. I was a little scared and I got up to go to the bathroom a minute. While I was in there I looked out the window, down toward the corner where the street light is. I saw something then that I knew Sis would want to know about.

"You know what?" I asked when I was back in the bed.

She was lying over close to the edge as she could get, stiff. She didn't answer.

"Tuck's car is parked down by the street light. Just drawn up to the curb. I could tell because of the box and the two tires on the back. I could see it from the bathroom window."

She didn't even move.

"He must be just sitting out there. What ails you and him?"

She didn't say anything at all.

"I couldn't see him but he's probably just sitting there in the car under the street light. Just sitting there."

It was like she didn't care or had known it all along. She was as far over the edge of the bed as she could get, her legs stretched out stiff and her hands holding tight to the edge and her face on one arm.

She used always to sleep all sprawled over on my side so I'd have to push at her when it was hot and sometimes turn on the light and draw the line down the middle and show her how she really was on my side. I wouldn't have to draw any line that night, I was thinking. I felt bad. I looked out at the moonlight a long time before I could get to sleep again.

The next day was Sunday and Mama and Dad went in the morning to church because it was the anniversary of the day my aunt died. Sis said she didn't feel well and stayed in bed. Dan was out and I was there by myself so naturally I went into our room where Sis was. Her face was white as the pillow and there were circles under her eyes. There was a muscle jumping on one side of her jaw like she was chewing. She hadn't combed her hair and it flopped over the pillow, glinty red and messy and pretty. She was reading with a book held up close to her face. Her eyes didn't move when I came in. I don't think they even moved across the page.

It was roasting hot that morning. The sun made everything blazing outside so that it hurt your eyes to look. Our room was so hot that you could almost touch the air with your finger. But Sis had the sheet pulled up clear to her shoulders.

"Is Tuck coming today?" I asked. I was trying to say something that would make her look more cheerful.

"Gosh! Can't a person have *any* peace in this house?"

She never did used to say mean things like that out of a clear sky. Mean things, maybe, but not grouchy ones.

"Sure," I said. "Nobody's going to notice you."

I sat down and pretended to read. When footsteps passed on the street Sis would hold onto the book tighter and I knew she was listening hard as she could. I can tell between footsteps easy. I can even tell without looking if the person who passes is colored or not. Colored people mostly make a slurry sound between the steps. When the steps would pass Sis would loosen the hold on the book and bite at her mouth. It was the same way with passing cars.

I felt sorry for Sis. I decided then and there that I never would let any fuss with any boy make me feel or look like that. But I wanted Sis and me to get back like we'd always been. Sunday mornings are bad enough without having any other trouble.

"We fuss a lots less than most sisters do," I said. "And when we do it's all over quick, isn't it?"

She mumbled and kept staring at the same spot on the book.

"That's one good thing," I said.

She was moving her head slightly from side to side—over and over again, with her face not changing. "We never do have any real long fusses like Bubber Davis's two sisters have—"

"No." She answered like she wasn't thinking about what I'd said.

"Not one real one like that since I can remember."

In a minute she looked up the first time. "I remember one," she said suddenly.

"When?"

Her eyes looked green in the blackness under them and like they were nailing themselves into what they saw. "You had to stay in every afternoon for a week. It was a long time ago."

All of a sudden I remembered. I'd forgotten it for a long time. I hadn't wanted to remember. When she said that it came back to me all complete.

It was really a long time ago—when Sis was about thirteen. If I remember right I was mean and even more hardboiled than I am now. My aunt who I'd liked better than all my other aunts put together had had a dead baby and she had died. After the funeral Mama had told Sis and me about it. Always the things I've learned new and didn't like have made me mad—mad clean through and scared.

That wasn't what Sis was talking about, though. It was a few mornings after that when Sis started with what every big girl has each month, and of course I found out and was scared to death. Mama then explained to me about it and what she had to wear. I felt then like I'd felt about my aunt, only ten times worse. I felt different toward Sis, too, and was so mad I wanted to pitch into people and hit.

I never will forget it. Sis was standing in our room before the dresser mirror. When I remembered her face it was white like Sis's there on the pillow and with the circles under her eyes and the glinty hair to her shoulders—it was only younger.

I was sitting on the bed, biting hard at my knee. "It shows," I said. "It does too!"

She had on a sweater and a blue pleated skirt and she was so skinny all over that it did show a little.

"Anybody can tell. Right off the bat. Just to look at you anybody can tell."

Her face was white in the mirror and did not move.

"It looks terrible. I wouldn't ever ever be like that. It shows and everything."

She started crying then and told Mother and said she wasn't going back to school and such. She cried a long time. That's how ugly and hardboiled I used to be and am still sometimes. That's why I had to stay in the house every afternoon for a week a long time ago . . .

Tuck came by in his car that Sunday morning before dinner time. Sis got up and dressed in a hurry and didn't even put on any lipstick. She said they were going out to dinner. Nearly every Sunday all of us in the family stay together all day, so that was a little funny. They didn't get home until almost dark. The rest of us were sitting on the front porch drinking ice tea because of the heat when the car drove up again. After they got out of the car Dad, who had been in a very good mood all day, insisted Tuck stay for a glass of tea.

Tuck sat on the swing with Sis and he didn't lean back and his heels didn't rest on the floor—as though he was all ready to get up again. He kept changing the glass from one hand to the other and starting new conversations. He and Sis didn't look at each other except on the sly, and then it wasn't at all like they were crazy about each other. It was a funny look. Almost like they were afraid of something. Tuck left soon.

"Come sit by your Dad a minute, Puss," Dad said. Puss is a nickname he calls Sis when he feels in a specially good mood. He still likes to pet us.

She went and sat on the arm of his chair. She sat stiff like Tuck had, holding herself off a little so Dad's arm hardly went around her waist. Dad smoked his cigar and looked out on the front yard and the trees that were beginning to melt into the early dark.

"How's my big girl getting along these days?" Dad still likes to hug us up when he feels good and treat us, even Sis, like kids.

"O.K.," she said. She twisted a little bit like she wanted to get up and didn't know how to without hurting his feelings.

"You and Tuck have had a nice time together this summer, haven't you, Puss?"

"Yeah," she said. She had begun to see-saw her lower jaw again. I wanted to say something but couldn't think of anything.

Dad said: "He ought to be getting back to Tech about now, oughtn't he? When's he leaving?"

"Less than a week," she said. She got up so quick that she knocked Dad's cigar out of his fingers. She didn't even pick it up but flounced on through the front door. I could hear her half running to our room and the sound the door made when she shut it. I knew she was going to cry.

It was hotter than ever. The lawn was beginning to grow dark and the locusts were droning out so shrill and steady that you wouldn't notice them unless you thought to. The sky was bluish grey and the trees in the vacant lot across the street were dark. I kept on sitting on the front porch with Mama and Papa and hearing their low talk without listening to the words. I wanted to go in our room with Sis but I was afraid to. I wanted to ask her what was really the matter. Was hers and Tuck's fuss so bad as that or was it that she was so crazy about him that she was sad because he was leaving? For a minute I didn't think it was either one of those things. I wanted to know but I was scared to ask. I just sat there with the grown people. I never have been so lonesome as I was that night. If ever I think about being sad I just remember how it was then—sitting there looking at the long bluish shadows across the lawn and feeling like I was the only child left in the family and that Sis and Dan were dead or gone for good.

It's October now and the sun shines bright and a little cool and the sky is the color of my turquoise ring. Dan's gone to Tech. So has Tuck gone. It's not at all like it was last fall, though. I come in from High School (I go there now) and Sis maybe is just sitting by the window reading or writing to Tuck or just looking out. Sis is thinner and sometimes to me she looks in the face like a grown person. Or like, in a way, something has suddenly hurt her hard. We don't do any of the things we used to. It's good weather for fudge or for doing so many things. But no she just sits around or goes for long walks in the chilly late afternoon by herself. Sometimes she'll smile in a way that really gripes—like I was such a kid and all. Sometimes I want to cry or to hit her.

But I'm hardboiled as the next person. I can get along by myself if Sis or anybody else wants to. I'm glad I'm thirteen and still wear socks and can do what I please. I don't want to be any older if I'd get like Sis has. But I wouldn't. I wouldn't like any boy in the world as much as she does Tuck. I'd never let any boy or any thing make me act like she does. I'm not going to waste my time and try to make Sis be like she used to be. I get lonesome—sure—but I don't care. I know there's no way I can make myself stay thirteen all my life, but I know I'd never let anything really change me at all—no matter what it is.

I skate and ride my bike and go to the school football games every Friday. But when one afternoon the kids all got quiet in the gym basement and then started telling certain things—about being married and all—I got up quick so I wouldn't hear and went up and played basketball. And when some of the kids said they were going to start wearing lipstick and stockings I said I wouldn't for a hundred dollars.

You see I'd never be like Sis is now. I wouldn't. Anybody could know that if they knew me. I just wouldn't, that's all. I don't want to grow up—if it's like that.

—1936

HELENA MARÍA VIRAMONTES

B. 1954

Helena María Viramontes was born in East Los Angeles. After attending California State University, Los Angeles, she received an MFA from the University of California, Irvine, in 1984, and published her first book of stories, The Moths and Other Stories, *the next year. She has also edited, with Maria Herrera Sobek, two collections of essays:* Chicana (W)rites: On Word and Film *(1995) and* Chicana Creativity and Criticism: Charting New Frontiers in American Literature *(1988), both of which have been highly influential in gaining critical attention for the writings of contemporary Hispanics. In 1995, she published a novel,* Under the Feet of Jesus, *which traces the life of a young girl in a migrant family. Viramontes currently lives and teaches in Los Angeles.*

MISS CLAIROL

Arlene and Champ walk to K-Mart. The store is full of bins mounted with bargain buys from T-shirts to rubber sandals. They go to aisle 23, Cosmetics. Arlene, wearing bell bottom jeans two sizes too small, can't bend down to the Miss Clairol boxes, asks Champ.

—Which one amá—asks Champ, chewing her thumb nail.

—Shit, mija, I dunno,—Arlene smacks her gum, contemplating the decision.— Maybe I need a change, tú sabes. What do you think?—She holds up a few blond strands with black roots. Arlene has burned the softness of her hair with peroxide; her hair is stiff, breaks at the ends and she needs plenty of Aqua Net hairspray to tease and tame her ratted hair, then folds it back into a high lump behind her head. For the last few months she has been a platinum "Light Ash" blond, before that a Miss Clairol "Flame" redhead, before that Champ couldn't even identify the color—somewhere between orange and brown, a "Sun Bronze." The only way Champ knows her mother's true hair color is by her roots which, like death, inevitably rise to the truth.

—I hate it, tú sabes, when I can't decide.—Arlene is wearing a pink, strapless tube top. Her stomach spills over the hip hugger jeans. Spits the gum onto the floor.—Fuck it.—And Champ follows her to the rows of nailpolish, next to the Maybelline rack of make-up, across the false eyelashes that look like insects on display in clear, plastic boxes. Arlene pulls out a particular color of nailpolish, looks at the bottom of the bottle for the price, puts it back, gets another. She has a tattoo of purple XXX's on her left finger like a ring. She finally settles for a purple-blackish color, Ripe Plum, that Champ thinks looks like the color of Frankenstein's nails. She looks at her own stubby nails, chewed and gnawed.

Walking over to the eyeshadows, Arlene slowly slinks out another stick of gum from her back pocket, unwraps and crumbles the wrapper into a little ball, lets it drop on the floor. Smacks the gum.

—Grandpa Ham used to make chains with these gum wrappers—she says, toe-ing the wrapper on the floor with her rubber sandals, her toes dotted with old nailpolish.—He started one, tú sabes, that went from room to room. That was before he went nuts—she says, looking at the price of magenta eyeshadow.—Sabes que? What do you think?—lifting the eyeshadow to Champ.

—I dunno know—responds Champ, shrugging her shoulders the way she always does when she is listening to something else, her own heartbeat, what Gregorio said on the phone yesterday, shrugs her shoulders when Miss Smith says OFELIA, answer my question. She is too busy thinking of things people otherwise dismiss like parentheses, but sticks to her like gum, like a hole on a shirt, like a tattoo, and sometimes she wishes she weren't born with such adhesiveness. The chain went from room to room, round and round like a web, she remembers. That was before he went nuts.

—Champ. You listening? Or in lala land again?—Arlene has her arms akimbo on a fold of flesh, pissed.

—I said, I dunno know.—Champ whines back, still looking at the wrapper on the floor.

—Well you better learn, tú sabes, and fast too. Now think, will this color go good with Pancha's blue dress?—Pancha is Arlene's comadre. Since Arlene has a special date tonight, she lent Arlene her royal blue dress that she keeps in a plastic bag at the end of her closet. The dress is made of chiffon, with satin-like material under-lining, so that when Arlene first tried it on and strutted about, it crinkled sounds of elegance. The dress fits too tight. Her plump arms squeeze through, her hips breathe in and hold their breath, the seams do all they can to keep the body con-tained. But Arlene doesn't care as long as it sounds right.

—I think it will—Champ says, and Arlene is very pleased.

—Think so? So do I mija.—

They walk out the double doors and Champ never remembers her mother paying.

It is four in the afternoon, but already Arlene is preparing for the date. She scrubs the tub, Art Labo on the radio, drops crystals of Jean Nate into the running water, lemon scent rises with the steam. The bathroom door ajar, she removes her top and her breasts flop and sag, pushes her jeans down with some difficulty, kicks them off, and steps in the tub.

—Mija. MIJA—she yells.—Mija, give me a few bobby pins.—She is worried about her hair frizzing and so wants to pin it up.

Her mother's voice is faint because Champ is in the closet. There are piles of clothes on the floor, hangers thrown askew and tangled, shoes all piled up or thrown on the top shelf. Champ is looking for her mother's special dress. Pancha says every girl has one at the end of her closet.

—Goddamn it Champ.—

Amidst the dirty laundry, the black hole of the closet, she finds nothing.

—NOW—

—Alright, ALRIGHT. Cheeze amá, stop yelling—says Champ, and goes in the steamy bathroom, checks the drawers, hairbrushes jump out, rollers, strands of hair, rummages through bars of soap, combs, eyeshadows, finds nothing; pulls open another drawer, powder, empty bottles of oil, manicure scissors, kotex, dye instruc-tions crinkled and botched, finally, a few bobby pins.

After Arlene pins up her hair, she asks Champ,—Sabes que? Should I wear my hair up? Do I look good with it up?— Champ is sitting on the toilet.

—Yea, amá, you look real pretty.—

—Thanks mija—says Arlene, Sabes que? When you get older I'll show you how you can look just as pretty—and she puts her head back, relaxes, like the Calgon commercials.

Champ lays on her stomach, T.V. on to some variety show with pogo stick dancers dressed in outfits of stretchy material and glitter. She is wearing one of Gregorio's white T-shirts, the ones he washes and bleaches himself so that the whiteness is impeccable. It drapes over her deflated ten year old body like a dress. She is busy cutting out Miss Breck models from the stacks of old magazines Pancha found in the back of her mother's garage. Champ collects the array of honey colored haired women, puts them in a shoe box with all her other special things.

Arlene is in the bathroom, wrapped in a towel. She has painted her eyebrows so that the two are arched and even, penciled thin and high. The magenta shades her eyelids. The towel slips, reveals one nipple blind from a cigarette burn, a date to forget. She rewraps the towel, likes her reflection, turns to her profile for additional inspection. She feels good, turns up the radio to . . . your love. For your loveeeee, I will do anything, I will do anything, forrr your love. For your kiss . . .

Champ looks on. From the open bathroom door, she can see Arlene, anticipation burning like a cigarette from her lips, sliding her shoulders to the ahhhh ahhhhh, and pouting her lips until the song ends. And Champ likes her mother that way.

Arlene carefully stretches black eyeliner, like a fallen question mark, outlines each eye. The work is delicate, her hand trembles cautiously, stops the process to review the face with each line. Arlene the mirror is not Arlene the face who has worn too many relationships, gotten too little sleep. The last touch is the chalky, beige lipstick.

By the time she is finished, her ashtray is full of cigarette butts, Champ's variety show is over, and Jackie Gleason's dancing girls come on to make kaleidoscope patterns with their long legs and arms. Gregorio is still not home, and Champ goes over to the window, checks the houses, the streets, corners, roams the sky with her eyes.

Arlene sits on the toilet, stretches up her nylons, clips them to her girdle. She feels good thinking about the way he will unsnap her nylons, and she will unroll them slowly, point her toes when she does.

Champ opens a can of Campbell soup, finds a perfect pot in the middle of a stack of dishes, pulls it out to the threatening rumbling of the tower. She washes it out, pours the contents of the red can, turns the knob. After it boils, she puts the pot on the sink for it to cool down. She searches for a spoon.

Arlene is romantic. When Champ begins her period, she will tell her things that only women can know. She will tell her about the first time she made love with a boy, her awkwardness and shyness forcing them to go under the house, where the cool, refined soil made a soft mattress. How she closed her eyes and wondered what to expect, or how the penis was the softest skin she had ever felt against her, how it tickled her, searched for a place to connect. She was eleven and his name was Harry.

She will not not tell Champ that her first fuck was a guy named Puppet who ejaculated prematurely, at the sight of her apricot vagina, so plump and fuzzy.—Pendejo—she said—you got it all over me.—She rubbed the gooey substance off her legs, her belly in disgust. Ran home to tell Rat and Pancha, her mouth open with laughter.

Arlene powder puffs under her arms, between her breasts, tilts a bottle of *Love Cries* perfume and dabs behind her ears, neck and breasts for those tight caressing songs which permit them to grind their bodies together until she can feel a bulge in his pants and she knows she's in for the night.

Jackie Gleason is a bartender in a saloon. He wears a black bow tie, a white apron, and is polishing a glass. Champ is watching him, sitting in the radius of the gray light, eating her soup from the pot.

Arlene is a romantic. She will dance until Pancha's dress turns a different color, dance until her hair becomes undone, her hips jiggering and quaking beneath a new pair of hosiery, her mascara shadowing under her eyes from the perspiration of the ritual, dance spinning herself into Miss Clairol, and stopping only when it is time to return to the sewing factory, time to wait out the next date, time to change hair color. Time to remember or to forget.

Champ sees Arlene from the window. She can almost hear Arlene's nylons rubbing against one another, hear the crinkling sound of satin when she gets in the blue and white shark-finned Dodge. Champ yells goodbye. It all sounds so right to Arlene who is too busy cranking up the window to hear her daughter.

—1987

RICHARD WRIGHT

1908-1960

Richard Wright was born in Natchez, Mississippi, lived in New York City and Chicago, and died in Paris. Wright was among a generation of expatriate black artists who migrated to Europe after World War II because he felt racism was less a negative factor in his life and career there. The autobiographical narratives Black Boy *(1945) and* American Hunger *(1977) detail the oppressive social and economic power of white supremacy based on the experiences of his youth and early adulthood in Chicago. Wright's intellectual range spanned fiction and political writing. His involvement with the Communist Party in the 1930s led Wright to critique communism's limited engagement with issues of race in* Native Son *(1940), his most influential novel which chronicled the doomed path of Bigger Thomas, an impoverished urban black youth. Although he is most known for his depiction and indictment of racial injustice in the years before the black power movement of the 1950s and '60s, Wright consistently presented scenarios of the interrelation of race and gender. His other publications include* Uncle Tom's Children *(1938),* The Outsider *(1953),* The Long Dream *(1958), and* Eight Men *(1961).*

THE MAN WHO WAS ALMOST A MAN

Dave struck out across the fields, looking homeward through paling light. Whut's the use talkin wid em niggers in the field? Anyhow, his mother was putting supper on the table. Them niggers can't understan nothing. One of these days he was going to get a gun and practice shooting, then they couldn't talk to him as though he were a little boy. He slowed, looking at the ground. Shucks, Ah ain scareda them even ef they are biggern me! Aw, Ah know whut Ahma do. Ahm going by ol Joe's sto n git that Sears Roebuck catlog n look at them guns. Mebbe Ma will lemme buy one when she gits mah pay from ol man Hawkins. Ahma beg her t gimme some money. Ahm ol ernough to hava gun. Ahm seventeen. Almost a man. He strode, feeling his long loose-jointed limbs. Shucks, a man oughta hava little gun aftah he done worked hard all day.

He came in sight of Joe's store. A yellow lantern glowed on the front porch. He mounted steps and went through the screen door, hearing it bang behind him. There was a strong smell of coal oil and mackerel fish. He felt very confident until he saw fat Joe walk in through the rear door, then his courage began to ooze.

"Howdy, Dave! Whutcha want?"

"How yuh, Mistah Joe? Aw, Ah don wanna buy nothing. Ah jus wanted t see ef yuhd lemme look at tha catlog erwhile."

"Sure! You wanna see it here?"

"Nawsuh. Ah wants t take it home wid me. Ah'll bring it back termorrow when Ah come in from the fiels."

"You plannin on buying something?"

"Yessuh."

"Your ma lettin you have your own money now?"

"Shucks. Mistah Joe, Ahm gittin t be a man like anybody else!"

Joe laughed and wiped his greasy white face with a red bandanna.

"Whut you plannin on buyin?"

Dave looked at the floor, scratched his head, scratched his thigh, and smiled. Then he looked up shyly.

"Ah'll tell yuh, Mistah Joe, ef yuh promise yuh won't tell."

"I promise."

"Waal, Ahma buy a gun."

"A gun? What you want with a gun?"

"Ah wanna keep it."

"You ain't nothing but a boy. You don't need a gun."

"Aw, lemme have the catlog, Mistah Joe. Ah'll bring it back."

Joe walked through the rear door. Dave was elated. He looked around at barrels of sugar and flour. He heard Joe coming back. He craned his neck to see if he were bringing the book. Yeah, he's got it. Gawddog, he's got it!

"Here, but be sure you bring it back. It's the only one I got."

"Sho, Mistah Joe."

"Say, if you wanna buy a gun, why don't you buy one from me? I gotta gun to sell."

"Will it shoot?"

"Sure it'll shoot."

"Whut kind is it?"

"Oh, it's kinda old . . . a left-hand Wheeler. A pistol. A big one."

"Is it got bullets in it?"

"It's loaded."

"Kin Ah see it?"

"Where's your money?"

"Whut yuh wan fer it?"

"I'll let you have it for two dollars."

"Just two dollahs? Shucks, Ah could buy tha when Ah git mah pay."

"I'll have it here when you want it."

"Awright, suh. Ah be in fer it."

He went through the door, hearing it slam again behind him. Ahma git some money from Ma n buy me a gun! Only two dollahs! He tucked the thick catalogue under his arm and hurried.

"Where yuh been, boy?" His mother held a steaming dish of black-eyed peas.

"Aw, Ma, Ah jus stopped down the road t talk wid the boys."

"Yuh know bettah t keep suppah waitin."

He sat down, resting the catalogue on the edge of the table.

"Yuh git up from there and git to the well n wash yosef! Ah ain feedin no hogs in mah house!"

She grabbed his shoulder and pushed him. He stumbled out of the room, then came back to get the catalogue.

"Whut this?"

"Aw, Ma, it's jusa catlog."

"Who yuh git it from?"

"From Joe, down at the sto."

"Waal, thas good. We kin use it in the outhouse."

"Naw, Ma." He grabbed for it. "Gimme ma catlog, Ma."

She held onto it and glared at him.

"Quit hollerin at me! Whut's wrong wid yuh? Yuh crazy?"

"But Ma, please. It ain mine! It's Joe's! He tol me t bring it back t im termorrow."

She gave up the book. He stumbled down the back steps, hugging the thick book under his arm. When he had splashed water on his face and hands, he groped back to the kitchen and fumbled in a corner for the towel. He bumped into a chair; it clattered to the floor. The catalogue sprawled at his feet. When he had dried his eyes he snatched up the book and held it again under his arm. His mother stood watching him.

"Now, ef yuh gonna act a fool over that ol book, Ah'll take it n burn it up."

"Naw, Ma, please."

"Waal, set down n be still!"

He sat down and drew the oil lamp close. He thumbed page after page, unaware of the food his mother set on the table. His father came in. Then his small brother.

"Whutcha got there, Dave?" his father asked.

"Jusa catlog," he answered, not looking up.

"Yeah, here they is!" His eyes glowed at blue-and-black revolvers. He glanced up, feeling sudden guilt. His father was watching him. He eased the book under the table and rested it on his knees. After the blessing was asked, he ate. He scooped up peas and swallowed fat meat without chewing. Buttermilk helped to wash it down. He did not want to mention money before his father. He would do much better by cornering his mother when she was alone. He looked at his father uneasily out of the edge of his eye.

"Boy, how come yuh don quit foolin wid tha book n eat yo suppah?"

"Yessuh."

"How you n ol man Hawkins gitten erlong?"

"Suh?"

"Can't yuh hear? Why don yuh lissen? Ah ast yu how wuz yuh n ol man Hawkins gittin erlong?"

"Oh, swell, Pa. Ah plows mo lan than anybody over there."

"Waal, yuh oughta keep yo mind on what yuh doin."

"Yessuh."

He poured his plate full of molasses and sopped it up slowly with a chunk of cornbread. When his father and brother had left the kitchen, he still sat and looked again at the guns in the catalogue, longing to muster courage enough to present his case to his mother. Lawd, ef Ah only had tha pretty one! He could almost feel the slickness of the weapon with his fingers. If he had a gun like that he would polish it and keep it shining so it would never rust! N Ah'd keep it loaded, by Gawd!

"Ma?" His voice was hesitant.

"Hunh?"

"Ol man Hawkins give yuh mah money yit?"

"Yeah, but ain no usa yuh thinking bout throwin nona it erway. Ahm keeping tha money sos yuh kin have cloes t go to school this winter."

He rose and went to her side with the open catalogue in his palms. She was washing dishes, her head bent low over a pan. Shyly he raised the book. When he spoke, his voice was husky, faint.

"Ma, Gawd knows Ah wans one of these."

"One of whut?" she asked, not raising her eyes.

"One of these," he said again, not daring even to point. She glanced up at the page, then at him with wide eyes.

"Nigger, is yuh gone plumb crazy?"

"Aw, Ma—"

"Git outta here! Don yuh talk t me bout no gun! Yuh a fool!"

"Ma, Ah kin buy one fer two dollahs."

"Not ef Ah knows it, yuh ain!"

"But yuh promised me one—"

"Ah don care what Ah promised! Yuh ain nothing but a boy yit!"

"Ma, ef yuh lemme buy one Ah'll *never* ast yuh fer nothing no mo."

"Ah tol yuh t git outta here! Yuh ain gonna toucha penny of tha money fer no gun! Thas how come Ah has Mistah Hawkins t pay yo wages t me, cause Ah knows yuh ain got no sense."

"But, Ma, we needa gun. Pa ain got no gun. We needa gun in the house. Yuh kin never tell whut might happen."

"Now don yuh try to maka fool outta me, boy! Ef we did hava gun, yuh wouldn't have it!"

He laid the catalogue down and slipped his arm around her waist.

"Aw, Ma, Ah done worked hard alla summer n ain ast yuh fer nothing, is Ah, now?"

"Thas what yuh spose t do!"

"But Ma, Ah wans a gun. Yuh kin lemme have two dollahs outta mah money. Please, Ma. I kin give it to Pa . . . Please, Ma! Ah loves yuh, Ma!"

When she spoke her voice came soft and low.

"What yu wan wida gun, Dave? Yuh don need no gun. Yuh'll git in trouble. N ef yo pa jus thought Ah let yuh have money t buy a gun he'd hava fit."

"Ah'll hide it, Ma. It ain but two dollahs."

"Lawd, chil, whut's wrong wid yuh?"

"Ain nothin wrong, Ma. Ahm almos a man now. Ah wans a gun."

"Who gonna sell yuh a gun?"

"Ol Joe at the sto."

"N it don cos but two dollahs?"

"Thas all, Ma. Jus two dollahs. Please, Ma."

She was stacking the plates away; her hands moved slowly, reflectively. Dave kept an anxious silence. Finally, she turned to him.

"Ah'll let yuh git tha gun ef yuh promise me one thing."

"What's tha, Ma?"

"Yuh bring it straight back t me, yuh hear? It be fer Pa."

"Yessum! Lemme go now, Ma."

She stooped, turned slightly to one side, raised the hem of her dress, rolled down the top of her stocking, and came up with a slender wad of bills.

"Here," she said. "Lawd knows yuh don need no gun. But yer pa does. Yuh bring it right back t me, yuh hear? Ahma put it up. Now ef yuh don, Ahma have yuh pa lick yuh so hard yuh won fergit it."

"Yessum."

He took the money, ran down the steps, and across the yard.

"Dave! Yuuuuuh Daaaaave!"

He heard, but he was not going to stop now. "Naw, Lawd!"

The first movement he made the following morning was to reach under his pillow for the gun. In the gray light of dawn he held it loosely, feeling a sense of power. Could kill a man with a gun like this. Kill anybody, black or white. And if he were holding his gun in his hand, nobody could run over him; they would have to respect him. It was a big gun, with a long barrel and a heavy handle. He raised and lowered it in his hand, marveling at its weight.

He had not come straight home with it as his mother had asked; instead he had stayed out in the fields, holding the weapon in his hand, aiming it now and then at some imaginary foe. But he had not fired it; he had been afraid that his father might hear. Also he was not sure he knew how to fire it.

To avoid surrendering the pistol he had not come into the house until he knew that they were all asleep. When his mother had uptoed to his bedside late that night and demanded the gun, he had first played possum; then he had told her that the gun was hidden outdoors, that he would bring it to her in the morning. Now he lay turning it slowly in his hands. He broke it, took out the cartridges, felt them, and then put them back.

He slid out of bed, got a long strip of old flannel from a trunk, wrapped the gun in it, and tied it to his naked thigh while it was still loaded. He did not go in to breakfast. Even though it was not yet daylight, he started for Jim Hawkins' plantation. Just as the sun was rising he reached the barns where the mules and plows were kept.

"Hey! That you, Dave?"

He turned. Jim Hawkins stood eyeing him suspiciously.

"What're yuh doing here so early?"

"Ah didn't know Ah wuz gittin up so early, Mistah Hawkins. Ah wuz fixin t hitch up ol Jenny n take her t the fiels."

"Good. Since you're so early, how about plowing that stretch down by the woods?"

"Suits me, Mistah Hawkins."

"O.K. Go to it!"

He hitched Jenny to a plow and started across the fields. Hot dog! This was just what he wanted. If he could get down by the woods, he could shoot his gun and nobody would hear. He walked behind the plow, hearing the traces creaking, feeling the gun tied tight to his thigh.

When he reached the woods, he plowed two whole rows before he decided to take out the gun. Finally, he stopped, looked in all directions, then untied the gun and held it in his hand. He turned to the mule and smiled.

"Know whut this is, Jenny? Naw, yuh wouldn know! Yuhs jusa ol mule! Anyhow, this is a gun, n it kin shoot, by Gawd!"

He held the gun at arm's length. Whut t hell, Ahma shoot this thing! He looked at Jenny again.

"Lissen here, Jenny! When Ah pull this ol trigger, Ah don wan yuh t run n acka fool now!"

Jenny stood with head down, her short ears pricked straight. Dave walked off about twenty feet, held the gun far out from him at arm's length, and turned his head. Hell, he told himself, Ah ain afraid. The gun felt loose in his fingers; he waved it wildly for a moment. Then he shut his eyes and tightened his forefinger. Bloom! A report half deafened him and he thought his right hand was torn from his arm. He heard Jenny whinnying and galloping over the field, and he found himself on his knees, squeezing his fingers hard between his legs. His hand was numb; he jammed it into his mouth, trying to warm it, trying to stop the pain. The gun lay at his feet. He did not quite know what had happened. He stood up and stared at the gun as though it were a living thing. He gritted his teeth and kicked the gun. Yuh almos broke mah arm! He turned to look for Jenny; she was far over the fields, tossing her head and kicking wildly.

"Hol on there, ol mule!"

When he caught up with her she stood trembling, walling her big white eyes at him. The plow was far away; the traces had broken. Then Dave stopped short, looking, not believing. Jenny was bleeding. Her left side was red and wet with blood. He went closer. Lawd, have mercy! Wondah did Ah shoot this mule? He grabbed for Jenny's mane. She flinched, snorted, whirled, tossing her head.

"Hol on now! Hol on."

Then he saw the hole in Jenny's side, right between the ribs. It was round, wet, red. A crimson stream streaked down the front leg, flowing fast. Good Gawd! Ah wuzn't shootin at tha mule. He felt panic. He knew he had to stop that blood, or Jenny would bleed to death. He had never seen so much blood in all his life. He chased the mule for half a mile, trying to catch her. Finally she stopped, breathing hard, stumpy tail half arched. He caught her mane and led her back to where the plow and gun lay. Then he stopped and grabbed handfuls of damp black earth and tried to plug the bullet hole. Jenny shuddered, whinnied, and broke from him.

"Hol on! Hol on now!"

He tried to plug it again, but blood came anyhow. His fingers were hot and sticky. He rubbed dirt into his palms, trying to dry them. Then again he attempted to plug the bullet hole, but Jenny shied away, kicking her heels high. He stood helpless. He had to do something. He ran at Jenny; she dodged him. He watched a red stream of blood flow down Jenny's leg and form a bright pool at her feet.

"Jenny . . . Jenny," he called weakly.

His lips trembled. She's bleeding t death! He looked in the direction of home, wanting to go back, wanting to get help. But he saw the pistol lying in the damp black clay. He had a queer feeling that if he only did something, this would not be; Jenny would not be there bleeding to death.

When he went to her this time, she did not move. She stood with sleepy, dreamy eyes; and when he touched her she gave a low-pitched whinny and knelt to the ground, her front knees slopping in blood.

"Jenny . . . Jenny . . ." he whispered.

For a long time she held her neck erect; then her head sank, slowly. Her ribs swelled with a mighty heave and she went over.

Dave's stomach felt empty, very empty. He picked up the gun and held it gingerly between his thumb and forefinger. He buried it at the foot of a tree. He took a stick and tried to cover the pool of blood with dirt—but what was the use? There was Jenny lying with her mouth open and her eyes walled and glassy. He could not tell Jim Hawkins he had shot his mule. But he had to tell something. Yeah, Ah'll tell em Jenny started gittin wil n fell on the joint of the plow. . . . But that would hardly happen to a mule. He walked across the field slowly, head down.

It was sunset. Two of Jim Hawkins' men were over near the edge of the woods digging a hole in which to bury Jenny. Dave was surrounded by a knot of people, all of whom were looking down at the dead mule.

"I don't see how in the world it happened," said Jim Hawkins for the tenth time.

The crowd parted and Dave's mother, father, and small brother pushed into the center.

"Where Dave?" his mother called.

"There he is," said Jim Hawkins.

His mother grabbed him.

"Whut happened, Dave? Whut yuh done?"

"Nothin."

"C mon, boy, talk," his father said.

Dave took a deep breath and told the story he knew nobody believed.

"Waal," he drawled. "Ah brung ol Jenny down here sos Ah could do mah plowin. Ah plowed bout two rows, just like yuh see." He stopped and pointed at the long rows of upturned earth. "Then somethin musta been wrong wid ol Jenny. She wouldn ack right a-tall. She started snortin n kickin her heels. Ah tried t hol her, but she pulled erway, rearin n goin in. Then when the point of the plow was stickin up in the air, she swung erroun n twisted herself back on it . . . She stuck herself n started t bleed. N fo Ah could do anything, she wuz dead."

"Did you ever hear of anything like that in all of your life?" asked Jim Hawkins.

There were white and black standing in the crowd. They murmured. Dave's mother came close to him and looked hard into his face. "Tell the truth, Dave," she said.

"Looks like a bullet hole to me," said one man.

"Dave, whut yuh do wid the gun?" his mother asked.

The crowd surged in, looking at him. He jammed his hands into his pockets, shook his head slowly from left to right, and backed away. His eyes were wide and painful.

"Did he hava gun?" asked Jim Hawkins.

"By Gawd, Ah tol yuh tha wuz a gun wound," said a man, slapping his thigh.

His father caught his shoulders and shook him till his teeth rattled.

"Tell whut happened, yuh rascal! Tell whut . . ."

Dave looked at Jenny's stiff legs and began to cry.

"Whut yuh do wid tha gun?" his mother asked.

"What wuz he doin wida gun?" his father asked.

"Come on and tell the truth," said Hawkins. "Ain't nobody going to hurt you . . ."

His mother crowded close to him.

"Did yuh shoot tha mule, Dave?"

Dave cried, seeing blurred white and black faces.

"Ahh ddinn gggo tt sshooot hher . . . Ah sssswear ffo Gawd Ahh ddin . . . Ah wuz a-tryin t sssee ef the old gggun would sshoot—"

"Where yuh git the gun from?" his father asked.

"Ah got it from Joe, at the sto."

"Where yuh git the money?"

"Ma give it t me."

"He kept worryin me, Bob. Ah had t. Ah tol im t bring the gun right back t me . . . It was fer yuh, the gun."

"But how yuh happen to shoot that mule?" asked Jim Hawkins.

"Ah wuzn shootin at the mule, Mistah Hawkins. The gun jumped when Ah pulled the trigger . . . N fo Ah knowed anythin Jenny was there a-bleedin."

Somebody in the crowd laughed. Jim Hawkins walked close to Dave and looked into his face.

"Well, looks like you have bought you a mule, Dave."

"Ah swear fo Gawd, Ah didn go t kill the mule, Mistah Hawkins!"

"But you killed her!"

All the crowd was laughing now. They stood on tiptoe and poked heads over one another's shoulders.

"Well, boy, looks like yuh done bought a dead mule! Hahaha!"

"Ain tha ershame."

"Hohohohoho."

Dave stood, head down, twisting his feet in the dirt.

"Well, you needn't worry about it, Bob," said Jim Hawkins to Dave's father. "Just let the boy keep on working and pay me two dollars a month."

"Whut yuh wan fer yo mule, Mistah Hawkins?"

Jim Hawkins screwed up his eyes.

"Fifty dollars."

"Whut yuh do wid tha gun?" Dave's father demanded.

Dave said nothing.

"Yuh wan me t take a tree n beat yuh till yuh talk!"

"Nawsuh!"

"Whut yuh do wid it?"

"Ah throwed it erway."

"Where?"

"Ah . . . Ah throwed it in the creek."

"Waal, c mon home. N firs thing in the mawnin git to tha creek n fin tha gun."

"Yessuh."

"Whut yuh pay fer it?"

"Two dollahs."

"Take tha gun n git yo money back n carry it t Mistah Hawkins, yuh hear? N don fergit Ahma lam you black bottom good fer this! Now march yosef on home, suh!"

Dave turned and walked slowly. He heard people laughing. Dave glared, his eyes welling with tears. Hot anger bubbled in him. Then he swallowed and stumbled on.

That night Dave did not sleep. He was glad that he had gotten out of killing the mule so easily, but he was hurt. Something hot seemed to turn over inside him each time he remembered how they had laughed. He tossed on his bed, feeling his hard pillow. N Pa says he's gonna beat me . . . He remembered other beatings, and his back quivered. Naw, naw, Ah sho don wan im t beat me tha way no mo. Dam em all! Nobody ever gave him anything. All he did was work. They treat me like a mule, n then they beat me. He gritted his teeth. N Ma had t tell on me.

Well, if he had to, he would take old man Hawkins that two dollars. But that meant selling the gun. And he wanted to keep that gun. Fifty dollars for a dead mule.

He turned over, thinking how he had fired the gun. He had an itch to fire it again. Ef other men kin shoota gun, by Gawd, Ah kin! He was still, listening. Mebbe they all sleepin now. The house was still. He heard the soft breathing of his brother. Yes, now! He would go down and get that gun and see if he could fire it! He eased out of bed and slipped into overalls.

The moon was bright. He ran almost all the way to the edge of the woods. He stumbled over the ground, looking for the spot where he had buried the gun. Yeah, here it is. Like a hungry dog scratching for a bone, he pawed it up. He puffed his black cheeks and blew dirt from the trigger and barrel. He broke it and found four cartridges unshot. He looked around; the fields were filled with silence and moonlight. He clutched the gun stiff and hard in his fingers. But, as soon as he wanted to pull the trigger, he shut his eyes and turned his head. Naw, Ah can't shoot wid mah eyes closed n mah head turned. With effort he held his eyes open; then he squeezed. *Blooooom!* He was stiff, not breathing. The gun was still in his hands. Dammit, he'd done it! He fired again. *Blooooom!* He smiled. *Bloooom! Blooooom! Click, click.* There! It was empty. If anybody could shoot a gun, he could. He put the gun into his hip pocket and started across the fields.

When he reached the top of a ridge he stood straight and proud in the moonlight, looking at Jim Hawkins' big white house, feeling the gun sagging in his pocket. Lawd, ef Ah had just one mo bullet Ah'd taka shot at tha house. Ah'd like t scare ol man Hawkins jusa little . . . Jusa enough t let im know Dave Saunders is a man.

To his left the road curved, running to the tracks of the Illinois Central. He jerked his head, listening. From far off come a faint *hoooof-hoooof; hoooof-hoooof.* . . . He stood rigid. Two dollahs a mont. Les see now . . . Tha means it'll take bout two years. Shucks! Ah'll be dam!

He started down the road, toward the tracks. Yeah, here she comes! He stood beside the track and held himself stiffly. Here she comes, erroun the ben . . . C mon, yuh slow poke! C mon! He had his hand on his gun; something quivered in his stomach. Then the train thundered past, the gray and brown box cars rumbling and clinking. He gripped the gun tightly; then he jerked his hand out of his pocket. Ah betcha

Bill wouldn't do it! Ah betcha . . . The cars slid past, steel grinding upon steel. Ahm ridin yuh ternight, so hep me Gawd! He was hot all over. He hesitated just a moment; then he grabbed, pulled atop of a car, and lay flat. He felt his pocket; the gun was still there. Ahead the long rails were glinting in the moonlight, stretching away, away to somewhere, somewhere where he could be a man . . .

—1940

DRAMA

CHERRÍE MORAGA

B. 1952

Cherríe Moraga was born in California and is a playwright, educator, and Latina and lesbian activist and essayist. Her works include loving in the War Years *(1983),* Giving Up the Ghost *(1986),* Heroes and Saints *(1992), and* Watsonville *(1995). In 1981, she coedited with Gloria Anzaldua the highly influential anthology of lesbian writers of color* This Bridge Called My Back *(1981). She currently lives in San Francisco, where she teaches at the University of California, Berkeley, and is active in community politics. Her most recent publication is* Waiting in the Wings: Portrait of a Queer Motherhood *(1997), a nonfiction account of the creation of a non-heterosexual or "alternative" reproductive family.*

GIVING UP THE GHOST
A Stage Play in Three Portraits

If I had wings like an angel
over these prison walls
I would fly
(*song my mother would sing to me*)

CHARACTERS
MARISA, *Chicana in her late 20s*
CORKY, MARISA *as a teenager*
AMALIA, *Mexican-born, a generation older than* MARISA
THE PEOPLE, *those viewing the performance or reading the play*

SET

The stage set should be simple, with as few props as possible. A crate is used for street scenes downstage. A raised platform, stage left, serves as the bed in a variety of settings, including a hotel room, a mental hospital, and both AMALIA's *and* MARISA's *apartments. A simple wooden table and two chairs, stage right, represent* AMALIA's *kitchen. Windows, doorways, and furniture appear in the imagination when needed. The suggestion of a Mexican desert landscape is illuminated upstage during scenes evoking indigenous México. Scrims can be used for the dreamlike sequences. Aside from the minimal set pieces mentioned above, lighting and music should be the main features in providing setting. Music should be used to re-create the "streetwise ritmo" of the urban life of these Chicanas, spanning a generation of Motown, soul, Tex-Mex, and Latin rock. It should also reflect the profound influence of traditional Mexican folk music—rancheras, corridos, mariachi, etc.—as well as the more ancient indigenous sounds of the flauta, concha, and tambor. Throughout the long monologues (unless otherwise indicated) when the non-speaking actors remain on stage, the lighting and direction should give the impression that the characters both disappear and remain within hearing range of the speaker. In short, direction should reflect that each character knows, on an intuitive level, the minds of the other characters.*

R E T R A T O I

"La Pachuca"

Prologue

This is the urban Southwest, a Chicano barrio within the sprawling Los Angeles basin. Street sounds fill the air: traffic, children's schoolyard voices, street repairs, etc. MARISA *sits on a wooden crate, centerstage. She wears a pair of Levi's, tennis shoes and a bright-colored shirt. Her black hair is pulled back, revealing a face of dark intensity and definite Indian features. She holds a large sketchbook on her lap.* CORKY *enters upstage. Their eyes meet. As* MARISA's *younger self,* CORKY *tries to act tough but displays a wide open-heartedness in her face which betrays the toughness. She dresses "Cholo style"—khaki pants with razor-sharp creases, pressed white undershirt. Her hair is cut short and slicked back. She approaches the upstage wall, spray can in hand, feigning the false bravado of her teenage male counterparts. She writes in large, Chicano graffiti-style letters, as* MARISA *writes in her sketchbook.*

Dedicación

Don't know where this woman
and I will find each other again,
but I am grateful to her   to something
that feels like a blessing

that I am, in fact, not trapped

      which brings me to the question of prisons
      politics
      sex.

CORKY *tosses the spray can to* MARISA.

CORKY (*with* MARISA): I'm only telling you this to stay my hand.
MARISA: But why, cheezus, why me?
    Why'd I hafta get into a situation where all my ghosts come to visit?
    I always see that man . . . thick-skinned, dark, muscular.
    He's a boulder between us.
    I can't lift him and her, too . . . carrying him.

    He's a ghost, always haunting her . . .
    lingering.

Fade out.

Scene One

A Chicano "oldie" rises. Crossfade to CORKY *coming downstage, moving "low and slow" to the tune.*

CORKY: the smarter I get the older I get the meaner I get
    tough a tough cookie my mom calls me
    sometimes I even pack a blade
    no one knows I never use it or nut'ing
    but can feel it there there in my pants pocket
    run the pad of my thumb over it to remind me I carry somet'ing
    am sharp secretly
    always envy those batos who get all cut up at the weddings
    getting their rented tuxes all bloody
    that red 'n' clean color
    against the white starched collars
    I love that shit!

    the best part is the chicks all climbing into the ball of the fight
    "Chuy, déjalo! Leave him go, Güero!" tú sabes
    you know how the chicks get all excited 'n' upset 'n' stuff
    they always pulling on the carnales 'n' getting nowhere
    'cept messed up themselves 'n' everybody looks so
    like they digging the whole t'ing tú sabes
    their dresses ripped here 'n' there . . . like a movie
    it's all like a movie

    when I was a real little kid I useta love the movies
    every Saturday you could find me there

my eyeballs glued to the screen
then later my friend Arturo and me
we'd make up our own movies
one was where we'd be out in the desert
'n' we'd capture these chicks 'n' hold 'em up for ransom
we'd string 'em up 'n' make 'em take their clothes off
"strip" we'd say to the wall all cool-like
funny . . . now when I think about how little I was at the time
and a girl but in my mind I was big 'n' tough 'n' a dude
in my *mind* I had all their freedom
the freedom to see a girl   kina
the way   you see
an animal   you know?

like imagining
they got a difernt set
of blood vessels or somet'ing   like   so
when you mess with 'em
it don' affect 'em the way   it do   you
like like they got a difernt gland system or somet'ing that
that makes their pain cells
more dense

hell I dunno

but you see
I never could
quite
pull it off

always knew I was a girl
deep down inside
no matter how I tried to pull the other off

I knew
always knew
I was an animal that kicked back . . .

(*with* MARISA) . . . cuz it hurt! (CORKY *exits.*)

MARISA (*from the platform, coming downstage*): I never wanted to be a man, only
    wanted a woman to want me that bad. And they have, you know, plenty of
    them, but there's always that one you can't pin down, who's undecided. (*Beat.*)
    My mother was a heterosexual, I couldn't save her. My failures follow there-
    after.

AMALIA (*entering*): I am a failure.

AMALIA *is visibly "soft" in just the ways that* MARISA *appears "hard." She chooses her clothes with an artist's eye for color and placement. They appear to be draped over her, rather than worn: a rebozo wrapped around her shoulders, a blouse falling over the waist of an embroidered skirt. Her hair is long and worn down or loosely braided. As a woman nearing fifty, she gives the impression of someone who was once a rare beauty, now trading that for a fierce dignity in bearing.*

AMALIA: I observe the Americans. Their security. Their houses. Their dogs. Their children are happy. They are not *un* . . . happy. Sure, they have their struggles, their problemas, but . . . it's a life. I always say this, it's a life. (*She sits at the table stacked with art books, puts on a pair of wire-rim glasses, leafs through a book.*)

MARISA: My friend Marta bought her mother a house. I admire her. Even after the family talked bad about her like that for leaving home with a gabacha, she went back cash in hand and bought her mother a casita kina on the outskirts of town. Ten grand was all it took, that's nothing here, but it did save her mother from the poverty her dead father left behind. I envy her. For the first time wished my father'd die so I could do my mother that kind of rescue routine.

I wanna talk about betrayal, about a battle I will never win and never stop fighting. The dick beats me every time. I know I'm not supposed to be sayin' this cuz it's like confession, like still cryin' your sins to a priest you long ago stopped believing was god or god's sit-in, but still confessing what you'd hoped had been forgiven in you. . . . (*Looking to* AMALIA.) That prison . . . that passion to beat men at their own game.

AMALIA: I worry about La Pachuca. That's my nickname for her. I have trouble calling her by her Christian name. (*Savoring it.*) Marisa. ("*Rain sticks*" *in the background.*) I worry about La Pachuca. I worry what will happen to the beautiful corn she is growing if it continues to rain so hard and much.

CORKY (*entering*): one time Tury 'n' me stripped for real
there was this minister 'n' his family down the street
they was presbyterians or methodists or somet'ing
you know one of those gringo religions
'n' they had a bunch a kids
the oldest was named Lisa or somet'ing lightweight like that
'n' the littlest was about three or so, named Chrissy
I mean you couldn't really complain about Chrissy
cuz she wasn't old enough yet to be a pain in the cola
but you knew that was coming

Lisa'd be hassling me 'n' my sister Patsy all the time
telling us how we wernt really christians
cuz cath-lics worshipped the virgin mary or somet'ing
I dint let this worry me though cuz we was being tole at school
how being cath-lic was the one true numero uno church 'n' all
so I jus' let myself be real cool with her
'n' the rest of her little pagan baby brothers 'n' sisters
that's all they was to me as far as I was concerned

they dint even have no mass
jus' some paddy preaching up there with a dark suit on
very weird
not a damn candle for miles
dint seem to me that there was any god happening in that place at all

so one day Tury comes up with this idea how we should strip
"for real"
I wasn't that hot on the idea but still go along with him
checkin' out the neighborhood looking for prey
then we run into Chrissy 'n' Tury 'n' me eye each other
the trouble is I'm still not completely sold on the idea
pero ni modo cuz I already hear comin' outta my mouth
real syrupy-like
"come heeeeere Chrissy, we got somet'ing to shooooow, you"
well, a'course she comes cuz I was a big kid 'n' all
'n' we take her into this shed

I have her hand 'n' Tury tells her . . .
no *I* tole her this
I tell her we think she's got somet'ing wrong with her
"down there"
I think . . . I think I said she had a cut or somet'ing
'n' Tury 'n' me had to check it out
so I pull her little shorts down 'n' then her chones
'n' then jus' as I catch a glimpse of her little fuchi fachi . . .
it was so tender-looking all pink 'n' real sweet like a bun
then stupid Tury like a menso goes 'n' sticks his dirty finger on it
like it was burning hot

'n' jus' at that moment . . . I see this little Chrissy-kid
look up at me like . . . like I was her mom or somet'ing
like tú sabes she has this little kid's frown on her face
the chubby skin on her forehead all rumpled up
like . . . like she knew somet'ing was wrong with what we was doing
'n' was looking to me to reassure her
that everyt'ing was cool 'n' regular 'n' all
what a jerk I felt like!
(*She pushes "Tury" away, bends down to "Chrissy".*)

so, I pull up her shorts 'n' whisper to her
"no no you're fine really there's nut'ing wrong with you
but don' tell nobody we looked
we don' want nobody to worry about you"
what else was I supposed to say? ¡Tonta!
'n' Tury 'n' me make a beeline into the alley 'n' outta there!
(*She exits.*)

Scene Two

Crossfade to AMALIA *rising from the bed. It is morning.*

AMALIA: I remember the first time I met her, the day she first began to bring me her work. It was early morning, too early really, and there was someone at the door. At first I think it is my son, Che. Like him to appear at my doorstep with the least amount of warning. (*She goes to the "window," looks down to the front steps.* MARISA *appears, carrying a portfolio.*) But it was Marisa, standing there with a red jacket on, I remember, a beautiful color of red. Maybe if I had not dreamed the color the night before I might not even have bothered to open the door so early, such a hermit I am. (*To* MARISA:) ¿Sí?

MARISA: Hello. I got these . . . paintings. I . . . heard you could help me.

AMALIA: ¿Quién eres?

MARISA: Marisa. Marisa Moreno.

AMALIA: It's a little early, ¿qué no?

MARISA: I'm sorry. Frank Delgado—

AMALIA: Súbete.

AMALIA *"buzzes"* MARISA *in.* AMALIA *puts on a robe, brushes back her hair.* MARISA *enters.*

MARISA: Good morning.

AMALIA: It's too early to tell.

MARISA: I'm sorry.

AMALIA: That's two "sorrys" already and I don't even got my eyes on yet.

MARISA: Sor . . .

AMALIA (*smiling*): Pásale. Pásale.

MARISA (*handing her a small paper sack*): Here, this is for you.

AMALIA: Siéntate.

MARISA: It's pandulce.

AMALIA (*looking inside*): Conchas. They're my favorites.

AMALIA *puts the pastry on the table.* MARISA *sits down, holds the portfolio awkwardly in her lap. During the following scene there are brief lapses in the conversation.*

AMALIA: ¿Quieres café?

MARISA: Gracias. No.

AMALIA: Pues, yo . . . sí. (*Goes to prepare the coffee.*) I can't even talk before I have a cup of coffee in me. Help yourself to the pandulce.

MARISA (*indicating the books on the table*): Are all these yours?

AMALIA: The books? Claro.

MARISA: They're wonderful.

AMALIA: Take a look at them if you want.

MARISA *carefully props up her portfolio onto a chair and begins to leaf through one of the books.* AMALIA *reenters, looking for her glasses.*

MARISA: You got a lotta . . . things.

AMALIA: What? Yes. Too much. My son, Che, he calls me a . . . rat pack.

MARISA: A pack rat.

AMALIA: Whatever you call it, I can't even find my glasses.

MARISA (*pointing to the painting on the upstage wall*): And this?

AMALIA: Well, I couldn't afford a room with a view, so . . . bueno, pues I improvised a little. ¿Te gusta? (*She finds her glasses in her robe pocket, puts them on.*)

MARISA: Yeah. Mucho.

AMALIA (*observing her*): You don't seem quite as awesome as Delgado described you.

MARISA: He told you about me?

AMALIA: Ay, all los boys at El Centro were talking about you, telling me how I should see your work . . . this new "Eastlos import."

MARISA: I didn't think they liked me.

AMALIA: Pues, I didn't say they *liked* you.

MARISA: Oh.

AMALIA: I think you scared them a little. Una pintora bien chingona, me dijo Frank.

MARISA: That's what he said?

AMALIA: Más o menos. Bueno . . . (*Indicating the portfolio.*) Abrélo. Let's see what makes those machos shake in their botas so much.

As MARISA *opens the portfolio, the lights crossfade to* CORKY *entering.*

CORKY: the weird thing was that after that episode with Chrissy
   I was like a maniac all summer
   snotty Lisa kept harassing me about the virgin mary 'n' all
   'n' jus' in general being a pain in the coolie
   things began to break down with her 'n' her minister's family
   when me 'n' Patsy stopped going to their church meetings
   on wednesday nights
   we'd only go cuz they had cookies 'n' treats after all the bible stuff
   'n' sometimes had arts 'n' crafts where you got to paint
   little clay statues of blond jesus in a robe
   'n' the little children coming to him
   the drag was that you also had to do these prayer sessions
   where everybody'd stand in a circle squeezing hands
   'n' each kid'd say a little prayer
   you know like "for the starving people in china"
   Patsy 'n' me always passed when we got squeezed
   jus' shaked our heads no
   cuz it was against our religion to pray with them
   well, one time, this Lisa punk has the nerve to pray that Patsy 'n' me
   would (*mimicking*) "come to the light of the one true Christian faith"
   shi-it can you get to that? 'course we never went again

AMALIA *puts on an apron, becomes* CORKY's *"mother."*

CORKY: but I remember coming home 'n' telling my mom . . .

"MOTHER": It's better mi'jitas, I think, it you don' go no more.
CORKY: 'n' it was so nice to hear her voice so warm
   like she loved us a lot
   'n' that night being cath-lic felt like my mom
   real warm 'n' dark 'n' kind

Fade out.

Scene Three

At rise, MARISA *straddles the kitchen chair, addresses* THE PEOPLE. AMALIA *is upstage by the bed. During* MARISA's *monologue,* AMALIA *ties her hair back into a tight bun, applies a grey powder to her face, and draws dark circles under her eyes.*

MARISA: The women I have loved the most have always loved the man more than
   me, even in their hatred of him. I'm queer I am. Sí, soy jota because I have never
   been crazy about a man. (*Pause.*) My friend Sally the hooker told me the day she
   decided to stop tricking was when once, by accident, a john made her come. That
   was strictly forbidden. She'd forgotten to resist, to keep business business. It
   was very unprofessional . . . and dangerous. No, I've never been in love with a
   man and I never understood women who were, although I've certainly been
   around to pick up the pieces. My sister was in love with my brother.
CORKY (*entering*): My mother loved her father.
MARISA: My first woman—
CORKY: The man who put her away.
MARISA: The crazy house. Camarillo, Califas. Sixteen years old.

   Blue light. Haunting music. AMALIA *becomes* "NORMA," MARISA's *"first woman."*
   She sits on the bed in a kind of psychotic stupor. CORKY *goes over to her.* MARISA
   narrates.

MARISA: When I come to get my cousin Norma, she has eyes like saucers, spinning
   black and glass. I can see through them, my face, my name. She says . . .
"NORMA": I am Buddha.
CORKY: How'd you get that black eye? ¿Quién te pegó?
"NORMA": I am Buddha.

   Fade out.

Scene Four

CORKY *is alone on stage. She takes out a yo-yo, tries a few tricks. She is quite good.*

CORKY: since that prayer meeting night
   when Patsy 'n' me wouldn't get squeezed into the minister's jesus
   Lisa's nose was gettin' higher 'n' higher in the air

   one day Patsy 'n' her are playing dolls up

on the second story porch of Mrs. Rodríguez's house
it was nice up there cuz Mrs. R would let you move the tables
'n' chairs 'n' stuff around to play "pertend"

my sister had jus' gotten this nice doll for her birthday
with this great curly hair
Lisa only had this kina stupid doll
with plastic painted-on hair 'n' only one leg
she'd always put long dresses on it to disguise the missing leg
but we all knew it was gone

anyway, one day this brat Lisa throws my sister's new doll
into this mud puddle right down from Mrs. R's porch
(*She lets out the yo-yo. It dangles helplessly.*)

Patsy comes back into our yard crying like crazy
her doll's all muddy 'n' the hair has turned bone straight
I mean like an arrow!
I wanted to kill that punk Lisa!
so me 'n' Patsy go over to Lisa's house
where we find the little creep all pleased with herself
I mean not even feeling bad
suddenly I see her bike which is really a trike
but it's huge . . . I mean hu-u-uge!
to this day, I never seen a trike that big
it useta bug me to no end that she wasn't even *trying*
to learn to ride a two-wheeler
so all of a sudden . . . (*Winding up with the yo-yo like a pitcher.*)
that trike 'n' Lisa's wimpiness come together in my mind
'n' I got that thing (*Throwing the pitch.*)
'n' I threw the sucker into the street

I dint even wreck it none (*She stuffs the yo-yo in her back pocket.*)
but it was the principle of the thing

a'course she goes 'n' tells her mom on me
'n' this lady who by my mind don' even seem like a mom
she dint wear no makeup 'n' was real skinny 'n' tall
'n' wore her hair in some kina dumb bun
she has the nerve to call my mom 'n' tell her what I done

AMALIA, *as* CORKY's *"mom," appears upstage in an apron. She is stirring a pot in her arms. She observes* CORKY.

CORKY: so a'course my mom calls me on the carpet
wants to know the story
'n' I tell her 'bout the doll 'n' Patsy 'n' the principle of the thing

'n' Patsy's telling the same story 'n' I can see in my mom's eyes
   she don' believe I did nut'ing so bad but she tells me . . .
"MOTHER": We got to keep some peace in the neighborhood, hija.
CORKY: cuz we was already getting pedo from the paddy neighbors
   'bout how my mom hollered too much at her kids . . . her own kids!
   I mean if you can't yell at your own kids who *can* you yell at?
   but she don' let on that this is the real reason
   I hafta go over to the minister's house and apologize
   she jus' kina turns back to the stove 'n' keeps on
   with what she was doing
"MOTHER": Andale, mija, dinner's almost ready. (CORKY *hesitates.*) Andale. Andale.
CORKY (*coming downstage*): so, a'course I go
   I go by myself
   with no one to watch me to see if I really do it
   but my mom knows I will cuz she tole me to
   'n' I ring the doorbell 'n' Mrs. Minister answers
   'n' as I begin to talk that little wimp Lisa runs up
   'n' peeks out at me from behind her mother's skirt
   with the ugliest most snottiest shit-eating grin
   I'd ever seen in a person
   while all the while *I* say *I'm* sorry
   'n' as the door shuts in front of my face
   I vow I'll never make that mistake again . . .

(*with* MARISA) I'll never show nobody how mad I can get!

Black out.

Scene Five

MARISA *is pacing about* AMALIA's *room.* AMALIA *sits on the floor mixing paints. She wears a paint-splattered apron.*

MARISA (*to* THE PEOPLE): I have a very long memory. I try to warn people that when I get hurt, I don't forget it—I use it against them. I blame women for everything. My mistakes. Missed opportunities. My grief. I usually leave just when I wanna lay a woman flat. When I feel that vengeance rise up in me, I split. I desert.
AMALIA: Desert. Desierto. For some reason, I could always picture mi cholita in the desert, amid the mesquite y nopal. Always when I closed my eyes to search for her, it was in the Mexican desert that I found her. I *had* intended to take her . . . to México. She would never have gone alone, sin gente allá.
MARISA: This is México! What are you talking about? It was those gringos that put up those fences between us!

AMALIA *brings* MARISA *to the table, takes out a piece of charcoal from her apron, puts it into* MARISA's *hand.* MARISA *begins to sketch.*

AMALIA: She was hardly convincing. Her nostalgia for the land she had never seen was everywhere. In her face, her drawings, her love of the hottest sand by the sea.

Coming around behind her, AMALIA *wraps her arms around* MARISA's *neck. Indigenous flutes and drums can be heard in the background.*

AMALIA: Desierto de Sonora. Tierra de tu memoria. (*Turning* MARISA's *face to her.*) Same chata face. Yaqui. (*They hesitate, then kiss their first kiss.*)
MARISA: I've just never believed a woman capable of loving a man was capable of loving . . . me. Some part of me remains amazed that I'm not the only lesbian in the world and that I can always manage to find someone to love me. (*Pause.*) But I am never satisfied because there are always those women left alone . . . and unloved.

Lights slowly fade to black. Musical interlude.

RETRATO II

"La Loca"

Scene Six

A sunny morning. AMALIA *is kneeling on a chair, bent over the table, painting in thick strokes and occasionally sipping at a cup of coffee. Her hair is combed into a braid and tied up.* MARISA *lies on the bed, hands behind her head.*

AMALIA: I've only been crazy over one man in my life. Alejandro was nothing special. Era pescador, indio. Once we took a drive out of the small town he lived in, and he was terrified, like a baby. I'm driving through the mountains and he's squirming in his seat, "¿Amalia, pá dónde vamos? Are you sure you know where we're going?" I was so amused to see this big macho break out into a cold sweat just from going no more than twenty miles from his home town. Pero, ¡Ay, Dios! How I loved that man! I still ask myself what I saw in him, really. (*Pause.*) He was one of the cleanest people I had ever met. Took two, three baths a day. You have to, you know. That part of la costa is like steam baths some seasons. I remember how he'd even put powder in his shorts and under his huevos to keep dry. He was that clean. I always loved knowing that when I touched him I would find him like a saint. Pure somehow . . . that no matter where he had been or who he had been with, he would always have washed himself for me. He always smelled . . . so clean. (*She wipes her hands, sits at the foot of the bed.*) When I went back home that first time, after my son was already grown, I had never dreamed of falling in love. Too many damn men under the bridge. I can see them all floating down the river like so many sacks of potatoes. "Making love," they call it, was like having sex with children. They rub your chi-chis a little, then they stick it in you. Nada más. It's all over in a few minutes. ¡Un río de cuerpos muertos!

MARISA: Sometimes I only see the other river on your face. I see it running behind your eyes. Remember the time we woke up together and your eye was a bowl of blood? I thought the river had broken open inside you.

AMALIA: I was crazy about Alejandro. But what I loved was not so much him . . . I loved his children. I loved the way he had made México my home again. (*Pause.*) He was not a strong man really. He was soft. An inside softness, I could feel even as his desire swelled into a rock hardness. Once he said that with me he felt as though he were "a heart that knew no sex." No man-woman, he meant, only heat and a heart and that even a man could be entered in this way. (*Indigenous music rises in the background.*) I, on the other hand, was *not* clean, forgot sometimes to wash. Not when I was around others, pero con mí misma, I became like the animals. Uncombed. El olor del suelo.

MARISA: I remember the story you told me about the village children, how they had put una muñeca at the door of your casita. How you had found it there . . . there, in your likeness and you thought—

AMALIA: I must be mad.

Suddenly, the beat of tambores. CORKY enters, wearing a native bruja mask. She dances across the stage with rattles in her hand. As she exits, MARISA goes to AMALIA, unbraids her hair.

MARISA: So we take each other in doses. I learn to swallow my desire, work my fear slowly through the strands of your hair.

MARISA *bends to kiss* AMALIA *on the neck.* AMALIA *pulls away, comes downstage.*

AMALIA: Of course, soon after, Alejandro ran to every whore he could find, but not without first calling me that: "puta, bruja." He claimed I was trying to work some kind of mala suerte on him, that I was trying to take from him his manhood, make him something less than a man. (*Pause, to* MARISA:) I have always felt like an outsider.

MARISA *starts toward her, then changes her mind and exits.*

AMALIA (*to* THE PEOPLE): Ni de aquí, ni de allá. Ask me in one word to describe to you the source of all my loneliness and I will tell you, "México." Not that I would have been any happier staying there. How *could* I have stayed there, been some man's wife . . . after so many years in this country, so many years on my own? (*Pause.*) I'll never forget the trip, the day our whole tribe left para el norte.

Sudden spiritedness. A Mexican mariachi instrumental rises. AMALIA ties a bandana around her head. She is a young girl.

AMALIA: All of us packed into the old blue Chevy. I was thirteen and la regla had started, the bleeding, and I was ashamed to tell my mother. Tía Fita had been the one to warn me that at my age, any day, I could expect to become sick. "Mala," she said, and that when it happened I should come to her and she would bless me and tell me how to protect myself. It came the morning of our long jornada to California.

AMALIA *sees the "blood" coming down her leg. She takes the bandana from her head, looks around nervously, then stuffs it under her skirt, flattening it back into place.*

AMALIA: Tía Fita was not speaking to my mother so angry was she for all of us leaving. We had asked her to come with us. "What business do I have up there with all those pochos y gringos?" My father said she had no sense. It broke her heart to see us go. So, there was no running to Tía Fita that morning. It seemed too selfish to tell her my troubles when *I* was the one leaving *her.*

Southwestern desert and distant highway sounds can be heard. AMALIA, *trying to hide from the others, pulls the bandana out from under her skirt. Kneeling by the "river," she secretly begins to wash the blood from it. Sound and lights gradually fade out.*

Scene Seven

MARISA *sits at the table in soft light sipping at a beer. She is dressed for the evening in a man's suit jacket. She wears a kind of classic androgynous look.* AMALIA *enters in a slip, crosses to the bed where she begins to dress.*

MARISA: If I were a man, things would've been a lot simpler between us, except . . . she never would've wanted me. I mean, she would've seen me more and all, fit me more conveniently into her life, but she never would've, tú sabes . . . wanted me.

AMALIA: Sometimes I think, with me, that she only wanted to feel herself so much a woman that she would no longer be hungry for one. Pero, siempre tiene hambre. Siempre tiene pena.

MARISA: She'd come to me sometimes I swear like heat on wheels. I'd open the door and find her there, wet from the outta nowhere June rains, and, without her even opening her mouth, I knew what she had come for. I never knew when to expect her this way, just like the rains. Never ever when I wanted it, asked for it, begged for it, only when she decided.

AMALIA: I always had to have a few traguitos and then things would cloud between us a little and I could feel her as if underwater, my hands swimming towards her in the darkness, discovering breasts, not mine . . . not these empty baldes, pero senos firmes, like small stones of heat. Y como un recién nacido, I drink and drink and drink y no me traga la tierra.

Lights suggest memory. Nighttime freeway sounds, car radio music. MARISA *and* AMALIA *hold each other's eyes. Voice over.*

MARISA: I'll keep driving if you promise not to stop touching me.
AMALIA: You want me to stop touching you?
MARISA: No, if you promise *not* to stop.

AMALIA *crosses in front of* MARISA. *She prepares herself a drink.* MARISA *watches her.*

MARISA: It's odd being queer. It's not that you don't want a man, you just don't want a man in a man. You want a man in a woman. The woman part goes without saying. That's what you always learn to want first. Maybe the first time you see your dad touch your mom in that way . . .
CORKY (*entering*): ¡Hiiiijo! I remember the first time I got hip to that! My mom standing at the stove making chile colorado and flippin' tortillas. She asks my dad . . .
AMALIA (*as "MOM" to* MARISA): ¿Quieres otra, viejo?
CORKY: Kina like she's sorta hassled 'n' being poquita fría, tú sabes, but she's really digging my dad to no end. 'N' jus' as she comes over to him, kina tossing the tort onto the plate, he slides his hand, real suave-like, up the inside of her thigh. Cheezus! I coulda died! I musta been only about nine or so, but I got that tingling, tú sabes, that now I know what it means.

As CORKY *exits, she throws her chin out to* MARISA *"bato style."* MARISA, *amused, returns the gesture. The lights shift.* MARISA *puts on a tape. A Mexican ballad is played—"Adios Paloma" by Chavela Vargas.* AMALIA *hums softly along with it.*

MARISA: Hay un hombre en esta mujer. Lo he sentido. La miro, cocinando para nosotras. Pienso . . . ¿comó puede haber un hombre en una persona, tan feminina? Su pelo, sus movimientos de una serenidad imposible de describir.
AMALIA (*softly singing*):
  'Ya se va tu paloma, mi vida
  lleva en sus alas dolor
  lleva en sus ojos tristeza
  y es till lamento su voz.'
MARISA (*going to her*): Tu voz que me acaricia con cada palabra . . . tan suave . . . tan rica. (*Takes her by the hand.*) Vente.

The music rises. They dance for a few moments, then MARISA *takes* AMALIA *to the bed. The music fades as* MARISA *slowly removes* AMALIA's *blouse.*

MARISA: Con ella, me siento como un joven lleno de deseo. I move on top of her. She wants this. The worn denim and metal buttons are cotton and cool ice on my skin. And she is full of slips and lace and stockings . . .
AMALIA: Quítate los pantalones.

MARISA: And yet it is she who's taking me.

A soft jazz rises. MARISA *takes off her jacket. They kiss each other, at first tenderly, then passionately. They hold and caress each other.* MARISA *takes* AMALIA's *hand, brings it to her chest. The music softens.*

MARISA: I held the moment. Prayed that if I looked long and hard enough at your hand full inside me, if I could keep this pictured forever in my mind . . . how beneath that moon blasting through the window, . . . how everything was changing at that moment in both of us.
AMALIA: How everything was changing . . . in both of us.

The jazz rises again. The lights slowly fade as they hold a deep kiss.

RETRATO III

"La Salvadora"

Scene Eight

CORKY *writes graffiti-style on upstage wall.*

> I have this rock in my hand
> it is my memory
> the weight is solid
> in my palm   it cannot fly away
>
> because I still remember
> that woman
> not my savior, but an angel
> with wings
> that did once lift me
> to another
> self.

MARISA *and* AMALIA *appear in shadow on opposite ends of the stage.*

AMALIA: You have the rest of your life to forgive me.
MARISA: Forgive you for what?
AMALIA: Por lo que soy.

Black out.

Scene Nine

AMALIA *enters carrying a small suitcase. She sets it down at the foot of the bed, removes her rebozo and holds it in her lap.*

AMALIA: All I was concerned about was getting my health back together. It was not so much that I had been sick, only I lacked . . . energy. My body felt like a rag, squeezed dry of any feeling. Possibly it was the "change" coming on. But the women in my family did not go through the change so young. I wasn't even fifty. I thought . . . maybe it was the American influence that causes the blood to be sucked dry from you so early. Nothing was wrong with me, really. My bones ached. I needed rest. Nothing México couldn't cure.

She lies down, covers herself with the rebozo. MARISA *enters, barefoot.*

MARISA: For the whole summer, I watched the people fly in bright-colored sails over the Califas sea, waiting for her. Red- and gold- and blue-striped wings blazing the sky. Lifting off the sandy cliffs, dangling gringo legs. Always imagined myself up there in their place, flying for real. Never ever coming back down to earth, just leaving my body behind. (*Pause.*) One morning I awoke to find a bird dead on the beach. I knew it wasn't a rock because it was light enough to roll with the tide . . . I saw this from a distance. Later that day, they found a woman dead there at the very same spot, I swear. Una viejita. (*A soft grey light washes over* AMALIA.) A crowd gathered 'round her as a young man in a blue swimsuit tried to spoon the sand from her throat with his finger. Putting his breath to her was too late. She was so very very grey and wet, como la arena . . . y una mexicana, I could tell by her house dress. How did she drown? Then I remembered what Amalia had told me about bad omens. (*A sudden ominous tambor,* AMALIA *bolts up in bed.*) I stopped going. I stopped waiting.

MARISA *exits.*

AMALIA: When I learned of Alejandro's death, I died too. I just started bleeding and the blood wouldn't stop, not until his ghost had passed through me or was born in me. I don't know which. That Mexican morning I had awakened to find the hotel sheets red with blood. It had come out in torrents and thick clots that looked like a fetus. But I was not pregnant, my tubes had been tied for years. Yet, lying there in the cool dampness of my own blood, I felt my womanhood leave me. And it was Alejandro being born in me. Does this make sense? I can't say exactly how I knew this, except . . . again . . . for the smell, the unmistakable smell of the man, as if we had just made love. And coming from my mouth was *his* voice. . . . "¡Ay mi Marisa! ¡Te deseo! ¡Te deseo!" (*Her eyes search for* MARISA.) Marisa!

Lights rise. Morning in Mexico City. AMALIA *gets up from the bed.*

AMALIA: It is barely dawn and the sun has already entered my hotel window. Afuera los hombres are already at work tearing up the Mexican earth with their steel claws. (*Indigenous music.*) Pero La Tierra is not as passive as they think. "Regresaré," Ella nos recuerda. "Regresaré," nos promete. When they "discovered" El Templo Mayor beneath the walls of this city, they had not realized that it was She who discovered them. Nothing remains buried forever. Not even memory. Especially not memory.

Fade out.

Scene Ten

The indigenous music blends into Chicano urban sounds. MARISA *enters. Her posture is noticeably more guarded than in the previous scene. The music fades. There is a pause as* MARISA *scans the faces of* THE PEOPLE.

MARISA: Got raped once. When I was a kid. Taken me a long to say that was exactly what happened, but that was exactly what happened. Makes you more aware than ever that you are one hunerd percent female, just in case you had any doubts. One hunerd percent female whether you act it . . . or like it . . . or not. Y'see, I never ever really let myself think about it, the possibility of rape, even after it happened. Not like other girls, I didn't walk down the street like there were men lurking everywhere, every corner, to devour me. Yeah, the street was a war zone, but for different reasons, . . . for muggers, mexicanos sucking their damn lips at you, gringo stupidity, drunks like old garbage socks thrown around the street, and the rape of other women and the people I loved. They weren't safe and I worried each time they left the house . . . but never, never me. I guess I never wanted to believe I was raped. If someone took me that bad, I wouldn't really want to think I was took, you follow me? But the truth is . . .
CORKY (*entering*): I was took

MARISA *crosses to the platform.* CORKY *"stakes out the territory."*

CORKY: I was about twelve years old
    I was still going to cath-lic school then
    'n' we wore those stupid checkered jumpers
    they looked purty shitty on the seventh 'n' eighth grade girls
    cuz here we was getting chi-chis 'n' all
    'n' still trying to shove 'em into the tops of these play suits
    I wasn't too big pero the big girls looked terrible!

    anyway in the seventh grade I was trying to mend my ways
    so would hang after school 'n' try to be helpful 'n' all to the nuns
    I guess cuz my cousin Norma got straight A's
    'n' was taking me into her bed by then
    so I figured . . . that was the way to go
    she'd get really pissed when I fucked up in school

threatened to "take it away" tú sabes if I dint behave
can you get to that? ¡Qué fría! ¿no?

anyway Norma was the only one I ever tole
about the janitor doing it to me
'n' then she took it away for good
I'd still like to whip her butt for that
her 'n' her goddamn hubby 'n' kids now   shi-it
puros gabachos, little blond-haired blue-eyed things
the oldest is a little joto if you ask me
sure he's barely four years old but you can already tell
the way he goes around primping all over the place
pleases me to no end
what goes around comes around
"Jason" they call him
no, not "Ha-són" pero "Jay-sun"
puro gringo

anyway so I was walking by Sister Mary Dominic's classroom
"the Hawk" we called her cuz she had a nose 'n' attitude like one
when this man a mexicano motions to me to come on inside
"Ven p'aca," he says
I dint recognize him but the parish was always hiring
mexicanos to work around the grounds 'n' stuff
I guess cuz they dint need to know English
'n' the priests dint need to pay 'em much
they'd do it "por Dios" tú sabes
so he asks me, "Señorita, ¿hablas español?" muy polite y todo
'n' I answer, "Sí poquito," which I always say to strangers
cuz I dunno how much they're gonna expect outta me
"Ven p'aca," he says otra vez
'n' I do outta respect for my primo Enrique
cuz he looks a lot like him but somet'ing was funny
his Spanish   I couldn't quite make it out cuz he mumbled alot
which made me feel kina bad about myself tú sabes
that I was Mexican too but couldn't understand him that good

he's trying to fix this drawer that's loose in the Hawk's desk
I knew already about the drawer
cuz she was always bitchin' 'n' moanin'
about it getting stuck cuz the bottom kept falling out
so he tells me he needs someone to hold the bottom of the drawer up
so he can screw the sides in
(*She goes to the "desk," demonstrates.*)
so standing to the side I lean over
and hold the drawer in place así
then he says all frustrated-like, "No, así, así"

it turns out he wants me to stand in front of the drawer
with my hands holding each side up así
(*She stands with her legs apart, her pelvis pressed up
against the edge of the "desk."*)
'n' believe it or not this cabrón sits behind me on the floor
'n' reaches his arm up between my legs
that I'm straining to keep closed
even though he keeps saying all business-like
"Abrete más por favor las piernas. Abretelas un poco más"
'n' like a pendeja   I do

(*She grips the edge of the "desk."*)
I feel my face getting hotter
'n' I can kina feel him jiggling the drawer
pressed up against me down there
I'm staring straight ahead don' wanna look at what's happening
then worry how someone would see us like this
this guy's arm up between my legs
'n' then it begins to kina brush past the inside of my thigh
I can feel the hair   that first
then the heat of his skin
(*Almost tenderly.*) the skin is so soft I hafta admit
young kina like a girl's like Norma's shoulder
I try to think about Norma 'n' her shoulders
to kina pass the time hoping to hurry things along
while he keeps saying, "Casi termino. Casi termino."
'n' I keep saying back, "Señor me tengo que ir, mi mamá me espera"
still all polite como mensa!
until finally I feel the screwdriver by my leg like ice
then suddenly the tip of it   it feels like to me
is against the cotton of my chones

"Don't move:" he tells me. In English. His accent gone. 'n' I don'

from then on all I see in my mind's eye . . .
were my eyes shut?
is this screwdriver he's got in his sweaty palm
yellow   glass   handle
shiny metal
the kind my father useta use to fix things around the house
remembered how I'd help him how he'd take me on his jobs with him
'n' I kept getting him confused in mind
this man 'n' his arm with my father
kept imagining he was my father returned come back
the arm was so soft but this other thing . . .
hielo   hielo   ice!
I wanted to cry, "Papi! Papi!"

'n' then I started crying for real
cuz I knew I musta done somet'ing real wrong
to get myself in this mess

I figure he's gonna shove the damn thing up me
he's trying to get my chones down, "Por favor señor please don'."
but I can hear my voice through my own ears
not from the inside out but the other way around
'n' I know I'm not fighting this one
I know I don' even sound convinced
"¿Dónde 'stás, Papi? ¿Dónde 'stás?"
'n' finally I hear the man answering, "Aquí estoy. Soy tu papá."
'n' this gives me permission to go 'head to not hafta fight

by the time he gets my chones down to my knees
I suddenly feel like I'm floating in the air
my thing kina attached to no body
flapping in the wind like a bird a wounded bird
I'm relieved when I hear the metal drop to the floor
only worry *who will see me doing this?*
(*Gritting her teeth.*) *get-this-over-with-get-this-over-with*
'n' he does gracias a dios bringing me down to earth

linoleum floor   cold
the smell of wax
polish

y ya 'stoy lista for what long ago waited for me
there is no surprise
'n' I open my legs wide wide open
for the angry animal that springs outta the opening in his pants
'n' all I wanna do is have it over so I can go back to being myself
'n' a kid again

then he hit me with it
into what was supposed to be a hole
(*Tenderly.*) that I remembered had to be
cuz Norma had found it once wet 'n' forbidden
'n' showed me too how wide 'n' deep like a cueva hers got
when she wanted it to only with me she said

MARISA: Only with you, Corky.
CORKY: but with this one there was no hole he had to make it
    'n' I saw myself down there like a face with no opening
    a face with no features
    no eyes no nose no mouth
    only little lines where they shoulda been

so I dint cry
I never cried as he shoved the thing
into what was supposed to be a mouth
with no teeth
with no hate
with no voice
only a hole
a hole!

He made me a hole!

MARISA *approaches, wraps a rebozo around* CORKY's *shoulders, holds her.*

MARISA: I don't regret it. I don't regret nuthin'. He only convinced me of my own name. From an early age you learn to live with it, being a woman. I just got a head start over some. And then, years later, after I got to be with some other men, I admired how their things had no opening . . . only a tiny tiny pinhole dot to pee from, to come from. I thought . . . how lucky they were, that they could release all that stuff, all that pent-up shit from the day, through a hole that *nobody* could get into.

Scene Eleven

MARISA *and* CORKY *remain on stage. The lighting slowly shifts. Indigenous music, lively tambores.* AMALIA *enters wearing a rebozo. She covers* MARISA's *shoulders with one as well. All three, now in rebozos, have become indias. They enter a dream.* CORKY *comes downstage, kneels. She begins making tortillas, slapping her hands together.* MARISA *and* AMALIA *join her on each side, forming a half circle. They, too, clap tortillas to the rhythm of the tambores. They are very happy. The rhythm quickens, accelerates.*

MARISA *and* AMALIA *slowly bend toward each other, their faces crossing in front of* CORKY's. *They kiss. Suddenly the scene darkens, the drumming becomes sinister . . . the clapping frantic. Thunder. Lightning. The gods have been angered. The three scatter. The stage is a maze of colliding lights, searching out the women.* CORKY *has disappeared.* AMALIA *cowers beneath her rebozo.* MARISA *appears upstage in shadow. She is out of breath. She is being hunted, her arms spread, her body pressed up against an invisible wall.*

MARISA: Amalia, let me in! ¡Abre la puerta! ¡Vienen a agarrarme!

AMALIA *wrestles in bed with her "pesadilla."*

MARISA: ¡No me dejes, Amalia! ¡No me dejes sola! Let me in!

AMALIA *can't bear to hear her, covers her ears.*

MARISA: Amalia! . . . Amalia! . . . Let . . . me . . . in!

The lights fade out and rise again. CORKY *can be seen in shadow standing where* MARISA *had been seconds before. She holds a beer bottle in the air above her head. She comes down with it, like a weapon. The sound of glass breaking. Black out.*

AMALIA (*in the darkness*): ¿Quién es? ¿Quién es? Who is it? ¿Eres tú Che?

Lights rise. AMALIA *is sitting up in bed. There is an opened, unpacked suitcase on the floor and a photo of a man with a candle next to it on the table.* MARISA *appears in the doorway. She is very drunk, almost in a stupor.*

AMALIA: Marisa.
MARISA: Where the . . . where have you been? (AMALIA *gets out of bed, puts on a robe.*)
AMALIA: What are you doing here?
MARISA (*menacingly*): I'm asking you a question.
AMALIA: Don't come near me.
MARISA: I said, where have you been?
AMALIA: What do you want?
MARISA: I wanna know . . . (*She stalks* AMALIA.) I wanna know where you been.
AMALIA: You're drunk.
MARISA: Good observation, maestra. Now are you gonna answer me?
AMALIA: Stay away from me. Don't touch me.
MARISA: I'm not gonna touch you. No, no. These hands? No, no, Doña Amalia . . . us jotas learn to keep our hands to ourselves.
AMALIA: ¡Aidó!
MARISA: Answer me!
AMALIA: You know where I was.
MARISA: I waited for you. I waited three goddamn months! Count them! June, July—
AMALIA: I can count.
MARISA: Well, jus' cuz it aint all hanging out on the outside don' mean I don' feel nuthin'. What did you expect from me anyway?
AMALIA: Well, not this.
MARISA: Well, honey, this is what you got. Aint I a purty picture?
AMALIA: Estás borracha. Estás loca.
MARISA. Bueno, 'stoy loca. Tal vez quieres que te hable en español, eh? A lo mejor you could understand me then. I'm sorry, y'know, us pochas don' speak it as purty as you do.
AMALIA: What are you talking about?
MARISA: I'm talking about going to the goddamn mailbox every day, thinking every llamadita would be you. "Ven, Chatita. Meet me in México." You lied to me.
AMALIA: I didn't lie.
MARISA: No?
AMALIA: No. (*She turns away.*)
MARISA: What then?

There is a pause.

MARISA: Look at you. You don' got nuthin' to say to me. You don' feel a thing.

AMALIA: It's three o'clock in the morning, what am I supposed to feel?

MARISA (*after a beat*): Nuthin'. You're supposed to feel nuthin'.

AMALIA: I'm going to get you some coffee.

MARISA: I don' want no coffee! You went back to him, didn't you?

AMALIA: Ay, Marisa, por favor no empieces.

MARISA (*seeing the photo*): What is this? A little altar we have for the man? (*She picks it up.*)

AMALIA: Don't.

MARISA: ¡Vela y todo! What is he, a saint now?

AMALIA: ¡Déjalo!

MARISA: You're still in love with him, aren't you?

AMALIA: Put it down, te digo.

MARISA (*approaching*): I'm asking you a question.

AMALIA: Stay away from me.

MARISA: Answer me! (*Grabs* AMALIA.) Are you in love with him or not?

AMALIA: ¡Déjame!

MARISA (*shaking her*): Did you sleep with him?

AMALIA: No! Stop it!

MARISA: Did you? Tell me the truth!

AMALIA: No! ¡Déjame! (*They struggle. The picture falls to the floor.* AMALIA *breaks* MARISA's *hold.*) I'm not an animal! What gives you the right to come in here like this? Do you think you're the only person in the world who's ever been left waiting?

MARISA: What was I supposed to think . . . that you were dead? That you were dead or you were with him, those were my two choices.

AMALIA (*bitterly*): He's the one who's dead.

MARISA (*after a pause*): What?

AMALIA: He's dead.

AMALIA *slowly walks over to the picture, picks it up, replaces it by the candle. She sits down on the bed, her face impassive.*

AMALIA (*after a pause*): When I got the news, I was in a hotel in Mexico City. I didn't stop to think about it, I took a bus right away to la Costa. Then I hired a boy to give me a lift in a truck. When I got to the river, I knew where to go. The exact spot. The place under the tamarindo where we used to make love. And for hours until dark I sat there by la orilla as I imagined he had that last time.

MARISA: He drowned.

AMALIA: He drowned himself.

MARISA (*going to her*): It's not your fault, Amalia.

AMALIA (*after a pause*): Whose face do you think he saw in the belly of that river moments before it swallowed him?

MARISA: It's not your fault. (*There is a long silence.* MARISA *makes a gesture to touch* AMALIA, *but is unable to.*) I shouldn't have come. I'm sorry.

AMALIA: No, stay. Stay and keep an old woman company.

MARISA: I'll come back tomorrow . . . fix the window. (*She starts to exit.*)
AMALIA: Soñé contigo.
MARISA: You did?
AMALIA: Last night. (*Pause.*) I dreamed we were indias. In our village, some terrible taboo had been broken. There was thunder and lightning. I am crouched down in terror, unable to move when I realize it is *you* who have gone against the code of our people. But I was not afraid of being punished. I did not fear that los dioses would enact their wrath against el pueblo for the breaking of the taboo. It was merely that the taboo *could* be broken. And if this law nearly transcribed in blood could go, then what else? What *was* there to hold to? What immutable truths were left? (*Pause. She turns to* MARISA.) I never wanted you the way I wanted a man. With a man, I just would have left him. Punto. (*Pause.*) Like I left Alejandro.

The lights slowly fade to black.

Scene Twelve

MARISA *sits on the platform.* AMALIA's *rebozo has been left there.*

MARISA: I must admit I wanted to save her. That's probably the whole truth of the story. And the problem is . . . sometimes I actually believed I could, and *sometimes* she did too.

She was like no woman I had ever had. I think it was in the quality of her skin. Some people, you know, their skin is like a covering. They're supposed to be showing you something when the clothes fall into a heap around your four ankles, but nothing is lost, y'know what I mean? They jus' don' give up nuthin'. Pero, Amalia . . . ¡Híjole!

She picks up AMALIA's *rebozo, fingers it.*

She was never ever fully naked in front of me, always had to keep some piece of clothing on, a shirt or something always wrapped up around her throat, her arms all outta it and flying. What she did reveal, though, each item of clothing removed was a gift, I swear, a small offering, a suggestion of all that could be lost and found in our making love together. It was like she was saying to me, "I'll lay down my underslip. ¿Y tú? ¿Qué me vas a dar?" And I'd give her the palm of my hand to warm the spot she had just exposed. Everything was a risk. Everything took time. Was slow and deliberate.

I'll never forget after the first time we made love, I was feeling muy orgullosa y todo, like a good lover, and she says to me—
AMALIA (*voice-over, memory*): You make love to me like worship.
MARISA: And I nearly died, it was so powerful what she was saying. And I wanted to answer, "Sí, la mujer es mi religion." If only sex coulda saved us.

Y'know, sometimes when me and her were in the middle of it, making love, I'd look up at her face, kinda grey from being indoors so much with all those books of hers, and I'd see it change, turn this real deep color of brown and olive, like she was cooking inside. Tan linda. Kind. Very very very kind to me, to herself, to the pinche planet . . . and I'd watch it move from outside the house where that crazy espíritu of hers had been out makin' tracks. I'd watch it come inside, through the door, watch it travel all through her own private miseries and settle itself, finally, right there in the room with us. This bed. This fucking dreary season. This cement city. With us. With me. No part of her begging to have it over . . . forget. And I could feel all the parts of her move into operation. Waiting. Held. Suspended. Praying for me to put my tongue to her and I knew and she knew we would find her . . . como fuego. And just as I pressed my mouth to her, I'd think . . . *I could save your life.*

(*Coming downstage.*) It's not often you get to see people this way in all their pus and glory and still love them. It makes you feel so good, like your hands are weapons of war. And as they move up into el corazón de esta mujer, you are making her body remember, it didn't have to be that hurt. ¿Me entiendes? It was not natural or right that she got beat down so damn hard, and that all those crimes had nothing to do with the girl she once was two, three, four decades ago.

Pause. Music rises softly in the background.

MARISA: It's like making familia from scratch
    each time all over again . . .
    with strangers, if I must.
    If I must, I will.

    I am preparing myself for the worst
    so I cling to her in my heart
    my daydream with pencil in my mouth

    when I put my fingers
    to my own forgotten places.

The lights gradually fade out. Music.

END

                                                                   –1986

Part

II

How are our everyday lives shaped by
gender? What social institutions—law,
religion, education, marriage, family, work,
the military, the media—produce and
regulate gender? How is power gendered?

LIVING

Gender pervades our everyday lives. Almost everything we do or think is linked to gender: the way we experience our bodies, the way we speak, the way we interact with others, and the way we are perceived. Yet because gender is so deep and pervasive an **ideology**, it may not be foremost in our minds.

Try to imagine yourself without a gender identity. What would you look like? How would you respond to the world? Try to recall images of humans who are not gendered. Babies, you say? How often have we seen these diapered beings transformed by a quick application of a bow or the parting of a forelock? Try movie monsters? Even the extension of *Alien* to *Aliens* genders the monster female, with her eggs and womb-like goo. In sci-fi TV we typically encounter men in space suits or humanoids who just happen to feature visible male and female differentiation. As we have seen so often on shows like *Star Trek,* the universe is full of an infinite variety of species, yet no planet seems to lack gender.

If we ask where this reliance on gender comes from, many of us would say "society," and to an extent that is right. But society is more than an abstraction; it is also quite clearly us. In our engagements with the business of living—in the ways we interact in public and in private, in the ways we labor, spend money, make families, and get in and out of daily trouble—we are part of the institutions that maintain and even revise the meanings and effects of gender. By turning from learning to living gender, the texts in this section extend our consideration to the daily life practices through which gender roles, ideals, and realities are both made and contested.

What are these institutions and how do they operate in terms of gender? Societal institutions can be divided into roughly two kinds: 1) state and national forms of power such as citizenship, the military, law enforcement, the penal system, and education; and 2) ideological forms of power such as motherhood and fatherhood, the family, romance, literature, and most important for our purposes, gender. State institutions operate through elaborate and codified laws and are part of the communities in which we live (the voting booth, the police station, the courthouse, the prison, the school). Ideological institutions are far less visible and tangible; for this very reason, they are also more difficult to study. Together these two types of institutions produce daily life.

Many of the texts in this section analyze the impact of state institutions as they affect individual lives. For instance, in Charles Fuller's drama *A Soldier's Play*, the role of the military comes under intense scrutiny, allowing us to explore the various ways in which **race** shapes and transforms norms of **masculinity**. Richard Rodriguez's fiction essay "Proofs" extends the conversation about masculinity by depicting the power of gender and race to condition economic patterns of employment across the U.S.–Mexico border. His use of the border as simultaneously a real place and a **metaphor** for identity enables us to understand how institutions both condition and frame the ways we come to perceive ourselves.

For explorations of the construction of **femininity**, this section offers a range of texts, including e. e. cummings's "she being Brand," which associates women with pleasure by gendering one kind of **commodity**, the automobile, and celebrating the masculine power the driver thereby achieves. Sylvia Plath's "The Applicant" is a kind of biting rejoinder to this scenario of woman as machine. Making fun of the way that housewifery is akin to machine-like devotion and efficiency, Plath manipulates **tone** in order to compel her readers to think about the dehumanizing effects of the **sexual division of labor**, modern life, and consumer culture for the white middle class. A woman's struggle with her lover's ability to associate parts and images of women with pleasure is the theme that Alice Walker explores in "Porn." As a backdrop to all of these pieces are those that focus on the threat and actuality of physical violence, as in Wanda Coleman's "Rape" and Hisaye Yamamoto's "The High-Heeled Shoes: A Memoir."

The relationship between gender and the ideological institution of the family concerns an overwhelming number of U.S. writers. The mixed pleasures and burdens of fatherhood and masculinity are the subject of Charles Johnson's "Moving Pictures" and William Carlos Williams's "Danse Russe." The demands of motherhood are explored in Gwendolyn Brooks's "the mother," which uses a pattern of **rhyme** familiar from literature written for children in order to reinforce the poem's complex exploration of an abortion.

Marriage too is an almost obsessive topic of modern literature, one variously represented here. Stephen Crane's "The Bride Comes to Yellow Sky" asks us to consider the effect of marriage on larger patterns of U.S. history such as continental expansion. Zora Neale Hurston's "The Gilded Six-Bits" presents marriage as a special economic arrangement of gender while Langston Hughes in "Deferred" and John Updike's "The Rumor" focus on marriage as a domestic or privatized institution by examining how communication in marriage often breaks down along gender lines.

The most challenging piece in this section, "Eyes of Zapata," narrates a love story between a mistress of lower **class** standing and her politically powerful male lover in the context of the Mexican Revolution and Civil War in the period between 1911 and 1917. While the mistress's passivity and forbearance, even her worship of her lover's body, fulfill gendered stereotypes of the "double standard" of **heterosexual** relationships, the **narration** from the mistress's **point of view** revises Mexican history. In this way Sandra Cisneros explores both the state and ideological forms of power, and she does so by foregrounding issues of both race and class.

As you read these selections, we want you to think about power. Who has power and who does not? What social forces affect individual lives and limit individual opportunities or choices? How are relationships between men and women part of broader social and historical contexts? To what extent is the individual shaped by ideas and institutions outside of individual control? In what ways do individuals garner control of their own lives from within such constraints?

POETRY

GWENDOLYN BROOKS

B. 1917

Gwendolyn Brooks was born in Topeka, Kansas, and raised on Chicago's South Side. A precocious student, Brooks attended poetry readings by such famous writers as Langston Hughes and James Weldon Johnson, becoming schooled in the oral traditions of African-American literature early on. Her poetry is characterized by keen attention to rhythm and by form that interacts with everyday language. Throughout her career, Brooks has remained active in her community, forging links between the creative life and broader issues of social transformation. Her books include A Street in Bronzeville *(1945),* The Bean Eaters *(1960),* In the Mecca *(1968),* Riot *(1969),* Report from Part I *(1972), and* Report from Part II *(1996). She received the Pulitzer Prize for poetry in 1950 for her collection* Annie Allen.

THE MOTHER

Abortions will not let you forget.
You remember the children you got that you did not get,
The damp small pulps with a little or with no hair,
The singers and workers that never handled the air.
You will never neglect or beat
Them, or silence or buy with a sweet.
You will never wind up the sucking-thumb
Or scuttle off ghosts that come.
You will never leave them, controlling your luscious sigh,
Return for a snack of them, with gobbling mother-eye.

I have heard in the voices of the wind the voices of my dim killed
    children.
I have contracted. I have eased
My dim dears at the breasts they could never suck.
I have said, Sweets, if I sinned, if I seized
Your luck
And your lives from your unfinished reach,
If I stole your births and your names,
Your straight baby tears and your games,
Your stilted or lovely loves, your tumults, your marriages, aches,

and your deaths,
If I poisoned the beginnings of your breaths,
Believe that even in my deliberateness I was not deliberate.
Though why should I whine,
Whine that the crime was other than mine?—
Since anyhow you are dead.
Or rather, or instead,
You were never made.
But that too, I am afraid,
Is faulty: oh, what shall I say, how is the truth to be said?
You were born, you had body, you died.
It is just that you never giggled or planned or cried.

Believe me, I loved you all.
Believe me, I knew you, though faintly, and I loved, I loved you
All.

—1945

WANDA COLEMAN

B. 1945

Wanda Coleman was born and raised in Los Angeles. A sharp social critic of Los Angeles society, Coleman was inspired to write professionally by workshops sponsored in the wake of the Watts Rebellion in 1965. Her vibrant and incisive poetry captures the inner complexities of contemporary urban identities. Her books of poetry include Mad Dog Black Lady *(1979),* Imagoes *(1983),* Heavy Daughter Blues: Poems and Stories 1968-1986 *(1987), and* Hand Dance *(1993). Coleman has also published a collection of short fiction,* A War of Eyes *(1988), and most recently a volume of essays focusing on inter-ethnic relations in L.A.,* Native in a Strange Land: Trials and Tremors *(1996).*

RAPE

Thanx, Kika Warfield

i am here to help you

he laughed. and his partner laughed. she squeezed
her palms/triggers. their uniforms bled
the laughter became screams of horror and she
dragged the bodies of the white blond cop and

his chinese bunky down stairs
and buried them in her eyes/hatred
sprang up and blossomed

talk about it

tell me every detail, said the doctor
they broke in on me. every detail. they took me
in the bedroom, one at a time. next detail
i was scared they'd find my purse—i lied about
having no money. detail, detail. they undressed me,
asked me to tell them how it felt. did it feel
good? yes. did you cum? they were gentle lovers
did you cum? yes. both times? yes

the boyfriend

came in. she was feeling shrunken dirty suicide
she hadn't douched. the wetness still pouring
out/a sticky riverlet on her inner thighs
he got indignant. why didn't she call the police
why didn't she call her mama. why didn't she die
fighting. she remained silent. he asked her where
it happened. she showed him the spot. he
pulled down his pants, forced her back onto the sheets
i haven't cleaned up, she whined. but he was
full saddle hard dicking and cumming torrents

the two burglars

kicked the door in. she woke. she thought, he's
drunk again. she slipped into her thin pink
gown, got up and went to see. it wasn't him. we
have guns, the dark one announced
there's no one here but me and the kids she said

there was little

for them to steal. the dark one took her into
the bedroom while his partner searched. he turned
out the lights and stripped. he laid her gently on
the bed. this is my name. when you cum, call
my name. she agreed. and he entered. your pussy's
hot and tight. where's your old man? he's
a fool not to be here with you. you're pretty
you're soft. you fuck good. kiss me. and she did
as told. we don't want to hurt you. you like

the way i kiss. tell the truth. it's good,
she said and after a while she moaned his name

the other one

came in and took off his clothes in the dark
i'm really sorry to do this, he said, but
i can't help myself. strange, she thought. such
polite rapists. i wonder if they'll kill me
somehow it must make them care enough not
to kill me. he told her his name and sucked
hungry at her nipples, parted her legs
he was very thick long hard. his friend's seed
eased the pain. i want your tongue he said
give me your tongue. she gave and gave
jesus! he cried and shot into her, long spastic jerks
he trembled and fell into her arms. shit
that was good

in the kitchen

her few valuables were piled neatly mid-floor
she promised not to call the police
what could they do, save her?
the other one, the jesus-man took her typewriter
and put it back, and all the other stuff they
had planned to take. even the television

here is my number, said the dark one
when you get lonely, call

and she walked

them to the door. the dark one took her in his arms
kissed her goodbye

she waited

until she was sure they wouldn't
come back and kill

she picked up the phone

and made the mistake of thinking the world
would understand

—1983

E. E. CUMMINGS

1894-1962

*e. e. cummings was born in Cambridge, Massachusetts. His poetry combined
the influence of metaphysical and pre-Raphaelite verse with the innovative
techniques extolled by his contemporary, the poet Ezra Pound. A popular and
accessible poet, cummings balanced the demanding stylistic experimentation
characteristic of modernist poetry with a sense of whimsy and eroticism that
most often celebrated the stance of the individual (always represented by
the lowercase "i") against mass society. cummings served in World War I,
painted seriously, lived in Paris and New York City, and traveled in the
U.S.S.R. His major works include* Tulips and Chimneys *(1923),* The Enormous
Room *(1922),* Is 5 *(1926),* 1 x 1 *(1944), and* Selected Poems *(1959).*

SHE BEING BRAND

-new;and you
know consequently a
little stiff i was
careful of her and(having

thoroughly oiled the universal
joint tested my gas felt of
her radiator made sure her springs were O.

K.)i went right to it flooded-the-carburetor cranked her

up,slipped the
clutch(and then somehow got into reverse she
kicked what
the hell)next
minute I was back in neutral tried and

again slo-wly;bare,ly nudg.   ing(my

lev-er Right-
oh and her gears being in
A 1 shape passed
from low through
second-in-to-high like
greasedlightning)just as we turned the corner of Divinity

avenue i touched the accelerator and give

her the juice,good

                    (it

was the first ride and believe i we was
happy to see how nice she acted right up to
the last minute coming back by the Public
Gardens i slammed on

the
internalexpanding
&
externalcontracting
brakes Bothatonce and

brought allofher tremB
-ling
to a:dead.

stand-
;Still)

                              —1926

ROBERT FROST

1874-1963

Robert Frost was born in California, but moved in 1885 with his mother, a schoolteacher, to New England. Frost studied briefly at Dartmouth College in New Hampshire and at Harvard University, holding odd jobs and occasionally teaching. Although he was well-read in English and American classics, had traveled in England, and built a serious career as a writer, Frost preferred to cultivate the image of the vernacular farmer-poet. In his role as Poet Laureate of the United States, Frost read at John F. Kennedy's 1961 presidential inauguration. His major works include A Boy's Will *(1915),* New Hampshire *(1923),* Two Tramps in Mud-Time *(1935), and* The Gift Outright *(1961). He received the Pulitzer Prize in poetry in 1924, 1931, 1937, and 1943.*

HOME BURIAL

He saw her from the bottom of the stairs
Before she saw him. She was starting down,
Looking back over her shoulder at some fear.
She took a doubtful step and then undid it
To raise herself and look again. He spoke
Advancing toward her: "What is it you see
From up there always?—for I want to know."
She turned and sank upon her skirts at that,
And her face changed from terrified to dull.
He said to gain time: "What is it you see?"
Mounting until she cowered under him.
"I will find out now—you must tell me, dear."
She, in her place, refused him any help,
With the least stiffening of her neck and silence.
She let him look, sure that he wouldn't see,
Blind creature; and awhile he didn't see.
But at last he murmured, "Oh," and again, "Oh."

"What is it—what?" she said.

                "Just that I see."

"You don't," she challenged. "Tell me what it is."

"The wonder is I didn't see at once.
I never noticed it from here before.
I must be wonted to it—that's the reason.
The little graveyard where my people are!
So small the window frames the whole of it.
Not so much larger than a bedroom, is it?
There are three stones of slate and one of marble,
Broad-shouldered little slabs there in the sunlight
On the sidehill. We haven't to mind *those.*
But I understand: it is not the stones,
But the child's mound——"

              "Don't, don't, don't, don't," she cried.

She withdrew, shrinking from beneath his arm
That rested on the banister, and slid downstairs;
And turned on him with such a daunting look,
He said twice over before he knew himself:
"Can't a man speak of his own child he's lost?"

"Not you!—Oh, where's my hat? Oh, I don't need it!
I must get out of here. I must get air.—
I don't know rightly whether any man can."

"Amy! Don't go to someone else this time.
Listen to me. I won't come down the stairs."
He sat and fixed his chin between his fists.
"There's something I should like to ask you, dear."

"You don't know how to ask it."

"Help me, then."

Her fingers moved the latch for all reply.

"My words are nearly always an offense.
I don't know how to speak of anything
So as to please you. But I might be taught,
I should suppose. I can't say I see how.
A man must partly give up being a man
With womenfolk. We could have some arrangement
By which I'd bind myself to keep hands off
Anything special you're a-mind to name.
Though I don't like such things 'twixt those that love.
Two that don't love can't live together without them.
But two that do can't live together with them."
She moved the latch a little. "Don't—don't go.
Don't carry it to someone else this time.
Tell me about it if it's something human.
Let me into your grief. I'm not so much
Unlike other folks as your standing there
Apart would make me out. Give me my chance.
I do think, though, you overdo it a little.
What was it brought you up to think it the thing
To take your mother-loss of a first child
So inconsolably—in the face of love.
You'd think his memory might be satisfied——"

"There you go sneering now!"

"I'm not, I'm not!
You make me angry. I'll come down to you.
God, what a woman! And it's come to this,
A man can't speak of his own child that's dead."

"You can't because you don't know how to speak.
If you had any feelings, you that dug
With your own hand—how could you?—his little grave;
I saw you from that very window there,
Making the gravel leap and leap in air,
Leap up, like that, like that, and land so lightly
And roll back down the mound beside the hole.

I thought, Who is that man? I didn't know you.
And I crept down the stairs and up the stairs
To look again, and still your spade kept lifting.
Then you came in. I heard your rumbling voice
Out in the kitchen, and I don't know why,
But I went near to see with my own eyes.
You could sit there with the stains on your shoes
Of the fresh earth from your own baby's grave
And talk about your everyday concerns.
You had stood the spade up against the wall
Outside there in the entry, for I saw it."

"I shall laugh the worst laugh I ever laughed.
I'm cursed. God, if I don't believe I'm cursed."

"I can repeat the very words you were saying:
'Three foggy mornings and one rainy day
Will rot the best birch fence a man can build.'
Think of it, talk like that at such a time!
What had how long it takes a birch to rot
To do with what was in the darkened parlor?
You *couldn't* care! The nearest friends can go
With anyone to death, comes so far short
They might as well not try to go at all.
No, from the time when one is sick to death,
One is alone, and he dies more alone.
Friends make pretense of following to the grave,
But before one is in it, their minds are turned
And making the best of their way back to life
And living people, and things they understand.
But the world's evil. I won't have grief so
If I can change it. Oh, I won't, I won't!"

"There, you have said it all and you feel better.
You won't go now. You're crying. Close the door.
The heart's gone out of it: why keep it up?
Amy! There's someone coming down the road!"

"*You*—oh, you think the talk is all. I must go—
Somewhere out of this house. How can I make you——"

"If—you—do!" She was opening the door wider.
"Where do you mean to go? First tell me that.
I'll follow and bring you back by force. I *will!*—"

—1914

JOY HARJO

B. 1951

Joy Harjo was born in Tulsa, Oklahoma, of Creek, French, and Cherokee ancestry. A saxophonist, poet, and screenplay writer, Harjo's work forcefully confronts the social issues facing contemporary Native peoples. She is the author of five books of poetry, including Secrets from the Center of The World *(1987),* In Mad Love and War *(1990),* Fishing *(1992), and* The Woman Who Fell from the Sky *(1994). Her screenplays and TV play include* The Gaan Story *(1984),* We Are One, Umonho *(1984), and* The Runaway *(1986). Her band, "Poetic Justice," has attracted attention in North America and Europe for its compelling combination of poetry and music. Harjo teaches creative writing at the University of New Mexico.*

THE WOMAN HANGING FROM THE THIRTEENTH FLOOR WINDOW

She is the woman hanging from the 13th floor
window. Her hands are pressed white against the
concrete molding of the tenement building. She
hangs from the 13th floor window in east Chicago,
with a swirl of birds over her head. They could
be a halo, or a storm of glass waiting to crush her.

She thinks she will be set free.

The woman hanging from the 13th floor window
on the east side of Chicago is not alone.
She is a woman of children, of the baby, Carlos,
and of Margaret, and of Jimmy who is the oldest.
She is her mother's daughter and her father's son.
She is several pieces between the two husbands
she has had. She is all the women of the apartment
building who stand watching her, watching themselves.

When she was young she ate wild rice on scraped down
plates in warm wood rooms. It was in the farther
north and she was the baby then. They rocked her.

She sees Lake Michigan lapping at the shores of
herself. It is a dizzy hole of water and the rich
live in tall glass houses at the edge of it. In some
places Lake Michigan speaks softly, here, it just sputters
and butts itself against the asphalt. She sees
other buildings just like hers. She sees other
women hanging from many-floored windows

counting their lives in the palms of their hands
and in the palms of their children's hands.

She is the woman hanging from the 13th floor window
on the Indian side of town. Her belly is soft from
her children's births, her worn levis swing down below
her waist, and then her feet, and then her heart.
She is dangling.

The woman hanging from the 13th floor hears voices.
They come to her in the night when the lights have gone
dim. Sometimes they are little cats mewing and scratching
at the door, sometimes they are her grandmother's voice,
and sometimes they are gigantic men of light whispering
to her to get up, to get up, to get up. That's when she wants
to have another child to hold on to in the night, to be able
to fall back into dreams.

And the woman hanging from the 13th floor window
hears other voices. Some of them scream out from below
for her to jump, they would push her over. Others cry softly
from the sidewalks, pull their children up like flowers and gather
them into their arms. They would help her, like themselves.

But she is the woman hanging from the 13th floor window,
and she knows she is hanging by her own fingers, her
own skin, her own thread of indecision.

She thinks of Carlos, of Margaret, of Jimmy.
She thinks of her father, and of her mother.
She thinks of all the women she has been, of all
the men. She thinks of the color of her skin, and
of Chicago streets, and of waterfalls and pines.
She thinks of moonlight nights, and of cool spring storms.
Her mind chatters like neon and northside bars.
She thinks of the 4 a.m. lonelinesses that have folded
her up like death, discordant, without logical and
beautiful conclusion. Her teeth break off at the edges.
She would speak.

The woman hangs from the 13th floor window crying for
the lost beauty of her own life. She sees the
sun falling west over the gray plain of Chicago.
She thinks she remembers listening to her own life
break loose, as she falls from the 13th floor
window on the east side of Chicago, or as she
climbs back up to claim herself again.

—1983

LANGSTON HUGHES

1902-1967

Langston Hughes was born in Joplin, Missouri, and died in New York City. He was one of the key figures of the African-American cultural explosion known as the Harlem Renaissance of the 1920s and early '30s. Erudite and well-traveled, Hughes favored deceptively simple lyric forms borrowed from traditional African-American forms such as spiritual, blues, and jazz; using these, he critiqued the limitations and contradictions inherent in American democracy under white supremacy. Hughes's cultural production is varied and immense. Highlights include The Weary Blues *(1926),* One-Way Ticket *(1949),* Simple Speaks His Mind *(1950), and* Montage of A Dream Deferred *(1951).*

DEFERRED

This year, maybe, do you think I can graduate?
I'm already two years late.
Dropped out six months when I was seven,
a year when I was eleven,
then got put back when we come North.
To get through high at twenty's kind of late—
But maybe this year I can graduate.

Maybe now I can have that white enamel stove
I dreamed about when we first fell in love
eighteen years ago.
But you know,
rooming and everything
then kids,
cold-water flat and all that.
But now my daughter's married
And my boy's most grown—
quit school to work—
and where we're moving
there ain't no stove—
Maybe I can buy that white enamel stove!

Me, I always did want to study French.
It don't make sense—
I'll never go to France,
but night schools teach French.
Now at last I've got a job
where I get off at five,
in time to wash and dress,
so, s'il-vous plait, I'll study French!

Someday,
I'm gonna buy two new suits
at once!

All I want is
one more bottle of gin.

All I want is to see
my furniture paid for.

All I want is a wife who will
work with me and not against me. Say,
baby, could you see your way clear?

Heaven, heaven, is my home!
This world I'll leave behind
When I set my feet in glory
I'll have a throne for mine!

I want to pass the civil service.

I want a television set.

You know, as old as I am,
I ain't never
owned a decent radio yet?

I'd like to take up Bach.

>   *Montage*
>   *of a dream*
>   *deferred.*

Buddy, have you heard?

—1951

YUSEF KOMUNYAKAA

B. 1947

Yusef Komunyakaa was born in Bogalusa, Louisiana. Immediately after graduating from high school Komunyakaa served in Vietnam, where he earned a bronze star as a correspondent and editor of the army newspaper The Southern Cross. *After the war, he continued his education, receiving a Ph.D. from the University of California, Irvine. Employing short lines and mixing vernacular and unusual words, Komunyakaa often writes about African-American culture in the South and the psychic and material violence of the Vietnam War. His books of poetry include* Lost in the Bonewheel Factory *(1979),* Copacetic *(1983),* I Apologize for the Eyes in My Head *(1986), and* Dien Cai Dau *(1988). He won a Pushcart Prize for the poem "Tu Do Street" and received the Pulitzer Prize for* Neon Vernacular *in 1994. He currently teaches creative writing at Princeton University.*

MORE GIRL THAN BOY

You'll always be my friend.
Is that clear, Robert Lee?
We go beyond the weighing
of each other's words,
hand on a shoulder,
go beyond the color of hair.
Playing Down the Man on the Field
we embraced each other before
I discovered girls.
You taught me a heavy love
for jazz, how words can hurt
more than a quick jab.
Something there's no word for
saved us from the streets.

Night's pale horse
rode you past common sense,
but you made it home from Chicago.
So many dreams dead.
All the man-sweet gigs
meant absolutely nothing.
Welcome back to earth, Robert.
You always could make that piano
talk like somebody's mama.

—1993

PHILIP LEVINE

B. 1928

Philip Levine was born to Russian-Jewish immigrant parents in Detroit, Michigan, and attended Wayne State University and the University of Iowa Writers' Workshop. A child of the Depression, Levine is concerned in his poetry to give voice to the working classes; many of his poems pay particular attention to the conflicts and emotional textures of work environments. Levine was on the faculty of California State University, Fresno, from 1958 to 1992 and won the Pulitzer Prize in 1995. His works include One for the Roses *(1981),* What Work Is *(1991), and* The Simple Truth *(1994).*

MAKING SODA POP

The big driver said
he only fucked Jews. Eddie smiled
and folded his glasses
into their little blue
snap case and put the case
into his lunch bag. Last night
I think she was your sister.
This was noon
on the loading docks
at Mavis-Nu-Icy Bottling,
Eddie and I side by side
our backs to the wall,
our legs stretched out
before us the way children
do on a sofa. Ain't got
no sister, Eddie said.
Must have been
your mother then. Eddie
landed first
and the man, older and slower,
fell back out of the shade
into the cinders
of the rail yard. The guy
beside me went on chewing.
Eddie came slowly forward
crouching, his weak eyes
wide, and swung
again, again, and the man
went down heavier
this time and didn't

try to get up. Eddie
came back to his place
beside me, no smile on
his face, nothing, and opened
a peanut butter sandwich.
Alvin, the foreman, looked up
and said, OK, you guys,
this afternoon cream soda.

SYLVIA PLATH

1932-1963

Sylvia Plath was born in Boston and graduated in 1955 from Smith College for women. A highly successful student, Plath won a Fulbright Scholarship to England. There, she married the poet Ted Hughes, had two children, and wrote poetry with increasing assurance and urgency. Among her books of poetry are The Collosus and Other Poems *(1960) and* Ariel *(1965). She also wrote a best-selling novel,* The Bell Jar *(1963), chronicling the nervous breakdown and recovery of a young career woman in New York City. After a long struggle with mental illness, Plath committed suicide in 1963. Her posthumous* Collected Poems, *edited by Ted Hughes, received the Pulitzer Prize in 1982.*

THE APPLICANT

First, are you our sort of a person?
Do you wear
A glass eye, false teeth or a crutch,
A brace or a hook,
Rubber breasts or a rubber crotch,

Stitches to show something's missing? No, no? Then
How can we give you a thing?
Stop crying.
Open your hand.
Empty? Empty. Here is a hand

To fill it and willing
To bring teacups and roll away headaches

And do whatever you tell it.
Will you marry it?
It is guaranteed

To thumb shut your eyes at the end
And dissolve of sorrow.
We make new stock from the salt.
I notice you are stark naked.
How about this suit——

Black and stiff, but not a bad fit.
Will you marry it?
It is waterproof, shatterproof, proof
Against fire and bombs through the roof
Believe me, they'll bury you in it.

Now your head, excuse me, is empty.
I have the ticket for that.
Come here sweetie, out of the closet.
Well, what do you think of *that?*
Naked as paper to start

But in twenty-five years she'll be silver,
In fifty, gold.
A living doll, everywhere you look.
It can sew, it can cook,
It can talk, talk, talk.

It works, there is nothing wrong with it.
You have a hole, it's a poultice.
You have an eye, it's an image.
My boy, it's your last resort.
Will you marry it, marry it, marry it.

—1962

WILLIAM CARLOS WILLIAMS
1883-1963

William Carlos Williams practiced medicine in Rutherford, New Jersey, in the days when doctors still made house calls. He was educated in prep schools in New Jersey and Switzerland and studied medicine at the University of Pennsylvania, maintaining his ties to the New York City bohemian literati. His first book, Poems, *appeared in 1909, to be followed by many others, including* Spring and All *(1923), the four-volume* Paterson *(1946-1951), and* Pictures from Brueghel *(1963). Williams received the National Book Award (1950), the Bollingen Prize (1953), and a Pulitzer Prize (1963). He wrote frankly about the body and sexuality, often drawing on his experiences with poor patients and with the women who worked in the houses he visited.*

DANSE RUSSE

If when my wife is sleeping
and the baby and Kathleen
are sleeping
and the sun is a flame-white disc
in silken mists
above shining trees.—
if I in my north room
dance naked, grotesquely
before my mirror
waving my shirt round my head
and singing softly to myself:
"I am lonely, lonely.
I was born to be lonely,
I am best so!"
If I admire my arms, my face,
my shoulders, flanks, buttocks
against the yellow drawn shades,—

Who shall say I am not
the happy genius of my household?

—1938

FICTION

SANDRA CISNEROS

B. 1954

Sandra Cisneros was born in Chicago to a Mexican father and a Mexican-American mother. Her poetry and fiction explore the productive disjuncture between American and Mexican culture in prose marked by "poetic" diction and compression and in an English inflected by Spanish words and syntax. She is the author of The House on Mango Street *(1983), which was awarded the Before Columbus Foundation Book Award in 1985 and two books of poetry,* My Wicked Wicked Ways *(1987) and* Loose Woman *(1994). Cisneros's short story collection* Woman Hollering Creek *(1991) received the Lannan Award for Fiction and the PEN Center West Award for Fiction. A recent recipient of a MacArthur "genius" Award, Cisneros lives in San Antonio, Texas.*

EYES OF ZAPATA

I put my nose to your eyelashes. The skin of the eyelids as soft as the skin of the penis, the collarbone with its fluted wings, the purple knot of the nipple, the dark, blue-black color of your sex, the thin legs and long thin feet. For a moment I don't want to think of your past nor your future. For now you are here, you are mine.

Would it be right to tell you what I do each night you sleep here? After your cognac and cigar, after I'm certain you're asleep, I examine at my leisure your black trousers with the silver buttons—fifty-six pairs on each side; I've counted them—your embroidered sombrero with its horsehair tassel, the lovely Dutch linen shirt, the fine braid stitching on the border of your *charro* jacket, the handsome black boots, your tooled gun belt and silver spurs. Are you my general? Or only that boy I met at the country fair in San Lázaro?

Hands too pretty for a man. Elegant hands, graceful hands, fingers smelling sweet as your Havanas. I had pretty hands once, remember? You used to say I had the prettiest hands of any woman in Cuautla. *Exquisitas* you called them, as if they were something to eat. It still makes me laugh remembering that.

Ay, but now look. Nicked and split and callused—how is it the hands get old first? The skin as coarse as the wattle of a hen. It's from the planting in the *tlacolol,* from the hard man's work I do clearing the field with the hoe and the machete, dirty work that leaves the clothes filthy, work no woman would do before the war.

But I'm not afraid of hard work or of being alone in the hills. I'm not afraid of dying or jail. I'm not afraid of the night like other women who run to the sacristy at the first call of *el gobierno*. I'm not other women.

Look at you. Snoring already? *Pobrecito.* Sleep, *papacito.* There, there. It's only me—Inés. *Duerme, mi trigueño, mi chulito, mi bebito. Ya, ya, ya.*

You say you can't sleep anywhere like you sleep here. So tired of always having to be *el gran general* Emiliano Zapata. The nervous fingers flinch, the long elegant bones shiver and twitch. Always waiting for the assassin's bullet.

Everyone is capable of becoming a traitor, and traitors must be broken, you say. A horse to be broken. A new saddle that needs breaking in. To break a spirit. Something to whip and lasso like you did in the *jaripeos* years ago.

Everything bothers you these days. Any noise, any light, even the sun. You say nothing for hours, and then when you do speak, it's an outburst, a fury. Everyone afraid of you, even your men. You hide yourself in the dark. You go days without sleep. You don't laugh anymore.

I don't need to ask; I've seen for myself. The war is not going well. I see it in your face. How it's changed over the years, Miliano. From so much watching, the face grows that way. These wrinkles new, this furrow, the jaw clenched tight. Eyes creased from learning to see in the night.

They say the widows of sailors have eyes like that, from squinting into the line where the sky and sea dissolve. It's the same with us from all this war. We're all widows. The men as well as the women, even the children. *All clinging to the tail of the horse of our* jefe Zapata. All of us scarred from these nine years of *aguantando—* enduring.

Yes, it's in your face. It's always been there. Since before the war. Since before I knew you. Since your birth in Anenecuilco and even before then. Something hard and tender all at once in those eyes. You knew before any of us, didn't you?

This morning the messenger arrived with the news you'd be arriving before nightfall, but I was already boiling the corn for your supper tortillas. I saw you riding in on the road from Villa de Ayala. Just as I saw you that day in Anenecuilco when the revolution had just begun and the government was everywhere looking for you. You were worried about the land titles, went back to dig them up from where you'd hidden them eighteen months earlier, under the altar in the village church— am I right?—reminding Chico Franco to keep them safe. *I'm bound to die,* you said, *someday. But our titles stand to be guaranteed.*

I wish I could rub the grief from you as if it were a smudge on the cheek. I want to gather you up in my arms as if you were Nicolás or Malena, run up to the hills. I know every cave and crevice, every back road and ravine, but I don't know where I could hide you from yourself. You're tired. You're sick and lonely with this war, and I don't want any of those things to ever touch you again, Miliano. It's enough for now you are here. For now. Under my roof again.

Sleep, *papacito.* It's only Inés circling above you, wide-eyed all night. The sound of my wings like the sound of a velvet cape crumpling. A warm breeze against your skin, the wide expanse of moon-white feathers as if I could touch all the walls of the house at one sweep. A rustling, then weightlessness, light scattered out the window until it's the moist night wind beneath my owl wings. Whorl of stars like the filigree earrings you gave me. Your tired horse still as tin, there, where you tied it to a guamuchil tree. River singing louder than ever since the time of the rains.

I scout the hillsides, the mountains. My blue shadow over the high grass and slash of *barrancas,* over the ghosts of haciendas silent under the blue night. From this height, the village looks the same as before the war. As if the roofs were still intact, the walls still whitewashed, the cobbled streets swept of rubble and weeds. Nothing blistered and burnt. Our lives smooth and whole.

Round and round the blue countryside, over the scorched fields, giddy wind barely ruffling my stiff, white feathers, above the two soldiers you left guarding our door, one asleep, the other dull from a day of hard riding. But I'm awake, I'm always awake when you are here. Nothing escapes me. No coyote in the mountains, or scorpion in the sand. Everything clear. The trail you rode here. The night jasmine with its frothy scent of sweet milk. The makeshift roof of cane leaves on our adobe house. Our youngest child of five summers asleep in her hammock—*What a little woman you are now, Malenita.* The laughing sound of the river and canals, and the high, melancholy voice of the wind in the branches of the tall pine.

I slow-circle and glide into the house, bringing the night-wind smell with me, fold myself back into my body. I haven't left you. I don't leave you, not ever. Do you know why? Because when you are gone I re-create you from memory. The scent of your skin, the mole above the broom of your mustache, how you fit in my palms. Your skin dark and rich as *piloncillo.* This face in my hands. I miss you. I miss you even now as you lie next to me.

To look at you as you sleep, the color of your skin. How in the half-light of moon you cast your own light, as if you are all made of amber, Miliano. As if you are a little lantern, and everything in the house is golden too.

You used to be *tan chistoso. Muy bonachón, muy bromista.* Joking and singing off-key when you had your little drinks. *Tres vicios tengo y los tengo muy arraigados; de ser borracho, jugador, y enamorado . . .* Ay, my life, remember? Always *muy enamorado,* no? Are you still that boy I met at the San Lázaro country fair? Am I still that girl you kissed under the little avocado tree? It seems so far away from those days, Miliano.

We drag these bodies around with us, these bodies that have nothing at all to do with you, with me, with who we really are, these bodies that give us pleasure and pain. Though I've learned how to abandon mine at will, it seems to me we never free ourselves completely until we love, when we lose ourselves inside each other. Then we see a little of what is called heaven. When we can be that close that we no longer are Inés and Emiliano, but something bigger than our lives. And we can forgive, finally.

You and I, we've never been much for talking, have we? Poor thing, you don't know how to talk. Instead of talking with your lips, you put one leg around me when we sleep, to let me know it's all right. And we fall asleep like that, with one arm or a leg or one of those long monkey feet of yours touching mine. Your foot inside the hollow of my foot.

Does it surprise you I don't let go little things like that? There are so many things I don't forget even if I would do well to.

Inés, for the love I have for you. When my father pleaded, you can't imagine how I felt. How a pain entered my heart like a current of cold water and in that current were the days to come. But I said nothing.

Well then, my father said, *God help you. You've turned out just like the* perra *that bore you.* Then he turned around and I had no father.

I never felt so alone as that night. I gathered my things in my *rebozo* and ran out into the darkness to wait for you by the jacaranda tree. For a moment, all my courage left me. I wanted to turn around, call out, *apá,* beg his forgiveness, and go back to sleeping on my *petate* against the cane-rush wall, waking before dawn to prepare the corn for the day's tortillas.

Perra. That word, the way my father spat it, as if in that one word I were betraying all the love he had given me all those years, as if he were closing all the doors to his heart.

Where could I hide from my father's anger? I could put out the eyes and stop the mouths of all the saints that wagged their tongues at me, but I could not stop my heart from hearing that word *perra.* My father, my love, who would have nothing to do with me.

You don't like me to talk about my father, do you? I know, you and he never, well . . . Remember that thick scar across his left eyebrow? Kicked by a mule when he was a boy. Yes, that's how it happened. Tía Chucha said it was the reason he sometimes acted like a mule—but you're as stubborn as he was, aren't you, and no mule kicked you.

It's true, he never liked you. Since the days you started buying and selling livestock all through the *rancheritos.* By the time you were working the stables in Mexico City there was no mentioning your name. Because you'd never slept under a thatch roof, he said. Because you were a *charro,* and didn't wear the cotton whites of the *campesino.* Then he'd mutter, loud enough for me to hear, *That one doesn't know what it is to smell his own shit.*

I always thought you and he made such perfect enemies because you were so much alike. Except, unlike you, he was useless as a soldier. I never told you how the government forced him to enlist. Up in Guanajuato is where they sent him when you were busy with the Carrancistas, and Pancho Villa's boys were giving everyone a rough time up north. My father, who'd never been farther than Amecameca, grayhaired and broken as he was, they took him. It was during the time the dead were piled up on the street corners like stones, when it wasn't safe for anyone, man or woman, to go out into the streets.

There was nothing to eat, Tía Chucha sick with the fever, and me taking care of us all. My father said better he should go to his brother Fulgencio's in Tenexcapán and see if they had corn there. *Take Malenita,* I said. *With a child they won't bother you.*

And so my father went out toward Tenexcapán dragging Malenita by the hand. But when night began to fall and they hadn't come back, well, imagine. It was the widow Elpidia who knocked on our door with Malenita howling and with the story they'd taken the men to the railroad station. *South to the work camps, or north to fight?* Tía Chucha asked. *If God wishes,* I said, *he'll be safe.*

That night Tía Chucha and I dreamt this dream. My father and my Tío Fulgencio standing against the back wall of the rice mill. *Who lives?* But they don't answer, afraid to give the wrong *viva. Shoot them; discuss politics later.*

At the moment the soldiers are about to fire, an officer, an acquaintance of my father's from before the war, rides by and orders them set free.

Then they took my father and my Tío Fulgencio to the train station, shuttled them into box cars with others, and didn't let them go until they reached Guanajuato where they were each given guns and orders to shoot at the Villistas.

With the fright of the firing squad and all, my father was never the same. In Guanajuato, he had to be sent to the military hospital, where he suffered a collapsed lung. They removed three of his ribs to cure him, and when he was finally well enough to travel, they sent him back to us.

All through the dry season my father lived on like that, with a hole in the back of his chest from which he breathed. Those days I had to swab him with a sticky pitch pine and wrap him each morning in clean bandages. The opening oozed a spittle like the juice of the prickly pear, sticky and clear and with a smell both sweet and terrible like magnolia flowers rotting on the branch.

We did the best we could to nurse him, my Tía Chucha and I. Then one morning a *chachalaca* flew inside the house and battered against the ceiling. It took both of us with blankets and the broom to get it out. We didn't say anything but we thought about it for a long time.

Before the next new moon, I had a dream I was in church praying a rosary. But what I held between my hands wasn't my rosary with the glass beads, but one of human teeth. I let it drop, and the teeth bounced across the flagstones like pearls from a necklace. The dream and the bird were sign enough.

When my father called my mother's name one last time and died, the syllables came out sucked and coughed from that other mouth, like a drowned man's, and he expired finally in one last breath from that opening that killed him.

We buried him like that, with his three missing ribs wrapped in a handkerchief my mother had embroidered with his initials and with the hoofmark of the mule under his left eyebrow.

For eight days people arrived to pray the rosary. All the priests had long since fled, we had to pay a *rezandero* to say the last rites. Tía Chucha laid the cross of lime and sand, and set out flowers and a votive lamp, and on the ninth day, my *tía* raised the cross and called out my father's name—Remigio Alfaro—and my father's spirit flew away and left us.

But suppose he won't give us his permission.

That old goat, we'll be dead by the time he gives his permission. Better we just run off. He can't be angry forever.

Not even on his deathbed did he forgive you. I suppose you've never forgiven him either for calling in the authorities. I'm sure he only meant for them to scare you a little, to remind you of your obligations to me since I was expecting your child. Who could imagine they would force you to join the cavalry.

I can't make apologies on my father's behalf, but, well, what were we to think, Miliano? Those months you were gone, hiding out in Puebla because of the protest signatures, the political organizing, the work in the village defense. Me as big as a boat, Nicolás waiting to be born at any moment, and you nowhere to be found, and no money sent, and not a word. I was so young, I didn't know what else to do but abandon our house of stone and adobe and go back to my father's. Was I wrong to do that? You tell me.

I could endure my father's anger, but I was afraid for the child. I placed my hand on my belly and whispered—Child, be born when the moon is tender; even a tree must be pruned under the full moon so it will grow strong. And at the next full moon, I gave light, Tía Chucha holding up our handsome, strong-lunged boy.

Two planting seasons came and went, and we were preparing for the third when you came back from the cavalry and met your son for the first time. I thought you'd forgotten all about politics, and we could go on with our lives. But by the end of the year you were already behind the campaign to elect Patricio Leyva governor, as if all the troubles with the government, with my father, had meant nothing.

You gave me a pair of gold earrings as a wedding gift, remember? *I never said I'd marry you, Inés. Never.* Two filagree hoops with tiny flowers and fringe. I buried them when the government came, and went back for them later. But even these I had to sell when there was nothing to eat but boiled corn silk. They were the last things I sold.

Never. It made me feel a little crazy when you hurled that at me. That word with all its force.

But, Miliano, I thought . . .

You were foolish to have thought then.

That was years ago. We're all guilty of saying things we don't mean. *I never said . . .* I know. You don't want to hear it.

What am I to you now, Miliano? When you leave me? When you hesitate? Hover? The last time you gave a sigh that would fit into a spoon. What did you mean by that?

If I complain about these woman concerns of mine, I know you'll tell me—Inés, these aren't times for that—wait until later. But, Miliano, I'm tired of being told to wait.

Ay, you don't understand. Even if you had the words, you could never tell me. You don't know your own heart, men. Even when you are speaking with it in your hand.

I have my livestock, a little money my father left me. I'll set up a house for us in Cuautla of stone and adobe. We can live together, and later we'll see.

Nicolás is crazy about his two cows, La Fortuna y La Paloma. Because he's a man now, you said, when you gave him his birthday present. When you were thirteen, you were already buying and reselling animals throughout the ranches. To see if a beast is a good worker, you must tickle it on the back, no? If it can't bother itself to move, well then, it's lazy and won't be of any use. See, I've learned that much from you.

Remember the horse you found in Cuernavaca? Someone had hidden it in an upstairs bedroom, wild and spirited from being penned so long. She had poked her head from between the gold fringe of velvet drapery just as you rode by, just at that moment. A beauty like that making her appearance from a balcony like a woman waiting for her serenade. You laughed and joked about that and named her La Coquetona, remember? La Coquetona, yes.

When I met you at the country fair in San Lázaro, everyone knew you were the best man with horses in the state of Morelos. All the hacienda owners wanted you to work for them. Even as far as Mexico City. A *charro* among *charros*. The livestock, the horses bought and sold. Planting a bit when things were slow. Your brother Eufemio borrowing time and time again because he'd squandered every peso of his inheritance, but you've always prided yourself in being independent, no? You once confessed one of the happiest days of your life was the watermelon harvest that produced the 600 pesos.

And *my* happiest memory? The night I came to live with you, of course. I remember how your skin smelled sweet as the rind of a watermelon, like the fields after it has rained. I wanted my life to begin there, at that moment when I balanced that thin boy's body of yours on mine, as if you were made of balsa, as if you were boat and I river. The days to come, I thought, erasing the bitter sting of my father's good-bye.

There's been too much suffering, too much of our hearts hardening and drying like corpses. We've survived, eaten grass and corn cobs and rotten vegetables. And the epidemics have been as dangerous as the *federales*, the deserters, the bandits. Nine years.

In Cuautla it stank from so many dead. Nicolás would go out to play with the bullet shells he'd collected, or to watch the dead being buried in trenches. Once five federal corpses were piled up in the *zócalo*. We went through their pockets for money, jewelry, anything we could sell. When they burned the bodies, the fat ran off them in streams, and they jumped and wiggled as if they were trying to sit up. Nicolás had terrible dreams after that. I was too ashamed to tell him I did, too.

At first we couldn't bear to look at the bodies hanging in the trees. But after many months, you get used to them, curling and drying into leather in the sun day after day, dangling like earrings, so that they no longer terrify, they no longer mean anything. Perhaps that is worst of all.

Your sister tells me Nicolás takes after you these days, nervous and quick with words, like a sudden dust storm or shower of sparks. When you were away with the Seventh Cavalry, Tía Chucha and I would put smoke in Nicolás's mouth, so he would learn to talk early. All the other babies his age babbling like monkeys, but Nicolás always silent, always following us with those eyes all your kin have. Those are not Alfaro eyes, I remember my father saying.

The year you came back from the cavalry, you sent for us, me and the boy, and we lived in the house of stone and adobe. From your silences, I understood I was not to question our marriage. It was what it was. Nothing more. Wondering where you were the weeks I didn't see you, and why it was you arrived only for a few slender nights, always after nightfall and leaving before dawn. Our lives ran along as they had before. What good is it to have a husband and not have him? I thought.

When you began involving yourself with the Patricio Leyva campaign, we didn't see you for months at a time. Sometimes the boy and I would return to my father's house where I felt less alone. *Just for a few nights,* I said, unrolling a *petate* in my old corner against the cane-rush wall in the kitchen. *Until my husband returns.* But a few nights grew into weeks, and the weeks into months, until I spent more time under my father's thatch roof than in our house with the roof of tiles.

That's how the weeks and months passed. Your election to the town council. Your work defending the land titles. Then the parceling of the land when your name began to run all along the villages, up and down the Cuautla River. Zapata this and Zapata that. I couldn't go anywhere without hearing it. And each time, a kind of fear entered my heart like a cloud crossing the sun.

I spent the days chewing on this poison as I was grinding the corn, pretending to ignore what the other women washing at the river said. That you had several *pastimes.* That there was a certain María Josefa in Villa de Ayala. Then they would just laugh. It was worse for me those nights you did arrive and lay asleep next to me. I lay awake watching and watching you.

In the day, I could support the grief, wake up before dawn to prepare the day's tortillas, busy myself with the chores, the turkey hens, the planting and collecting of herbs. The boy already wearing his first pair of trousers and getting into all kinds of trouble when he wasn't being watched. There was enough to distract me in the day. But at night, you can't imagine.

Tía Chucha made me drink heart-flower tea—*yoloxochitl,* flower from the magnolia tree-petals soft and seamless as a tongue. *Yoloxochitl, flor de corazón,* with its breath of vanilla and honey. She prepared a tonic with the dried blossoms and applied a salve, mixed with the white of an egg, to the tender skin above my heart.

It was the season of rain. *Plum . . . plum plum.* All night I listened to that broken string of pearls, bead upon bead upon bead rolling across the waxy leaves of my heart.

I lived with that heartsickness inside me, Miliano, as if the days to come did not exist. And when it seemed the grief would not let me go, I wrapped one of your handkerchiefs around a dried hummingbird, went to the river, whispered, *Virgencita, ayúdame,* kissed it, then tossed the bundle into the waters where it disappeared for a moment before floating downstream in a dizzy swirl of foam.

That night, my heart circled and fluttered against my chest, and something beneath my eyelids palpitated so furiously, it wouldn't let me sleep. When I felt myself whirling against the beams of the house, I opened my eyes. I could see perfectly in the darkness. Beneath me—all of us asleep. Myself, there, in my *petate* against the kitchen wall, the boy asleep beside me. My father and my Tía Chucha sleeping in their corner of the house. Then I felt the room circle once, twice, until I found myself under the stars flying above the little avocado tree, above the house and the corral.

I passed the night in a delirious circle of sadness, of joy, reeling round and round above our roof of dried sugarcane leaves, the world as clear as if the noon sun shone. And when dawn arrived I flew back to my body that waited patiently for me where I'd left it, on the *petate* beside our Nicolás.

Each evening I flew a wider circle. And in the day, I withdrew further and further into myself, living only for those night flights. My father whispered to my Tía Chucha, *Ojos que no ven, corazón que no siente.* But my eyes did see and my heart suffered.

One night over *milpas* and beyond the *tlacolol,* over *barrancas* and thorny scrub forests, past the thatch roofs of the *jacales* and the stream where the women do the wash, beyond bright bougainvillea, high above canyons and across fields of rice and corn, I flew. The gawky stalks of banana trees swayed beneath me. I saw rivers of cold water and a river of water so bitter they say it flows from the sea. I didn't stop until I reached a grove of high laurels rustling in the center of a town square where all the whitewashed houses shone blue as abalone under the full moon. And I remember my wings were blue and soundless as the wings of a *tecolote.*

And when I alighted on the branch of a tamarind tree outside a window, I saw you asleep next to that woman from Villa de Ayala, that woman who is your wife sleeping beside you. And her skin shone blue in the moonlight and you were blue as well.

She wasn't at all like I'd imagined. I came up close and studied her hair. Nothing but an ordinary woman with her ordinary woman smell. She opened her mouth and gave a moan. And you pulled her close to you, Miliano. Then I felt a terrible grief inside me. The two of you asleep like that, your leg warm against hers, your foot inside the hollow of her foot.

They say I am the one who caused her children to die. From jealousy, from envy. What do you say? Her boy and girl both dead before they stopped sucking teat. She won't bear you any more children. But my boy, my girl are alive.

When a customer walks away after you've named your price, and then he comes back, that's when you raise your price. When you know you have what he wants. Something I learned from your horse-trading years.

You married her, that woman from Villa de Ayala, true. But see, you came back to me. You always come back. In between and beyond the others. That's my magic. You come back to me.

You visited me again Thursday last. I yanked you from the bed of that other one. I dreamt you, and when I awoke I was sure your spirit had just fluttered from the room. I have yanked you from your sleep before into the dream I was dreaming. Twisted you like a spiral of hair around a finger. Love, you arrived with your heart full of birds. And when you would not do my bidding and come when I commanded, I turned into the soul of a *tecolote* and kept vigil in the branches of a purple jacaranda outside your door to make sure no one would do my Miliano harm while he slept.

You sent a letter by messenger how many months afterward? On paper thin and crinkled as if it had been made with tears.

I burned copal in a clay bowl. Inhaled the smoke. Said a prayer in *mexicano* to the old gods, an Ave María in Spanish to La Virgen, and gave thanks. You were on your way home to us. The house of stone and adobe aired and swept clean, the night sweet with the scent of candles that had been burning continually since I saw you in the dream. Sometime after Nicolás had fallen asleep, the hoofbeats.

A silence between us like a language. When I held you, you trembled, a tree in rain. Ay, Miliano, I remember that, and it helps the days pass without bitterness.

What did you tell her about me? *That was before I knew you, Josefa. That chapter of my life with Inés Alfaro is finished.* But I'm a story that never ends. Pull one string and the whole cloth unravels.

Just before you came for Nicolás, he fell ill with the symptoms of the jealousy sickness, big boy that he was. But it was true, I was with child again. Malena was born without making a sound, because she remembered how she had been conceived—nights tangled around each other like smoke.

You and Villa were marching triumphantly down the streets of Mexico City, your hat filled with flowers the pretty girls tossed at you. The brim sagging under the weight like a basket.

I named our daughter after my mother. María Elena. Against my father's wishes.

You have your *pastimes.* That's how it's said, no? Your many *pastimes.* I know you take to your bed women half my age. Women the age of our Nicolás. You've left many mothers crying, as they say.

They say you have three women in Jojutla, all under one roof. And that your women treat each other with *a most extraordinary harmony, sisters in a cause who believe in the greater good of the revolution.* I say they can all go to hell, those newspaper journalists and the mothers who bore them. Did they ever ask me?

These stupid country girls, how can they resist you? The magnificent Zapata in his elegant *charro* costume, riding a splendid horse. Your wide sombrero a halo around your face. You're not a man for them; you're a legend, a myth, a god. But you are as well my husband. Albeit only sometimes.

How can a woman be happy in love? To love like this, to love as strong as we hate. That is how we are, the women of my family. We never forget a wrong. We know how to love and we know how to hate.

I've seen your other children in the dreams. María Luisa from that Gregoria Zúñiga in Quilamula after her twin sister Luz died on you childless. Diego born in Tlatizapán of that woman who calls herself *Missus* Jorge Piñeiro. Ana María in Cuautla from that she-goat Petra Torres. Mateo, son of that nobody, Jesusa Pérez of Temilpa. All your children born with those eyes of Zapata.

I know what I know. How you sleep cradled in my arms, how you love me with a pleasure close to sobbing, how I still the trembling in your chest and hold you, hold you, until those eyes look into mine.

Your eyes. Ay! Your eyes. Eyes with teeth. Terrible as obsidian. The days to come in those eyes, *el porvenir,* the days gone by. And beneath that fierceness, something ancient and tender as rain.

Miliano, Milianito. And I sing you that song I sang Nicolás and Malenita when they were little and would not sleep.

Seasons of war, a little half-peace now and then, and then war and war again. Running up to the hills when the *federales* come, coming back down when they've gone.

Before the war, it was the *caciques* who were after the young girls and the married women. They had their hands on everything it seems—the land, law, women. Remember when they found that *desgraciado* Policarpo Cisneros in the arms of the Quintero girl? *¡Virgen purísima!* She was only a little thing of twelve years. And he, what? At least eighty, I imagine.

Desgraciados. All members of one army against us, no? The *federales,* the *caciques,* one as bad as the other, stealing our hens, stealing the women at night. What long sharp howls the women would let go when they carried them off. The next morning the women would be back, and we would say *Buenos días,* as if nothing had happened.

Since the war began, we've gotten used to sleeping in the corral. Or in the hills, in trees, in caves with the spiders and scorpions. We hide ourselves as best we can when the *federales* arrive, behind rocks or in *barrancas,* or in the pine and tall grass when there is nothing else to hide behind. Sometimes I build a shelter for us with cane branches in the mountains. Sometimes the people of the cold lands give us boiled water sweetened with cane sugar, and we stay until we can gather a little strength, until the sun has warmed our bones and it is safe to come back down.

Before the war, when Tía Chucha was alive, we passed the days selling at all the town markets—chickens, turkey hens, cloth, coffee, the herbs we collected in the hills or grew in the garden. That's how our weeks and months came and went.

I sold bread and candles. I planted corn and beans back then and harvested coffee at times too. I've sold all kinds of things. I even know how to buy and resell animals. And now I know how to work the *tlacolol*, which is the worst of all—your hands and feet split and swollen from the machete and hoe.

Sometimes I find sweet potatoes in the abandoned fields, or squash, or corn. And this we eat raw, too tired, too hungry to cook anything. We've eaten like the birds, what we could pluck from the trees—guava, mango, tamarind, almond when in season. We've gone without corn for the tortillas, made do when there were no kernels to be had, eaten the cobs as well as the flower.

My *metate,* my good shawl, my fancy *huipil,* my filigree earrings, anything I could sell, I've sold. The corn sells for one peso and a half a *cuartillo* when one can find a handful. I soak and boil and grind it without even letting it cool, a few tortillas to feed Malenita, who is always hungry, and if there is anything left, I feed myself.

Tía Chucha caught the sickness of the wind in the hot country. I used all her remedies and my own, *guacamaya* feathers, eggs, cocoa beans, chamomile oil, rosemary, but there was no help for her. I thought I would finish myself crying, all my mother's people gone from me, but there was the girl to think about. Nothing to do but go on, *aguantar,* until I could let go that grief. Ay, how terrible those times.

I go on surviving, hiding, searching if only for Malenita's sake. Our little plantings, that's how we get along. The government run off with the *maíz,* the chickens, my prize turkey hens and rabbits. Everyone has had his turn to do us harm.

Now I'm going to tell you about when they burned the house, the one you bought for us. I was sick with the fever. Headache and a terrible pain in the back of my calves. Fleas, babies crying, gunshots in the distance, someone crying out *el gobierno,* a gallop of horses in my head, and the shouting of those going off to join troops and of those staying. I could barely manage to drag myself up the hills. Malenita was suffering one of her *corajes* and refused to walk, sucking the collar of her blouse and crying. I had to carry her on my back with her little feet kicking me all the way until I gave her half of a hard tortilla to eat and she forgot about her anger and fell asleep. By the time the sun was strong and we were far away enough to feel safe, I was weak. I slept without dreaming, holding Malenita's cool body against my burning. When I woke the world was filled with stars, and the stars carried me back to the village and showed me.

It was like this. The village did not look like our village. The trees, the mountains against the sky, the land, yes, that was still as we remembered it, but the village was no longer a village. Everything pocked and in ruins. Our house with its roof tiles gone. The walls blistered and black. Pots, pans, jugs, dishes axed into shards, our shawls and blankets torn and trampled. The seed we had left, what we'd saved and stored that year, scattered, the birds enjoying it.

Hens, cows, pigs, goats, rabbits, all slaughtered. Not even the dogs were spared and were strung from the trees. The Carrancistas destroyed everything, because, as they say, *Even the stones here are Zapatistas.* And what was not destroyed was carried off by their women, who descended behind them like a plague of vultures to pick us clean.

It's *her* fault, the villagers said when they returned. *Nagual. Bruja.* Then I understood how alone I was.

Miliano, what I'm about to say to you now, only to you do I tell it, to no one else have I confessed it. It's necessary I say it; I won't rest until I undo it from my heart.

They say when I was a child I caused a hailstorm that ruined the new corn. When I was so young I don't even remember. In Tetelcingo that's what they say.

That's why the years the harvest was bad and the times especially hard, they wanted to burn me with green wood. It was my mother they killed instead, but not with green wood. When they delivered her to our door, I cried until I finished myself crying. I was sick, sick, for several days, and they say I vomited worms, but I don't remember that. Only the terrible dreams I suffered during the fever.

My Tía Chucha cured me with branches from the pepper tree and with the broom. And for a long time afterward, my legs felt as if they were stuffed with rags, and I kept seeing little purple stars winking and whirling just out of reach.

It wasn't until I was well enough to go outside again that I noticed the crosses of pressed *pericón* flowers on all the village doorways and in the *milpa* too. From then on the villagers avoided me, as if they meant to punish me by not talking, just as they'd punished my mother with those words that thumped and thudded like the hail that killed the corn.

That's why we had to move the seven kilometers from Tetelcingo to Cuautla, as if we were from that village and not the other, and that's how it was we came to live with my Tía Chucha, little by little taking my mother's place as my teacher, and later as my father's wife.

My Tía Chucha, she was the one who taught me to use my sight, just as her mother had taught her. The women in my family, we've always had the power to see with more than our eyes. My mother, my Tía Chucha, me. Our Malenita as well.

It's only now when they murmur *bruja, nagual,* behind my back, just as they hurled those words at my mother, that I realize how alike my mother and I are. How words can hold their own magic. How a word can charm, and how a word can kill. This I've understood.

Mujeriego. I dislike the word. Why not *hombreriega?* Why not? The word loses its luster. *Hombreriega.* Is that what I am? My mother? But in the mouth of men, the word is flint-edged and heavy, makes a drum of the body, something to maim and bruise, and sometimes kill.

What is it I am to you? Sometime wife? Lover? Whore? Which? To be one is not so terrible as being all.

I've needed to hear it from you. To verify what I've always thought I knew. You'll say I've grown crazy from living on dried grass and corn silk. But I swear I've never seen more clearly than these days.

Ay, Miliano, don't you see? The wars begin here, in our hearts and in our beds. You have a daughter. How do you want her treated? Like you treated me?

All I've wanted was words, that magic to soothe me a little, what you could not give me.

The months I disappeared, I don't think you understood my reasons. I assumed I made no difference to you. Only Nicolás mattered. And that's when you took him from me.

When Nicolás lost his last milk tooth, you sent for him, left him in your sister's care. He's lived like deer in the mountains, sometimes following you, sometimes meeting you ahead of your campaigns, always within reach. I know. I let him go. I agreed, yes, because a boy should be with his father, I said. But the truth is I wanted a part of me always hovering near you. How hard it must be for you to keep letting Nicolás go. And yet, he is always yours. Always.

When the *federales* captured Nicolás and took him to Tepaltzingo, you arrived with him asleep in your arms after your brother and Chico Franco rescued him. If anything happens to this child, you said, if anything . . . and started to cry. I didn't say anything, Miliano, but you can't imagine how in that instant, I wanted to be small and fit inside your heart, I wanted to belong to you like the boy, and know you loved me.

If I am a witch, then so be it, I said. And I took to eating black things—*huitlacoche* the corn mushroom, coffee, dark chiles, the bruised part of fruit, the darkest, blackest things to make me hard and strong.

You rarely talk. Your voice, Miliano, thin and light as a woman's, almost delicate. Your way of talking is sudden, quick, like water leaping. And yet I know what that voice of yours is capable of.

I remember after the massacre of Tlatizapán, 286 men and women and children slaughtered by the Carrancistas. Your thin figure, haggard and drawn, your face small and dark under your wide sombrero. I remember even your horse looked half-starved and wild that dusty, hot June day.

It was as if misery laughed at us. Even the sky was sad, the light leaden and dull, the air sticky and everything covered with flies. Women filled the streets searching among the corpses for their dead.

Everyone was tired, exhausted from running from the Carrancistas. The government had chased us almost as far as Jojutla. But you spoke in *mexicano,* you spoke to us in our language, with your heart in your hand, Miliano, which is why we listened to you. The people were tired, but they listened. Tired of surviving, of living, of enduring. Many were deserting and going back to their villages. *If you don't want to fight anymore, you said, we'll all go to the devil. What do you mean you are tired? When you elected me, I said I would represent you if you backed me. But now you must back me, I've kept my word. You wanted a man who wore pants, and I've been that man. And now, if you don't mean to fight, well then, there's nothing I can do.*

We were filthy, exhausted, hungry, but we followed you.

Under the little avocado tree behind my father's house is where you first kissed me. A crooked kiss, all wrong, on the side of the mouth. *You belong to me now,* you said, and I did.

The way you rode in the morning of the San Lázaro fair on a pretty horse as dark as your eyes. The sky was sorrel-colored, remember? Everything swelled and smelled of rain. A cool shadow fell across the village. You were dressed all in black as is your custom. A graceful, elegant man, thin and tall.

You wore a short black linen *charro* jacket, black trousers of cashmere adorned with silver buttons, and a lavender shirt knotted at the collar with a blue silk neckerchief. Your sombrero had a horsehair braid and tassel and a border of carnations embroidered along the wide brim in gold and silver threads. You wore the sombrero set forward—not at the back of the head as others do—so it would shade those eyes of yours, those eyes that watched and waited. Even then I knew it was an animal to match mine.

Suppose my father won't let me?
We'll run off, he can't be angry for always.
Wait until the end of the harvest.
You pulled me toward you under the little avocado tree and kissed me. A kiss tasting of warm beer and whiskers. *You belong to me now.*

It was during the plum season we met. I saw you at the country fair at San Lázaro. I wore my braids up away from the neck with bright ribbons. My hair freshly washed and combed with oil prepared with the ground bone of the mamey. And the neckline of my *huipil*, a white one, I remember, showed off my neck and collarbones.

You were riding a fine horse, silver-saddled with a fringe of red and black silk tassels, and your hands, beautiful hands, long and sensitive, rested lightly on the reins. I was afraid of you at first, but I didn't show it. How pretty you made your horse prance.

You circled when I tried to cross the *zócalo*, I remember. I pretended not to see you until you rode your horse in my path, and I tried to dodge one way, then the other, like a calf in a *jaripeo*. I could hear the laughter of your friends from under the shadows of the arcades. And when it was clear there was no avoiding you, I looked up at you and said, *With your permission.* You did not insist, you touched the brim of your hat, and let me go, and I heard your friend Francisco Franco, the one I would later know as Chico, say, *Small, but bigger than you, Miliano.*

So is it yes? I didn't know what to say, I was still so little, just laughed, and you kissed me like that, on my teeth.
Yes? and pressed me against the avocado tree. *No, is it?* And I said yes, then I said no, and yes, your kisses arriving in between.

Love? We don't say that word. For you it has to do with stroking with your eyes what catches your fancy, then lassoing and harnessing and corraling. Yanking home what is easy to take.

But not for me. Not from the start. You were handsome, yes, but I didn't like handsome men, thinking they could have whomever they wanted. I wanted to be, then, the one you could not have. I didn't lower my eyes like the other girls when I felt you looking at me.

I'll set up a house for us. We can live together, and later we'll see.
But suppose one day you leave me.
Never.
Wait at least until the end of the harvest.

I remember how your skin burned to the touch. How you smelled of lemongrass and smoke. I balanced that thin boy's body of yours on mine.
Something undid itself—gently, like a braid of hair unraveling. And I said, *Ay, mi chulito, mi chulito, mi chulito,* over and over.

Mornings and nights I think your scent is still in the blankets, wake remembering you are tangled somewhere between the sleeping and the waking. The scent of
your skin, the mole above the broom of your thick mustache, how you fit in my
hands.

Would it be right to tell you, each night you sleep here, after your cognac and
cigar, when I'm certain you are finally sleeping, I sniff your skin. Your fingers sweet
with the scent of tobacco. The fluted collarbones, the purple knot of the nipple, the
deep, plum color of your sex, the thin legs and long, thin feet.

I examine at my leisure your black trousers with the silver buttons, the lovely
shirt, the embroidered sombrero, the fine braid stitching on the border of your
charro jacket, admire the workmanship, the spurs, leggings, the handsome black
boots.

And when you are gone, I re-create you from memory. Rub warmth into your fingertips. Take that dimpled chin of yours between my teeth. All the parts are there
except your belly. I want to rub my face in its color, say no, no, no. Ay. Feel its
warmth from my left cheek to the right. Run my tongue from the hollow in your
throat, between the smooth stones of your chest, across the trail of down below the
navel, lose myself in the dark scent of your sex. To look at you as you sleep, the
color of your skin. How in the half-light of moon you cast your own light, as if you
are a man made of amber.

Are you my general? Or only my Milianito? I think, I don't know what you say,
you don't belong to me nor to that woman from Villa de Ayala. You don't belong to
anyone, no? Except the land. *La madre tierra que nos mantiene y cuida.* Every one
of us.

I rise high and higher, the house shutting itself like an eye. I fly farther than I've ever
flown before, farther than the clouds, farther than our Lord Sun, husband of the
moon. Till all at once I look beneath me and see our lives, clear and still, far away
and near.

And I see our future and our past, Miliano, one single thread already lived and
nothing to be done about it. And I see the face of the man who will betray you. The
place and the hour. The gift of a horse the color of gold dust. A breakfast of warm
beer swirling in your belly. The hacienda gates opening. The pretty bugles doing the
honors. *TirriLEE tirREE.* Bullets like a sudden shower of stones. And in that instant,
a feeling of relief almost. And loneliness, just like that other loneliness of being born.

And I see my clean *huipil* and my silk Sunday shawl. My rosary placed between
my hands and a palm cross that has been blessed. Eight days people arriving to
pray. And on the ninth day, the cross of lime and sand raised, and my name called
out—Inés Alfaro. The twisted neck of a rooster. Pork tamales wrapped in corn
leaves. The masqueraders dancing, the men dressed as women, the women as men.
Violins, guitars, one loud drum.

And I see other faces and other lives. My mother in a field of cempoaxúchitl flowers with a man who is not my father. Her *rebozo de bolita* spread beneath them. The
smell of crushed grass and garlic. How, at a signal from her lover, the others
descend. The clouds scurrying away. A machete-sharp cane stake greased with lard
and driven into the earth. How the men gather my mother like a bundle of corn. Her

sharp cry against the infinity of sky when the cane stake pierces her. How each waiting his turn grunts words like hail that splits open the skin, just as before they'd whispered words of love.

The star of her sex open to the sky. Clouds moving soundlessly, and the sky changing colors. Hours. Eyes still fixed on the clouds the morning they find her—braids undone, a man's sombrero tipped on her head, a cigar in her mouth, as if to say, this is what we do to women who try to act like men.

The small black bundle that is my mother delivered to my father's door. My father without a "who" or "how." He knows as well as everyone.

How the sky let go a storm of stones. The corn harvest ruined. And how we move from Tetelcingo to my Tía Chucha's in Cuautla.

And I see our children. Malenita with her twins, who will never marry, two brave *solteronas* living out their lives selling herbs in La Merced in Mexico City.

And our Nicolás, a grown man, the grief and shame Nicolás will bring to the Zapata name when he kicks up a fuss about the parcel of land the government gives him, how it isn't enough, how it's never enough, how the son of a great man should not live like a peasant. The older Anenecuilcans shaking their heads when he sells the Zapata name to the PRI campaign.

And I see the ancient land titles the smoky morning they are drawn up in Náhuatl and recorded on tree-bark paper—*conceded to our pueblo the 25th of September of 1607 by the Viceroy of New Spain*—the land grants that prove the land has always been our land.

And I see that dappled afternoon in Anenecuilco when the government has begun to look for you. And I see you unearth the strong box buried under the main altar of the village church, and hand it to Chico Franco—*if you lose this, I'll have you dangling from the tallest tree,* compadre. *Not before they fill me with bullets,* Chico said and laughed.

And the evening, already as an old man, in the Canyon of the Wolves, Chico Franco running and running, old wolf, old cunning, the government men Nicolás sent shouting behind him, his sons Vírulo and Julián, young, crumpled on the cool courtyard tiles like bougainvillea blossoms, and how useless it all is, because the deeds are buried under the floorboards of a *pulquería* named La Providencia, and no one knowing where they are after the bullets pierce Chico's body. Nothing better or worse than before, and nothing the same or different.

And I see rivers of stars and the wide sea with its sad voice, and emerald fish fluttering on the sea bottom, glad to be themselves. And bell towers and blue forests, and a store window filled with hats. A burnt foot like the inside of a plum. A lice comb with two nits. The lace hem of a woman's dress. The violet smoke from a cigarette. A boy urinating into a tin. The milky eyes of a blind man. The chipped finger of a San Isidro statue. The tawny bellies of dark women giving life.

And more lives and more blood, those being born as well as those dying, the ones who ask questions and the ones who keep quiet, the days of grief and all the flower colors of joy.

Ay papacito, cielito de mi corazón, now the burros are complaining. The rooster beginning his cries. Morning already? Wait, I want to remember everything before you leave me.

How you looked at me in the San Lázaro plaza. How you kissed me under my father's avocado tree. Nights you loved me with a pleasure close to sobbing, how I stilled the trembling in your chest and held you, held you. Miliano, Milianito.

My sky, my life, my eyes. Let me look at you. Before you open those eyes of yours. The days to come, the days gone by. Before we go back to what we'll always be.

—1991

STEPHEN CRANE
1871-1900

Stephen Crane was born in New Jersey and died in Germany of tuberculosis. Abandoning conventional studies at Syracuse University in favor of journalism in New York City, Crane published a remarkable volume of writing in his short life, including essays, novels, poetry, and short fiction. His unembellished yet frank account of urban poverty in Maggie: A Girl of the Streets *(1893) attracted critical attention not only for its daring topic but for its spare stylistics. Best known for his realist war fiction* The Red Badge of Courage: An Episode of the American Civil War *(1895), Crane brilliantly depicted the conflicts and insecurities inherent in masculinity in a number of other texts, including his collection* The Open Boat and Other Stories, *which appeared in 1898.*

THE BRIDE COMES TO YELLOW SKY

I

The great Pullman was whirling onward with such dignity of motion that a glance from the window seemed simply to prove that the plains of Texas were pouring eastward. Vast flats of green grass, dull-hued spaces of mesquit and cactus, little groups of frame houses, woods of light and tender trees, all were sweeping into the east, sweeping over the horizon, a precipice.

A newly married pair had boarded this coach at San Antonio. The man's face was reddened from many days in the wind and sun, and a direct result of his new black clothes was that his brick-coloured hands were constantly performing in a most conscious fashion. From time to time he looked down respectfully at his attire. He sat with a hand on each knee, like a man waiting in a barber's shop. The glances he devoted to other passengers were furtive and shy.

The bride was not pretty, nor was she very young. She wore a dress of blue cashmere, with small reservations of velvet here and there, and with steel buttons abounding. She continually twisted her head to regard her puff sleeves, very stiff, straight, and high. They embarrassed her. It was quite apparent that she had cooked, and that she expected to cook, dutifully. The blushes caused by the care-less scrutiny of some passengers as she had entered the car were strange to see upon this plain, under-class countenance, which was drawn in placid, almost emo-tionless lines.

They were evidently very happy. "Ever been in a parlour-car before?" he asked, smiling with delight.

"No," she answered; "I never was. It's fine, ain't it?"

"Great! And then after a while we'll go forward to the diner, and get a big lay-out. Finest meal in the world. Charge a dollar."

"Oh, do they?" cried the bride. "Charge a dollar? Why, that's too much—for us—ain't it, Jack?"

"Not this trip, anyhow," he answered bravely. "We're going to go the whole thing."

Later he explained to her about the trains. "You see, it's a thousand miles from one end of Texas to the other; and this train runs right across it, and never stops but four times." He had the pride of an owner. He pointed out to her the dazzling fittings of the coach; and in truth her eyes opened wider as she contemplated the sea-green figured velvet, the shining brass, silver, and glass, the wood that gleamed as darkly brilliant as the surface of a pool of oil. At one end a bronze figure sturdily held a support for a separated chamber, and at convenient places on the ceiling were frescos in olive and silver.

To the minds of the pair, their surroundings reflected the glory of their marriage that morning in San Antonio; this was the environment of their new estate; and the man's face in particular beamed with an elation that made him appear ridiculous to the negro porter. This individual at times surveyed them from afar with an amused and superior grin. On other occasions he bullied them with skill in ways that did not make it exactly plain to them that they were being bullied. He subtly used all the manners of the most unconquerable kind of snobbery. He oppressed them; but of this oppression they had small knowledge, and they speedily forgot that infrequently a number of travellers covered them with stares of derisive enjoyment. Historically there was supposed to be something infinitely humorous in their situation.

"We are due in Yellow Sky at 3:42," he said, looking tenderly into her eyes.

"Oh, are we?" she said, as if she had not been aware of it. To evince surprise at her husband's statement was part of her wifely amiability. She took from a pocket a little silver watch; and as she held it before her, and stared at it with a frown of attention, the new husband's face shone.

"I bought it in San Anton' from a friend of mine," he told her gleefully.

"It's seventeen minutes past twelve," she said, looking up at him with a kind of shy and clumsy coquetry. A passenger, noting this play, grew excessively sardonic, and winked at himself in one of the numerous mirrors.

At last they went to the dining-car. Two rows of negro waiters, in glowing white suits, surveyed their entrance with the interest, and also the equanimity, of men who had been forewarned. The pair fell to the lot of a waiter who happened to feel pleasure in steering them through their meal. He viewed them with the manner of a fatherly pilot, his countenance radiant with benevolence. The patronage, entwined with the ordinary deference, was not plain to them. And yet, as they returned to their coach, they showed in their faces a sense of escape.

To the left, miles down a long purple slope, was a little ribbon of mist where moved the keening Rio Grande. The train was approaching it at an angle, and the apex was Yellow Sky. Presently it was apparent that, as the distance from Yellow Sky grew shorter, the husband became commensurately restless. His brick-red hands were more insistent in their prominence. Occasionally he was even rather absent-minded and far-away when the bride leaned forward and addressed him.

As a matter of truth, Jack Potter was beginning to find the shadow of a deed weigh upon him like a leaden slab. He, the town marshal of Yellow Sky, a man known, liked, and feared in his corner, a prominent person, had gone to San Antonio to meet a girl he believed he loved, and there, after the usual prayers, had actually induced her to marry him, without consulting Yellow Sky for any part of the transaction. He was now bringing his bride before an innocent and unsuspecting community.

Of course people in Yellow Sky married as it pleased them, in accordance with a general custom; but such was Potter's thought of his duty to his friends, or of their idea of his duty, or of an unspoken form which does not control men in these matters, that he felt he was heinous. He had committed an extraordinary crime. Face to face with this girl in San Antonio, and spurred by his sharp impulse, he had gone headlong over all the social hedges. At San Antonio he was like a man hidden in the dark. A knife to sever any friendly duty, any form, was easy to his hand in that remote city. But the hour of Yellow Sky—the hour of daylight—was approaching.

He knew full well that his marriage was an important thing to his town. It could only be exceeded by the burning of the new hotel. His friends could not forgive him. Frequently he had reflected on the advisability of telling them by telegraph, but a new cowardice had been upon him. He feared to do it. And now the train was hurrying him toward a scene of amazement, glee, and reproach. He glanced out of the window at the line of haze swinging slowly in toward the train.

Yellow Sky had a kind of brass band, which played painfully, to the delight of the populace. He laughed without heart as he thought of it. If the citizens could dream of his prospective arrival with his bride, they would parade the band at the station and escort them, amid cheers and laughing congratulations, to his adobe home.

He resolved that he would use all the devices of speed and plainscraft in making the journey from the station to his house. Once within that safe citadel, he could issue some sort of vocal bulletin, and then not go among the citizens until they had time to wear off a little of their enthusiasm.

The bride looked anxiously at him. "What's worrying you, Jack?"

He laughed again. "I'm not worrying, girl; I'm only thinking of Yellow Sky."

She flushed in comprehension.

A sense of mutual guilt invaded their minds and developed a finer tenderness. They looked at each other with eyes softly aglow. But Potter often laughed the same nervous laugh; the flush upon the bride's face seemed quite permanent.

The traitor to the feelings of Yellow Sky narrowly watched the speeding landscape. "We're nearly there," he said.

Presently the porter came and announced the proximity of Potter's home. He held a brush in his hand, and, with all his airy superiority gone, he brushed Potter's new clothes as the latter slowly turned this way and that way. Potter fumbled out a coin and gave it to the porter, as he had seen others do. It was a heavy and muscle-bound business, as that of a man shoeing his first horse.

The porter took their bag, and as the train began to slow they moved forward to the hooded platform of the car. Presently the two engines and their long string of coaches rushed into the station of Yellow Sky.

"They have to take water here," said Potter, from a constricted throat and in mournful cadence, as one announcing death. Before the train stopped his eye had swept the length of the platform, and he was glad and astonished to see there was none upon it but the station agent, who, with a slightly hurried and anxious air, was walking toward the water-tanks. When the train had halted, the porter alighted first, and placed in position a little temporary step.

"Come on, girl," said Potter, hoarsely. As he helped her down they each laughed on a false note. He took the bag from the negro, and bade his wife cling to his arm. As they slunk rapidly away, his hang-dog glance perceived that they were unloading the two trunks, and also that the station-agent, far ahead near the baggage-car, had turned and was running toward him, making gestures. He laughed, and groaned as he laughed, when he noted the first effect of his marital bliss upon Yellow Sky. He gripped his wife's arm firmly to his side, and they fled. Behind them the porter stood, chuckling fatuously.

II

The California express on the Southern Railway was due at Yellow Sky in twenty-one minutes. There were six men at the bar of the Weary Gentleman saloon. One was a drummer who talked a great deal and rapidly; three were Texans who did not care to talk at that time; and two were Mexican sheep-herders, who did not talk as a general practice in the Weary Gentleman saloon. The barkeeper's dog lay on the board walk that crossed in front of the door. His head was on his paws, and he glanced drowsily here and there with the constant vigilance of a dog that is kicked on occasion. Across the sandy street were some vivid green grass-plots, so wonderful in appearance, amid the sands that burned near them in a blazing sun, that they caused a doubt in the mind. They exactly resembled the grass mats used to represent lawns on the stage. At the cooler end of the railway station, a man without a coat sat in a tilted chair and smoked his pipe. The fresh-cut bank of the Rio Grande circled near the town, and there could be seen beyond it a great plum-coloured plain of mesquit.

Save for the busy drummer and his companions in the saloon, Yellow Sky was dozing. The new-comer leaned gracefully upon the bar, and recited many tales with the confidence of a bard who has come upon a new field.

"—and at the moment that the old man fell downstairs with the bureau in his arms, the old woman was coming up with two scuttles of coal, and of course—"

The drummer's tale was interrupted by a young man who suddenly appeared in the open door. He cried: "Scratchy Wilson's drunk, and has turned loose with both hands." The two Mexicans at once set down their glasses and faded out of the rear entrance of the saloon.

The drummer, innocent and jocular, answered: "All right, old man. S'pose he has? Come in and have a drink, anyhow."

But the information had made such an obvious cleft in every skull in the room that the drummer was obliged to see its importance. All had become instantly solemn.

"Say," said he, mystified, "what is this?" His three companions made the introductory gesture of eloquent speech; but the young man at the door forestalled them.

"It means, my friend," he answered, as he came into the saloon, "that for the next two hours this town won't be a health resort."

The barkeeper went to the door, and locked and barred it; reaching out of the window, he pulled in heavy wooden shutters, and barred them. Immediately a solemn, chapel-like gloom was upon the place. The drummer was looking from one to another.

"But say," he cried, "what is this, anyhow? You don't mean there is going to be a gun-fight?"

"Don't know whether there'll be a fight or not," answered one man, grimly; "but there'll be some shootin'—some good shootin'."

The young man who had warned them waved his hand. "Oh, there'll be a fight fast enough, if any one wants it. Anybody can get a fight out there in the street. There's a fight just waiting."

The drummer seemed to be swayed between the interest of a foreigner and a perception of personal danger.

"What did you say his name was?" he asked.

"Scratchy Wilson," they answered in chorus.

"And will he kill anybody? What are you going to do? Does this happen often? Does he rampage around like this once a week or so? Can he break in that door?"

"No; he can't break down that door," replied the barkeeper. "He's tried it three times. But when he comes you'd better lay down on the floor, stranger. He's dead sure to shoot at it, and a bullet may come through."

Thereafter the drummer kept a strict eye upon the door. The time had not yet been called for him to hug the floor, but, as a minor precaution, he sidled near to the wall. "Will he kill anybody?" he said again.

The men laughed low and scornfully at the question.

"He's out to shoot, and he's out for trouble. Don't see any good in experimentin' with him."

"But what do you do in a case like this? What do you do?"

A man responded: "Why, he and Jack Potter—"

"But," in chorus the other men interrupted, "Jack Potter's in San Anton'."

"Well, who is he? What's he got to do with it?"

"Oh, he's the town marshal. He goes out and fights Scratchy when he gets on one of these tears."

"Wow!" said the drummer, mopping his brow. "Nice job he's got."

The voices had toned away to mere whisperings. The drummer wished to ask further questions, which were born of an increasing anxiety and bewilderment; but when he attempted them, the men merely looked at him in irritation and motioned him to remain silent. A tense waiting hush was upon them. In the deep shadows of the room their eyes shone as they listened for sounds from the street. One man made three gestures at the barkeeper; and the latter, moving like a ghost, handed him a glass and a bottle. The man poured a full glass of whisky, and set down the bottle noiselessly. He gulped the whisky in a swallow, and turned again toward the door in immovable silence. The drummer saw that the barkeeper, without a sound, had taken a Winchester from beneath the bar. Later he saw this individual beckoning to him, so he tiptoed across the room.

"You better come with me back of the bar."

"No, thanks," said the drummer, perspiring; "I'd rather be where I can make a break for the back door."

Whereupon the man of bottles made a kindly but peremptory gesture. The drummer obeyed it, and, finding himself seated on a box with his head below the level of the bar, balm was laid upon his soul at sight of various zinc and copper fittings that bore a resemblance to armour-plate. The barkeeper took a seat comfortably upon an adjacent box.

"You see," he whispered, "this here Scratchy Wilson is a wonder with a gun—a perfect wonder; and when he goes on the war-trail, we hunt our holes—naturally. He's about the last one of the old gang that used to hang out along the river here. He's a terror when he's drunk. When he's sober he's all right—kind of simple—wouldn't hurt a fly—nicest fellow in town. But when he's drunk—whoo!"

There were periods of stillness. "I wish Jack Potter was back from San Anton'," said the barkeeper. "He shot Wilson up once—in the leg—and he would sail in and pull out the kinks in this thing."

Presently they heard from a distance the sound of a shot, followed by three wild yowls. It instantly removed a bond from the men in the darkened saloon. There was a shuffling of feet. They looked at each other. "Here he comes," they said.

III

A man in a maroon-coloured flannel shirt, which had been purchased for purposes of decoration, and made principally by some Jewish women on the East Side of New York, rounded a corner and walked into the middle of the main street of Yellow Sky. In either hand the man held a long, heavy, blue-black revolver. Often he yelled, and these cries rang through a semblance of a deserted village, shrilly flying over the roofs in a volume that seemed to have no relation to the ordinary vocal strength of a man. It was as if the surrounding stillness formed the arch of a tomb over him. These cries of ferocious challenge rang against walls of silence. And his boots had red tops with gilded imprints, of the kind beloved in winter by little sledding boys on the hillsides of New England.

The man's face flamed in a rage begot of whisky. His eyes, rolling, and yet keen for ambush, hunted the still doorways and windows. He walked with the creeping movement of the midnight cat. As it occurred to him, he roared menacing information. The long revolvers in his hands were as easy as straws; they were moved with an electric swiftness. The little fingers of each hand played sometimes in a musician's way. Plain from the low collar of the shirt, the cords of his neck straightened and sank, straightened and sank, as passion moved him. The only sounds were his terrible invitations. The calm adobes preserved their demeanour at the passing of this small thing in the middle of the street.

There was no offer of fight—no offer of fight. The man called to the sky. There were no attractions. He bellowed and fumed and swayed his revolvers here and everywhere.

The dog of the barkeeper of the Weary Gentleman saloon had not appreciated the advance of events. He yet lay dozing in front of his master's door. At sight of the dog, the man paused and raised his revolver humorously. At sight of the man, the dog sprang up and walked diagonally away, with a sullen head, and growling.

The man yelled, and the dog broke into a gallop. As it was about to enter an alley, there was a loud noise, a whistling, and something spat the ground directly before it. The dog screamed, and, wheeling in terror, galloped headlong in a new direction. Again there was a noise, a whistling, and sand was kicked viciously before it. Fear-stricken, the dog turned and flurried like an animal in a pen. The man stood laughing, his weapons at his hips.

Ultimately the man was attracted by the closed door of the Weary Gentleman saloon. He went to it and, hammering with a revolver, demanded drink.

The door remaining imperturbable, he picked a bit of paper from the walk, and nailed it to the framework with a knife. He then turned his back contemptuously upon this popular resort and, walking to the opposite side of the street and spinning there on his heel quickly and lithely, fired at the bit of paper. He missed it by a half-inch. He swore at himself, and went away. Later he comfortably fusilladed the windows of his most intimate friend. The man was playing with this town; it was a toy for him.

But still there was no offer of fight. The name of Jack Potter, his ancient antagonist, entered his mind, and he concluded that it would be a glad thing if he should go to Potter's house, and by bombardment induce him to come out and fight. He moved in the direction of his desire, chanting Apache scalp-music.

When he arrived at it, Potter's house presented the same still front as had the other adobes. Taking up a strategic position, the man howled a challenge. But this house regarded him as might a great stone god. It gave no sign. After a decent wait, the man howled further challenges, mingling with them wonderful epithets.

Presently there came the spectacle of a man churning himself into deepest rage over the immobility of a house. He fumed at it as the winter wind attacks a prairie cabin in the North. To the distance there should have gone the sound of a tumult like the fighting of two hundred Mexicans. As necessity bade him, he paused for breath or to reload his revolvers.

IV

Potter and his bride walked sheepishly and with speed. Sometimes they laughed together shamefacedly and low.

"Next corner, dear," he said finally.

They put forth the efforts of a pair walking bowed against a strong wind. Potter was about to raise a finger to point the first appearance of the new home when, as they circled the corner, they came face to face with a man in a maroon-coloured shirt, who was feverishly pushing cartridges into a large revolver. Upon the instant the man dropped his revolver to the ground and, like lightning, whipped another from its holster. The second weapon was aimed at the bridegroom's chest.

There was a silence. Potter's mouth seemed to be merely a grave for his tongue. He exhibited an instinct to at once loosen his arm from the woman's grip, and he dropped the bag to the sand. As for the bride, her face had gone as yellow as old cloth. She was a slave to hideous rites, gazing at the apparitional snake.

The two men faced each other at a distance of three paces. He of the revolver smiled with a new and quiet ferocity.

"Tried to sneak up on me," he said. "Tried to sneak up on me!" His eyes grew more baleful. As Potter made a slight movement, the man thrust his revolver venomously forward. "No; don't you do it, Jack Potter. Don't you move a finger toward a gun just yet. Don't you move an eyelash. The time has come for me to settle with you, and I'm goin' to do it my own way, and loaf along with no interferin'. So if you don't want a gun bent on you, just mind what I tell you."

Potter looked at his enemy. "I ain't got a gun on me Scratchy," he said. "Honest, I ain't." He was stiffening and steadying, but yet somewhere at the back of his mind a vision of the Pullman floated: the sea-green figured velvet, the shining brass, silver, and glass, the wood that gleamed as darkly brilliant as the surface of a pool of oil—all the glory of the marriage, the environment of the new estate. "You know I fight when it comes to fighting, Scratchy Wilson; but I ain't got a gun on me. You'll have to do all the shootin' yourself."

His enemy's face went livid. He stepped forward, and lashed his weapon to and fro before Potter's chest. "Don't you tell me you ain't got no gun on you, you whelp. Don't tell me no lie like that. There ain't a man in Texas ever seen you without no gun. Don't take me for no kid." His eyes blazed with light, and his throat worked like a pump.

"I ain't takin' you for no kid," answered Potter. His heels had not moved an inch backward. "I'm takin' you for a damn fool. I tell you I ain't got a gun, and I ain't. If you're goin' to shoot me up, you better begin now; you'll never get a chance like this again."

So much enforced reasoning had told on Wilson's rage; he was calmer. "If you ain't got a gun, why ain't you got a gun?" he sneered. "Been to Sunday-school?"

"I ain't got a gun because I've just come from San Anton' with my wife. I'm married," said Potter. "And if I'd thought there was going to be any galoots like you prowling around when I brought my wife home, I'd had a gun, and don't you forget it."

"Married!" said Scratchy, not at all comprehending.

"Yes, married. I'm married," said Potter, distinctly.

"Married?" said Scratchy. Seemingly for the first time, he saw the drooping, drowning woman at the other man's side. "No!" he said. He was like a creature allowed a glimpse of another world. He moved a pace backward, and his arm, with the revolver, dropped to his side. "Is this the lady?" he asked.

"Yes; this is the lady," answered Potter.

There was another period of silence.

"Well," said Wilson at last, slowly, "I s'pose it's all off now."

"It's all off if you say so, Scratchy. You know I didn't make the trouble." Potter lifted his valise.

"Well, I 'low it's off, Jack," said Wilson. He was looking at the ground. "Married!" He was not a student of chivalry; it was merely that in the presence of this foreign condition he was a simple child of the earlier plains. He picked up his starboard revolver, and, placing both weapons in their holsters, he went away. His feet made funnel-shaped tracks in the heavy sand.

—1897

Z O R A N E A L E H U R S T O N
1891-1960

Zora Neale Hurston was trained under Franz Boas as an anthropologist at Barnard College. Her writing was recovered from critical neglect through the 1979 collection I Love Myself When I Am Laughing, *edited by Alice Walker. A folklorist, Hurston drew on the oral tradition she studied in her hometown of Eatonville, Florida, for much of the vernacular language and plot found in her fiction, as evidenced in her best-known novel,* Their Eyes Were Watching God *(1937). Her other work includes a play,* Singing Steel *(1934); an autobiography,* Dust Tracks on a Road *(1942); a collection of folklore,* Mules and Men *(1935); and several other novels, including* Jonah's Gourd Vine *(1934),* Moses, Man of the Mountain *(1939), and* Seraph on the Suwanee *(1948). Some ethnographic photography shot by Hurston has recently been found as well.*

T H E G I L D E D S I X - B I T S

It was a Negro yard around a Negro house in a Negro settlement that looked to the payroll of the G. and G. Fertilizer works for its support.

But there was something happy about the place. The front yard was parted in the middle by a sidewalk from gate to door-step, a sidewalk edged on either side by quart bottles driven neck down into the ground on a slant. A mess of homey flowers planted without a plan but blooming cheerily from their helter-skelter places. The fence and house were whitewashed. The porch and steps scrubbed white.

The front door stood open to the sunshine so that the floor of the front room could finish drying after its weekly scouring. It was Saturday. Everything clean from the front gate to the privy house. Yard raked so that the strokes of the rake would make a pattern. Fresh newspaper cut in fancy edge on the kitchen shelves.

Missie May was bathing herself in the galvanized washtub in the bedroom. Her dark-brown skin glistened under the soapsuds that skittered down from her wash rag. Her stiff young breasts thrust forward aggressively like broad-based cones with the tips lacquered in black.

She heard men's voices in the distance and glanced at the dollar clock on the dresser.

"Humph! Ah'm way behind time t'day! Joe gointer be heah 'fore Ah git mah clothes on if Ah don't make haste."

She grabbed the clean meal sack at hand and dried herself hurriedly and began to dress. But before she could tie her slippers, there came the ring of singing metal on wood. Nine times.

Missie May grinned with delight. She had not seen the big tall man come stealing in the gate and creep up the walk grinning happily at the joyful mischief he was about to commit. But she knew that it was her husband throwing silver dollars in the door for her to pick up and pile beside her plate at dinner. It was this way every Saturday afternoon. The nine dollars hurled into the open door, he scurried to a hiding place behind the cape jasmine bush and waited.

Missie May promptly appeared at the door in mock alarm.

"Who dat chunkin' money in mah do'way?" she demanded. No answer from the yard. She leaped off the porch and began to search the shrubbery. She peeped under the porch and hung over the gate to look up and down the road. While she did this, the man behind the jasmine darted to the china berry tree. She spied him and gave chase.

"Nobody ain't gointer be chunkin' money at me and Ah not do 'em nothin'," she shouted in mock anger. He ran around the house with Missie May at his heels. She overtook him at the kitchen door. He ran inside but could not close it after him before she crowded in and locked with him in a rough and tumble. For several minutes the two were a furious mass of male and female energy. Shouting, laughing, twisting, turning, tussling, tickling each other in the ribs; Missie May clutching onto Joe and Joe trying, but not too hard, to get away.

"Missie May, take yo' hand out mah pocket!" Joe shouted out between laughs.

"Ah ain't, Joe, not lessen you gwine gimme whateve' it is good you got in yo' pocket. Turn it go, Joe, do Ah'll tear yo' clothes."

"Go on tear 'em. You de one dat pushes de needles round heah. Move yo' hand Missie May."

"Lemme git dat paper sack out yo' pocket. Ah bet it's candy kisses."

"Tain't. Move yo' hand. Woman ain't got no business in a man's clothes nohow. Go way."

Missie May gouged way down and gave an upward jerk and triumphed.

"Unhhunh! Ah got it. It 'tis so candy kisses. Ah knowed you had somethin' for me in yo' clothes. Now Ah got to see whut's in every pocket you got."

Joe smiled indulgently and let his wife go through all of his pockets and take out the things that he had hidden there for her to find. She bore off the chewing gum, the cake of sweet soap, the pocket handkerchief as if she had wrested them from him, as if they had not been bought for the sake of this friendly battle.

"Whew! dat play-fight done got me all warmed up," Joe exclaimed. "Got me some water in de kittle?"

"Yo' water is on de fire and yo' clean things is cross de bed. Hurry up and wash yo'self and git changed so we kin eat. Ah'm hongry." As Missie said this, she bore the steaming kettle into the bedroom.

"You ain't hongry, sugar," Joe contradicted her. "Youse jes' a little empty. Ah'm de one whut's hongry. Ah could eat up camp meetin', back off 'ssociation, and drink Jurdan dry. Have it on de table when Ah git out de tub."

"Don't you mess wid mah business, man. You git in yo' clothes. Ah'm a real wife, not no dress and breath. Ah might not look lak one, but if you burn me, you won't git a thing but wife ashes."

Joe splashed in the bedroom and Missie May fanned around in the kitchen. A fresh red and white checked cloth on the table. Big pitcher of buttermilk beaded with pale drops of butter from the churn. Hot fried mullet, crackling bread, ham hock atop a mound of string beans and new potatoes, and perched on the windowsill a pone of spicy potato pudding.

Very little talk during the meal but that little consisted of banter that pretended to deny affection but in reality flaunted it. Like when Missie May reached for a second helping of the tater pone, Joe snatched it out of her reach.

After Missie May had made two or three unsuccessful grabs at the pan, she begged, "Aw, Joe gimme some mo' dat tater pone."

"Nope, sweetenin' is for us men-folks. Y'all pritty lil frail eels don't need nothin' lak dis. You too sweet already."

"Please, Joe."

"Naw, naw. Ah don't want you to git no sweeter than whut you is already. We goin' down de road a lit piece t'night so you go put on yo' Sunday-go-to-meetin' things."

Missie May looked at her husband to see if he was playing some prank. "Sho nuff, Joe?"

"Yeah. We goin' to de ice cream parlor."

"Where de ice cream parlor at, Joe?"

"A new man done come heah from Chicago and he done got a place and took and opened it up for a ice cream parlor, and bein' as it's real swell, Ah wants you to be one de first ladies to walk in dere and have some set down."

"Do Jesus, Ah ain't knowed nothin' 'bout it. Who de man done it?"

"Mister Otis D. Slemmons, of spots and places—Memphis, Chicago, Jacksonville, Philadelphia and so on."

"Dat heavy-set man wid his mouth full of gold teethes?"

"Yeah. Where did you see 'im at?"

"Ah went down to de sto' tuh git a box of lye and Ah seen 'im standin' on de corner talkin' to some of de mens, and Ah come on back and went to scrubbin' de floor, and he passed and tipped his hat whilst Ah was scourin' de steps. Ah thought Ah never seen *him* befo'."

Joe smiled pleasantly. "Yeah, he's up to date. He got de finest clothes Ah ever seen on a colored man's back."

"Aw, he don't look no better in his clothes than you do in yourn. He got a puzzlegut on 'im and he so chuckle-headed, he got a pone behind his neck."

Joe looked down at his own abdomen and said wistfully, "Wisht Ah had a build on me lak he got. He ain't puzzle-gutted, honey. He jes' got a corperation. Dat make 'm look lak a rich white man. All rich mens is got some belly on 'em."

"Ah seen de pitchers of Henry Ford and he's a spare-built man and Rockefeller look lak he ain't got but one gut. But Ford and Rockefeller and dis Slemmons and all de rest kin be as many-gutted as dey please, Ah'm satisfied wid you jes lak you is, baby. God took pattern after a pine tree and built you noble. Youse a pritty man, and if Ah knowed any way to make you mo' pritty still Ah'd take and do it."

Joe reached over gently and toyed with Missie May's ear. "You jes' say dat cause you love me, but Ah know Ah can't hold no light to Otis D. Slemmons. Ah ain't never been nowhere and Ah ain't got nothin' but you."

Missie May got on his lap and kissed him and he kissed back in kind. Then he went on. "All de womens is crazy 'bout 'im everywhere he go."

"How you know dat, Joe?"

"He tole us so hisself."

"Dat don't make it so. His mouf is cut cross-ways, ain't it? Well, he kin lie jes' lak anybody else."

"Good Lawd, Missie! You womens sho is hard to sense into things. He's got a five-dollar gold piece for a stick-pin and he got a ten-dollar gold piece on his watch chain and his mouf is jes' crammed full of gold teethes. Sho wisht it wuz mine. And whut make it so cool, he got money 'cumulated. And womens give it all to 'im."

"Ah don't see whut de womens see on 'im. Ah wouldn't give 'im a wink if de sheriff wuz after 'im."

"Well, he tole us how de white womens in Chicago give 'im all dat gold money. So he don't 'low nobody to touch it at all. Not even put dey finger on it. Dey tole 'im not to. You kin make 'miration at it, but don't tetch it."

"Whyn't he stay up dere where dey so crazy 'bout 'im?"

"Ah reckon dey done made 'im vast-rich and he wants to travel some. He say dey wouldn't leave 'im hit a lick of work. He got mo' lady people crazy 'bout him than he kin shake a stick at."

"Joe, Ah hates to see you so dumb. Dat stray nigger jes' tell y'all anything and y'all b'lieve it."

"Go 'head on now, honey and put on yo' clothes. He talkin' 'bout his pritty womens—Ah want 'im to see *mine*."

Missie May went off to dress and Joe spent the time trying to make his stomach punch out like Slemmons' middle. He tried the rolling swagger of the stranger, but found that his tall bone-and-muscle stride fitted ill with it. He just had time to drop back into his seat before Missie May came in dressed to go.

On the way home that night Joe was exultant. "Didn't Ah say ole Otis was swell? Can't he talk Chicago talk? Wuzn't dat funny whut he said when great big fat ole Ida Armstrong come in? He asted me, 'Who is dat broad wid de forte shake?' Dat's a new word. Us always thought forty was a set of figgers but he showed us where it means a whole heap of things. Sometimes he don't say forty, he jes' say thirty-eight and two and dat mean de same thing. Know whut he tole me when Ah wuz payin' for our ice cream? He say, 'Ah have to hand it to you, Joe. Dat wife of yours is jes' thirty-eight and two. Yessuh, she's forte!' Ain't he killin'?"

"He'll do in case of a rush. But he sho is got uh heap uh gold on 'im. Dat's de first time Ah ever seed gold money. It lookted good on him sho nuff, but it'd look a whole heap better on you."

"Who, me? Missie May youse crazy! Where would a po' man lak me git gold money from?"

Missie May was silent for a minute, then she said, "Us might find some goin' long de road some time. Us could."

"Who would be losin' gold money round heah? We ain't even seen none dese white folks wearin' no gold money on dey watch chain. You must be figgerin' Mister Packard or Mister Cadillac goin' pass through heah."

"You don't know whut been lost 'round heah. Maybe somebody way back in memorial times lost they gold money and went on off and it ain't never been found. And then if we wuz to find it, you could wear some 'thout havin' no gang of womens lak dat Slemmons say he got."

Joe laughed and hugged her. "Don't be so wishful 'bout me. Ah'm satisfied de way Ah is. So long as Ah be yo' husband, Ah don't keer 'bout nothin' else. Ah'd ruther all de other womens in de world to be dead than for you to have de toothache. Less we go to bed and git our night rest."

It was Saturday night once more before Joe could parade his wife in Slemmons' ice cream parlor again. He worked the night shift and Saturday was his only night off. Every other evening around six o'clock he left home, and dying dawn saw him hustling home around the lake where the challenging sun flung a flaming sword from east to west across the trembling water.

That was the best part of life—going home to Missie May. Their white-washed house, the mock battle on Saturday, the dinner and ice cream parlor afterwards, church on Sunday nights when Missie out-dressed any woman in town—all, everything was right.

One night around eleven the acid ran out at the G. and G. The foreman knocked off the crew and let the steam die down. As Joe rounded the lake on his way home, a lean moon rode the lake in a silver boat. If anybody had asked Joe about the moon on the lake, he would have said he hadn't paid it any attention. But he saw it with his feelings. It made him yearn painfully for Missie. Creation obsessed him. He thought about children. They had been married more than a year now. They had money put away. They ought to be making little feet for shoes. A little boy child would be about right.

He saw a dim light in the bedroom and decided to come in through the kitchen door. He could wash the fertilizer dust off himself before presenting himself to Missie May. It would be nice for her not to know that he was there until he slipped into his place in bed and hugged her back. She always liked that.

He eased the kitchen door open slowly and silently, but when he went to set his dinner bucket on the table he bumped it into a pile of dishes, and something crashed to the floor. He heard his wife gasp in fright and hurried to reassure her.

"Iss me, honey. Don't git skeered."

There was a quick, large movement in the bedroom. A rustle, a thud, and a stealthy silence. The light went out.

What? Robbers? Murderers? Some varmint attacking his helpless wife, perhaps. He struck a match, threw himself on guard and stepped over the door-sill into the bedroom.

The great belt on the wheel of Time slipped and eternity stood still. By the match light he could see the man's legs fighting with his breeches in his frantic desire to get them on. He had both chance and time to kill the intruder in his helpless condition—half in and half out of his pants—but he was too weak to take action. The shapeless enemies of humanity that live in the hours of Time had waylaid Joe. He was assaulted in his weakness. Like Samson awakening after his haircut. So he just opened his mouth and laughed.

The match went out and he struck another and lit the lamp. A howling wind raced across his heart, but underneath its fury he heard his wife sobbing and Slemmons pleading for his life. Offering to buy it with all that he had. "Please, suh, don't kill me. Sixty-two dollars at de sto'. Gold money."

Joe just stood. Slemmons looked at the window, but it was screened. Joe stood out like a rough-backed mountain between him and the door. Barring him from escape, from sunrise, from life.

He considered a surprise attack upon the big clown that stood there laughing like a chessy cat. But before his fist could travel an inch, Joe's own rushed out to crush him like a battering ram. Then Joe stood over him.

"Git into yo' damn rags, Slemmons, and dat quick."

Slemmons scrambled to his feet and into his vest and coat. As he grabbed his hat, Joe's fury overrode his intentions and he grabbed at Slemmons with his left hand and struck at him with his right. The right landed. The left grazed the front of his vest. Slemmons was knocked a somersault into the kitchen and fled through the open door. Joe found himself alone with Missie May, with the golden watch charm clutched in his left fist. A short bit of broken chain dangled between his fingers.

Missie May was sobbing. Wails of weeping without words. Joe stood, and after awhile he found out that he had something in his hand. And then he stood and felt without thinking and without seeing with his natural eyes. Missie May kept on crying and Joe kept on feeling so much and not knowing what to do with all his feelings, he put Slemmons' watch charm in his pants pocket and took a good laugh and went to bed.

"Missie May, whut you cryin' for?"

"Cause Ah love you so hard and Ah know you don't love *me* no mo'."

Joe sank his face into the pillow for a spell then he said huskily, "You don't know de feelings of dat yet, Missie May."

"Oh Joe, honey, he said he wuz gointer give me dat gold money and he jes' kept on after me——"

Joe was very still and silent for a long time. Then he said, "Well, don't cry no mo', Missie May. Ah got yo' gold piece for you."

The hours went past on their rusty ankles. Joe still and quiet on one bed-rail and Missie May wrung dry of sobs on the other. Finally the sun's tide crept upon the shore of night and drowned all its hours. Missie May with her face stiff and streaked towards the window saw the dawn come into her yard. It was day. Nothing more. Joe wouldn't be coming home as usual. No need to fling open the front door and sweep off the porch, making it nice for Joe. Never no more breakfast to cook; no more washing and starching of Joe's jumper-jackets and pants. No more nothing. So why get up?

With this strange man in her bed, she felt embarrassed to get up and dress. She decided to wait till he had dressed and gone. Then she would get up, dress quickly and be gone forever beyond reach of Joe's looks and laughs. But he never moved. Red light turned to yellow, then white.

From beyond the no-man's land between them came a voice. A strange voice that yesterday had been Joe's.

"Missie May, ain't you gonna fix me no breakfus'?"

She sprang out of bed. "Yeah, Joe. Ah didn't reckon you wuz hongry."

No need to die today. Joe needed her for a few more minutes anyhow.

Soon there was a roaring fire in the cook stove. Water bucket full and two chickens killed. Joe loved fried chicken and rice. She didn't deserve a thing and good Joe was letting her cook him some breakfast. She rushed hot biscuits to the table as Joe took his seat.

He ate with his eyes in his plate. No laughter, no banter.

"Missie May, you ain't eatin' yo' breakfus'."

"Ah don't choose none, Ah thank yuh."

His coffee cup was empty. She sprang to refill it. When she turned from the stove and bent to set the cup beside Joe's plate, she saw the yellow coin on the table between them.

She slumped into her seat and wept into her arms.

Presently Joe said calmly, "Missie May, you cry too much. Don't look back lak Lot's wife and turn to salt."

The sun, the hero of every day, the impersonal old man that beams as brightly on death as on birth, came up every morning and raced across the blue dome and dipped into the sea of fire every evening. Water ran down hill and birds nested.

Missie knew why she didn't leave Joe. She couldn't. She loved him too much, but she could not understand why Joe didn't leave her. He was polite, even kind at times, but aloof.

There were no more Saturday romps. No ringing silver dollars to stack beside her plate. No pockets to rifle. In fact the yellow coin in his trousers was like a monster hiding in the cave of his pockets to destroy her.

She often wondered if he still had it, but nothing could have induced her to ask nor yet to explore his pockets to see for herself. Its shadow was in the house whether or no.

One night Joe came home around midnight and complained of pains in the back. He asked Missie to rub him down with liniment. It had been three months since Missie had touched his body and it all seemed strange. But she rubbed him. Grateful for the chance. Before morning, youth triumphed and Missie exulted. But the next day, as she joyfully made up their bed, beneath her pillow she found the piece of money with the bit of chain attached.

Alone to herself, she looked at the thing with loathing, but look she must. She took it into her hands with trembling and saw first thing that it was no gold piece. It was a gilded half dollar. Then she knew why Slemmons had forbidden anyone to touch his gold. He trusted village eyes at a distance not to recognize his stick-pin as a gilded quarter, and his watch charm as a four-bit piece.

She was glad at first that Joe had left it there. Perhaps he was through with her punishment. They were man and wife again. Then another thought came clawing at her. He had come home to buy from her as if she were any woman in the long house. Fifty cents for her love. As if to say that he could pay as well as Slemmons. She slid the coin into his Sunday pants pocket and dressed herself and left his house.

Half way between her house and the quarters she met her husband's mother, and after a short talk she turned and went back home. Never would she admit defeat to that woman who prayed for it nightly. If she had not the substance of marriage she had the outside show. Joe must leave *her.* She let him see she didn't want his old gold four-bits too.

She saw no more of the coin for some time though she knew that Joe could not help finding it in his pocket. But his health kept poor, and he came home at least every ten days to be rubbed.

The sun swept around the horizon, trading its robes of weeks and days. One morning as Joe came in from work, he found Missie May chopping wood. Without a word he took the ax and chopped a huge pile before he stopped.

"You ain't got no business choppin' wood, and you know it."

"How come? Ah been choppin' it for de last longest."

"Ah ain't blind. You makin' feet for shoes."

"Won't you be glad to have a lil baby chile, Joe?"

"You know dat 'thout astin' me."

"Iss gointer be a boy chile and de very spit of you."

"You reckon, Missie May?"

"Who else could it look lak?"

Joe said nothing, but he thrust his hand deep into his pocket and fingered something there.

It was almost six months later Missie May took to bed and Joe went and got his mother to come wait on the house.

Missie May was delivered of a fine boy. Her travail was over when Joe came in from work one morning. His mother and the old women were drinking great bowls of coffee around the fire in the kitchen.

The minute Joe came into the room his mother called him aside.

"How did Missie May make out?" he asked quickly.

"Who, dat gal? She strong as a ox. She gointer have plenty mo'. We done fixed her wid de sugar and lard to sweeten her for dee nex' one."

Joe stood silent awhile.

"You ain't ast 'bout de baby, Joe. You oughter be mighty proud cause he sho is de spittin' image of yuh, son. Dat's yourn all right, if you never git another one, dat un is yourn. And you know Ah'm mighty proud too, son, cause Ah never thought well of you marryin' Missie May cause her ma used tuh fan her foot round right smart and Ah been mighty skeered dat Missie May wuz gointer git misput on her road."

Joe said nothing. He fooled around the house till late in the day then just before he went to work, he went and stood at the foot of the bed and asked his wife how she felt. He did this every day during the week.

On Saturday he went to Orlando to make his market. It had been a long time since he had done that.

Meat and lard, meal and flour, soap and starch. Cans of corn and tomatoes. All the staples. He fooled around town for awhile and bought bananas and apples. Way after while he went around to the candy store.

"Hello, Joe," the clerk greeted him. "Ain't seen you in a long time."

"Nope, Ah ain't been heah. Been round in spots and places."

"Want some of them molasses kisses you always buy?"

"Yessuh." He threw the gilded half dollar on the counter. "Will dat spend?"

"Whut is it, Joe? Well, I'll be doggone! A gold-plated four-bit piece. Where'd you git it, Joe?"

"Often a stray nigger dat come through Eatonville. He had it on his watch chain for a charm—goin' round making out iss gold money. Ha ha! He had a quarter on his tie pin and it wuz all golded up too. Tryin' to fool people. Makin' out he so rich and everything. Ha! Ha! Tryin' to tole off folkses wives from home."

"How did you git it, Joe? Did he fool you, too?"

"Who, me? Naw suh! He ain't fooled me none. Know whut Ah done? He come round me wid his smart talk. Ah hauled off and knocked 'im down and took his old four-bits way from 'im. Gointer buy my wife some good ole lasses kisses wid it. Gimme fifty cents worth of dem candy kisses."

"Fifty cents buys a mighty lot of candy kisses, Joe. Why don't you split it up and take some chocolate bars, too. They eat good, too."

"Yessuh, dey do, but Ah wants all dat in kisses. Ah got a lil boy chile home now. Tain't a week old yet, but he kin suck a sugar tit and maybe eat one them kisses hisself."

Joe got his candy and left the store. The clerk turned to the next customer. "Wisht I could be like these darkies. Laughin' all the time. Nothin' worries 'em."

Back in Eatonville, Joe reached his own front door. There was the ring of singing metal on wood. Fifteen times. Missie May couldn't run to the door, but she crept there as quickly as she could.

"Joe Banks, Ah hear you chunkin' money in mah do'way. You wait till Ah got mah strength back and Ah'm gointer fix you for dat."

—1933

CHARLES JOHNSON
B. 1948

Charles Johnson was born in Evanston, Illinois, and educated at Southern Illinois University where he received a BA in 1971. Initially pursuing journalism, Johnson later became a cartoonist and editor. Presently a professor of English at the University of Washington in Seattle, he is also a martial artist and a practicing Buddhist. His books, which include Faith and the Good Thing *(1974),* Oxherding Tale *(1982), and* The Sorcerer's Apprentice *(1986), develop a philosophy of African-American life and literature. Johnson has published shorter pieces in* Mother Jones, Callaloo, Indiana Review, *and* Obsidian.

MOVING PICTURES

You sit in the Neptune Theater waiting for the thin, overhead lights to dim with a sense of respect, perhaps even reverence, for American movie houses are, as everyone knows, the new cathedrals, their stories better remembered than legends, totems, or mythologies, their directors more popular than novelists, more influential than saints—enough people, you've been told, have seen the James Bond adventures to fill the entire country of Argentina. Perhaps you have written this movie. Perhaps not. Regardless, you come to it as everyone does, as a seeker groping in the darkness for light, hoping something magical will be beamed from above, and no matter how bad this matinee is, or silly, something deep and maybe even too dangerous to talk loudly about will indeed happen to you and the others, before this drama reels to its last transparent frame.

Naturally, you have left your life outside the door. Like any life, it's a messy thing, hardly as orderly as art, what some call life in the fast lane: the Sanka and sugar-doughnut breakfasts, bumper-to-bumper traffic downtown, the business lunches, and a breakneck schedule not to get ahead but simply to stay in one place, which is peculiar, because you grew up in the sixties speeding on methadone and despising all this, knowing your Age (Aquarian) was made for finer stuff. But no matter. Outside, across town, you have put away for ninety minutes the tedious, repetitive job that is, obviously, beneath your talents, sensitivity, and education (a degree in English), the once beautiful woman—or wife—a former model (local), college dancer, or semiprofessional actress named Megan or Daphne, who has grown tired of you, or you of her, and talks now of legal separation and finding herself, the children from a former, frighteningly brief marriage whom you don't want to lose, the mortgage, alimony, IRS audit, the aging, gin-fattened face that once favored a rock star's but now frowns back at you in the bathroom mirror, the young woman at work born in 1960 and unable to recall John Kennedy who, after the Christmas party, took you to bed in her spacious downtown loft, perhaps out of pity because your mother, God bless her, died and left you with $1,000 in debt before you could get the old family house clear—all that shelved, mercifully, as the film starts, first that frosty mountaintop ringed by stars, or a lion roaring or floodlights bathing the tips of buildings in a Hollywood skyline: stable trademarks in a world of flux, you think, surefire signs that whatever follows—tragedy or farce—is made by people who are accomplished dream merchants. Perhaps more: masters of vision, geniuses of the epistemological Murphy.

If you have written this film, which is possible, you look for your name in the credits, and probably frown at the names of the Crew, each recalling some disaster during the production, first at the studio, then later on location for five weeks in Oklahoma cow towns during the winter, which was worse than living on the moon, the days boiling and nights so cold. Nevertheless, you'd seen it as a miracle, an act of God when the director, having read your novel, called, offering you the project— a historical romance—then walked you patiently through the first eight drafts, suspicious of you at first (there was real money riding on this; it wasn't poetry), of your dreary, novelistic pretensions to Deep Profundity, and you equally suspicious of him, his background in sitcoms, obsession with "keeping it sexy," and love of Laurel and Hardy films. For this you wrote a dissertation on Derrida? Yet you'd listened. He was right, in the end. He was good, you admitted, grudgingly. He knew, as you— with your liberal arts degree—didn't, the meaning of Entertainment. You'd learned. With his help, you got good, too. You gloated. And lost friends. "A movie?" said your poet friends. "That's wonderful, it's happening for you," and then they avoided you as if you had AIDS. What *was* happening was this:

You'd shelved the novel, the Big Book, for bucks monitored by the Writers Guild (West), threw yourself into fast-and-dirty scripts, the instant gratification of quick deadlines and fat checks because the Book, with its complexity and promise of critical praise, the Book, with its long-distance demands and no financial reward whatsoever, was impossible, and besides, you didn't have it anymore, not really, the gift for narrative or language, while the scripts were easy, like writing shorthand, and soon—way sooner than you thought—the films, with their life span shorter than a mayfly's, were all you could do. It's a living, you said. Nothing lasts forever. And you pushed on.

The credits crawl up against a montage of Oklahoma farm life, and in this you read a story, too, even before the film begins. For the audience, the actors are stars, the new Olympians, but oh, you know them, this one—the male lead—whose range is boundless, who could be a Brando, but who hadn't seen work in two years before this role and survived by doing voice-overs for a cartoon villain in *The Smurfs;* that one—the female supporting role—who can play the full scale of emotions, but whose last memorable performance was a commercial for Rolaids, all of them; all, including you, fighting for life in a city where the air is so corrupt joggers spit black after a two-mile run; failing, trying desperately to keep up the front of doing-well, these actors, treating you shabbily sometimes because your salary was bigger than theirs, even larger than the producer's, though he wasn't exactly hurting—no, he was richer than a medieval king, a complex man of remarkable charm and cunning, someone both to admire for his Horatio Alger orphan-boy success and to fear for his worship at the altar of power. You won't forget the evening he asked you to his home after a long conference, served you scotch, and then, from inside a drawer in his desk removed an envelope, dumped its contents out, and you saw maybe fifty snapshots of beautiful, naked women on his bed—all of them second-rate actresses, though the female supporting role was there, too—and he watched you closely for your reaction, sipping his drink, smiling, then asked, "You ever sleep with a woman like that?" No, you hadn't. And no, you didn't trust him either. You didn't turn your back. But, then again, nobody in this business did, and in some ways he was, you knew, better than most.

You'd compromised, given up ground, won a few artistic points, but generally you agreed to the producer's ideas—it *was* his show—and then the small army of badly paid performers and production people took over, you trailing behind them in Oklahoma, trying to look writerly, wearing a Panama hat, holding your notepad ready for rewrites, surviving the tedium of eight or nine takes for difficult scenes, the fights, fallings-out, bad catered food, and midnight affairs, watching your script change at each level of interpretation—director, actor—until it was unrecognizable, a new thing entirely, a celebration of the Crew. Not you. Does anyone suspect how bad this thing really looked in rough cut? How miraculous it is that its rags of shots, conflicting ideas, and scraps of footage actually cohere? You sneak a look around at the audience, the faces lit by the glow of the screen. No one suspects. You've managed to fool them again, you old fox.

No matter whether the film is yours or not, it pulls you in, reels in your perception like a trout. On the narrow screen, the story begins with an establishing wide shot of an Oklahoma farm, then in close-up shows the face of a big, tow-headed, brown-freckled boy named Bret, and finally settles on a two-shot of Bret and his blond, bosomy girl friend, Bess. No margin for failure in a formula like that. In the opening funeral scene at a tiny whitewashed church, camera favors Bret, whose father has died. Our hero must seek his fortune in the city. Bess just hates to see him go. Dissolve to cemetery gate. As they leave the cemetery, and the coffin is lowered, she squeezes his hand, and something inside you shivers, the sense of ruin you felt at your own mother's funeral, the irreversible feeling of abandonment. There was no girl with you, but you wished to heaven there had been, the one named Sondra you knew in high school who wouldn't see you for squat, preferring basketball players to weird little wimps and geeks, which is pretty much what you were back then, a washout to those who knew you, but you give all that to Bret and Bess, the pain of parental loss, the hopeless, quiet love never to be, which thickens the screen so thoroughly that when Bess kisses Bret, your nose is clogged with tears and mucus, and then you have your handkerchief out, honking shamelessly, your eyes streaming, locked—even you—in a cycle of emotion (yours) which their images have borrowed, intensified, then given back to you, not because the images or sensations are sad, but because, at bottom, all you have known these last few minutes are the workings of your own nervous system. That is all you have ever known. You yourself have been supplying the grief and satisfaction all along, from within. But even that is not the true magic of film.

As Bret rides away, you remember sitting in the studio's tiny editing room amidst reels of film hanging like stockings in a bathroom, the editor, a fat, friendly man named Coates, tolerating your curiosity, letting you peer into his viewer as he patched the first reel together, figuring he owed you, a semifamous scriptwriter, that much. Each frame, you recall, was a single frozen image, like an individual thought, complete in itself, with no connection to the others, as if time stood still; but then the frames came faster as the viewer sped up, chasing each other, surging forward and creating a linear, continuous motion that outstripped your perception, and presto: a sensuously rich world erupted and took such nerve-knocking reality that you shielded your eyes when the harpsichord music came up and Bret stepped into a darkened Oklahoma shed seen only from his point of view—oh, yes, at times even your body responded, the sweat glands swaling, but it was lunchtime then and Coates wanted to go to the cafeteria for coffee and clicked off his viewer; the images flipped less quickly, slowed finally to a stop, the drama disappearing again into frames, and you saw, pulling on your coat, the nerve racking, heart-thumping vision for what it really was: the illusion of speed.

But is even that the magic of film? Sitting back in your seat, aware of your right leg falling asleep, you think so, for the film has no capacity to fool you anymore. You do not give it your feelings to transfigure. All that you see with godlike detachment are your own decisions, the lines that were dropped, and the microphone just visible in a corner of one scene. Nevertheless, it's gratifying to see the audience laugh out loud at the funny parts, and blubber when Bret rides home at last to marry Bess (actually, they hated each other on the set), believing, as you can't, in a dream spun from accelerated imagery. It almost makes a man feel superior, like knowing how Uri Geller bends all those spoons.

And then it is done, the theater emptying, the hour and a half of illusion over. You file out with the others, amazed by how so much can be projected onto the tabula rasa of the Big Screen—grief, passion, fire, death—yet it remains, in the end, untouched. Dragging on your overcoat, the images still an afterglow in your thoughts, you step outside to the street. It takes your eyes, still in low gear, a moment to adjust to the light of late afternoon, traffic noise, and the things around you as you walk to your Fiat, feeling good, the objects on the street as flat and dimensionless at first as props on a stage. And then you stop.

The Fiat, you notice, has been broken into. The glove compartment has been rifled, and this is where you keep a checkbook, an extra key to the house, and where—you remember—you put the report due tomorrow at nine sharp. The glove compartment, how does it look? Like a part of your body, yes? A wound? From it spills a crumpled photo of your wife, who has asked you to move out so she can have the house, and another one of the children, who haven't the faintest idea how empty you feel getting up every morning to finance their lives at a job that is a ghastly joke, given your talents, where you can't slow down and at least four competitors stand waiting for you to step aside, fall on your face, or die, and the injustice of all this, what you see in the narrow range of radiation you call vision, in the velocity of thought, is necessary and sufficient—as some logicians say—to bring your fists down again and again on the Fiat's roof. You climb inside, sit, furiously cranking the starter, then swear and lower your forehead to the steering wheel, which is, as anyone in Hollywood can tell you, conduct unbecoming a triple-threat talent like yourself: producer, star, and director in the longest, most fabulous show of all.

—1985

JOYCE CAROL OATES

B. 1938

Joyce Carol Oates was born in Lockport, New York, and received her education at Syracuse University and the University of Wisconsin. She has taught at Princeton University since 1978. A prolific essayist, literary and cultural critic, novelist, poet, short story writer, and editor, Oates has published over a dozen novels (not counting those written under a pseudonym) and one hundred short stories. Her abiding interest in female adolescent rebellion is evidenced by Foxfire: Confessions of a Girl Gang *(1993). Her many awards include the National Book Award for* them *(1970), the 1996 PEN/Malamud Award for lifetime achievement in the short story, and the 1988 O. Henry Award for Continuing Achievement.*

STALKING

*T*he Invisible Adversary *is fleeing across a field.*

Gretchen, walking slowly, deliberately, watches with her keen unblinking eyes the figure of the Invisible Adversary some distance ahead. The Adversary has run boldly in front of all that traffic—on long spiky legs brisk as colts' legs—and jumped up onto a curb of new concrete, and now is running across a vacant field. The Adversary glances over his shoulder at Gretchen.

Bastard, Gretchen thinks.

Saturday afternoon. November. A cold gritty day. Gretchen is out stalking. She has hours for her game. Hours. She is dressed for the hunt, her solid legs crammed into old blue jeans, her big, square, strong feet jammed into white leather boots that cost her mother forty dollars not long ago, but are now scuffed and filthy with mud.

Hopeless to get them clean again, Gretchen doesn't give a damn. She is wearing a dark green corduroy jacket that is worn out at the elbows and the rear, with a zipper that can be zipped swiftly up or down, attached to a fringed leather strip. On her head nothing, though it is windy today.

She has hours ahead.

Cars and trucks and buses from the city and enormous interstate trucks hauling automobiles pass by on the highway; Gretchen waits until the way is nearly clear, then starts out. A single car is approaching. *Slow down, you bastard,* Gretchen thinks; and like magic he does.

Following the footprints of the Invisible Adversary. There is no sidewalk here yet, so she might as well cut right across the field. A gigantic sign announces the site of the new Pace & Fischbach Building, an office building of fifteen floors to be completed the following year. The land around here is all dug up and muddy; she can see the Adversary's footsteps leading right past the gouged-up area . . . and there he is, smirking back at her, pretending panic.

I'll get you. Don't worry, Gretchen thinks carefully.

Because the Adversary is so light-footed and invisible, Gretchen doesn't make any effort to be that way. She plods along as she does at school, passing from classroom to classroom, unhurried and not even sullen, just unhurried. She knows she is very visible. She is thirteen years old and weighs one hundred and thirty-five pounds. She's only five feet three—stocky, muscular, squat in the torso and shoulders, with good strong legs and thighs. She could be good at gym, if she bothered; instead, she just stands around, her face empty, her arms crossed and her shoulders a little slumped. If forced, she takes part in the games of volleyball and basketball, but she runs heavily, without spirit, and sometimes bumps into other girls, hurting them. *Out of my way,* she thinks; at such times her face shows no expression.

And now? . . . The Adversary is peeking out at her from around the corner of a gas station. Something flickers in her brain. *I see you,* she thinks, with quiet excitement. The Adversary ducks back out of sight. Gretchen heads in his direction, plodding through a jumbled, bulldozed field of mud and thistles and debris that is mainly rocks and chunks of glass. The gas station is brand new and not yet opened for business. It is all white tile, white concrete, perfect plate-glass windows with whitewashed X's on them, a large driveway and eight gasoline pumps, all proudly erect and ready for business. But the gas station has not opened since Gretchen and her family moved here—about six months ago. Something must have gone wrong. Gretchen fixes her eyes on the corner where the Adversary was last seen. He can't escape.

One wall of the gas station's white tile has been smeared with something like tar. Dreamy, snakelike, thick twistings of black. Black tar. Several windows have been broken. Gretchen stands in the empty driveway, her hands jammed into her pockets. Traffic is moving slowly over here. A barricade has been set up that directs traffic out onto the shoulder of the highway, on a narrow, bumpy, muddy lane that loops out and back again onto the pavement. Cars move slowly, carefully. Their bottoms scrape against the road. The detour signs are great rectangular things, bright yellow with black zigzag lines. SLOW. DETOUR. In the two center lanes of the highway are bulldozers not being used today, and gigantic concrete pipes to be used for storm sewers. Eight pipes. They are really enormous; Gretchen's eyes crinkle with awe, just to see them.

She remembers the Adversary.

There he is—headed for the shopping plaza. *He won't get away in the crowds,* Gretchen promises herself. She follows. Now she is approaching an area that is more completed, though there are still no sidewalks and some of the buildings are brand-new and yet unoccupied, vacant. She jumps over a concrete ditch that is stained with rust-colored water and heads up a slight incline to the service drive of the Federal Savings Bank. The drive-in tellers' windows are all dark today, behind their green-tinted glass. The whole bank is dark, closed. Is this the bank her parents go to now? It takes Gretchen a minute to recognize it.

Now a steady line of traffic, a single lane, turns onto the service drive that leads to the shopping plaza. BUCKINGHAM MALL. 101 STORES. Gretchen notices a few kids her own age, boys or girls, trudging in jeans and jackets ahead of her, through the mud. They might be classmates of hers. Her attention is captured again by the Invisible Adversary, who has run all the way up to the Mall and is hanging around the entrance of the Cunningham Drug Store, teasing her.

You'll be sorry for that, you bastard, Gretchen thinks with a smile.

Automobiles pass her slowly. The parking lot for the Mall is enormous, many acres. A city of cars on a Saturday afternoon. Gretchen sees a car that might be her mother's, but she isn't sure. Cars are parked slanted here, in lanes marked LOT K, LANE 15; LOT K, LANE 16. The signs are spheres, bubbles, perched up on long slender poles. At night they are illuminated.

Ten or twelve older kids are hanging around the drugstore entrance. One of them is sitting on top of a mailbox, rocking it back and forth. Gretchen pushes past them—they are kidding around, trying to block people—and inside the store her eye darts rapidly up and down the aisles, looking for the Invisible Adversary.

Hiding here? Hiding?

She strolls along, cunning and patient. At the cosmetics counter a girl is showing an older woman some liquid make-up. She smears a small oval onto the back of the woman's hand, rubs it in gently. "That's Peach Pride," the girl says. She has shimmering blond hair and eyes that are penciled to show a permanent exclamatory interest. She does not notice Gretchen, who lets one hand drift idly over a display of marked-down lipsticks, each for only $1.59.

Gretchen slips the tube of lipstick into her pocket. Neatly. Nimbly. Ignoring the Invisible Adversary, who is shaking a finger at her, she drifts over to the newsstand, looks at the magazine covers without reading them, and edges over to another display. Packages in a cardboard barrel, out in the aisle. Big bargains. Gretchen doesn't even glance in the barrel to see what is being offered . . . she just slips one of the packages in her pocket. No trouble.

She leaves by the other door, the side exit. A small smile tugs at her mouth.

The Adversary is trotting ahead of her. The Mall is divided into geometric areas, each colored differently; the Adversary leaves the blue pavement and is now on the green. Gretchen follows. She notices the Adversary going into a Franklin Joseph store.

Gretchen enters the store, sniffs in the perfumy, overheated smell, sees nothing that interests her on the counters or at the dress racks, and so walks right to the back of the store, to the Ladies Room. No one inside. She takes the tube of lipstick out of her pocket, opens it, examines the lipstick. It has a tart, sweet smell. A very light pink: *Spring Blossom.* Gretchen goes to the mirror and smears the lipstick onto it, at first lightly, then coarsely; part of the lipstick breaks and falls into a hair-littered sink. Gretchen goes into one of the toilet stalls and tosses the tube into the toilet bowl. She takes handfuls of toilet paper and crumbles them into a ball and throws them into the toilet. Remembering the package from the drugstore, she takes it out of her pocket—just toothpaste. She throws it, cardboard package and all, into the toilet bowl, then, her mind glimmering with an idea, she goes to the apparatus that holds the towel—a single cloth towel on a roll—and tugs at it until it comes loose, then pulls it out hand over hand, patiently, until the entire towel is out. She scoops it up and carries it to the toilet. She pushes it in and flushes the toilet.

The stuff doesn't go down, so she tries again. This time it goes part-way down before it gets stuck.

Gretchen leaves the rest room and strolls unhurried through the store. The Adversary is waiting for her outside—peeking through the window—wagging a finger at her. *Don't you wag no finger at me,* she thinks, with a small tight smile. Outside, she follows him at a distance. Loud music is blaring around her head. It is rock music, piped out onto the colored squares and rectangles of the Mall, blown everywhere by the November wind, but Gretchen hardly hears it.

Some boys are fooling around in front of the record store. One of them bumps into Gretchen and they all laugh as she is pushed against a trash can. "Watch it, babe!" the boy sings out. Her leg hurts. Gretchen doesn't look at them but, with a cold, swift anger, her face averted, she knocks the trash can over onto the sidewalk. Junk falls out. The can rolls. Some women shoppers scurry to get out of the way and the boys laugh.

Gretchen walks away without looking back.

She wanders through Sampson Furniture, which has two entrances. In one door and out the other, as always; it is a ritual with her. Again she notices the sofa that is like the sofa in their family room at home—covered with black and white fur, real goatskin. All over the store there are sofas, chairs, tables, beds. A jumble of furnishings. People stroll around them, in and out of little displays, displays meant to be living rooms, dining rooms, bedrooms, family rooms. . . . It makes Gretchen's eyes squint to see so many displays: like seeing the inside of a hundred houses. She slows down, almost comes to a stop. Gazing at a living-room display on a raised platform. Only after a moment does she remember why she is here—whom she is following—and she turns to see the Adversary beckoning to her.

She follows him outside again. He goes into Dodi's Boutique and, with her head lowered so that her eyes seem to move to the bottom of her eyebrows, pressing up against her forehead, Gretchen follows him. *You'll regret this,* she thinks. Dodi's Boutique is decorated in silver and black. Metallic strips hang down from a dark ceiling, quivering. Salesgirls dressed in pants suits stand around with nothing to do except giggle with one another and nod their heads in time to the music amplified throughout the store. It is music from a local radio station. Gretchen wanders over to the dress rack, for the hell of it. Size 14. "The time is now 2:35," a radio announcer says cheerfully. "The weather is 32 degrees with a chance of showers and possible sleet tonight. You're listening to WCKK, Radio Wonderful. . . ." Gretchen selects several dresses and a salesgirl shows her to a dressing room.

"Need any help?" the girl asks. She has long swinging hair and a high-shouldered, indifferent, bright manner.

"No," Gretchen mutters.

Alone, Gretchen takes off her jacket. She is wearing a navy blue sweater. She zips one of the dresses open and it falls off the flimsy plastic hanger before she can catch it. She steps on it, smearing mud onto the white wool. *The hell with it.* She lets it lie there and holds up another dress, gazing at herself in the mirror.

She has untidy, curly hair that looks like a wig set loosely on her head. Light brown curls spill out everywhere, bouncy, a little frizzy, a cascade, a tumbling of curls. Her eyes are deep set, her eyebrows heavy and dark. She has a stern, staring look, like an adult man. Her nose is perfectly formed, neat and noble. Her upper lip is long, as if it were stretched to close with difficulty over the front teeth. She wears no make-up, her lips are perfectly colorless, pale, a little chapped, and they are usually held tight, pursed tightly shut. She has a firm, rounded chin. Her facial structure is strong, pensive, its features stern and symmetrical as a statue's, blank, neutral, withdrawn. Her face is attractive. But there is a blunt, neutral, sexless stillness to it, as if she were detached from it and somewhere else, uninterested.

She holds the dress up to her body, smooths it down over her breasts, staring.

After a moment she hangs the dress up again, and runs down the zipper so roughly that it breaks. The other dress she doesn't bother with. She leaves the dressing room, putting on her jacket.

At the front of the store the salesgirl glances at her . . . "—Didn't fit?—"

"No," says Gretchen.

She wanders around for a while, in and out of Carmichael's, the Mall's big famous store, where she catches sight of her mother on an escalator going up. Her mother doesn't notice her. She pauses by a display of "winter homes." Her family owns a home like this, in the Upper Peninsula, except theirs is larger. This one comes complete for only $5330: PACKAGE ERECTED ON YOUR LOT—YEAR-ROUND HOME FIBER GLASS INSULATION—BEAUTIFUL ROUGH-SAWN VERTICAL B. C. CEDAR SIDING WITH DEEP SIMULATED SHADOW LINES FOR A RUGGED EXTERIOR.

Only 3:15. For the hell of it, Gretchen goes into the Big Boy restaurant and orders a ground-round hamburger with French fries. Also a Coke. She sits at the crowded counter and eats slowly, her jaws grinding slowly, as she glances at her reflection in the mirror directly in front of her—her mop of hair moving almost imperceptibly with the grinding of her jaws—and occasionally she sees the Adversary waiting outside, coyly. *You'll get yours,* she thinks.

She leaves the Big Boy and wanders out into the parking lot, eating from a bag of potato chips. She wipes her greasy hands on her thighs. The afternoon has turned dark and cold. Shivering a little, she scans the maze of cars for the Adversary—yes, there he is—and starts after him. He runs ahead of her. He runs through the parking lot, waits teasingly at the edge of a field, and as she approaches he runs across the field, trotting along with a noisy crowd of four or five loose dogs that don't seem to notice him.

Gretchen follows him through that field, trudging in the mud, and through another muddy field, her eyes fixed on him. Now he is at the highway—hesitating there—now he is about to run across in front of traffic—now, now—now he darts out—

Now! He is struck by a car! His body knocked backward, spinning backward. Ah, now, *now how does* it *feel?* Gretchen asks.

He picks himself up. Gets to his feet. Is he bleeding? Yes, bleeding! He stumbles across the highway to the other side, where there is a sidewalk. Gretchen follows him as soon as the traffic lets up. He is staggering now, like a drunken man. *How does it feel? Do you like it now?*

The Adversary staggers along the sidewalk. He turns onto a side street, beneath an archway. *Piney Woods.* He is leading Gretchen into the Piney Woods subdivision. Here the homes are quite large, on artificial hills that show them to good advantage. Most of the homes are white colonials with attached garages. There are no sidewalks here, so the Adversary has to walk in the street, limping like an old man, and Gretchen follows him in the street, with her eyes fixed on him.

Are you happy now? Does it hurt? Does it?

She giggles at the way he walks. He looks like a drunken man. He glances back at her, white-faced, and turns up a flagstone walk . . . goes right up to a big white colonial house. . . .

Gretchen follows him inside. She inspects the simulated brick of the foyer: yes, there are blood spots. He is dripping blood. Entranced, she follows the splashes of blood into the hall, to the stairs . . . forgets her own boots, which are muddy . . . but she doesn't feel like going back to wipe her feet. The hell with it.

Nobody seems to be home. Her mother is probably still shopping, her father is out of town for the weekend. The house empty. Gretchen goes into the kitchen, opens the refrigerator, takes out a Coke, and wanders to the rear of the house, to the family room. It is two steps down from the rest of the house. She takes off her jacket and tosses it somewhere. Turns on the television set. Sits on the goatskin sofa and stares at the screen: a return of a Shotgun Steve show, which she has already seen.

If the Adversary comes crawling behind her, groaning in pain, weeping, she won't even bother to glance at him.

—1972

RICHARD RODRIGUEZ

B. 1944

Richard Rodriguez was born in San Francisco of Mexican immigrant parents. A graduate of Stanford and Columbia Universities, Rodriguez writes provocatively about biculturalism and assimilation as well as masculinity and sexuality. Rodriguez is an editor at Pacific News Service and a contributing editor for such major publications as Harper's Magazine *and* U.S. News and World Report. *His collections of essays are* Hunger of Memory: The Education of Richard Rodriguez *(1982) and* Days of Obligation: An Argument with My Mexican Father *(1992). "Proofs" comes from a photo essay focusing on the border between Mexico and the United States. Rodriguez lives in San Francisco.*

PROOFS

You stand around. You smoke. You spit. You are wearing your two shirts, two pants, two underpants. Jesús says if they chase you, throw that bag down. Your plastic bag is your mama, all you have left: the yellow cheese she wrapped has formed a translucent rind; the laminated scapular of the Sacred Heart nestles, flame in its cleft. Put it in your pocket. Inside. Put it in your underneath pants' pocket. The last hour of Mexico is twilight, the shuffling of feet. Jesús says they are able to see in the dark. They have X-rays and helicopters and searchlights. Jesús says wait, just wait, till he says. Though most of the men have started to move. You feel the hand of Jesús clamp your shoulder, fingers cold as ice. *Venga, corre.* You run. All the rest happens without words. Your feet are tearing dry grass, your heart is lashed like a mare. You trip, you fall. You are now in the United States of America. You are a boy from a Mexican village. You have come into the country on your knees with your head down. You are a man.

Papa, what was it like?
I am his second son, his favorite child, his confidant. After we have polished the DeSoto, we sit in the car and talk. I am sixteen years old. I fiddle with the knobs of the radio. He is fifty.
He will never say. He was an orphan there. He had no mother, he remembered none. He lived in a village by the ocean. He wanted books and he had none.
You are lucky, boy.

In the nineteenth century, American contractors reached down into Mexico for cheap labor. Men were needed to build America: to lay track, to mine, to dredge, to harvest. It was a man's journey. And, as a year's contract was extended, as economic dependence was established, sons followed their fathers north. When American jobs turned scarce—during the Depression, as today—Mexicans were rounded up and thrown back over the border. But for generations it has been the rite of passage for the poor Mexican male.
I will send for you or I will come home rich.

In the fifties, Mexican men were contracted to work in America as *braceros,* farm workers. I saw them downtown in Sacramento. I saw men my age drunk in Plaza Park on Sundays, on their backs on the grass. I was a boy at sixteen, but I was an American. At sixteen, I wrote a gossip column, "The Watchful Eye," for my school paper.
Or they would come into town on Monday nights for the wrestling matches or on Tuesdays for boxing. They worked over in Yolo county. They were men without women. They were Mexicans without Mexico.
On Saturdays, they came into town to the Western Union office where they sent money—money turned into humming wire and then turned back into money—all the way down into Mexico. They were husbands, fathers, sons. They kept themselves poor for Mexico.
Much that I would come to think, the best I would think about male Mexico, came as much from those chaste, lonely men as from my own father who made false teeth

and who—after thirty years in America—owned a yellow stucco house on the east side of town.

The male is responsible. The male is serious. A man remembers.

Fidel, the janitor at church, lived over the garage at the rectory. Fidel spoke Spanish and was Mexican. He had a wife down there, people said; some said he had grown children. But too many years had passed and he didn't go back. Fidel had to do for himself. Fidel had a clean piece of linoleum on the floor, he had an iron bed, he had a table and a chair. He had a coffee pot and a frying pan and a knife and a fork and a spoon, I guess. And everything else Fidel sent back to Mexico. Sometimes, on summer nights, I would see his head through the bars of the little window over the garage at the rectory.

The migration of Mexico is not only international, South to North. The epic migration of Mexico, and throughout Latin America, is from the village to the city. And throughout Latin America, the city has ripened, swollen with the century. Lima. Caracas. Mexico City. So the journey to Los Angeles is much more than a journey from Spanish to English. It is the journey from *tu*—the familiar, the erotic, the intimate pronoun—to the repellent *usted* of strangers' eyes.

Most immigrants to America came from villages. The America that Mexicans find today, at the decline of the century, is a closed-circuit city of ramps and dark towers, a city without God.

It is 1986 and I am a journalist. I am asking questions of a Mexican woman in her East L.A. house. She is watchful and pretty, in her thirties, she wears an apron. Her two boys—Roy and Danny—are playing next door. Her husband is a tailor. He is sewing in a bright bedroom at the back of the house. His feet work the humming treadle of an old Singer machine as he croons Mexican love songs by an open window.

For attribution, mama says she is grateful for America. This country has been so good to her family. They have been here ten years and look, already they have this nice house. Outside the door is Mexican Los Angeles; in the distance, the perpetual orbit of traffic. Here old women walk slowly under lace parasols. The Vietnam vet pushes his tinkling ice cream cart past little green lawns. Teenagers in this neighborhood have scorpions tattooed onto their biceps.

The city is evil. Turn. Turn.

At 16th and Mission in San Francisco, young Mexican Americans in dark suits preach to the passing city from perfectbound Bibles. They pass leaflets for Victory Outreach—"the junkie church."

In Latin America, Catholicism remains the religion of the village. But in the city now, in Lima as in Los Angeles, more and more souls rap upon the skin of the tambourine for the promise of evangelical Protestantism: you can be cleansed of the city, you can become a new man, you can be born again.

The raven-haired preacher with a slash on his neck tells me his grandmother is from Jalisco, Mexico. His mother understood Spanish but she couldn't speak it. She couldn't do anything right. She was a junkie. She had him when she was seventeen. She disappeared.

"I lived out on the streets. Didn't go past seventh grade. Grass, crack, dust—I've had it all; messed up with gangs, rolled queers. I've stabbed people, man, I've stuck the blade all the way in and fell a heart flutter like a pigeon.

"I was a sinner, I was alone in the city. Until I found Jesus Christ. . . ."

The U.S. Border Patrol station at Chula Vista has a P.R. officer who handles journalists; he says he is glad to have us—"helps in Washington if the public can get a sense of the scope of the problem."

Right now he is occupied with a West German film crew. They were promised a helicopter. Where is the helicopter? Two journalists from a Tokyo daily—with five canvas bags of camera equipment between them—lean against the wall, arms folded. One of them brings up his wrist to look at his watch. A reporter from Chicago catches my sleeve, says, Did I hear about the other night? What? There was a carload of Yugoslavians caught coming over.

The Japanese reporter who is not looking at his watch is popping CHEEZITS into his mouth. The Border Patrol secretary has made some kind of mistake. She has me down as a reporter for *American Farmer*. Fat red steer in clover. Apologies. Whiteout. "I . . . agree to abide by any oral directions given to me during the operation by the officer in charge of the unit. . . ." Having signed the form, I am soon assigned a patrolman with whom I will spend the night.

We stop for coffee at a donut shop along the freeway. The patrolman tells me about growing up Tex-Mex in Dallas. After City College, he worked with an anti-poverty agency. Then he was a probation officer. He got married, needed money, moved to California and took this job with the *migra*.

Once into the dark, I cannot separate myself from the patrolman's intention. We ride through the dark in a Ram Charger, both intent upon finding people who do not want to be found.

We come upon a posse of Border Patrolmen preparing to ride into the canyon on horseback. I get out of the truck; ask the questions; pet the horses in the dark, prickly, moist, moving in my hand. The officers call me sir. It is as though I am being romanced at some sort of cowboy cotillion. "Here," says one, "have a look." He invites me so close to his chin I can smell cologne as I peer through his night-vision scope.

Mexico is on the phone—long distance.

A crow alights upon a humming wire, bobs up and down, needles the lice within his vest, surveys with clicking eyes the field, the cloud of mites, then dips into the milky air and flies away.

Juanito killed! My mother shrieks, drops the phone in the dark. She cries for my father. For light.

The earth quakes. The peso flies like chaff in the wind. The police chief purchases his mistress a mansion on the hill.

The door bell rings. I split the blinds to see three nuns standing on our front porch.

Mama. Mama.

Monsignor Lyons has sent three Mexican nuns over to meet my parents. The nuns have come to Sacramento to beg for Mexico at the eleven o'clock mass. We are the one family in the parish that speaks Spanish. As they file into our living room, the nuns smell pure, not sweet, pure like candles or like laundry.

The nun with a black mustache sighs at the end of each story the other two tell. Orphan. Leper. Crutch. Dry land. One eye. Casket.

¡Que lastima!

But the Mexican poor are not bent. They are proof of a refining fire.

The Mexican nuns smile with dignity as they stand after mass with their baskets extended, begging for Mexico.

A dusty black car pulls up in front of our house. My uncle has brought his family all the way from Ciudad Juarez. During their visit, my mother keeps trying to give them things to take back. There is a pair of lamps in the living room with porcelain roses. My aunt's eyes demur with pleasure to my uncle. My uncle says no. My uncle says his sister's children (I am the only one watching) would get the wrong impression of Mexico.

Mexico is poor. But my mama says there are no love songs like the love songs of Mexico. She hums a song she can't remember. The ice cream there is creamier than here. Someday we will see. The people are kinder—poor, but kinder to each other.

My mother's favorite record is *"Mariachis de Mexico y Pepe Villa con Orchestra."* Every Sunday she plays her record (*"Rosas de Plata"; "Madrecita Linda"*) while she makes us our pot-roast dinner.

Men sing in Mexico. Men are strong and silent. But in song the Mexican male is granted license he is otherwise denied. The male can admit longing, pain, desire.

HAIII—EEEE—a cry like a comet rises over the song. A cry like mock-weeping tickles the refrain of Mexican love songs. The cry is meant to encourage the balladeer—it is the raw edge of his sentiment. HAIII-EEEE. It is the man's sound. A ticklish arching of semen, a node wrung up a guitar string, until it bursts in a descending cascade of mockery. HAI. HAI. HAI. The cry of a jackal under the moon, the whistle of the phallus, the maniacal song of the skull.

Tell me, Papa.
    What?
    About Mexico.
    I lived with the family of my uncle. I was the orphan in the village. I used to ring the church bells in the morning, many steps up in the dark. When I'd get up to the tower I could see the ocean.
    The village, Papa, the houses too. . . .
    The ocean. He studies the polished hood of our beautiful blue DeSoto.

Mexico was not the past. People went back and forth. People came up for work. People went back home, to mama or wife or village. The poor had mobility. Men who were too poor to take a bus walked from Sonora to Sacramento.

Relatives invited relatives. Entire Mexican villages got recreated in three stories of a single house. In the fall, after the harvest in the Valley, families of Mexican adults and their American children would load up their cars and head back to Mexico in caravans, for weeks, for months. The school teacher said to my mother what a shame it was the Mexicans did that—took their children out of school.

Like wandering Jews. They carried their home with them, back and forth; they had no true home but the tabernacle of memory.

Each year the American kitchen takes on a new appliance.

The children are fed and grow tall. They go off to school with children from Vietnam, from Kansas, from Hong Kong. They get into fights. They come home and they say dirty words.

The city will win. The city will give the children all the village could not—VCRs, hairstyles, drum beat. The city sings mean songs, dirty songs. But the city will sing the children a great Protestant hymn.

You can be anything you want to be.

We are parked. The patrolman turns off the lights of the truck—"back in a minute"—a branch scrapes the door as he rolls out of the van to take a piss. The brush crackles beneath his receding steps. It is dark. Who? Who is out there? The faces I have seen in San Diego—dishwashers, janitors, gardeners. They come all the time, no big deal. There are other Mexicans who tell me the crossing is dangerous.

The patrolman returns. We drive again. I am thinking of epic migrations in history books—pan shots of orderly columns of paleolithic peoples, determined as ants, heeding some trumpet of history, traversing miles and miles . . . of paragraph.

The patrolman has turned off the headlights. He can't have to piss again? Suddenly the truck accelerates, pitches off the rutted road, banging, slamming a rock, faster, ignition is off, the truck is soft-pedalled to a stop in the dust: the patrolman is out like a shot. The cab light is on. I sit exposed for a minute. I can't hear anything. Cautiously, I decide to follow—I leave my door open as the patrolman has done. There is a boulder in the field. Is that it? The patrolman is barking in Spanish. His flashlight is trained on the boulder like a laser, he weaves it along the grain as though he is untying a knot. He is: Three men and a woman stand up. The men are young—sixteen, seventeen. The youngest is shivering. He makes a fist. He looks down. The woman is young too. Or she could be the mother? Her legs are very thin. She wears a man's digital wristwatch. They come from somewhere. And somewhere—San Diego, Sacramento—somebody is waiting for them.

The patrolman tells them to take off their coats and their shoes, throw them in a pile. Another truck rolls up.

As a journalist, I am allowed to come close. I can even ask questions.

There are no questions.

You can take pictures, the patrolman tells me.

I stare at the faces. They stare at me. To them I am not bearing witness; I am part of the process of being arrested. I hold up my camera. Their eyes swallow the flash, a long tunnel, leading back.

Your coming of age. It is early. From your bed you watch your mama moving back and forth under the light. The bells of the church ring in the dark. Mama crosses herself. From your bed you watch her back as she wraps the things you will take.

You are sixteen. Your father has sent for you. That's what it means: He has sent an address in Nevada. He is there with your uncle. You remember your uncle remembering snow with his beer.

You dress in the shadows. You move toward the table, the circle of light. You sit down. You force yourself to eat. Mama stands over you to make the sign of the cross on your forehead with her thumb. You are a man. You smile. She puts the bag of food in your hands. She says she has told *La Virgin*.

Then you are gone. It is gray. You hear a little breeze. It is the rustle of your old black *Dueña*, the dog, taking her short-cuts through the weeds, crazy *Dueña*, her pads on the dust. She is following you.

You pass the houses of the village, each window is a proper name. You pass the store. The bar. The lighted window of the clinic where the pale medical student from Monterrey lives alone and reads his book full of sores late into the night.

You want to be a man. You have the directions in your pocket: an address in Tijuana, and a map with a yellow line that leads from the highway to an "X" on a street in Reno. You are afraid, but you have never seen snow.

You are just beyond the cemetery. The breeze has died. You turn and throw a rock back at *La Dueña*, where you know she is—where you will always know where she is. She will not go past the cemetery. She will turn in circles like a *loca* and bite herself.

The dust takes on gravel, the path becomes a rutted road which leads to the highway. You walk north. The sky has turned white overhead. Insects click in the fields. In time, there will be a bus.

I will send for you or I will come home rich.

—1988

JOHN UPDIKE

B. 1932

John Updike grew up in in Shillington, Pennsylvania. After receiving a BA in 1954 from Harvard University, where he edited the Harvard Lampoon, *he studied at Oxford University in England and became a reporter at* The New Yorker. *In 1959, Updike published his first book of stories,* The Same Door, *and also his first novel,* The Poorhouse Fair; *the next year he published* Rabbit, Run, *the first novel in an enormously successful series—* Rabbit Redux *(1971),* Rabbit Is Rich *(1981), and* Rabbit at Rest *(1990)— whose protagonist, "Rabbit" Angstrom, is an icon of white middle-class masculinity. Both the first and last Rabbit books won the Pulitzer Prize. His most recent publications include three novels,* Brazil *(1994),* In the Beauty of the Lillies *(1996), and* Toward the End of Time *(1997); a collection of short stories,* The Afterlife and Other Stories *(1993);* A Helpful Alphabet of Friendly Objects: Poems *(1995); and* Golf Dreams: Writings on Golf *(1996).*

THE RUMOR

Frank and Sharon Whittier had come from the Cincinnati area and, with an inheritance of hers and a sum borrowed from his father, had opened a small art gallery on the fourth floor of a narrow brown building on West 57th Street. They had known each other as children; their families had been in the same country-club set. They had married in 1970, when Frank was freshly graduated from Oberlin and Vietnam-vulnerable and Sharon was only nineteen, a sophomore at Antioch majoring in dance. By the time, six years later, they arrived in New York, they had two small children; the birth of a third led them to give up their apartment and the city struggle and to move to a house in Hastings, a low stucco house with a wide-eaved Wright-style roof and a view, through massive beeches at the bottom of the yard, of the leaden ongliding Hudson. They were happy, surely. They had dry Midwestern taste, and by sticking to representational painters and abstract sculptors they managed to survive the uglier Eighties styles—faux graffiti, Germanic-*brut* expressionism, cathode-ray prole-play, ecological-protest trash art—and bring their quiet, chaste string of fourth-floor rooms into the calm lagoon of Nineties eclectic revivalism and subdued recession chic. They prospered; their youngest child turned twelve, their oldest was filling out college applications.

When Sharon first heard the rumor that Frank had left her for a young homosexual with whom he was having an affair, she had to laugh, for, far from having left her, there he was, right in the lamplit study with her, ripping pages out of *ARTnews.*

"I don't think so, Avis," she said, to the graphic artist on the other end of the line. "He's right here with me. Would you like to say hello?" The easy refutation was made additionally sweet by the fact that, some years before, there had been a brief (Sharon thought) romantic flareup between her husband and this caller, an over-animated redhead with protuberant cheeks and chin. Avis was a second-wave appropriationist, who made colored Xeroxes of masterpieces out of art books and then signed them in an ink mixed of her own blood and urine. How could she, who had actually slept with Frank, be imagining this grotesque thing?

The voice on the phone gushed as if relieved and pleased. "I know, it's wildly absurd, but I heard it from two sources, with absolutely solemn assurances."

"Who were these sources?"

"I'm not sure they'd like you to know. But it was Ed Jaffrey and then that boy who's been living with Walton Forney, oh, what does he call himself, one of those single names like Madonna—Jojo!"

"Well, then," Sharon began.

"But I've heard it from still others," Avis insisted. "All over town—it's in the air. Couldn't you and Frank do something about it, if it's not true?"

"If," Sharon protested, and her thrust of impatience carried, when she put down the receiver, into her conversation with Frank. "Avis says you're supposed to have run off with your homosexual lover."

"I don't have a homosexual lover," Frank said, too calmly, ripping an auction ad out of the magazine.

"She says all New York says you do."

"Well, what are you going to believe, all New York or your own experience? Here I sit, faithful to a fault, straight as a die, whatever that means. We made love just two nights ago."

It seemed possibly revealing to her that he so distinctly remembered, as if heterosexual performance were a duty he checked off. He was—had always been, ever since she had met him—a slim blond man several inches under six feet tall, with a narrow head he liked to keep trim, even in those years when long hair was in fashion, and frosty blue eyes set at a slight tilt, such as you see on certain taut Slavic or Norwegian faces, and a small precise mouth he kept pursed over teeth a shade too prominent and yellow. He was reluctant to smile, let alone laugh. He was vain of his flat belly and lithe collegiate condition; he weighed himself every morning on the bathroom scale and, if he weighed a pound more than yesterday, skipped lunch. In this, and in his general attention to his own person, he was as quietly fanatic as—it for the first time occurred to her—a woman.

"You know I've never liked the queer side of this business," he went on. "I've just gotten used to it. I don't even think any more, who's gay and who isn't."

"Avis was *jubilant*," Sharon said. "How *could* she think it?"

It took him a moment to focus on the question, and realize that his answer was important to her. He became nettled. "Ask *her* how," he said. "Our brief and regrettable relationship, if that's what interests you, seemed satisfactory to me at least. I mean, the moving parts all functioned. What troubles and amazes me, if I may say so, is how *you* can be taking this ridiculous rumor so seriously."

"I'm *not*, Frank," she insisted, and then backtracked. "But why would such a rumor come out of thin air? Doesn't there have to be something? Since we moved up here, we're not together so much, naturally; some days when I can't come into town you're gone sixteen hours. . . ."

"But, *Sha*ron," he said, like a teacher restoring discipline, removing his reading glasses from his almond-shaped eyes, with their stubby fair lashes. "Don't you *know* me? Ever since that time after the dance when we parked by the river? How old were you? Seventeen?"

She didn't want to reminisce. Their early sex had been difficult for her; she had submitted to his advances out of a larger, more social, rather idealistic attraction: she knew that together they would have the strength to get out of Cincinnati and, singly, or married to others, they would stay. "Well," she said, enjoying this sensation, despite the chill the rumor had awakened in her, of descending with Frank to a deeper level of intimacy than usual, "how well do you know even your own spouse? People are fooled all the time. Peggy Jacobson, for instance, when Henry ran off with the au pair, couldn't believe, even when the evidence was right there in front of her—"

"I'm *deeply* insulted," Frank interrupted, his mouth tense in that way of his when making a joke but not wanting to show his teeth. "My masculinity is insulted." But he couldn't deny himself a downward glance into his magazine; his tidy white hand jerked, as if wanting to tear out yet another item that might be useful to their business. Intimacy had always made him nervous. She kept at it. "Avis said two separate people had solemnly assured her."

"Who, exactly?"

When she told him, he said, just as she had done, "Well, then." He added, "You know how gays are. Malicious. Mischievous. They have all that time and money on their hands."

"You sound jealous." Something about the way he was arguing with her strengthened Sharon's suspicion that, outrageous as the rumor was—indeed, *because* it was outrageous—it was true.

In the days that followed, now that Sharon was alert to the rumor's vaporous presence, she imagined it everywhere—on the poised young faces of their staff, in the delicate negotiatory accents of their artists' agents, in the heartier tones of their repeat customers, even in the gruff, self-preoccupied ramblings of the artists themselves. People seemed startled when she and Frank entered a room together: the desk receptionist and the security guard in their gallery halted their daily morning banter, and the waiters in their pet restaurant, over on 59th Street, appeared especially effusive and attentive. Handshakes lasted a second too long; women embraced her with an extra squeeze; she felt herself ensnared in a net of unspoken pity.

Frank sensed her discomfort and took a certain malicious pleasure in it, enacting all the while his perfect innocence. He composed himself to appear, from her angle, aloof above the rumor. Dealing professionally in so much absurdity—the art world's frantic attention-getting grotesquerie—he merely intensified the fastidious dryness that had sustained their gallery through wave after wave of changing fashion, and that had, like a rocket's heat-resistant skin, insulated their launch, their escape from the comfortable riverine smugness of semi-Southern, puritanical Cincinnati to this capital of dreadful freedom. The rumor amused him, and it amused him, too, to notice how she helplessly watched to see if in the metropolitan throngs his eyes now followed young men as once they had noticed and followed young women. She observed his gestures—always a bit excessively graceful and precise—distrustfully, and listened for the buttery, reedy tone of voice that might signal an invisible sex change.

That she even in some small fraction of her was willing to believe the rumor justified a certain maliciousness on his part. He couldn't help teasing her—glancing over at her, say, when an especially lithe and magnetic young waiter served them, or, at home, in their bedroom, pushing more brusquely than was his style at her increasing sexual unwillingness. At last away from the countless knowing eyes of their New York milieu, in the privacy of their Hastings upstairs, beneath the wide Midwestern eaves, she would on occasion burst into tears and strike out at him, at his infuriating impervious apparent blamelessness. He was like one of those photo-realist nudes, merciless in every detail and yet subtly, defiantly not there, not human. "You're distant," she accused him. "You've always been."

"I don't mean to be. Sharon, you didn't use to mind my manner. You thought it was quietly masterful."

"I was a teenaged girl. I deferred to you."

"It worked out," he pointed out, lifting his hands in an effete, disclaiming way to indicate their large bedroom, their expensive house, their joint career. "What is it that bothers you, my dear? The idea of losing me? Or the insult to your female pride? The people who started this ridiculous rumor don't even *see* women—women to them are just background noise."

"It's *not* ridiculous—if it were, why does it keep on and on, even though we're seen together all the time?"

For, ostensibly to quiet her, and to quench the rumor, he had all but ceased to go to the city alone, and took her with him even though it meant some neglect of the house and their still-growing sons.

Frank asked, "Who *says* it keeps on all the time? I've *never* heard it, never once, except from you. Who's mentioned it lately?"

"Nobody."

"Well, then." He smiled, his lips not quite parting on his curved teeth, tawny like a beaver's.

"You bastard!" Sharon burst out. "You have some stinking little secret!"

"I don't," he serenely half-lied.

The rumor had no factual basis. But might there be, Frank asked himself, some truth to it after all? Not circumstantial truth, but some higher, inner truth? As a young man, slight of build, with artistic interests, had he not been fearful of being mistaken for a homosexual? Had he not responded to homosexual overtures as they arose, in bars and locker rooms, with a disproportionate terror and repugnance? Had not his early marriage, and then, ten years later, his flurry of adulterous womanizing, been an escape of sorts, into safe, socially approved terrain? When he fantasized, or saw a pornographic movie, was not the male organ the hero of the occasion for him, at the center of every scene? Were not those slavish, lapping, sucking starlets his robotlike delegates, with glazed eyes and undisturbed coiffures venturing where he did not dare? Did he not, perhaps, envy women their privilege of worshipping the phallus? And did he not, when the doctor gave him his annual prostate exam with a greased finger, have to fight getting an erection, right there in a passive curled position on the examining table? But, Frank further asked himself, in fairness arguing both sides of the case, can homosexual strands be entirely disentangled from heterosexual in that pink muck of carnal excitement, of dream made flesh, of return to the pre-sexual womb?

More broadly, had he not felt more comfortable with his father than with his mother? Was not this in itself a sinister reversal of the usual biology? His father had been a genteel Fourth Street lawyer, of no particular effectuality save that most of his clients were from the same social class, with the same accents and comfortably narrowed aspirations, here on this plateau by the swelling Ohio. Darker and taller than Frank, with the same long teeth and primly set mouth, his father had had the lawyer's gift of silence, of judicious withholding, and in his son's scattered memories of times together—a trip downtown in the Packard to buy Frank his first suit, each summer's one or two excursions to see the Reds play at old Crosley Field—the man said little; but this prim reserve, letting so much go unstated and unacknowledged, was a relief, after the daily shower of words and affection and advice that Frank received from his mother. As an adult he was attracted, he had noticed, to stoical men, taller than he, gravely sealed around an unexpressed sadness. His favorite college roommate had been of this saturnine type, and his pet tennis partner in Hastings, and artists he especially favored and encouraged—dour, weathered landscapists and virtually illiterate sculptors, welded solid into their crafts and stubborn obsessions. With these men he became a catering, wifely, subtly agitated presence that Sharon would scarcely recognize.

Frank's mother, once a fluffy belle from Louisville, had been gaudy, strident, sardonic, volatile, needy, demanding, loving; from her he had inherited his "artistic" side, as well as his blondness and "interesting" almond-shaped eyes, but he was not especially grateful. Less—as was proposed by a famous formula he didn't know as a boy—would have been more. His mother had given him an impression of women as complex, brightly colored traps, attractive but treacherous, their petals apt to harden in an instant into knives. A certain wistful passivity had drawn him to Sharon and, after the initial dazzlement of the Avises of the world faded and fizzled, always drew him back. Other women asked more than he could provide; he was aware of other, bigger, hotter men they had had. But with Sharon he had been a rescuer; he had slain the dragon of the Ohio; he had got her out of Cincinnati. What more devastatingly, and less forgivably, confirmed the rumor's essential truth than the willingness of the one who knew him best and owed him most to entertain it? Sharon's instinct had been to believe Avis even though, far from running off, he was sitting there right in front of her eyes.

He was unreal to her, he could not help but conclude: all those years of cohabitation and husbandly service were now thanklessly dismissed because of an apparition, a shadow of gossip. On the other hand, now that the rumor existed, Frank had become more real in the eyes of José, the younger, slier of the two security guards, whose daily greetings had subtly moved beyond the perfunctory; a certain mischievous dance in the boy's velvety features had come to enrich their employer-employee courtesies. And Jennifer, too, the severely beautiful receptionist, with her neo-hippie bangs and shawls and serapes, now treated him more relaxedly, even offhandedly. She assumed with him a comradely slanginess—"The boss was in earlier but she went out to exchange something at Bergdorf's"—as if both he and she were in roughly parallel bondage to "the boss." Frank's heart felt a reflex of loyalty to Sharon, a single sharp beat, but then he, too, relaxed, as if his phantom male lover and the weightless life he led with him in some nonexistent apartment had bestowed at last what the city had withheld from the overworked, child-burdened married couple who had arrived fifteen years ago—a halo of glamour, of debonair mystery.

In Hastings, when he and his wife attended a suburban party, the effect was less flattering. The other couples, he imagined, were slightly unsettled by the Whittiers' stubbornly appearing together, and became disjointed in their presence, the men drifting off in distaste, the women turning supernormal and laying up a chinkless wall of conversation about children's college applications, local zoning, and Wall Street layoffs. The women, it seemed to Frank, edged, with an instinctive animal movement, a few inches closer to Sharon and touched her with a deft, protective flicking on the shoulder or forearm, to express solidarity and sympathy.

Wes Robertson, Frank's favorite tennis partner, came over to him and grunted, "How's it going?"

"Fine," Frank gushed, staring up at Wes with what he hoped weren't unduly starry eyes. Wes, who had recently turned fifty, had an old motorcycle-accident scar on one side of his chin, a small pale rose of discoloration, which seemed to concentrate the man's self-careless manliness. Frank gave him more of an answer than he might have wanted: "In the art game we're feeling the slowdown like everybody else, but the Japanese are keeping the roof from caving in. The trouble with the Japanese, though, is, from the standpoint of a personal gallery like ours, they aren't adventurous—they want blue chips, they want guaranteed value, they can't grasp that in art value has to be subjective to an extent. Look at their own stuff—it's all standardized. Who the hell but the experts can tell a Hiroshige from a Hokusai? When you think about it, their whole society, their whole success really, is based on everybody being alike, everybody agreeing. The notion of art as an individualistic struggle, a gamble, as the dynamic embodiment of an existential problem—they just don't get it." He was talking too much, he knew, but he couldn't help it; Wes's scowling presence, his melancholy scarred face and stringy alcoholic body, which nevertheless could still whip a backhand right across the forecourt, perversely excited Frank, made him want to flirt.

Wes grimaced and contemplated Frank glumly. "Be around for a game Sunday?" Meaning, had he really run off?

"Of course. Why wouldn't I be?" This was teasing the issue, and Frank tried to sober up, to rein in. He felt a flush on his face, and a stammer coming on. He asked, "The usual hour? Ten-forty-five, more or less?"

Wes nodded. "Sure."

Frank chattered on: "Let's try to get Court Four this time. Those brats having their lessons on Court One drove me crazy last time. We had to keep retrieving their damn balls. And listening to their moronic chatter."

Wes didn't grant this attempt at evocation of past liaisons even a word, just continued his melancholy, stoical nodding. This was one of the things, it occurred to Frank, that he liked about men: their relational minimalism, their gender-based realization that the cupboard of life, emotionally speaking, was pretty near bare. There wasn't that tireless, irksome, bright-eyed *hope* women kept fluttering at you.

Once, years ago, on a stag golfing trip to Portugal, he and Wes had shared a room, with two single beds, and Wes had fallen asleep within a minute and started snoring, keeping Frank awake for much of the night. Contemplating the unconscious male body on its moonlit bed, Frank had been struck by the tragic dignity of this supine form, like a stone knight eroding on a tomb—the snoring profile in motionless gray silhouette, the massive, scarred warrior weight helpless, as his breathing struggled from phase to phase of the sleep cycle—from deep to REM to a near-wakefulness that brought a few merciful minutes of silence. The next morning, Wes said Frank should have reached over and poked him in the side; that's what his wife did. But he wasn't his wife, Frank thought, though he had felt, in the course of that night's ordeal, his heart make many curious motions, among them the heaving, all but impossible effort women's hearts make in overcoming men's heavy grayness and achieving—a rainbow born of drizzle—love.

At the opening of Ned Forschheimer's show—Forschheimer, a shy, rude, stubborn, and now elderly painter of tea-colored, wintry Connecticut landscapes, was one of the Whittier Gallery's pets, unfashionable yet sneakily sellable—none other than Walton Forney came up to Frank, his round face lit by white wine and his odd unquenchable self-delight, and said, "Say, Frank old boy. Methinks I owe you an apology. It was Charlie Whit*field,* who used to run that framing shop down on Eighth

Street, who left his wife suddenly, with some little Guatemalan boy he was putting through CCNY on the side. They took off for Mexico and left the missus sitting with the shop mortgaged up to its attic and about a hundred prints of wild ducks left unframed. The thing that must have confused me, Charlie came from Ohio, too—Columbus or Cleveland, one of those. I knew it began with a C. It was, what do they call it, a Freudian slip, an understandable confusion. Avis Wasserman told me Sharon wasn't all that thrilled to get the word a while ago, and you must have wondered yourself what the hell was up."

"We ignored it," Frank said, in a voice firmer and less catering than his usual one. "We rose above it." Walton was a number of inches shorter than Frank, with yet a bigger head; his gleaming, thin-skinned face, bearing smooth jowls that had climbed into his sideburns, was shadowed blue here and there, like the moon. His bruised and powdered look somehow went with his small spaced teeth and the horizontal red tracks his glasses had left in the fat in front of his ears.

The man gazed at Frank with a gleaming, sagging lower lip, his nearsighted eyes trying to assess the damage, the depth of the grudge. "Well, *mea culpa, mea culpa,* I guess, though I *didn't* tell Jojo and that *poisonous* Ed Jaffrey to go blabbing it all over town."

"Well, Wally, thanks for filling me in," Frank said resonantly. Depending on what type of man he was with, Frank felt large and straight and sonorous or, as with Wes, gracile and flighty. Sharon, scenting blood amid the vacuous burble of the party, pushed herself through the crowd and joined them. Frank quickly told her, "Wally just confessed to me he started the rumor because Charlie Whitfield downtown, who *did* run off with somebody, came from Ohio, too. Toledo, as I remember."

"I said Cleveland or Columbus," Wally murmured, not sure Frank was being satirical.

Sharon asked, "What rumor, honey?"

Frank blushed. "You know, the one that said I ran off with a boy."

"Oh, *that* rumor," Sharon said, blinking once, as if her party mascara were sticking. "I'd totally forgotten it. Who could believe it," she asked Wally, "of Frank?"

"Everybody, evidently," Frank said. It was possible, given the strange willful ways of women, that she had forgotten it, even while he had been brooding over its possible justice. If the rumor were truly quenched—and Walton would undoubtedly tell the story of his "Freudian slip" around town, as a self-promoting joke on himself—Frank would feel diminished. He would feel emasculated, if his wife no longer thought he had a secret.

Yet that night, at the party, Walton Forney's Jojo came up to him. He seemed, despite an earring the size of a faucet washer and a magenta stripe in the center of his "rise" hairdo, unexpectedly intelligent and low-key, offering, not in so many words, a kind of apology, and praising the tea-colored landscapes being offered for sale. "I've been thinking, in my own work, of going, you know, more traditional. You get this feeling of, like, a dead end with total abstraction." The boy had a bony, humorless face, with a silvery line of a scar under one eye, and seemed uncertain in manner, hesitant, as if he had reached a point in life where he needed direction. That fat fool Forney could certainly not provide direction, and it pleased Frank to imagine that Jojo was beginning to realize it.

"All that abstract-expressionist fuss about *paint*," he told the boy. "A person looking at a Rembrandt knows he's looking at *paint*. The question is, What *else* is he looking at?"

As he and Sharon drove home together along the Hudson, the car felt close; the heater fan blew oppressively, parchingly. "*You* were willing to believe it at first," he reminded her.

"Well, Avis seemed so definite. But you convinced me."

"How?"

She placed her hand high on his thigh and dug her fingers in, annoyingly, infuriatingly. "*You* know," she said, in a lower register, meant to be sexy, but almost inaudible over the roar of the heater fan. The Hudson glowered far beneath them, like the dark Ohio when he used to drive her home from a date across the river in honky-tonk Kentucky.

"That could be mere performance," he warned her. "Women are fooled that way all the time."

"Who says?"

"Everybody. Books. Proust. People aren't that simple."

"They're simple enough," Sharon said, in a neutral, defensive tone, removing her hand.

"If you say so, my dear," Frank said, somewhat stoically, his mind drifting. That silvery line of a scar under Jojo's left eye . . . lean long muscles snugly wrapped in white skin . . . lofts with a Spartan, masculine tang to their spaces . . . Hellenic fellowship, exercise machines . . . direct negotiations, between equals . . . no more dealing with this pathetic, maddening race of *others* . . .

The rumor might be dead in the world, but in him it had come alive.

−1994

ALICE WALKER

B. 1944

Alice Walker, poet, novelist, short story writer, editor, political activist, and essayist, was born in rural Georgia. She attended historically African-American Spelman College and Sarah Lawrence College for women. Her novel The Color Purple *(1982) won the National Book Award, the Pulitzer Prize, and the American Book Award, before becoming a controversial film directed by Steven Spielberg in 1985. An essay collection,* In Search of Our Mothers' Gardens, *appeared in 1983 and established Walker as a major feminist voice in the United States. Her publications include several books of poetry, including* Once *(1968) and* Revolutionary Petunias *(1973), and numerous novels:* The Third Life of Grange Copeland *(1970),* Meridian *(1976),* The Temple of My Familiar *(1989), and* Possessing the Secret of Joy *(1992). Her most recent writing is* Alice Walker Banned *(1996).*

PORN

Like many thoughtful women of the seventies, she had decided women were far more interesting than men. But, again like most thoughtful women, she rarely admitted this aloud. Besides, again like her contemporaries, she maintained a close connection with a man.

It was a sexual connection.

They had met in Tanzania when it was still Tanganyika; she was with an international group of students interested in health care in socialist African countries; he with an American group intent upon building schools. They met. Liked each other. Wrote five or six letters over the next seven years. Married other people. Had children. Lived in different cities. Divorced. Met again to discover they now shared a city and lived barely three miles apart.

A strong bond between them was that they respected their former spouses and supported their children. They had each arranged a joint custody settlement and many of their favorite outings were amid a clash of children. Still, her primary interest in him was sexual. It was not that she did not respect his mind; she did. It was a fine mind. More scientific than hers, more given to abstractions. But also a mind curious about nature and the hidden workings of things (it was probably this, she thought, that made him such a good lover) and she enjoyed following his thoughts about the distances of stars and whole galaxies from the earth, the difference between low clouds and high fog, and the complex survival mechanisms of the snail.

But sex together was incredibly good: like conversation with her women friends, who were never abstract, rarely distant enough from nature to be critical in their appraisal of it, and whose own mechanisms for survival were hauled out in discussion for all to see. The touch of his fingers—sensitive, wise, exploring the furthest reaches of sensation—were like the tongues of women, talking, questing, searching for the *true* place, the place which, when touched, has no choice but to respond.

She was aflame with desire for him.

On those evenings when all the children were with their other parents, he would arrive at the apartment at seven. They would walk hand in hand to a Chinese restaurant a mile away. They would laugh and drink and eat and touch hands and knees over and under the table. They would come home. Smoke a joint. He would put music on. She would run water in the tub with lots of bubbles. In the bath they would lick and suck each other, in blissful delight. They would admire the rich candle glow on their wet, delectably earth-toned skins. Sniff the incense—the odor of sandal and redwood. He would carry her in to bed.

Music. Emotion. Sensation. Presence.
Satisfaction like rivers
flowing and silver.

On the basis of their sexual passion they built the friendship that sustained them through the outings with their collective children, through his loss of a job (temporarily), through her writer's block (she worked as a free-lance journalist), through her bouts of frustration and boredom when she perceived that, in conversation, he could only *be* scientific, only *be* abstract, and she was, because of her intrepid, garrulous women friends—whom she continued frequently, and often in desperation, to see—used to so much more.

In short, they had devised an almost perfect arrangement.

One morning at six o'clock they were making "morning love." "Morning love" was relaxed, clearheaded. Fresh. No music but the birds and cars starting. No dope.

They came within seconds of each other.

This inspired him. He thought they could come together.

She was sated, indifferent, didn't wish to think about the strain.

But then he said: "Did I ever show you [he knew he hadn't] my porn collection?"

"What could it be?" she inevitably wondered. Hooked.

His hands are cupping her ass. His fingers like warm grass or warm and supple vines. One thumb—she fancies she feels the whorled print—makes a circle in the wetness of her anus. She shivers. His tongue gently laps her vulva as it enters her, his top lip caressing the clitoris. For five minutes she is moving along as usual. Blissed *out,* she thinks to herself. Then she stops.

"What have you got?" she has asked him.

"This," he replied. "And this."

A gorgeous black woman who looks like her friend Fannie has a good friend (white boy from her hometown down South) who is basically gay. Though—. "Fannie" and let us call him "Fred" pick up a hick tourist in a bar. They both dig him, the caption says. He is not gorgeous. He is short, pasty, dirty blond. Slightly cross-eyed. In fact, looks retarded. Fred looks very much the same. "Fannie" invites them to her place where without holding hands or eating or bathing or putting on music, they strip and begin to fondle each other. "Fannie" looks amused as they take turns licking and suck- ing her. She smiles benignly as they do the same things to each other. . . .

"And this."

A young blonde girl from Minnesota [probably kidnapped, she thinks, reading] is *far from home in New York, lonely and very horny. She is befriended by two of the black- est men on the East Coast. (They had been fighting outside a bar and she had stopped them by flinging her naive white self into the fray.) In their gratitude for her peace- making they take her to their place and do everything they can think of to her. She grinning liberally the whole time. Finally they make a sandwich of her: one filling the anus and the other the vagina, so that all that is visible of her body between them is a sliver of white thighs.* [And we see that these two pugilists have finally come together on something.]

She is sitting with her back against the headboard of the bed so that her breasts hang down. This increases sensation in her already very aroused nipples. He crawls up to her on all fours like a gentle but ravenous bear and begins to nuzzle her. He nuzzles and nuzzles until her nipples virtually aim themselves at him. He takes one into his mouth. She begins to flow.

But the flow stops.

Once he said to her: "I could be turned on by bondage." No, he said "by 'a little *light* bondage.'" She had told him of a fantasy in which she lay helpless, bound, waiting for the pleasure worse than death.

There is no plot this time. No story of an improbable friendship down South, no goldilocks from the Midwestern plains. Just page after page of women: yellow, red, white, brown, black [she had let him tie her up very loosely once; it was not like her fantasy at all. She had wanted to hold him, caress him, snuggle and cuddle] *bound, often gagged. Their legs open. Forced to their knees.*

He is massaging the back of her neck, her shoulders. Her buttocks. The backs of her thighs. She has bent over a hot typewriter all day and is tired. She sinks into the feeling of being desired and pampered. Valued. Loved. Soon she is completely restored. Alert. She decides to make love to him. She turns over. She cradles his head in her arms. Kisses his forehead. His eyes. Massages his scalp with her fingers. Buries her nose in his neck. Kisses his neck. Caresses his chest. Flicks his nipples, back and forth, with her tongue. Slowly she moves down his body. His penis (which he thinks should not be called "penis"—"a white boy's word"; he prefers "cock") is standing. She takes it—she is on her knees—into her mouth.

She gags.

The long-term accommodation that protects marriage and other such relationships is, she knows, forgetfulness. She will forget what turns him on.

"No, no," he says, very sorry he has shown her his collection; in fact, vowing passionately to throw it away. "The point is for *you* to be turned on by it *too!*"

She thinks of the lovely black girl—whom she actually thinks of as her friend Fannie—and is horrified. What is Fannie doing in such company? she wonders. She panics as he is entering her. Wait! she says, and races to the phone.

The phone rings and rings.

Her friend Fannie is an out-of-work saleswoman. She is also a lesbian. She proceeds to write in her head a real story about Fannie based on what she knows. Her lover at work on her body the whole time.

Fannie and *Laura share a tiny loft apartment. They almost never make love. Not because they are not loving—they do a lot of caressing and soothing—but they are so guilty about what they feel that sexuality has more or less dried* up. [She feels her own juices drying up at this thought.]

They have both been out of work for a long time. Laura's mother is sick. Fannie's young brother has entered Howard University. There is only Fannie to send him money for books, clothes and entertainment. Fannie is very pretty but basically unskilled in anything but selling, and salespersons by the thousands have been laid off in the recession. Unemployment is not enough.

But Fannie is really very beautiful. Men stop her on the street all the time to tell her so. It is the way they chose to tell her so, when she was barely pubescent, that makes her return curses for "compliments" even today.

*But these men would still stop her on the street, offer her money "for a few hours'
work."...*

By now she has faked all kinds of things, and exhausted her lover. He is sound
asleep. She races to Fannie and Laura's apartment. Sits waiting for them on the
stoop. Finally they come home from seeing a Woody Allen movie. They are in high
spirits, and besides, because she shares part of her life with a man, care much less
for her than she does for them. They yawn loudly, kiss her matronizingly on both
cheeks, and send her home again.

Now, when he makes love to her, she tries to fit herself into the white-woman,
two-black-men story. But who will she be? The men look like her brothers, Bobo and
Charlie. She is disgusted, and worse, bored, by Bobo and Charlie. The white woman
is like the young girl who, according to the *Times, was* seduced off a farm in
Minnesota by a black pimp and turned out on 42nd Street. She cannot stop herself
from thinking: *Poor: Ignorant: Sleazy: Depressing.* This does not excite or stimulate.

He watches her face as he makes expert love to her. He knows his technique is virtually flawless, but he thinks perhaps it can be improved. Is she moving less rhyth-
mically under him? Does she seem distracted? There seems to be a separate activity in her body, to which she is attentive, and which is not connected to the current
he is sending through his fingertips. He notices the fluttering at the corners of her
eyelids. Her eyes could fly open at any moment, he thinks, and look objectively at
him. He shudders. Holds her tight.
   He thinks frantically of what she might be thinking of him. Realizes he is moving in her *desperately,* as if he is climbing the walls of a closed building. As if she
reads his mind, she moans encouragingly. But it is a distracted moan—that offends
him.
   He bites the pillow over her head: Where *is* she? he thinks. Is she into fantasy or
not?
   He must be.
   He slips her into the role of "Fannie" with some hope. But nothing develops. As
"Fannie" she refuses even to leave her Southern town. Won't speak to, much less go
down on, either of the two gays.
   He races back and forth between an image of her bound and on her knees, to
two black men and a white woman becoming acquainted outside a bar.
   This does not help.
   Besides, she is involved in the activity inside herself and holding him—
nostalgically.
   He feels himself sliding down the wall that is her body, and expelled from inside
her.

—1981

Tobias Wolff

B. 1945

*Tobias Wolff was born in Birmingham, Alabama, and educated at Oxford
University in England and Stanford University. He was a lieutenant in the
United States Army Special Forces from 1964 to 1968, stationed in Vietnam.
He published his first book,* Ugly Rumours, *in 1975. His first collection of
short stories,* In the Garden of the North American Martyrs, *appeared in
1981, followed by* The Barracks Thief *(1984),* Back in the World *(1985), and
his autobiographical novel,* This Boy's Life: A Memoir *(1990), which was
made into a major film starring Leonardo DiCaprio and Robert DeNiro in
1993. His most recent works are* In Pharaoh's Army: Memories of the Lost
War *(1994) and* The Night in Question: Stories *(1996). Wolff currently
teaches at Stanford University.*

Hunters in the Snow

Tub had been waiting for an hour in the falling snow. He paced the sidewalk to
keep warm and stuck his head out over the kerb whenever he saw lights approaching. The fall of snow thickened. Tub stood below the overhang of a building. Across
the road the clouds whitened just above the rooftops, and the street lights went out.
He shifted the rifle strap to his other shoulder. The whiteness seeped up the sky.

A truck slid around the corner, horn blaring, rear end sashaying. Tub moved to
the sidewalk and held up his hand. The truck jumped the kerb and kept coming, half
on the street and half on the sidewalk. It wasn't slowing down at all. Tub stood for
a moment, still holding up his hand, then jumped back. His rifle slipped off his
shoulder and clattered on the ice, a sandwich fell out of his pocket. He ran for the
steps of the building. Another sandwich and a package of cookies tumbled onto the
new snow. He made the steps and looked back.

The truck had stopped several feet beyond where Tub had been standing. He
picked up his sandwiches and his cookies and slung the rifle and went up to the driver's window. The driver was bent against the steering wheel, slapping his knees
and drumming his feet on the floorboards. He looked like a cartoon of a person
laughing. 'You ought to see yourself,' the driver said. 'He looks just like a beach ball
with a hat on, doesn't he? Doesn't he, Frank?'

The man beside him smiled and looked off.

'You almost ran me down,' Tub said. 'You could've killed me.'

'Come on, Tub,' said the man beside the driver. 'Be mellow. Kenny was just mess-
ing around.' He opened the door and slid over to the middle of the seat.

Tub took the bolt out of his rifle and climbed in beside him. 'I waited an hour,'
he said. 'If you meant ten o'clock why didn't you say ten o'clock?'

'Tub, you haven't done anything but complain since we got here,' said the man
in the middle. 'If you want to piss and moan all day you might as well go home and

bitch at your kids. Take your pick.' When Tub didn't say anything he turned to the driver. 'Okay, Kenny, let's hit the road.'

Some juvenile delinquents had heaved a brick through the windshield on the driver's side, so the cold and snow funnelled right into the cab. The heater didn't work. They covered themselves with a couple of blankets Kenny had brought along and pulled down the muffs on their caps. Tub tried to keep his hands warm by rubbing them under the blanket but Frank made him stop.

They left Spokane and drove deep into the country, running along black lines of fences. The snow let up, but still there was no edge to the land where it met the sky. Nothing moved in the chalky fields. The cold bleached their faces and made the stubble stand out on their cheeks and along their upper lips. They stopped twice for coffee before they got to the woods where Kenny wanted to hunt.

Tub was for trying someplace different; two years in a row they'd been up and down this land and hadn't seen a thing. Frank didn't care one way or the other, he just wanted to get out of the goddamned truck. 'Feel that,' Frank said, slamming the door. He spread his feet and closed his eyes and leaned his head way back and breathed deeply. 'Tune in on that energy.'

'Another thing,' Kenny said. 'This is open land. Most of the land around here is posted.'

'I'm cold,' Tub said.

Frank breathed out. 'Stop bitching, Tub. Get centred.'

'I wasn't bitching.'

'Centred,' Kenny said. 'Next thing you'll be wearing a nightgown, Frank. Selling flowers out at the airport.'

'Kenny,' Frank said, 'you talk too much.'

'Okay,' Kenny said. 'I won't say a word. Like I won't say anything about a certain babysitter.'

'What babysitter?' Tub asked.

'That's between us,' Frank said, looking at Kenny. 'You keep your mouth shut.'

Kenny laughed.

'You're asking for it,' Frank said.

'Asking for what?'

'You'll see.'

'Hey,' Tub said, 'are we hunting or what?'

They started off across the field. Tub had trouble getting through the fences. Frank and Kenny could have helped him; they could have lifted up the top wire and stepped on the bottom wire, but they didn't. They stood and watched him. There were a lot of fences and Tub was puffing when they reached the woods.

They hunted for over two hours and saw no deer, no tracks, no sign. Finally they stopped by the creek to eat. Kenny had several slices of pizza and a couple of candy bars; Frank had a sandwich, an apple, two carrots, and a square of chocolate; Tub ate one hard-boiled egg and a stick of celery.

'You ask me how I want to die today,' Kenny said, 'I'll tell you burn me at the stake.' He turned to Tub. 'You still on that diet?' He winked at Frank.

'What do you think? You think I like hard-boiled eggs?'

'All I can say is, it's the first diet I ever heard of where you gained weight from it.'

'Who said I gained weight?'

'Oh, pardon me. I take it back. You're just wasting away before my very eyes. Isn't he, Frank?'

Frank had his fingers fanned out on the stump where he'd laid his food. His knuckles were hairy. He wore a heavy wedding band and on his right pinky another gold ring with a flat face and an 'F' in what looked like diamonds. 'Tub,' he said, 'you haven't seen your own balls in ten years.'

Kenny doubled over laughing. He took off his hat and slapped his leg with it.

'What am I supposed to do?' Tub said. 'It's my glands.'

They left the woods and hunted along the creek. Frank and Kenny worked one bank and Tub worked the other, moving upstream. The snow was light but the drifts were deep and hard to move through. Wherever Tub looked the surface was smooth, undisturbed, and after a time he lost interest. He stopped looking for tracks and just tried to keep up with Frank and Kenny on the other side. A moment came when he realized he hadn't seen them in a long time. The breeze was moving from him to them; when it stilled he could sometimes hear Kenny laughing but that was all. He quickened his pace, breasting the drifts, fighting away the snow. He heard his heart and felt the flush on his face but he never once stopped.

Tub caught up with Frank and Kenny at a bend of the creek. They were standing on a log that stretched from their bank to his. Ice had backed up behind the log. Frozen reeds stuck out.

'See anything?' Frank asked.

Tub shook his head.

There wasn't much daylight left and they decided to head back towards the road. Frank and Kenny crossed the log and they started downstream, using the trail Tub had broken. Before they had gone very far Kenny stopped. 'Look at that,' he said, and pointed to some tracks going from the creek back into the woods. Tub's footprints crossed right over them. There on the bank, plain as day, were several mounds of deer shit. 'What do you think that is, Tub?' Kenny kicked at it. 'Walnuts on vanilla icing?'

'I guess I didn't notice.'

Kenny looked at Frank.

'I was lost.'

'You were lost. Big deal.'

They followed the tracks into the woods. The deer had gone over a fence half buried in drifting snow. A no hunting sign was nailed to the top of one of the posts. Frank laughed and said the son of a bitch could read. Kenny wanted to go after him but Frank said no way, the people out here didn't mess around. He thought maybe the farmer who owned the land would let them use it if they asked. Kenny wasn't so sure. Anyway, he figured that by the time they walked to the truck and drove up the road and doubled back it would be almost dark.

'Relax,' Frank said. 'You can't hurry nature. If we're meant to get that deer, we'll get it. If we're not, we won't.'

They started back towards the truck. This part of the woods was mainly pine. The snow was shaded and had a glaze on it. It held up Kenny and Frank but Tub kept falling through. As he kicked forward, the edge of the crust bruised his shins. Kenny and Frank pulled ahead of him, to where he couldn't even hear their voices any more. He sat down on a stump and wiped his face. He ate both the sandwiches and half the cookies, taking his own sweet time. It was dead quiet.

When Tub crossed the last fence into the road the truck started moving. Tub had to run for it and just managed to grab hold of the tailgate and hoist himself into the bed. He lay there, panting. Kenny looked out the rear window and grinned. Tub crawled into the lee of the cab to get out of the freezing wind. He pulled his earflaps low and pushed his chin into the collar of his coat. Someone rapped on the window but Tub would not turn around.

He and Frank waited outside while Kenny went into the farmhouse to ask permission. The house was old and paint was curling off the sides. The smoke streamed westward off the top of the chimney, fanning away into a thin grey plume. Above the ridge of the hills another ridge of blue clouds was rising.

'You've got a short memory,' Tub said.

'What?' Frank said. He had been staring off.

'I used to stick up for you.'

'Okay, so you used to stick up for me. What's eating you?'

'You shouldn't have just left me back there like that.'

'You're a grown-up, Tub. You can take care of yourself. Anyway, if you think you're the only person with problems I can tell you that you're not.'

'Is something bothering you, Frank?'

Frank kicked at a branch poking out of the snow. 'Never mind,' he said.

'What did Kenny mean about the babysitter?'

'Kenny talks too much,' Frank said. 'You just mind your own business.'

Kenny came out of the farmhouse and gave the thumbs-up and they began walking back towards the woods. As they passed the barn a large black hound with a grizzled snout ran out and barked at them. Every time he barked he slid backwards a bit, like a cannon recoiling. Kenny got down on all fours and snarled and barked back at him, and the dog slunk away into the barn, looking over his shoulder and peeing a little as he went.

'That's an old-timer,' Frank said. 'A real greybeard. Fifteen years if he's a day.'

'Too old,' Kenny said.

Past the barn they cut off through the fields. The land was unfenced and the crust was freezing up thick and they made good time. They kept to the edge of the field until they picked up the tracks again and followed them into the woods, farther and farther back toward the hills. The trees started to blur with the shadows and the wind rose and needled their faces with the crystals it swept off the glaze. Finally they lost the tracks.

Kenny swore and threw down his hat. 'This is the worst day of hunting I ever had, bar none.' He picked up his hat and brushed off the snow. 'This will be the first season since I was fifteen I haven't got my deer.'

'It isn't the deer,' Frank said. 'It's the hunting. There are all these forces out here and you just have to go with them.'

'You go with them,' Kenny said. 'I came out here to get me a deer, not listen to a bunch of hippie bullshit. And if it hadn't been for dimples here I would have, too.'

'That's enough,' Frank said.

'And you—you're so busy thinking about that little jailbait of yours you wouldn't know a deer if you saw one.'

'Drop dead,' Frank said, and turned away.

Kenny and Tub followed him back across the fields. When they were coming up to the barn Kenny stopped and pointed. 'I hate that post,' he said. He raised his rifle and fired. It sounded like a dry branch cracking. The post splintered along its right side, up towards the top. 'There,' Kenny said. 'It's dead.'

'Knock it off,' Frank said, walking ahead.

Kenny looked at Tub. He smiled. 'I hate that tree,' he said, and fired again. Tub hurried to catch up with Frank. He started to speak but just then the dog ran out of the barn and barked at them. 'Easy, boy,' Frank said.

'I hate that dog.' Kenny was behind them.

'That's enough,' Frank said. 'You put that gun down.'

Kenny fired. The bullet went in between the dog's eyes. He sank right down into the snow, his legs splayed out on each side, his yellow eyes open and staring. Except for the blood he looked like a small bearskin rug. The blood ran down the dog's muzzle into the snow.

They all looked at the dog lying there.

'What did he ever do to you?' Tub asked. 'He was just barking.'

Kenny turned to Tub. 'I hate you.'

Tub shot from the waist. Kenny jerked backwards against the fence and buckled to his knees. He folded his hands across his stomach. 'Look,' he said. His hands were covered with blood. In the dusk his blood was more blue than red. It seemed to belong to the shadows. It didn't seem out of place. Kenny eased himself onto his back. He sighed several times, deeply. 'You shot me,' he said.

'I had to,' Tub said. He knelt beside Kenny. 'Oh God,' he said. 'Frank. Frank.'

Frank hadn't moved since Kenny killed the dog.

'Frank!' Tub shouted.

'I was just kidding around,' Kenny said. 'It was a joke. Oh!' he said, and arched his back suddenly. 'Oh!' he said again, and dug his heels into the snow and pushed himself along on his head for several feet. Then he stopped and lay there, rocking back and forth on his heels and head like a wrestler doing warm-up exercises.

Frank roused himself. 'Kenny,' he said. He bent down and put his gloved hand on Kenny's brow. 'You shot him,' he said to Tub.

'He made me,' Tub said.

'No no no,' Kenny said.

Tub was weeping from the eyes and nostrils. His whole face was wet. Frank closed his eyes, then looked down at Kenny again. 'Where does it hurt?'

'Everywhere,' Kenny said, 'just everywhere.'

'Oh God,' Tub said.

'I mean where did it go in?' Frank said.

'Here.' Kenny pointed at the wound in his stomach. It was welling slowly with blood.

'You're lucky,' Frank said. 'It's on the left side. It missed your appendix. If it had hit your appendix you'd really be in the soup.' He turned and threw up onto the snow, holding his sides as if to keep warm.

'Are you all right?' Tub said.

'There's some aspirin in the truck,' Kenny said.

'I'm all right,' Frank said.

'We'd better call an ambulance,' Tub said.

'Jesus,' Frank said. 'What are we going to say?'

'Exactly what happened,' Tub said. 'He was going to shoot me but I shot him first.'

'No sir!' Kenny said. 'I wasn't either!'

Frank patted Kenny on the arm. 'Easy does it, partner.' He stood. 'Let's go.'

Tub picked up Kenny's rifle as they walked down toward the farmhouse. 'No sense leaving this around,' he said. 'Kenny might get ideas.'

'I can tell you one thing,' Frank said. 'You've really done it this time. This definitely takes the cake.'

They had to knock on the door twice before it was opened by a thin man with lank hair. The room behind him was filled with smoke. He squinted at them. 'You get anything?' he asked.

'No,' Frank said.

'I knew you wouldn't. That's what I told the other fellow.'

'We've had an accident.'

'The man looked past Frank and Tub into the gloom. 'Shoot your friend, did you?'

Frank nodded.

'I did,' Tub said.

'I suppose you want to use the phone.'

'If it's okay.'

The man in the doorway looked behind him, then stepped back. Frank and Tub followed him into the house. There was a woman sitting by the stove in the middle of the room. The stove was smoking badly. She looked up and then down again at the child asleep in her lap. Her face was white and damp; strands of hair were pasted across her forehead. Tub warmed his hands over the stove while Frank went into the kitchen to call. The man who had let them in stood at the window, his hands in his pockets.

'My friend shot your dog,' Tub said.

The man nodded without turning around. 'I should have done it myself. I just couldn't.'

'He loved that dog so much,' the woman said. The child squirmed and she rocked it.

'You asked him to?' Tub said. 'You asked him to shoot your dog?'

'He was old and sick. Couldn't chew his food any more. I would have done it myself but I don't have a gun.'

'You couldn't have anyway,' the woman said. 'Never in a million years.'

The man shrugged.

Frank came out of the kitchen. 'We'll have to take him ourselves. The nearest hospital is fifty miles from here and all their ambulances are out anyway.'

The woman knew a shortcut but the directions were complicated and Tub had to write them down. The man told them where they could find some boards to carry Kenny on. He didn't have a flashlight but he said he would leave the porch light on.

It was dark outside. The clouds were low and heavy-looking and the wind blew in shrill gusts. There was a screen loose on the house and it banged slowly and then quickly as the wind rose again. They could hear it all the way to the barn. Frank went for the boards while Tub looked for Kenny, who was not where they had left him. Tub found him farther up the drive, lying on his stomach. 'You okay?' Tub said.

'It hurts.'

'Frank says it missed your appendix.'

'I already had my appendix out.'

'All right,' Frank said, coming up to them. 'We'll have you in a nice warm bed before you can say Jack Robinson.' He put the two boards on Kenny's right side.

'Just as long as I don't have one of those male nurses,' Kenny said.

'Ha ha,' Frank said. 'That's the spirit. Get ready, set, *over you go*,' and he rolled Kenny onto the boards. Kenny screamed and kicked his legs in the air. When he quieted down Frank and Tub lifted the boards and carried him down the drive. Tub had the back end, and with the snow blowing into his face he had trouble with his footing. Also he was tired and the man inside had forgotten to turn the porch light on. Just past the house Tub slipped and threw out his hands to catch himself. The boards fell and Kenny tumbled out and rolled to the bottom of the drive, yelling all the way. He came to rest against the right front wheel of the truck.

'You fat moron,' Frank said. 'You aren't good for diddly.'

Tub grabbed Frank by the collar and backed him hard up against the fence. Frank tried to pull his hands away but Tub shook him and snapped his head back and forth and finally Frank gave up.

'What do you know about fat,' Tub said. 'What do you know about glands.' As he spoke he kept shaking Frank. 'What do you know about me.'

'All right,' Frank said.

'No more,' Tub said.

'All right.'

'No more talking to me like that. No more watching. No more laughing.'

'Okay, Tub. I promise.'

Tub let go of Frank and leaned his forehead against the fence. His arms hung straight at his sides.

'I'm sorry, Tub.' Frank touched him on the shoulder. 'I'll be down at the truck.'

Tub stood by the fence for a while and then got the rifles off the porch. Frank had rolled Kenny back onto the boards and they lifted him into the bed of the truck. Frank spread the seat blankets over him. 'Warm enough?' he asked.

Kenny nodded.

'Okay. Now how does reverse work on this thing?'

'All the way to the left and up.' Kenny sat up as Frank started forward to the cab. 'Frank!'

'What?'

'If it sticks don't force it.'

The truck started right away. 'One thing,' Frank said, 'you've got to hand it to the Japanese. A very ancient, very spiritual culture and they can still make a hell of a truck.' He glanced over at Tub. 'Look, I'm sorry. I didn't know you felt that way, honest to God I didn't. You should have said something.'

'I did.'

'When? Name one time.'

'A couple of hours ago.'

'I guess I wasn't paying attention.'

'That's true, Frank,' Tub said. 'You don't pay attention very much.'

'Tub,' Frank said, 'what happened back there, I should have been more sympathetic. I realize that. You were going through a lot. I just want you to know it wasn't your fault. He was asking for it.'

'You think so?'

'Absolutely. It was him or you. I would have done the same thing in your shoes, no question.'

The wind was blowing into their faces. The snow was a moving white wall in front of their lights; it swirled into the cab through the hole in the windshield and settled on them. Tub clapped his hands and shifted around to stay warm, but it didn't work.

'I'm going to have to stop,' Frank said. 'I can't feel my fingers.'

Up ahead they saw some lights off the road. It was a tavern. Outside in the parking lot there were several jeeps and trucks. A couple of them had deer strapped across their hoods. Frank parked and they went back to Kenny. 'How you doing, partner?' Frank said.

'I'm cold.'

'Well, don't feel like the Lone Ranger. It's worse inside, take my word for it. You should get that windshield fixed.'

'Look,' Tub said, 'he threw the blankets off.' They were lying in a heap against the tailgate.

'Now look, Kenny,' Frank said, 'it's no use whining about being cold if you're not going to try and keep warm. You've got to do your share.' He spread the blankets over Kenny and tucked them in at the corners.

'They blew off.'

'Hold on to them then.'

'Why are we stopping, Frank?'

'Because if me and Tub don't get warmed up we're going to freeze solid and then where will you be?' He punched Kenny lightly in the arm. 'So just hold your horses.'

The bar was full of men in coloured jackets, mostly orange. The waitress brought coffee. 'Just what the doctor ordered,' Frank said, cradling the steaming cup in his hand. His skin was bone white. 'Tub, I've been thinking. What you said about me not paying attention, that's true.'

'It's okay.'

'No. I really had that coming. I guess I've just been a little too interested in old number one. I've had a lot on my mind. Not that that's any excuse.'

'Forget it, Frank. I sort of lost my temper back there. I guess we're all a little on edge.'

Frank shook his head. 'It isn't just that.'

'You want to talk about it?'

'Just between us, Tub?'

'Sure, Frank. Just between us.'

'Tub, I think I'm going to be leaving Nancy.'

'Oh, Frank. Oh, Frank.' Tub sat back and shook his head.

Frank reached out and laid his hand on Tub's arm. 'Tub, have you ever been really in love?'

'Well—'

'I mean *really* in love.' He squeezed Tub's wrist. 'With your whole being.'

'I don't know. When you put it like that, I don't know.'

'You haven't then. Nothing against you, but you'd know it if you had.' Frank let go of Tub's arm. 'This isn't just some bit of fluff I'm talking about.'

'Who is she, Frank?'

Frank paused. He looked into his empty cup. 'Roxanne Brewer.'

'Cliff Brewer's kid? The babysitter?'

'You can't just put people into categories like that, Tub. That's why the whole system is wrong. And that's why this country is going to hell in a rowboat.'

'But she can't be more than—' Tub shook his head.

'Fifteen. She'll be sixteen in May.' Frank smiled. 'May fourth, three twenty-seven p.m. Hell, Tub, a hundred years ago she'd have been an old maid by that age. Juliet was only thirteen.'

'Juliet? Juliet Miller? Jesus, Frank, she doesn't even have breasts. She doesn't even wear a top to her bathing suit. She's still collecting frogs.'

'Not Juliet Miller. The real Juliet. Tub, don't you see how you're dividing people up into categories? He's an executive, she's a secretary, he's a truck driver, she's fifteen years old. Tub, this so-called babysitter, this so-called fifteen-year-old has more in her little finger than most of us have in our entire bodies. I can tell you this little lady is something special.'

Tub nodded. 'I know the kids like her.'

'She's opened up whole worlds to me that I never knew were there.'

'What does Nancy think about all this?'

'She doesn't know.'

'You haven't told her?'

'Not yet. It's not so easy. She's been damned good to me all these years. Then there's the kids to consider.' The brightness in Frank's eyes trembled and he wiped quickly at them with the back of his hand. 'I guess you think I'm a complete bastard.'

'No, Frank. I don't think that.'

'Well, you *ought* to.'

'Frank, when you've got a friend it means you've always got someone on your side, no matter what. That's the way I feel about it, anyway.'

'You mean that, Tub?'

'Sure I do.'

Frank smiled. 'You don't know how good it feels to hear you say that.'

Kenny had tried to get out of the truck but he hadn't made it. He was jackknifed over the tailgate, his head hanging above the bumper. They lifted him back into the bed and covered him again. He was sweating and his teeth chattered. 'It hurts, Frank.'

'It wouldn't hurt so much if you just stayed put. Now we're going to the hospital. Got that? Say it—I'm going to the hospital.'

'I'm going to the hospital.'

'Again.'

'I'm going to the hospital.'

'Now just keep saying that to yourself and before you know it we'll be there.'

After they had gone a few miles Tub turned to Frank. 'I just pulled a real boner,' he said.

'What's that?'

'I left the directions on the table back there.'

'That's okay. I remember them pretty well.'

The snowfall lightened and the clouds began to roll back off the fields, but it was no warmer and after a time both Frank and Tub were bitten through and shaking. Frank almost didn't make it around a curve, and they decided to stop at the next roadhouse.

There was an automatic hand-dryer in the bathroom and they took turns standing in front of it, opening their jackets and shirts and letting the jet of hot air breathe across their faces and chests.

'You know,' Tub said, 'what you told me back there, I appreciate it. Trusting me.'

Frank opened and closed his fingers in front of the nozzle. 'The way I look at it, Tub, no man is an island. You've got to trust someone.'

'Frank—'

Frank waited.

'When I said that about my glands, that wasn't true. The truth is I just shovel it in.'

'Well, Tub—'

'Day and night, Frank. In the shower. On the freeway.' He turned and let the air play over his back. 'I've even got stuff in the paper towel machine at work.'

'There's nothing wrong with your glands at all?' Frank had taken his boots and socks off. He held first his right, then his left foot up to the nozzle.

'No. There never was.'

'Does Alice know?' The machine went off and Frank started lacing up his boots.

'Nobody knows. That's the worst of it, Frank. Not the being fat, I never got any big kick out of being thin, but the lying. Having to lead a double life like a spy or a hit man. This sounds strange but I feel sorry for those guys, I really do. I know what they go through. Always having to think about what you say and do. Always feeling like people are watching you, trying to catch you at something. Never able to just be yourself. Like when I make a big deal about only having an orange for breakfast and then scarf all the way to work. Oreos, Mars Bars, Twinkies. Sugar Babies. Snickers.' Tub glanced at Frank and looked quickly away. 'Pretty disgusting, isn't it?'

'Tub. Tub.' Frank shook his head. 'Come on.' He took Tub's arm and led him into the restaurant half of the bar. 'My friend is hungry,' he told the waitress. 'Bring four orders of pancakes, plenty of butter and syrup.'

'Frank—'

'Sit down.'

When the dishes came Frank carved out slabs of butter and just laid them on the pancakes. Then he emptied the bottle of syrup, moving it back and forth over the plates. He leaned forward on his elbows and rested his chin in one hand. 'Go on, Tub.'

Tub ate several mouthfuls, then started to wipe his lips. Frank took the napkin away from him. 'No wiping,' he said. Tub kept at it. The syrup covered his chin; it dripped to a point like a goatee. 'Weigh in, Tub,' Frank said, pushing another fork across the table. 'Get down to business.' Tub took the fork in his left hand and lowered his head and started really chowing down. 'Clean your plate,' Frank said when the pancakes were gone, and Tub lifted each of the four plates and licked it clean. He sat back, trying to catch his breath.

'Beautiful,' Frank said. 'Are you full?'

'I'm full,' Tub said. 'I've never been so full.'

Kenny's blankets were bunched up against the tailgate again.

'They must have blown off,' Tub said.

'They're not doing him any good,' Frank said. 'We might as well get some use out of them.'

Kenny mumbled. Tub bent over him. 'What? Speak up.'

'I'm going to the hospital,' Kenny said.

'Attaboy,' Frank said.

The blankets helped. The wind still got their faces and Frank's hands but it was much better. The fresh snow on the road and the trees sparkled under the beam of the headlight. Squares of light from farmhouse windows fell onto the blue snow in the fields.

'Frank,' Tub said after a time, 'you know that farmer? He told Kenny to kill the dog.'

'You're kidding!' Frank leaned forward, considering. 'That Kenny. What a card.' He laughed and so did Tub. Tub smiled out the back window. Kenny lay with his arms folded over his stomach, moving his lips at the stars. Right overhead was the Big Dipper, and behind, hanging between Kenny's toes in the direction of the hospital, was the North Star, Pole Star, Help to Sailors. As the truck twisted through the gentle hills the star went back and forth between Kenny's boots, staying always in his sight. 'I'm going to the hospital,' Kenny said. But he was wrong. They had taken a different turn a long way back.

—1981

HISAYE YAMAMOTO

B. 1921

Hisaye Yamamoto, born in Redondo Beach, California, is a fiction writer and journalist. During World War II, Yamamoto was interned in a Japanese-American detention camp in Poston, Arizona, where she wrote for The Poston Chronicle, *the camp newspaper.* Seventeen Syllables and Other Stories *(1988) collects the stories she wrote in the 1940s and '50s. In 1988, the collection received the Award for Literature from the Association for Asian American Studies, and in 1991, "Seventeen Syllables" and "Yoneko's Earthquake" (Best American Short Stories 1952) served as the basis of the American Playhouse/PBS film* Hot Summer Winds, *directed by Emiko Omori. In 1986, Yamamoto won the prestigious American Book Award for Lifetime Achievement from the Before Columbus Foundation.*

THE HIGH-HEELED SHOES:
A MEMOIR

In the middle of the morning, the telephone rings. I am the only one at home. I answer it. A man's voice says softly, "Hello, this is Tony."

I don't know anyone named Tony. Nobody else in the house has spoken of knowing any Tony. But the greeting is very warm. It implies, "There is a certain thing which you and I alone know." Evidently he has dialed a wrong number. I tell him so, "You must have the wrong number," and prepare to hang up as soon as I know that he understands.

But the man says this is just the number he wants. To prove it, he recites off the pseudonym by which this household, Garbo-like, goes in the directory; the address, and the phone number. It is a unique name and I know there is probably no such person in the world. I merely tell him a fragment of the truth, that there is no such person at the address, and I am ready to hang up again.

But the man stalls. If there is no such person available, it appears he is willing to talk to me, whoever I am. I am suddenly in a bad humor, suspecting a trap in which I shall be imprisoned uncomfortably by words, words, words, earnestly begging me to try some product or another, the like of which is unknown anywhere else in the world. It isn't that I don't appreciate the unrapturous life a salesman must often lead. And I like to buy things. If I had the money, I would buy a little from every salesman who comes along, after I had permitted him to run ably or ineptly (it doesn't really matter) through the words he has been coached to repeat. Then, not only in the pride of the new acquisition, but in the knowledge that he was temporarily encouraged, my own spirits would gently rise, lifted by the wings of the dove. At each week's end, surrounded kneedeep by my various purchases—the Fuller toothbrush, the receipt for the magazine subscription which will help a girl obtain a nine-week flying course which she eagerly, eagerly wants, the one dozen white eggs fresh from the farm and cheaper than you can get at the corner grocery, the first volume in the indispensable 12-volume Illustrated Encyclopaedia of Home Medicine, the drug sundries totalling at least two dollars which will help guarantee a youngish veteran a permanent job—I could sigh and beam. That would be nice. But I don't have the money, and this coming of ill temper is just as much directed at myself for not having it as it is at the man for probably intending to put me in a position where I shall have to make him a failure.

"And just what is it you want?" I ask impatiently.

The man tells me, as man to woman. In the stark phrasing of his urgent need, I see that the certain thing alluded to by the warmth of his voice is a secret not of the past, but, with my acquiescence, of the near future. I let the receiver take a plunge down onto the book from approximately a one-foot height. Then, I go outside and pick some pansies for Margarita, as I had been intending to do just before the phone rang. Margarita is the seven-year-old girl next door. She has never known any mother or father, only *tias* and *tios* who share none of her blood. She has a face that looks as if it had been chiseled with utter care out of cream and pale pink marble. Her soft brown hair hangs in plaits as low as her waist. And these days, because the Catholic school is full and cannot take her, she wanders lonesomely about, with plenty of time for such amenities as dropping in to admire a neighbor's flowers. The pansies I pick for her, lemon yellow, deep purple, clear violet, mottled brown, were transplanted here last year by Wakako and Chester, a young couple we know who have a knack for getting things wholesale, and they are thriving like crazy this spring, sprawling untidily over their narrow bed and giving no end of blooms.

Later, there is a small, timid rat-tat-tat at the door. It's Margarita, bearing two calla lilies, a couple of clove pinks, and one tall amaryllis stalk with three brilliant brick-red flowers and a bud. She dashes off the porch, down the steps, and around the ivy-sprawled front fence before I can properly thank her. Oh, well. Taking the gift to the service porch, I throw out the wilting brown-edged callas she dashed over with last week, rinse out the blue potato glass, fill it with water, and stick in the new bouquet. But all the time the hands are occupied with these tokens of arrived spring and knowing Margarita, the mind recalls unlovely, furtive things.

When Mary lived with us, there was a time she left for work in the dark hours of the morning. On one of these mornings, about midway in her lonely walk past the cemetery to the P-car stop, a man came from behind and grabbed her, stopped her mouth with his hand, and, rather arbitrarily, gave her a choice between one kiss and rape. Terrified, she indicated what seemed to be the somewhat lesser requirement. He allowed her to go afterwards, warning her on no account to scream for help or look back, on penalty of death. When she arrived at her place of work, trembling and pale green, her office friends asked whether she was ill, and she told them of her encounter. They advised her to go to the police immediately.

She doubted whether that would help, since she had been unable to see the man. But, persuaded that a report, even incomplete, to the police was her duty to the rest of womankind, she reluctantly went to the nearest station with her story. She came back with the impression that the police had been much amused, that they had actually snickered as she left with their officially regretful shrug over her having given them nothing to go on. She told her boss and he called the police himself and evidently made his influence felt, for we had a caller that evening.

It was I who answered the knock. A policeman stepped in, and, without any preliminaries, asked, "Are you the girl that was raped?"

Making up with enough asperity for a sudden inexplicable lack of aplomb, I said, no, and no one had been raped, *yet,* and called Mary. She and the officer went out on the porch and talked in near whispers for a while. After he left, Mary identified him and his companion as the night patrol for our section of the city. He had promised that they would tell the dawn patrol to be hovering around about the time she left for work each morning. But Mary, nervously trying the dim walk a couple of more times, caught no sign of any kind of patrol. Thereafter, she and the rest of the women of the household took to traveling in style, by taxi, when they were called on to go forth at odd hours. This not only dented our budgets, but made us considerably limit our unescorted evening gadding.

There were similar episodes, fortunately more fleeting. What stayed with me longer than Mary's because it was mine, was the high-heeled shoes. Walking one bright Saturday morning to work along the same stretch that Mary had walked, I noticed a dusty blue, middle-aged sedan parked just ahead. A pair of bare, not especially remarkable legs was crossed in the open doorway, as though the body to them were lying on the front seat, relaxing. I presumed they were a woman's legs, belonging to the wife of some man who had business in the lumberyard just opposite, because they were wearing black high-heeled shoes. As I passed, I glanced at the waiting woman.

My presumption had been rash. It wasn't a woman, but a man, unclothed (except for *the high-heeled shoes, the high-heeled shoes*), and I saw that I was, with frantic gestures, being enjoined to linger awhile. Nothing in my life before had quite prepared for this: some Freud, a smattering of Ellis, lots of Stekel, and fat Krafft-Ebing, in red covers, were on my bookshelves, granted; conversation had explored curiously, and the imagination conjured bizarre scenes at the drop of a casual word. But reading is reading, talking is talking, thinking is thinking, and living is different. Improvising hastily on behavior for the occasion, I chose to pretend as though my heart were repeating Pippa's song, and continued walking, possibly a little faster and a little straighter than I had been, up to the P-car stop. When I got to the print shop, the boss said, "You look rather put upon this morning." I mustered up a feeble smile and nodded, but I couldn't bring myself to speak of the high-heeled shoes. This was nothing so uncomplicated as pure rape, I knew, and the need of the moment was to go away by myself, far from everybody, and think about things for awhile. But there were galleys and page proofs waiting to be read, and I set to with a sort of dedicated vengeance, for I had recently been reprimanded for getting sloppy again. When the hectic morning of poring over small print was over and my elbows black, letting my thoughts go cautiously but wholly back to the time between leaving the house and boarding the P-car, I found there was not much to think about. I had seen what I had seen. I had, admit it now, been thrown for a sickening loop. That was all. But the incongruity of a naked man in black high-heeled shoes was something the mind could not entirely dismiss, and there were times afterwards when he, never seen again, contributed to a larger perplexity that stirred the lees around and around, before more immediate matters, claiming attention, allowed them to settle again.

There was a man in the theatre with groping hands. There was a man on the streetcar with insistent thighs. There was a man who grinned triumphantly and walked quickly away after he trailed one down a drizzly street at dusk and finally succeeded in his aim of thrusting an unexpected hand under one's raincoat.

I remembered them as I plucked the pansies, took them over to Margarita's house, came back home, answered the door, received the amaryllis, the callas, the pinks, and arranged them in the blue potato glass on top of the buffet. I remembered another man, Mohandas Gandhi, probably a stranger to this company, not only because I had been reading on him of late, but because he seemed to be the only unimpeachable authority who had ever been called on to give public advice in this connection. When someone had delicately asked Gandhi, "What is a woman to do when she is attacked by miscreants?" naming the alternatives of violent self-defense and immediate flight, he had replied, "For me, there can be no preparation for violence. All preparation must be for non-violence if courage of the highest type is to be developed. Violence can only be tolerated as being preferable always to cowardice. Therefore I would have no boats ready for flight. . . ." Then he had soared on to the nobler implications of non-violence, reproaching the world for its cowardice in arming itself with the atomic bomb.

I understood. When I first read these words, I had said, "Why, of course," smiling at the unnecessary alarms of some people. But I had read the words at a rarefied period, forgetting Mary, forgetting the high-heeled shoes. I decided now that the inspiration they gave to his probably feminine questioner was small potatoes. Of all the men suspected of sainthood, Gandhi, measured by his own testimony, should have been able to offer the most concrete comfort here. But he had evaded the issue. In place of the tangible example, vague words. Gandhi, in face of the ubiquitous womanly fear, was a failure. All he had really said was: don't even think about it. Then (I guessed), holding up his strong, bony brown hand, he had shaken his white-fuzzed, compactly-shaped head slowly back and forth and declined to hear the ifs and buts. The rest, as they say, was silence.

But could I have momentarily borrowed Gandhi's attitude to life and death, what would I have done as the man who called himself Tony rang my number? With enough straining, with maybe a resort to urgent, concentrated prayer, could I have found the gentle but effective words to make Tony see that there were more charming ways to spend a morning? I practiced this angle for awhile:

"I'm afraid you *do* have the wrong number." Soberly, hang up. Disconcerting enough, but rather negative.

"It's a nice day for the beach, sir. Why don't you go swimming?—might help you cool off a little." The voice with a compassionate smile. Too flippant.

"There are many lonely women in the world, and there are more acceptable ways to meet them than this. Have you tried joining a Lonely Hearts club? Don't you have any kind of hobby?" Condescending, as though I were forever above his need. Ambiguously worded, too, that last, fraught with the possibility of an abrupt answer.

"Listen, you know you aren't supposed to go around doing things like this. I think I know what made you do it, though, and I think a psychiatrist would help you quite a bit, if you'd cooperate." The enlightened woman's yap. Probably'd hang up on me.

Anyway, it was too late. And, after all, Gandhi was Gandhi, an old man, moreover dead, and I was I, a young woman, more or less alive. Since I was unable to hit on the proper pacifist approach, since, indeed, I doubted the efficacy of the pacifist approach in this crisis, should I, eschewing cowardice, have shouted bitter, indignant words to frighten Tony? Not that, either. Besides, I hadn't gauged his mood. He had spoken casually enough, but there had been an undertone of something. Restrained glee? Playfulness? Confidence? Desperation? I didn't know.

Then, to help protect my sisters, should I have turned toward the official avenues? Was it my responsibility to have responded with pretended warmth, invited him over, and had the police waiting with me when he arrived? Say I had sorrowfully pressed the matter, say Tony were consequently found guilty (of abusing his communication privileges, of course)—the omnipotent they (representing us) would have merely restricted his liberty for a while, in the name of punishment. What would he have done when he was let go, his debt to society as completely repaid as society, who had created his condition, could make him repay? Telephones in working order abound, with telephone books conveniently alongside them, containing any number of women's names, addresses, and numbers.

And what did Tony do when the sound of my receiver crashed painfully in his ear? Did he laugh and proceed to some other number? His vanity bruised, did he curse? Or perhaps he felt shame, thinking, "My God, what am I doing, what am I doing?" Whatever, whatever—I knew I had discovered yet another circle to put away with my collection of circles. I was back to what I had started with, the helpless, absolutely useless knowledge that the days and nights must surely be bleak for a man who knew the compulsion to thumb through the telephone directory for a woman's name, any woman's name; that this bleakness, multiplied infinite times (see almost any daily paper), was a great, dark sickness on the earth that no amount of pansies, pinks, or amaryllis, thriving joyously in what garden, however well-ordered and pointed to with pride, could ever begin to assuage.

The telephone rings. Startled, I go warily, wondering whether it might not be Tony again, calling perhaps to avenge the blow to pride by anonymous invective, to raise self-esteem by letting it be known that he is a practical joker. I hold my breath after I say, "Hello?"

It is the familiar voice, slightly querulous but altogether precious, of my aunt Miné. She says I am not to plan anything for supper. She has made something special, ricecakes with Indian bean frosting, as well as pickled fish on vinegared rice. She has also been able to get some yellowtail, to slice and eat raw. All these things she and Uncle are bringing over this evening. Is about five o'clock too early?

It is possible she wonders at my enthusiastic appreciation, which is all right, but all out of proportion.

—1948

DRAMA

CHARLES FULLER

B. 1939

Charles Fuller was born in Philadelphia, the city with which he remains closely associated today. Fuller attended Villanova University and LaSalle College, both in Philadelphia, and held jobs ranging from bank loan collector, college counselor, and city housing inspector to cofounder and director of the Afro-American Arts Theatre. Fuller served in the United States military in Japan and Korea from 1959 to 1962. His plays include The Village: A Party *(1968),* Candidate *(1974),* The Brownsville Raid *(1975),* Zooman and the Sign *(1982),* A Soldier's Play *(1982), and* Jonquil *(1990). Fuller has also written screenplays for television in the* Roots, Resistance, *and* Renaissance *series and for* A Gathering of Old Men *(1987).* A Soldier's Play, *which won the Pulitzer Prize in drama, was made into a highly successful film,* A Soldier's Story, *in 1985.*

A SOLDIER'S PLAY

CHARACTERS

TECH/SERGEANT VERNON C. WATERS
CORPORAL BERNARD COBB
PRIVATE JAMES WILKIE
PRIVATE LOUIS HENSON
PFC MELVIN PETERSON
PRIVATE TONY SMALLS
CORPORAL ELLIS
CAPTAIN CHARLES TAYLOR
CAPTAIN RICHARD DAVENPORT
PRIVATE C. J. MEMPHIS
LIEUTENANT BYRD
CAPTAIN WILCOX

ACT ONE

TIME: 1944

PLACE: Fort Neal, Louisiana

SCENE: *The inner shell of the stage is black. On the stage, in a horseshoe-like half circle, are several platforms at varying levels.*

On the left side of this horseshoe is a military office arrangement with a small desk (a nameplate on the desk reads: CAPTAIN CHARLES TAYLOR), *two office-type chairs, one straight-backed, a regimental, and an American flag. A picture of F.D.R. is on the wall.*

On the right side of the horseshoe, and curved toward the rear, is a barracks arrangement, with three bunk beds and footlockers set in typical military fashion. The exit to this barracks is a freestanding doorway on the far right. (This barracks should be changeable—these bunks with little movement can look like a different place.) On the edge of this barracks is a poster, semi-blown up, of Joe Louis in an army uniform, helmet, rifle, and bayonet. It reads: PVT. JOE LOUIS SAYS, "WE'RE GOING TO DO OUR PART—AND WE'LL WIN BECAUSE WE'RE ON GOD'S SIDE."

On the rear of the horseshoe, upstage center, is a bare platform, raised several feet above everything else. It can be anything we want it to be—a limbo if you will.

The entire set should resemble a courtroom. The sets, barracks and office, will both be elevated, so that from anywhere on the horseshoe one may look down onto a space at center stage that is on the stage floor. The levels should have easy access by either stairs or ramps, and the entire set should be raked ever so slightly so that one does not perceive much difference between floor and set, and the bottom edges of the horseshoe. There must also be enough area on both sides of the horseshoe to see exits and entrances.

Lighting will play an intergral part in the realization of the play. It should there-fore be sharp, so that areas are clearly defined, with as little spill into other areas as possible. Lights must also be capable of suggesting mood, time, and place.

As the play opens, the stage is black. In the background, rising in volume, we hear the song "Don't Sit under the Apple Tree," sung by the Andrews Sisters. Quite sud-denly, in a sharp though narrow beam of light, in limbo, TECH/SERGEANT VERNON C. WATERS, a well-built, light-brown-skinned man in a World War II, winter army uni-form, is seen down on all fours. He is stinking drunk, trying to stand and mumbling to himself.

WATERS (*repeating*): They'll still hate you! They still hate you . . . They still hate you!

WATERS is laughing as suddenly someone steps into the light. (We never see this person.) He is holding a .45 caliber pistol. He lifts it swiftly and ominously toward WATERS's head and fires. WATERS is knocked over backward. He is dead. The music has stopped and there is a strong silence onstage.

VOICE: Le's go!

The man with the gun takes a step, then stops. He points the gun at WATERS again and fires a second time. There is another silence as limbo is plunged into darkness, and the barracks is just as quickly lit.

We are in the barracks of Company B, 221st Chemical Smoke Generating Company, at Fort Neal. Five black enlisted men stand at "parade rest" with their hands above their heads and submit to a search. They are: CORPORAL BERNARD COBB, a man in his mid to late twenties, dressed in a T-shirt, dog tags, fatigues, and slippers. PRIVATE JAMES WILKIE, a man in his early forties, a career soldier, is dressed in fatigues from which the stripes have been removed, with a baseball cap on, and smoking a cigar. PRIVATE LOUIS HENSON, thin, in his late twenties or early thirties, is wearing a baseball T-shirt that reads "Fort Neal" on the front and "#4" on the back with fatigues and boots on. PFC MELVIN PETERSON, a man in his late twenties, wearing glasses, looks angelic. His shirt is open but he does not look sloppy; of all the men, his stripe is the most visible, his boots the most highly polished. PRIVATE TONY SMALLS, a man in his late thirties, a career man, is as small as his name feels. All five men are being searched by CORPORAL ELLIS, a soldier who is simply always "spit and polish." ELLIS is also black, and moves from man to man, patting them down in a police-like search. CAPTAIN CHARLES TAYLOR, a young white man in his mid to late thirties, looks on, a bit disturbed. All the men's uniforms are from World War II.

TAYLOR: I'm afraid this kind of thing can't be helped, men—you can put your arms down when Ellis finishes. (*Several men drop their arms. ELLIS is searching PVT. HENSON*) We don't want anyone from Fort Neal going into Tynin looking for red-necks.
COBB: May I speak, sir? (*TAYLOR nods*) Why do this, Captain? They got M.P.'s sur-rounding us, and hell, the Colonel must know nobody colored killed the man!

TAYLOR: This is a precaution, Cobb. We can't have revenge killings, so we search for weapons.

PETERSON: Where'd they find the Sarge, sir?

TAYLOR: In the woods out by the Junction—and so we don't have any rumors. Sergeant Waters was shot twice—we don't know that he was lynched! (*Pause*) Twice. Once in the chest, and a bullet in the head. (ELLIS *finishes with the last man*) You finished the footlockers?

ELLIS: Yes, sir! There aren't any weapons.

TAYLOR (*relaxes*): I didn't think there would be. At ease, men! (*The men relax*) Tech/Sergeant Waters, in my opinion, served the 221st and this platoon in particular with distinction, and I for one shall miss the man. (*Slight pause*) But no matter what we think of the Sergeant's death, we will not allow this incident to make us forget our responsibility to this uniform. We are soldiers, and our war is with the Nazis and Japs, not the civilians in Tynin. Any enlisted man found with unauthorized weapons will be immediately subject to summary court-martial. (*Softens*) Sergeant Waters's replacement won't be assigned for several weeks. Until that time, you will all report to Sergeant Dorsey of C Company. Corporal Cobb will be barracks N.C.O.—any question?

PETERSON: Who do they think did it, sir?

TAYLOR: At this time there are no suspects.

HENSON: You know the Klan did it, sir.

TAYLOR: Were you an eyewitness, soldier?

HENSON: Who else goes around killin' Negroes in the South?—They lynched Jefferson the week I got here, sir! And that Signal Corps guy, Daniels, two months later!

TAYLOR: Henson, unless you saw it, keep your opinions to yourself! Is that clear? (HENSON *nods*) And that's an order! It also applies to everybody else!

ALL (*almost simultaneously*): Yes, sir!

TAYLOR: You men who have details this afternoon, report to the orderly room for your assignments. The rest of you are assigned to the Colonel's quarters—clean-up detail. Cobb, I want to see you in my office at 1350 hours.

COBB: Yes, sir.

TAYLOR: As of 0600 hours this morning, the town of Tynin was placed off-limits to all military personnel. (*Slight groan from the men*) The Friday night dance has also been canceled—(*All the men moan.* TAYLOR *is sympathetic*) O.K., O.K.! Some of the officers are going to the Colonel—I can't promise anything. Right now, it's canceled.

ELLIS: Tenn-hut!

The men snap to. The CAPTAIN *salutes. Only* COBB *salutes him back. The* CAPTAIN *starts out.*

TAYLOR: As you were!

The CAPTAIN *and* ELLIS *exit the barracks. The men move to their bunks or footlockers.* WILKIE *goes to the rear of the bunks and looks out.*

COBB: They still out there, Wilkie?

WILKIE: Yeah. Got the whole place surrounded.

HENSON: I don't know what the hell they thought we'd go into that town with— mops and dishrags?

WILKIE: Y'all recruits know what Colonel's clean-up detail is, don't you? Shovelin' horseshit in his stables—

COBB: Ain't no different from what we been doin'. (*He lies down and begins scratching around his groin area*)

PETERSON (*to* COBB): Made you the barracks Commander-in-Chief, huh? (COBB *nods*) Don't git like ole Stone-ass—what are you doin'?

COBB: Scratchin'!

HENSON (*overlapping*): Taylor knows the Klan did it—I hope y'all know that!

SMALLS (*sudden*): Then why are the M.P.'s outside with rifles? Why hold us prisoner?

PETERSON: They scared we may kill a couple peckerwoods, Smalls. Calm down, man!

WILKIE (*quickly*): Smalls, you wanna play some coon-can?

SMALLS *shakes his head no. He is quiet, staring.*

COBB (*examining himself*): Peterson, you know I think Eva gave me the crabs.

HENSON: Cobb, the kinda women you find, it's a wonda your nuts ain't fell off— crabs? You probably got lice, ticks, bedbugs, fleas—tapeworms—

COBB: Shut up, Henson! Pete—I ain't foolin', man! (*He starts to open his pants*)

PETERSON: Get some powder from the PX.

WILKIE (*almost simultaneously*): Which one of y'all feels like playin' me some cards? (*He looks at* HENSON)

HENSON: Me and Peterson's goin' down the mess hall—you still goin', Pete?

PETERSON (*nods*): Wilkie? I thought all you could do was play go-fer?

HENSON (slyly): Yeah, Wilkie—whose ass can you kiss, now that your number-one ass is dead?

COBB (*laughing*): That sounds like something C.J. would sing! (*Looks at himself again*) Ain't this a bitch? (*Picks at himself*)

WILKIE (*overlapping, to* HENSON): You know what you can do for me, Henson—you too, Peterson!

PETERSON: Naughty, naughty!

WILKIE *moves to his bunk, justifying.*

WILKIE: I'm the one lost three stripes—and I'm the only man in here with kids, so when the man said jump, I jumped!

HENSON (*derisively*): Don't put your wife and kids between you and Waters's ass, man!

WILKIE: I wanted my stripes back!

COBB: I'm goin' to sick call after chow.

WILKIE (*continuing*): Y'all ain't neva' had nothin', that's why you can't understand a man like me! There was a time I was a sergeant major, you know!

HENSON *waves disdainfully at him, turning his attention to* COBB.

HENSON: Ole V-girl slipped Cobb the crabs! How you gonna explain that to the girl back home, Corporal? How will that fine, big-thighed Moma feel, when the only ribbon you bring home from this war is the Purple Heart for crab bites? (HENSON *laughs as* SMALLS *stands suddenly*)

SMALLS: Don't any of you guys give a damn?

PETERSON: What's the matta', Smalls?

SMALLS: The man's dead! We saw him alive last night!

COBB (*quickly*): I saw him, too. At least I know he died good and drunk!

SMALLS (*loud*): What's the matter with y'all?

HENSON: The man got hisself lynched! We're in the South, and we can't do a god-damn thing about it—you heard the Captain! But don't start actin' like we guilty of somethin'. (*Softens*) I just hope we get lucky enough to get shipped outta this hell-hole to the war! (*To himself*) Besides, whoever did it, didn't kill much anyway.

SMALLS: He deserved better than that!

COBB: Look, everbody feels rotten, Smalls. But it won't bring the man back, so let's forget about it!

PETERSON *moves to pat* SMALLS *on the back.*

PETERSON: Why don't you walk it off, man?

SMALLS *moves away to his bunk.* PETERSON *shrugs.*

HENSON: Yeah—or go turn on a smoke machine, let the fog make you think you in London!

SMALLS *sits down on his bunk and looks at them for a moment, then lays down, his face in the pillow.*

WILKIE (*overlapping*): Let Cobb bring his Eva over, she'll take his mind off Waters plus give him a bonus of crabs!

The men laugh, but SMALLS *doesn't move as the lights begin slowly to fade out.*

HENSON (*counting*):—an' blue-balls. Clap. Syphilis. Pimples! (COBB *throws a pillow at* HENSON) Piles! Fever blisters. Cockeyes. Cooties!

The men are laughing as the lights go out. As they do, a rather wiry black officer wearing glasses, CAPTAIN RICHARD DAVENPORT, *walks across the stage from the wings, dressed sharply in an M.P. uniform, his hat cocked to the side and strapped down, the way airmen wear theirs. He is carrying a briefcase, and we are aware of a man who is very confident and self-assured. He is smiling as he faces the audience, cleaning his glasses as he begins to speak.*

DAVENPORT: Call me Davenport—Captain, United States Army, attached to the 343rd Military Police Corps Unit, Fort Neal, Louisiana. I'm a lawyer the segregated Armed Services couldn't find a place for. My job in this war? Policing colored troops. (*Slight pause*) One morning, during mid-April 1944, a colored tech/sergeant, Vernon C. Waters, assigned to the 221st Chemical Smoke Generating Company, stationed here before transfer to Europe, was brutally shot to death in a wooded section off the New Post Road and the junction of Highway 51—just two hundred yards from the colored N.C.O. club—by a person or persons unknown. (*Pauses a little*) Naturally, the unofficial consensus was the local Ku Klux Klan, and for that reason, I was told at the time, Colonel Barton Nivens ordered the Military Police to surround the enlisted men's quarters—then instructed all his company commanders to initiate a thorough search of all personal property for unauthorized knives, guns—weapons of any kind. (*Slight pause*) You see, ninety percent of the Colonel's command—all of the enlisted men stationed here are Negroes, and the Colonel felt—and I suppose justly—that once word of the Sergeant's death spread among his troops, there might be some retaliation against the white citizens of Tynin. (*Shrugs*) What he did worked—there was no retaliation and no racial incidents. (*Pause*) The week after the killing took place, several correspondents from the Negro press wrote lead articles about it. But the headlines faded—(*Smiles*) The NAACP got me involved in this. Rumor has it, Thurgood Marshall ordered an immediate investigation of the killing, and the army, pressured by Secretary of War Stimson, rather randomly ordered Colonel Nivens to initiate a preliminary inquiry into the Sergeant's death. Now, the Colonel didn't want to rehash the murder, but he complied with the army's order by instructing the Provost Marshal, my C.O., Major Hines, to conduct a *few* question-and-answer sessions among the men of Sergeant Waters's platoon and file a report. The matter was to be given the lowest priority. (*Pause*) The case was mine, five minutes later. It was four to five weeks after his death—the month of May. (*He pauses as the light builds in* CAPTAIN TAYLOR's *office.* TAYLOR *is facing* DAVENPORT, *expressionless.* DAVENPORT *is a bit puzzled*) Captain?

TAYLOR: Forgive me for occasionally staring, Davenport, you're the first colored officer I've ever met. I'd heard you had arrived a month ago, and you're a bit startling. (*Quickly*) I mean you no offense. (*Starts back to his desk and sits on the edge of it, as* DAVENPORT *starts into the office a bit cautiously*) We'll be getting some of you as replacements, but we don't expect them until next month. Sit down, Davenport. (DAVENPORT *sits*) You came out of Fort Benning in '43?

DAVENPORT: Yes.

TAYLOR: And they assigned a lawyer to the Military Police? I'm Infantry and I've been with the Engineers, Field Artillery, and Signal Corps—this is some army. Where'd you graduate law school?

DAVENPORT: Howard University.

TAYLOR: Your daddy a rich minister or something? (DAVENPORT *shakes his head no*) I graduated the Point—(*Pause*) We didn't have any Negroes at the Point. I never saw a Negro until I was twelve or thirteen. (*Pause*) You like the army, I suppose, huh?

DAVENPORT: Captain, did you see my orders?

TAYLOR (*bristling slightly*): I saw them right after Colonel Nivens sent them to Major Hines. I sent my orderly to the barracks and told him to have the men waiting for you.

DAVENPORT: Thank you.

TAYLOR: I didn't know at the time that Major Hines was assigning a Negro, Davenport. (DAVENPORT *stiffens*) My preparations were made in the belief that you'd be a white man. I think it only fair to tell you that had I known what Hines intended I would have requested the immediate suspension of the investigation—May I speak freely?

DAVENPORT: You haven't stopped yet, Captain.

TAYLOR: Look—how far could you get even if you succeed? These local people aren't going to charge a white man in this parish on the strength of an investigation conducted by a Negro!—and Nivens and Hines know that! The Colonel doesn't give a damn about finding the men responsible for this thing! And they're making a fool of you—can't you see that?—and—take off those sunglasses!

DAVENPORT: I intend to carry out my orders—and I like these glasses—they're like MacArthur's.

TAYLOR: You go near that sheriff's office in Tynin in your uniform—carrying a briefcase, looking and sounding white, and charging local people—and you'll be found just as dead as Sergeant Waters! People around here don't respect the colored!

DAVENPORT: I know that.

TAYLOR (*annoyed*): You know how many times I've asked Nivens to look into this killing? Every day, since it happened, Davenport. Major Hines didn't tell you that!

DAVENPORT: Do you suspect someone, Captain?

TAYLOR: Don't play cat-and-mouse with me, soldier!

DAVENPORT (*calmly*): Captain, like it or not, I'm all you've got. I've been ordered to look into Sergeant Waters's death, and I intend to do exactly that.

There is a long pause.

TAYLOR: Can I tell you a little story? (DAVENPORT *nods*) Before you were assigned here? Nivens got us together after dinner one night, and all we did was discuss Negroes in the officer ranks. We all commanded Negro troops, but nobody had ever come face to face with colored officers—there were a lot of questions that night—for example, your quarters—had to be equal to ours, but we had none—no mess hall for you! (*Slight pause*) Anyway, Jed Harris was the only officer who defended it—my own feelings were mixed. The only Negroes I've ever known were subordinates—My father hired the first Negro I ever saw—man named Colfax—to help him fix the shed one summer. Nice man—worked hard—did a good job, too. (*Remembering; smiles thoughtfully*) But I never met a Negro with any education until I graduated the Point—hardly an officer of equal rank. So I frankly wasn't sure how I'd feel—until right now—and—(*Struggles*) I don't want to offend you, but I just cannot get used to it—the bars, the uniform—being in charge just doesn't look right on Negroes!

DAVENPORT (*rises*): Captain, are you through?

TAYLOR: You could ask Hines for another assignment—this case is not for you! By the time you overcome the obstacles to your race, this case would be dead!

DAVENPORT (*sharply*): I got it. And I *am* in charge! All your orders instruct you to do is cooperate!

There is a moment of silence.

TAYLOR: I won't be made a fool of, Davenport. (*Straightens*) Ellis! You're right, there's no need to discuss this any further.

ELLIS *appears on the edge of the office.*

ELLIS: Yes, sir!

TAYLOR: Captain Davenport will need assistance with the men—I can't prevent that, Davenport, but I intend to do all I can to have this so-called investigation stopped.

DAVENPORT: Do what you like. If there's nothing else, you'll excuse me, won't you, Captain?

TAYLOR (*sardonically*): Glad I met you, Captain.

DAVENPORT *salutes and* TAYLOR *returns salute. For an instant the two men trade cold stares, then* DAVENPORT *gestures to* ELLIS, *and the two of them start out of the office by way of the stage.* DAVENPORT *follows* ELLIS *out. Behind them,* TAYLOR *stares after them as the lights in his office fade out.* DAVENPORT *removes his glasses.*

ELLIS: We heard it was you, sir—you know how the grapevine is. Sad thing—what happened to the Sarge.

DAVENPORT: What's on the grapevine about the killing?

The two men stop as slowly, almost imperceptibly, on the right the barracks area is lit. In it, a small table and two chairs have been set up. ELLIS *shrugs.*

ELLIS: We figure the Klan. They ain't crazy about us tan yanks in this part of the country.

DAVENPORT: Is there anything on the grapevine about trouble in the town before Sergeant Waters was killed?

ELLIS: None that I know of before—after, there were rumors around the post—couple our guys from the Tank Corps wanted to drive them Shermans into Tynin— then I guess you heard that somebody said two officers did it—I figure that's why the Colonel surrounded our barracks.

DAVENPORT: Was the rumor confirmed—I didn't hear that! Did anything ever come of it?

ELLIS: Not that I know of, sir.

DAVENPORT: Thanks, Ellis—I'd better start seeing the men. (*They start into the barracks from the stage floor*) Did you set this up? (ELLIS *nods*) Good—(*He sets his briefcase on the table*) Are they ready?

ELLIS: The Captain instructed everybody in the Sarge's platoon to be here, sir. He told them you'd be starting this morning.

DAVENPORT *smiles.*

DAVENPORT (*to himself*): Before he found out, huh?
ELLIS (*puzzled*): Sir?
DAVENPORT: Nothing. Call the first man in, Corporal—and stay loose, I might need you.
ELLIS: Yes, sir! Sir, may I say something? (DAVENPORT *nods*) It sure is good to see one of us wearin' them Captain's bars, sir.
DAVENPORT: Thank you.

ELLIS *salutes, does a sharp about-face, and starts out.*

ELLIS (*loud*): Private Wilkie!
WILKIE (*offstage*): Yes, sir! (*Almost immediately,* WILKIE *appears in the doorway. He is dressed in proper uniform of fatigues, boots, and cap.*)
ELLIS: Cap'n wants to see you!
WILKIE: Yes indeedy! (*Moves quickly to the table, where he comes to attention and salutes*) Private James Wilkie reporting as ordered, sir.
DAVENPORT: At ease, Private. Have a seat. (*To* ELLIS *as* WILKIE *sits*) That will be all, Corporal.
ELLIS! Yes, sir.

ELLIS *salutes and exits.* DAVENPORT *waits until he leaves before speaking.*

DAVENPORT: Private Wilkie, I am Captain Davenport—
WILKIE (*interjecting*): Everybody knows that, sir. You all we got down here. (*Smiles broadly*) I was on that first detail got your quarters togetha', sir.

DAVENPORT *nods.*

DAVENPORT (*coldly*): I'm conducting an investigation into the events surrounding Sergeant Waters's death. Everything you say to me will go in my report, but that report is confidential.
WILKIE: I understand, sir.

DAVENPORT *removes pad and pencil from the briefcase.*

DAVENPORT: How long did you know Sergeant Waters?
WILKIE: 'Bout a year, sir. I met him last March—March 5th—I remember the date, I had been a staff sergeant exactly two years the day after he was assigned. This company was basically a baseball team then, sir. See, most of the boys had played for the Negro League, so naturally the army put us all together. (*Chuckles at the memory*) We'd be assigned to different companies—Motor Pool—Dump Truck all week long—made us do the dirty work on the post—garbage, clean-up—but on Saturdays we were whippin' the hell out of 'em on the baseball diamond! I was hittin' .352 myself! And we had a boy, C.J. Memphis? He coulda

hit a ball from Fort Neal to Berlin, Germany—or Tokyo—if he was battin'
right-handed. (*Pauses, catches* DAVENPORT's *impatience*) Well, the army sent
Waters to manage the team. He had been in Field Artillery—Gunnery Sergeant.
Had a croix de guerre from the First War, too.

DAVENPORT: What kind of man was he?

WILKIE: All spit and polish, sir.

At that moment, in limbo, a spotlight hits SERGEANT WATERS. *He is dressed in a
well-creased uniform, wearing a helmet liner and standing at parade-rest, facing
the audience. The light around him, however, is strange—it is blue-gray like the
past. The light around* DAVENPORT *and* WILKIE *abates somewhat. Dialogue is
continuous.*

DAVENPORT: Tell me about him.

WILKIE: He took my stripes! (*Smiles*) But I was in the wrong, sir!

WATERS *stands at ease. His voice is crisp and sharp, his movements minimal. He
is the typical hard-nosed N.C.O.—strict, soldierly.*

WATERS: Sergeant Wilkie! You are a noncommissioned officer in the army of a country at war—the penalty for being drunk on duty is severe in peacetime, so
don't bring me no po'colored-folks-can't-do-nothin'-unless-they-drunk shit as an
excuse! You are supposed to be an example to your men—so, I'm gonna send
you to jail for ten days *and* take them goddamn stripes, Teach you a lesson—
You in the army! (*Derisively*) Colored folks always runnin' off at the mouth 'bout
what y'all gonna do if the white man gives you a chance—and you get it, and
what do you do with it? You wind up drunk on guard duty—I don't blame
the white man—why the hell should he put colored and white together in this
war? You can't even be trusted to guard your own quarters—no wonder they
treat us like dogs—Get outta' my sight, *Private!*

Light fades at once on WATERS.

DAVENPORT: What about the other men?

WILKIE: Sometimes the Southern guys caught a little hell—Sarge always said he was
from up North somewhere. He was a good soldier, sir. I'm from Detroit myself—
born and raised there. Joe Louis started in Detroit—did you know that, sir?

DAVENPORT: What about the Southerners?

WILKIE: Sarge wasn't exactly crazy 'bout 'em—'cept for C.J. Now C.J. was from the
South, but with him Sarge was different—probably because C.J. was the best ball
player we had. He could sing too! (*Slight pause*) Sarge never got too close to
nobody—maybe me—but he didn' mess with C.J., you know what I mean? Not
like he did with everybody else.

In limbo, the spotlight illuminates C.J. MEMPHIS, *a young, handsome black man.
He is in a soldier's uniform, cap on the side. He is strumming a guitar.* WATERS *is
watching him, smiling. Their light is the strange light of the past.* C.J. *begins to
sing, his voice deep, melodious, and bluesy.*

C.J.: It's a low / it's a low, low / lowdown dirty shame! Yeah, it's a low / it's a low, low / lowdown dirty shame!

WILKIE (*before* C.J. *finishes*): Big Mississippi boy!

WILKIE *and* C.J. *simultaneously sing.*

C.J. AND WILKIE: They say we fightin' Hitler! But they won't let us in the game!

C.J. *strums and hums as* WATERS *looks on.*

WILKIE: Worked harder and faster than everybody—wasn' a man on the team didn't like him. Sarge took to him the first time he saw him. "Wilkie," he says.

WILKIE AND WATERS (*simultaneously*): What have we got here?

WATERS: A guitar-playin' man! Boy, you eva' heard of Blind Willie Reynolds? Son House? Henry Sims?

C.J. *nods to everything.*

C.J.: You heard them play, Sarge?

WATERS: Every one of 'em. I was stationed in Mississippi couple years ago—you from down that way, ain't you?

C.J.: Yes, sah!

WATERS: Well, they use ta play over at the Bandana Club outside Camp J. J. Reilly.

C.J.: I played there once!

WATERS (*smiles*): Ain't that somethin'? I'd go over there from time to time—people use ta come from everywhere! (*To* WILKIE) Place was always dark, Wilkie— smoky. Folks would be dancin'—sweatin'—guitar pickers be strummin', shoutin'—it would be wild in there sometimes. Reminded me of a place I use ta go in France durin' the First War—the women, the whiskey—place called the Café Napoleon.

C.J.: You really like the blues, huh?

WATERS: No other kind of music—where'd you learn to play so good? I came by here yesterday and heard this pickin'—one of the men tol' me it was you.

C.J.: My daddy taught me, Sarge.

WATERS: You play pretty good, boy. Wilkie, wasn' that good?

WILKIE: Yes indeed, Sarge.

WILKIE (*to Davenport*): I mostly agreed with the Sarge, sir. He was a good man. Good to his men. Talked about his wife and kids all the time—(WATERS *starts down from the limbo area, as the lights around C.J. fade out.* WATERS *pulls a pipe from his pocket, lights it as he moves to the edge of the* CAPTAIN's *office and sits on the edge of the platform supporting it. He puffs a few times.* WILKIE's *talk is continuous*) Use ta write home every day. I don't see why nobody would want to kill the Sarge, sir.

WATERS *smiles.*

WATERS: Wilkie? (WILKIE *rises and walks into the blue-gray light and the scene with* WATERS. DAVENPORT *will watch*) You know what I'ma get that boy of mine for

his birthday? One of them Schwinn bikes. He'll be twelve—time flies, don't it? Let me show you something?
WILKIE (*to* DAVENPORT): He was always pullin' out snapshots, sir.

WATERS *hands him a snapshot.*

WATERS: My wife let a neighbor take this a couple weeks ago—ain't he growin' fast?
WILKIE: He's over your wife's shoulder! (*Hands it back.* WATERS *looks at the photo*)
WATERS: I hope this kid never has to be a soldier.
WILKIE: It was good enough for you.
WATERS: I couldn't do any better—and this army was the closest I figured the white man would let me get to any kind of authority. No, the army ain't for this boy. When this war's over, things are going to change, Wilkie—and I want him to be ready for it—my daughter, too! I'm sendin' bot' of 'em to some big white college—let 'em rub elbows with the whites, learn the white man's language—how he does things. Otherwise, we'll be left behind—you can see it in the army. White man runnin' rings around us.
WILKIE: A lot of us didn't get the chance or the schoolin' the white folks got.
WATERS: That ain't no excuse, Wilkie. Most niggahs just don't care—tomorrow don't mean nothin' to 'em. My daddy shoveled coal from the back of a wagon all his life. He couldn't read or write, but he saw to it we did! Not havin' ain't no excuse for not gettin'.
WILKIE: Can't get pee from a rock, Sarge.

WATERS *rises abruptly.*

WATERS: You just like the rest of 'em, Wilkie—I thought bustin' you would teach you something—we got to challenge this man in his arena—use his weapons, don't you know that? We need lawyers, doctors—generals—senators! Stop thinkin' like a niggah!
WILKIE: All I said—
WATERS: Is the equipment ready for tomorrow's game?
WILKIE: Yeah.
WATERS: Good. You can go now, Wilkie. (WILKIE *is stunned*) That's an order!

WILKIE *turns toward* DAVENPORT. *In the background, the humming of C.J. rises a bit as the light around* WATERS *fades out.*

WILKIE: He could be two people sometimes, sir. Warm one minute—ice the next.
DAVENPORT: How did you feel about him?
WILKIE: Overall—I guess he was all right. You could always borrow a ten-spot off him if you needed it.
DAVENPORT: Did you see the Sergeant any time immediately preceding his death?
WILKIE: I don't know how much before it was, but a couple of us had been over the N.C.O. club that night and Sarge had been juicin' pretty heavy.
DAVENPORT: Did Waters drink a lot?
WILKIE: No more than most—(*Pause*) Could I ask you a question, sir? (DAVENPORT

nods) Is it true, when they found Sarge all his stripes and insignia were still on his uniform?

DAVENPORT: I don't recall it being mentioned in my preliminary report. Why?

WILKIE: If that's the way they found him, something's wrong, ain't it, sir? Them Klan boys don't like to see us in these uniforms. They usually take the stripes and stuff off, before they lynch us.

DAVENPORT *is quiet, thoughtful for a moment.*

DAVENPORT: Thank you, Private—I might want to call you again, but for now you're excused.

WILKIE *rises.*

WILKIE: Yes, sir! (*Sudden mood swing, hesitant*) Sir?

DAVENPORT: Yes?

WILKIE: Can you do anything about allotment checks? My wife didn' get hers last month.

DAVENPORT: There's nothing I can do directly—did you see the finance officer? (WILKIE *nods*) Well—I'll—I'll mention it to Captain Taylor.

WILKIE: Thank you, sir. You want me to send the next man in?

DAVENPORT *nods.* WILKIE *salutes, does an about-face, and exits.* DAVENPORT *returns the salute, then leans back in his chair thoughtfully. In the background, the humming of C.J. rises again as the next man,* PFC MELVIN PETERSON, *enters. Dressed in fatigues, he is the model soldier. He walks quickly to the table, stands at attention, and salutes. The humming fades out as* DAVENPORT *returns the salute.*

PETERSON: Private First Class Melvin Peterson reporting as ordered, sir!

DAVENPORT: Sit down, Private. (PETERSON *sits*) Do you know why I'm here?

PETERSON: Yes, sir.

DAVENPORT: Fine. Now, everything you tell me is confidential, so I want you to speak as freely as possible. (PETERSON *nods*) Where are you from?

PETERSON: Hollywood, California—by way of Alabama, sir. I enlisted in '42— thought we'd get a chance to fight.

DAVENPORT (*ignores the comment*): Did you know Sergeant Waters well?

PETERSON: No, sir. He was already with the company when I got assigned here. And us common G.I.'s don't mix well with N.C.O.'s.

DAVENPORT: Were you on the baseball team?

PETERSON: Yes, sir—I played shortstop.

DAVENPORT: Did you like the Sergeant?

PETERSON: No, sir.

Before DAVENPORT *can speak,* ELLIS *enters.*

ELLIS: Beg your pardon, sir. Captain Taylor would like to see you in his office at once.

DAVENPORT: Did he say why?

ELLIS: No, sir—just that you should report to him immediately.

DAVENPORT (*annoyed*): Tell the men to stick around. When I finish with the Captain, I'll be back.

ELLIS: Yes, sir!

ELLIS *exits*.

DAVENPORT (to PETERSON): Feel like walking, Private? We can continue this on the way. (*Begins to put his things in his briefcase*) Why didn't you like the Sergeant?

DAVENPORT *and* PETERSON *start out as the light begins to fade in the barracks. They go through doorway, exit, and reenter the stage in full view.*

PETERSON: It goes back to the team, sir. I got here in—baseball season had started, so it had to be June—June of last year. The team had won maybe nine—ten games in a row, there was a rumor that they would even get a chance to play the Yankees in exhibition. So when I got assigned to a team like that, sir—I mean, I felt good. Anyway, ole Stone-ass—

DAVENPORT: Stone-ass?

PETERSON: I'm the only one called him that—Sergeant Waters, sir.

As the two of them pass in front of the barracks area, the light begins to rise very slowly, but it is the blue-gray light of the past. The chairs and table are gone, and the room looks different.

DAVENPORT: Respect his rank, with me, Private.

PETERSON: I didn't mean no offense, sir. (*Slight pause*) Well, the Sergeant and that brown-nosin' Wilkie? They ran the team—and like it was a chain gang, sir. A chain gang!

The two men exit the stage. As they do, C.J. MEMPHIS, HENSON, COBB, *and* SMALLS *enter in their baseball uniforms. T-shirts with "Fort Neal" stamped on the fronts, and numbers on the back, and baseball caps. They are carrying equipment—bats, gloves.* C.J. *is carrying his guitar.* SMALLS *enters tossing a baseball into the air and catching it. They almost all enter at once, with the exuberance of young men. Their talk is locker-room loud, and filled with bursts of laughter.*

HENSON: You see the look on that umpire's face when C.J. hit that home run? I thought he was gonna die on the spot, he turned so pale!

They move to their respective bunks.

SMALLS: Serves the fat bastard right! Some of them pitches he called strikes were well ova' my head!

C.J. *strums his guitar.* COBB *begins to brush off his boots.*

COBB: C.J.? Who was that fine, river-hip thing you was talkin' to, homey?

C.J. *shrugs and smiles.*

HENSON: Speakin' of women, I got to write my Lady a letter. (*He begins to dig for his writing things*)

COBB: She looked mighty good to me, C.J.

SMALLS (*overlapping*): Y'all hear Henson? Henson, you ain't had a woman since a woman had you!

HENSON *makes an obscene gesture.*

C.J. (*overlapping* SMALLS): Now, all she did was ask me for my autograph.

COBB: Look like she was askin' you fo' mor'n that. (*To* SMALLS) You see him, Smalls? Leanin' against the fence, all in the woman's face, breathin' heavy—

HENSON: If Smalls couldn't see enough to catch a ground ball right in his glove, how the hell could he see C.J. ova' by the fence?

SMALLS: That ball got caught in the sun!

HENSON: On the ground?

COBB (*at once*): We beat 'em nine to one! Y'all be quiet, I'm askin' this man 'bout a woman he was with had tits like two helmets!

C.J.: If I had'a give that gal what she asked fo'—she'da give me somethin' I didn' want! Them V-gals git you a bad case a' clap. 'Sides, she wasn' but sixteen.

SMALLS: You shoulda introduced her to Henson—sixteen's about his speed.

HENSON *makes a farting sound in retaliation.*

C.J.: Aroun' home? There's a fella folks use ta call, Lil' Jimmy One Leg—on account of his thing was so big? Two years ago—ole young pretty thing laid clap on Jimmy so bad, he los' the one good leg he had! Now folks jes' call him Little!

Laughter.

C.J.: That young thing talkin' to me ain' look so clean.

HENSON: Dirty or clean, she had them white boys lookin'.

COBB: Eyes popin' out they sockets, wasn' they? Remind me of that pitcher las' week! The one from 35th Ordnance? The one everybody claimed was so good? Afta' twelve straight hits, he looked the same way!

PETERSON *enters, carrying two baseball bats.*

SMALLS: It might be funny ta y'all, but when me and Pete had duty in the Ordnance mess hall, that same white pitcher was the first one started the name-callin'—

HENSON: Forget them dudes in Ordnance—lissen to this! (HENSON *begins to read from a short letter*) "Dear, Louis"—y'all hear that? The name is Louis—

COBB: Read the damn letter!

HENSON (*makes obscene gesture*): "Dear, Louis. You and the boys keep up the good work. All of us here at home are praying for you and inspired in this great cause by you. We know the Nazis and the Japs can't be stopped unless we all work together, so tell your buddies to press forward and win this war. All our hopes for the future go with you, Louis. Love Mattie." I think I'm in love with the sepia Winston Churchill—what kinda' letter do you write a nut like this?

COBB: Send her a round of ammunition and a bayonet, *Louis!*

HENSON *waves disdainfully.*

PETERSON: Y'all oughta listen to what Smalls said. Every time we beat them at base-ball, they get back at us every way they can.

COBB: It's worth it to me just to wipe those superior smiles off they faces.

PETERSON: I don't know—seems like it makes it that much harder for us.

C.J.: They tell me, coupla them big-time Negroes is on the verge a' gittin' all of us togetha'—colored and white—say they want one army.

PETERSON: Forget that, C.J.! White folks'll neva' integrate no army!

C.J. (*strums*): If they do—I'ma be ready for 'em! (*Sings*) Well, I got me a bright red zoot suit / And a pair a' patent-leatha' shoes / And my woman she sittin' waitin' / Fo' the day we hea' the news! Lawd, lawd, lawd, lawd, / Lawd, lawd, lawd, lawd!

SERGEANT WATERS, *followed by* WILKIE, *enters, immediately crossing to the center of the barracks, his strident voice abruptly cutting off* C.J.'s *singing and playing.*

WATERS: Listen up! (*To* C.J.) We don't need that guitar playin'-sittin'-round-the-shack music today, C.J.! (*Smiles*) I want all you men out of those baseball uni-forms and into work clothes! You will all report to me at 1300 hours in front of the Officers Club. We've got a work detail. We're painting the lobby of the club.

Collective groan.

SMALLS: The officers can't paint their own club?

COBB: Hell no, Smalls! Let the great-colored-clean-up company do it! Our motto is: Anything you don't want to do, the colored troops will do for you!

HENSON (*like a cheer*): Anything you don't want to do, the colored troops will do for you! (*He starts to lead the others*)

OTHERS: Anything you don't—

WATERS: That's enough!

The men are instantly silent.

HENSON: When do we get a rest? We just played nine innings of baseball, Sarge!

SMALLS: We can't go in the place, why the hell should we paint it?

COBB: Amen, brother!

There is a moment of quiet before WATERS *speaks.*

WATERS: Let me tell you fancy-assed ball-playin' Negroes somethin'! The *reasons* for any orders given by a superior officer is none of y'all's business! You obey them! This country is at war, and you niggahs are soldiers—nothin' else! So baseball teams—win or lose—get no special privileges! They need to work some of you niggahs till your legs fall off! (*Intense*) And something else—from now on, when I tell you to do something, I want it done—is that clear? (*The men are quiet*) Now, Wilkie's gonna' take all them funky shirts you got on over to the laundry. I could smell you suckers before I hit the field!

PETERSON: What kinda colored man are you?

WATERS: I'm a soldier, Peterson! First, last, and always! I'm the kinda colored man that don't like lazy, shiftless Negroes!

PETERSON: You ain't got to come in here and call us names!

WATERS: The Nazis call you schvatza! You gonna tell them they hurt your little feelings?

C.J.: Don't look like to me we could do too much to them Nazis wit' paint brushes, Sarge.

The men laugh. The moment is gone, and though WATERS is angry, his tone becomes overly solicitous, smiling.

WATERS: You tryin' to mock me, C.J.?

C.J.: No, sah, Sarge.

WATERS: Good, because whatever an ignorant, low-class geechy like you has to say isn't worth paying attention to, is it? (*Pause*) Is it?

C.J.: I reckon not, Sarge.

PETERSON: You' a creep, Waters!

WATERS: Boy, you are something—ain't been in the company a month, Wilkie, and already everybody's champion!

C.J. (*interjecting*): Sarge was just jokin', Pete—he don't mean no harm!

PETERSON: He does! We take enough from the white boys!

WATERS: Yes, you do—and if it wasn' for you Southern niggahs, yessahin', bowin' and scrapin', scratchin' your heads, white folks wouldn' think we were all fools!

PETERSON: Where you from, England?

Men snicker.

HENSON (*at once*): Peterson!

WATERS (*immediately*): You got somethin' to say, Henson?

HENSON: Nothin', Sarge.

HENSON *shakes his head as* WATERS *turns back to* PETERSON.

WATERS: Peterson, you got a real comic streak in you. Wilkie, looks like we got us a wise-ass Alabama boy here! (*He moves toward* PETERSON) Yes, sir—(*He snatches* PETERSON *in the collar*) Don't get smart, niggah!

PETERSON *yanks away.*

PETERSON: Get your fuckin' hands off me!

WATERS smiles, leans forward.

WATERS: You wanna hit ole Sergeant Waters, boy? (*Whispers*) Come on! Please! Come on, niggah!

CAPTAIN TAYLOR enters the barracks quite suddenly, unaware of what is going on.

HENSON: Tenn-hut!

All the men snap to.

TAYLOR: At ease! (*He moves toward* WATERS, *feeling the tension*) What's going on here, Sergeant?
WATERS: Nothin', sir—I was going over the *Manual of Arms.* Is there something in particular you wanted, sir? Something I can do?
TAYLOR (*relaxed somewhat*): Nothing—(*To the men*) Men, I congratulate you on the game you won today. We've only got seven more to play, and if we win them, we'll be the first team in Fort Neal history to play the Yanks in exhibition. Everyone in the regiment is counting on you. In times like these, morale is important—and winning can help a lot of things. (*Pause*) Sergeant, as far as I'm concerned, they've got the rest of the day off.

The men are pleased.

WATERS: Begging your pardon, sir, but these men need all the work they can get. They don't need time off—our fellas aren't getting time off in North Africa—besides, we've got orders to report to the Officers Club for a paint detail at 1300 hours.
TAYLOR: Who issued that order?
WATERS: Major Harris, sir.
TAYLOR: I'll speak to the Major.
WATERS: Sir, I don't think it's such a good idea to get a colored N.C.O. mixed up in the middle of you officers, sir.
TAYLOR: I said, I'd speak to him, Sergeant.
WATERS: Yes, sir!
TAYLOR: I respect the men's duty to service, but they need time off.
WATERS: Yes, sir.

Pause.

TAYLOR: You men played a great game of baseball out there today—that catch you made in center field, Memphis—how the hell'd you get up so high?
C.J. (*shrugs, smiles*): They say I got "Bird" in mah blood, sir.

TAYLOR is startled by the statement, his smile is an uncomfortable one. WATERS is standing on "eggs."

TAYLOR: American eagle, I hope. (*Laughs a little*)

C.J.: No, sah, crow—(WATERS *starts to move, but C.J. stops him by continuing. Several of the men are beginning to get uncomfortable*) Man tol' my daddy the day I was born, the shadow of a crow's wings—

TAYLOR (*cutting him off*): Fine—men, I'll say it again—you played superbly. (*Turns to WATERS*) Sergeant. (*He starts out abruptly*)

WATERS: Tenn-hut!

WATERS *salutes as the men snap to.*

TAYLOR (*exiting*): As you were.

TAYLOR *salutes as he goes. There is an instant of quiet. The men relax a little, but their focus is C.J.*

WATERS (*laughing*): Ain't these geechies somethin'? How long a story was you gonna tell the man, C.J.? My God! (*The men join him, but as he turns toward PETERSON, he stiffens*) Peterson! Oh, I didn't forget you, boy. (*The room quiets*) It's time to teach you a lesson!

PETERSON: Why don't you drop dead, Sarge?

WATERS: Nooo! I'ma drop you, boy! Out behind the barracks—Wilkie, you go out and make sure it's all set up.

WILKIE: You want all the N.C.O.'s?

WATERS *nods.* WILKIE *goes out smiling.*

WATERS: I'm going outside and wait for you, geechy! And when you come out, I'm gonna whip your black Southern ass—let the whole company watch it, too! (*Points*) You need to learn respect, boy—how to talk to your betters. (*Starts toward the door*) Fight hard, hea'? I'ma try to bust your fuckin' head open—the rest of you get those goddamn shirts off like I said!

He exits. The barracks is quiet for a moment.

COBB: You gonna fight him?

HENSON (*overlapping*): I tried to warn you!

PETERSON: You ain't do nothin'!

SMALLS: He'll fight you dirty, Pete—don't do it!

PETERSON *goes to his bunk and throws his cap off angrily.*

COBB: You don't want to do it?

PETERSON: You wanna fight in my place, Cobb? (*He sits*) Shit!

Slight pause. HENSON *pulls off his shirt.*

C.J.: I got some Farmers Dust—jes' a pinch'll make you strong as a bull—they say it comes from the city of Zar. (*Removes a pouch from his neck*) I seen a man use this stuff and pull a mule outta a sinkhole by hisself!

PETERSON: Get the hell outta here with that backwater crap—can't you speak up for yourself—let that bastard treat you like a dog!

C.J.: 'Long as his han's ain't on me—he ain't done me no harm, Pete. Callin' names ain't nothin', I know what I is. (*Softens*) Sarge ain't so bad—been good to me.

PETERSON: The man despises you!

C.J.: Sarge? You wrong, Pete—plus I feel kinda sorry for him myself. Any man ain't sure where he belongs must be in a whole lotta pain.

PETERSON: Don't y'all care?

HENSON: Don't nobody like it, Pete—but when you here a little longer—I mean, what can you do? This hea's the army and Sarge got all the stripes.

PETERSON *rises, disgusted, and starts out.* SMALLS *moves at once.*

SMALLS: Peterson, look, if you want me to, I'll get the Captain. You don't have to go out there and get your head beat in!

PETERSON: Somebody's got to fight him.

He exits. There is quiet as SMALLS *walks back to his bunk.*

C.J. (*singing*): It's a low / it's a low, low / lowdown dirty shame! It's a low / it's a low, low / lowdown dirty shame! Been playin' in this hea' army / an ain't even learned the game! Lawd, lawd, lawd, lawd—

C.J. *begins to hum as the lights slowly fade out over the barracks. As they do, the lights come up simultaneously in the* CAPTAIN's *office. It is empty.* PETERSON (*in proper uniform*) *and* DAVENPORT *enter from off-stage. They stop outside the* CAPTAIN'S *office.*

PETERSON: He beat me pretty bad that day, sir. The man was crazy!

DAVENPORT: Was the incident ever reported?

PETERSON: I never reported it, sir—I know I should have, but he left me alone after that. (*Shrugs*) I just played ball.

DAVENPORT: Did you see Waters the night he died?

PETERSON: No, sir—me and Smalls had guard duty.

DAVENPORT: Thank you, Private. That'll be all for now. (PETERSON *comes to attention*) By the way, did the team ever get to play the Yankees?

PETERSON: No, sir. We lost the last game to a Sanitation Company.

He salutes. DAVENPORT *returns salute.* PETERSON *does a crisp about-face and exits. Slowly* DAVENPORT *starts into the* CAPTAIN's *office, surprised that no one is about.*

DAVENPORT: Captain? (*There is no response. For a moment or two,* DAVENPORT *looks around. He is somewhat annoyed*) Captain?

He starts out. TAYLOR *enters. He crosses the room to his desk, where he sits.*

TAYLOR: I asked you back here because I wanted you to see the request I've sent to Colonel Nivens to have your investigation terminated. (*He picks up several sheets of paper on his desk and hands them to* DAVENPORT, *who ignores them*)

DAVENPORT: What?

TAYLOR: I wanted you to see that my reasons have nothing to do with you personally—my request will not hurt your army record in any way! (*Pause*) There are other things to consider in this case!

DAVENPORT: Only the color of my skin, Captain.

TAYLOR (*sharply*): I want the people responsible for killing one of my men found and jailed, Davenport!

DAVENPORT: So do I!

TAYLOR: Then give this up! (*Rises*) Whites down here won't see their duty—or justice. They'll see *you!* And once they do, the law—due process—it all goes! And what is the point of continuing an investigation that can't possibly get at the truth?

DAVENPORT: Captain, my orders are very specific, so unless you want charges brought against you for interfering in a criminal investigation, stay the hell out of my way and leave me and my investigation alone!

TAYLOR (*almost sneering*): Don't take yourself too seriously, Davenport. You couldn't find an officer within five hundred miles who would convey charges to a court-martial board against me for something like that, and you know it!

DAVENPORT: Maybe not, but I'd—I'd see to it that your name, rank, and duty station got into the Negro press! Yeah, let a few colored newspapers call you a Negro-hater! Make you an embarrassment to the United States Army, Captain— like Major Albright at Fort Jefferson, and you'd never command troops again— or wear more than those captain's bars on that uniform, Mr. West Point!

TAYLOR: I'll never be more than a captain, Davenport, because I won't let them get away with dismissing things like Waters's death. I've been the commanding officer of three outfits! I raised hell in all of them, so threatening me won't change my request. Let the Negro press print that I don't like being made a fool of with phony investigations!

DAVENPORT (*studies* TAYLOR *for a moment*): There are two white officers involved in this, Captain—aren't there?

TAYLOR: I want them in jail—out of the army! And there is no way *you* can get them charged, or court-martialed, or put away! The white officers on this post won't let you—they won't let me!

DAVENPORT: Why wasn't there any mention of them in your preliminary report? I checked my own summary on the way over here, Captain—nothing! You think I'ma let you get away with this? (*There is a long silence.* TAYLOR *walks back to his desk as* DAVENPORT *watches him.* TAYLOR *sits*) Why?

TAYLOR: I couldn't prove the men in question had anything to do with it.

DAVENPORT: Why didn't you report it?

TAYLOR: I was ordered not to. (*Pause*) Nivens and Hines. The doctors took two .45 caliber bullets out of Waters—army issue. But remember what it was like that morning? If these men had thought a white officer killed Waters, there would have been a slaughter! (*Pause*) Cobb reported the incident innocently the night before—then suddenly it was all over the Fort.

DAVENPORT: Who were they, Captain? I want their names!

TAYLOR: Byrd and Wilcox. Byrd's in Ordnance—Wilcox's with the 12th Hospital Group. I was Captain of the Guard the night Waters was killed. About 2100 hours, Cobb came into my office and told me he'd just seen Waters and two white officers fighting outside the colored N.C.O. club. I called *your* office, and when I couldn't get two M.P.'s, I started over myself to break it up. When I got there—no Waters, no officers. I checked the officers' billet and found Byrd and Wilcox in bed. Several officers verified they'd come in around 2130. I then told Cobb to go back to the barracks and forget it.

DAVENPORT: What made you do that?

TAYLOR: At the time there was no reason to believe anything was wrong! Waters wasn't found until the following morning. I told the Colonel what had happened the previous night, and about the doctor's report, and I was told, since the situation at the Fort was potentially dangerous, to keep my mouth shut until it blew over. He agreed to let me question Byrd and Wilcox, but I've asked him for a follow-up investigation every day since it happened. (*Slight pause*) When I saw you, I exploded—it was like he was laughing at me.

DAVENPORT: Then you never believed the Klan was involved?

TAYLOR: No. Now, can you see why this thing needs—someone else?

DAVENPORT: What did they tell you, Captain? Byrd and Wilcox?

TAYLOR: They're not going to let you charge those two men!

DAVENPORT (*snaps*): Tell me what they told you!

> TAYLOR *is quiet for a moment. At this time, on center stage in limbo,* SERGEANT WATERS *is staggering. He is dressed as we first saw him. Behind him a blinking light reads: 221st N.C.O. Club. As he staggers toward the stairs leading to center stage, two white officers,* LIEUTENANT BYRD, *a spit-and-polish soldier in his twenties, and* CAPTAIN WILCOX, *a medical officer, walk on-stage. Both are in full combat gear—rifles, pistol belts, packs—and both are tired.* TAYLOR *looks out as if he can see them.*

TAYLOR: They were coming off bivouac.

> *The two men see* WATERS. *In the background is the faint hum of* C.J.'s *music.*

TAYLOR: They saw him outside the club.

> *He rises, as* WATERS *sees* BYRD *and* WILCOX, *and smiles.*

WATERS: Well, if it ain't the white boys!

WATERS *straightens and begins to march in a mock circle and then down in their direction. He is mumbling, barely audibly:* "One, two, three, four! Hup, hup, three, four! Hup, hup, three, four!" BYRD's *speech overlaps* WATERS's.

BYRD: And it wasn't like we were looking for trouble, Captain. Were we, Wilcox?

WILCOX *shakes his head no, but he is astonished by* WATERS's *behavior and stares at him, disbelieving.*

WATERS: White boys! All starched and stiff! Wanted everybody to learn all that symphony shit! That's what you were saying in France—and you know, I listened to you? Am I all right now? Am I?

BYRD: Boy, you'd better straighten up and salute when you see an officer, or you'll find yourself without those stripes! (*To* WILCOX *as* WATERS *nears them, smiling the "coon" smile and doing a juba*) Will you look at this niggah? (*Loud*) Come to attention, Sergeant! That's an order!

WATERS: No, sah! I ain't straightenin' up for y'all no more! I ain't doin' nothin' white folks say do, no more! (*Sudden change of mood, smiles, sings*) No more, no more / no more, no more, noooo! No more, no more / no more, no more, noooooo!

BYRD *faces* TAYLOR *as* WATERS *continues to sing.*

BYRD (*overlapping*): Sir, I thought the man was crazy!
TAYLOR: And what did you think, Wilcox?

BYRD *moves toward* WATERS, *and* WATERS, *still singing low, drunk and staggering, moves back and begins to circle* BYRD, *stalk him, shaking his head no as he sings.* WILCOX *watches apprehensively.*

WILCOX (*at once*): He did appear to be intoxicated, sir—out of his mind almost! (*He turns to* BYRD) Byrd, listen—
BYRD *ignores him.*
DAVENPORT (*suddenly*): Did they see anyone else in the area?
TAYLOR: No. (*To* BYRD) I asked them what they did next.
BYRD: I told that niggah to shut up!
WATERS (*sharply*): No! (*Change of mood*) Followin' behind y'all? Look what it's done to me!—I hate myself!
BYRD: Don't blame us, boy! God made you black, not me!
WATERS (*smiles*): My daddy use ta say—
WILCOX: Sergeant, get hold of yourself!
WATERS (*points*): Listen!

BYRD *steps toward him and shoves him in the face.*

BYRD: I gave you an order, niggah!

WILCOX *grabs* BYRD, *and stops him from advancing, as* WATERS *begins to cry.*

WATERS: My daddy said, "Don't talk like dis'—talk like that!" "Don't live hea'—live there!" (*To them*) I've killed for you! (*To himself; incredulous*) And nothin' changed!

BYRD *pulls free of* WILCOX *and charges* WATERS.

BYRD: He needs to be taught a lesson!

He shoves WATERS *onto the ground, where he begins to beat and kick the man, until he is forcibly restrained by* WILCOX. WATERS *moans.*

WILCOX: Let him be! You'll kill the man! He's sick—leave him alone!

BYRD *pulls away; he is flush.* WATERS *tries to get up.*

WATERS: Nothin' changed—see? And I've tried everything! Everything!
BYRD: I'm gonna bust his black ass to buck private!—I should blow his coward's head off! (*Shouts*) There are good men killing for you, niggah! Gettin' their guts all blown to hell for you!

WILCOX *pulls him away. He pulls* BYRD *off-stage as the light around* WATERS *and that section of the stage begins to fade out. As it does, a trace of* C.J.'s *music is left on the air.* WATERS *is on his knees, groveling, as the lights go out around him.*

DAVENPORT: Did they shove Waters again?
TAYLOR: No. But Byrd's got a history of scrapes with Negroes. They told me they left Waters at 2110—and everyone in the officers' billet verifies they were both in by 2130. And neither man left—Byrd had duty the next morning, and Wilcox was scheduled at the hospital at 0500 hours—both men reported for duty.
DAVENPORT: I don't believe it.
TAYLOR: I couldn't shake their stories.
DAVENPORT: That's nothing more than officers lying to protect two of their own and you know it! I'm going to arrest and charge both of them, Captain—and you may consider yourself confined to your quarters pending my charges against you!
TAYLOR: What charges?
DAVENPORT: It was *your* duty to go over Nivens's head if you had to!
TAYLOR: Will you arrest Colonel Nivens too, Davenport? Because he's part of their alibi—he was there when they came in—played poker—from 2100 to 0300 hours the following morning, the Colonel—your Major Hines, "Shack" Callahan—Major Callahan, and Jed Harris—and Jed wouldn't lie for either of them!
DAVENPORT: They're all lying!
TAYLOR: Prove it, hotshot—I told you all I know, now you go out and prove it!
DAVENPORT: I will, Captain! You can bet your sweet ass on that! I will!

DAVENPORT *starts out as the lights begin to fade, and* TAYLOR *looks after him and shakes his head. In the background, the sound of "Don't Sit under the Apple Tree" comes up again and continues to play as the lights fade to black.*

ACT TWO

SCENE: *As before.*

Light rises slowly over limbo. We hear a snippet of "Don't Sit under the Apple Tree" as DAVENPORT, *seated on the edge of a bunk, finishes dressing. He is putting on a shirt, tie, bars, etc., and addresses the audience as he does so.*

DAVENPORT: During May of '44, the Allies were making final preparations for the invasion of Europe. Invasion! Even the sound of it made Negroes think we'd be in it—be swept into Europe in the waves of men and equipment—I know I felt it. (*Thoughtfully*) We hadn't seen a lot of action except in North Africa—or Sicily. But the rumor in orderly rooms that spring was, pretty soon most of us would be in combat—somebody said Ike wanted to find out if the colored boys could fight—shiiit, we'd been fighting all along—right here, in these small Southern towns—(*Intense*) I don't have the authority to arrest a white *private* without a white officer present! (*Slight pause*) Then I get a case like this? There was no way I wouldn't see this through to its end. (*Smiles*) And after my first twenty-four hours, I wasn't doing too badly. I had two prime suspects—a motive, and opportunity! (*Pause*) I went to Colonel Nivens and convinced him that word of Byrd's and Wilcox's involvement couldn't be kept secret any longer. However, before anyone in the press could accuse him of complicity—I would silence all suspicions by pursuing the investigation openly—on his orders—(*Mimics himself*) "Yes, sir, Colonel, you can even send along a white officer—not Captain Taylor, though—I think he's a little too close to the case, sir." Colonel Nivens gave me permission to question Byrd and Wilcox, and having succeeded sooo easily, I decided to spend some time finding out more about Waters and Memphis. Somehow the real drama seemed to be there, and my curiosity wouldn't allow me to ignore it.

DAVENPORT *is dressed and ready to go as a spotlight in the barracks area opens on PRIVATE HENSON. He is seated on a footlocker. He rises as DAVENPORT descends to the stage. He will not enter the barracks, but will almost handle this like a courtroom interrogation. He returns HENSON's salute.*

DAVENPORT: Sit down, Private. Your name is Louis Henson, is that right?
HENSON: Yes, sir.

HENSON *sits, as DAVENPORT paces.*

DAVENPORT: Tell me what you know about Sergeant Waters and C.J. Memphis. (HENSON *looks at him strangely*) Is there something wrong?
HENSON: No, sir—I was just surprised you knew about it.
DAVENPORT: Why?
HENSON: You're an officer.
DAVENPORT (*quickly*): And?

HENSON (*hesitantly*): Well—officers are up here, sir—and us enlisted men—down here. (*Slight pause*) C.J. and Waters—that was just between enlisted men, sir. But I guess ain't nothin' a secret around colored folks—not that it was a secret. (*Shrugs*) There ain't that much to tell—sir. Sarge ain't like C.J. When I got to the company in May of las' year, the first person I saw Sarge chew out was C.J.! (*He is quiet*)

DAVENPORT: Go on.

HENSON's *expression is pained.*

HENSON: Is that an order, sir?

DAVENPORT: Does it have to be?

HENSON: I don't like tattle-talin', sir—an' I don't mean no offense, but I ain't crazy 'bout talkin' to officers—colored or white.

DAVENPORT: It's an order, Henson!

HENSON *nods.*

HENSON: C.J. wasn' movin' fast enough for *him*. Said C.J. didn' have enough *fire-under-his-behind* out on the field.

DAVENPORT: You were on the team?

HENSON: Pitcher. (*Pause.* DAVENPORT *urges with a look*) He jus' *stayed* on C.J. all the time—every little thing, it seemed like to me—then the shootin' went down, and C.J. caught all the hell.

DAVENPORT: What shooting?

HENSON: The shootin' at Williams's Golden Palace, sir—here, las' year!—way before you got here. Toward the end of baseball season. (DAVENPORT *nods his recognition*) The night it happened, a whole lotta gunshots went off near the barracks. I had gotten drunk over at the enlisted men's club, so when I got to the barracks I just sat down in a stupor!

Suddenly shots are heard in the distance and grow ever closer as the eerie blue-gray light rises in the barracks over the sleeping figures of men in their bunks. HENSON is seated, staring at the ground. He looks up once as the gunshots go off, and as he does, someone—we cannot be sure who—sneaks into the barracks as the men begin to shift and awaken. This person puts something under C.J.'s bed and rushes out. HENSON watches—surprised at first, rising, then disbelieving. He shakes his head, then sits back down as several men wake up. DAVENPORT recedes to one side of the barracks, watching.

COBB: What the hell's goin' on? Don't they know a man needs his sleep? (*He is quickly back to sleep*)

SMALLS (*simultaneously*): Huh? Who is it? (*Looks around, then falls back to sleep*)

DAVENPORT: Are you sure you saw someone?

HENSON: Well—I saw something, sir.

DAVENPORT: What did you do?

The shooting suddenly stops and the men settle down.

HENSON: I sat, sir—I was juiced—(*Shrugs*) The gunshots weren't any of my business—plus I wasn't sure what I had seen in the first place, then out of nowhere Sergeant Waters, he came in.

WATERS *enters the barracks suddenly, followed by* WILKIE. HENSON *stands immediately, staggering a bit.*

WATERS: All right, all right! Everybody up! Wake them, Wilkie!

WILKIE *moves around the bunks, shaking the men.*

WILKIE: Let's go! Up! Let's go, you guys!

COBB *shoves* WILKIE's *hand aside angrily as the others awaken slowly.*

WATERS: Un-ass them bunks! Tenn-hut! (*Most of the men snap to.* SMALLS *is the last one, and* WATERS *moves menacingly toward him*) There's been a shooting! One of ours bucked the line at Williams's pay phone and three soldiers are dead! Two colored and one white M.P. (*Pauses*) Now, the man who bucked the line, he killed the M.P., and the white boys started shootin' everybody—that's how our two got shot. And this lowdown niggah we lookin' for got chased down here—and was almost caught, 'til somebody in these barracks started shootin' at the men chasin' him. So, we got us a vicious, murderin' piece of black trash in here somewhere—and a few people who helped him. If any of you are in this, I want you to step forward. (*No one moves*) All you baseball niggahs are innocent, huh? Wilkie, make the search. (PETERSON *turns around as* WILKIE *begins*) Eyes front!
PETERSON: I don't want that creep in my stuff!
WATERS: You don't talk at attention!

WILKIE *will search three bunks, top and bottom, along with footlockers. Under* C.J.'s *bed he will find what he is looking for.*

WATERS: I almost hope it is some of you geechies—get rid of you Southern niggahs! (*To* WILKIE) Anything yet?
WILKIE: Nawwww!
WATERS: Memphis, are you in this?
C.J.: No, sah, Sarge.
WATERS: How many of you were out tonight?
SMALLS: I was over at Williams's around seven—got me some Lucky Strikes—I didn't try to call home, though.
COBB: I was there, this mornin'!
WATERS: Didn't I say *tonight*—uncle?
WILKIE: Got somethin'!

WILKIE *is holding up a .45 caliber automatic pistol, army issue. Everyone's attention focuses on it. The men are surprised, puzzled.*

WATERS: Where'd you find it?

WILKIE *points to* C.J., *who recoils at the idea.*

C.J.: Naaaawww, man!
WATERS: C.J.? This yours?
C.J.: You know it ain't mine, Sarge!
WATERS: It's still warm—how come it's under your bunk?
C.J.: Anybody coulda' put it thea', Sarge!
WATERS: Who? Or maybe this .45 crawled in through an open window—looked around the whole room—passed Cobb's bunk, and decided to snuggle up under yours? Must be voodoo, right, boy? Or some of that Farmers Dust round that neck of yours, huh?
C.J.: That pistol ain't mine!
WATERS: Liar!
C.J.: No, Sarge—I hate guns! Make me feel bad jes' to see a gun!
WATERS: You're under arrest—Wilkie, escort this man to the stockade!

PETERSON *steps forward.*

PETERSON: C.J. couldn't hurt a fly, Waters, you know that!
WATERS: I found a gun, soldier—now get out of the way!
PETERSON: Goddammit, Waters, you know it ain't him!
WATERS: How do I know?
HENSON: Right before you came in, I thought I saw somebody sneak in.
WATERS: You were drunk when you left the club—I saw you myself!
WILKIE: Besides, how you know it wasn't C.J.?
COBB: I was here all night. C.J. didn't go out.

WATERS *looks at them, intense.*

WATERS: We got the right man. (*Points at* C.J., *impassioned*) You think he's innocent, don't you? C.J. Memphis, playin' cotton-picker singin' the blues, bowin' and scrapin'—smilin' in everybody's face—this man undermined us! You and me! The description of the man who did the shooting fits C.J.! (*To* HENSON) You saw C.J. sneak in here! (*Points*) Don't be fooled—that yassah boss is hidin' some-thing—niggahs ain't like that today! This is 1943—he shot that white boy!

C.J. *is stunned, then suddenly the enormity of his predicament hits him and he breaks free of* WILKIE *and hits* WATERS *in the chest. The blow knocks* WATERS *down, and* C.J. *is immediately grabbed by the other men in the barracks.* COBB *goes to* WATERS *and helps him up slowly. The blow hurt* WATERS, *but he forces a smile at* C.J., *who has suddenly gone immobile, surprised by what he has done.*

WATERS: What did you go and do now, boy? Hit a noncommissioned officer.
COBB: Sarge, he didn't mean it!
WATERS: Shut up! (*Straightens*) Take him out, Wilkie.

WILKIE *grabs* C.J. *by the arm and leads him out.* C.J. *goes calmly, almost passively.* WATERS *looks at all the men quietly for a moment, then walks out without saying a word. There is a momentary silence in the barracks.*

SMALLS: Niggah like that can't have a mother.

HENSON: I know I saw something!

PETERSON: C.J. was sleepin' when I came in! It's Waters—can't y'all see that? I've seen him before—we had 'em in Alabama! White man gives them a little ass job as a servant—close to the big house, and when the boss ain't lookin', old copycat niggahs act like they the new owner! They take to soundin' like the boss—shoutin', orderin' people aroun'—and when it comes to you and me—they sell us to continue favor. They think the high-jailers like that. Arrestin' C.J.—that'll get Waters another stripe! Next it'll be you—or you. He can't look good unless he's standin' on you! Cobb tol' him C.J. was in all evening—Waters didn't even listen! Turning somebody in (*mimics*): "Look what I done, Captain Boss!" They let him in the army 'cause they know he'll do anything they tell him to—I've seen his kind of fool before. Someone's going to kill him.

SMALLS: I heard they killed a sergeant at Fort Robinson—recruit did it—

COBB: It'll just be our luck, Sarge'll come through the whole war without a scratch.

PETERSON: Maybe—but I'm goin' over to the stockade—tell the M.P.'s what I know—C.J. was here all evening. (*He starts dressing*)

SMALLS: I'll go with you!

COBB: Me too, I guess.

They all begin to dress as the light fades slowly in the barracks area. HENSON *rises and starts toward* DAVENPORT. *In the background,* C.J.'s *music comes up a bit.*

DAVENPORT: Could the person you thought you saw have stayed in the barracks—did you actually see someone go out?

HENSON: Yes, sir!

DAVENPORT: Was Wilkie the only man out of his bunk that night?

HENSON: Guess so—he came in with Sarge.

DAVENPORT: And Peterson—he did most of the talking?

HENSON: As I recall. It's been a while ago—an' I was juiced!

DAVENPORT *rises.*

DAVENPORT: Ellis!

ELLIS *appears at the door.*

ELLIS: Sir!

DAVENPORT: I want Private Wilkie and Pfc Peterson to report to me at once.

ELLIS: They're probably on work detail, sir.

DAVENPORT: Find them.

ELLIS: Yes, sir!

ELLIS *exits quickly and* DAVENPORT *lapses into a quiet thoughtfulness.*

HENSON: Is there anything else?—Sir?
DAVENPORT (*vexed*): No! That'll be all—send in the next man.

HENSON *comes to attention and salutes.* DAVENPORT *returns salute as* HENSON *exits through the barracks.* C.J.'s *music plays in background. There is a silence.* DAVENPORT *rises, mumbling something to himself.* COBB *appears suddenly at the doorway. He watches* DAVENPORT *for a moment.*

COBB: Sir? (DAVENPORT *faces him*) Corporal Cobb reporting as ordered, sir. (*He salutes*)
DAVENPORT: Have a seat, Corporal (COBB *crosses the room and sits*) And let's get something straight from the beginning—I don't care whether you like officers or not—is that clear?

COBB *looks at him strangely.*

COBB: Sir?

Pause. DAVENPORT *calms down somewhat.*

DAVENPORT: I'm sorry—Did you know Sergeant Waters well?
COBB: As well as the next man, sir—I was already with the team when he took over. Me and C.J., we made the team the same time.
DAVENPORT: Were you close to C.J.?
COBB: Me and him were "homeys," sir! Both came from Mississippi. C.J. from Carmella—me, I'm from up 'roun' Jutlerville, what they call snake county. Plus, we both played for the Negro League before the war.
DAVENPORT: How did you feel about his arrest?
COBB: Terrible—C.J. didn't kill nobody, sir.
DAVENPORT: He struck Sergeant Waters—
COBB: Waters made him, sir! He called that boy things he had never heard of before—C.J., he was so confused he didn't know what else to do—(*Pause*) An' when they put him in the stockade, he jus' seemed to go to pieces. (*Lowly in the background,* C.J.'s *music comes up*) See, we both lived on farms and even though C.J.'s daddy played music, C.J., he liked the wide-open spaces. (*Shakes his head*) That cell? It started closin' in on him right away. (*Blue-gray light rises in limbo, where* C.J. *is sitting on the edge of a bunk. A shadow of bars cuts across the space. His guitar is on the bunk beside him*) I went to see him, the second day he was in there. He looked pale and ashy, sir—like something dead.

C.J. *faces* COBB.

C.J.: It's hard to breathe in these little spaces, Cobb—man wasn' made for this hea'—nothin' was! I don't think I'll eva' see a' animal in a cage agin' and not feel sorry for it. (*To himself*) I'd rather be on the chain gang.

COBB *looks up at him.*

COBB: Come on, homey! (*He rises, moves toward* C.J.)

C.J.: I don't think I'm comin' outta here, Cobb—feels like I'm goin' crazy. Can't walk in hea'—can't see the sun! I tried singin', Cobb, but nothin' won't come out. I sure don't wanna die in this jail!

COBB (*moving closer*): Ain't nobody gonna die, C.J.!

C.J.: Yesterday I broke a guitar string—lost my Dust! I got no protection—nothin' to keep the dog from tearin' at my bones!

COBB: Stop talkin' crazy!

C.J. *is quiet for a moment. He starts forward. Slowly, in center stage,* WATERS *emerges. He faces the audience.*

C.J.: You know, he come up hea' las' night? Sergeant Waters?

WATERS *smiles, pulls out his pipe, lights it.*

WATERS (*calmly*): You should learn never to hit sergeants, boy—man can get in a lot of trouble doin' that kinda thing durin' wartime—they talkin' 'bout givin' you five years—they call what you did mutiny in the navy. Mutiny, boy.

C.J.: That gun ain't mine!

WATERS: Oh, we know that, C.J.! (C.J. *is surprised*) That gun belonged to the niggah did the shootin' over at Williams's place—me and Wilkie caught him hidin' in the Motor Pool, and he confessed his head off. You're in here for striking a superior officer, boy. And I got a whole barracks full of your friends to prove it! (*Smiles broadly, as* C.J. *shakes his head*)

DAVENPORT (*to* COBB, *at once*): Memphis wasn't charged with the shooting?

COBB: No, sir—

WATERS: Don't feel too bad, boy. It's not your fault entirely—it has to be this way. The First War, it didn't change much for us, boy—but this one—it's gonna change a lot of things. Them Nazis ain't all crazy—a whole lot of people just can't fit into where things seem to be goin'—like you, C.J. The black race can't afford you no more. There use ta be a time when we'd see somebody like you, singin', clownin'—yas-sah-bossin'—and we wouldn't do anything. (*Smiles*) Folks liked that—you were good—homey kinda' niggah—they needed somebody to mistreat—call a name, they paraded you, reminded them of the old days—corn-bread bakin', greens and ham cookin'—Daddy out pickin' cotton, Grandmammy sit on the front porch smokin' a pipe. (*Slight pause*) Not no more. The day of the geechy is gone, boy—the only thing that can move the race is power. It's all the white respects—and people like you just make us seem like fools. And we can't let nobody go on believin' we all like you! You bring us down—make people think the whole race is unfit! (*Quietly pleased*) I waited a long time for you, boy, but I gotcha! And I try to git rid of you wherever I go. I put two geechies in jail at Fort Campbell, Kentucky—three at Fort Huachuca. Now I got you—one less fool for the race to be ashamed of! (*Points*) And I'ma git that ole boy Cobb next! (*Light begins to fade around* WATERS)

DAVENPORT (*at once*): You?

COBB: Yes, sir. (*Slight pause*)

DAVENPORT: Go on.

C.J.: You imagin' anybody sayin' that? I know I'm not gittin' outta' hea', Cobb! (*Quiets*) You remember I tol' you 'bout a place I use ta go outside Carmella? When I was a little ole tiny thing? Place out behind O'Connell's Farm? Place would be stinkin' of plums, Cobb. Shaded—that ripe smell be weavin' through the cotton fields and clear on in ta town on a warm day. First time I had Evelyn? I had her unda' them plum trees. I wrote song a for her—(*Talks, sings*) My ginger-colored Moma—she had thighs the size of hams! (*Chuckles*) And when you spread them, Momaaaa! / (*Talks*) You let me have my jelly roll and jam! (*Pause, mood swing*) O'Connell, he had a dog—meanes' dog I *eva'* did see! An' the only way you could enjoy them plum trees was to outsmart that dog. Waters is like that ole dog, Cobb—you gotta run circles roun' ole Windy—that was his name. They say he tore a man's arm off once, and got to likin' it. So, you had to cheat that dog outta' bitin' you every time. Every time. (*Slowly the light begins to fade around* C.J.)

COBB: He didn't make sense, sir. I tried talkin' about the team—the war—ain't nothin' work—seem like he jes' got worse.

DAVENPORT: What happened to him?

COBB *looks at him incredulously.*

COBB: The next day—afta' the day I saw him? C.J., he hung hisself, sir! Suicide—jes' couldn't stand it. M.P.'s found him hung from the bars.

DAVENPORT *is silent for a moment.*

DAVENPORT: What happened after that?

COBB: We lost our last game—we jes' threw it—we did it for C.J.—Captain, he was mad 'cause we ain't git ta play the Yankees. Peterson was right on that one—somebody needed to protest that man!

DAVENPORT: What did Waters do?

COBB: Well, afta' we lost, the commanding officer, he broke up the team, and we all got reassigned to this Smoke Company. Waters, he started actin' funny, sir—stayed drunk—talked to hisself all the time.

DAVENPORT: Did you think you were next?

COBB: I ain't sure I eva' believed Waters said that, sir—C.J. had to be outta' his head or he wouldna' killed hisself—Sarge, he neva' came near me afta' C.J. died.

DAVENPORT: What time did you get back the night Waters was killed?

COBB: I'd say between 2120 and 9:30.

DAVENPORT: And you didn't go out again?

COBB: No, sir—me and Henson sat and listened to the radio till Abbott and Lou Costello went off, then I played checkers with Wilkie for 'notha' hour, then everybody went to bed. What C.J. said about Waters? It ain't botha' me, sir.

DAVENPORT *is silent.*

DAVENPORT: Who were the last ones in that night?
COBB: Smalls and Peterson—they had guard duty.

TAYLOR *enters the barracks area and stops just inside the door when he sees* DAVENPORT *isn't quite finished.*

DAVENPORT: Thank you, Corporal.

COBB *rises at attention and salutes.* DAVENPORT *returns salute and* COBB *starts out. He nods to* TAYLOR, *who advances toward* DAVENPORT.

TAYLOR (*smiling*): You surprise me, Davenport—I just left Colonel Nivens. He's given you permission to question Byrd and Wilcox? (DAVENPORT *nods*) How'd you manage that? You threatened him with an article in the Chicago *Defender*, I suppose.
DAVENPORT: I convinced the Colonel it was in his best interests to allow it.
TAYLOR: Really? Did he tell you I would assist you?
DAVENPORT: I told him I especially didn't want you.
TAYLOR: That's precisely why he sent me—he didn't want you to think you could get your way entirely—not with him. Then neither Byrd or Wilcox would submit to it without a white officer present. That's how it is. (*There is a rather long silence*) But there's something else, Davenport. The Colonel began talking about the affidavits he and the others signed—and the discrepancies in their statements that night. (*Mimics*) He wants me with you because he doesn't want Byrd and Wilcox giving you the wrong impression—he never elaborated on what he meant by the wrong impression. I want to be there!
DAVENPORT: So you're not on *that* side anymore—you're on *my* side now, right?
TAYLOR (*bristles*): I want whoever killed my sergeant, Davenport!
DAVENPORT: Bullshit! Yesterday you were daring me to try! And today we're allies? Besides, you don't give that much of a damn about your men! I've been around you a full day and you haven't uttered a word that would tell me you had any more than a minor acquaintance with Waters! He managed your baseball team— was an N.C.O. in your company, and you haven't offered *any* opinion of the man as a soldier—sergeant—platoon leader! Who the hell was he?
TAYLOR: He was one of my men! On my roster—a man these bars make me responsible for! And no, I don't know a helluva lot about him—or a lot of their names or where they come from, but I'm still their commanding officer and in a little while I may have to trust them with my life! And I want them to know they can trust me with theirs—here and now! (*Pause*) I have Byrd and Wilcox in my office. (DAVENPORT *stares at him for a long moment, then rises and starts out toward center stage*) Why didn't you tell Nivens that you'd placed me under arrest?

DAVENPORT *stops.*

DAVENPORT: I didn't find it necessary.

They stare at one another. TAYLOR *is noticeably strained.*

DAVENPORT (*starts away*): What do you know about C.J. Memphis?

TAYLOR *follows.*

TAYLOR (*shrugs*): He was a big man as I recall—more a boy than a man, though. Played the guitar sometimes at the Officers Club—there was something embarrassing about him. Committed suicide in the stockade. Pretty good center fielder—

DAVENPORT *stops.*

DAVENPORT: Did you investigate his arrest—the charges against him?
TAYLOR: He was charged with assaulting a noncommissioned officer—I questioned him—he didn't say much. He admitted he struck Waters—I started questioning several of the men in the platoon and he killed himself before I could finish—open-and-shut case.
DAVENPORT: I think Waters tricked C.J. into assaulting him.
TAYLOR: Waters wasn't that kind of a man! He admitted he might have provoked the boy—he accused him of that Golden Palace shooting—

Behind them, the CAPTAIN's *office is lit. In two chairs facing* TAYLOR's *desk are* LIEUTENANT BYRD *and* CAPTAIN WILCOX, *both in dress uniform.*

TAYLOR: Listen, Waters didn't have a fifth-grade education—he wasn't a schemer! And colored soldiers aren't devious like that.
DAVENPORT: What do you mean we aren't devious?
TAYLOR (*sharply*): You're not as devious—! (DAVENPORT *stares as* TAYLOR *waves disdainfully and starts into the office*) Anyway, what has that to do with this? (*He is distracted by* BYRD *and* WILCOX *before* DAVENPORT *can answer.* TAYLOR *speaks as he moves to his desk*) This is Captain Davenport—you've both been briefed by Colonel Nivens to give the Captain your full cooperation.

DAVENPORT *puts on his glasses.* TAYLOR *notices and almost smiles.*

BYRD (*to* DAVENPORT): They tell me you a lawyer, huh?
DAVENPORT: I am not here to answer your questions, Lieutenant. And I am Captain Davenport, is that clear?
BYRD (*to* TAYLOR): Captain, is he crazy?
TAYLOR: You got your orders.
BYRD: Sir, I vigorously protest as an officer—
TAYLOR (*cuts him off*): You answer him the way he wants you to, Byrd, or I'll have your ass in a sling so tight you won't be able to pee, soldier!

BYRD *backs off slightly.*

DAVENPORT: When did you last see Sergeant Waters?
BYRD: The night he was killed, but I didn' kill him—I should have blown his head off, the way he spoke to me and Captain Wilcox here.

DAVENPORT: How did he speak to you, Captain?

WILCOX: Well, he was very drunk—and he said a lot of things he shouldn't have. I told the Lieutenant here not to make the situation worse and he agreed, and we left the Sergeant on his knees, wallowing in self-pity. (*Shrugs*)

DAVENPORT: What exactly did he say?

WILCOX: Some pretty stupid things about us—I mean white people, sir.

BYRD *reacts to the term "sir."*

DAVENPORT: What kind of things?

BYRD (*annoyed*): He said he wasn't going to obey no white man's orders! And that me and Wilcox here were to blame for him being black, and not able to sleep or keep his food down! And I didn't even know the man! Never even spoke to him before that night!

DAVENPORT: Anything else?

WILCOX: Well—he said he'd killed somebody.

DAVENPORT: Did he call a name—or say who?

WILCOX: Not that I recall, sir.

DAVENPORT *looks at* BYRD.

BYRD: No—(*Sudden and sharp*) Look—the goddamn Negro was disrespectful! He wouldn't salute! Wouldn't come to attention! And where I come from, colored don't talk the way he spoke to us—not to white people they don't!

DAVENPORT: Is that the reason you killed him?

BYRD: I killed nobody! I said "where I come from," didn't I? You'd be dead yourself, where I come from! But I didn't kill the—the *Negro!*

DAVENPORT: But you hit him, didn't you?

BYRD: I knocked him down!

DAVENPORT (*quickens pace*): And when you went to look at him, he was dead, wasn't he?

BYRD: He was alive when we left!

DAVENPORT: You're a liar! You beat Waters up—you went back and you shot him!

BYRD: No! (*Rises*) But you better get outta my face before I kill you!

DAVENPORT *stands firm.*

DAVENPORT: Like you killed Waters?

BYRD: No! (*He almost raises a hand to* DAVENPORT)

TAYLOR (*at once*): Soldier!

BYRD: He's trying to put it on me!

TAYLOR: Answer his questions, Lieutenant.

DAVENPORT: You were both coming off bivouac, right?

WILCOX: Yes.

DAVENPORT: So you both had weapons?

BYRD: So what? We didn't fire them!

DAVENPORT: Were the weapons turned in immediately?

WILCOX: Yes, sir—Colonel Nivens took our .45's to Major Hines. It was all kept quiet because the Colonel didn't want the colored boys to know that anyone white from the Fort was involved in any way—ballistics cleared them.

DAVENPORT: We can check.

BYRD: Go ahead.

TAYLOR: I don't believe it—why wasn't I told?

WILCOX: The weapons had cleared—and the Colonel felt if he involved you further, you'd take the matter to Washington and there'd be a scandal about colored and white soldiers—as it turned out, he thinks you went to Washington anyway. (*To* DAVENPORT) I'd like to say, Captain, that neither Lieutenant Byrd or myself had anything whatsoever to do with Sergeant Waters's death—I swear that as an officer and a gentleman. He was on the ground when we left him, but very much alive.

TAYLOR: Consider yourselves under arrest, gentlemen!

BYRD: On what charge?

TAYLOR: Murder! You think I believe that crap—

DAVENPORT: Let them go, Captain.

TAYLOR: You've got motive—a witness to their being at the scene—

DAVENPORT: Let them go! This is still my investigation—you two are dismissed!

BYRD *rises quickly.* WILCOX *follows his lead.*

WILCOX: Are we being charged, sir?

DAVENPORT: Not by me.

WILCOX: Thank you.

WILCOX *comes to attention, joined by a reluctant* BYRD. *They both salute.* DAVENPORT *returns salute.*

BYRD: I expected more from a white man, Captain.

TAYLOR: Get out of here, before I have you cashiered out of the army, Byrd!

Both men exit quietly, and for a moment TAYLOR *and* DAVENPORT *are quiet.*

TAYLOR: What the hell is the matter with you? You could have charged both of them—Byrd for insubordination—Wilcox, tampering with evidence.

DAVENPORT: Neither charge is murder—you think Wilcox would tell a story like that if he didn't have Hines and Nivens to back it up? (*Slightly tired*) They've got a report.

TAYLOR: So what do you do now?

DAVENPORT: Finish the investigation.

TAYLOR: They're lying, dammit! So is the Colonel! You were ordered to investigate and charge the people responsible—charge them! I'll back you up!

DAVENPORT: I'm not satisfied yet, Captain.

TAYLOR: I am! Dammit!—I wish they'd sent somebody else! I do—you—you're afraid! You thought you'd accuse the Klan, didn't you?—and that would be the end of it, right? Another story of midnight riders for your Negro press! And now it's officers—white men in the army. It's too much for you—what will happen when Captain Davenport comes up for promotion to major if he accuses white officers, right?

DAVENPORT: I'm not afraid of white men, Captain.

TAYLOR: Then why the hell won't you arrest them?

DAVENPORT: Because I do what the facts tell me, Captain—not you!

TAYLOR: You don't know what a fact is, Davenport!

ELLIS *enters suddenly and salutes.*

ELLIS: Begging your pardon, sir.

TAYLOR: What is it, Corporal?

ELLIS: Ah—it's for Captain Davenport—(*To* DAVENPORT) We found Private Wilkie, sir. We haven't located Pfc Peterson yet. Seems him and Private Smalls went out on detail together, and neither one of 'em showed up—but I got a few men from the company lookin' for 'em around the N.C.O. club and in the PX, sir.

DAVENPORT: Where's Wilkie?

ELLIS: He's waiting for you in the barracks, Captain.

DAVENPORT *nods, and* ELLIS *goes out after saluting. The lights come up around* WILKIE, *who is seated in a chair in the barracks reading a Negro newspaper.* DAVENPORT *is thoughtful for a moment.*

TAYLOR: Didn't you question Wilkie and Peterson yesterday? (DAVENPORT *starts out*) Davenport? (DAVENPORT *does not answer*) Don't you ignore me!

DAVENPORT: Get off my back! What I do—how I do it—who I interrogate is my business, Captain! This investigation is mine! (*Holds out the back of his hand, showing* TAYLOR *the color of his skin*) Mine!

TAYLOR: Don't treat me with that kind of contempt—I'm not some red-neck cracker!

DAVENPORT: And I'm not your yessirin' colored boy either!

TAYLOR: I asked you a question!

DAVENPORT: I don't have to answer it!

There is a long silence. The two men glare at one another—TAYLOR *in another time, disturbed.*

TAYLOR: Indeed you don't—*Captain.*

Pause.

DAVENPORT: Now, *Captain*—what if Byrd and Wilcox are telling the truth?

TAYLOR: Neither one of us believes that.

DAVENPORT: What if they are?

TAYLOR: Then who killed the goddamn man?

DAVENPORT: I don't know yet. (*Slight pause*) Is there anything else?

TAYLOR *shakes his head no as* DAVENPORT *starts toward center stage, headed toward* WILKIE.

TAYLOR: No, hotshot. Nothing.

> DAVENPORT *enters the barracks area.* WILKIE *quickly puts his paper aside and snaps to attention and salutes.* DAVENPORT *returns salute but remains silent, going right to the desk and removing his pad and pencil. The light around the office fades out.*

DAVENPORT (*snapping at* WILKIE): When did you lose your stripes? (*He is standing over* WILKIE)

WILKIE: Couple months before they broke up the team—right after Sergeant Waters got assigned to us, sir.

DAVENPORT: Nervous, Wilkie?

WILKIE (*smiles haltingly*): I couldn't figure out why you called me back, sir? (*Laughs nervously*)

DAVENPORT: You lost your stripes for being drunk on duty, is that correct?

WILKIE: Yes, sir.

DAVENPORT: You said Waters busted you, didn't you?

WILKIE: He got me busted—he's the one reported me to the Captain.

DAVENPORT: How did you feel? Must have been awful—(DAVENPORT *paces*) Weren't you and the Sergeant good friends? Didn't you tell me he was all right? A nice guy?

WILKIE: Yes, sir.

DAVENPORT: Would a nice guy have gotten a friend busted?

WILKIE: No, sir.

DAVENPORT: So you lied when you said he was a nice guy, right?

WILKIE: No, sir—I mean—

DAVENPORT: Speak up! Speak up! Was the Sergeant a nice guy or not?

WILKIE: No, sir.

DAVENPORT: Why not? Answer me!

WILKIE: Well, you wouldn't turn somebody in over something like that!

DAVENPORT: Not a good friend, right?

WILKIE: Right, sir—I mean, a friend would give you extra duty—I would have—or even call you a whole buncha' names—you'd expect that, sir—but damn! Three stripes? They took ten years to get in this army, sir! Ten years! I started out with the 24th Infantry—I—

DAVENPORT: Made you mad, didn't it?

WILKIE: Yeah, it made me mad—all the things I did for him!

DAVENPORT (*quickly*): That's right! You were his assistant, weren't you? Took care of the team—(WILKIE *nods*) Ran all his errands, looked at his family snapshots (WILKIE *nods again*), policed his quarters, put the gun under C.J.'s bed—

> WILKIE *looks up suddenly.*

WILKIE: No!

DAVENPORT (*quickly*): It was you Henson saw, wasn't it, Wilkie?

WILKIE: No, sir!

DAVENPORT: Liar! You lied about Waters, and you're lying now! You were the only person out of the barracks that night, and the only one who knew the layout well enough to go straight to C.J.'s bunk! Not even Waters knew the place that well! Henson didn't see who it was, but he saw what the person did—he was positive about that—only you knew the barracks in the dark!

WILKIE (*pleadingly*): It was the Sarge, Captain—he ordered me to do it—he said I'd get my stripes back—he wanted to scare that boy C.J.! Let him stew in jail! Then C.J. hit him—and he had the boy right where he wanted him—(*Confused*) But it backfired—C.J. killed hisself—Sarge didn't figure on that.

DAVENPORT: Why did he pick Memphis?

WILKIE: He despised him, Captain—he'd hide it, 'cause everybody in the company liked that boy so much. But underneath—it was a crazy hate, sir—he'd go cold when he talked about C.J. You could feel it.

In limbo, the blue-gray light rises on C.J. *and* WATERS. C.J. *is humming a blues song and* WATERS *is standing smiling, smoking a pipe as he was in Act One.* WATERS *turns away from* C.J. *His speech takes place over* C.J.'s *humming.*

WATERS: He's the kinda boy seems innocent, Wilkie. Got everybody around the post thinking he's a strong, black buck! Hits home runs—white boys envy his strength—his speed, the power in his swing. Then this colored champion lets those same white boys call him Shine—or Sambo at the Officers Club. They laugh at his blues songs, and he just smiles—can't talk, barely read or write his own name—and don't care! He'll tell you they like him—or that colored folks ain't supposed to have but so much sense. (*Intense*) Do you know the damage one ignorant *Negro* can do? (*Remembering*) We were in France during the First War, Wilkie. We had won decorations, but the white boys had told all the French gals we had tails. And they found this ignorant colored soldier. Paid him to tie a tail to his ass and parade around naked making monkey sounds. (*Shakes his head*) They sat him on a big, round table in the Café Napoleon, put a reed in his hand, a crown on his head, a blanket on his shoulders, and made him eat bananas in front of them Frenchies. And ohhh, the white boys danced that night—passed out leaflets with that boy's picture on them—called him Moonshine, King of the Monkeys. And when we slit his throat, you know that fool asked us what he had done wrong? (*Pause*) My daddy told me, we got to turn our backs on his kind, Wilkie. Close our ranks to the chittlin's, the collard greens—the corn-bread style. We are men—soldiers, and I don't intend to have our race cheated out of its place of honor and respect in this war because of fools like C.J.! You watch everything he does—*everything!*

Light fades slowly around WATERS *and* C.J., *and as it does,* C.J. *stops humming.*

WILKIE: And I watched him, sir—but Waters—he couldn't wait! He wouldn't talk about nothin' else—it was C.J. this—C.J. all the time!

DAVENPORT (*troubled*): Why didn't he pick Peterson—they fought—

WILKIE: They fought all the time, sir—but the Sarge, he likes Peterson. (*Nods*) Peterson fought back, and Waters admired that. He promoted Pete! Imagine that—he thought Peterson would make a fine soldier!

DAVENPORT: What was Peterson's reaction—when C.J. died?

WILKIE: Like everybody else, he was sad—he put together that protest that broke up the team, but afta' that he didn' say much. And he usually runs off at the mouth. Kept to himself—or with Smalls.

Slight pause.

DAVENPORT: The night Waters was killed, what time did you get in?
WILKIE: Around nine forty-five—couple of us came from the club and listened to the radio awhile—I played some checkers, then I went to bed. Sir? I didn't mean to do what I did—it wasn't my fault—he promised me my stripes!

Suddenly, out of nowhere, in the near distance, is the sound of gunfire, a bugle blaring, something like a cannon going off. The noise is continuous through scene. DAVENPORT *rises, startled.*

DAVENPORT: I'm placing you under arrest, Private!

ELLIS *bursts into the room.*

ELLIS: Did you hear, sir? (DAVENPORT, *surprised, shakes his head no*) Our orders! They came down from Washington, Captain! We're shippin' out! They finally gonna let us Negroes fight!

DAVENPORT *is immediately elated, and almost forgets* WILKIE *as he shakes* ELLIS's *hand.*

DAVENPORT: Axis ain't got a chance!
ELLIS: Surrrre—we'll win this mother in six months now! Afta' what Jesse Owens did to them people? Joe Louis?

HENSON *bursts in.*

HENSON: Did y'all hear it? Forty-eight-hour standby alert? We goin' into combat! (*Loud*) Look out, Hitler, the niggahs is comin' to git your ass through the fog!
ELLIS: With real rifles—it's really O.K., you know?
HENSON: They tell me them girls in England—woooow!

DAVENPORT *faces* WILKIE *as* COBB *enters, yelling.*

COBB: They gonna let us git in it! We may lay so much smoke the Germans may never get to see what a colored soldier looks like 'til the war's over! (*To* HENSON) I wrote my woman jes' the otha' day that we'd be goin' soon!
ELLIS: Go on!
HENSON (*overlapping*): Man, you ain't nothin'!

DAVENPORT *begins to move* WILKIE *toward* ELLIS.

HENSON: If the army said we was all discharged, you'd claim you wrote that! (*He quiets, watching* DAVENPORT)

COBB (*quickly*): You hea' this fool, sir?

HENSON: Shhhhh!

DAVENPORT (*To* ELLIS): Corporal, escort Private Wilkie to the stockade.

ELLIS (*surprised*): Yes, sir!

ELLIS *starts* WILKIE *out, even though he is bewildered by it. They exit.*

HENSON: Wilkie's under arrest, sir? (DAVENPORT *nods*) How come? I apologize, sir— I didn't mean that.

DAVENPORT: Do either of you know where Smalls and Peterson can be located?

HENSON *shrugs.*

COBB: Your men got Smalls in the stockade, sir!

DAVENPORT: When?

COBB: I saw two colored M.P.'s takin' him through the main gate. Jes' a while ago— I was on my way ova' hea'!

DAVENPORT *goes to the desk and picks up his things and starts out.*

COBB: Tenn-hut.

DAVENPORT *stops and salutes.*

DAVENPORT: As you were. By the way—congratulations!

DAVENPORT *exits the barracks through the doorway.*

HENSON: Lookout, Hitler!

COBB: The niggahs is coming to get yo' ass.

HENSON AND COBB: Through the fog.

The lights in the barracks go down at once. Simultaneously, they rise in limbo, where SMALLS *is pacing back and forth. He is smoking a cigarette. There is a bunk, and the shadow of a screen over his cell. In the background, the sounds of celebration continue.* DAVENPORT *emerges from the right, and begins to speak immediately as the noises of celebration fade.*

DAVENPORT: Why'd you go AWOL, soldier?

SMALLS *faces him, unable to see* DAVENPORT *at first. When he sees him, he snaps to attention and salutes.*

SMALLS: Private Anthony Smalls, sir!

DAVENPORT: At ease—answer my question!

SMALLS: I didn't go AWOL, sir—I—I got drunk in Tynin and fell asleep in the bus depot—it was the only public place I could find to sleep it off.

DAVENPORT: Where'd you get drunk? Where in Tynin?

SMALLS: Jake's—Jake's and Lilly's Golden Slipper—on Melville Street—

DAVENPORT: Weren't you and Peterson supposed to be on detail? (SMALLS *nods*) Where was Peterson? Speak up!

SMALLS: I don't know, sir!

DAVENPORT: You're lying! You just walked off your detail and Peterson did nothing?

SMALLS: No, sir—he warned me, sir—"Listen, Smalls!" he said—

DAVENPORT (*cutting him off*): You trying to make a fool of me, Smalls? Huh? (*Loud*) Are you?

SMALLS: No, sir!

DAVENPORT: The two of you went A-W-O-L together, didn't you? (SMALLS *is quiet*) Answer me!

SMALLS: Yes!

DAVENPORT: You left together because Peterson knew I would find out the two of you killed Waters, didn' you? (SMALLS *suddenly bursts into quiet tears, shaking his head*) What? I can't hear you! (SMALLS *is sobbing*) You killed Waters, didn't you? I want an answer!

SMALLS: I can't sleep—I can't sleep!

DAVENPORT: Did you kill Sergeant Waters?

SMALLS: It was Peterson, sir! (*As if he can see it*) I watched! It wasn't me!

The blue-gray light builds in center stage. As it does, SERGEANT WATERS staggers forward and falls on his knees. He can't get up, he is drunk. He has been beaten, and looks the way we saw him in the opening of Act One.

SMALLS: We were changing the guard.

WATERS: Can't be trusted—no matter what we do, there are no guarantees—and your mind won't let you forget it. (*Shakes his head repeatedly*) No, no, no!

SMALLS (*overlapping*): On our way back to the Captain's office—and Sarge, he was on the road. We just walked into him! He was ranting, and acting crazy, sir!

PETERSON emerges from the right. He is dressed in a long coat, pistol belt and pistol, rifle, helmet, his pants bloused over his boots. He sees WATERS and smiles. WATERS continues to babble.

PETERSON: Smalls, look who's drunk on his ass, boy! (*He begins to circle WATERS*)

SMALLS (*to DAVENPORT*): I told him to forget Waters!

PETERSON: Noooo! I'm gonna' enjoy this, Smalls—big, bad Sergeant Waters down on his knees? No, sah—I'm gonna' love this! (*Leans over WATERS*) Hey, Sarge—need some help? (WATERS *looks up; almost smiles. He reaches for PETERSON, who pushes him back down*) That's the kinda help I'll give yah, boy! Let me help you again—all right? (*Kicks WATERS*) Like that, Sarge? Huh? Like that, dog?

SMALLS (*shouts*): Peterson!

PETERSON: No! (*Almost pleading*) Smalls—some people, man— If this was a German, would you kill it? If it was Hitler—or that fuckin' Tojo? Would you kill him? (*Kicks* WATERS *again*)

WATERS (*mumbling throughout*): There's a trick to it, Peterson—it's the only way you can win—C.J. could never make it—he was a clown! (*Grabs at* PETERSON) A clown in blackface! A niggah!

PETERSON *steps out of reach. He is suddenly expressionless as he easily removes his pistol from his holster.*

WATERS: You got to be like them! And I was! I was—but the rules are fixed. (*Whispers*) Shhhh! Listen. It's C.J.—(*Laughs*) I made him do it, but it doesn't make any difference! They still hate you! (*Looks at* PETERSON, *who has moved closer to him*) They still hate you! (WATERS *laughs*)

PETERSON (*to* SMALLS): Justice, Smalls. (*He raises the pistol*)

DAVENPORT (*suddenly, harshly*): That isn't justice!

SMALLS *almost recoils.*

PETERSON (*simultaneously, continuing*): For C.J.! Everybody!

PETERSON *fires the gun at* WATERS's *chest, and the shot stops everything. The celebration noise stops. Even* DAVENPORT *in his way seems to hear it.* PETERSON *fires again. There is a moment of quiet on stage.* DAVENPORT *is angered and troubled.*

DAVENPORT: You call that justice?

SMALLS: No, sir.

DAVENPORT (*enraged*): Then why the fuck didn't you do something?

SMALLS: I'm scared of Peterson—just scared of him!

PETERSON *has been looking at* WATERS's *body throughout. He now begins to lift* WATERS *as best he can, and pull him off-stage. It is done with some difficulty.*

SMALLS: I tried to get him to go, sir, but he wanted to drag the Sergeant's body back into the woods—

Light fades quickly around PETERSON, *as* DAVENPORT *paces.*

SMALLS: Said everybody would think white people did it.

DAVENPORT (*somewhat drained*): Then what happened?

SMALLS: I got sick, sir—and Peterson, when he got done, he helped me back to the barracks and told me to keep quiet. (*Slight pause*) I'm sorry, sir.

There is a long pause, during which DAVENPORT *stares at* SMALLS *with disgust, then abruptly starts out without saluting. He almost flees.* SMALLS *rises quickly.*

SMALLS: Sir?

DAVENPORT *turns around.* SMALLS *comes to attention and salutes.* DAVENPORT *returns salute and starts out of the cell and down toward center stage. He is thoughtful as the light fades around* SMALLS. DAVENPORT *removes his glasses and begins to clean them as he speaks.*

DAVENPORT: Peterson was apprehended a week later in Alabama. Colonel Nivens called it "just another black mess of cuttin', slashin', and shootin'!" He was delighted there were no white officers mixed up in it, and his report to Washington characterized the events surrounding Waters's murder as "the usual, common violence any commander faces in Negro Military units." It was the kind of "mess" that turns up on page 3 in the colored papers—the Cain and Abel story of the week—the headline we Negroes can't quite read in comfort. (*Shakes head and paces*) For me? Two colored soldiers are dead—two on their way to prison. Four less men to fight with—and none of their reasons—nothing anyone said, or did, would have been worth a life to men with larger hearts—men less split by the madness of race in America. (*Pause*) The case got little attention. The details were filed in my report and I was quickly and rather unceremoniously ordered back to my M.P. unit. (*Smiles*) A style of guitar pickin' and a dance called the C.J. caught on for a while in Tynin saloons during 1945. (*Slight pause*) In northern New Jersey, through a military foul-up, Sergeant Waters's family was informed that he had been killed in action. The Sergeant was, therefore, thought and unofficially rumored to have been the first colored casualty of the war from that county and under the circumstances was declared a hero. Nothing could be done officially, but his picture was hung on a Wall of Honor in the Dorie Miller VFW Post #978. (*Pause*) The men of the 221st Chemical Smoke Generating Company? The entire outfit—officers and enlisted men—was wiped out in the Ruhr Valley during a German advance. (*He turns toward* TAYLOR, *who enters quietly*) Captain?
TAYLOR: Davenport—I see you got your man.
DAVENPORT: I got him—what is it, Captain?
TAYLOR: Will you accept my saying, you did a splendid job?
DAVENPORT: I'll take the praise—but how did I manage it?
TAYLOR: Dammit, Davenport—I didn't come here to be made fun of—(*Slight pause*) The men—the regiment—we all ship out for Europe tomorrow, and (*hesitates*) I was wrong, Davenport—about the bars—the uniform—about Negroes being in charge. (*Slight pause*) I guess I'll have to get used to it.
DAVENPORT: Oh, you'll get used to it—you can bet your ass on that. Captain—you will get used to it.

Lights begin to fade slowly as the music "Don't Sit under the Apple Tree" rises in the background, and the house goes to black.

—1981

Part
III

How do we resist gender norms and beliefs? What new genders and new gender relations do writers imagine in place of the old?

RESISTING

Gender **ideology**, like any system of cultural belief, is not entirely neat and tidy. It cannot account for all the possibilities of gendered behavior and interaction. In fact, gender resistance is as much a part of the gender system as gender normativity. The critique and revision of gender ideologies goes on continuously, if unevenly, in everyday life; even as we adhere in some instances to normative gender roles, we may diverge from accepted roles in the next instance. Despite the severe social prohibitions against questioning gender difference, you probably can recall occasions and situations in which you found gender ideologies too constricting, when as a girl you wanted to put on pads and play tackle football or perhaps as a boy when you didn't but weren't allowed the choice not to play.

Have you ever considered that biology cannot account for the fact that in the United States more girls than boys desire ballet training, or that the growing numbers of women in medical school probably has less to do with a basic shift in women's brain capacity than with expansion of educational opportunities for women? Have you ever wondered why it is so often expected that men pay for romantic outings with women, even when the men may not earn more than the women? The selections assembled in this last section all question the assumptions of gender ideologies. As you will see, once the questions are cast, the answers typically implicate deep structures of society not immediately connected to gender (such as economy, language, race, and law) that are beyond the scope of any individual to address adequately.

Dissatisfaction with gender can occur on the level of the individual who questions the roles in which he is cast by the institutions of gender. For instance, Sharon Olds quietly critiques the distortions of gender produced by the Hollywood star industry in "The Death of Marilyn Monroe," which presents a portrait of the woman behind the international sex symbol. Edna St. Vincent Millay's seemingly more docile adaptation of the sonnet, the traditional form of love poetry, is a strong critique of a male-dominated cultural legacy. With "Phantasia for Elvira Shatayev," Adrienne Rich transforms both the form and force of the traditional elegy for the dead, while Olga Broumas revises familiar fairy tales in accordance with modern feminist principles. In jazz-inflected yet tightly controlled verse, Michael Harper meditates on the limiting roles allowed to fatherhood in "Nightmare Begins Responsibility." As the title might suggest, David Mura's "Notes on Pornography Abandoned" narrates one character's struggle for a personal ethics about gender and power.

While many of the pieces in this section rebel in some way against gender norms, some show how a self-conscious use of those very norms can be a form of rebellion as well. Of these, Susan Glaspell's play *Trifles* demonstrates how one woman is able to manipulate potentially debilitating patriarchal assumptions about women's nature to her own defense, getting away with murder, or so it seems. Her use of foreshadowing is matched only by Charlotte Perkins Gilman's "The Yellow Wall-Paper," where the unsavory color and condition of the narrator's new bedroom predicts the less than sanitary effect of the "rest cure" ordered by John, her doctor and husband, for her nervous condition.

The romance **narrative**, that most powerful and recognizable pattern of human expectation—boy meets girl, boy loses girl, boy gets girl back, boy and girl live happily ever after—serves as a template to be revised for some authors or, for others, to be completely rejected and replaced by alternative kinds of relationships. Ernest Hemingway's "The Sea Change" revises the heterosexual romance by exploring the exciting and yet destructive effects of the loosening of gendered roles. Rebecca Brown disturbs her reader by pointedly refusing gendered pronouns in her bitter love story, "Forgiveness," while Matthew Stadler's "Love Problem" asks us to disconnect sex, gender, and sexuality in ways that seem initially beyond imagining. Finally, in science fiction, we encounter a **genre** in which radical revisions of all the institutions of earth life are the norm. Both Octavia Butler's "Bloodchild" and Joanna Russ's "When It Changed" construct cultures whose histories and biological arrangements defy the sex/gender system, thereby providing exciting new questions about bodies, human capacity, and the ideals of masculine and feminine. At the same time, Ursula Le Guin's "Sur" takes us back in time to imagine a different kind of history, one in which women explorers make a pact with nature to preserve the earth.

In a number of the texts included here, resistance is coded along lines that intersect with other kinds of social **hierarchy**, and in ways that privilege direct and at times untidy emotion. In Audre Lorde's "Eulogy for Alvin Frost," the poet takes aim at the landscape of human waste she sees around her, forcefully lamenting the early deaths of black men. Like Dorothy Allison's "The Women Who Hate Me," Lorde's poem grieves the absence of justice, hoping to find in the emotion of anger the energy and power to change the world. In a very different way, Michael Lassell's "How to watch your brother die" also grieves, but here its focus on loss is not simply for those who have died, but for the living—characterized by the bemused, unsure but surviving brother—who cannot fully feel their relationship to others.

All of us have resisted at one time or another gendered ideologies, depending on our different levels of comfort and pain with the norms of gender. As the selections in this section demonstrate, resistance takes many forms. While some of us will feel pushed to imagine whole new worlds, others might only manage more partial and we might even say more timid interventions into the assumptions and practices that underlie gender norms and ideals. What matters for the **critical thinker** is not the mere fact of resistance, but the way that such resistance demonstrates once again the centrality of gender to our everyday lives, social relations, and personal identities.

POETRY

DOROTHY ALLISON

B. 1949

Dorothy Allison was born in Greenville, South Carolina, and has lived in Florida, Washington, D.C., and New York City, where she pursued a degree in anthropology at The New School. Her first book, a collection of poetry called The Women Who Hate Me, *was published in 1983, followed by* Trash, *a collection of short fiction, in 1988. Her novel,* Bastard Out of Carolina *(1992), received wide critical attention and was made into a TV movie in 1996. Because of her straightforward portrayals of lesbian sex and the violence of incest, Allison has been a focus of debate among feminists, religious conservatives, and anti-pornography groups. Her 1994 collection of essays,* Skin, *offers polemics on sexual politics, class, and the publishing industry. Her most recent novel is* Cave Dweller *(1997).*

The Women Who Hate Me

1

The women who do not know me.

The women who, not knowing me, hate me
mark my life, rise in my dreams and shake their loose hair
throw out their thin wrists, narrow their already sharp eyes
say   "Who do you think you are?"

"Lazy, useless, cuntsucking, scared, stupid
What you scared of anyway?"
Their eyes, their hands, their voices
Terrifying.

The women who hate me cut me
as men can't.   Men don't count.
I can handle men. Never expected better
of any man   anyway.
                                    But the women,
shallow-cheeked young girls the world was made for
safe little girls who think nothing of bravado
who never got over by playing it tough.

What do they know of my fear?

What do they know of the women in my body?
My weakening hips, sharp good teeth
angry nightmares, scarred cheeks,
fat thighs, fat everything.

"Don't smile too wide. You look like a fool."
"Don't want too much. You an't gonna get it."
An't   gonna   get   it.
Goddamn.

Say Goddamn and kick somebody's ass
that I am not even half what I should be,
full of terrified angry bravado
                                    BRAVADO.

The women who hate me
don't know
can't imagine
life-saving, precious bravado.

2

God on their right shoulder
righteousness on their left,
the women who hate me never use words
like hate,   speak instead of nature
of the spirit not housed in the flesh
as if my body, a temple of sin,
didn't mirror their own.

Their measured careful words echo
earlier coarser stuff,   say

"What do you think you're doing?"
"Who do you think you are?"

"Whitetrash
no-count
bastard
mean-eyed
garbage-mouth
cuntsucker
cuntsucker
no good to anybody, never did diddlyshit anyway."

"You figured out yet who you an't gonna be?"

The women who hate me hate
their insistent desires, their fat lusts
swallowed and hidden, disciplined to nothing
narrowed to bone and dry hot dreams.
The women who hate me deny
hunger and appetite,
the cream delight
of a scream
that arches the thighs and fills
the mouth with singing.

3

Something hides here
a secret thing shameful and complicated.
Something hides in a tight mouth
a life too easily rendered
a childhood of inappropriate longing
girl's desire to grow into a man
a boyish desire to stretch and sweat

Every three years I discover again
that   No   I knew nothing before.
Everything must be dragged out,
looked over again. The unexamined life
is the lie, but still
must I every time deny
everything I knew before?

<h1 style="text-align:center">4</h1>

My older sister tells me flatly
she don't care who I take to my bed
what I do there.   Tells me finally
she sees no difference between
her husbands, my lovers. Behind it all
we are too much the same to deny.

My little sister thinks my older crazy
thinks me sick
more shameful to be queer than crazy
as if her years hustling ass,
her pitiful junky whiteboy
saved through methadone and marriage, all that
asslicking interspersed with asskicking
all those pragmatic family skills we share mean nothing
measured against the little difference
of who and what I am.

My little sister too
is one of the women who hate me.

<h1 style="text-align:center">5</h1>

I measure it differently, what's shared,
what's denied, what no one wants recognized.
My first lover's skill at mystery,
how one day she was there, the next gone;
the woman with whom I lived for eight years
but slept with less than one;
the lover who tied me to the foot of her bed
when I didn't really want that
but didn't really know
what else I could get.

What else can I get?
Must I rewrite my life
edit it down to a parable where everything
turns out for the best?

But then what would I do with the lovers
too powerful to disappear,   the women
too hard to melt to soft stuff?
Now that I know that soft stuff
was never where I wanted to put my hand.

6

The women who hate me
hate too my older sister
with her many children, her weakness for
good whiskey, country music, bad men.
She says the thing "women's lib" has given her
is a sense she don't have to stay too long
though she does
still she does
much too long.

7

I am not so sure anymore of the difference.
I do not believe anymore in the natural superiority
of the lesbian, the difference between my sisters and me.

Fact is, for all I tell my sisters
I turned out terrific at it myself:
sucking cunt, stroking ego, provoking
manipulating, comforting and keeping.
Plotting my life around mothering
other women's desperation
the way my sisters
build their lives
around their men.
Til I found myself   sitting at the kitchen table
shattered glass, blood in my lap and her
the good one with her stern insistence
just standing there wanting me
to explain it to her,   save her from being
alone with herself.

Or that other one
another baby-butch wounded girl
                    How can any of us forget how wounded
                    any of us   have to be   to get that hard?
Never to forget that working class says nothing
does not say who she was   how she was
fucking me helpless.   Her hand on my arm
raising lust to my throat,   that lust
everyone says does not happen

though it goes on happening
all the time.

How can I speak of her, us together?
Her touch drawing heat from my crotch to my face
her face, terrifying, wonderful.
Me saying, *"Yeah, goddamn it, yeah,*
put it to me, ease me, fuck me, anything . . ."
til the one thing I refused
then back up against a wall
her rage ugly in the muscles of her neck
her fist swinging up to make a wind,
a wind blowing back to my mama's cheek
past my stepfather's arm

I ask myself over and over how I
came to be standing in such a wind?
How I came to be held up like my mama
with my jeans, my shoes locked in a drawer
and the woman I loved breathing on me
    "You bitch.   You damned fool."

    "You want to try it?"
    "You want to walk to Brooklyn
       barefooted?"
    "You want to try it
       mothernaked?"

Which meant,   of course,   I had to decide
how naked   I was willing to go   where.

Do I forget all that?
Deny all that?
Pretend I am not
my mama's daughter
my sisters' mirror.
Pretend I have not
at least as much lust
in my life   as pain?

Where then will I find the country
where women never wrong women
where we will sit knee to knee
finally listening
to the whole
naked truth
of our lives?

                 —1983

OLGA BROUMAS

B. 1949

Olga Broumas was born in Syros, Greece, and has lived in the United States since 1967. Her first book of poetry, Beginning With O, *received the prestigious 1977 Yale Younger Poets Award. A collection of highly lyrical poems, this volume melded lesbian erotics with overt feminist political intention and received special acclaim for its poetic revisions of familiar fairy tales and ancient myths. Subsequent publications continued to rework classical mythology for contemporary situations, as in* Perpetua *(1989) and* Ithaca—Little Summer in Winter *(1996). Her other volumes include* Caritas *(1976),* Soie Savage *(1979), and* Pastoral Jazz *(1983). She currently lives and writes in Provincetown, Massachusetts.*

LITTLE RED RIDING HOOD

I grow old, old
without you, Mother, landscape
of my heart. No child, no daughter between my bones
has moved, and passed
out screaming, dressed in her mantle of blood

as I did
once through your pelvic scaffold, stretching it
like a wishbone, your tenderest skin
strung on its bow and tightened
against the pain. I slipped out like an arrow, but not before

the midwife
plunged to her wrist and guided
my baffled head to its first mark. High forceps
might, in that one instant, have accomplished
what you and that good woman failed
in all these years to do: cramp
me between the temples, hobble
my baby feet. Dressed in my red hood, howling, I went—

evading
the white-clad doctor and his fancy claims: microscope,
stethoscope, scalpel, all
the better to see with, to hear,
and to eat—straight from your hollowed basket
into the midwife's skirts. I grew up

good at evading, and when you said,
"Stick to the road and forget the flowers, there's
wolves in those bushes, mind
where you got to go, mind
you get there," I
minded. I kept

to the road, kept
the hood secret, kept what it sheathed more
secret still. I opened
it only at night, and with other women
who might be walking the same road to their own
grandma's house, each with her basket of gifts, her small hood
safe in the same part. I minded well. I have no daughter

to trace that road, back to your lap with my laden
basket of love. I'm growing
old, old
without you. Mother, landscape
of my heart, architect of my body, what other gesture
can I conceive

to make with it
that would reach you, alone
in your house and waiting, across this improbable forest
peopled with wolves and our lost, flower-gathering
sisters they feed on.

—1977

RITA DOVE

B. 1952

Rita Dove was born in Akron, Ohio, and educated at Miami University of Ohio, Universität Tübingen in Germany, and the University of Iowa. She has published the poetry collections The Yellow House on the Corner *(1980),* Museum *(1983),* Thomas and Beulah *(1986),* Grace Notes *(1989),* Selected Poems *(1993), and* Mother Love *(1995), along with a book of short stories,* Fifth Sunday *(1985); a novel,* Through the Ivory Gate *(1992); a collection of essays,* The Poet's World *(1995); and a verse drama,* The Darker Face of the Earth *(1994). She has received numerous literary and academic honors, among them the 1987 Pulitzer Prize in poetry. From 1993 to 1995 she served as Poet Laureate of the United States and Consultant in Poetry to the Library of Congress. She is Commonwealth Professor of English at the University of Virginia in Charlottesville.*

THE GREAT PALACES OF VERSAILLES

Nothing nastier than a white person!
She mutters as she irons alterations
in the backroom of Charlotte's Dress Shoppe.
The steam rising from a cranberry wool
comes alive with perspiration
and stale Evening of Paris.
Swamp she born from, swamp
she swallow, swamp she got to sink again.

The iron shoves gently
into a gusset, waits until
the puckers bloom away. Beyond
the curtain,
the white girls are all
wearing shoulder pads to make their faces
delicate. That laugh would be Autumn,
tossing her hair in imitation of Bacall.

Beulah had read in the library
how French ladies at court would tuck
their fans in a sleeve
and walk in the gardens for air. Swaying
among lilies, lifting shy layers of silk,
they dropped excrement as daintily
as handkerchieves. Against all rules

she had saved the lining from a botched coat
to face last year's gray skirt. She knows
whenever she lifts a knee
she flashes crimson. That seems legitimate;
but in the book she had read
how the *cavaliere* amused themselves
wearing powder and perfume and spraying
yellow borders knee-high on the stucco
of the *Orangerie.*

A hanger clatters
in the front of the shoppe.
Beulah remembers how
even Autumn could lean into a settee
with her ankles crossed, sighing
I need a man who'll protect me
while smoking her cigarette down to the very end.

—1986

MICHAEL HARPER

B. 1938

Michael Harper was born and raised in New York. He has taught at Brown University since 1970 and was the first Poet Laureate of the state of Rhode Island, from 1988 to 1993. Harper has published ten books of poetry, including Dear John, Dear Coltrane *(1970) and* Images of Kin, New and Selected Poems *(1977), both nominated for the National Book Award. His most recent book of poems is* Honorable Amendments *(1995). Harper is also an editor, most recently of* Every Shut Eye Ain't Asleep, *an anthology of poetry by African Americans since 1945. In 1995, he was elected to the American Academy of Arts and Science.*

NIGHTMARE BEGINS RESPONSIBILITY

I place these numbed wrists to the pane
watching white uniforms whisk over
him in the tube-kept
prison
fear what they will do in experiment
watch my gloved stickshifting gasolined hands
breathe *boxcar-information-please* infirmary tubes
distrusting white-pink mending paperthin
silkened end hairs, distrusting tubes
shrunk in his *trunk-skincapped*
shaven head, in thighs
distrusting-white-hands-picking-baboon-light
on this son who will not make his second night
of this wardstrewn intensive airpocket
where his father's asthmatic
hymns of *night-train,* train done gone
his mother can only know that he has flown
up into essential calm unseen corridor
going boxscarred home, *mamaborn, sweetsonchild
gonedowntown* into *researchtestingwarehousebatteryacid
mama-son-done-gone*/me telling her 'nother
train tonight, no music, no breathstroked
heartbeat in my infinite distrust of them:

and of my distrusting self
white-doctor-who-breathed-for-him-all-night
say it for two sons gone,
say nightmare, say it loud
panebreaking heartmadness:
nightmare begins responsibility.

—1977

MICHAEL LASSELL

B. 1947

Michael Lassell was born in New York City. Educated at Colgate University, California Institute of Arts, and the Yale School of Drama, Lassell has been a culture and arts critic in Los Angeles and presently is managing editor of Interview, *a New York City publication specializing in culture and style. His book,* Poems for Lost and Unlost Boys, *received the Amelia Chapbook Award for 1985, while his novel,* Decade Dance, *won the Lambda Literary Award for 1990. His most recent novel,* The Hard Way, *appeared in 1995. Along with Lawrence Schimel, he has edited a collection,* Two Hearts Desire: Gay Couples and Their Love. *His poetry has appeared in many journals and in collections. The piece selected here explores the ways in which heterosexual masculinity defends itself against the emotional connections and affections of brotherhood.*

HOW TO WATCH YOUR BROTHER DIE

For Carl Morse

When the call comes, be calm.
Say to your wife, "My brother is dying. I have to fly
to California."
Try not to be shocked that he already looks like
a cadaver.
Say to the young man sitting by your brother's side,
"I'm his brother."
Try not to be shocked when the young man says,
"I'm his lover. Thanks for coming."

Listen to the doctor with a steel face on.
Sign the necessary forms.
Tell the doctor you will take care of everything.
Wonder why doctors are so remote.

Watch the lover's eyes as they stare into
your brother's eyes as they stare into
space.
Wonder what they see there.
Remember the time he was jealous and
opened your eyebrow with a sharp stick.
Forgive him out loud
even if he can't
understand you.
Realize the scar will be
all that's left of him.

Over coffee in the hospital cafeteria
say to the lover, "You're an extremely good-looking
young man."
Hear him say,
"I never thought I was good enough looking to
deserve your brother."

Watch the tears well up in his eyes. Say,
"I'm sorry. I don't know what it means to be
the lover of another man."
Hear him say,
"It's just like a wife, only the commitment is
deeper because the odds against you are so much
greater."
Say nothing, but
take his hand like a brother's.

Drive to Mexico for unproven drugs that might
help him live longer.
Explain what they are to the border guard.
Fill with rage when he informs you,
"You can't bring those across."
Begin to grow loud.
Feel the lover's hand on your arm
restraining you. See in the guard's eye
how much a man can hate another man.
Say to the lover, "How can you stand it?"
Hear him say, "You get used to it."
Think of one of your children getting used to
another man's hatred.

Call your wife on the telephone. Tell her,
"He hasn't much time.
I'll be home soon." Before you hang up say,
"How could anyone's commitment be deeper than
a husband and wife?" Hear her say,
"Please. I don't want to know all the details."

When he slips into an irrevocable coma,
hold his lover in your arms while he sobs,
no longer strong. Wonder how much longer
you will be able to be strong.
Feel how it feels to hold a man in your arms
whose arms are used to holding men.
Offer God anything to bring your brother back.
Know you have nothing God could possibly want.

Curse God, but do not
abandon Him.

Stare at the face of the funeral director
when he tells you he will not
embalm the body for fear of
contamination. Let him see in your eyes
how much a man can hate another man.

Stand beside a casket covered in flowers,
white flowers. Say,
"Thank you for coming," to each of several hundred
    men
who file past in tears, some of them
holding hands. Know that your brother's life
was not what you imagined. Overhear two
mourners say, "I wonder who'll be next?" and
"I don't care anymore,
as long as it isn't you."

Arrange to take an early flight home.
His lover will drive you to the airport.
When your flight is announced say,
awkwardly, "If I can do anything, please
let me know." Do not flinch when he says,
"Forgive yourself for not wanting to know him
after he told you. He did."
Stop and let it soak in. Say,
"He forgave me, or he knew himself?"
"Both," the lover will say, not knowing what else
to do. Hold him like a brother while he
kisses you on the cheek. Think that
you haven't been kissed by a man since
your father died. Think,
"This is no moment not to be strong."

Fly first class and drink Scotch. Stroke
your split eyebrow with a finger and
think of your brother alive. Smile
at the memory and think
how your children will feel in your arms,
warm and friendly and without challenge.

                      —1990

AUDRE LORDE

1934-1992

Audre Lorde was born in New York City, where she lived, wrote, and taught her entire life. Since the 1970s, Lorde has been the most influential black lesbian-feminist voice in the United States. Her literary works include From a Land Where Other People Live *(1973),* The Black Unicorn *(1978),* Our Dead Behind Us *(1986), and the collection* Undersong: Chosen Poems, Old and New *(1992). In 1982, she published her "mytho-biography,"* Zami: A New Spelling of My Name *(1982), and two years later a collection of critical writings on race, sexuality, gender, and power called* Sister Outsider: Essays and Speeches *(1984). Her powerful text* The Cancer Journals *(1980) chronicles her struggle with breast cancer.*

EULOGY FOR ALVIN FROST

I.

Black men bleeding to death inside themselves
inside their fine strong bodies
inside their stomachs
inside their heads
a hole
as large as a dum-dum bullet
eaten away from the inside
death at 37.

Windows are holes to let in the light
in Newark airport at dawn I read
of your death by illumination
the carpets are dark and the windows are smoky
to keep out the coming sun
I plummet down through a hole in the carpet
seeking immediate ground for my feet to embrace
my toes have no wisdom no strength
to resist
they curl in a spasm of grief
of fury uprooted
It is dawn in the airport and nothing is open
I cannot even plant you a tree
the earth is still frozen
I write a card saying
machines grew the flowers I send
to throw into your grave.

On occasion we passed in the hallway
usually silent and hurried but fighting
on the same side.
You congratulate me on my latest book
in a Black Caucus meeting
you are distinguished
by your genuine laughter
and you might have been my long lost
second grade seat-mate named Alvin
grown into some other magic
but we never had time enough
just to talk.

II.

From an airplane heading south
the earth grows slowly greener
we pass the first swimming pool
filled with blue water
this winter is almost over
I don't want to write a natural poem
I want to write about the unnatural death
of a young man at 37
eating himself for courage in secret
until he vanished
bleeding to death inside.
He will be eulogized in echoes
by a ghost of these winters
that haunt morning people
wearing away our days like smiling water
in southern pools
leaving psychic graffiti
clogging the walls of our hearts
carving out ulcers inside our stomachs
from which we explode
or bleed to death.

III.

The day after your burial
John Wade slid off his chair
onto the carpet in the student cafeteria
and died there on the floor
between Abnormal Psychology and a half-finished
cup of black coffee.
Cafeteria guards rushed him out
the back door between classes

and we never knew until a week later
that he had even been ill.

I am tired of writing memorials to black men
whom I was on the brink of knowing
weary like fig trees
weighted like a crepe myrtle
with all the black substance poured into earth
before earth is ready to bear.
I am tired of holy deaths
of the ulcerous illuminations the cerebral accidents
the psychology of the oppressed
where mental health is the ability
to repress
knowledge of the world's cruelty.

IV.

Dear Danny who does not know me
I am
writing to you for your father
whom I barely knew
except at meetings where he was
distinguished
by his genuine laughter
and his kind bright words
Danny son of Alvin
please cry
whenever it hurts
remember to laugh
even when you do battle
stay away from coffee and fried plastic
even when it looks like chicken
and grow up
black and strong and beautiful
but not too soon.

We need you
and there are so few
left.

                                        —1978

Edna St. Vincent Millay
1892-1950

Edna St. Vincent Millay was born in Rockland, Maine, and educated at Vassar College for women. Taught to write verse at age four by her mother, Millay achieved a wide popularity by the time she was 20 years old. Working within the constraints of a traditional verse form, Millay nevertheless epitomized the new sexual freedom of the bohemians in New York's Greenwich Village. Her works of poetry include Renascence, and Other Poems *(1912),* A Few Figs and Thistles: Poems and Four Sonnets *(1920), and* Huntsman, What Quarry? *(1939). She has a collection of plays called simply* Three Plays *(1926) and a book of prose sketches,* Distressing Dialogues, *published under a pseudonym in 1924. She received the Pulitzer Prize in poetry in 1923.*

I Too Beneath Your Moon, Almighty Sex

I too beneath your moon, almighty Sex,
Go forth at nightfall crying like a cat,
Leaving the lofty tower I laboured at
For birds to foul and boys and girls to vex
With tittering chalk; and you, and the long necks
Of neighbours sitting where their mothers sat
Are well aware of shadowy this and that
In me, that's neither noble nor complex.
Such as I am, however, I have brought
To what it is, this tower; it is my own;
Though it was reared To Beauty, it was wrought
From what I had to build with: honest bone
Is there, and anguish; pride; and burning thought;
And lust is there, and nights not spent alone.

—1939

DAVID MURA

David Mura has taught at the University of Minnesota, the Loft, St. Olaf's College, and the University of Oregon. He is artistic director of the Asian American Renaissance, a multidisciplinary educational group that promotes pan-Asian culture and arts. His books include A Male Grief: Notes on Pornography and Addiction *(1987),* After We Lost Our Way *(1989),* Turning Japanese: Memoirs of a Sansei *(1991),* The Colors of Desire *(1995), and* Where the Body Meets Memory: An Odyssey of Race, Sexuality, and Identity *(1995). Many of his poems meditate on issues of personal responsibility and social ethics, especially in the context of contemporary perspectives on race, gender, and sexuality.*

NOTES ON PORNOGRAPHY ABANDONED

1

Yesterday, past the oak, the wicker chairs,
friends kept knocking wooden balls; shouts,
laughter, echoing on the lawn. On the tape player
a cello concerto ballooned upwards to
an endless blue. Watching I felt like some count
in Chekhov, wry, foolish, Russian. Later,
picking up the plates, like tiny moons gathered
in her grasp, my wife floated through the dark,
beautiful, ghostly in gauze white pleats.
A shudder swept through me, half guilt, half fear,
nothing I could quite name: just a chill,
as if nothing had changed . . .

2

Always there's this memory cut open like a fig, bursting with seeds.
There's the late spring when the sheets like a flock of doves
scatter and rush with the wind on the lines. There's
an apartment complex across the alley, moths
battering the screen with tiny wings, and I, sixteen,
look up from the *Genealogy:*
Of course, I see it, her window. She pulls the pins
from her hair, pulls off her uniform,
and there's a falling, a slicing of the cord
so some cry can break free, and her bra slides
off like the slow tilting of snow, sliding to an avalanche,
just above the valley where desire sleeps. Rooted tight,
I stare and stare,

and even when her lights go off, when I start to tell myself—
go to sleep, forget it, you'll never do this again . . .—it
dropped like a plummet in my conscience:

No, no, no, no. You cannot stop . . .

3

It was in the bookstore, another endless session:
Settled in a booth, putting in quarter after quarter
for film, I turned, saw an eye peering through
this hole cut in the wall, and then,
like a flag of surrender, a penis: ridiculous, pathetic,
hard. As the woman on the screen shouted, coming
again and again, pounding the bed, her face
twisted like an astronaut pulled by G's,
I felt this rush, this fix at the center.
And found myself kneeling, unable to stop . . .
Then a warm saltiness spread on my tongue; slipping
off the shaft, soft, sticky as taffy, I knew I'd
crossed one more line. And nothing, nothing happened . . .

4

What gain does the pimp, the devourer of pornography,
seek through the nerves, the depositions and debits,

the checks of the brain? He fills an emptiness in himself
through creating emptiness elsewhere. But where is

that elsewhere? In his empathy, his wish to see others
suffer exactly what he suffers, he finds a face, a body,

a blank moan; a woman who must remain mute so his
pleasure can exist—And in that muteness his pleasure, his power, hides . . .

5

Four years ago today, believing
The "I" who I was has been leveled as by a great wind,

I poured them in the dumpster, the glossy pages unfolding, spilling
like liquid dreams. Doused them with gas.

A mother called in the dark, *Jimmy, Jimmy Lee . . .* The match
            popped.
And faces, naked bodies, flamed, curled

to ash, smoke sifting through my lungs, blood, brain.
And something caved inside me, some long, slow, unrepentant sigh.

I thought of how, during the war, the Vietnamese communists
took the southern prostitutes to a camp

where all day they would play games, sing songs, run races,
eat and sleep like children, exactly like children.

I'd read—but didn't quite believe—that some, some did recover . . .

—1994

SHARON OLDS
B. 1942

*Sharon Olds was born in San Francisco and is a widely published poet who
writes unflinchingly about sex and the body, violence, parenting, marriage,
and the tensions between mothers and daughters. She has numerous volumes of poetry:* Satan Says *(1980),* The Dead and the Living *(1984),* The
Gold Cell *(1987),* The Matter of This World: New and Selected Poems
(1987), The Sign of Saturn: Poems, 1980-1987 *(1991), and* The Father
*(1992). Among her many awards is the National Book Critics Circle Award,
a National Endowment for the Arts grant, a James Laughlin Award from
the Academy of American Poets, and a Guggenheim Foundation Fellowship.
Olds has directed the creative writing program at New York University
since 1991.*

THE DEATH OF MARILYN MONROE

The ambulance men touched her cold
body, lifted it, heavy as iron,
onto the stretcher, tried to close the
mouth, closed the eyes, tied the
arms to the sides, moved a caught
strand of hair, as if it mattered,
saw the shape of her breasts, flattened by
gravity, under the sheet,
carried her, as if it were she,
down the steps.

These men were never the same. They went out
afterwards, as they always did,
for a drink or two, but they could not meet
each other's eyes.

Their lives took
a turn—one had nightmares, strange

pains, impotence, depression. One did not
like his work, his wife looked
different, his kids. Even death
seemed different to him—a place where she
would be waiting,

And one found himself standing at night
in the doorway to a room of sleep, listening to
a woman breathing, just an ordinary
woman
breathing.

—1983

ADRIENNE RICH

B. 1929

Adrienne Rich, born in Baltimore, is one of the best-known poets of this day. Rich has been involved as a teacher and lecturer in civil rights and antiwar activism, and more recently, as a lesbian in the women's liberation movement. Beginning with the Yale Younger Poets Award for A Change of World *(1951) and a National Book Award for* Diving into the Wreck *(1973), Rich has received many awards, including a MacArthur "genius" Award in 1995 and the Academy of American Poets' highest honor, the Tanning Prize, in 1996. She has also been an influential essayist of feminist and lesbian thought in works such as* Of Woman Born *(1976), and* On Lies, Secrets, and Silences *(1979). Her most recent works include* An Atlas of the Difficult World *(1991),* Collected Early Poems *(1993),* What Is Found There: Notebook on Poetry and Politics *(1993), and* Dark Fields of the Republic: Poems 1991–1995 *(1995).*

PHANTASIA FOR ELVIRA SHATAYEV

(leader of a women's climbing team, all of whom died in a storm on Lenin Peak, August 1974. Later, Shatayev's husband found and buried the bodies.)

The cold felt cold until our blood
grew colder   then the wind
died down and we slept

If in this sleep I speak
it's with a voice no longer personal

(I want to say   *with voices*)
When the wind tore   our breath from us at last
we had no need of words
For months   for years   each one of us
had felt her own *yes*   growing in her
slowly forming   as she stood at windows   waited
for trains   mended her rucksack   combed her hair
What we were to learn   was simply what we had
up here   as out of all words   that *yes*   gathered
its forces   fused itself   and only just in time
to meet a *No* of no degrees
the black hole   sucking the world in

I feel you climbing toward me
your cleated bootsoles leaving   their geometric bite
colossally embossed   on microscopic crystals
as when I trailed you in the Caucasus
Now I am further
ahead   than either of us dreamed   anyone would be
I have become
the white snow packed like asphalt by the wind
the women I love   lightly flung   against the mountain
that blue sky
our frozen eyes unribboned   through the storm
we could have stitched that blueness   together   like a quilt

You come (I know this)   with your love   your loss
strapped to your body   with your tape-recorder   camera
ice-pick   against advisement
to give us burial in the snow   and in your mind
While my body lies out here
flashing like a prism   into your eyes
how could you sleep   You climbed here for yourself
we climbed for ourselves

When you have buried us   told your story,
ours does not end   we stream
into the unfinished   the unbegun
the possible
Every cell's core of heat   pulsed out of us
into the thin air   of the universe
the armature of rock beneath these snows
this mountain   which has taken   the imprint of our minds
through changes elemental and minute
as those we underwent
to bring each other here
choosing ourselves   each other   and this life

whose every breath   and grasp   and further foothold
is somewhere   still enacted   and continuing

In the diary I wrote: *Now we are ready*
and each of us knows it   I have never loved
like this   I have never seen
my own forces so taken up and shared
and given back
After the long training   the early sieges
we are moving almost effortlessly in our love

In the diary as the wind   began to tear
at the tents over us   I wrote:
We know now we have always been in danger
down in our separateness
and now up here together   but till now
we had not touched our strength

In the diary torn from my fingers I had written:
What does love mean
what does it mean   "to survive"
A cable of blue fire ropes our bodies
burning together in the snow   We will not live
to settle for less   We have dreamed of this
all of our lives

—1974

GREGG SHAPIRO

B. 1959

Gregg Shapiro is a poet, editor, and fiction writer whose work has begun to receive national critical attention. He has published in a variety of small but important literary journals, including Christopher Street, The Washington Blade, Gargoyle, Thing, The Quarterly, Widener Review, Lip Service, *and* Plum Review. *He is a coeditor of* Queer Planet Review. *A volume of his short stories,* Indiscretion, *is available on disk from Sheridan Square Press. The poem included here originally appeared in* Mondo Barbie *(1993), a collection of poetry and prose focusing—often to hilarious effect—on the famous doll. Shapiro currently lives and writes in Chicago.*

CALL ME BARBIE

For Denise

When my mother bought me a Ken doll,
my Aunt Darlene almost had a stroke.
Years later, she forbade my cousin Joel
to talk to me. My father said it was
because I was always badmouthing the family.
I think it was because I kissed my male
friends hello, wore Salvation Army clothes
and let Ken kiss my cousin's GI Joe.

I learned to braid hair on my sister
Dana's Barbie doll. None of her friends'
brothers could make a pigtail so tight,
not a strand of synthetic hair out of place.
I organized fashion shoots, gynecological
exams, and shopping sprees for her dolls.
My sister never complained. She had an older
brother who wanted to be her older sister.

My boyfriend's name is Ken. Even though
he doesn't have plastic-injection-molded
hair, I love him anyway. He has perfect
teeth, a deep voice, green eyes, and genitals
that leave nothing to the imagination.
Look, I even shaved my chest, just to make us
a more perfect match. As soon as I get used
to walking on my toes, you can call me Barbie.

—1992

FICTION

SHERMAN ALEXIE

B. 1966

Sherman Alexie grew up on the Wellpinit Indian reservation outside Spokane, Washington. A member of the Spokane and Couer d'Alene tribes, Alexie attended Washington State University in Pullman and was an NEA poetry fellow in 1992. A prolific author of novels, short stories, and poetry, his books include The Business of Fancy Dancing *(1992),* First Indian on the Moon *(1993),* The Lone Ranger and Tonto Fist Fight in Heaven *(1993),* Reservation Blues *(1995), and most recently,* Indian Killer *(1996) and* The Summer of Black Widows *(1996). Alexie wrote the screenplay for a major independent film,* Smoke Signals *(1998), produced and directed by and featuring Native Americans. His fiction chronicles contemporary reservation life, noting its limitations and brutalities with a critical intelligence marked equally by sociological accuracy and humanistic poignancy.*

JESUS CHRIST'S HALF-BROTHER IS ALIVE AND WELL ON THE SPOKANE INDIAN RESERVATION

1966

Rosemary MorningDove gave birth to a boy today and seeing as how it was nearly Christmas and she kept telling everyone she was still a virgin even though Frank Many Horses said it was his we all just figured it was an accident. Anyhow she gave birth to him but he came out all blue and they couldn't get him to breathe for a long time but he finally did and Rosemary MorningDove named him ——— which is unpronounceable in Indian and English but it means: *He Who Crawls Silently Through the Grass with a Small Bow and One Bad Arrow Hunting for Enough Deer to Feed the Whole Tribe.*

We just call him James.

1967

Frank Many Horses and Lester FallsApart and I were drinking beers in the Break-away Bar playing pool and talking stories when we heard the sirens. Indians get all excited when we hear sirens because it means fires and it means they need firefighters to put out the fires and it means we get to be firefighters and it means we get paid to be firefighters. Hell somebody always starts a fire down at the Indian burial grounds and it was about time for the Thirteenth Annual All-Indian Burial Grounds Fire so Frank and Lester and I ran down to the fire station expecting to get hired but we see smoke coming from Commodity Village where all the really poor Indians live so we run down there instead and it was Rosemary MorningDove's house that was on fire. Indians got buckets of water but this fire was way too big and we could hear a baby crying and Frank Many Horses gets all excited even though it's Lillian Many's baby right next to us. But Frank knows James is in the house so he goes running in before any of us can stop him and pretty soon I see Frank leaning out the upstairs window holding James and they're both a little on fire and Frank throws James out the window and I'm running my ass over to catch him before he hits the ground making like a high school football hero again but I miss him just barely slipping through my fingers and James hits the ground hard and I pick him up right away and slap the flames out with my hands all the while expecting James to be dead but he's just looking at me almost normal except the top of his head looks all dented in like a beer can.

He wasn't crying.

1967

I went down to the reservation hospital to see how James and Frank and Rosemary were doing and I got drunk just before I went so I wouldn't be scared of all the white walls and the sound of arms and legs getting sawed off down in the basement. But I heard the screams anyway and they were Indian screams and those can travel forever like all around the world and sometimes from a hundred years ago so I close my ears and hide my eyes and just look down at the clean clean floors. Oh Jesus I'm so drunk I want to pray but I don't and before I can change my mind about coming here Moses MorningDove pulls me aside to tell me Frank and Rosemary have died and since I saved James's life I should be the one who raises him. Moses says it's Indian tradition but somehow since Moses is going on about two hundred years old and still drinking and screwing like he was twenty I figure he's just trying to get out of his grandfatherly duties. I don't really want any of it and I'm sick and the hospital is making me sicker and my heart is shaking and confused like when the nurse wakes you up in the middle of the night to give you a sleeping pill but I know James will end up some Indian kid at a welfare house making baskets and wearing itchy clothes and I'm only twenty myself but I take one look at James all lumpy and potato looking and I look in the mirror and see myself holding him and I take him home.

Tonight the mirror will forgive my face.

1967

All dark tonight and James couldn't sleep and just kept looking at the ceiling so I walk on down to the football field carrying James so we can both watch the stars looking down at the reservation. I put James down on the fifty-yard line and I run and run across the frozen grass wishing there was snow enough to make a trail and let the world know I was there in the morning. Thinking I could spell out my name or James's name or every name I could think of until I stepped on every piece of snow on the field like it was every piece of the world or at least every piece of this reservation that has so many pieces it might just be the world. I want to walk circles around James getting closer and closer to him in a new dance and a better kind of healing which could make James talk and walk before he learns to cry. But he's not crying and he's not walking and he's not talking and I see him sometimes like an old man passed out in the back of a reservation van with shit in his pants and a battered watch in his pocket that always shows the same damn time. So I pick James up from the cold and the grass that waits for spring and the sun to change its world but I can only walk home through the cold with another future on my back and James's future tucked in my pocket like an empty wallet or a newspaper that feeds the fire and never gets read.

Sometimes all of this is home.

1968

The world changing the world changing the world. I don't watch the TV anymore since it exploded and left a hole in the wall. The woodpile don't dream of me no more. It sits there by the ax and they talk about the cold that waits in corners and surprises you on a warm almost spring day. Today I stood at the window for hours and then I took the basketball from inside the wood stove and shot baskets at the hoop nailed to a pine tree in the yard. I shot and shot until the cold meant I was protected because my skin was too warm to feel any of it. I shot and shot until my fingertips bled and my feet ached and my hair stuck to the skin of my bare back. James waited by the porch with his hands in the dirt and his feet stuck into leather shoes I found in the dump under a washing machine. I can't believe the details I am forced to remember with each day that James comes closer to talking. I change his clothes and his dirty pants and I wash his face and the crevices of his little body until he shines like a new check.

This is my religion.

1968

Seems like the cold would never go away and winter would be like the bottom of my feet but then it is gone in one night and in its place comes the sun so large and laughable. James sitting up in his chair so young and he won't talk and the doctors at the Indian clinic say it's way too early for him to be talking anyhow but I see in his eyes something and I see in his eyes a voice and I see in his eyes a whole new set of words. It ain't Indian or English and it ain't cash register and it ain't traffic light or speed bump and it ain't window or door. Late one day James and I watch the sun fly across the sky like a basketball on fire until it falls down completely and lands in Benjamin Lake with a splash and shakes the ground and even wakes up Lester FallsApart who thought it was his father come back to slap his face again.

Summer coming like a car from down the highway.

1968

James must know how to cry because he hasn't cried yet and I know he's waiting for that one moment to cry like it was five hundred years of tears. He ain't walked anywhere and there are no blisters on his soles but there are dreams worn clean into his rib cage and it shakes and shakes with each breath and I see he's trying to talk when he grabs at the air behind his head or stares up at the sky so hard. All of this temperature rising hot and I set James down in the shade by the basketball court and I play and I play until the sweat of my body makes it rain everywhere on the reservation. I play and I play until the music of my shoes against pavement sounds like every drum. Then I'm home alone and I watch the cockroaches live their complicated lives.

I hold James with one arm and my basketball with the other arm and I hold everything else inside my whole body.

1969

I take James to the Indian clinic because he ain't crying yet and because all he does sometimes is stare and stare and sometimes he'll wrap his arms around the stray dogs and let them carry him around the yard. He's strong enough to hold his body off the ground but he ain't strong enough to lift his tongue from the bottom of his mouth to use the words for love or anger or hunger or good morning. Maybe he's only a few years old but he's got eyes that are ancient and old and dark like a castle or a lake where the turtles go to die and sometimes even to live. Maybe he's going to howl out the words when I least expect it or want it and he'll yell out a cuss word in church or a prayer in the middle of a grocery store. Today I moved through town and walked and walked past the people who hadn't seen me in so long maybe for months and they asked questions about me and James and no one bothered to knock on the door and look for the answers. It's just me and James walking and walking except he's on my back and his eyes are looking past the people who are looking past us for the coyote of our soul and the wolverine of our heart and the crazy crazy man that touches every Indian who spends too much time alone. I stand in the Trading Post touching the canned goods and hoping for a vision of all the miles until Seymour comes in with a twenty-dollar bill and buys a couple cases of beer and we drink and drink all night long. James gets handed from woman to woman and from man to man and a few children hold this child of mine who doesn't cry or recognize the human being in his own body. All the drunks happy to see me drunk again and back from the wagon and I fell off that wagon and broke my ass and dreams and I wake up the next morning in a field watching a cow watch me. With piss in my pants I make the long walk home past the HUD houses and abandoned cars and past the powwow grounds and the Assembly of God where the sinless sing like they could forgive us all. I get home and James is there with Suzy Song feeding him and rocking him like a boat or a three-legged chair.

I say no and I take James away and put him in his crib and I move into Suzy's arms and let her rock and rock me away from my stomach and thin skin.

1969

Long days and nights mean the sky looks the same all the time and James has no words yet but he dreams and kicks in his sleep and sometimes kicks his body against my body as he sleeps in my arms. Nobody dreams all the time because it would hurt too much but James keeps dreaming and sleeping through a summer rainstorm and heat lightning reaching down a hand and then a fist to tear a tree in half and then to tear my eyes in half with the light. We had venison for dinner. We ate deer and its wild taste shook me up and down my spine. James spit his mouthful out on the floor and the dogs came to finish it up and I ate and ate and the dogs ate and ate what they could find and the deer grew in my stomach. The deer grew horns and hooves and skin and eyes that pushed at my rib cage and I ate and ate until I could not feel anything but my stomach expanding and stretched full.

All my life the days I remember most with every detail sharp and clear are the days when my stomach was full.

1969

We played our first basketball game of the season tonight in the community center and I had Suzy Song watch James while I played and all of us warriors roaring against the air and the nets and the clock that didn't work and our memories and our dreams and the twentieth-century horses we called our legs. We played some Nez Percé team and they ran like they were still running from the cavalry and they were kicking the shit out of us again when I suddenly steal the ball from their half-white point guard and drive all the way to the bucket. I jump in the air planning to dunk it when the half-white point guard runs under me knocking my ass to the floor and when I land I hear a crunch and my leg bends in half the wrong way. They take me to the reservation hospital and later on they tell me my leg has exploded and I can't play ball for a long time or maybe forever and when Suzy comes by with James and they ask me if this is my wife and son and I tell them yes and James still doesn't make a noise and so they ask me how old he is. I tell them he's almost four years old and they say his physical development is slow but that's normal for an Indian child. Anyhow I have to have an operation and all but since I don't have the money or the strength or the memory and it's not covered by Indian Health I just get up and walk home almost crying because my leg and life hurt so bad. Suzy stays with me that night and in the dark she touches my knee and asks me how much it hurts and I tell her it hurts more than I can talk about so she kisses all my scars and she huddles up close to me and she's warm and she talks into my ear close. She isn't always asking questions and sometimes she has the answers. In the morning I wake up before her and I hobble into the kitchen and make some coffee and fix a couple of bowls of cornflakes and we sit in bed eating together while James lies still in his crib watching the ceiling so Suzy and I watch the ceiling too.

The ordinary can be like medicine.

1970

Early snow this year and James and I sit at home by the stove because I can't walk anywhere with my bad knee and since it is snowing so hard outside nobody could drive out to get us but I know somebody must be thinking about us because if they weren't we'd just disappear just like those Indians who used to climb the pueblos. Those Indians disappeared with food still cooking in the pot and air waiting to be breathed and they turned into birds or dust or the blue of the sky or the yellow of the sun.

There they were and suddenly they were forgotten for just a second and for just a second nobody thought about them and then they were gone.

1970

I took James down to the reservation hospital again because he was almost five years old and still hadn't bothered to talk yet or crawl or cry or even move when I put him on the floor and once I even dropped him and his head was bleeding and he didn't make a sound. They looked him over and said there was nothing wrong with him and that he's just a little slow developing and that's what the doctors always say and they've been saying that about Indians for five hundred years. Jesus I say don't you know that James wants to dance and to sing and to pound a drum so hard it hurts your ears and he ain't ever going to drop an eagle feather and he's always going to be respectful to elders at least the Indian elders and he's going to change the world. He's going to dynamite Mount Rushmore or hijack a plane and make it land on the reservation highway. He's going to be a father and a mother and a son and a daughter and a dog that will pull you from a raging river.

He'll make gold out of commodity cheese.

1970

Happy birthday James and I'm in the Breakaway Bar drinking too many beers when the Vietnam war comes on television. The white people always want to fight someone and they always get the dark-skinned people to do the fighting. All I know about this war is what Seymour told me when he came back from his tour of duty over there and he said all the gooks he killed looked like us and Seymour said every single gook he killed looked exactly like someone he knew on the reservation. Anyhow I go to a Christmas party over at Jana Wind's house and leave James with my auntie so I could get really drunk and not have to worry about coming home for a few days or maybe for the rest of my life. We all get really drunk and Jana's old man Ray challenges me to a game of one-on-one since he says I'm for shit now and was never any good anyway but I tell him I can't since my knee is screwed up and besides there's two feet of snow on the ground and where are we going to play anyhow? Ray says I'm chickenshit so I tell him come on and we drive over to the high school to the outside court and there's two feet of snow on the court and we can't play but Ray smiles and pulls out a bottle of kerosene and pours it all over the court and lights it up and pretty soon the snow is all melted down along with most of Lester FallsApart's pants since he was standing too close to the court when Ray lit the fire. Anyhow the court is clear and Ray and I go at it and my knee only hurts a little and everyone was cheering us on and I can't remember who won since I was too drunk and so was everyone else. Later I hear how Ray and Joseph got arrested for beating some white guy half to death and I say that Ray and Joseph are just kids but Suzy says nobody on the reservation is ever a kid and that we're all born grown up anyway. I look at James and I think maybe Suzy is wrong about Indian kids being born adults and that maybe James was born this way and wants to stay this way like a baby because he doesn't want to grow up and see and do everything we all do?

There are all kinds of wars.

1971

So much time alone with a bottle of one kind or another and James and I remember nothing except the last drink and a drunk Indian is like the thinker statue except nobody puts a drunk Indian in a special place in front of a library. For most Indians the only special place in front of a library might be a heating grate or a piece of sun-warmed cement but that's an old joke and I used to sleep with my books in piles all over my bed and sometimes they were the only thing keeping me warm and always the only thing keeping me alive.

Books and beer are the best and worst defense.

1971

Jesse WildShoe died last night and today was the funeral and usually there's a wake but none of us had the patience or energy to mourn for days so we buried Jesse right away and dug the hole deep because Jesse could fancydance like God had touched his feet. Anyhow we dug the hole all day and since the ground was still a little frozen we kept doing the kerosene trick and melting the ice and frost and when we threw a match into the bottom of the grave it looked like I suppose hell must look and it was scary. There we were ten little Indians making a hell on earth for a fancydancer who already had enough of that shit and probably wouldn't want to have any more of it and I kept wondering if maybe we should just take his body high up in the mountains and bury him in the snow that never goes away. Maybe we just sort of freeze him so he doesn't have to feel anything anymore and especially not some crazy ideas of heaven or hell. I don't know anything about religion and I don't confess my sins to anybody except the walls and the wood stove and James who forgives everything like a rock. He ain't talking or crying at all and sometimes I shake him a little too hard or yell at him or leave him in his crib for hours all alone but he never makes a sound. One night I get so drunk I leave him at somebody's house and forget all about him and can you blame me? The tribal police drag me into the cell for abandonment and I'm asking them who they're going to arrest for abandoning me but the world is spinning and turning back on itself like a snake eating its own tail. Like a snake my TV dinner rises from the table the next day and snaps at my eyes and wrists and I ask the tribal cop how long I've been drunk and he tells me for most of a year and I don't remember any of it. I've got the DT's so bad and the walls are Nazis making lampshades out of my skin and the toilet is a white man in a white hood riding me down on horseback and the floor is a skinny man who wants to teach me a trick he's learned to do with a knife and my shoes squeal and kick and pull me down into the dead pig pit of my imagination. Oh Jesus I wake up on the bottom of that mass grave with the bones of generations of slaughter and I crawl and dig my way up through layers and years of the lunch special. I dig for hours through the skin and eyes and the fresh blood soon enough and pull myself through the eye of a sow and pluck the maggots from my hair and I want to scream but I don't want to open my mouth and taste and taste and taste.

Like the heroin addict said I just want to be pure.

1971

Been in A.A. for a month because that was the only way to keep James with me and my auntie and Suzy Song both moved into the house with me to make sure I don't drink and to help take care of James. They show the same old movies in A.A. and it's always the same white guy who almost destroys his life and his wife and his children and his job but finally realizes the alcohol is killing him and he quits overnight and spends the rest of the movie and the rest of his whole life at a picnic with his family and friends and boss all laughing and saying we didn't even recognize you back then Bob and we're glad to have you back Daddy and we'll hire you back at twice the salary you old dog you. Yesterday I get this postcard from Pine Ridge and my cousin says all the Indians there are gone and do I know where they went? I write back and tell him to look in the A.A. meeting and then I ask him if there are more birds with eyes that look like his and I ask him if the sky is more blue and the sun more yellow because those are the colors we all become when we die. I tell him to search his dreams for a man dressed in red with a red tie and red shoes and a hawk head. I tell him that man is fear and will eat you like a sandwich and will eat you like an ice cream cone and will never be full and he'll come for you in your dreams like he was a bad movie. I tell him to turn his television toward the wall and to study the walls for imperfections and those could be his mother and father and the stain on the ceiling could be his sisters and maybe the warped floorboard squeaking and squeaking is his grandfather talking stories.

Maybe they're all hiding on a ship in a bottle.

1972

Been sober so long it's like a dream but I feel better somehow and Auntie was so proud of me she took James and me into the city for James's checkup and James still wasn't talking but Auntie and James and I ate a great lunch at Woolworth's before we headed back to the reservation. I got to drive and Auntie's uranium money Cadillac is a hell of a car and it was raining a little and hot so there were rainbows rainbows rainbows and the pine trees looked like wise men with wet beards or at least I thought they did. That's how I do this life sometimes by making the ordinary just like magic and just like a card trick and just like a mirror and just like the disappearing. Every Indian learns how to be a magician and learns how to misdirect attention and the dark hand is always quicker than the white eye and no matter how close you get to my heart you will never find out my secrets and I'll never tell you and I'll never show you the same trick twice.

I'm traveling heavy with illusions.

1972

Every day I'm trying not to drink and I pray but I don't know who I'm praying to and if it's the basketball gathering ash on the shelf or the blank walls crushing me into the house or the television that only picks up public channels, I've seen only painters and fishermen and I think they're both the same kind of men who made a different choice one time in their lives. The fisherman held a rod in his hand and said yes and the painter held a brush in his hand and said yes and sometimes I hold a beer in my hand and say yes. At those moments I want to drink so bad that it aches and I cry which is a strange noise in our house because James refuses tears and he refuses words but sometimes he holds a hand up above his head like he's reaching for something. Yesterday I nearly trip over Lester FallsApart lying drunk as a skunk in front of the Trading Post and I pick him up and he staggers and trembles and falls back down. Lester I say you got to stand up on your own and I pick him up and he falls down again.

Only a saint would have tried to pick him up the third time.

1972

The streetlight outside my house shines on tonight and I'm watching it like it could give me vision. James ain't talked ever and he looks at that streetlight like it was a word and maybe like it was a verb. James wanted to streetlight me and make me bright and beautiful so all the moths and bats would circle me like I was the center of the world and held secrets. Like Joy said that everything but humans keeps secrets. Today I get my mail and there's a light bill and a postcard from an old love from Seattle who asks me if I still love her like I used to and would I come to visit?

I send her my light bill and tell her I don't ever want to see her again.

1973

James talked today but I had my back turned and I couldn't be sure it was real. He said potato like any good Indian would because that's all we eat. But maybe he said I love you because that's what I wanted him to say or maybe he said geology or mathematics or college basketball. I pick him up and ask him again and again what did you say? He just smiles and I take him to the clinic and the doctors say it's about time but are you sure you didn't imagine his voice? I said James's voice sounded like a beautiful glass falling off the shelf and landing safely on a thick shag carpet.

The doctor said I had a very good imagination.

1973

I'm shooting hoops again with the younger Indian boys and even some Indian girls who never miss a shot. They call me old man and elder and give me a little bit of respect like not running too fast or hard and even letting me shoot a few more than I should. It's been a long time since I played but the old feelings and old moves are there in my heart and in my fingers. I see these Indian kids and I know that basketball was invented by an Indian long before that Naismith guy ever thought about it. When I play I don't feel like drinking so I wish I could play twenty-four hours a day seven days a week and then I wouldn't wake up shaking and quaking and needing just one more beer before I stop for good. James knows it too and he sits on the sideline clapping when my team scores and clapping when the other team scores too. He's got a good heart. He always talks whenever I'm not in the room or I'm not looking at him but never when anybody else might hear so they all think I'm crazy. I am crazy. He says things like I can't believe. He says $E = MC^2$ and that's why all my cousins drink themselves to death. He says the earth is an oval marble that nobody can win. He says the sky is not blue and the grass is not green.

He says everything is a matter of perception.

1973

Christmas and James gets his presents and he gives me the best present of all when he talks right at me. He says so many things and the only thing that matters is that he says he and I don't have the right to die for each other and that we should be living for each other instead. He says the world hurts. He says the first thing he wanted after he was born was a shot of whiskey. He says all that and more. He tells me to get a job and to grow my braids. He says I better learn how to shoot left-handed if I'm going to keep playing basketball. He says to open a fireworks stand.

Every day now there are little explosions all over the reservation.

1974

Today is the World's Fair in Spokane and James and I drive to Spokane with a few cousins of mine. All the countries have exhibitions like art from Japan and pottery from Mexico and mean-looking people talking about Germany. In one little corner there's a statue of an Indian who's supposed to be some chief or another. I press a little button and the statue talks and moves its arms over and over in the same motion. The statue tells the crowd we have to take care of the earth because it is our mother. I know that and James says he knows more. He says the earth is our grand-mother and that technology has become our mother and that they both hate each other. James tells the crowd that the river just a few yards from where we stand is all we ever need to believe in. One white woman asks me how old James is and I tell her he's seven and she tells me that he's so smart for an Indian boy. James hears this and tells the white woman that she's pretty smart for an old white woman. I know this is how it will all begin and how the rest of my life will be. I know when I am old and sick and ready to die that James will wash my body and take care of my wastes. He'll carry me from HUD house to sweathouse and he will clean my wounds. And he will talk and teach me something new every day.

But all that is so far ahead.

—1993

LUIS ALFARO

B. 1961

Luis Alfaro was born in Los Angeles. He is a poet, dramatist, fiction writer, essayist, and performance artist who describes himself as a "community-based artist." His signature performance-art piece, Down/Town, *challenges contemporary perspectives on race relations, sexual orientation, gender, and poverty. His work has been published in a number of anthologies, including* The United States of Poetry *(1995) and* His: Brilliant New Fiction by Gay Writers *(1995). In 1996, Alfaro wrote and starred in "The L.A. Plays" for PBS in Los Angeles. Codirector of the Latino Theater Initiative at the Mark Taper Forum in Los Angeles and founder and project codirector of VIVA/Lesbian and Gay Latino Artists, he was awarded a MacArthur "genius" grant in 1997. Alfaro teaches in the Writer's Program at the University of California, Los Angeles Extension.*

BITTER HOMES AND GARDENS

1. Daughter

There is a great deal you do not know about me.
You only know me as the hostess at a world famous casino in downtown Las Vegas. A woman with perfect posture who hands out free miniature hot dogs to the millions of visitors at an oasis in the desert.

But I am more. So much more.

True, I have worked at this posture all my life, but when I turned thirty, I went to an experimental clinic in Frankfurt, Germany. I paid a scientist my life savings and he broke my back in fifteen different places. He then reset it perfectly and I briefly worked as a model for the J. C. Penney catalogue. My operation ensured a back as straight as a line. This, of course, is enough to constitute a life fulfilled, but I have lived more. So much more.

I had a house once.

A stationary in a trailer park that was cable accessible.

I knew I had climbed a ladder when we got the cable.

Not a big one, but a ladder nevertheless.

My husband, the day laborer and heroin addict, was ignorant about the world but smart about holding up liquor stores. I accepted him as a fact of my life because men, they need this rush, this liquor store robbing, this adrenaline. Especially if it isn't football season. I am sure that if I had not met my husband I would now be working on the Strip. But that's life. A series of choices.

I killed a chicken when I was ten.

I had a dream one night. I think it was the queen of England. Yes, it was the queen who told me to kill a chicken for England. So I did. The next morning I awoke and killed poultry. That was the beginning of my days as a murderess. Little did I know that I would kill and kill again. And furthermore, little did I know that it would make me a feminist. A feminist! Can you believe that? All my life I slept on wooden boards in my efforts to have perfect posture in hopes that one day at the height of my desirability I could become a hostess. All I ever wanted to be was a hostess. But the queen of England told me to kill a chicken and I became a feminist.

It was a cereal box.

My husband, the day laborer and heroin addict, collected cereal boxes for leisure reading. One morning I awoke to find a kitchen loaded with cereal boxes. So, I poured myself a large bowl of milk. And the rage set in. You see, the milk had been poured. There was no going back.

Cheerios. Empty. Leisure reading.

Rice Krispies. Empty. Leisure reading.

Trix, Corn Puffs, Frosted Flakes. All empty. All leisure reading. In a fit of rage I killed my husband with my bare hands. Blood on my hands. The beginnings of my feminism. How did it happen? What drove me to it? I don't know. Only that something about being a housewife led me to murder. Sweeping the same floor that dirtied itself over and over again. Washing the same dirty dishes, picking up my husband's used syringes. It was a life of lies, empty promises. Hopes that never fulfilled themselves in the form of empty cereal boxes. I killed him like I killed that chicken.

In my own defense I must say that I prayed to the Holy Virgin for guidance. She confirmed that my husband, one of society's undesirables, must be killed. I couldn't be a housewife, a feminist and a hostess all at the same time. That ended a chapter in the life of a woman with perfect posture.

I was going to talk about the murder of my second husband, the insurance broker and street mime, but I have decided not to. One of the joys of being a feminist is that I don't have to talk, about anything that I don't want to talk about.

Las Vegas has been good to me.

One day I hope to work in the Roman palace on the Strip. A backless toga is what I would be honored to wear. This causes much distress in my hostess/feminist support group. But I've worked so hard on this back. It deserves to be seen.

My mother says that I've paid more attention to my back than my husbands. It's silly and it's rubbish. These are the issues that women face in the modern world. When are my life and back mine and when are they my husband's? I don't know. The vertebrae is a very special gift. A series of bones that God puts together very carefully and distinctly. I was born imperfectly. But a clinic in Frankfurt saved my life. Never as a housewife or person with an imperfect back did I think of killing myself. Did Liberace kill himself? Did Mr. Wayne Newton kill himself? Did Siegfried and Roy kill themselves? Of course not. These are leaders in our community. Pillars in the entertainment industry. Of course they have not killed themselves and believe me, they have lots of reasons to want to kill themselves.

There are but three things that I have been in my life: a murderess, a feminist and a woman with perfect posture. Look at my back. Straight as a line. The vertebrae. A delicate little gift inching up our backs. I have always been poised for perfection.

2. Father

Has anybody ever killed a moose with their bare hands? Well, neither have I. I grew up in the middle of East L.A. and they don't have mooses over there. I don't even know what the hell a moose looks like.

Has anybody read *Iron John*? It's one of those men books. Sort of a *Fear of Flying* for us guys. I bought it because it's a best-seller. I wouldn't know what to buy if they didn't have those best-seller lists.

So, I've been having a dream about this book.

I'm killing a moose with my bare hands.

This moose is just a moose. Just one of the many stupid mooses in the wilderness and I'm killing it with my bare hands. And standing behind me are those ethical animal people and they're all white. And so of course, I pay them no mind, cause you know I work on a printing press and that's all I got on my back all day is white people. I ain't saying white people are bad. I'm just saying that all the Mexicans at work got white people on their backs. And maybe it's just coincidence but you just don't pay them no mind.

So, I'm tearing the moose apart and standing there in front of all the white people are John Bradshaw and Robert Bly. People healers. White Indians, I call them. Just standing there watching me. And they're crying. Sad tears rolling down their cheeks. And Bly looks at me and says, "Boy, you've really changed." And Bradshaw says, "Yes, you're a different man." And I feel real guilty for a few minutes there, but I finish killing the moose anyway. Cause the truth of it is, you have to make choices, and I know they're healers and all, but they're white people.

So, I don't know if the moose is the environment or white people or what. But what I do know is that things have changed. The woman I married is not the same woman I live with now. Changed.
The house I built. Built it with my own hands. Changed.
And this world. This world is changing. I don't understand it and I most certainly don't agree with it, but I know we have to live with it ONE-DAY-AT-A-TIME.
But I can see it.
I'm alive and I know what's going on. Okay?
I'm alive, I can see it and I know what's going on.

3. Mother

I wanna talk a little bit about desire.

Desire is memory. A time bomb that ticks with the kind of power that can blow up buildings. And one day it just fizzles out. Nothing.
And you forget just when it blew or how, and it doesn't really matter because all that really mattered was that it was ticking.

Yesterday, I turned forty.

I thought getting older meant getting wiser, but that's simply not true.
Because it doesn't matter, when you're a housewife nobody cares that you're smarter.
Not your husband.
Not the kids.
Not the Betty Crocker cake mix.
No one.

I thought that my body was changing in the way it looked at the world, but I was wrong.
The change is in the way the world looks at my body.

Well, I just want to say that somebody lied.

Somebody promised that being a housewife, being a mother, has its payoffs. But it doesn't.

I tried so hard not to be a broad and now I can't wait to be one, because the only women with real control in their lives are the broads.
The women with the tube tops.
The no makeup.
The no pedicure.
The no Summer's Eve.

The broads who kick in the T.V. set when that asshole, that role model for all women, Sally Jesse Raphael, tells me I think too much, I haven't cared enough, I haven't cleaned enough.

I bet you she's never made tortillas.

Well listen Sally fucking Jesse, Maybe you've got the pulse on how rotten your life is, but you don't know shit about America.

Look at these hands.

Look at these.

Do you know what I've done with these hands?

I made a house with these.

Did anybody notice?

Not my father.

Not my husband.

Not my God.

None of those *men.*

These hands have done a lot. They used to make love to my husband. The other day I took one of these fingers deep inside of me and gave myself a Fourth of July fireworks in the living room at four o'clock in the afternoon. Right in the middle of "Geraldo."

These hands made these tortillas. Do you know how hard I worked on these? Do you know how many dozens of these I've made in my lifetime? DID ANYBODY NOTICE MY TORTILLAS?

Just feel these things, goddammit. I've got nothing else to show for my life but these tortillas.

Well, my kids but . . . never mind.

Tortillas are my biggest accomplishment and, believe me, I know that this body doesn't make them like she used to.

Can you hear the ticking time bomb?

What about you, Miss America?

What are you going to do when it all starts to droop?

Well I turned forty yesterday and my body is dying to be a broad. I guess I wouldn't be feeling this way if I hadn't married my childhood sweetheart. But I'm not bitter. Do you hear me? I'm not bitter. I'm miserable. That's a big difference. The difference between being a woman and being a housewife. Never forget that.

It's all here. Traces of America everywhere in this house. Talk show hosts and T.V. evangelists are deeply woven into the fabric of this house. "News at Eleven" is sitting on the love seat.

I saw two visions.

One was an old lady and the other was a little boy. They came to me in the same day, and that night I checked myself into Edgewood. That's why I love the world, 'cause it talks to you all the time. "The Home Shopping Club," it's talking to me. The guy down the street with the kiddie porn. I bet you he's got something to say to me. They all do. If I just open myself up to it.

The other day when I was taking the bus to see the ocean, I saw this little boy. Jumping up and down and banging himself on the head, real hard. Like the Ayatollah's funeral. And he was laughing, like he enjoyed it. Down on Olympic I saw an old lady. A bag lady that looked like my Grandma Consuelo out at the dump in Tijuana. She was crying. One of those long, painful cries of death. And she was banging herself on the head. Really hard. And you know what I thought? I thought to myself, that's me all right.
Not the old lady.
Not the little boy.
Something in between.
That's the nite I checked myself in.
That's the nite I made the Kraft Macaroni and Cheese.
I'm getting better all the time. I even have a daughter who's half nuts. Someone to talk to. She's gonna pull me over to the other side. And when she does I'm gonna put on one of those *quincinera* dresses with the hoop and the lace and I'm gonna have myself a coming out. I'm gonna go down and rent that dress from the bridal place with the mural on Broadway. It'll be my coming out. Just like the guys in the gay bars. I'm gonna call my mom and everybody on the block and say, "Hey, you guys, guess what? I'm back. Just like I was in 1969. I went to somewhere like hell, like Hollywood and Western, and I'm back."

I lived to tell.
I saw the El Pollo Locos and the 99 Cent stores and the girls who throw up their dinners to stay skinny.
I saw the T.V. evangelists and the kiddie porno rings.
The Winchell's beggars and the Bob's Big Boy massacre.
I saw it all.
I saw anger and loneliness.
Sadness.
Ooh, the sadness.
I saw desperation and isolation.
I saw America. I saw America all over the place.

I saw my cunt.
The power that is my cunt. I reached down there and I tasted a force of nature. And it opened itself up to a pain. Something bigger and more painful than my four kids who raced through me.
I saw my mother and my dead father. I saw the roof cave in at my wedding. People crushed under centerpieces, wedding cakes and big slabs of marble.

I saw an interview with the top ten serial killers on "Hard Copy."
I did.
They were celebrities and we were nobody.

I saw this poor house with its carved wood and drooping arches. This house with its rooms full of memories and that attic full of sadness. I looked in the den and I saw my first kiss. Holding hands on the porch. Walking in the backyard. I saw my husband fucking me in the kitchen. That beautiful round ass of his. His body on top of mine in the breakfast nook.

I saw my daughter and she was smiling. God, how long has that been?

I saw it alright.
All of it. I saw America.

−1995

REBECCA BROWN
B. 1956

*Rebecca Brown is a novelist, short story writer, and AIDS activist based in Seattle and London. Considered one of the most important fiction writers of her generation, Brown uses surrealist prose to depict the overwhelming nature of family relations and of romance. As the selection included here demonstrates, she is also interested in challenging the gendered nature of the English language. Her publications include three novels—*The Haunted House *(1987),* The Children's Crusade *(1991), and* Annie Oakley's Girl *(1993)—and four volumes of short fiction:* The Evolution of Darkness *(1984),* The Terrible Girls *(1992), from which comes "Forgiveness,"* The Gifts of the Body *(1994), and* What Keeps Me Here: A Book of Stories *(1996). Her social activism is reflected in her coediting with Jill Hyland and Andrea Kane* Incentives and Supports for the Employment of Welfare Recipients *(1997).*

FORGIVENESS

When I said I'd give my right arm for you, I didn't think you'd ask me for it, but you did.

You said, Give it to me.

And I said OK.

There were lots of reasons I gave it to you.

First of all, I didn't want to be made a liar of. (I had never lied to you.) So when you reminded me that I'd said it and asked me if I really meant it, I didn't want to seem like I was copping out by saying that I'd only spoken figuratively. (It is an old saying, after all.) Also, I had the feeling you didn't think I would really do it, that you were testing me to see if I would, and I wanted you to know I would.

Also, I believed you wouldn't have asked me for it unless you really wanted it, and needed it.

But then, when you got it, you bronzed it and put it on the mantel over the fireplace in the den.

The night you took it, I dreamt of arms. I slept on the couch in the den because I was still bleeding, even through the bandages, and I knew I'd stir during the night and need to put on more bandages and we didn't want me to wake you up. So I stayed on the couch and when I slept, I dreamt of arms: red arms, blue arms, golden arms. And arms made out of jade. Arms with tattoos, arms with stripes. Arms waving, sleeping, holding. Arms that rested up against my ribs.

We kept my arm in the bathtub, bleeding like a fish. When I went to bed, the water was the color of rose water, with thick red lines like strings. And when I woke up the first time to change my bandages, it was colored like salmon. Then it was carnation red, and then maroon, then burgundy, then purple, thick, and almost black by morning.

In the morning, you took it out. I watched you pat it dry with my favorite big fat terry cloth towel and wrap it in saran wrap and take it out to get it bronzed.

I learned to do things differently, To button my shirts, to screw and unscrew the toothpaste cap, to tie my shoes. We didn't think of this. Together, we were valiant, brave and stoic. Though I couldn't quite keep up with you at tennis anymore.

In a way, it was fun. Things I once took for granted became significant. Cutting a steak with a knife and fork, or buttoning my fly, untying a knot around a bag, adding milk while stirring.

After a while, I developed a scab and you let me come back to bed. But sometimes in the night, I'd shift or have a nightmare, jolt, and suddenly, I'd open up again, and bleed all over uncontrollably. The first time this happened neither of us could go back to sleep. But after a while, you got used to it and you'd be back asleep in a minute. It didn't seem to bother you at all.

But I guess after a while it started bothering you, because one day when I was washing out the sheets I'd bloodied the night before, you said, You sleep too restless. I don't like it when your bleeding wakes me up. I think you're sick. I think it's sick to cut off your own arm.

I looked at you, your sweet brown eyes, innocent as a puppy. But you cut it off, I said. You did it. You didn't blink. You asked me for it, so I said OK.

Don't try to make me feel guilty, you said, your pretty brown eyes looking at me. It was your arm.

You didn't blink.

I closed my eyes.

That night I bled again. I woke up and the bed was red, all full of blood and wet. I reached over to touch you and to wake you up and tell you I was sorry, but you were not there.

I learned more. To cook and clean, to eat a quarter pounder with one fist, to balance my groceries on my knee while my hand fumbled with the front door key.

My arm got strong. My left sleeve on my shirts got tight and pinched. My right shirt sleeve was lithe and open, carefree, like a pretty girl.

But then the novelty wore off. I had to convince myself. I read about those valiant cases, one-legged heroes who run across the continent to raise money for causes, and paraplegic mothers of four, one-eyed pool sharks. I wanted these stories to inspire me, but they didn't. I didn't want to be like those people. I didn't want to be cheery and valiant. I didn't want to have to rise above my situation. What I wanted was my arm.

Because I missed it. I missed everything about it. I missed the long solid weight of it in my sleeve. I missed clapping and waving and putting my hand in my pocket. I missed waking up at night with it twisted behind my head, asleep and heavy and tingling.

And then I realized that I had missed these things all along, the whole time my arm had been over the mantel, but that I'd never said anything or even let myself feel anything bad because I didn't want to dwell on those feelings because I didn't want to make you feel bad and I didn't want you to think I wanted you to feel bad.

I decided to look for it. Maybe you'd sold it. You were always good with things like that.

I hit the pawnshops. I walked into them and they'd ask me could they help me and I'd say, I'm looking for an arm. And they'd stare at me, my empty sleeve pinned to my shirt, or flapping in the air. I never have liked acting like things aren't the way they are.

When I searched all the local pawnshops, I started going to ones further away. I saw a lot of the country. It was nice. And I got good at it. The more I did, the more I learned to do. The braver ones would look at me directly in the eye. They'd give me the names and addresses of outlets selling artificial limbs, or reconstructive surgeons. But I didn't want another one, I wanted mine. And then, the more I looked for it, the more I wondered if I wasn't looking more for something else besides my severed arm. I wondered was I really searching for you?

It all came clear to me. Like something hacked away from me; you'd done this to me as a test. To show me things. To show me what things meant to me, how much my arm was part of me, but how I could learn to live without it. How, if I was forced to, I could learn to get by with only part of me, with next to nothing. You'd done this to me to teach me something.

And then I thought how, if you were testing me, you must be watching me, to see if I was passing.

So I started acting out my life for you. And then I felt you watching all my actions. I whistled with bravado, jaunted, rather than walked. I had a confident swagger. I slapped friendly pawnshop keepers on their shoulders and told them jokes. I was fun, an inspiration they'd remember after I'd passed through.

I acted like I couldn't care less about my old arm. Like I liked the breezes in my sleeve.

I began to think in perfect sentences, as if you were listening to me. I thought clear sentences inside myself. I said, I get along just fine without my arm. I think that I convinced myself, in trying to convince you, that I had never had an arm I'd lost.

Soon I didn't think the word inside me any more. I didn't think about the right hand gloves buried in my bottom drawer.

I made myself not miss it. I tested myself. I sat in the den and stared at the empty space above the mantel. I spent the night on the couch. I went into the bathroom and looked in the tub. I felt nothing. I went to bed.

I thought my trips to pawnshops, my wanderlust, were only things I did to pass the time. I thought of nothing almost happily.

I looked at my shoulder. The tissue was smooth. I ran my fingers over it. Round and slightly puffed, pink and shiny and slick. As soft as pimento, as cool as a spoon, the tenderest flesh of my body.

My beautiful empty sleeve and I were friends, like intimates.

So everything was fine.
      For a while.
      Then you came back.
      Then everything did.

But I was careful. It had been a long time. I had learned how to live. Why, hadn't I just forgotten what used to fill my empty sleeve entirely? I was very careful. I acted like nothing had ever been different, that you had never ripped it out of me, then bronzed it, put it on the mantel, left with it. I wanted things to stay forgot.

And besides, it was so easy, so familiar having you around. It was nice.

I determined to hold on to what I'd learned. About the strength of having only one.

Maybe I should have told you then. Maybe I should have told you then. But then, I told myself, if you knew to leave it alone, then good. And if you didn't know, we needed to find that out.

So we were sitting in the den. You looked at me with your big sweet pretty brown eyes and you said, you whispered it softly like a little girl, you said, Oh, I'm so sorry. You started crying softly, your lips quivering. Can you ever forgive me? You said it slow and sweet like a foreign language. I watched you, knowing you knew the way I was watching you. You leaned into me and pulled my arm around you and ran your pretty fingers down the solid muscle in my sleeve. Just hold me, darling, you said. Just hold me again.

I ran my wet palm, shaking, on your gorgeous back. Your hair smelled sweet.

I looked at your beautiful tear-lined face and tried to pretend that I had never seen you before in my life.

Why did you do it? I whispered.

You looked at me, your eyes all moist and sweet like you could melt anything in the world. You didn't answer.

What did you do with it?

You shrugged your shoulders, shook your head and smiled at me sweeter than an angel.

Say something, I whispered into your pretty hair. Say something, goddammit.

You looked up at me and your sweet brown eyes welled up with tears again. You put your head against my breast and sobbed.

You made me rock you and I did and then you cried yourself to sleep as innocent as a baby. When you were asleep I walked you to the bedroom and put you to bed. You slept. I watched you all night. You remembered nothing in the morning.

In the morning we had coffee. You chatted to me about your adventures. You cocked your head at just the right places, the way I remembered you did. You told me you'd worked hard in the time you'd been away. You told me you had grown. You told me how much you had learned about the world, about yourself, about honor, faith and trust, etc. You looked deep into my eyes and said, I've changed. You said how good and strong and true and truly different you were. How you had learned that it is not our acts, but our intents, that make us who we are.

I watched your perfect teeth.

I felt your sweet familiar hands run up my body, over the empty sleeve that rumpled on the exposed side of me. I closed my eyes and couldn't open them. My mouth was closed. I couldn't tell you anything.

I couldn't tell you that you can't re-do a thing that's been undone. I couldn't tell you anything that you would understand. I couldn't tell you that it wasn't just the fact that you had ripped it out of me and taken it and mounted it, then left with it then lost it, how it wasn't only that, but it was more. How it was that when you asked me, I believed you and I told you yes. How, though I had tried a long time to replace what you had hacked away from me, I never could undo the action of your doing so, that I had, and only ever would have, more belief in your faulty memory, your stupid sloppy foresight, than in your claims of change. How I believed, yes, I believed with all my heart, that given time, you'd do something else again, some new and novel variant to what you'd done to me, again. And then I thought, but this was only half a thought, that even if you had changed, no *really* changed, truly and at last, and even if you knew me better than I know myself, and even if I'm better off than I've ever been, and even if this was the only way we could have gotten to this special place where we are now, and even if there's a reason, darling, something bigger than both of us, and even if all these even if's are true, that I would never believe you again, never forget what I know of you, never forget what you've done to me, what you will do, I'll never believe the myth of forgiveness between us.

                                                                      −1990

OCTAVIA BUTLER

B. 1947

Octavia Butler was born in Pasadena, California. She attended Pasadena College and California State University, Los Angeles, graduating in 1969. Butler has made a living as a freelance writer, collecting such prizes as science fiction's Hugo and Nebula Awards and in 1995 the MacArthur "genius" grant. Her early interest in the genre of science fiction was tempered by her desire to see better female characterizations and more imaginative renderings of the possibilities and histories of race, class, and sexuality. These issues are all central to the story selected here. Her books include Patternmaster *(1976),* Survivor *(1978),* Wild Seed *(1980),* Dawn *(1987), and* Bloodchild and Other Stories *(1995). Butler currently lives and writes in Los Angeles.*

BLOODCHILD

My last night of childhood began with a visit home. T'Gatoi's sister had given us two sterile eggs. T'Gatoi gave one to my mother, brother, and sisters. She insisted that I eat the other one alone. It didn't matter. There was still enough to leave everyone feeling good. Almost everyone. My mother wouldn't take any. She sat, watching everyone drifting and dreaming without her. Most of the time she watched me.

I lay against T'Gatoi's long, velvet underside, sipping from my egg now and then, wondering why my mother denied herself such a harmless pleasure. Less of her hair would be gray if she indulged now and then. The eggs prolonged life, prolonged vigor. My father, who had never refused one in his life, had lived more than twice as long as he should have. And toward the end of his life, when he should have been slowing down, he had married my mother and fathered four children.

But my mother seemed content to age before she had to. I saw her turn away as several of T'Gatoi's limbs secured me closer. T'Gatoi liked our body heat and took advantage of it whenever she could. When I was little and at home more, my mother used to try to tell me how to behave with T'Gatoi—to be respectful and always obedient because T'Gatoi was the Tlic government official in charge of the Preserve, and thus the most important of her kind to deal directly with Terrans. It was an honor, my mother said, that such a person had chosen to come into the family. My mother was at her most formal and severe when she was lying.

I had no idea why she was lying, or even what she was lying about. It *was* an honor to have T'Gatoi in the family, but it was hardly a novelty. T'Gatoi and my mother had been friends all my mother's life, and T'Gatoi was not interested in being honored in the house she considered her second home. She simply came in, climbed onto one of her special couches, and called me over to keep her warm. It was impossible to be formal with her while lying against her and hearing her complain as usual that I was too skinny.

"You're better," she said this time, probing me with six or seven of her limbs. "You're gaining weight finally. Thinness is dangerous." The probing changed subtly, became a series of caresses.

"He's still too thin," my mother said sharply.

T'Gatoi lifted her head and perhaps a meter of her body off the couch as though she were sitting up. She looked at my mother, and my mother, her face lined and old looking, turned away.

"Lien, I would like you to have what's left of Gan's egg."

"The eggs are for the children," my mother said.

"They are for the family. Please take it."

Unwillingly obedient, my mother took it from me and put it to her mouth. There were only a few drops left in the now-shrunken, elastic shell, but she squeezed them out, swallowed them, and after a few moments some of the lines of tension began to smooth from her face.

"It's good," she whispered. "Sometimes I forget how good it is."

"You should take more," T'Gatoi said. "Why are you in such a hurry to be old?"

My mother said nothing.

"I like being able to come here," T'Gatoi said. "This place is a refuge because of you, yet you won't take care of yourself."

T'Gatoi was hounded on the outside. Her people wanted more of us made available. Only she and her political faction stood between us and the hordes who did not understand why there was a Preserve—why any Terran could not be courted, paid, drafted, in some way made available to them. Or they did understand, but in their desperation, they did not care. She parceled us out to the desperate and sold us to the rich and powerful for their political support. Thus, we were necessities, status symbols, and an independent people. She oversaw the joining of families, putting an end to the final remnants of the earlier system of breaking up Terran families to suit impatient Tlic. I had lived outside with her. I had seen the desperate eagerness in the way some people looked at me. It was a little frightening to know that only she stood between us and that desperation that could so easily swallow us. My mother would look at her sometimes and say to me, "Take care of her." And I would remember that she too had been outside, had seen.

Now T'Gatoi used four of her limbs to push me away from her onto the floor. "Go on, Gan," she said. "Sit down there with your sisters and enjoy not being sober. You had most of the egg. Lien, come warm me."

My mother hesitated for no reason that I could see. One of my earliest memories is of my mother stretched alongside T'Gatoi, talking about things I could not understand, picking me up from the floor and laughing as she sat me on one of T'Gatoi's segments. She ate her share of eggs then. I wondered when she had stopped, and why.

She lay down now against T'Gatoi, and the whole left row of T'Gatoi's limbs closed around her, holding her loosely, but securely. I had always found it comfortable to lie that way, but except for my older sister, no one else in the family liked it. They said it made them feel caged.

T'Gatoi meant to cage my mother. Once she had, she moved her tail slightly, then spoke. "Not enough egg, Lien. You should have taken it when it was passed to you. You need it badly now."

T'Gatoi's tail moved once more, its whip motion so swift I wouldn't have seen it if I hadn't been watching for it. Her sting drew only a single drop of blood from my mother's bare leg.

My mother cried out—probably in surprise. Being stung doesn't hurt. Then she sighed and I could see her body relax. She moved languidly into a more comfortable position within the cage of T'Gatoi's limbs. "Why did you do that?" she asked, sounding half asleep.

"I could not watch you sitting and suffering any longer."

My mother managed to move her shoulders in a small shrug. "Tomorrow," she said.

"Yes. Tomorrow you will resume your suffering—if you must. But just now, just for now, lie here and warm me and let me ease your way a little."

"He's still mine, you know," my mother said suddenly.

"Nothing can buy him from me." Sober, she would not have permitted herself to refer to such things.

"Nothing," T'Gatoi agreed, humoring her.

"Did you think I would sell him for eggs? For long life? My son?"

"Not for anything," T'Gatoi said, stroking my mother's shoulders, toying with her long, graying hair.

I would like to have touched my mother, shared that moment with her. She would take my hand if I touched her now. Freed by the egg and the sting, she would smile and perhaps say things long held in. But tomorrow, she would remember all this as a humiliation. I did not want to be part of a remembered humiliation. Best just be still and know she loved me under all the duty and pride and pain.

"Xuan Hoa, take off her shoes," T'Gatoi said. "In a little while I'll sting her again and she can sleep."

My older sister obeyed, swaying drunkenly as she stood up. When she had finished, she sat down beside me and took my hand. We had always been a unit, she and I.

My mother put the back of her head against T'Gatoi's underside and tried from that impossible angle to look up into the broad, round face. "You're going to sting me again?"

"Yes, Lien."

"I'll sleep until tomorrow noon."

"Good. You need it. When did you sleep last?"

My mother made a wordless sound of annoyance. "I should have stepped on you when you were small enough," she muttered.

It was an old joke between them. They had grown up together, sort of, though T'Gatoi had not, in my mother's lifetime, been small enough for any Terran to step on. She was nearly three times my mother's present age, yet would still be young when my mother died of age. But T'Gatoi and my mother had met as T'Gatoi was coming into a period of rapid development—a kind of Tlic adolescence. My mother was only a child, but for a while they developed at the same rate and had no better friends than each other.

T'Gatoi had even introduced my mother to the man who became my father. My parents, pleased with each other in spite of their different ages, married as T'Gatoi was going into her family's business—politics. She and my mother saw each other less. But sometime before my older sister was born, my mother promised T'Gatoi one of her children. She would have to give one of us to someone, and she preferred T'Gatoi to some stranger.

Years passed. T'Gatoi traveled and increased her influence. The Preserve was hers by the time she came back to my mother to collect what she probably saw as her just reward for her hard work. My older sister took an instant liking to her and wanted to be chosen, but my mother was just coming to term with me and T'Gatoi liked the idea of choosing an infant and watching and taking part in all the phases of development. I'm told I was first caged within T'Gatoi's many limbs only three minutes after my birth. A few days later, I was given my first taste of egg. I tell Terrans that when they ask whether I was ever afraid of her. And I tell it to Tlic when T'Gatoi suggests a young Terran child for them and they, anxious and ignorant, demand an adolescent. Even my brother who had somehow grown up to fear and distrust the Tlic could probably have gone smoothly into one of their families if he had been adopted early enough. Sometimes, I think for his sake he should have been. I looked at him, stretched out on the floor across the room, his eyes open, but glazed as he dreamed his egg dream. No matter what he felt toward the Tlic, he always demanded his share of egg.

"Lien, can you stand up?" T'Gatoi asked suddenly.

"Stand?" my mother said. "I thought I was going to sleep."

"Later. Something sounds wrong outside." The cage was abruptly gone.

"What?"

"Up, Lien!"

My mother recognized her tone and got up just in time to avoid being dumped on the floor. T'Gatoi whipped her three meters of body off her couch, toward the door, and out at full speed. She had bones—ribs, a long spine, a skull, four sets of limb bones per segment. But when she moved that way, twisting, hurling herself into controlled falls, landing running, she seemed not only boneless, but aquatic—something swimming through the air as though it were water. I loved watching her move.

I left my sister and started to follow her out the door, though I wasn't very steady on my own feet. It would have been better to sit and dream, better yet to find a girl and share a waking dream with her. Back when the Tlic saw us as not much more than convenient, big, warm-blooded animals, they would pen several of us together, male and female, and feed us only eggs. That way they could be sure of getting another generation of us no matter how we tried to hold out. We were lucky that didn't go on long. A few generations of it and we would have *been* little more than convenient, big animals.

"Hold the door open, Gan," T'Gatoi said. "And tell the family to stay back."

"What is it?" I asked.

"N'Tlic."

I shrank back against the door. "Here? Alone?"

"He was trying to reach a call box, I suppose." She carried the man past me, unconscious, folded like a coat over some of her limbs. He looked young—my brother's age perhaps—and he was thinner than he should have been. What T'Gatoi would have called dangerously thin.

"Gan, go to the call box," she said. She put the man on the floor and began stripping off his clothing.

I did not move.

After a moment, she looked up at me, her sudden stillness a sign of deep impatience.

"Send Qui," I told her. "I'll stay here. Maybe I can help."

She let her limbs begin to move again, lifting the man and pulling his shirt over his head. "You don't want to see this," she said. "It will be hard. I can't help this man the way his Tlic could."

"I know. But send Qui. He won't want to be of any help here. I'm at least willing to try."

She looked at my brother—older, bigger, stronger, certainly more able to help her here. He was sitting up now, braced against the wall, staring at the man on the floor with undisguised fear and revulsion. Even she could see that he would be useless.

"Qui, go!" she said.

He didn't argue. He stood up, swayed briefly, then steadied, frightened sober.

"This man's name is Bram Lomas," she told him, reading from the man's armband. I fingered my own armband in sympathy. "He needs T'Khotgif Teh. Do you hear?"

"Bram Lomas, T'Khotgif Teh," my brother said. "I'm going." He edged around Lomas and ran out the door.

Lomas began to regain consciousness. He only moaned at first and clutched spasmodically at a pair of T'Gatoi's limbs. My younger sister, finally awake from her egg dream, came close to look at him, until my mother pulled her back.

T'Gatoi removed the man's shoes, then his pants, all the while leaving him two of her limbs to grip. Except for the final few, all her limbs were equally dexterous. "I want no argument from you this time, Gan," she said.

I straightened. "What shall I do?"

"Go out and slaughter an animal that is at least half your size."

"Slaughter? But I've never—"

She knocked me across the room. Her tail was an efficient weapon whether she exposed the sting or not.

I got up, feeling stupid for having ignored her warning, and went into the kitchen. Maybe I could kill something with a knife or an ax. My mother raised a few Terran animals for the table and several thousand local ones for their fur. T'Gatoi would probably prefer something local. An achti, perhaps. Some of those were the right size, though they had about three times as many teeth as I did and a real love of using them. My mother, Hoa, and Qui could kill them with knives. I had never killed one at all, had never slaughtered any animal. I had spent most of my time with T'Gatoi while my brother and sisters were learning the family business. T'Gatoi had been right. I should have been the one to go to the call box. At least I could do that.

I went to the corner cabinet where my mother kept her large house and garden tools. At the back of the cabinet there was a pipe that carried off waste water from the kitchen—except that it didn't anymore. My father had rerouted the waste water below before I was born. Now the pipe could be turned so that one half slid around the other and a rifle could be stored inside. This wasn't our only gun, but it was our most easily accessible one. I would have to use it to shoot one of the biggest of the achti. Then T'Gatoi would probably confiscate it. Firearms were illegal in the Preserve. There had been incidents right after the Preserve was established—Terrans shooting Tlic, shooting N'Tlic. This was before the joining of families began, before everyone had a personal stake in keeping the peace. No one had shot a Tlic in my lifetime or my mother's, but the law still stood—for our protection, we were told. There were stories of whole Terran families wiped out in reprisal back during the assassinations.

I went out to the cages and shot the biggest achti I could find. It was a handsome breeding male, and my mother would not be pleased to see me bring it in. But it was the right size, and I was in a hurry.

I put the achti's long, warm body over my shoulder—glad that some of the weight I'd gained was muscle—and took it to the kitchen. There, I put the gun back in its hiding place. If T'Gatoi noticed the achti's wounds and demanded the gun, I would give it to her. Otherwise, let it stay where my father wanted it.

I turned to take the achti to her, then hesitated. For several seconds, I stood in front of the closed door wondering why I was suddenly afraid. I knew what was going to happen. I hadn't seen it before but T'Gatoi had shown me diagrams and drawings. She had made sure I knew the truth as soon as I was old enough to understand it.

Yet I did not want to go into that room. I wasted a little time choosing a knife from the carved, wooden box in which my mother kept them. T'Gatoi might want one, I told myself, for the tough, heavily furred hide of the achti.

"Gan!" T'Gatoi called, her voice harsh with urgency.

I swallowed. I had not imagined a single moving of the feet could be so difficult. I realized I was trembling and that shamed me. Shame impelled me through the door.

I put the achti down near T'Gatoi and saw that Lomas was unconscious again. She, Lomas, and I were alone in the room—my mother and sisters probably sent out so they would not have to watch. I envied them.

But my mother came back into the room as T'Gatoi seized the achti. Ignoring the knife I offered her, she extended claws from several of her limbs and slit the achti from throat to anus. She looked at me, her yellow eyes intent. "Hold this man's shoulders, Gan."

I stared at Lomas in panic, realizing that I did not want to touch him, let alone hold him. This would not be like shooting an animal. Not as quick, not as merciful, and, I hoped, not as final, but there was nothing I wanted less than to be part of it.

My mother came forward. "Gan, you hold his right side," she said. "I'll hold his left." And if he came to, he would throw her off without realizing he had done it. She was a tiny woman. She often wondered aloud how she had produced, as she said, such "huge" children.

"Never mind," I told her, taking the man's shoulders. "I'll do it." She hovered nearby.

"Don't worry," I said. "I won't shame you. You don't have to stay and watch."

She looked at me uncertainly, then touched my face in a rare caress. Finally, she went back to her bedroom.

T'Gatoi lowered her head in relief. "Thank you, Gan," she said with courtesy more Terran than Tlic. "That one . . . she is always finding new ways for me to make her suffer."

Lomas began to groan and make choked sounds. I had hoped he would stay unconscious. T'Gatoi put her face near his so that he focused on her.

"I've stung you as much as I dare for now," she told him. "When this is over, I'll sting you to sleep and you won't hurt anymore."

"Please," the man begged. "Wait . . ."

"There's no more time, Bram. I'll sting you as soon as it's over. When T'Khotgif arrives she'll give you eggs to help you heal. It will be over soon."

"T'Khotgif!" the man shouted, straining against my hands.

"Soon, Bram." T'Gatoi glanced at me, then placed a claw against his abdomen slightly to the right of the middle, just below the left rib. There was movement on the right side—tiny, seemingly random pulsations moving his brown flesh, creating a concavity here, a convexity there, over and over until I could see the rhythm of it and knew where the next pulse would be.

Lomas's entire body stiffened under T'Gatoi's claw, though she merely rested it against him as she wound the rear section of her body around his legs. He might break my grip, but he would not break hers. He wept helplessly as she used his pants to tie his hands, then pushed his hands above his head so that I could kneel on the cloth between them and pin them in place. She rolled up his shirt and gave it to him to bite down on.

And she opened him.

His body convulsed with the first cut. He almost tore himself away from me. The sound he made . . . I had never heard such sounds come from anything human. T'Gatoi seemed to pay no attention as she lengthened and deepened the cut, now and then pausing to lick away blood. His blood vessels contracted, reacting to the chemistry of her saliva, and the bleeding slowed.

I felt as though I were helping her torture him, helping her consume him. I knew I would vomit soon, didn't know why I hadn't already. I couldn't possibly last until she was finished.

She found the first grub. It was fat and deep red with his blood—both inside and out. It had already eaten its own egg case but apparently had not yet begun to eat its host. At this stage, it would eat any flesh except its mother's. Let alone, it would have gone on excreting the poisons that had both sickened and alerted Lomas. Eventually it would have begun to eat. By the time it ate its way out of Lomas's flesh, Lomas would be dead or dying—and unable to take revenge on the thing that was killing him. There was always a grace period between the time the host sickened and the time the grubs began to eat him.

T'Gatoi picked up the writhing grub carefully and looked at it, somehow ignoring the terrible groans of the man.

Abruptly, the man lost consciousness.

"Good." T'Gatoi looked down at him. "I wish you Terrans could do that at will." She felt nothing. And the thing she held . . .

It was limbless and boneless at this stage, perhaps fifteen centimeters long and two thick, blind and slimy with blood. It was like a large worm. T'Gatoi put it into the belly of the achti, and it began at once to burrow. It would stay there and eat as long as there was anything to eat.

Probing through Lomas's flesh, she found two more, one of them smaller and more vigorous. "A male!" she said happily. He would be dead before I would. He would be through his metamorphosis and screwing everything that would hold still before his sisters even had limbs. He was the only one to make a serious effort to bite T'Gatoi as she placed him in the achti.

Paler worms oozed to visibility in Lomas's flesh. I closed my eyes. It was worse than finding something dead, rotting, and filled with tiny animal grubs. And it was far worse than any drawing or diagram.

"Ah, there are more," T'Gatoi said, plucking out two long, thick grubs. You may have to kill another animal, Gan. Everything lives inside you Terrans."

I had been told all my life that this was a good and necessary thing Tlic and Terran did together—a kind of birth. I had believed it until now. I knew birth was painful and bloody, no matter what. But this was something else, something worse. And I wasn't ready to see it. Maybe I never would be. Yet I couldn't not see it. Closing my eyes didn't help.

T'Gatoi found a grub still eating its egg case. The remains of the case were still wired into a blood vessel by their own little tube or hook or whatever. That was the way the grubs were anchored and the way they fed. They took only blood until they were ready to emerge. Then they ate their stretched, elastic egg cases. Then they ate their hosts.

T'Gatoi bit away the egg case, licked away the blood. Did she like the taste? Did childhood habits die hard—or not die at all?

The whole procedure was wrong, alien. I wouldn't have thought anything about her could seem alien to me.

"One more, I think," she said. "Perhaps two. A good family. In a host animal these days, we would be happy to find one or two alive." She glanced at me. "Go out-side, Gan, and empty your stomach. Go now while the man is unconscious."

I staggered out, barely made it. Beneath the tree just beyond the front door, I vomited until there was nothing left to bring up. Finally, I stood shaking, tears streaming down my face. I did not know why I was crying, but I could not stop. I went further from the house to avoid being seen. Every time I closed my eyes I saw red worms crawling over redder human flesh.

There was a car coming toward the house. Since Terrans were forbidden motor-ized vehicles except for certain farm equipment, I knew this must be Lomas's Tlic with Qui and perhaps a Terran doctor. I wiped my face on my shirt, struggled for control.

"Gan," Qui called as the car stopped. "What happened?" He crawled out of the low, round, Tlic-convenient car door. Another Terran crawled out the other side and went into the house without speaking to me. The doctor. With his help and a few eggs, Lomas might make it.

"T'Khotgif Teh?" I said.

The Tlic driver surged out of her car, reared up half her length before me. She was paler and smaller than T'Gatoi—probably born from the body of an animal. Tlic from Terran bodies were always larger as well as more numerous.

"Six young," I told her. "Maybe seven, all alive. At least one male."

"Lomas?" she said harshly. I liked her for the question and the concern in her voice when she asked it. The last coherent thing he had said was her name.

"He's alive," I said.

She surged away to the house without another word.

"She's been sick," my brother said, watching her go. "When I called, I could hear people telling her she wasn't well enough to go out even for this."

I said nothing. I had extended courtesy to the Tlic. Now I didn't want to talk to anyone. I hoped he would go in—out of curiosity if nothing else.

"Finally found out more than you wanted to know, eh?"

I looked at him.

"Don't give me one of *her* looks," he said. "You're not her. You're just her property."

One of her looks. Had I picked up even an ability to imitate her expressions?

"What'd you do, puke?" He sniffed the air. "So now you know what you're in for."

I walked away from him. He and I had been close when we were kids. He would let me follow him around when I was home, and sometimes T'Gatoi would let me bring him along when she took me into the city. But something had happened when he reached adolescence. I never knew what. He began keeping out of T'Gatoi's way. Then he began running away—until he realized there was no "away." Not in the Preserve. Certainly not outside. After that he concentrated on getting his share of every egg that came into the house and on looking out for me in a way that made me all but hate him—a way that clearly said, as long as I was all right, he was safe from the Tlic.

"How was it, really?" he demanded, following me.

"I killed an achti. The young ate it."

"You didn't run out of the house and puke because they ate an achti."

"I had . . . never seen a person cut open before." That was true, and enough for him to know. I couldn't talk about the other. Not with him.

"Oh," he said. He glanced at me as though he wanted to say more, but he kept quiet.

We walked, not really headed anywhere. Toward the back, toward the cages, toward the fields.

"Did he say anything?" Qui asked. "Lomas, I mean."

Who else would he mean? "He said 'T'Khotgif.'"

Qui shuddered. "If she had done that to me, she'd be the last person I'd call for."

"You'd call for her. Her sting would ease your pain without killing the grubs in you."

"You think I'd care if they died?"

No. Of course he wouldn't. Would I?

"Shit!" He drew a deep breath. "I've seen what they do. You think this thing with Lomas was bad? It was nothing."

I didn't argue. He didn't know what he was talking about.

"I saw them eat a man," he said.

I turned to face him. "You're lying!"

"*I saw them eat a man.*" He paused. "It was when I was little. I had been to the Hartmund house and I was on my way home. Halfway here, I saw a man and a Tlic and the man was N'Tlic. The ground was hilly. I was able to hide from them and watch. The Tlic wouldn't open the man because she had nothing to feed the grubs. The man couldn't go any further and there were no houses around. He was in so much pain, he told her to kill him. He begged her to kill him. Finally, she did. She cut his throat. One swipe of one claw. I saw the grubs eat their way out, then burrow in again, still eating."

His words made me see Lomas's flesh again, parasitized, crawling. "Why didn't you tell me that?" I whispered.

He looked startled as though he'd forgotten I was listening. "I don't know."

"You started to run away not long after that, didn't you?"

"Yeah. Stupid. Running inside the Preserve. Running in a cage."

I shook my head, said what I should have said to him long ago. "She wouldn't take you, Qui. You don't have to worry."

"She would . . . if anything happened to you."

"No. She'd take Xuan Hoa. Hoa . . . wants it." She wouldn't if she had stayed to watch Lomas.

"They don't take women," he said with contempt.

"They do sometimes." I glanced at him. "Actually, they prefer women. You should be around them when they talk among themselves. They say women have more body fat to protect the grubs. But they usually take men to leave the women free to bear their own young."

"To provide the next generation of host animals," he said, switching from contempt to bitterness.

"It's more than that!" I countered. Was it?

"If it were going to happen to me, I'd want to believe it was more, too."

"It *is* more!" I felt like a kid. Stupid argument.

"Did you think so while T'Gatoi was picking worms out of that guy's guts?"

"It's not supposed to happen that way."

"Sure it is. You weren't supposed to see it, that's all. And his Tlic was supposed to do it. She could sting him unconscious and the operation wouldn't have been as painful. But she'd still open him, pick out the grubs, and if she missed even one, it would poison him and eat him from the inside out."

There was actually a time when my mother told me to show respect for Qui because he was my older brother. I walked away, hating him. In his way, he was gloating. He was safe and I wasn't. I could have hit him, but I didn't think I would be able to stand it when he refused to hit back, when he looked at me with contempt and pity.

He wouldn't let me get away. Longer legged, he swung ahead of me and made me feel as though I were following him.

"I'm sorry," he said.

I strode on, sick and furious.

"Look, it probably won't be that bad with you. T'Gatoi likes you. She'll be careful."

I turned back toward the house, almost running from him.

"Has she done it to you yet?" he asked, keeping up easily. "I mean, you're about the right age for implantation. Has she—"

I hit him. I didn't know I was going to do it, but I think I meant to kill him. If he hadn't been bigger and stronger, I think I would have.

He tried to hold me off, but in the end, had to defend himself. He only hit me a couple of times. That was plenty. I don't remember going down, but when I came to, he was gone. It was worth the pain to be rid of him.

I got up and walked slowly toward the house. The back was dark. No one was in the kitchen. My mother and sisters were sleeping in their bedrooms—or pretending to.

Once I was in the kitchen, I could hear voices—Tlic and Terran from the next room. I couldn't make out what they were saying—didn't want to make it out.

I sat down at my mother's table, waiting for quiet. The table was smooth and worn, heavy and well crafted. My father had made it for her just before he died. I remembered hanging around underfoot when he built it. He didn't mind. Now I sat leaning on it, missing him. I could have talked to him. He had done it three times in his long life. Three clutches of eggs, three times being opened up and sewed up. How had he done it? How did anyone do it?

I got up, took the rifle from its hiding place, and sat down again with it. It needed cleaning, oiling.

All I did was load it.

"Gan?"

She made a lot of little clicking sounds when she walked on bare floor, each limb clicking in succession as it touched down. Waves of little clicks.

She came to the table, raised the front half of her body above it, and surged onto it. Sometimes she moved so smoothly she seemed to flow like water itself. She coiled herself into a small hill in the middle of the table and looked at me.

"That was bad," she said softly. "You should not have seen it. It need not be that way."

"I know."

"T'Khotgif—Ch'Khotgif now—she will die of her disease. She will not live to raise her children. But her sister will provide for them and for Bram Lomas." Sterile sister. One fertile female in every lot. One to keep the family going. That sister owed Lomas more than she could ever repay.

"He'll live then?"

"Yes."

"I wonder if he would do it again."

"No one would ask him to do that again."

I looked into the yellow eyes, wondering how much I saw and understood there, and how much I only imagined. "No one ever asks us," I said. "You never asked me."

She moved her head slightly. "What's the matter with your face?"

"Nothing. Nothing important." Human eyes probably wouldn't have noticed the swelling in the darkness. The only light was from one of the moons, shining through a window across the room.

"Did you use the rifle to shoot the achti?"

"Yes."

"And do you mean to use it to shoot me?"

I stared at her, outlined in the moonlight—coiled, graceful body. "What does Terran blood taste like to you?"

She said nothing.

"What are you?" I whispered. "What are we to you?"

She lay still, rested her head on her topmost coil. "You know me as no other does," she said softly. "You must decide."

"That's what happened to my face," I told her.

"What?"

"Qui goaded me into deciding to do something. It didn't turn out very well." I moved the gun slightly, brought the barrel up diagonally under my own chin. "At least it was a decision I made."

"As this will be."

"Ask me, Gatoi."

"For my children's lives?"

She would say something like that. She knew how to manipulate people, Terran and Tlic. But not this time.

"I don't want to be a host animal," I said. "Not even yours."

It took her a long time to answer. "We use almost no host animals these days," she said. "You know that."

"You use us."

"We do. We wait long years for you and teach you and join our families to yours."
She moved restlessly. "You know you aren't animals to us."

I stared at her, saying nothing.

"The animals we once used began killing most of our eggs after implantation
long before your ancestors arrived," she said softly. "You know these things, Gan.
Because your people arrived, we are relearning what it means to be a healthy, thriving people. And your ancestors, fleeing from their homeworld, from their own kind
who would have killed or enslaved them—they survived because of us. We saw them
as people and gave them the Preserve when they still tried to kill us as worms."

At the word "worms," I jumped. I couldn't help it, and she couldn't help noticing it.

"I see," she said quietly. "Would you really rather die than bear my young, Gan?"

I didn't answer.

"Shall I go to Xuan Hoa?"

"Yes!" Hoa wanted it. Let her have it. She hadn't had to watch Lomas. She'd be
proud. . . . Not terrified.

T'Gatoi flowed off the table onto the floor, startling me almost too much.

"I'll sleep in Hoa's room tonight," she said. "And sometime tonight or in the
morning, I'll tell her."

This was going too fast. My sister Hoa had had almost as much to do with raising me as my mother. I was still close to her—not like Qui. She could want T'Gatoi
and still love me.

"Wait! Gatoi!"

She looked back, then raised nearly half her length off the floor and turned to
face me. "These are adult things, Gan. This is my life, my family!"

"But she's . . . my sister."

"I have done what you demanded. I have asked you!"

"But—"

"It will be easier for Hoa. She has always expected to carry other lives inside her."

Human lives. Human young who should someday drink at her breasts, not at her
veins.

I shook my head. "Don't do it to her, Gatoi." I was not Qui. It seemed I could
become him, though, with no effort at all. I could make Xuan Hoa my shield. Would
it be easier to know that red worms were growing in her flesh instead of mine?

"Don't do it to Hoa," I repeated.

She stared at me, utterly still.

I looked away, then back at her. "Do it to me."

I lowered the gun from my throat and she leaned forward to take it.

"No," I told her.

"It's the law," she said.

"Leave it for the family. One of them might use it to save my life someday."

She grasped the rifle barrel, but I wouldn't let go. I was pulled into a standing
position over her.

"Leave it here!" I repeated. "If we're not your animals, if these are adult things,
accept the risk. There is risk, Gatoi, in dealing with a partner."

It was clearly hard for her to let go of the rifle. A shudder went through her and
she made a hissing sound of distress. It occurred to me that she was afraid. She was

old enough to have seen what guns could do to people. Now her young and this gun would be together in the same house. She did not know about the other guns. In this dispute, they did not matter.

"I will implant the first egg tonight," she said as I put the gun away. "Do you hear, Gan?"

Why else had I been given a whole egg to eat while the rest of the family was left to share one? Why else had my mother kept looking at me as though I were going away from her, going where she could not follow? Did T'Gatoi imagine I hadn't known?

"I hear."

"Now!" I let her push me out of the kitchen, then walked ahead of her toward my bedroom. The sudden urgency in her voice sounded real. "You would have done it to Hoa tonight!" I accused.

"I must do it to someone tonight."

I stopped in spite of her urgency and stood in her way. "Don't you care who?"

She flowed around me and into my bedroom. I found her waiting on the couch we shared. There was nothing in Hoa's room that she could have used. She would have done it to Hoa on the floor. The thought of her doing it to Hoa at all disturbed me in a different way now, and I was suddenly angry.

Yet I undressed and lay down beside her. I knew what to do, what to expect. I had been told all my life. I felt the familiar sting, narcotic, mildly pleasant. Then the blind probing of her ovipositor. The puncture was painless, easy. So easy going in. She undulated slowly against me, her muscles forcing the egg from her body into mine. I held on to a pair of her limbs until I remembered Lomas holding her that way. Then I let go, moved inadvertently, and hurt her. She gave a low cry of pain and I expected to be caged at once within her limbs. When I wasn't, I held on to her again, feeling oddly ashamed.

"I'm sorry," I whispered.

She rubbed my shoulders with four of her limbs.

"Do you care?" I asked. "Do you care that it's me?"

She did not answer for some time. Finally, "You were the one making the choices tonight, Gan. I made mine long ago."

"Would you have gone to Hoa?"

"Yes. How could I put my children into the care of one who hates them?"

"It wasn't . . . hate."

"I know what it was."

"I was afraid."

Silence.

"I still am." I could admit it to her here, now.

"But you came to me . . . to save Hoa."

"Yes." I leaned my forehead against her. She was cool velvet, deceptively soft. "And to keep you for myself," I said. It was so. I didn't understand it, but it was so.

She made a soft hum of contentment. "I couldn't believe I had made such a mistake with you," she said. "I chose you. I believed you had grown to choose me."

"I had, but . . ."

"Lomas."

"Yes."

"I had never known a Terran to see a birth and take it well. Qui has seen one, hasn't he?"

"Yes."

"Terrans should be protected from seeing."

I didn't like the sound of that—and I doubted that it was possible. "Not protected," I said. "Shown. Shown when we're young kids, and shown more than once. Gatoi, no Terran ever sees a birth that goes right. All we see is N'Tlic—pain and terror and maybe death."

She looked down at me. "It is a private thing. It has always been a private thing."

Her tone kept me from insisting—that and the knowledge that if she changed her mind, I might be the first public example. But I had planted the thought in her mind. Chances were it would grow, and eventually she would experiment.

"You won't see it again," she said. "I don't want you thinking any more about shooting me."

The small amount of fluid that came into me with her egg relaxed me as completely as a sterile egg would have, so that I could remember the rifle in my hands and my feelings of fear and revulsion, anger and despair. I could remember the feelings without reviving them. I could talk about them.

"I wouldn't have shot you," I said. "Not you." She had been taken from my father's flesh when he was my age.

"You could have," she insisted.

"Not you." She stood between us and her own people, protecting, interweaving.

"Would you have destroyed yourself?"

I moved carefully, uncomfortable. "I could have done that. I nearly did. That's Qui's 'away.' I wonder if he knows."

"What?"

I did not answer.

"You will live now."

"Yes." *Take care of her,* my mother used to say. Yes.

"I'm healthy and young," she said. "I won't leave you as Lomas was left—alone, N'Tlic. I'll take care of you."

—1985

CHARLOTTE PERKINS GILMAN

1860-1935

Charlotte Perkins Gilman was born in Hartford, Connecticut, and raised primarily by her mother in impoverished conditions. She briefly attended the Rhode Island School of Design before working as a commercial artist, art teacher, and governess. In 1885, Gilman had a nervous breakdown. Her decision to have her daughter live with her ex-husband prompted newspaper assaults on her character. In 1892, "The Yellow Wall-Paper" appeared in The New England Magazine. *Her* Women and Economics *(1898) and* The Man-Made World *(1911) are hailed as major feminist tracts linking issues of capitalist organization to women's subordination in patriarchy. Her novel,* Herland *(1915), featured a world of parthenogenetic women. Neglected after her death, Perkins Gilman's works were finally collected in 1979.*

THE YELLOW WALL-PAPER

It is very seldom that mere ordinary people like John and myself secure ancestral halls for the summer.

A colonial mansion, a hereditary estate, I would say a haunted house, and reach the height of romantic felicity—but that would be asking too much of fate!

Still I will proudly declare that there is something queer about it.

Else, why should it be let so cheaply? And why have stood so long untenanted?

John laughs at me, of course, but one expects that in marriage.

John is practical in the extreme. He has no patience with faith, an intense horror of superstition, and he scoffs openly at any talk of things not to be felt and seen and put down in figures.

John is a physician, and *perhaps*—(I would not say it to a living soul, of course, but this is dead paper and a great relief to my mind)—*perhaps* that is one reason I do not get well faster.

You see he does not believe I am sick!

And what can one do?

If a physician of high standing, and one's own husband, assures friends and relatives that there is really nothing the matter with one but temporary nervous depression—a slight hysterical tendency—what is one to do?

My brother is also a physician, and also of high standing, and he says the same thing.

So I take phosphates or phosphites—whichever it is, and tonics, and journeys, and air, and exercise, and am absolutely forbidden to "work" until I am well again.

Personally, I disagree with their ideas.

Personally, I believe that congenial work, with excitement and change, would do me good.

But what is one to do?

I did write for a while in spite of them; but it *does* exhaust me a good deal—having to be so sly about it, or else meet with heavy opposition.

I sometimes fancy that in my condition if I had less opposition and more society and stimulus—but John says the very worst thing I can do is to think about my condition, and I confess it always makes me feel bad.

So I will let it alone and talk about the house.

The most beautiful place! It is quite alone, standing well back from the road, quite three miles from the village. It makes me think of English places that you read about, for there are hedges and walls and gates that lock, and lots of separate little houses for the gardeners and people.

There is a *delicious* garden! I never saw such a garden—large and shady, full of box-bordered paths, and lined with long grape-covered arbors with seats under them.

There were greenhouses, too, but they are all broken now.

There was some legal trouble, I believe, something about the heirs and coheirs; anyhow, the place has been empty for years.

That spoils my ghostliness, I am afraid, but I don't care—there is something strange about the house—I can feel it.

I even said so to John one moonlight evening, but he said what I felt was a *draught,* and shut the window.

I get unreasonably angry with John sometimes. I'm sure I never used to be so sensitive. I think it is due to this nervous condition.

But John says if I feel so, I shall neglect proper self-control; so I take pains to control myself—before him, at least, and that makes me very tired.

I don't like our room a bit. I wanted one downstairs that opened on the piazza and had roses all over the window, and such pretty old-fashioned chintz hangings! but John would not hear of it.

He said there was only one window and not room for two beds, and no near room for him if he took another.

He is very careful and loving, and hardly lets me stir without special direction.

I have a schedule prescription for each hour in the day; he takes all care from me, and so I feel basely ungrateful not to value it more.

He said we came here solely on my account, that I was to have perfect rest and all the air I could get. "Your exercise depends on your strength, my dear," said he, "and your food somewhat on your appetite; but air you can absorb all the time." So we took the nursery at the top of the house.

It is a big, airy room, the whole floor nearly, with windows that look all ways, and air and sunshine galore. It was nursery first and then playroom and gymnasium, I should judge; for the windows are barred for little children, and there are rings and things in the walls.

The paint and paper look as if a boys' school had used it. It is stripped off—the paper—in great patches all around the head of my bed, about as far as I can reach, and in a great place on the other side of the room low down. I never saw a worse paper in my life.

One of those sprawling flamboyant patterns committing every artistic sin.

It is dull enough to confuse the eye in following, pronounced enough to constantly irritate and provoke study, and when you follow the lame uncertain curves for a little distance they suddenly commit suicide—plunge off at outrageous angles, destroy themselves in unheard of contradictions.

The color is repellent, almost revolting; a smouldering unclean yellow, strangely faded by the slow-turning sunlight.

It is a dull yet lurid orange in some places, a sickly sulphur tint in others.

No wonder the children hated it! I should hate it myself if I had to live in this room long.

There comes John, and I must put this away,—he hates to have me write a word.

We have been here two weeks, and I haven't felt like writing before, since that first day.

I am sitting by the window now, up in this atrocious nursery, and there is nothing to hinder my writing as much as I please, save lack of strength.

John is away all day, and even some nights when his cases are serious.

I am glad my case is not serious!

But these nervous troubles are dreadfully depressing.

John does not know how much I really suffer. He knows there is no *reason* to suffer, and that satisfies him.

Of course it is only nervousness. It does weigh on me so not to do my duty in any way!

I meant to be such a help to John, such a real rest and comfort, and here I am a comparative burden already!

Nobody would believe what an effort it is to do what little I am able,—to dress and entertain, and order things.

It is fortunate Mary is so good with the baby. Such a dear baby!

And yet I *cannot* be with him, it makes me so nervous.

I suppose John never was nervous in his life. He laughs at me so about this wall-paper!

At first he meant to repaper the room, but afterwards he said that I was letting it get the better of me, and that nothing was worse for a nervous patient than to give way to such fancies.

He said that after the wall-paper was changed it would be the heavy bedstead, and then the barred windows, and then that gate at the head of the stairs, and so on.

"You know the place is doing you good," he said, "and really, dear, I don't care to renovate the house just for a three months' rental."

"Then do let us go downstairs," I said, "there are such pretty rooms there."

Then he took me in his arms and called me a blessed little goose, and said he would go down to the cellar, if I wished, and have it whitewashed into the bargain.

But he is right enough about the beds and windows and things.

It is an airy and comfortable room as any one need wish, and, of course, I would not be so silly as to make him uncomfortable just for a whim.

I'm really getting quite fond of the big room, all but that horrid paper.

Out of one window I can see the garden, those mysterious deep shaded arbors, the riotous old-fashioned flowers, and bushes and gnarly trees.

Out of another I get a lovely view of the bay and a little private wharf belonging to the estate. There is a beautiful shaded lane that runs down there from the house. I always fancy I see people walking in these numerous paths and arbors, but John has cautioned me not to give way to fancy in the least. He says that with my imaginative power and habit of story-making, a nervous weakness like mine is sure to lead to all manner of excited fancies, and that I ought to use my will and good sense to check the tendency. So I try.

I think sometimes that if I were only well enough to write a little it would relieve the press of ideas and rest me.

But I find I get pretty tired when I try.

It is so discouraging not to have any advice and companionship about my work. When I get really well, John says we will ask Cousin Henry and Julia down for a long visit; but he says he would as soon put fireworks in my pillow-case as to let me have those stimulating people about now.

I wish I could get well faster.

But I must not think about that. This paper looks to me as if it *knew* what a vicious influence it had!

There is a recurrent spot where the pattern lolls like a broken neck and two bulbous eyes stare at you upside down.

I get positively angry with the impertinence of it and the everlastingness. Up and down and sideways they crawl, and those absurd, unblinking eyes are everywhere. There is one place where two breadths didn't match, and the eyes go all up and down the line, one a little higher than the other.

I never saw so much expression in an inanimate thing before, and we all know how much expression they have! I used to lie awake as a child and get more entertainment and terror out of blank walls and plain furniture than most children could find in a toy-store.

I remember what a kindly wink the knobs of our big, old bureau used to have, and there was one chair that always seemed like a strong friend.

I used to feel that if any of the other things looked too fierce I could always hop into that chair and be safe.

The furniture in this room is no worse than inharmonious, however, for we had to bring it all from downstairs. I suppose when this was used as a playroom they had to take the nursery things out, and no wonder! I never saw such ravages as the children have made here.

The wall-paper, as I said before, is torn off in spots, and it sticketh closer than a brother—they must have had perseverance as well as hatred.

Then the floor is scratched and gouged and splintered, the plaster itself is dug out here and there, and this great heavy bed which is all we found in the room, looks as if it had been through the wars.

But I don't mind it a bit—only the paper.

There comes John's sister. Such a dear girl as she is, and so careful of me! I must not let her find me writing.

She is a perfect and enthusiastic housekeeper, and hopes for no better profession. I verily believe she thinks it is the writing which made me sick!

But I can write when she is out, and see her a long way off from these windows.

There is one that commands the road, a lovely shaded winding road, and one that just looks off over the country. A lovely country, too, full of great elms and velvet meadows.

This wall-paper has a kind of sub-pattern in a different shade, a particularly irritating one, for you can only see it in certain lights, and not clearly then.

But in the places where it isn't faded and where the sun is just so—I can see a strange, provoking, formless sort of figure, that seems to skulk about behind that silly and conspicuous front design.

There's sister on the stairs!

Well, the Fourth of July is over! The people are all gone and I am tired out. John thought it might do me good to see a little company, so we just had mother and Nellie and the children down for a week.

Of course I didn't do a thing. Jennie sees to everything now.

But it tired me all the same.

John says if I don't pick up faster he shall send me to Weir Mitchell in the fall.

But I don't want to go there at all. I had a friend who was in his hands once, and she says he is just like John and my brother, only more so!

Besides, it is such an undertaking to go so far.

I don't feel as if it was worth while to turn my hand over for anything, and I'm getting dreadfully fretful and querulous.

I cry at nothing, and cry most of the time.

Of course I don't when John is here, or anybody else, but when I am alone.

And I am alone a good deal just now. John is kept in town very often by serious cases, and Jennie is good and lets me alone when I want her to.

So I walk a little in the garden or down that lovely lane, sit on the porch under the roses, and lie down up here a good deal.

I'm getting really fond of the room in spite of the wall-paper. Perhaps *because* of the wall-paper.

It dwells in my mind so!

I lie here on this great immovable bed—it is nailed down, I believe—and follow that pattern about by the hour. It is as good as gymnastics, I assure you. I start, we'll say, at the bottom, down in the corner over there where it has not been touched, and I determine for the thousandth time that I *will* follow that pointless pattern to some sort of a conclusion.

I know a little of the principle of design, and I know this thing was not arranged on any laws of radiation, or alternation, or repetition, or symmetry, or anything else that I ever heard of.

It is repeated, of course, by the breadths, but not otherwise.

Looked at in one way each breadth stands alone, the bloated curves and flourishes—a kind of "debased Romanesque" with *delirium tremens*—go waddling up and down in isolated columns of fatuity.

But, on the other hand, they connect diagonally, and the sprawling outlines run off in great slanting waves of optic horror, like a lot of wallowing seaweeds in full chase.

The whole thing goes horizontally, too, at least it seems so, and I exhaust myself in trying to distinguish the order of its going in that direction.

They have used a horizontal breadth for a frieze, and that adds wonderfully to the confusion.

There is one end of the room where it is almost intact, and there, when the crosslights fade and the low sun shines directly upon it, I can almost fancy radiation after all,—the interminable grotesques seem to form around a common centre and rush off in headlong plunges of equal distraction.

It makes me tired to follow it. I will take a nap I guess.

I don't know why I should write this.

I don't want to.

I don't feel able.

And I know John would think it absurd. But I *must* say what I feel and think in some way—it is such a relief!

But the effort is getting to be greater than the relief.

Half the time now I am awfully lazy, and lie down ever so much.

John says I mustn't lose my strength, and has me take cod liver oil and lots of tonics and things, to say nothing of ale and wine and rare meat.

Dear John! He loves me very dearly, and hates to have me sick. I tried to have a real earnest reasonable talk with him the other day, and tell him how I wish he would let me go and make a visit to Cousin Henry and Julia.

But he said I wasn't able to go, nor able to stand it after I got there; and I did not make out a very good case for myself, for I was crying before I had finished.

It is getting to be a great effort for me to think straight. Just this nervous weakness I suppose.

And dear John gathered me up in his arms, and just carried me upstairs and laid me on the bed, and sat by me and read to me till it tired my head.

He said I was his darling and his comfort and all he had, and that I must take care of myself for his sake, and keep well.

He says no one but myself can help me out of it, that I must use my will and self-control and not let any silly fancies run away with me.

There's one comfort, the baby is well and happy, and does not have to occupy this nursery with the horrid wall-paper.

If we had not used it, that blessed child would have! What a fortunate escape! Why, I wouldn't have a child of mine, an impressionable little thing, live in such a room for worlds.

I never thought of it before, but it is lucky that John kept me here after all, I can stand it so much easier than a baby, you see.

Of course I never mention it to them any more—I am too wise,—but I keep watch of it all the same.

There are things in that paper that nobody knows but me, or ever will.

Behind that outside pattern the dim shapes get clearer every day.

It is always the same shape, only very numerous.

And it is like a woman stooping down and creeping about behind that pattern. I don't like it a bit. I wonder—I begin to think—I wish John would take me away from here!

It is so hard to talk with John about my case, because he is so wise, and because he loves me so.

But I tried it last night.

It was moonlight. The moon shines in all around just as the sun does.

I hate to see it sometimes, it creeps so slowly, and always comes in by one window or another.

John was asleep and I hated to waken him, so I kept still and watched the moonlight on that undulating wall-paper till I felt creepy.

The faint figure behind seemed to shake the pattern, just as if she wanted to get out.

I got up softly and went to feel and see if the paper *did* move, and when I came back John was awake.

"What is it, little girl?" he said. "Don't go walking about like that—you'll get cold."

I thought it was a good time to talk, so I told him that I really was not gaining here, and that I wished he would take me away.

"Why darling!" said he, "our lease will be up in three weeks, and I can't see how to leave before.

"The repairs are not done at home, and I cannot possibly leave town just now. Of course if you were in any danger, I could and would, but you really are better, dear, whether you can see it or not. I am a doctor, dear, and I know. You are gaining flesh and color, your appetite is better, I feel really much easier about you."

"I don't weigh a bit more," said I, "nor as much; and my appetite may be better in the evening when you are here, but it is worse in the morning when you are away!"

"Bless her little heart!" said he with a big hug, "she shall be as sick as she pleases! But now let's improve the shining hours by going to sleep, and talk about it in the morning!"

"And you won't go away?" I asked gloomily.

"Why, how can I, dear? It is only three weeks more and then we will take a nice little trip of a few days while Jennie is getting the house ready. Really dear you are better!"

"Better in body perhaps—" I began, and stopped short, for he sat up straight and looked at me with such a stern, reproachful look that I could not say another word.

"My darling," said he, "I beg of you, for my sake and for our child's sake, as well as for your own, that you will never for one instant let that idea enter your mind! There is nothing so dangerous, so fascinating, to a temperament like yours. It is a false and foolish fancy. Can you not trust me as a physician when I tell you so?"

So of course I said no more on that score, and we went to sleep before long. He thought I was asleep first, but I wasn't, and lay there for hours trying to decide whether that front pattern and the back pattern really did move together or separately.

On a pattern like this, by daylight, there is a lack of sequence, a defiance of law, that is a constant irritant to a normal mind.

The color is hideous enough, and unreliable enough, and infuriating enough, but the pattern is torturing.

You think you have mastered it, but just as you get well underway in following, it turns a back-somersault and there you are. It slaps you in the face, knocks you down, and tramples upon you. It is like a bad dream.

The outside pattern is a florid arabesque, reminding one of a fungus. If you can imagine a toadstool in joints, an interminable string of toadstools, budding and sprouting in endless convolutions—why, that is something like it.

That is, sometimes!

There is one marked peculiarity about this paper, a thing nobody seems to notice but myself, and that is that it changes as the light changes.

When the sun shoots in through the east window—I always watch for that first long, straight ray—it changes so quickly that I never can quite believe it.

That is why I watch it always.

By moonlight—the moon shines in all night when there is a moon—I wouldn't know it was the same paper.

At night in any kind of light, in twilight, candle light, lamplight, and worst of all by moonlight, it becomes bars! The outside pattern I mean, and the woman behind it is as plain as can be.

I didn't realize for a long time what the thing was that showed behind, that dim sub-pattern, but now I am quite sure it is a woman.

By daylight she is subdued, quiet. I fancy it is the pattern that keeps her so still. It is so puzzling. It keeps me quiet by the hour.

I lie down ever so much now. John says it is good for me, and to sleep all I can. Indeed he started the habit by making me lie down for an hour after each meal.

It is a very bad habit I am convinced, for you see I don't sleep.

And that cultivates deceit, for I don't tell them I'm awake—O no!

The fact is I am getting a little afraid of John.

He seems very queer sometimes, and even Jennie has an inexplicable look.

It strikes me occasionally, just as a scientific hypothesis,—that perhaps it is the paper!

I have watched John when he did not know I was looking, and come into the room suddenly on the most innocent excuses, and I've caught him several times *looking at the paper!* And Jennie too. I caught Jennie with her hand on it once.

She didn't know I was in the room, and when I asked her in a quiet, a very quiet voice, with the most restrained manner possible, what she was doing with the paper—she turned around as if she had been caught stealing, and looked quite angry—asked me why I should frighten her so!

Then she said that the paper stained everything it touched, that she had found yellow smooches on all my clothes and John's, and she wished we would be more careful!

Did not that sound innocent? But I know she was studying that pattern, and I am determined that nobody shall find it out but myself!

Life is very much more exciting now than it used to be. You see I have something more to expect, to look forward to, to watch. I really do eat better, and am more quiet than I was.

John is so pleased to see me improve! He laughed a little the other day, and said I seemed to be flourishing in spite of my wall-paper.

I turned it off with a laugh. I had no intention of telling him it was *because* of the wall-paper—he would make fun of me. He might even want to take me away.

I don't want to leave now until I have found it out. There is a week more, and I think that will be enough.

I'm feeling ever so much better! I don't sleep much at night, for it is so interesting to watch developments; but I sleep a good deal in the daytime.

In the daytime it is tiresome and perplexing.

There are always new shoots on the fungus, and new shades of yellow all over it. I cannot keep count of them, though I have tried conscientiously.

It is the strangest yellow, that wall-paper! It makes me think of all the yellow things I ever saw—not beautiful ones like buttercups, but old foul, bad yellow things.

But there is something else about that paper—the smell! I noticed it the moment we came into the room, but with so much air and sun it was not bad. Now we have had a week of fog and rain, and whether the windows are open or not, the smell is here.

It creeps all over the house.

I find it hovering in the dining-room, skulking in the parlor, hiding in the hall, lying in wait for me on the stairs.

It gets into my hair.

Even when I go to ride, turn my head suddenly and surprise it—there is that smell!

Such a peculiar odor, too! I have spent hours in trying to analyze it, to find what it smelled like.

It is not bad—at first, and very gentle, but quite the subtlest, most enduring odor I ever met.

In this damp weather it is awful, I wake up in the night and find it hanging over me.

It used to disturb me at first. I thought seriously of burning the house—to reach the smell.

But now I am used to it. The only thing I can think of that it is like is the *color* of the paper! A yellow smell.

There is a very funny mark on this wall, low down, near the mopboard. A streak that runs round the room. It goes behind every piece of furniture, except the bed, a long, straight, even smooch, as if it had been rubbed over and over.

I wonder how it was done and who did it, and what they did it for. Round and round and round—round and round and round—it makes me dizzy!

I really have discovered something at last.

Through watching so much at night, when it changes so, I have finally found out.

The front pattern *does* move—and no wonder! The woman behind shakes it!

Sometimes I think there are a great many women behind, and sometimes only one, and she crawls around fast, and her crawling shakes it all over.

Then in the very bright spots she keeps still, and in the very shady spots she just takes hold of the bars and shakes them hard.

And she is all the time trying to climb through. But nobody could climb through that pattern—it strangles so; I think that is why it has so many heads.

They get through, and then the pattern strangles them off and turns them upside down, and makes their eyes white!

If those heads were covered or taken off it would not be half so bad.

I think that woman gets out in the daytime!

And I'll tell you why—privately—I've seen her!

I can see her out of every one of my windows!

It is the same woman, I know, for she is always creeping, and most women do not creep by daylight.

I see her on that long road under the trees, creeping along, and when a carriage comes she hides under the blackberry vines.

I don't blame her a bit. It must be very humiliating to be caught creeping by daylight!

I always lock the door when I creep by daylight. I can't do it at night, for I know John would suspect something at once.

And John is so queer now, that I don't want to irritate him. I wish he would take another room! Besides, I don't want anybody to get that woman out at night but myself.

I often wonder if I could see her out of all the windows at once.

But, turn as fast as I can, I can only see out of one at one time.

And though I always see her, she *may* be able to creep faster than I can turn!

I have watched her sometimes away off in the open country, creeping as fast as a cloud shadow in a high wind.

If only that top pattern could be gotten off from the under one! I mean to try it, little, by little.

I have found out another funny thing, but I shan't tell it this time! It does not do to trust people too much.

There are only two more days to get this paper off, and I believe John is beginning to notice. I don't like the look in his eyes.

And I heard him ask Jennie a lot of professional questions about me. She had a very good report to give.

She said I slept a good deal in the daytime.

John knows I don't sleep very well at night, for all I'm so quiet!

He asked me all sorts of questions, too, and pretended to be very loving and kind. As if I couldn't see through him!

Still, I don't wonder he acts so, sleeping under this paper for three months.

It only interests me, but I feel sure John and Jennie are secretly affected by it.

Hurrah! This is the last day, but it is enough. John is to stay in town over night, and won't be out until this evening.

Jennie wanted to sleep with me—the sly thing! but I told her I should undoubtedly rest better for a night all alone.

That was clever, for really I wasn't alone a bit! As soon as it was moonlight and that poor thing began to crawl and shake the pattern, I got up and ran to help her.

I pulled and she shook, I shook and she pulled, and before morning we had peeled off yards of that paper.

A strip about as high as my head and half around the room.

And then when the sun came and that awful pattern began to laugh at me, I declared I would finish it to-day!

We go away to-morrow, and they are moving all my furniture down again to leave things as they were before.

Jennie looked at the wall in amazement, but I told her merrily that I did it out of pure spite at the vicious thing.

She laughed and said she wouldn't mind doing it herself, but I must not get tired.

How she betrayed herself that time!

But I am here, and no person touches this paper but me,—not *alive!*

She tried to get me out of the room—it was too patent! But I said it was so quiet and empty and clean now that I believed I would lie down again and sleep all I could; and not to wake me even for dinner—I would call when I woke.

So now she is gone, and the servants are gone, and the things are gone, and there is nothing left, but that great bedstead nailed down, with the canvas mattress we found on it.

We shall sleep downstairs to-night, and take the boat home to-morrow.

I quite enjoy the room, now it is bare again.

How those children did tear about here!

This bedstead is fairly gnawed!

But I must get to work.

I have locked the door and thrown the key down into the front path.

I don't want to go out, and I don't want to have anybody come in, till John comes.

I want to astonish him.

I've got a rope up here that even Jennie did not find. If that woman does get out, and tries to get away, I can tie her!

But I forgot I could not reach far without anything to stand on!

This bed will *not* move!

I tried to lift and push it until I was lame, and then I got so angry I bit off a little piece at one corner—but it hurt my teeth.

Then I peeled off all the paper I could reach standing on the floor. It sticks horribly and the pattern just enjoys it! All those strangled heads and bulbous eyes and waddling fungus growths just shriek with derision!

I am getting angry enough to do something desperate. To jump out of the window would be admirable exercise, but the bars are too strong even to try.

Besides I wouldn't do it. Of course not. I know well enough that a step like that is improper and might be misconstrued.

I don't like to *look* out of the windows even—there are so many of those creeping women, and they creep so fast.

I wonder if they all come out of that wall-paper as I did?

But I am securely fastened now by my well-hidden rope—you don't get me out in the road there!

I suppose I shall have to get back behind the pattern when it comes night, and that is hard!

It is so pleasant to be out in this great room and creep around as I please!

I don't want to go outside. I won't, even if Jennie asks me to.

For outside you have to creep on the ground, and everything is green instead of yellow.

But here I can creep smoothly on the floor, and my shoulder just fits in that long smooch around the wall, so I cannot lose my way.

Why there's John at the door!

It is no use, young man, you can't open it!

How he does call and pound!

Now he's crying for an axe.

It would be a shame to break down that beautiful door!

"John dear!" said I in the gentlest voice, "the key is down by the front steps, under a plantain leaf!"

That silenced him for a few moments.

Then he said—very quietly indeed, "Open the door, my darling!"

"I can't," said I. "The key is down by the front door under a plantain leaf!"

And then I said it again, several times, very gently and slowly, and said it so often that he had to go and see, and he got it of course, and came in. He stopped short by the door.

"What is the matter?" he cried. "For God's sake what are you doing!"

I kept on creeping just the same, but I looked at him over my shoulder.

"I've got out at last," said I, "in spite of you and Jane. And I've pulled off most of the paper, so you can't put me back!"

Now why should that man have fainted? But he did, and right across my path by the wall, so that I had to creep over him every time!

−1892

ERNEST HEMINGWAY

1899-1961

Ernest Hemingway was born in Oak Park, Illinois, but spent the greater part of his life in France after World War I as an expatriate writer. With a laconic, journalistic style that suited U.S. culture's need for a masculine literary representative voice, Hemingway became famous for depictions of sport, nature, and "exotic" European and Latin American locales. More recently, Hemingway's fiction has been mined for its more complex treatment of gender conflict within and between characters. The texts that established his reputation include the novels The Sun Also Rises *(1926),* A Farewell to Arms *(1929), and* The Old Man and the Sea *(1952), and such short story collections as* Men Without Women *(1927) and* Winner Take Nothing *(1933). Hemingway won the Pulitzer Prize for fiction in 1953 and the Nobel Prize for literature in 1954. He committed suicide in 1961.*

THE SEA CHANGE

"All right," said the man. "What about it?"

"No," said the girl, "I can't."

"You mean you won't."

"I can't," said the girl. "That's all that I mean."

"You mean that you won't."

"All right," said the girl. "You have it your own way."

"I don't have it my own way. I wish to God I did."

"You did for a long time," the girl said.

It was early, and there was no one in the café except the barman and these two who sat together at a table in the corner. It was the end of the summer and they were both tanned, so that they looked out of place in Paris. The girl wore a tweed suit, her skin was a smooth golden brown, her blonde hair was cut short and grew beautifully away from her forehead. The man looked at her.

"I'll kill her," he said.

"Please don't," the girl said. She had very fine hands and the man looked at them. They were slim and brown and very beautiful.

"I will. I swear to God I will."

"It won't make you happy."

"Couldn't you have gotten into something else? Couldn't you have gotten into some other jam?"

"It seems not," the girl said. "What are you going to do about it?"

"I told you."

"No; I mean really."

"I don't know," he said. She looked at him and put out her hand. "Poor old Phil," she said. He looked at her hands, but he did not touch her hand with his.

"No, thanks," he said.

"It doesn't do any good to say I'm sorry?"

"No."

"Nor to tell you how it is?"

"I'd rather not hear."

"I love you very much."

"Yes, this proves it."

"I'm sorry," she said, "if you don't understand."

"I understand. That's the trouble. I understand."

"You do," she said. "That makes it worse, of course."

"Sure," he said, looking at her. "I'll understand all the time. All day and all night. Especially all night. I'll understand. You don't have to worry about that."

"I'm sorry," she said.

"If it was a man——"

"Don't say that. It wouldn't be a man. You know that. Don't you trust me?"

"That's funny," he said. "Trust you. That's really funny."

"I'm sorry," she said. "That's all I seem to say. But when we do understand each other there's no use to pretend we don't."

"No," he said. "I suppose not."

"I'll come back if you want me."

"No. I don't want you."

Then they did not say anything for a while.

"You don't believe I love you, do you?" the girl asked.

"Let's not talk rot," the man said.

"Don't you really believe I love you?"

"Why don't you prove it."

"You didn't use to be that way. You never asked me to prove anything. That isn't polite."

"You're a funny girl."

"You're not. You're a fine man and it breaks my heart to go off and leave you——"

"You have to, of course."

"Yes," she said. "I have to and you know it."

He did not say anything and she looked at him and put her hand out again. The barman was at the far end of the bar. His face was white and so was his jacket. He knew these two and thought them a handsome young couple. He had seen many handsome young couples break up and new couples form that were never so hand-some long. He was not thinking about this, but about a horse. In half an hour he could send across the street to find if the horse had won.

"Couldn't you just be good to me and let me go?" the girl asked.

"What do you think I'm going to do?"

Two people came in the door and went up to the bar.

"Yes, sir," the barman took the orders.

"You can't forgive me? When you know about it?" the girl asked.

"No."

"You don't think things we've had and done should make any difference in understanding?"

"'Vice is a monster of such fearful mien,'" the young man said bitterly, "that to be something or other needs but to be seen. Then we something, something, then embrace." He could not remember the words. "I can't quote," he said.

"Let's not say vice," she said. "That's not very polite."

"Perversion," he said.

"James," one of the clients addressed the barman, "you're looking very well."

"You're looking very well yourself," the barman said.

"Old James," the other client said. "You're fatter, James."

"It's terrible," the barman said, "the way I put it on."

"Don't neglect to insert the brandy, James," the first client said.

"No, sir," said the barman. "Trust me."

The two at the bar looked over at the two at the table, then looked back at the barman again. Towards the barman was the comfortable direction.

"I'd like it better if you didn't use words like that," the girl said. "There's no necessity to use a word like that."

"What do you want me to call it?"

"You don't have to call it. You don't have to put any name to it."

"That's the name for it."

"No," she said. "We're made up of all sorts of things. You've known that. You've used it well enough."

"You don't have to say that again."

"Because that explains it to you."

"All right," he said. "All right."

"You mean all wrong. I know. It's all wrong. But I'll come back. I told you I'd come back. I'll come back right away."

"No, you won't."

"I'll come back."

"No, you won't. Not to me."

"You'll see."

"Yes," he said. "That's the hell of it. You probably will."

"Of course I will."

"Go on, then."

"Really?" She could not believe him, but her voice was happy.

"Go on," his voice sounded strange to him. He was looking at her, at the way her mouth went and the curve of her cheek bones, at her eyes and at the way her hair grew on her forehead and at the edge of her ear and at her neck.

"Not really. Oh, you're too sweet," she said. "You're too good to me."

"And when you come back tell me all about it." His voice sounded very strange. He did not recognize it. She looked at him quickly. He was settled into something.

"You want me to go?" she asked seriously.

"Yes," he said seriously. "Right away." His voice was not the same, and his mouth was very dry. "Now," he said.

She stood up and went out quickly. She did not look back at him. He watched her go. He was not the same looking man as he had been before he had told her to go. He got up from the table, picked up the two checks and went over to the bar with them.

"I'm a different man, James," he said to the barman. "You see in me quite a different man."

"Yes, sir?" said James.

"Vice," said the brown young man, "is a very strange thing, James." He looked out the door. He saw her going down the street. As he looked in the glass, he saw he was really quite a different looking man. The other two at the bar moved down to make room for him.

"You're right there, sir," James said.

The other two moved down a little more, so that he would be quite comfortable. The young man saw himself in the mirror behind the bar. "I said I was a different man, James," he said. Looking into the mirror he saw that this was quite true.

"You look very well, sir," James said. "You must have had a very good summer."

—1933

URSULA K. LE GUIN

B. 1929

Ursula K. Le Guin was born in Berkeley, California, and resides by the Pacific Ocean in Oregon, the inspiration for the setting of many of her tales. She received her BA from Radcliffe College and her MA from Columbia College, spending a year in Paris on a Fulbright Scholarship. Often considered a science fiction writer, Le Guin's deep attention to the related structures of civilization and terrain might more accurately be termed ecological. Anthropological is another adjective to describe the detail with which Le Guin observes, for example, the workings of gender. Le Guin's many works include The Water is Wide *(1976), the* Earthsea Trilogy *(1968, 1971, 1972),* The Lefthand of Darkness *(1978),* The Beginning Place *(1980),* The Compass Rose *(1982),* Going Out With the Peacocks and Other Poems *(1994), and* Unlocking the Air and Other Stories *(1996). Her essays and talks appear in* Dancing at the Edge of the World *(1989).*

SUR

A Summary Report of the *Yelcho* Expedition to the Antarctic, 1909–1910

Although I have no intention of publishing this report, I think it would be nice if a grandchild of mine, or somebody's grandchild, happened to find it some day; so I shall keep it in the leather trunk in the attic, along with Rosita's christening dress and Juanito's silver rattle and my wedding shoes and finneskos.

The first requisite for mounting an expedition—money—is normally the hardest to come by. I grieve that even in a report destined for a trunk in the attic of a house in a very quiet suburb of Lima I dare not write the name of the generous benefactor, the great soul without whose unstinting liberality the *Yelcho* Expedition would never have been more than the idlest excursion into daydream. That our equipment was the best and most modern—that our provisions were plentiful and fine—that a ship of the Chilean Government, with her brave officers and gallant crew, was twice sent halfway round the world for our convenience: all this is due to that benefactor whose name, alas! I must not say, but whose happiest debtor I shall be till death.

When I was little more than a child my imagination was caught by a newspaper account of the voyage of the *Belgica*, which, sailing south from Tierra del Fuego, became beset by ice in the Bellingshausen Sea and drifted a whole year with the floe, the men aboard her suffering a great deal from want of food and from the terror of the unending winter darkness. I read and reread that account, and later followed with excitement the reports of the rescue of Dr. Nordenskjold from the South Shetland Isles by the dashing Captain Irizar of the *Uruguay*, and the adventures of the *Scotia* in the Weddell Sea. But all these exploits were to me but forerunners of the British National Antarctic Expedition of 1902–1904, in the *Discovery*, and the wonderful account of that expedition by Captain Scott. This book, which I ordered from London and reread a thousand times, filled me with longing to see with my own eyes that strange continent, last Thule of the South, which lies on our maps and globes like a white cloud, a void, fringed here and there with scraps of coastline, dubious capes, supposititious islands, headlands that may or may not be there: Antarctica. And the desire was as pure as the polar snows: to go, to see—no more, no less. I deeply respect the scientific accomplishments of Captain Scott's expedition, and have read with passionate interest the findings of physicists, meteorologists, biologists, etc.; but having had no training in any science, nor any opportunity for such training, my ignorance obliged me to forego any thought of adding to the body of scientific knowledge concerning Antarctica; and the same is true for all the members of my expedition. It seems a pity; but there was nothing we could do about it. Our goal was limited to observation and exploration. We hoped to go a little farther, perhaps, and see a little more; if not, simply to go and to see. A simple ambition, I think, and essentially a modest one.

Yet it would have remained less than an ambition, no more than a longing, but for the support and encouragement of my dear cousin and friend Juana ———. (I use no surnames, lest this report fall into strangers' hands at last, and embarrassment or unpleasant notoriety thus be brought upon unsuspecting husbands, sons, etc.) I had lent Juana my copy of *The Voyage of the Discovery*, and it was she who,

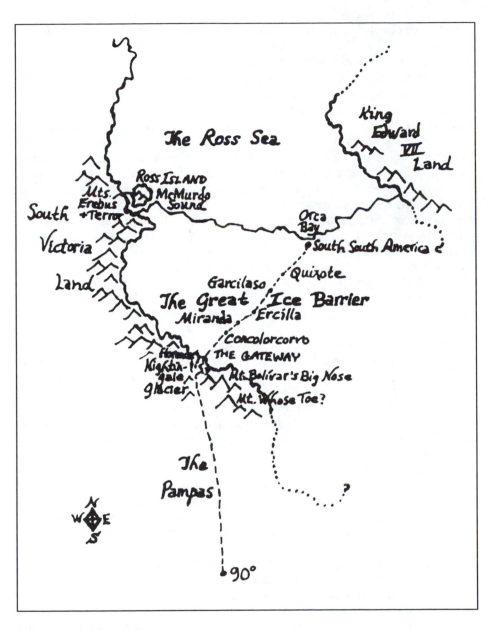

The Map in the Attic

as we strolled beneath our parasols across the Plaza de Armas after Mass one Sunday in 1908, said, "Well, if Captain Scott can do it, why can't we?"

It was Juana who proposed that we write Carlota ——— in Valparaiso. Through Carlota we met our benefactor, and so obtained our money, our ship, and even the plausible pretext of going on retreat in a Bolivian convent, which some of us were forced to employ (while the rest of us said we were going to Paris for the winter season). And it was my Juana who in the darkest moments remained resolute, unshaken in her determination to achieve our goal.

And there were dark moments, especially in the early months of 1909—times when I did not see how the Expedition would ever become more than a quarter ton of pemmican gone to waste and a lifelong regret. It was so very hard to gather our expeditionary force together! So few of those we asked even knew what we were talking about—so many thought we were mad, or wicked, or both! And of those few who shared our folly, still fewer were able, when it came to the point, to leave their daily duties and commit themselves to a voyage of at least six months, attended with not inconsiderable uncertainty and danger. An ailing parent; an anxious husband beset by business cares; a child at home with only ignorant or incompetent servants to look after it: these are not responsibilities lightly to be set aside. And those who wished to evade such claims were not the companions we wanted in hard work, risk, and privation.

But since success crowned our efforts, why dwell on the setbacks and delays, or the wretched contrivances and downright lies that we all had to employ? I look back with regret only to those friends who wished to come with us but could not, by any contrivance, get free—those we had to leave behind to a life without danger, without uncertainty, without hope.

On the seventeenth of August, 1909, in Punta Arenas, Chile, all the members of the Expedition met for the first time: Juana and I, the two Peruvians; from Argentina, Zoe, Berta, and Teresa; and our Chileans, Carlota and her friends Eva, Pepita, and Dolores. At the last moment I had received word that Maria's husband, in Quito, was ill, and she must stay to nurse him, so we were nine, not ten. Indeed, we had resigned ourselves to being but eight, when, just as night fell, the indomitable Zoe arrived in a tiny pirogue manned by Indians, her yacht having sprung a leak just as it entered the Strait of Magellan.

That night before we sailed we began to get to know one another; and we agreed, as we enjoyed our abominable supper in the abominable seaport inn of Punta Arenas, that if a situation arose of such urgent danger that one voice must be obeyed without present question, the unenviable honor of speaking with that voice should fall first upon myself: if I were incapacitated, upon Carlota: if she, then upon Berta. We three were then toasted as "Supreme Inca," "La Araucana," and "The Third Mate," among a lot of laughter and cheering. As it came out, to my very great pleasure and relief, my qualities as a "leader" were never tested; the nine of us worked things out amongst us from beginning to end without any orders being given by anybody, and only two or three times with recourse to a vote by voice or show of hands. To be sure, we argued a good deal. But then, we had time to argue. And one way or another the arguments always ended up in a decision, upon which action could be taken. Usually at least one person grumbled about the decision, sometimes bitterly. But what is life without grumbling, and the occasional opportunity to say, "I told you so"? How could one bear housework, or looking after babies, let alone the rigors of sledgehauling in Antarctica, without grumbling? Officers—as we came to understand aboard the *Yelcho*—are forbidden to grumble; but we nine were, and are, by birth and upbringing, unequivocally and irrevocably, all crew.

Though our shortest course to the southern continent, and that originally urged upon us by the captain of our good ship, was to the South Shetlands and the Bellingshausen Sea, or else by the South Orkneys into the Weddell Sea, we planned to sail west to the Ross Sea, which Captain Scott had explored and described, and from which the brave Ernest Shackleton had returned only the previous autumn. More was known about this region than any other portion of the coast of Antarctica, and though that more was not much, yet it served as some insurance of the safety of the ship, which we felt we had no right to imperil. Captain Pardo had fully agreed with us after studying the charts and our planned itinerary; and so it was westward that we took our course out of the Strait next morning.

Our journey half round the globe was attended by fortune. The little *Yelcho* steamed cheerily along through gale and gleam, climbing up and down those seas of the Southern Ocean that run unbroken round the world. Juana, who had fought bulls and the far more dangerous cows on her family's *estancia,* called the ship *"la vaca valiente,"* because she always returned to the charge. Once we got over being seasick we all enjoyed the sea voyage, though oppressed at times by the kindly but officious protectiveness of the captain and his officers, who felt that we were only "safe" when huddled up in the three tiny cabins which they had chivalrously vacated for our use.

We saw our first iceberg much farther south than we had looked for it, and saluted it with Veuve Clicquot at dinner. The next day we entered the ice pack, the belt of floes and bergs, broken loose from the land ice and winter-frozen seas of Antarctica, which drifts northward in the spring. Fortune still smiled on us: our little steamer, incapable, with her unreinforced metal hull, of forcing a way into the ice, picked her way from lane to lane without hesitation, and on the third day we were through the pack, in which ships have sometimes struggled for weeks and been obliged to turn back at last. Ahead of us now lay the dark grey waters of the Ross Sea, and beyond that, on the horizon, the remote glimmer, the cloud-reflected whiteness of the Great Ice Barrier.

Entering the Ross Sea a little east of Longitude West 160°, we came in sight of the Barrier at the place where Captain Scott's party, finding a bight in the vast wall of ice, had gone ashore and sent up their hydrogen-gas balloon for reconnaissance and photography. The towering face of the Barrier, its sheer cliffs and azure and violet water-worn caves, all were as described, but the location had changed: instead of a narrow bight there was a considerable bay, full of the beautiful and terrific orca whales playing and spouting in the sunshine of that brilliant southern spring.

Evidently masses of ice many acres in extent had broken away from the Barrier (which—at least for most of its vast extent—does not rest on land but floats on water) since the *Discovery*'s passage in 1902. This put our plan to set up camp on the Barrier itself in a new light; and while we were discussing alternatives, we asked Captain Pardo to take the ship west along the Barrier face towards Ross Island and McMurdo Sound. As the sea was clear of ice and quite calm, he was happy to do so, and, when we sighted the smoke plume of Mount Erebus, to share in our celebration—another half case of Veuve Clicquot.

The *Yelcho* anchored in Arrival Bay, and we went ashore in the ship's boat. I cannot describe my emotions when I set foot on the earth, on that earth, the barren, cold gravel at the foot of the long volcanic slope. I felt elation, impatience, gratitude, awe, familiarity. I felt that I was home at last. Eight Adélie penguins immediately came to greet us with many exclamations of interest not unmixed with disapproval. "Where on earth have you been? What took you so long? The Hut is around this way. Please come this way. Mind the rocks!" They insisted on our going to visit Hut Point, where the large structure built by Captain Scott's party stood, looking just as in the photographs and drawings that illustrate his book. The area about it, however, was disgusting—a kind of graveyard of seal skins, seal bones, penguin bones, and rubbish, presided over by the mad, screaming skua gulls. Our escorts waddled past the slaughterhouse in all tranquillity, and one showed me personally to the door, though it would not go in.

The interior of the hut was less offensive, but very dreary. Boxes of supplies had been stacked up into a kind of room within the room; it did not look as I had imagined it when the *Discovery* party put on their melodramas and minstrel shows in the long winter night. (Much later, we learned that Sir Ernest had rearranged it a good deal when he was there just a year before us.) It was dirty, and had about it a mean disorder. A pound tin of tea was standing open. Empty meat tins lay about; biscuits were spilled on the floor; a lot of dog turds were underfoot—frozen, of course, but not a great deal improved by that. No doubt the last occupants had had to leave in a hurry, perhaps even in a blizzard. All the same, they could have closed the tea tin. But housekeeping, the art of the infinite, is no game for amateurs.

Teresa proposed that we use the hut as our camp. Zoe counterproposed that we set fire to it. We finally shut the door and left it as we had found it. The penguins appeared to approve, and cheered us all the way to the boat.

McMurdo Sound was free of ice, and Captain Pardo now proposed to take us off Ross Island and across to Victoria Land, where we might camp at the foot of the Western Mountains, on dry and solid earth. But those mountains, with their storm-darkened peaks and hanging cirques and glaciers, looked as awful as Captain Scott had found them on his western journey, and none of us felt much inclined to seek shelter among them.

Aboard the ship that night we decided to go back and set up our base as we had originally planned, on the Barrier itself. For all available reports indicated that the clear way south was across the level Barrier surface until one could ascend one of the confluent glaciers to the high plateau which appears to form the whole interior of the continent. Captain Pardo argued strongly against this plan, asking what would become of us if the Barrier "calved"—if our particular acre of ice broke away and started to drift northward. "Well," said Zoe, "then you won't have to come so far to meet us." But he was so persuasive on this theme that he persuaded himself into leaving one of the *Yelcho*'s boats with us when we camped, as a means of escape. We found it useful for fishing, later on.

My first steps on Antarctic soil, my only visit to Ross Island, had not been pleasure unalloyed. I thought of the words of the English poet:

> *Though every prospect pleases,*
> *And only man is vile.*

But then, the backside of heroism is often rather sad; women and servants know that. They know also that the heroism may be no less real for that. But achievement is smaller than men think. What is large is the sky, the earth, the sea, the soul. I looked back as the ship sailed east again that evening. We were well into September now, with ten hours or more of daylight. The spring sunset lingered on the twelve-thousand-foot peak of Erebus and shone rosy gold on her long plume of steam. The steam from our own small funnel faded blue on the twilit water as we crept along under the towering pale wall of ice.

On our return to "Orca Bay"—Sir Ernest, we learned years later, had named it the Bay of Whales—we found a sheltered nook where the Barrier edge was low enough to provide fairly easy access from the ship. The *Yelcho* put out her ice anchor, and the next long, hard days were spent in unloading our supplies and setting up our camp on the ice, a half kilometer in from the edge: a task in which the *Yelcho*'s crew lent us invaluable aid and interminable advice. We took all the aid gratefully, and most of the advice with salt.

The weather so far had been extraordinarily mild for spring in this latitude; the temperature had not yet gone below –20° Fahrenheit, and there was only one blizzard while we were setting up camp. But Captain Scott had spoken feelingly of the bitter south winds on the Barrier, and we had planned accordingly. Exposed as our camp was to every wind, we built no rigid structures above ground. We set up tents to shelter in while we dug out a series of cubicles in the ice itself, lined them with hay insulation and pine boarding, and roofed them with canvas over bamboo poles, covered with snow for weight and insulation. The big central room was instantly named Buenos Aires by our Argentineans, to whom the center, wherever one is, is always Buenos Aires. The heating and cooking stove was in Buenos Aires. The storage tunnels and the privy (called Punta Arenas) got some back heat from the stove. The sleeping cubicles opened off Buenos Aires, and were very small, mere tubes into which one crawled feet first; they were lined deeply with hay and soon warmed by one's body warmth. The sailors called them "coffins" and "wormholes," and looked with horror on our burrows in the ice. But our little warren or prairie-dog village served us well, permitting us as much warmth and privacy as one could reasonably expect under the circumstances. If the *Yelcho* was unable to get through the ice in February, and we had to spend the winter in Antarctica, we certainly could do so, though on very limited rations. For this coming summer, our base—Sudamérica del Sur, South South America, but we generally called it the Base—was intended merely as a place to sleep, to store our provisions, and to give shelter from blizzards.

To Berta and Eva, however, it was more than that. They were its chief architect-designers, its most ingenious builder-excavators, and its most diligent and contented occupants, forever inventing an improvement in ventilation, or learning how to make skylights, or revealing to us a new addition to our suite of rooms, dug in the living ice. It was thanks to them that our stores were stowed so handily, that our stove drew and heated so efficiently, and that Buenos Aires, where nine people cooked, ate, worked, conversed, argued, grumbled, painted, played the guitar and banjo, and kept the Expedition's library of books and maps, was a marvel of comfort and convenience. We lived there in real amity; and if you simply had to be alone for a while, you crawled into your sleeping hole head first.

Berta went a little farther. When she had done all she could to make South South America livable, she dug out one more cell just under the ice surface, leaving a nearly transparent sheet of ice like a greenhouse roof; and there, alone, she worked at sculptures. They were beautiful forms, some like a blending of the reclining human figure with the subtle curves and volumes of the Weddell seal, others like the fantastic shapes of ice cornices and ice caves. Perhaps they are there still, under the snow, in the bubble in the Great Barrier. There where she made them they might last as long as stone. But she could not bring them north. That is the penalty for carving in water.

Captain Pardo was reluctant to leave us, but his orders did not permit him to hang about the Ross Sea indefinitely, and so at last, with many earnest injunctions to us to stay put—make no journeys—take no risks—beware of frostbite—don't use edge tools—look out for cracks in the ice—and a heartfelt promise to return to Orca Bay on the twentieth of February, or as near that date as wind and ice would permit, the good man bade us farewell, and his crew shouted us a great goodbye cheer as they weighed anchor. That evening, in the long orange twilight of October, we saw the topmast of the *Yelcho* go down the north horizon, over the edge of the world, leaving us to ice, and silence, and the Pole.

That night we began to plan the Southern Journey.

The ensuing month passed in short practice trips and depot-laying. The life we had led at home, though in its own way strenuous, had not fitted any of us for the kind of strain met with in sledge-hauling at ten or twenty degrees below freezing. We all needed as much working-out as possible before we dared undertake a long haul.

My longest exploratory trip, made with Dolores and Carlota, was southwest towards Mount Markham, and it was a nightmare—blizzards and pressure ice all the way out, crevasses and no view of the mountains when we got there, and white weather and sastrugi all the way back. The trip was useful, however, in that we could begin to estimate our capacities; and also in that we had started out with a very heavy load of provisions, which we depoted at 100 and 130 miles SSW of Base. Thereafter other parties pushed on farther, till we had a line of snow cairns and depots right down to Latitude 83° 43', where Juana and Zoe, on an exploring trip, had found a kind of stone gateway opening on a great glacier leading south. We established these depots to avoid, if possible, the hunger that had bedevilled Captain Scott's Southern Party, and the consequent misery and weakness. And we also established to our own satisfaction—intense satisfaction—that we were sledge-haulers at least as good as Captain Scott's husky dogs. Of course we could not have expected to pull as much or as fast as his men. That we did so was because we were favored by much better weather than Captain Scott's party ever met on the Barrier; and also the quantity and quality of our food made a very considerable difference. I am sure that the fifteen percent of dried fruits in our pemmican helped prevent scurvy; and the potatoes, frozen and dried according to an ancient Andean Indian method, were very nourishing yet very light and compact—perfect sledging rations. In any case, it was with considerable confidence in our capacities that we made ready at last for the Southern Journey.

The Southern Party consisted of two sledge teams: Juana, Dolores, and myself; Carlota, Pepita, and Zoe. The support team of Berta, Eva, and Teresa set out before us with a heavy load of supplies, going right up onto the glacier to prospect routes and leave depots of supplies for our return journey. We followed five days behind them, and met them returning between Depot Ercilla and Depot Miranda (see map). That "night"—of course there was no real darkness—we were all nine together in the heart of the level plain of ice. It was the fifteenth of November, Dolores's birthday. We celebrated by putting eight ounces of pisco in the hot chocolate, and became very merry. We sang. It is strange now to remember how thin our voices sounded in that great silence. It was overcast, white weather, without shadows and without visible horizon or any feature to break the level; there was nothing to see at all. We had come to that white place on the map, that void, and there we flew and sang like sparrows.

After sleep and a good breakfast the Base Party continued north, and the Southern Party sledged on. The sky cleared presently. High up, thin clouds passed over very rapidly from southwest to northeast, but down on the Barrier it was calm and just cold enough, five or ten degrees below freezing, to give a firm surface for hauling.

On the level ice we never pulled less than eleven miles, seventeen kilometers, a day, and generally fifteen or sixteen miles, twenty-five kilometers. (Our instruments, being British made, were calibrated in feet, miles, degrees Fahrenheit, etc., but we often converted miles to kilometers because the larger numbers sounded more encouraging.) At the time we left South America, we knew only that Mr. Shackleton had mounted another expedition to the Antarctic in 1908, had tried to attain the Pole but failed, and had returned to England in June of the current year, 1909. No coherent report of his explorations had yet reached South America when we left; we did not know what route he had gone, or how far he had got. But we were not altogether taken by surprise when, far across the featureless white plain, tiny beneath the mountain peaks and the strange silent flight of the rainbow-fringed cloud wisps, we saw a fluttering dot of black. We turned west from our course to visit it: a snow heap nearly buried by the winter's storms—a flag on a bamboo pole, a mere shred of threadbare cloth—an empty oilcan—and a few footprints standing some inches above the ice. In some conditions of weather the snow compressed under one's weight remains when the surrounding soft snow melts or is scoured away by the wind; and so these reversed footprints had been left standing all these months, like rows of cobbler's lasts—a queer sight.

We met no other such traces on our way. In general I believe our course was somewhat east of Mr. Shackleton's. Juana, our surveyor, had trained herself well and was faithful and methodical in her sightings and readings, but our equipment was minimal—a theodolite on tripod legs, a sextant with artificial horizon, two compasses, and chronometers. We had only the wheel meter on the sledge to give distance actually travelled.

In any case, it was the day after passing Mr. Shackleton's waymark that I first saw clearly the great glacier among the mountains to the southwest, which was to give us a pathway from the sea level of the Barrier up to the altiplano, ten thousand feet above. The approach was magnificent: a gateway formed by immense vertical domes and pillars of rock. Zoe and Juana had called the vast ice river that flowed through that gateway the Florence Nightingale Glacier, wishing to honor the British, who had been the inspiration and guide of our expedition; that very brave and very peculiar lady seemed to represent so much that is best, and strangest, in the island race. On maps, of course, this glacier bears the name Mr. Shackleton gave it, the Beardmore.

The ascent of the Nightingale was not easy. The way was open at first, and well marked by our support party, but after some days we came among terrible crevasses, a maze of hidden cracks, from a foot to thirty feet wide and from thirty to a thousand feet deep. Step by step we went, and step by step, and the way always upward now. We were fifteen days on the glacier. At first the weather was hot, up to 20° F., and the hot nights without darkness were wretchedly uncomfortable in our small tents. And all of us suffered more or less from snowblindness just at the time when we wanted clear eyesight to pick our way among the ridges and crevasses of the tortured ice, and to see the wonders about and before us. For at every day's advance more great, nameless peaks came into view in the west and southwest, summit beyond summit, range beyond range, stark rock and snow in the unending noon.

We gave names to these peaks, not very seriously, since we did not expect our discoveries to come to the attention of geographers. Zoe had a gift for naming, and it is thanks to her that certain sketch maps in various suburban South American attics bear such curious features as "Bolívar's Big Nose," "I Am General Rosas," "The Cloudmaker," "Whose Toe?" and "Throne of Our Lady of the Southern Cross." And when at last we got up onto the altiplano, the great interior plateau, it was Zoe who called it the pampa, and maintained that we walked there among vast herds of invisible cattle, transparent cattle pastured on the spindrift snow, their gauchos the restless, merciless winds. We were by then all a little crazy with exhaustion and the great altitude—twelve thousand feet—and the cold and the wind blowing and the luminous circles and crosses surrounding the suns, for often there were three or four suns in the sky, up there.

That is not a place where people have any business to be. We should have turned back; but since we had worked so hard to get there, it seemed that we should go on, at least for a while.

A blizzard came with very low temperatures, so we had to stay in the tents, in our sleeping bags, for thirty hours, a rest we all needed; though it was warmth we needed most, and there was no warmth on that terrible plain anywhere at all but in our veins. We huddled close together all that time. The ice we lay on is two miles thick.

It cleared suddenly and became, for the plateau, good weather: twelve below zero and the wind not very strong. We three crawled out of our tent and met the others crawling out of theirs. Carlota told us then that her group wished to turn back. Pepita had been feeling very ill; even after the rest during the blizzard, her temperature would not rise above 94°. Carlota was having trouble breathing. Zoe was perfectly fit, but much preferred staying with her friends and lending them a hand in difficulties to pushing on towards the Pole. So we put the four ounces of pisco which we had been keeping for Christmas into the breakfast cocoa, and dug out our tents, and loaded our sledges, and parted there in the white daylight on the bitter plain.

Our sledge was fairly light by now. We pulled on to the south. Juana calculated our position daily. On the twenty-second of December, 1909, we reached the South Pole. The weather was, as always, very cruel. Nothing of any kind marked the dreary whiteness. We discussed leaving some kind of mark or monument, a snow cairn, a tent pole and flag; but there seemed no particular reason to do so. Anything we could do, anything we were, was insignificant, in that awful place. We put up the tent for shelter for an hour and made a cup of tea, and then struck "90° Camp." Dolores, standing patient as ever in her sledging harness, looked at the snow; it was so hard frozen that it showed no trace of our footprints coming, and she said, "Which way?"

"North," said Juana.

It was a joke, because at that particular place there is no other direction. But we did not laugh. Our lips were cracked with frostbite and hurt too much to let us laugh. So we started back, and the wind at our backs pushed us along, and dulled the knife edges of the waves of frozen snow.

All that week the blizzard wind pursued us like a pack of mad dogs. I cannot describe it. I wished we had not gone to the Pole. I think I wish it even now. But I was glad even then that we had left no sign there, for some man longing to be first might come some day, and find it, and know then what a fool he had been, and break his heart.

We talked, when we could talk, of catching up to Carlota's party, since they might be going slower than we. In fact they had used their tent as a sail to catch the following wind and had got far ahead of us. But in many places they had built snow cairns or left some sign for us; once Zoe had written on the lee side of a ten-foot sastrugi, just as children write on the sand of the beach at Miraflores, "This Way Out!" The wind blowing over the frozen ridge had left the words perfectly distinct.

In the very hour that we began to descend the glacier, the weather turned warmer, and the mad dogs were left to howl forever tethered to the Pole. The distance that had taken us fifteen days going up we covered in only eight days going down. But the good weather that had aided us descending the Nightingale became a curse down on the Barrier ice, where we had looked forward to a kind of royal progress from depot to depot, eating our fill and taking our time for the last three hundred odd miles. In a tight place on the glacier I lost my goggles—I was swinging from my harness at the time in a crevasse—and then Juana had broken hers when we had to do some rock climbing coming down to the Gateway. After two days in bright sunlight with only one pair of snow goggles to pass amongst us, we were all suffering badly from snowblindness. It became acutely painful to keep lookout for landmarks or depot flags, to take sightings, even to study the compass, which had to be laid down on the snow to steady the needle. At Concolorcorvo Depot, where there was a particularly good supply of food and fuel, we gave up, crawled into our sleeping bags with bandaged eyes, and slowly boiled alive like lobsters in the tent exposed to the relentless sun. The voices of Berta and Zoe were the sweetest sound I ever heard. A little concerned about us, they had skied south to meet us. They led us home to Base.

We recovered quite swiftly, but the altiplano left its mark. When she was very little, Rosita asked if a dog "had bitted Mama's toes." I told her Yes, a great, white, mad dog named Blizzard! My Rosita and my Juanito heard many stories when they were little, about that fearful dog and how it howled, and the transparent cattle of the invisible gauchos, and a river of ice eight thousand feet high called Nightingale, and how Cousin Juana drank a cup of tea standing on the bottom of the world under seven suns, and other fairy tales.

We were in for one severe shock when we reached Base at last. Teresa was pregnant. I must admit that my first response to the poor girl's big belly and sheepish look was anger—rage—fury. That one of us should have concealed anything, and such a thing, from the others! But Teresa had done nothing of the sort. Only those who had concealed from her what she most needed to know were to blame. Brought up by servants, with four years' schooling in a convent, and married at sixteen, the poor girl was still so ignorant at twenty years of age that she had thought it was "the cold weather" that made her miss her periods. Even this was not entirely stupid, for all of us on the Southern Journey had seen our periods change or stop altogether as we experienced increasing cold, hunger, and fatigue. Teresa's appetite had begun to draw general attention; and then she had begun, as she said pathetically, "to get fat." The others were worried at the thought of all the sledge-hauling she had done, but she flourished, and the only problem was her positively insatiable appetite. As well as could be determined from her shy references to her last night on the hacienda with her husband, the baby was due at just about the same time as the *Yelcho,* the twentieth of February. But we had not been back from the Southern Journey two weeks when, on February 14, she went into labor.

Several of us had borne children and had helped with deliveries, and anyhow most of what needs to be done is fairly self-evident; but a first labor can be long and trying, and we were all anxious, while Teresa was frightened out of her wits. She kept calling for her José till she was as hoarse as a skua. Zoe lost all patience at last and said, "By God, Teresa, if you say 'José!' once more I hope you have a penguin!" But what she had, after twenty long hours, was a pretty little red-faced girl.

Many were the suggestions for that child's name from her eight proud midwife-aunts: Polita, Penguina, McMurdo, Victoria. . . . But Teresa announced, after she had had a good sleep and a large serving of pemmican, "I shall name her Rosa—Rosa del Sur," Rose of the South. That night we drank the last two bottles of Veuve Clicquot (having finished the pisco at 88° 30' South) in toasts to our little Rose.

On the nineteenth of February, a day early, my Juana came down into Buenos Aires in a hurry. "The ship," she said, "the ship has come," and she burst into tears—she who had never wept in all our weeks of pain and weariness on the long haul.

Of the return voyage there is nothing to tell. We came back safe.

In 1912 all the world learned that the brave Norwegian Amundsen had reached the South Pole; and then, much later, came the accounts of how Captain Scott and his men had come there after him, but did not come home again.

Just this year, Juana and I wrote to the captain of the *Yelcho,* for the newspapers have been full of the story of his gallant dash to rescue Sir Ernest Shackleton's men from Elephant Island, and we wished to congratulate him, and once more to thank him. Never one word has he breathed of our secret. He is a man of honor, Luis Pardo.

I add this last note in 1929. Over the years we have lost touch with one another. It is very difficult for women to meet, when they live so far apart as we do. Since Juana died, I have seen none of my old sledge-mates, though sometimes we write. Our little Rosa del Sur died of the scarlet fever when she was five years old. Teresa had many other children. Carlota took the veil in Santiago ten years ago. We are old women now, with old husbands, and grown children, and grandchildren who might some day like to read about the Expedition. Even if they are rather ashamed of having such a crazy grandmother, they may enjoy sharing in the secret. But they must not let Mr. Amundsen know! He would be terribly embarrassed and disappointed. There is no need for him or anyone else outside the family to know. We left no footprints, even.

—1981

JOANNA RUSS

B. 1937

Joanna Russ, born in New York City, is a short story writer and essayist edu-
cated at Cornell and Yale Universities. Best known as a science fiction
writer, Russ's early novel, The Female Man *(1975), became an instant fem-*
inist classic with its insistent questioning of the sex/gender system. Her
other fiction includes On Strike Against God *(1979),* The Zanzibar Cat
(1983), Extra (Ordinary) People *(1984), and* Magic Mommas, Trembling
Sisters, Puritans and Perverts *(1985). She has two critically important vol-*
umes of essays on women and writing, How to Suppress Women's Writing
(1983) and To Write Like a Woman: Essays in Feminist and Science Fiction
(1995). She currently lives in Tucson, Arizona.

WHEN IT CHANGED

Katy drives like a maniac; we must have been doing over 120 kilometers an hour
on those turns. She's good, though, extremely good, and I've seen her take the whole
car apart and put it together again in a day. My birthplace on Whileaway was largely
given to farm machinery and I refuse to wrestle with a five-gear shift at unholy
speeds, not having been brought up to it, but even on those turns in the middle of
the night on a country road as bad as only our district can make them, Katy's driving didn't scare me. The funny thing about my wife, though: she will not handle
guns. She has even gone hiking in the forests above the forty-eighth parallel without firearms for days at a time. And that *does* scare me.

Katy and I have three children between us, one of hers and two of mine. Yuriko,
my eldest, was asleep in the back seat, dreaming twelve-year-old dreams of love and
war: running away to sea, hunting in the North, dreams of strangely beautiful people in strangely beautiful places, all the wonderful guff you think up when you're
turning twelve and the glands start going. Someday soon, like all of them, she will
disappear for weeks on end to come back grimy and proud, having knifed her first
cougar or shot her first bear, dragging some abominably dangerous dead beastie
behind her, while I will never forgive for what it might have done to my daughter.
Yuriko says Katy's driving puts her to sleep.

For someone who has fought three duels, I am afraid of far, far too much. I'm
getting old. I told this to my wife.

"You're thirty-four," she said. Laconic to the point of silence, that one. She
flipped the lights on, on the dash—three kilometers to go and the road getting
worse all the time. Far out in the country. Electric-green trees rushed into our headlights and around the car. I reached down next to me where we bolt the carrier panel
to the door and eased my rifle into my lap. Yuriko stirred in the back. My height but
Katy's eyes, Katy's face. The car engine is so quiet, Katy says, that you can hear
breathing in the back seat. Yuki had been alone in the car when the message came,

enthusiastically decoding her dot-dashes (silly to mount a wide-frequency trans-
ceiver near an IC engine, but most of Whileaway is on steam). She had thrown herself out of the car, my gangly and gaudy offspring, shouting at the top of her lungs,
so of course she had had to come along. We've been intellectually prepared for this
ever since the colony was founded, ever since it was abandoned, but this is different. This is awful.

"Men!" Yuki had screamed, leaping over the car door. "They've come back! Real
Earth men!"

We met them in the kitchen of the farmhouse near the place where they had landed;
the windows were open, the night air very mild. We had passed all sorts of trans-
portation when we parked outside, steam tractors, trucks, an IC flatbed, even a bicycle. Lydia, the district biologist, had come out of her Northern taciturnity long
enough to take blood and urine samples and was sitting in a corner of the kitchen
shaking her head in astonishment over the results; she even forced herself (very big,
very fair, very shy, always painfully blushing) to dig up the old language manual—
though I can talk the old tongues in my sleep. And do. Lydia is uneasy with us; we're
Southerners and too flamboyant. I counted twenty people in that kitchen, all the
brains of North Continent. Phyllis Spet, I think, had come in by glider. Yuki was the
only child there.

Then I saw the four of them.

They are bigger than we are. They are bigger and broader. Two were taller than
me, and I am extremely tall, one meter, eighty centimeters in my bare feet. They are
obviously of our species but *off,* indescribably off, and as my eyes could not and still
cannot quite comprehend the lines of those alien bodies, I could not, then, bring
myself to touch them, though the one who spoke Russian—what voices they have!—
wanted to "shake hands," a custom from the past, I imagine. I can only say they were
apes with human faces. He seemed to mean well, but I found myself shuddering
back almost the length of the kitchen—and then I laughed apologetically—and then
to set a good example (*interstellar amity,* I thought) did "shake hands" finally. A
hard, hard hand. They are heavy as draft horses. Blurred, deep voices. Yuriko had
sneaked in between the adults and was gazing at *the men* with her mouth open.

He turned *his* head—those words have not been in our language for six hundred
years—and said, in bad Russian:

"Who's that?"

"My daughter," I said, and added (with that irrational attention to good manners
we sometimes employ in moments of insanity), "my daughter, Yuriko Janetson. We
use the matronymic. You would say patronymic."

He laughed, involuntarily. Yuki exclaimed, "I thought they would be good-looking!"
greatly disappointed at this reception of herself. Phyllis Helgason Spet, whom someday I shall kill, gave me across the room a cold, level, venomous look, as if to say:
Watch what you say. You know what I can do. It's true that I have little formal status,
but madam president will get herself in serious trouble with both me and her own staff
if she continues to consider industrial espionage good clean fun. Wars and rumors of
wars, as it says in one of our ancestors' books. I translated Yuki's words into *the man's*
dog-Russian, once our *lingua franca,* and *the man* laughed again.

"Where are all your people?" he said conversationally.

I translated again and watched the faces around the room; Lydia embarrassed (as usual), Spet narrowing her eyes with some damned scheme, Katy very pale.

"This is Whileaway," I said.

He continued to look unenlightened.

"Whileaway," I said. "Do you remember? Do you have records? There was a plague on Whileaway."

He looked moderately interested. Heads turned in the back of the room, and I caught a glimpse of the local professions-parliament delegate; by morning every town meeting, every district caucus, would be in full session.

"Plague?" he said. "That's most unfortunate."

"Yes," I said. "Most unfortunate. We lost half our population in one generation."

He looked properly impressed.

"Whileaway was lucky," I said. "We had a big initial gene pool, we had been chosen for extreme intelligence, we had a high technology and a large remaining population in which every adult was two-or-three experts in one. The soil is good. The climate is blessedly easy. There are thirty million of us now. Things are beginning to snowball in industry—do you understand?—give us seventy years and we'll have more than one real city, more than a few industrial centers, full-time professions, full-time radio operators, full-time machinists, give us seventy years and not everyone will have to spend three-quarters of a lifetime on the farm." And I tried to explain how hard it is when artists can practice full-time only in old age, when there are so few, so very few who can be free, like Katy and myself. I tried also to outline our government, the two houses, the one by professions and the geographic one; I told him the district caucuses handled problems too big for the individual towns. And that population control was not a political issue, not yet, though give us time and it would be. This was a delicate point in our history; give us time. There was no need to sacrifice the quality of life for an insane rush into industrialization. Let us go our own pace. Give us time.

"Where are all the people?" said that monomaniac.

I realized then that he did not mean people, he meant *men,* and he was giving the word the meaning it had not had on Whileaway for six centuries.

"They died," I said. "Thirty generations ago."

I thought we had poleaxed him. He caught his breath. He made as if to get out of the chair he was sitting in; he put his hand to his chest; he looked around at us with the strangest blend of awe and sentimental tenderness. Then he said, solemnly and earnestly:

"A great tragedy."

I waited, not quite understanding.

"Yes," he said, catching his breath again with that queer smile, that adult-to-child smile that tells you something is being hidden and will be presently produced with cries of encouragement and joy, "a great tragedy. But it's over." And again he looked around at all of us with the strangest deference. As if we were invalids.

"You've adapted amazingly," he said.

"To what?" I said. He looked embarrassed. He looked inane. Finally he said, "Where I come from, the women don't dress so plainly."

"Like you?" I said. "Like a bride?" for the men were wearing silver from head to foot. I had never seen anything so gaudy. He made as if to answer and then apparently thought better of it; he laughed at me again. With an odd exhilaration—as if we were something childish and something wonderful, as if he were doing us an enormous favor—he took one shaky breath and said, "Well, we're here."

I looked at Spet, Spet looked at Lydia, Lydia looked at Amalia, who is the head of the local town meeting, Amalia looked at I don't know who. My throat was raw. I cannot stand local beer, which the farmers swill as if their stomachs had iridium linings, but I took it anyway, from Amalia (it was her bicycle we had seen outside as we parked), and swallowed it all. This was going to take a long time. I said, "Yes, here you are," and smiled (feeling like a fool), and wondered seriously if male Earth people's minds worked so very differently from female Earth people's minds, but that couldn't be so or the race would have died out long ago. The radio network had got the news around-planet by now and we had another Russian speaker, flown in from Varna; I decided to cut out when *the man* passed around pictures of his wife, who looked like the priestess of some arcane cult. He proposed to question Yuki, so I barreled her into a back room in spite of her furious protests and went out on the front porch. As I left, Lydia was explaining the difference between parthenogenesis (which is so easy that anyone can practice it) and what we do, which is the merging of ova. That is why Katy's baby looks like me. Lydia went on to the Ansky Process and Katy Ansky, our one full-polymath genius and the great-great-I-don't-know-how-many-times-great-grandmother of my own Katharina.

A dot-dash transmitter in one of the outbuildings chattered faintly to itself: operators flirting and passing jokes down the line.

There was a man on the porch. The other tall man. I watched him for a few minutes—I can move very quietly when I want to—and when I allowed him to see me, he stopped talking into the little machine hung around his neck. Then he said calmly, in excellent Russian, "Did you know that sexual equality has been reestablished on Earth?"

"You're the real one," I said, "aren't you? The other one's for show." It was a great relief to get things cleared up. He nodded affably.

"As a people, we are not very bright," he said. "There's been too much genetic damage in the last few centuries. Radiation. Drugs. We can use Whileaway's genes, Janet." Strangers do not call strangers by the first name.

"You can have cells enough to drown in," I said. "Breed your own.

He smiled. "That's not the way we want to do it." Behind him I saw Katy come into the square of light that was the screened-in door. He went on, low and urbane, not mocking me, I think, but with the self-confidence of someone who has always had money and strength to spare, who doesn't know what it is to be second-class or provincial. Which is very odd, because the day before, I would have said that was an exact description of me.

"I'm talking to you, Janet," he said, "because I suspect you have more popular influence than anyone else here. You know as well as I do that parthenogenetic culture has all sorts of inherent defects, and we do not—if we can help it—mean to use you for anything of the sort. Pardon me; I should not have said 'use.' But surely you can see that this kind of society is unnatural."

"Humanity is unnatural," said Katy. She had my rifle under her left arm. The top of that silky head does not quite come up to my collarbone, but she is as tough as steel; he began to move, again with that queer, smiling deference (which his fellow had shown to me but he had not), and the gun slid into Katy's grip as if she had shot with it all her life.

"I agree," said the man. "Humanity is unnatural. I should know. I have metal in my teeth and metal pins here." He touched his shoulder. "Seals are harem animals," he added, "and so are men; apes are promiscuous and so are men; doves are monogamous and so are men; there are even celibate men and homosexual men. There are homosexual cows, I believe. But Whileaway is still missing something." He gave a dry chuckle. I will give him the credit of believing that it had something to do with nerves.

"I miss nothing," said Katy, "except that life isn't endless."

"You are—?" said the man, nodding from me to her.

"Wives," said Katy. "We're married." Again the dry chuckle.

"A good economic arrangement," he said, "for working and taking care of the children. And as good an arrangement as any for randomizing heredity, if your reproduction is made to follow the same pattern. But think, Katharina Michaelason, if there isn't something better that you might secure for your daughters. I believe in instincts, even in man, and I can't think that the two of you—a machinist, are you? and I gather you are some sort of chief of police—don't feel somehow what even you must miss. You know it intellectually, of course. There is only half a species here. Men must come back to Whileaway."

Katy said nothing.

"I should think, Katharina Michaelason," said the man gently, "that you, of all people, would benefit most from such a change," and he walked past Katy's rifle into the square of light coming from the door. I think it was then that he noticed my scar, which really does not show unless the light is from the side: a fine line that runs from temple to chin. Most people don't even know about it.

"Where did you get that?" he said, and I answered with an involuntary grin, "In my last duel." We stood there bristling at each other for several seconds (this is absurd but true) until he went inside and shut the screen door behind him. Katy said in a brittle voice, "You damned fool, don't you know when we've been insulted?" and swung up the rifle to shoot him through the screen, but I got to her before she could fire and knocked the rifle out of aim; it burned a hole through the porch floor. Katy was shaking. She kept whispering over and over, "That's why I never touched it, because I knew I'd kill someone, I knew I'd kill someone." The first man—the one I'd spoken with first—was still talking inside the house, something about the grand movement to recolonize and rediscover all that Earth had lost. He stressed the advantages to Whileaway: trade, exchange of ideas, education. He too said that sexual equality had been reestablished on Earth.

Katy was right, of course; we should have burned them down where they stood. Men are coming to Whileaway. When one culture has the big guns and the other has none, there is a certain predictability about the outcome. Maybe men would have come eventually in any case. I like to think that a hundred years from now my great-grandchildren could have stood them off or fought them to a standstill, but even that's no odds; I will remember all my life those four people I first met who were muscled like bulls and who made me—if only for a moment—feel small. A neurotic reaction, Katy says. I remember everything that happened that night; I remember

Yuki's excitement in the car, I remember Katy's sobbing when we got home as if her heart would break, I remember her lovemaking, a little peremptory as always, but wonderfully soothing and comforting. I remember prowling restlessly around the house after Katy fell asleep with one bare arm flung into a patch of light from the hall. The muscles of her forearms are like metal bars from all that driving and testing of her machines. Sometimes I dream about Katy's arms. I remember wandering into the nursery and picking up my wife's baby, dozing for a while with the poignant, amazing warmth of an infant in my lap, and finally returning to the kitchen to find Yuriko fixing herself a late snack. My daughter eats like a Great Dane.

"Yuki," I said, "do you think you could fall in love with a man?" and she whooped derisively. "With a ten-foot toad!" said my tactful child.

But men are coming to Whileaway. Lately I sit up nights and worry about the men who will come to this planet, about my two daughters and Betta Katharinason, about what will happen to Katy, to me, to my life. Our ancestors' journals are one long cry of pain and I suppose I ought to be glad now but one can't throw away six centuries, or even (as I have lately discovered) thirty-four years. Sometimes I laugh at the question those four men hedged about all evening and never quite dared to ask, looking at the lot of us, hicks in overalls, farmers in canvas pants and plain shirts: *Which of you plays the role of the man?* As if we had to produce a carbon copy of their mistakes! I doubt very much that sexual equality has been reestablished on Earth. I do not like to think of myself mocked, of Katy deferred to as if she were weak, of Yuki made to feel unimportant or silly, of my other children cheated of their full humanity or turned into strangers. And I'm afraid that my own achievements will dwindle from what they were—or what I thought they were—to the not-very-interesting curiosa of the human race, the oddities you read about in the back of the book, things to laugh at sometimes because they are so exotic, quaint but not impressive, charming but not useful. I find this more painful than I can say. You will agree that for a woman who has fought three duels, all of them kills, indulging in such fears is ludicrous. But what's around the corner now is a duel so big that I don't think I have the guts for it; in Faust's words: *Verweile doch, du bist so schön!* Keep it as it is. Don't change.

Sometimes at night I remember the original name of this planet, changed by the first generation of our ancestors, those curious women for whom, I suppose, the real name was too painful a reminder after the men died. I find it amusing, in a grim way, to see it all so completely turned around. This too shall pass. All good things must come to an end.

Take my life but don't take away the meaning of my life.

For-a-While.

—1972

MATTHEW STADLER

Matthew Stadler is a Seattle-based fiction writer, critic, and teacher. His novels include Landscape: Memory *(1990),* The Dissolution of Nicholas Dee *(1993),* The Sex Offender *(1994), and* Allan Stein *(1997). The piece included here, "Love Problem," first appeared in* His: Brilliant New Fiction by Gay Writers *(1995), edited by Robert Drake and Terry Wolverton. Its dizzying portrait of sexuality and gender purposely confuses a host of social norms and expectations.*

LOVE PROBLEM

Because I'm a man most people don't think of me as a lesbian. Technically, or whatever, I think they're right, but I like to call myself a lesbian. That is to say, I would like to call myself a lesbian here.

When I was a boy, a twelve-year-old boy living in a big house with my older sister and two brothers, and my sister had her best friend from school stay at our house for sleep-overs, I'd lie awake in my room listening to our drug-addicted neighbor playing Hendrix with his wah-wah. Late into the night, the various dogs were barking and the occasional sound of trucks rolled along the highway. Drunk kids in cars careened closer by, and their headlights shifted across my window. I lay there in bed, in the flickering darkness, trying to ascertain what my sister and her friend were up to. Hadn't they fallen asleep yet? It was almost two A.M. for god's sake, and they'd no TV or record player to keep them awake. I lay still under my blanket and listened intently to the empty sound of our house. The parents were asleep. Of course they were, with trust and a deep, abiding faith in the good nature of their children. They slept well, soundly and deep. My brothers were away somewhere, at parties or on trips, maybe sprawled and fucking in the backseats of those cars I heard swerving past our house. Where were they going? I wasn't interested. My sister was in bed, in the room next to me, with her girlfriend from school. Why did my heart beat so? It was only just becoming apparent to me that I had a body. The blanket was heavy against me. The house settled more deeply as the clock turned to three, and even our neighbor passed out and slept.

I crept from my bed wearing just underpants, wanting a friend just like me, and repeating an incantation: "We're lesbians, we're lesbians, we're lesbians." I felt I should be included too. I'd no dreams of bare breasts or glistening crotches, no strange postures or facial contortions burning in my mind. As I crept along the empty carpet toward my sister's room, rather, I think I imagined a sort of recognition and solidarity waiting for me behind her almost-closed door. I saw them leaning up from bed, naked and entangled, welcoming me into their club. I saw a moment of affirmation in their warm smiles, and their knowing glance toward me, their secret lesbian brother.

Later, when I had a love affair with my cousin, when he was fourteen, he told me he wished he could be a lesbian too. He said so after we'd made out in the toolshed of his family's house in Brooklyn the night I decided to quit college and move there. I was constantly alarmed by his precocious mind and gasped audibly, delighted by our shared interest in lesbians, and I wondered what it was that made the ladies so attractive to us. Sirens and dogs startled us, and we snuck back inside, careful not to wake the sleeping parents. We spent the night whispering and entangled in his bunk bed, crushing the small stuffed animals that had been his bedmates until I came along, and feeling not a little nervous because, well, I imagine you know why. I'm tempted to write only about him, because I love him so dearly, but my subject is lesbians. We were lesbians together, often proclaiming ourselves as such, and desperately waiting for others to proclaim it also. No one would. Convention and appearance conspired against us.

We tried disguises, employing makeup and mannish suits to complement our feminine faces, vying for attention at lesbian bars in New York and Boston. What we got we didn't want, and what we wanted was hard to ask for. "Hey, we're just a bunch of lesbians," I heard my poor cousin assert to a puzzled dyke, as he pushed her straying hand past his dead-give-away crotch. It wasn't an arousing stroke we'd gone there for, but an elusive inclusion, a shelter in some alternative to the manly strutting that seemed our lot in any male culture, gay or straight. Dateless, we returned to his bunk bed and undid our ties.

After my uncle found out and my cousin was taken to a psychiatrist I got a job serving drinks in a psychedelic bar on the West Side of Manhattan. I was miserable, shattered by the removal of my cousin, and unable to form coherent thoughts. It was a perfect job. I played sad Sam Cooke songs on the jukebox and shoveled cash into my pockets from the drunken teenagers I served beer to. They didn't know Sam Cooke from a lesbian, and I couldn't help them, inarticulate and deaf as I was to everything but the songs and the pay phone. Somehow, I figured, my cousin would call me on the pay phone. The cocktail waitress was straight, a sassy Barnard woman majoring in dance and French theory. "I'm in a sad mood tonight," I crooned to her each evening as we lit the pathetic table candles. At four A.M. the last band would stop playing and we'd shut the place, locking the door against the sour beer smell, and we'd walk down the street to the Empire Diner for a bite to eat. One night, while still rattling the door chains, we saw a car come careening down Twenty-ninth, knocking cans across the empty sidewalks, lurching and leaping at the curb. We stood near to the door and watched. The car slowed as it approached, and a drunk or drugged heavy-metal teen leaned out the passenger window, glaring at the two of us crouching together, and he yelled "Fucking lesbians!" I've never been so happy. Later the manager told me I was too gay and he fired me. Life isn't easy for lesbians.

It may simply be that I love my sister and envy her having a girlfriend, a big house and kitchen, loud friends, and a shelf of dog-eared lesbian fiction. I had a girlfriend (after my cousin left) but we didn't have a house. We lived in the meat market above a butcher in a building that used to be The Fuck Club. Men from Florida came each weekend in leather straps and boots, clutching xeroxed guidebooks, and asking us for drinks or a date. I apologized to each of them, and pointed them toward Hell Fire, across the street, where the bar was always open and wild dates could still be had. My girlfriend was a lesbian and I was inexperienced. She had a habit of dating any man our friend Oscar fell in love with. He loved me and lived with us, and we made him miserable. On summer Sundays we'd take the train to the beach together, fumbling through newspapers on the dirty platform, breathing the heavy smells of piss and exhaust in the stifling heat. Oscar and Debby wore colorful shorts and sunglasses, but I was still in mourning for my lost cousin. They took MDA and I took photographs and aspirin, setting my towel between them on the crowded sand, wondering where my affections lay.

Boyfriend to a lesbian, I lay in bed cherishing the taste of my own forearm, imagining it was the stomach of my cousin Max. Debby understood this, but it made her melancholy nonetheless. I spent my days bicycling aimlessly across the city, plotting an accidental rendezvous with Max, imagining what I'd say when we met. "Hi" seemed likely. Or "hello." The rest was tears and saliva. Jobless, I lived off the money my parents sent for therapy.

Debby wrote a play starring Oscar in his underpants with sad music I wrote grieving over Max. It was produced at a lesbian theater/bar/nightclub/bookstore/coffeehouse and attracted a large, diverse audience. *Home,* it was called, and Oscar spent most of the time gazing through a hung window frame into black fiddling with his shorts. Periodically actress/waitresses would billow tablecloths over a row of small round tables upstage while my sad music played. I had to press the tape button at exactly the right moment. One night Max came.

The girls were fluffing their tablecloths. The room was filled with that slightly nervous art-house silence. The music was sad. I saw him standing near the door, and thought of Sam Cooke and the pay phone. He was sixteen now and taller than before. His dark eyes and blushing face were so painfully handsome, and his loose T-shirt let me see the tender hollow at the base of his throat where I used to rest my tongue. His shirt had big black letters that read "No one knows I'm a Lesbian." But I knew, and I knew more, and nervously got up and left my station to go tell him. During the desperate months, in my darkest sadness, I'd lain in bed clutching his old shoe to my face, and written a cycle of stupid poems conjuring the flower of my frustrated love in sad phrases and arch line-breaks. Fragments came drifting to mind as I stumbled toward him, bumping tables in the hushed theater. I'd meant each word so deeply, but now they cluttered and clanked in the back of my throat like bitter metal chains. Why had I ever sent the villanelle beginning "I'd live in your mouth forever if you'd have me, and you've had me . . ."? I knew enough to keep quiet now and trust myself to his instincts. I needed only to make it across the room and reach him. I drew near and, wise child, he looked at me in silence for one brief moment, kissed me on each eye and stuck his hand down my pants.

Debby was so mad at me for leaving that night she got a new girlfriend whom she later dumped for a tattooed boyfriend with a habit. I couldn't help myself. Oscar was made to sing the sad tune during the billowy interludes the rest of that evening, and Debby had me replaced after that. I can't say that I blame her.

Max and I whispered in our embraces and went home to my place above the butcher's and made out. We arranged to go away for a weekend to my sister's house in Boston where we could talk all this over and understand what had happened.

These days we have books with stories of tender experimentation and discovery; characters are created who explore their sexuality, emerging from ambiguity into identity, clarity, whether gay or straight. It's all very uplifting. But my story isn't like that (and it's possible yours isn't either). Max wanted a last weekend of love because he'd decided never to see me again. I was too confusing. On the day we turned the clocks back he lay beside me covered with my sweat, pressing his face into my armpit and announced his departure. Now he lives in Buenos Aires and I have a new girlfriend, a golden retriever named Soda Pop, who's not nervous about love the way most people are. I cannot say what she means to me, but I welcome her eager affection, and always look forward to the times we spend together.

As a lesbian I can both tantalize men and stand apart from them; and while I know that is not the agenda of most women, it is, perhaps, mine.

−1995

DRAMA

SUSAN GLASPELL
1882-1948

Susan Glaspell was born and raised in Davenport, Iowa. She attended Drake Univeristy and worked for the Des Moines Daily News. *In 1915, she cofounded the Provincetown Players, a group of playwrights including Eugene O'Neill and Edna St. Vincent Millay based in New York City. In 1930, she won the Pulitzer Prize for her play* Alison's House *and published throughout the course of her life ten novels and more than forty short stories. Some of the most well-known volumes include* Plays *(1920),* The Verge *(1921),* The Comic Artist *(1927),* The Visioning *(1911),* Fidelity *(1915), and* The Morning is Near *(1937).* Trifles *was also written as a short story called "A Jury of Her Peers," which, like the dramatic version, has been widely anthologized.*

TRIFLES
A Play in One Act

CHARACTERS
GEORGE HENDERSON, *county attorney*
HENRY PETERS, *sheriff*
LEWIS HALE, *a neighboring farmer*
MRS. PETERS
MRS. HALE

SCENE

The kitchen in the now abandoned farmhouse of JOHN WRIGHT, a gloomy kitchen, and left without having been put in order—unwashed pans under the sink, a loaf of bread outside the breadbox, a dish towel on the table—other signs of incompleted work. At the rear the outer door opens and the SHERIFF comes in followed by the COUNTY ATTORNEY and HALE. The SHERIFF and HALE are men in middle life, the COUNTY ATTORNEY is a young man; all are much bundled up and go at once to the stove. They are followed by two women—the SHERIFF's wife first; she is a slight wiry woman, a thin nervous face. MRS. HALE is larger and would ordinarily be called more comfortable looking, but she is disturbed now and looks fearfully about as she enters. The women have come in slowly, and stand close together near the door.

COUNTY ATTORNEY (*Rubbing his hands*): This feels good. Come up to the fire, ladies.

MRS. PETERS (*After taking a step forward*): I'm not—cold.

SHERIFF (*Unbuttoning his overcoat and stepping away from the stove as if to mark the beginning of official business*): Now, Mr. Hale, before we move things about, you explain to Mr. Henderson just what you saw when you came here yesterday morning.

COUNTY ATTORNEY: By the way, has anything been moved? Are things just as you left them yesterday?

SHERIFF (*Looking about*): It's just the same. When it dropped below zero last night I thought I'd better send Frank out this morning to make a fire for us—no use getting pneumonia with a big case on, but I told him not to touch anything except the stove—and you know Frank.

COUNTY ATTORNEY: Somebody should have been left here yesterday.

SHERIFF: Oh—yesterday. When I had to send Frank to Morris Center for that man who went crazy—I want you to know I had my hands full yesterday. I knew you could get back from Omaha by today and as long as I went over everything here myself—

COUNTY ATTORNEY: Well, Mr. Hale, tell just what happened when you came here yesterday morning.

HALE: Harry and I had started to town with a load of potatoes. We came along the road from my place and as I got here I said, "I'm going to see if I can't get John Wright to go in with me on a party telephone." I spoke to Wright about it once before and he put me off, saying folks talked too much anyway, and all he asked was peace and quiet—I guess you know about how much he talked himself; but I thought maybe if I went to the house and talked about it before his wife, though I said to Harry that I didn't know as what his wife wanted made much difference to John—

COUNTY ATTORNEY: Let's talk about that later, Mr. Hale. I do want to talk about that, but tell now just what happened when you got to the house.

HALE: I didn't hear or see anything; I knocked at the door, and still it was all quiet inside. I knew they must be up, it was past eight o'clock. So I knocked again, and I thought I heard somebody say, "Come in." I wasn't sure, I'm not sure yet, but I opened the door—this door (*indicating the door by which the two women are still standing*) and there in that rocker—(*pointing to it*) sat Mrs. Wright.

They all look at the rocker.

COUNTY ATTORNEY: What—was she doing?

HALE: She was rockin' back and forth. She had her apron in her hand and was kind of—pleating it.

COUNTY ATTORNEY: And how did she—look?

HALE: Well, she looked queer.

COUNTY ATTORNEY: How do you mean—queer?

HALE: Well, as if she didn't know what she was going to do next. And kind of done up.

COUNTY ATTORNEY: How did she seem to feel about your coming?

HALE: Why, I don't think she minded—one way or other. She didn't pay much attention. I said, "How do, Mrs. Wright, it's cold, ain't it?" And she said, "Is it?"—and went on kind of pleating at her apron. Well, I was surprised; she didn't ask me to come up to the stove, or to set down, but just sat there, not even looking at me, so I said, "I want to see John." And then she—laughed. I guess you would call it a laugh. I thought of Harry and the team outside, so I said a little sharp: "Can't I see John?" "No," she says, kind o' dull like. "Ain't he home?" says I. "Yes," says she, "he's home." "Then why can't I see him?" I asked her, out of patience. "'Cause he's dead," says she. *"Dead?"* says I. She just nodded her head, not getting a bit excited, but rockin' back and forth. "Why—where is he?" says I, not knowing what to say. She just pointed upstairs—like that (*himself pointing to the room above*). I got up, with the idea of going up there. I walked from there to here—then I says, "Why, what did he die of?" "He died of a rope round his neck," says she, and just went on pleatin' at her apron. Well, I went out and called Harry. I thought I might—need help. We went upstairs and there he was lyin'—

COUNTY ATTORNEY: I think I'd rather have you go into that upstairs, where you can point it all out. Just go on now with the rest of the story.

HALE: Well, my first thought was to get that rope off. It looked . . . (*Stops, his face twitches*) . . . but Harry, he went up to him, and he said, "No, he's dead all right, and we'd better not touch anything." So we went back down stairs. She was still sitting that same way. "Has anybody been notified?" I asked. "No," says she, unconcerned. "Who did this, Mrs. Wright?" said Harry. He said it business-like— and she stopped pleatin' of her apron. "I don't know," she says. "You don't *know*?" says Harry. "No," says she. "Weren't you sleepin' in the bed with him?" says Harry. "Yes," says she, "but I was on the inside." "Somebody slipped a rope round his neck and strangled him and you didn't wake up?" says Harry. "I didn't wake up," she said after him. We must 'a looked as if we didn't see how that could be, for after a minute she said, "I sleep sound." Harry was going to ask her more questions but I said maybe we ought to let her tell her story first to the coroner, or the sheriff, so Harry went fast as he could to Rivers' place, where there's a telephone.

COUNTY ATTORNEY: And what did Mrs. Wright do when she knew that you had gone for the coroner?

HALE: She moved from that chair to this one over here (*Pointing to a small chair in the corner*) and just sat there with her hands held together and looking down. I got a feeling that I ought to make some conversation, so I said I had come in to see if John wanted to put in a telephone, and at that she started to laugh, and then she stopped and looked at me—scared. (*The* COUNTY ATTORNEY, *who has had his notebook out, makes a note.*) I dunno, maybe it wasn't scared. I wouldn't like to say it was. Soon Harry got back, and then Dr. Lloyd came, and you, Mr. Peters, and so I guess that's all I know that you don't.

COUNTY ATTORNEY (*Looking around*): I guess we'll go upstairs first—and then out to the barn and around there. (*To the* SHERIFF) You're convinced that there was nothing important here—nothing that would point to any motive.

SHERIFF: Nothing here but kitchen things.

The COUNTY ATTORNEY, *after again looking around the kitchen, opens the door of a cupboard closet. He gets up on a chair and looks on a shelf. Pulls his hand away, sticky.*

COUNTY ATTORNEY: Here's a nice mess.

The women draw nearer.

MRS. PETERS (*To the other woman*): Oh, her fruit; it did freeze. (*To the* COUNTY ATTORNEY) She worried about that when it turned so cold. She said the fire'd go out and her jars would break.

SHERIFF: Well, can you beat the women! Held for murder and worryin' about her preserves.

COUNTY ATTORNEY: I guess before we're through she may have something more serious than preserves to worry about.

HALE: Well, women are used to worrying over trifles.

The two women move a little closer together.

COUNTY ATTORNEY (*With the gallantry of a young politician*): And yet, for all their worries, what would we do without the ladies? (*The women do not unbend. He goes to the sink, takes a dipperful of water from the pail and pouring it into a basin, washes his hands. Starts to wipe them on the roller towel, turns it for a cleaner place.*) Dirty towels! (*Kicks his foot against the pans under the sink*) Not much of a housekeeper, would you say, ladies?

MRS. HALE (*Stiffly*): There's a great deal of work to be done on a farm.

COUNTY ATTORNEY: To be sure. And yet (*With a little bow to her*) I know there are some Dickson county farmhouses which do not have such roller towels.

He gives it a pull to expose its full length again.

MRS. HALE: Those towels get dirty awful quick. Men's hands aren't always as clean as they might be.

COUNTY ATTORNEY: Ah, loyal to your sex, I see. But you and Mrs. Wright were neighbors. I suppose you were friends, too.

MRS. HALE (*Shaking her head*): I've not seen much of her of late years. I've not been in this house—it's more than a year.

COUNTY ATTORNEY: And why was that? You didn't like her?

MRS. HALE: I liked her all well enough. Farmers' wives have their hands full, Mr. Henderson. And then—

COUNTY ATTORNEY: Yes—?

MRS. HALE (*Looking about*): It never seemed a very cheerful place.

COUNTY ATTORNEY: No—it's not cheerful. I shouldn't say she had the homemaking instinct.

MRS. HALE: Well, I don't know as Wright had, either.

COUNTY ATTORNEY: You mean that they didn't get on very well?

MRS. HALE: No, I don't mean anything. But I don't think a place'd be any cheerfuller for John Wright's being in it.

COUNTY ATTORNEY: I'd like to talk more of that a little later. I want to get the lay of things upstairs now.

He goes to the left, where three steps lead to a stair door.

SHERIFF: I suppose anything Mrs. Peters does'll be all right. She was to take in some clothes for her, you know, and a few little things. We left in such a hurry yesterday.

COUNTY ATTORNEY: Yes, but I would like to see what you take, Mrs. Peters, and keep an eye out for anything that might be of use to us.

MRS. PETERS: Yes, Mr. Henderson.

The women listen to the men's steps on the stairs, then look about the kitchen.

MRS. HALE: I'd hate to have men coming into my kitchen, snooping around and criticizing.

She arranges the pans under sink which the COUNTY ATTORNEY *had shoved out of place.*

MRS. PETERS: Of course it's no more than their duty.

MRS. HALE: Duty's all right, but I guess that deputy sheriff that came out to make the fire might have got a little of this on. (*Gives the roller towel a pull*) Wish I'd thought of that sooner. Seems mean to talk about her for not having things slicked up when she had to come away in such a hurry.

MRS. PETERS (*Who has gone to a small table in the left rear corner of the room, and lifted one end of a towel that covers a pan*): She had bread set.

Stands still.

MRS. HALE (*Eyes fixed on a loaf of bread beside the breadbox, which is on a low shelf at the other side of the room. Moves slowly toward it.*): She was going to put this in there. (*Picks up loaf, then abruptly drops it. In a manner of returning to familiar things*) It's a shame about her fruit. I wonder if it's all gone. (*Gets up on the chair and looks*) I think there's some here that's all right, Mrs. Peters. Yes—here; (*Holding it toward the window*) this is cherries, too. (*Looking again*) I declare I believe that's the only one. (*Gets down, bottle in her hand. Goes to the sink and wipes it off on the outside.*) She'll feel awful bad after all her hard work in the hot weather. I remember the afternoon I put up my cherries last summer.

She puts the bottle on the big kitchen table, center of the room. With a sigh, is about to sit down in the rocking-chair. Before she is seated realizes what chair it is; with a slow look at it, steps back. The chair which she has touched rocks back and forth.

MRS. PETERS: Well, I must get those things from the front room closet. (*She goes to the door at the right, but after looking into the other room, steps back.*) You coming with me, Mrs. Hale? You could help me carry them.

They go in the other room; reappear, MRS. PETERS carrying a dress and skirt, MRS. HALE following with a pair of shoes.

MRS. PETERS: My, it's cold in there.

She puts the clothes on the big table, and hurries to the stove.

MRS. HALE (*Examining the skirt*): Wright was close. I think maybe that's why she kept so much to herself. She didn't even belong to the Ladies Aid. I suppose she felt she couldn't do her part, and then you don't enjoy things when you feel shabby. She used to wear pretty clothes and be lively, when she was Minnie Foster, one of the town girls singing in the choir. But that—oh, that was thirty years ago. This all you was to take in?

MRS. PETERS: She said she wanted an apron. Funny thing to want, for there isn't much to get you dirty in jail, goodness knows. But I suppose just to make her feel more natural. She said they was in the top drawer in this cupboard. Yes, here. And then her little shawl that always hung behind the door. (*Opens stair door and looks*) Yes, here it is.

Quickly shuts door leading upstairs.

MRS. HALE (*Abruptly moving toward her*): Mrs. Peters?
MRS. PETERS: Yes, Mrs. Hale?
MRS. HALE: Do you think she did it?
MRS. PETERS (*In a frightened voice*): Oh, I don't know.
MRS. HALE: Well, I don't think she did. Asking for an apron and her little shawl. Worrying about her fruit.
MRS. PETERS (*Starts to speak, glances up, where footsteps are heard in the room above. In a low voice*): Mr. Peters says it looks bad for her. Mr. Henderson is awful sarcastic in a speech and he'll make fun of her sayin' she didn't wake up.
MRS. HALE: Well, I guess John Wright didn't wake when they was slipping that rope under his neck.
MRS. PETERS: No, it's strange. It must have been done awful crafty and still. They say it was such a—funny way to kill a man, rigging it all up like that.

MRS. HALE: That's just what Mr. Hale said. There was a gun in the house. He says that's what he can't understand.

MRS. PETERS: Mr. Henderson said coming out that what was needed for the case was a motive; something to show anger, or—sudden feeling.

MRS. HALE (*Who is standing by the table*): Well, I don't see any signs of anger around here. (*She puts her hand on the dish towel which lies on the table, stands looking down at table, one half of which is clean, the other half messy*) It's wiped to here. (*Makes a move as if to finish work, then turns and looks at loaf of bread outside the breadbox. Drops towel. In that voice of coming back to familiar things.*) Wonder how they are finding things upstairs. I hope she had it a little more red-up up there. You know, it seems kind of *sneaking.* Locking her up in town and then coming out here and trying to get her own house to turn against her!

MRS. PETERS: But Mrs. Hale, the law is the law.

MRS. HALE: I s'pose 'tis. (*Unbuttoning her coat*) Better loosen up your things, Mrs. Peters. You won't feel them when you go out.

MRS. PETERS *takes off her fur tippet, goes to hang it on hook at back of room, stands looking at the under part of the small corner table.*

MRS. PETERS: She was piecing a quilt.

She brings the large sewing basket and they look at the bright pieces.

MRS. HALE: It's a log cabin pattern. Pretty, isn't it? I wonder if she was goin' to quilt it or just knot it?

Footsteps have been heard coming down the stairs. The SHERIFF *enters followed by* HALE *and the* COUNTY ATTORNEY.

SHERIFF: They wonder if she was going to quilt it or just knot it!

The men laugh, the women look abashed.

COUNTY ATTORNEY: (*Rubbing his hands over the stove*): Frank's fire didn't do much up there, did it? Well, let's go out to the barn and get that cleared up.

The men go outside.

MRS. HALE (*Resentfully*): I don't know as there's anything so strange, our takin' up our time with little things while we're waiting for them to get the evidence. (*She sits down at the big table smoothing out a block with decision*) I don't see as it's anything to laugh about.

MRS. PETERS (*Apologetically*): Of course they've got awful important things on their minds.

Pulls up a chair and joins MRS. HALE *at the table.*

MRS. HALE (*Examining another block*): Mrs. Peters, look at this one. Here, this is one she was working on, and look at the sewing! All the rest of it has been so nice and even. And look at this! It's all over the place! Why, it looks as if she didn't know what she was about!

After she has said this they look at each other, then start to glance back at the door. After an instant MRS. HALE *has pulled at a knot and ripped the sewing.*

MRS. PETERS: Oh, what are you doing, Mrs. Hale?

MRS. HALE (*Mildly*): Just pulling out a stitch or two that's not sewed very good. (*Threading a needle.*) Bad sewing always made me fidgety.

MRS. PETERS (*Nervously*): I don't think we ought to touch things.

MRS. HALE: I'll just finish up this end. (*Suddenly stopping and leaning forward*) Mrs. Peters?

MRS. PETERS: Yes, Mrs. Hale?

MRS. HALE: What do you suppose she was so nervous about?

MRS. PETERS: Oh—I don't know. I don't know as she was nervous. I sometimes sew awful queer when I'm just tired. (MRS. HALE *starts to say something, looks at* MRS. PETERS, *then goes on sewing*) Well, I must get these things wrapped up. They may be through sooner than we think. (*Putting apron and other things together*) I wonder where I can find a piece of paper, and string.

MRS. HALE: In that cupboard, maybe.

MRS. PETERS (*Looking in cupboard*): Why, here's a bird-cage. (*Holds it up*) Did she have a bird, Mrs. Hale?

MRS. HALE: Why, I don't know whether she did or not—I've not been here for so long. There was a man around last year selling canaries cheap, but I don't know as she took one; maybe she did. She used to sing real pretty herself.

MRS. PETERS (*Glancing around*): Seems funny to think of a bird here. But she must have had one, or why would she have a cage? I wonder what happened to it.

MRS. HALE: I s'pose maybe the cat got it.

MRS. PETERS: No, she didn't have a cat. She's got that feeling some people have about cats—being afraid of them. My cat got in her room and she was real upset and asked me to take it out.

MRS. HALE: My sister Bessie was like that. Queer, ain't it?

MRS. PETERS (*Examining the cage*): Why, look at this door. It's broke. One hinge is pulled apart.

MRS. HALE (*Looking too*): Looks as if someone must have been rough with it.

MRS. PETERS: Why, yes.

She brings the cage forward and puts it on the table.

MRS. HALE: I wish if they're going to find any evidence they'd be about it. I don't like this place.

MRS. PETERS: But I'm awful glad you came with me, Mrs. Hale. It would be lonesome for me sitting here alone.

MRS. HALE: It would, wouldn't it? (*Dropping her sewing*) But I tell you what I do wish,

Mrs. Peters. I wish I had come over sometimes when *she* was here. I—(*Looking around the room*)—wish I had.

MRS. PETERS: But of course you were awful busy, Mrs. Hale—your house and your children.

MRS. HALE: I could've come. I stayed away because it weren't cheerful—and that's why I ought to have come. I—I've never liked this place. Maybe because it's down in a hollow and you don't see the road. I dunno what it is but it's a lonesome place and always was. I wish I had come over to see Minnie Foster sometimes. I can see now—

Shakes her head.

MRS. PETERS: Well, you mustn't reproach yourself, Mrs. Hale. Somehow we just don't see how it is with other folks until—something comes up.

MRS. HALE: Not having children makes less work—but it makes a quiet house, and Wright out to work all day, and no company when he did come in. Did you know John Wright, Mrs. Peters?

MRS. PETERS: Not to know him; I've seen him in town. They say he was a good man.

MRS. HALE: Yes—good; he didn't drink, and kept his word as well as most, I guess, and paid his debts. But he was a hard man, Mrs. Peters. Just to pass the time of day with him—(*Shivers*) Like a raw wind that gets to the bone. (*Pauses, her eye falling on the cage*) I should think she would 'a wanted a bird. But what do you suppose went with it?

MRS. PETERS: I don't know, unless it got sick and died.

She reaches over and swings the broken door, swings it again, both women watch it.

MRS. HALE: You weren't raised round here, were you? (MRS. PETERS *shakes her head*) You didn't know—her?

MRS. PETERS: Not till they brought her yesterday.

MRS. HALE: She—come to think of it, she was kind of a like a bird herself—real sweet and pretty, but kind of timid and—fluttery. How—she—did—change. (*Silence; then as if struck by a happy thought and relieved to get back to every-day things*) Tell you what, Mrs. Peters, why don't you take the quilt in with you? It might take up her mind.

MRS. PETERS: Why, I think that's a real nice idea, Mrs. Hale. There couldn't possibly be any objection to it, could there? Now, just what would I take? I wonder if her patches are in here—and her things.

They look in the sewing basket.

MRS. HALE: Here's some red. I expect this has got sewing things in it. (*Brings out a fancy box*) What a pretty box. Looks like something somebody would give you. Maybe her scissors are in here. (*Opens box. Suddenly puts her hand to her nose*) Why—(MRS. PETERS *bends nearer, then turns her face away*) There's something wrapped up in this piece of silk.

MRS. PETERS: Why, this isn't her scissors.

MRS. HALE (*Lifting the silk*): Oh, Mrs. Peters—it's—

MRS. PETERS *bends closer.*

MRS. PETERS: It's the bird.

MRS. HALE (*Jumping up*): But, Mrs. Peters—look at it! Its neck! Look at its neck! It's all—other side *to.*

MRS. PETERS: Somebody—wrung—its—neck.

Their eyes meet. A look of growing comprehension, of horror. Steps are heard outside. MRS. HALE slips box under quilt pieces, and sinks into her chair. Enter SHERIFF and COUNTY ATTORNEY. MRS. PETERS rises.

COUNTY ATTORNEY (*As one turning from serious things to little pleasantries*): Well, ladies, have you decided whether she was going to quilt it or knot it?

MRS. PETERS: We think she was going to—knot it.

COUNTY ATTORNEY: Well, that's interesting, I'm sure. (*Seeing the birdcage*) Has the bird flown?

MRS. HALE (*Putting more quilt pieces over the box*): We think the—cat got it.

COUNTY ATTORNEY: (*Preoccupied*): Is there a cat? (MRS. HALE *glances in a quick covert way at* MRS. PETERS)

MRS. PETERS: Well, not *now.* They're superstitious, you know. They leave.

COUNTY ATTORNEY: (*To* SHERIFF PETERS, *continuing an interrupted conversation*): No sign at all of anyone having come from the outside. Their own rope. Now let's go up again and go over it piece by piece. (*They start upstairs*) It would have to have been someone who knew just the—

MRS. PETERS *sits down. The two women sit there not looking at one another, but as if peering into something and at the same time holding back. When they talk now it is in the manner of feeling their way over strange ground, as if afraid of what they are saying, but as if they cannot help saying it.*

MRS. HALE: She liked the bird. She was going to bury it in that pretty box.

MRS. PETERS (*In a whisper*): When I was a girl—my kitten—there was a boy took a hatchet, and before my eyes—and before I could get there—(*Covers her face an instant*) If they hadn't held me back I would have—(*Catches herself, looks upstairs where steps are heard, falters weakly*)—hurt him.

MRS. HALE (*With a slow look around her*): I wonder how it would seem never to have had any children around. (*Pause*) No, Wright wouldn't like the bird—a thing that sang. She used to sing. He killed that, too.

MRS. PETERS (*Moving uneasily*): We don't know who killed the bird.

MRS. HALE: I knew John Wright.

MRS. PETERS: It was an awful thing was done in this house that night, Mrs. Hale. Killing a man while he slept, slipping a rope around his neck that choked the life out of him.

MRS. HALE: His neck. Choked the life out of him.

Her hand goes out and rests on the birdcage.

MRS. PETERS (*With rising voice*): We don't know who killed him. We don't *know*.

MRS. HALE (*Her own feeling not interrupted*): If there'd been years and years of nothing, then a bird to sing to you, it would be awful—still, after the bird was still.

MRS. PETERS (*Something within her speaking*): I know what stillness is. When we homesteaded in Dakota, and my first baby died—after he was two years old, and me with no other then—

MRS. HALE (*Moving*): How soon do you suppose they'll be through looking for the evidence?

MRS. PETERS: I know what stillness is. (*Pulling herself back*) The law has got to punish crime, Mrs. Hale.

MRS. HALE (*Not as if answering that*): I wish you'd seen Minnie Foster when she wore a white dress with blue ribbons and stood up there in the choir and sang. (*A look around the room*) Oh, I *wish* I'd come over here once in a while! That was a crime! That was a crime! Who's going to punish that?

MRS. PETERS (*Looking upstairs*): We mustn't—take on.

MRS. HALE: I might have known she needed help! I know how things can be—for women. I tell you, it's queer, Mrs. Peters. We live close together and we live far apart. We all go through the same things—it's all just a different kind of the same thing. (*Brushes her eyes, noticing the bottle of fruit, reaches out for it*) If I was you I wouldn't tell her her fruit was gone. Tell her it *ain't*. Tell her it's all right. Take this in to prove it to her. She—she may never know whether it was broke or not.

MRS. PETERS (*Takes the bottle, looks about for something to wrap it in; takes petticoat from the clothes brought from the other room, very nervously begins winding this around the bottle. In a false voice*): My, it's a good thing the men couldn't hear us. Wouldn't they just laugh! Getting all stirred up over a little thing like a—dead canary. As if that could have anything to do with—with—wouldn't they laugh!

The men are heard coming down stairs.

MRS. HALE (*Under her breath*): Maybe they would—maybe they wouldn't.

COUNTY ATTORNEY: No, Peters, it's all perfectly clear except a reason for doing it. But you know juries when it comes to women. If there was some definite thing. Something to show—something to make a story about—a thing that would connect up with this strange way of doing it—

The women's eyes meet for an instant. Enter HALE from outer door.

HALE: Well, I've got the team around. Pretty cold out there.

COUNTY ATTORNEY: I'm going to stay here a while by myself. (*To the* SHERIFF) You can send Frank out for me, can't you? I want to go over everything. I'm not satisfied that we can't do better.

SHERIFF: Do you want to see what Mrs. Peters is going to take in?

The COUNTY ATTORNEY *goes to the table, picks up the apron, laughs.*

COUNTY ATTORNEY: Oh, I guess they're not very dangerous things the ladies have picked out. (*Moves a few things about, disturbing the quilt pieces which cover the box. Steps back.*) No, Mrs. Peters doesn't need supervising. For that matter, a sheriff's wife is married to the law. Ever think of it that way, Mrs. Peters?
MRS. PETERS: Not—just that way.
SHERIFF (*Chuckling*): Married to the law. (*Moves toward the other room*) I just want you to come in here a minute, George. We ought to take a look at these windows.
COUNTY ATTORNEY (*Scoffingly*): Oh, windows!
SHERIFF: We'll be right out, Mr. Hale.

HALE *goes outside.* The SHERIFF *follows the* COUNTY ATTORNEY *into the other room. Then* MRS. HALE *rises, hands tight together, looking intensely at* MRS. PETERS, *whose eyes make a slow turn, finally meeting* MRS. HALE's. *A moment* MRS. HALE *holds her, then her own eyes point the way to where the box is concealed. Suddenly* MRS. PETERS *throws back quilt pieces and tries to put the box in the bag she is wearing. It is too big. She opens box, starts to take bird out, cannot touch it, goes to pieces, stands there helpless. Sound of a knob turning in the other room.* MRS. HALE *snatches the box and puts it in the pocket of her big coat. Enter* COUNTY ATTORNEY *and* SHERIFF.

COUNTY ATTORNEY (*Facetiously*): Well, Henry, at least we found out that she was not going to quilt it. She was going to—what is it you call it, ladies?
MRS. HALE (*Her hand against her pocket*): We call it—knot it, Mr. Henderson.

CURTAIN

—1916

Appendix

WRITING ABOUT LITERATURE AND CULTURE

This section of the book focuses on the relationship between critical thinking and effective writing. It provides an important linkage between the kinds of critical reading and interpretation skills and the necessary role that writing plays for thinking about literature and social issues.

It offers ideas, guidelines, strategies, and working principles for writing about literature. This appendix will accompany all the books in the Longman Literature and Culture series *(Literature and the Environment: A Reader on Nature and Culture; Literature, Culture, and Class: A Thematic Anthology; Literature, Race, and Ethnicity: Contested American Identities; Literature and Gender: Thinking Critically Through Fiction, Poetry, and Drama),* a series devoted to reading and thinking critically in ways that promote exploration and discovery. Writing about literature furthers these goals of critical analysis.

What I have attempted to do is focus on innovative approaches that will help you better analyze and understand the exciting and perhaps somewhat unfamiliar territory of writing about literature. I will begin by describing good writing—that is, writing that stays in the mind and positively influences readers. Next, I will offer some principles that underlie successful academic writing generally and critical work in literature classes more specifically. After that, I will discuss what it means to read for meaning, suggest how to get ready for class discussions, and then move to a consideration of the writing process with a particular focus on purpose, audience, drafting, and revising. Since one of the chief difficulties many writers face is "the blank page syndrome," I particularly address the problem of getting started on a writing project. The next section examines the various elements that comprise an essay, its various components. I then move to a brief consideration of the computer, with a particular focus on both word processing and electronic researching. Finally,

I offer a brief guide to research, with a listing of some of the most common bibliographic entries according to the Modern Language Association format.

What Is Good Writing?

Let's begin with some general principles that apply to all good academic writing. Many students equate academic writing with boredom, stuffiness, and abstraction. From their perspective, only academics write—and read—academic writing, which most others find dull, dry, and abstract. Now there is no doubt that writing of this kind exists, but most of it is not good writing, academic or otherwise.

Good writing has energy, clarity, and a liveliness of mind. It creates satisfaction by enlightening and persuading. It asks writers to place themselves at risk since they are making their ideas public. It changes minds because it illuminates its subject in a new light. It explores ideas thoughtfully, drawing upon research and other forms of evidence to persuade the reader.

Good writing has economy: it offers a thoughtful, efficient route toward increased understanding. No reader likes to read an essay that digresses or uses 35 words to state a 15-word idea. You may be assigned an essay with a required length, for example "Write a 2500-word essay that argues for a specific environmental policy to preserve western wilderness." Such essays can be challenging since students sometimes think they have to pad them to get the necessary words. This procedure is ill advised; no essay profits from repetition or flabby style. In this situation, the only choice is to do more reading, researching, and analyzing—subjects I will consider shortly.

Good writing leaves the author with a sense of accomplishment and satisfaction. Writing a passing essay may be easy, but unless writers are engaged in the hard struggle with the text and with their writing process, they are unlikely to experience a meaningful sense of accomplishment. Take your internal pulse after you complete an essay. Do you like it? Do you feel that it succeeds? Are you glad to have written it? Are you aware of your struggles, frustrations, and accomplishments? If you can answer "yes" to these questions, you stand a good chance of success. Good writing reveals insights that are often as surprising to the writer as they are to the reader. Good writing packs a punch. It stays in the memory. It makes a difference.

Although there is no single formula for good writing, certain general truths apply. First, writers need to capture their excitement, passion, and intellectual commitment. If a writer lacks those qualities—that is, writes simply to get done or to fill blank pages—the writing almost always is lackluster. Many times, writers get stuck and cannot complete a good draft, or work for hours and then throw up their hands in despair. If they possess an emotional and intellectual desire to produce a good piece of work, however, half the battle is won. They will try again, revise, seek the help of a teacher or tutor, research the subject more extensively, experiment, and otherwise redouble their effort. Most writers do not produce good first drafts, but if they care about the writing, they find ways to make it into something worth reading.

Good writing thus requires both time and effort. Even a short assignment ("Write a 500-word essay that explores why you think America is—or is not—a classless society") makes significant demands on any writer: time and effort to think, read, reflect, procrastinate, get started and get nowhere, draft, revise, edit, proofread. Few writers, be they students or professionals, can dash off two or three quick pages and achieve satisfying results.

Good writing generally exhibits active and descriptive verbs that perform "work" for the writer. Thus, instead of stating "John McPhee is a good writer and is my favorite author," try "John McPhee writes well and remains my favorite author" or "John McPhee is my favorite author because he writes so well" or "John McPhee, my favorite author, writes so well that reading one of his books is like seeing a movie" or some other version. Note the differences among these sentences: the ways that verbs get changed, altering sentence structure and meaning as well. Lackluster writing can often be traced to overdependence on the verb "to be" in its various forms: "am," "is," "are," "was," "were," "be," "been." If your writing is flat, examine it for overuse of the various "to be" verbs and try to find meaningful, accurate replacements.

Good writing conveys new information to readers. At first glance, this seems to pose a problem: after all, how can you write something "new" about literature when your instructor knows so much more? Although instructors do possess considerable knowledge, they by no means know everything about an essay, story, poem, drama, author, or subject. In fact, their love of literature can make them easy to write for, since they enjoy learning more. The key is to convey new information: an interpretation supported by quotes, analysis, and research; a historical exploration of a work or author; an argument about the meaning or significance of a literary subject; a personal assessment of why or how a literary work affects you; a well-documented research paper; and so on. Instructors respond positively to student work that teaches them something, that changes their interpretations, adds to their knowledge, or improves their appreciation. When students accomplish one or more of those objectives, they produce "good writing."

READING FOR MEANING

To be able to write, you—like any good writer—must find something to say. Too often, students receive an assignment and produce a quick and visceral response (sometimes just before class). One important key to succeeding in a literature class is to learn how to engage in sustained inquiry—that is, learning how to read for meaning and asking questions that lead toward improved understanding. Most literary works are sufficiently complex that at first they often frustrate readers. Success in this class will depend on learning how to read well.

Typically, we read to gain information. That is why we read many textbooks, newspapers, magazines, instructions, and the like. The kind of reading required in an English literature or composition course, however, requires a different set of strategies. Although most of us first read a story, essay, poem, or drama to find out what happens—that is, to gain some information and knowledge of how the "story" will end—the primary intent of literature is not simply to provide readers with information or a plot. Rather, its purpose is to give pleasure, to offer multiple possibilities for interpretation, to surprise, to shock, to amaze, to alter the reader's thinking. Works such as the ones in this book offer *more* than information, and figuring out that "more" takes effort, time, and critical analysis.

Here are some practical strategies and suggestions for how to get the most out of the selections in this anthology:

Sound Reading Strategies

1. Read when your concentration is at its peak. Many people do their reading when they are tired or distracted. They read at work or during television commercials. This is fine if you are skimming for information or pleasure—reading a newspaper, magazine, or the comic page, for example—but the selections in this book demand concentration. You need to read when you are focused and full of energy, alert and clear eyed.

2. Read for pleasure first. During your first time through a text, read for enjoyment. Every author in this book intends to give you pleasure—to make you enjoy exploring and analyzing ideas, language, form, structure, style, arguments.

3. Read actively, not passively. As you read, stop occasionally and imagine what will happen on the next page or in the next section; such a process helps to involve you in the ebb and flow of the text. Stop, occasionally, to write down your prediction, your emerging interpretation, your view of why you think the author wrote this work, what its strengths and weaknesses are. Compare your responses to those of your classmates.

4. Reread. Read the first time for pleasure; read the second time for increased understanding. Most of the selections in this anthology present complicated ideas in complicated ways; the reader's job is to figure out what the selection means beyond the obvious. How does the writer make her/his points? What kinds of similes, metaphors, and other figurative language does the writer use? Are there contradictions and paradoxes? What choices does the writer make—and why? Are the writer's arguments convincing and well supported? These kinds of questions often can only be answered through rereading.

5. Take notes. Underline passages that are memorable, surprising, confusing, provocative—that provoke a personal response. Opposite each underlined passage, write a marginal comment explaining why you underlined the passage, such as:

   "what is she saying here?"
   "why does he stumble—symbolic?"
   "empty purse—are they also empty emotionally?"
   "this desert is real but it is also symbolic of her despair"
   "who benefited from the slave trade?"
   "I can feel the author's love of his family here" etc.

   These comments along with the underlinings point the way toward a good, critical essay. Most importantly, they provide a written record of thoughts and impressions, some of which you may otherwise lose.

6. Discuss. Although reading is a solitary activity, understanding improves when students share interpretations. All readers bring their own experiences

to a text, their own strengths, weaknesses, experiences, insights, and blind spots. Perhaps the most important aspect of discussion is learning how to listen, comprehend, and respond thoughtfully. Listening is a parallel activity to reading; it requires us to be attentive and to work hard at understanding someone else's point of view.

GETTING READY FOR CLASS DISCUSSION

Class discussion is almost always a crucial and fundamental element of a literature or composition class. Most of us both enjoy and learn better when we engage in focused, thoughtful discussion with our peers. Aside from reading and rereading the assignment, certain other habits and practices can improve the quality of class conversation. What follows are some suggestions and strategies for preparing yourself to discuss literature in this class and the others you might take.

- Bring your textbook and notes to class. This may seem like obvious common-sense advice, but surprisingly many students do not follow it. It is especially important to have the text handy when enrolled in a class that focuses on literature, because frequently in discussion students need to quote from the assigned text in order to provide support for a comment or clarify an interpretation. Since many students (and faculty, for that matter) write marginal notes in the text as they read, they have an additional reason for wanting the book handy—namely, for ready reference.
- Do not read any out-of-class assignments in class. One of the fastest ways to sour instructors is if they observe you reading the assignment at your desk rather than participating in class activities. Bring your text, have it ready, but use it only for reference or clarification, unless instructed otherwise.
- Take notes. Both lecture and class discussion often produce creative and surprising insights. They trigger important questions that can lead directly to an essay or term paper. When that happens, it is crucial to write them down so that they can be remembered and reconsidered. Some faculty have been known to stop discussion in the middle of class in order to take hurried notes on something that was said. Students should do the same. Aside from having a record of useful comments, taking notes has the added benefit of focusing one's attention more on the discussion, thus keeping the mind from wandering off while others speak.
- Listen carefully. One of the best ways to improve listening is to write down a brief, succinct summary of what someone has said once he or she has finished. This technique is, of course, a form of note-taking. As others in the class speak, good listeners work hard to understand what they are saying and how it improves understanding of the text.
- In a class that centers on literature, discussion usually does not center on factual material ("In what year did Frederick Douglass first publish his autobiography?" "Who was Mother Jones?"). That kind of information, which is very important in terms of knowledge and mastery, is usually presented in a short lecture by the instructor or is something you are expected to learn

through reading and outside research. Rather, most class discussions emphasize interpretation, analysis, and argumentation ("Consider the concept of family in Gwendolyn Brooks's poem, 'Mother.'" "What images and associations of the city does Tom Wolfe invoke in 'O Rotten Gotham'—and what effect do they have on you as a reader?"). Meaningful class discussion requires not only offering an interpretation or analysis, but providing support if others in the class disagree. When class discussion goes well, it is usually because reasonable and thoughtful readers express differing interpretations and explanations equally supported by careful textual analysis.

- Be ready to explain yourself. The key to illuminating discussions is not just offering an opinion about a work of literature; it is possessing the knowledge and information to explain it. To do this, a reader should constantly be asking "why?" and then discovering the answer. For example, if a poem makes you feel exalted, it is important to know why and then pinpoint the language, ideas, and arguments that produce this result. Responses to literature are created through a combination of author intent, literary form and structure, social and historical contexts, the reader's personal history, and other factors. Thoughtful class participants learn how to explain themselves and their interpretations.

- Let others speak. When only the instructor or a few students dominate discussion, class soon becomes a bore. Although many instructors like to present short lectures in order to provide information efficiently, class discussion can only succeed if everyone limits his or her time and no one dominates. If you find yourself talking too much or too often, learn to love silence. Quite often, reticent students will begin to speak and participate if the "natural talkers" in the class restrain themselves.

- Be succinct. Students and teachers alike zone out when someone makes the same point repeatedly. Once you say it, don't repeat it. To say the same thing again and again is boring and repetitious—even redundant—even when there is slight variation. Like this paragraph.

- Focus. As you read an assignment, you may discover an interpretation or come up with questions. If so, write them out and bring them with you to class. Many instructors will welcome such written comments and provide class time for discussing them.

- Change the perspective from which you read and interpret the assignment. Put yourself in the place of the author: try to think why she wrote it, what she intended, why she made specific choices. Insert yourself in the role of a character or even that of a reviewer or critic. Write down your comments for use in class.

- Remember that not all interpretations or analyses are equally persuasive or insightful, but that does not mean they lack value, at least to the individual who offers them. This does not mean that anything goes; rather, that interpretation and analysis is a negotiation involving the reader, the author, the text, the class, historical circumstance, and the world of literary criticism. One of the major purposes of class discussion is to provide students and instructors with a rich and reasonable forum in which to test their hypotheses and participate in a collaborative give-and-take about meaning and understanding.

THE WRITING PROCESS

Preliminary Steps

Different writers write differently, and all writers must strive to find the composing process that best suits their needs. Professional writers demonstrate the diversity of composing processes. John McPhee, for example, plans extensively and creates an elaborate structure for his essays and books. This planning process can be extremely laborious, but once he develops the structure (which might take days, weeks, or longer), it provides a framework for the actual writing (and rewriting) that follows. When Jamaica Kincaid writes, she often spends a great deal of time deliberating and choosing. She might write down just one word in an hour, but once that word is on paper she knows it is the right one and seldom if ever changes it. Richard Selzer writes out of a sense almost of compulsion. He pours out many pages of prose every day longhand in his notebooks, only a small fraction of which ever makes its way to print. None of these writers would choose to follow the composing process of any other; what they do works for them.

The pages that follow offer a variety of approaches to writing, not all of which are likely to work for any one student. Even the order is somewhat arbitrary; my "Step One" might be someone else's "Step Four." What all writers must do is experiment, particularly if they are having trouble writing or are not achieving desired results. Although there is no one right way to write, there are wrong ways that can get someone stuck and frustrated. All writers, however, can alter their ways of composing and make the process more efficient and productive; it just takes time, practice, and the will to change.

Step One: Establish a Sense of Purpose

Frequently, instructors establish an outcome for their students in the assignment itself. For example:

> Analyze the metaphors that Barry Lopez uses to describe wilderness in his essay "The Stone Horse." In your essay, be sure to cite at least three metaphors and discuss their appropriateness to his themes of tenderness and fragility.

This instructor wants students to analyze Lopez's use of metaphors and offer reasons why they are—or are not—appropriate to two major themes in his work. Some students might prefer to write personal responses, but however satisfying to the writer, they are unlikely to fulfill the instructor's purpose (and will probably receive a poor grade).

Some instructors assign essays that allow more individual choice:

> Respond to Tillie Olsen's "I Stand Here Ironing." Can you relate your own experiences as either a parent or a child to this fictional monologue? In your essay, be sure and discuss who this speaker is—that is, describe in your own terms the speaker's values, feelings, and sense of self. Your essay should be at least 600 words, typed, and should include quotations from the story to support your interpretation.

This assignment asks students to present a written response, without specifying content. Students can write a personal reflection or an impersonal analysis, but they must analyze the speaker of the story in an essay of at least 600 typed words and include appropriate supporting quotations.

Whatever the assignment, students need to establish their own sense of purpose and commitment to their readers. Otherwise the writing becomes perfunctory.

Step Two: Analyze Your Audience's Expectations

Although audiences can vary, in most cases you will write essays that will be read by your instructor. My focus will thus be on writing for the teacher. Knowing that an essay is intended for an instructor does not necessarily help you successfully address this audience. What is more important is that your work satisfy the instructor's expectations. How can you accomplish this? Here are some suggestions.

- Study the assignment carefully and make sure that you understand what the instructor is asking you to do. Look for key words and phrases, especially those that are underlined or in boldface. Most assignments clearly state the instructor's expectations.
- Stuck? Then visit your instructor. A short conversation with an instructor can both clarify the situation and bolster confidence.
- Determine whether your instructor wants your essay to be a demonstration of knowledge (a synthesis of class discussion, an informed discussion of the ways a particular theory applies to a particular set of readings); a factual presentation (historical, biographical, a report); an interpretation (what a work means, why a student believes the meaning of the text to be "X"); an appreciation (why this work is so powerful and enduring); or something else. Asking detailed questions about expectations either in class or during an instructor's office hours is essential.
- Consider the assignment a form of conversation, of dialogue with the instructor. An essay offers each student an opportunity to have the instructor's exclusive attention. Successful essays engage readers because they bring a writer and reader together; they are a medium for the exchange of ideas.
- Try to state something new. Think of your audience as someone who is willing to try out your ideas and be surprised and informed by what you have to say. Instructors enjoy having their understanding and appreciation of a literary work enhanced because of something a student has written.
- Avoid plot summary. Because they want to learn something when they read student essays, most instructors do not like plot summary. When writing, assume that the reader already has read the work you are discussing. Plot summary is usually a surefire way to bore a reader—and write a pedestrian essay in the process.

Step Three: Draw On Your Resources

Student Resource List:

- conversations with other students in the class or others who have an interest in the topic

- the local Writing Center, where tutors can help you think through your subject, goals, possibilities, frustrations, structure, focus, and all the other aspects of writing
- the instructor, who is one of the best resources for getting comfortable with a topic and figuring out the best way to proceed
- the library research database, where you can look up primary material (that is, other works that the author has written, historical materials composed at the same time as the subject you are writing about) or secondary sources (books and articles written about your subject)
- electronic conversations over the Internet
- Web pages, which can be particularly helpful if you are researching a contemporary subject

Step Four: Start Early

The time to start writing an essay is immediately after an instructor hands out an assignment. The worst case scenario is to delay the writing until the day before it is due. To put it bluntly, this is a prescription for disaster.

Good ideas need to simmer. They need to be reflected upon, revised, researched, and explored. This takes time. Delay often results in ill-conceived work. Waiting too long to start can create a host of problems for writers, including: disliking what one has written but not having the time to change it; discovering that essential research materials are missing, stolen, or otherwise out of circulation; getting sick or stuck; or even deciding that one's argument no longer makes sense. There is no reason to have to create a panic situation every time a writing assignment is given.

Instead, good writers start early. That way, if something goes wrong, as it inevitably does in some situations, there is time to make adjustments.

Step Five: Share

Most professional writers share their work as they write: they produce a page or two, bring that work home, and read it to someone they trust to give an honest response. Students need to share their writing as well, and many instructors will create that possibility by setting up a rough draft workshop in the classroom or by reading drafts. Many times, an outside reader (not a roommate, spouse, or parent) can best tell a writer when an essay is making sense, where more support is needed, where the work is gaining or losing focus. Such readings can make a huge difference in the success of an essay; almost always, they provide a valuable road map for revision. Take advantage of this opportunity; it can make a world of difference.

Step Six: Revise

Virtually all successful writers spend the great majority of their time not drafting but revising, not writing but rewriting. In general, writing an essay is messy: It demands that writers explore a variety of ideas, go off on various tangents, explore various research sources, find appropriate examples and quotations, etc. As you write at this early stage, it is important not to spend much time editing and revising. Writing at this drafting stage should lead you forward; editing and revising are activities that require you constantly to look backward.

Only after you have finally produced a significant mass of words and ideas is it time to start pulling your essay together. This is revision: refocusing, deleting the unnecessary and repetitious, finding additional examples, cutting and pasting (using the computer, I hope), refining the essay so that it achieves its purpose. Sometimes revision means substantially changing the original; sometimes it means throwing out everything but two or three sentences! Whatever form it takes, revision is almost always the key to producing successful final essays.

Step Seven: Work Appropriately

At different points in the writing process, some kinds of attention are appropriate and others ill-advised. It is important to recognize that a first or second draft of an essay is just that: a draft. It is likely to have a variety of problems with focus, word usage, syntax, support, and other elements. Early in the composing process, writers need to concentrate on global issues: organization, development, finding examples, crafting the overall shape and scope of the essay. There is no sense editing and correcting sentences that may not make it into the final version. It makes no sense spell checking, correcting subject-verb agreement, or clarifying every phrase in the first draft. Instead, experienced writers focus on big ticket items such as building coherence or developing a cogent argument.

Only after a reasonably good draft has been achieved should you edit line by line for usage, correctness, and word choice. Correcting and editing are very important functions, but they should occur only when the writing is close to being finished.

GETTING STARTED

Many writers have trouble getting started; they defer the writing, often until too late. Then they do a poor job, excusing themselves because they ran out of time. Sometimes they sit down to write, but run out of steam after a few paragraphs: the essay lacks focus; everything written down seems dumb or obvious; the essay is too general and vague; the room is too hot; the paper is too white; the pencils are too sharp or not sharp enough. Almost all writers, even professional authors who make their living selling what they produce, have trouble at times getting started. John McPhee, who has written over twenty nonfiction books on sports, geology, wilderness, and many other topics, had so much trouble getting started early in his career that he would go into his office and tie himself into his chair with his bathrobe sash to force himself to get words down on paper. Although tying yourself to your chair may be an excellent technique, here are some less drastic strategies that can help.

Keep a reading log. Marginal notation is an excellent strategy, but many students want their notes and commentary collected in one place rather than distributed in the white space of various textbooks. They use a reading log, which is a written record of their interpretations, questions, and concerns. Your instructor may assign you to keep such a log or journal because it has proven to be so helpful to many students. To be successful, a log must be used consistently, at least three entries per week. When an essay is assigned, a reading log can become a great resource, since it is a repository of ideas and personal responses.

A typical entry might look like the following:

"The Horse"

I loved this poem. The horse is described as being so fluid, so full of power. But I don't understand why its hooves flash "blood red" in the last stanza. Why blood? Nor am I clear as to why it is "eternally riderless." After all, it is the "horseman's desire."

Rhythm. There's a kind of klop/klop rhythm to the lines, especially the last line of each stanza. Or am I imagining it?

Is this in some kind of form—like a sonnet? It isn't 14 lines, so that's not right—but I wonder if this is some form I should know (ask instructor) . . .

I'd love to write about the ways that this horse stands for freedom. Am I reading that into the poem? I don't think so. Freedom is mentioned in line 4 and once again in lines 15 and 26. That has to mean something, I think. . . .

As you can see, this is mostly a response that describes the feelings of the writer—as well as her ideas, confusions, and maybe even a possible essay topic. Even if this student does not choose to write about "The Horse," she is engaging in the kind of close and active reading that will help her throughout this course and beyond.

Write a letter, not an essay. Most writers find it much easier to write a personal letter than an essay. The reasons are fairly obvious: they know and like their audience; the letter is informal; they are used to writing in this format; they can usually find a congenial style for themselves; etc. Some students write their essay as a letter addressed to a friend or close relative, explaining why it is important to write about this story or poem, or why they are uncomfortable and then what it is they would like to say about this topic in an essay. Even though the letter is a fiction, writing it can be a great way to make that initial leap into the topic.

Create writing rituals. Like any sustained activity, writing can be hard to start unless it becomes part of another set of actions. In order to wash the car, for example, a person might gather together clean cloths, fill a pail with soapy water, park the car at the curb, and bring out the garden hose. Washing the car becomes an inevitable result of those preparations.

Writing benefits from the same kinds of ritualized activities. One writer gathers her research materials, reads them over several times, cleans off her desk, turns on her computer, and makes some notes about how she will structure her writing for the day. Other writers have other actions they must perform to write: they make a fresh pot of coffee, put on a certain baseball cap, take a dessert out of the freezer and leave it as a reward for a certain amount of writing (of course, the latter ritual can produce both pages and pounds). A friend of mine takes his laptop every weekday morning to a local coffeehouse, finds a quiet table, and writes for two hours; somehow he finds that ritual more productive than coming into the office where he gets distracted by mail, phone calls, and personal visits from me.

Productive writers discover or create rituals that get them in the mood for writing, that lead them toward pen and paper or the computer. Once you have devised such rituals, they can lead you toward writing.

Use index cards or some easily organizable form of note-taking. Many writers keep track of different ideas, quotations, references, and other pertinent information by listing each as a single entry so that they all can be stored and rearranged. Copying quotations and taping them on cards is one handy technique; another is using the computer to create and organize files, which then can be easily printed out during the drafting process. Each card should include not only a quotation or idea but also source information about where it was found.

Write before writing. Professor Donald Murray, a well-known writer and teacher, advocated that students "write before writing"—and this is excellent advice. How do you do that? One of the best strategies is to purchase a small notebook that fits handily in purse or pocket. As you read, think, and research about your assignments, write down ideas, insights, fragments, potential topics, words, quotations, and snatches of relevant conversations. Use the material in that notebook to jump-start your essay.

Try freewriting. Other writers use the technique of freewriting or quick writing to get started. First, of course, they have to do the necessary reading, rereading, and research. Once they possess some knowledge and ideas, they write nonstop for 10 or more minutes, not worrying about spelling, correctness, transitions, or even coherence. The purpose is to get ideas and sentences on paper; once that is done, the writer organizes, cuts and pastes, develops some ideas and discards others. Freewriting is an excellent way to write before writing, especially since it is low stress and produces a lot of words. Some writers begin their writing process this way, and then use successive and more focused freewritings to create later and longer drafts of an essay. Freewriting usually cannot be used to write a final draft, but with practice, this technique can help a writer get quite far along in the drafting process.

THE ELEMENTS OF A SUCCESSFUL ESSAY

Although there are many different kinds of essays, most of the good ones share certain features.

1. **A main point.** Most successful essays drive toward a central conclusion or major insight. It really does not matter if the essay is an appreciation, a critique, an argument, or a close reading: it collects around a main point like iron filings around a magnet. For example, let's say I am writing about William Stafford's poem "Traveling Through the Dark." After multiple readings, two entries in my reading log, and one freewriting, I begin to glimpse what makes this poem moving and powerful to me. I write a "discovery" draft, toward the end of which I compose the following sentence that defines my main point and thus becomes my thesis:

   "Traveling Through the Dark" is therefore a powerful poem that holds a central contradiction: it is a celebration of life that describes the poet's act of destroying the life of an innocent fawn. I think it reveals the speaker as tender and compassionate, perhaps in contrast to the unnamed, unseen other driver who first hit the doe.

   This is enough of a start for an essay because it is making a significant point that I can now develop over the course of an essay.

Please note: Not every writer knows the main point when first starting an essay. Oftentimes, writers discover their main point during the composing process. Thus good writers do not worry if they begin to write without a main point; if they are completing the assignment and still do not know their main point, however, that usually means real trouble.

2. **Specificity.** A successful essay examines a work of literature by analyzing a particular theme, meaning, image, use of language, argument, or interpretation. Too often, beginning writers attempt general and grandiose themes or generalized statements; they try to write, for example, about "the genius of Edward Abbey" or "That Perfect Poetic Form: The Ballad." Although there is much that can be said about both topics, they are too vague as stated to be covered in a short essay; indeed, they are more appropriate for entire books. An essay needs to examine more specific topics: *What Edward Abbey means by 'the Hoboken mystique' in his essay "Manhattan Twilight, Hoboken Night"* or *A Bittersweet Play of Voices in Langston Hughes's "Ballad of the Landlord."* An essay on either of these more focused topics is more likely to succeed.

3. **Complexity.** Good essays lock in on a complex subject and develop it thoughtfully. In general, this means that an essay must pursue a subject that is not superficially obvious to the most casual reader. To look for insights beyond the obvious, a writer must examine a work of literature for contradictions and paradox. Many literary authors use contradiction and paradox to put a spin on their creations. Theodore Roethke's "My Papa's Waltz," for example, is a poem that can be read simultaneously as a loving tribute and as a cry for help. Which interpretation is correct? Most critics would say that the poem can and should be read both ways at once, that it represents the complex and contradictory feelings a young boy has toward his father.

To achieve complexity, then, writers must be willing to explore seeming contradiction and not be afraid to take risks; they must be willing to explore questions that have no right answer. For example, to return to "Traveling Through the Dark," a student might at first compose the following focus sentence:

"Traveling Through the Dark" is a terrific poem because it is about a man in the wilderness.

This statement, though perhaps true, does not offer a writer any real purchase on a topic worth writing about. It is not very specific and does not offer a complex view of the poem. Why is the poem terrific? What is meant by "terrific"? Is every poem about a man and wilderness terrific? Other than finding a lot of different ways to repeat this main point, there is not much that can be said that would fill more than a page or so of text. This topic does not allow a very complicated or insightful essay to be written. After some struggle, this writer reformulates her main point as follows:

"Traveling Through the Dark" is about literal and figurative darkness, about the darkness of night and the darkness of death.

This statement is more specific, and it offers a thoughtful and complex inter-

pretation of "darkness," an important image in this poem. The statement
may need to be refined further, but it offers a useful starting point.

4. **Examples and illustrations.** Almost always, successful essays incorporate
   many examples, illustrative quotations, and statements that prove the
   point(s) that the writer is making. In English Studies, most successful essays
   put forward assertions that then have to be proven and supported. They
   move from the general to the specific and back again, weaving the particular
   constantly into the fabric of the overall argument. Clearly one of the most
   important ways to achieve this end is to use quotations, examples, and particular citations for support. Just as an economist uses statistics, a writer of
   essays about literature must nail down insights with an appropriate use of
   specific quotation. Quotes from the primary text (the actual work of literature being studied) or from secondary texts (criticism, history, biography,
   etc.) illustrate the points being made and persuade readers that the author
   knows what she is talking about. They also can inspire a writer to dig deeper
   into the meaning of a work of literature.

5. **Coherence.** All readers have formal expectations when they read. Although
   different in various cultures, these formal expectations guide readers and
   help them to understand what the writer is doing. They allow readers to
   anticipate where the writer is headed, a very important dimension to successful interaction between readers and writers. Typically, in United States
   higher education, successful essays have a beginning, middle, and end in
   some formal sense. They exhibit logical transitions between the various parts
   of the essay. They provide the reader with a sense of wholeness and com-
   pletion. Typically, a formal essay will:

   - articulate a main point
   - illustrate and exemplify that main point through several pages that
     develop and explore the theme of the essay through the use of analysis,
     appropriate quotation, assertions, insights
   - conclude by offering possibilities for additional exploration, returning to
     the image or argument presented at the beginning of the essay, summa-
     rizing and extending what has already been stated, or otherwise creating
     a sense of completion

6. **Style.** Instructors generally enjoy reading essays that express the voice, personal commitment, and investment of the writer—what we typically call
   "style." Style cannot be located in any one element; rather, it consists of a
   writer's individual perspective, phrasing, word choice, sentence construction,
   creation of paragraphs, organization, even formatting (font, type size, illustrations, spacing, etc.).

   One of the most important aspects of style is word and sentence variety.
   Successful writing keeps readers interested not just because of ideas, examples, and coherence, but also because of language use that pleases, surprises,
   and delights. Here is an example of a passage that has a lot of repetition and
   not much sentence variety:

Theodore Roethke's "My Papa's Waltz" is a powerful poem. It is a poem that draws its power from its theme of love and fear. The poem is written from the point of view of a young boy. The title of the poem . . .

This passage is likely to bore a reader because the sentences all have a similar subject-verb structure, use many of the same words, and express little sense of style. It is acceptable to write such sentences in a first draft, but once a writer starts moving toward the final draft, an improved version that achieves much more sentence variation is needed:

A powerful poem, Theodore Roethke's "My Papa's Waltz" expresses the love—and fear—that a young boy feels for his father. As is made clear from the title of the poem . . .

This revised version consolidates the sentences, cuts out the repetition of words ("is," "power," "of"), and expresses more vividly the stylistic personality of the writer. Successful writers create word and sentence variety in order to enhance their style.

Another key aspect to creating a successful style is not to overreach. That is, one of the worst decisions a writer can make is to refer constantly to a thesaurus while writing or to otherwise insert words and phrases that "sound good" because they are long, Latinate, or unfamiliar. A thesaurus is an excellent tool to rediscover a synonym that has slipped out of memory, but you should not use it to replace a familiar word with one you do not know. For example, a writer might state that he has "a great deal of empathy for a character's situation." But with the help of a thesaurus, he might revise that sentence to read that he has "a surfeit of vicarious emotion for a character's locale." Although brimming with excellent words, the second sentence makes little sense and sounds as though its author is living in the wrong century. It is far better to use words you know and can control.

7. **Correctness.** Correctness is easy to define but difficult to achieve: It consists of getting everything right. English instructors in particular urge their students to aim for correctness as part of what they do; after all, they are the educational caretakers of sentence structure, research format, spelling, grammar, and diction. Many writers have a difficult time achieving correctness on their own; they need the help of an outside reader (such as a tutor) to help them see error patterns or other areas where their essay needs to be edited and refashioned into standard academic English.

One of the best ways to get help with correctness is to go to the course instructor, who can provide professional help. Another good strategy is to buy a good handbook and then use it. Most handbooks have sections on grammar, usage, computers, footnoting, and other writing considerations. If a student possesses the motivation and knowledge to use such a handbook, it can be a great resource.

Here is a brief checklist that can help determine if an essay is ready to be handed in.

THE WRITER'S CHECKLIST

___ Essay has a title.

___ Writer's name is included on all the pages.

___ Spelling has been checked.

___ Footnotes are in proper form as determined by instructor.

___ Sentence structure has been checked, especially for fragments, run-on sentences, and comma splices (to obtain definitions of these terms, consult a handbook, or see instructor or Writing Center tutor).

___ Essay has been typed or completed on a word processor.

___ Pages are numbered.

___ Print is double-spaced with one-inch margins around all four borders.

___ Essay has been read carefully by a Writing Center tutor or some other informed and attentive reader.

___ Essay has been read carefully by the author at least one day after "finishing" it.

___ Quotation marks, semicolons, and colons are used properly and consistently (again, consult a handbook, or see instructor or Writing Center tutor).

___ Essay includes sufficient supporting material, such as quotations, examples, and narrative summaries.

A NOTE ABOUT USING COMPUTERS FOR WRITING AND RESEARCH

Another important resource is a computer. Students who know keyboarding and are familiar with word processing programs (such as Word or WordPerfect) have a strong advantage over those students who use less versatile technologies. Word processors allow writers to produce words relatively quickly and then revise them more easily. What with the "copy" and "cut and paste" functions on a computer, basic revision becomes easy, as long as the writer has a good sense of the essay's structure, purpose, and overall organization. A good word processing program can make a lot of editing easy, from spell-checking to formatting headers, footnotes, and page numbers.

Any writer who uses a computer to write an essay must *BACK THAT ESSAY UP CONTINUOUSLY* on a floppy disk during the entire writing process; too many tragedies occur when computers stall or otherwise eat up hours of work. Few events are more frustrating to a writer, especially one under deadline, than to write three or four effective paragraphs and then suddenly find that the computer has stalled or that the word processing program has crashed. The only remedy is to SAVE the writing to a floppy disk continuously during composing.

Once an essay is on disk, a good word processing program can make a lot of work easier, such as:

- adding and deleting sentences, paragraphs, ideas
- moving words and whole passages for improved focus and clarity
- revising passages until they are focused and coherent

- checking spelling (but be careful of misused words that are spelled correctly)
- making final copy look more presentable by formatting an essay in terms of margins, spacing, typeface, and related elements
- printing out rough drafts

Most writers who use computers agree that essays in progress should not just exist in virtual space, on screen. For one thing, a computer screen can hold only a small portion of the essay, even if it is single-spaced, making it hard to see how the different parts of the essay connect with one another. For another, many writers have a difficult time seeing errors or lapses on screen; somehow, the monitor display makes all writing look professionally presentable. Thus most writers find that they have to print out successive drafts of their essays; indeed, some of them revise the essay on paper the old-fashioned way, with pen, pencil, or scissors and paste, and then translate those revisions to the text via computer. Whatever revision method a writer chooses, printing drafts of the essay on paper is almost always a good idea.

Engaging in research on the World Wide Web via computer is much less beneficial, at least as of this writing, but it can be fun and it offers a dazzling array of images, texts, ideas, opinions, and information. To view material on the Web, users have to use a browser, the two chief competitors being Netscape's Navigator and Microsoft's Internet Explorer. The term "browser" is perfect for what these software programs do: They allow users to browse through an extraordinary array of verbal, audio, and visual presentations, from restaurant reviews and music CD catalogs to mapping programs and hobbyist bulletin boards. The materials available through the Web are seemingly infinite, but most of them are aimed toward the casual and commercial user.

The Web is much less useful to the student engaged in specific and narrow research on an author. Few long textual works have been scanned electronically, although there are sites that allow a user to access some classic works of literature, as well as dictionaries, thesauruses, handbooks, and the like. If a reader is looking for scholarly articles, however, the first and best resource is still the library. The library's electronic databases, including the Wilson Periodical Index, the PMLA Index, ERIC, and the Humanities Index, to name just a few, are extraordinarily rich electronic treasure-troves.

Starting one's research with the computer by accessing either library databases, the Internet, or the Web is an excellent way to initiate a project. Using search engines and search commands, a writer can build a useful bibliography of names, articles, and periodicals; the next step is to make use of the library stacks and spend some time reading the scholarship the old-fashioned way, in books, magazines, and journals. The mode of doing scholarship may change, but it is unlikely that the print medium will be replaced by the digitized computer file, if only because it is easier both to read longer texts on paper and to write marginal notes about them. The other great advantage that books have is that they are not battery operated and do not have to be plugged in, a real plus when on the bus or at the beach.

REFERENCE AND CITATION

One of the most frustrating moments in writing a research essay is discovering that you cannot find where a crucial quotation comes from. Almost always, it seems, that quotation is the I-beam on which the entire essay hangs, and no matter where you look, it has totally disappeared from sight. You vaguely remember that it came from an article but that's all, and now you need to know author, title, periodical, year and date of publication, and page number. So you spend an hour searching desperately through books, note cards, legal pads, computer files, bookshelves, desktops, briefcases, and wastebaskets while methodically beating your head against the nearest hard object.

There is no surefire way to prevent this from happening, other than careful researching. Each time you find a quotation or important item of source material, write it down, including essential information such as author, title, and page number; that way, you will almost always be able to find it again if you need to cite it. Thus every note card or piece of paper with a quotation should have a brief reference on it indicating where it came from. In addition, using either a copying machine, a word processor, or the old-fashioned pen and paper method, make sure you have all the necessary bibliographic material that you need to write a "Works Cited" page, something that I will discuss shortly. This means creating a separate file or folder where you keep full bibliographic information on all your sources. Researched essays require students to perform three related actions: to quote sources, to provide appropriate references for those sources, and then to indicate on a Works Cited page where those quotations can be found. Let's take these steps in order.

Quoting Sources

Whenever you are indebted to an author for a specific quotation, specific information, or a particular insight or idea, it is necessary to give that author credit through quotation and citation. This means that you have to know the difference between the knowledge gained through research and "common knowledge," which is what most people are expected to know. For example, if you were writing an essay about Amy Tan and you indicated that she is a popular contemporary author, such a statement would not need to be footnoted since it is common knowledge. If, however, you stated that she was born in 1952 in Oakland, California, and that both her parents are from China, you would need to indicate that you learned that information from, say, *Contemporary Authors*, since it is not general knowledge. Deciding what information you need to reference and what is common knowledge is a judgment call, one that your instructor can help you to determine. Remember, however, that if you are deeply indebted to an author for information or an interpretation, you need to state that in a footnote or a parenthetical citation.

The two primary ways of quoting material are through direct quotation and paraphrase. Direct quotation consists of putting specific words, phrases, or sentences within quotation marks followed by a parenthetical citation. For example:

```
In her autobiographical talk-story "White Tigers," Maxine Hong

Kingston writes: "My American life has been such a disappointment"

(45).
```

Note that the quotation from Kingston's essay/story appears in quotation marks and that it is followed by a parenthetical page citation so that the reader can turn to p. 45 in the cited book and find the quotation. The particular edition from which this quotation is taken will appear on the Works Cited page that appears at the end of every research essay. Whenever directly quoting an author or work, this kind of format is needed.

Indirect quotation is a bit trickier, in that it requires writers to decide whether the passage or idea that they are using is derived from a specific text or is common knowledge. If the idea or information is derived from a specific text, then it needs to be cited. For example:

> Many of us attribute great and even mystical powers to our mothers.
> This is certainly the case with Maxine Hong Kingston who endows her
> mother with supernatural powers within a world of ghosts and dark
> spirits as illustrated in "Shaman" (The Woman Warrior 57-109).

Even though the writer is not quoting directly from the book, this statement is derived from a reading of Kingston's story "Shaman," and therefore a citation is required. Whether the writer paraphrases an interpretation, summarizes the writer's life, or condenses several articles into a two- or three-sentence review, if the idea derives from a book or article, parenthetical citation is required.

Using Footnotes and Parenthetical Citation

Many of the newer word processors have a footnote feature which will organize, number, and format your footnotes. This is a useful aid, especially since footnotes are often hard to format. Unfortunately, many contemporary research essays (at least in English classes) do not require formal footnoting. About the only occasion when students are required to use them is if they need to comment on a statement or source and do not wish to put that comment in the main body of the essay, or if the essay is quoting from just one source and thus it is easier to cite it in a footnote than an entire page at the end of the essay. Check with your instructor to see if footnoting will be required.

The more common form of citation used today is parenthetical; that is, the citation is inserted between two parentheses as demonstrated in the quotations from *The Woman Warrior*. Parenthetical citation is advocated by the Modern Language Association, since it is efficient for both writers and readers. Footnotes drag a reader's eye down to the bottom of the page and break the flow of the text; parenthetical citations maintain the flow of the essay while providing necessary information about sources, page numbers, and research. Moreover, it is much easier for writers to use parenthetical citation since they do not have to worry about numbering their references in sequence and fitting them onto the page.

Parenthetical citation is formatted in slightly different ways, depending on whether the quotation appears within your sentence or as a block that is separated from your own writing. Note the differences below:

One of the more important genres that have recently received critical and popular attention are the narratives of slaves. One of the earliest and most influential collections of those narratives is <u>The Classic Slave Narratives</u> edited by Henry Louis Gates. Gates makes a good case for why these texts were created:

> The black slave narrators sought to indict both those who enslaved them and the metaphysical system drawn upon to justify their enslavement. They did so using the most enduring weapon at their disposal, the printing press. (ix)

Thus what we can see in the narratives is an account of the life they led as slaves, an account which by virtue of its own telling condemns the system of values that supports slavery for the sake of economic gain.

Note certain key conventions: Because the quotation is two or more sentences long, it gets set off in a block. Because it is set off, it does not need quotation marks around it. The page from which the quotation is taken appears at the very end within parentheses, after any end punctuation.

Here is a different version of the same student essay. In this case, the author is using only a part of the Gates quotation and is thus using internal parenthetical citation. It is called "internal" because the citation occurs within the student's own sentences:

One of the more important genres that have recently received critical and popular attention are the narratives of slaves. One of the earliest and most influential collections of those narratives is <u>The Classic Slave Narratives</u> edited by Henry Louis Gates. Gates makes a good case for why these texts were created, since he believes that the authors "sought to indict both those who enslaved them and the metaphysical system drawn upon to justify their enslavement" (ix). By that Gates means that what we can see in the narratives is an account of the life they led as slaves, an account which by virtue of its own telling condemns the system of values that supports slavery for the sake of economic gain.

Note the differences: Here the quotation is short, being less than a full sentence; thus it can be easily integrated into the student author's own paragraph. The page number still is cited, but now—since the citation occurs within the student's own sentence, it must be followed by a period since it ends a sentence.

Here is one more example of internal parenthetical citation:

In his Introduction to The Classic Slave Narratives, Henry Louis Gates writes that the slaves wanted to be "free and literate" (ix) and that is why they told their powerful and terrible stories. I agree, but only in part: I think we have to be equally aware that the slaves told these stories as a profound way of coming to terms with an experience that virtually defies language.

This internal parenthetical citation immediately follows the quotation it references, and no punctuation marks surround it since they would interfere with the grammar of the sentence.

Internal parenthetical citation provides necessary reference information with as little obstruction as possible. Thus it does not include abbreviations such as "p." for page or "2nd ed." for second edition; all the necessary bibliographic information goes onto the Works Cited page so that the reader can locate your sources. If you are citing a poem, your instructor will likely want your parenthetical reference to include line numbers; if citing a play, you will need to include act, scene, and line so that your instructor can find the quotation easily. Such inclusions follow the rule of thumb for parenthetical references: Include only the information a reader will need to find the quotation easily, neither more nor less.

Providing Full References: The Works Cited Page

Once you have filled in all the appropriate parenthetical citations, it is time to complete the project by writing a "Works Cited" page. Just as its name suggests, the Works Cited page is a bibliographic list that allows the reader to track down the specific books, articles, magazines, films, and other resources you cite in your essay.

No short guide can provide a complete list of proper forms; indeed, the Modern Language Association, to name just one such group, publishes an entire book devoted to forms and formats for references and bibliographies (see Joseph Gibaldi and Walter S. Achtert, *MLA Handbook for Writers of Research Papers*, 4th ed. [New York: MLA, 1995]). What I will include here is a brief listing of the more common forms for books, articles, periodicals, short works of literature, film, TV, and newspapers. These forms should provide proper formatting for most of the research sources that you will use.

Titles on the "Works Cited" page should be arranged alphabetically according to the first initial of the author's or editor's last name. You need only include the texts you actually cite; if for some reason you want to include every book or article that you read while researching your essay, even if you did not use all of them, title your page "List of Works Consulted," but first check with your instructor. You can use the model entries in the pages that follow to put your entries in the correct format. The entries do not correspond to real authors or real books or articles (for the most part), but the form (and explanations) should prove useful.

One last suggestion: even when an essay has proper references and a full "Works Cited" page, it is often helpful to the reader if the author opens with an Acknowledgments page. You can find a model in many scholarly books: the author begins her book by thanking those people who have helped in the formation of ideas, the reading of drafts, the revision of sentences. If your instructor allows it, writing an Acknowledgments page that leads off your essay can help establish the context for the essay that you have produced, and it is an excellent way of saying thank you to those students, staff members, and faculty who have helped you produce it, from conception to final draft.

Sample Citations for "Works Cited" from an Essay on Literature and Culture

A single book by a single author:

Auteur, Robin. <u>Literature and Culture</u>. New York: Knopf, 1997.

Note the order: author's name (last name first); then the title of the book, underlined, except for the final period. Then the place of publication, followed by a colon (if the city is not well known, include the state abbreviation as well. If the title page lists several cities, give only the first, as in Portsmouth, N.H. or Fargo, N.D.). Then the name of the publisher, followed by a comma. And then the year of publication.

A single book by two or more authors:

Auteur, Robin, and Chang Lee. <u>Literature and Culture</u>. Columbus, Ohio: Ohio

    State UP, 1949.

The first author appears with last name first, then the second author follows with first name first. If the book has more than three authors, give the name of the first author only (last name first) and follow it with "et al." (Latin for "and others"). The phrase "University Press" is abbreviated as "UP" for the sake of efficiency.

A book in several volumes:

Auteur, Robin, et al., eds. <u>Literature and Culture</u>. 4th ed. 3 vols. Chicago:

    Gilead UP, 1998.

Note that "eds." here means "editors" and not "edited by." The abbreviation "eds." always means "editors," whereas "ed." can mean either "editor" or "edited by," depending on its context.

Auteur, Robin. <u>Literature and Culture</u>. 11 vols. Ed. Chang Lee. Columbia,

S.C.: Wellman, 1955.

You will need to indicate the total number of volumes after the title. If you have used more than one volume, you can indicate which one as follows: (3:30), which means you are referring to page 30 of volume 3. If you have used only one volume of a multivolume work, in your entry in Works Cited indicate the volume number right after the period following the date, i.e., "Wellman, 1955. Vol. 2." You need only include the page reference in your parenthetical citations since readers will know all examples come from volume 2 when they consult the Works Cited page.

A book with a separate title in a set of volumes:

Auteur, Robin. <u>Literature and Culture</u>. Vol. 1 of <u>Encyclopedia of Literature</u>

<u>and Culture</u>. New York: Balloon, 1994.

Auteur, Robin. <u>Literature and Culture</u>. Ed. Chang Lee. Vol. 113 of <u>The</u>

<u>Literature and Culture Reader</u>. Princeton: Princeton UP, 1988.

A revised edition of a book:

Auteur, Robin. <u>Literature and Culture</u>. Rev. ed. Hamburg, Germany: Berlin

UP, 1974.

Auteur, Robin. <u>Literature and Culture</u>. Ed. Chang Lee. 5th ed. Norfolk:

Harcourt, 1997.

A reprint of an earlier edition:

Auteur, Robin. <u>Literature and Culture</u>. 1911. Ellis, Iowa: Central UP, 1993.

Note that the author is citing the original date (1911) but indicates that the writer is using the Iowa Central University Press reprint published in 1993.

An edited book other than an anthology:

Auteur, Robin. <u>Literature and Culture</u>. Ed. Chang Lee. 4 vols. Cambridge,

MA: Harvard UP, 1969.

An anthology:

<u>Literature and Culture</u>. Ed. Robin Auteur. 12 vols. Monrovia, La.: Literature

and Culture Books, 1918.

Or:

Auteur, Robin, ed. <u>Literature and Culture</u>. 12 vols. Monrovia, La.:

Literature and Culture Books, 1918.

Note that you have two choices: You can list it either by title or by editor.

A work by one author in a multivolume anthology:

Auteur, Robin. "Critical Studies." <u>Literature and Culture</u>. Ed. Chang Lee.

    5th ed. 3 vols. New York: Farrar, 1997. 3:145-98.

This entry indicates that you are citing Auteur's essay, entitled "Critical Studies," which appears in volume 3 of a five-volume anthology entitled *Literature and Culture*, edited by Chang Lee. Note that the page numbers of Auteur's complete essay are cited.

A work in an anthology that includes a number of authors:

Auteur, Robin. "Critical Studies." <u>Literature and Culture</u>. Ed. Chang Lee.

    Fargo, N.D.: Houghton, 1888. 243-76.

Start by listing the author and the title of the work you are citing, not the title of the anthology or the name of the editor. The entry ends by citing the pages of the selection you are citing. Note that the title of the short work you are citing is in quotation marks; if it is a long work (book length), the title is underlined. If the work is translated, after the period that follows the title, write "Trans." and give the name of the translator, followed by a period and then the name of the anthology.

Citing other works in the same anthology:

Auteur, Robin. <u>Literature and Culture</u>. Lee 301-46.

To avoid repetition, under each author's name (in the appropriate alphabetical order), list the author, the title of the work, then a period, one space, and the name of the editor of the anthology, followed by the page numbers for the selection.

Two or more works by the same author:

Auteur, Robin. <u>Critical Studies</u>. Boulder, Colo.: U of Harriman P, 1948.

---. <u>Literature and Culture</u>. Seattle: Jacob H. Library, 1955.

Note that the works are given in alphabetical order on the Works Cited page, so that *Critical Studies* comes before *Literature and Culture*. In the second listing, the author's name is represented by three dashes followed by a period. If the author is the translator or editor of a volume, the three dashes are followed by a comma, then a space, then the appropriate abbreviation (trans. or ed.), then (one space after the period) the title.

The Bible:

<u>The HarperCollins Study Bible</u>. Wayne A. Meeks, Gen. ed. New York:

    HarperCollins, 1989.

Note: If using the King James version, do not list the Bible in your Works Cited page, since it is familiar and available. In your essay, cite chapter and verse parenthetically as follows: (Isaiah 52.7-12 or Gen. 19.1-11).

A translated book:

Auteur, Robin. <u>Literature and Culture</u>. Trans. Chang Lee. New York: Culture

    Studies Press, 1990.

Note that "Trans." can mean "translated by" (just as "ed." can mean "edited by"). It is also the abbreviation for "translator."

An introduction, foreword, afterword, or other editorial apparatus:

Auteur, Robin. Introduction. <u>Literature and Culture</u>. By Chang Lee. New

    York: Epicurean, 1990, vii-x.

Use this form if you are specifically referring to the Introduction, Foreword, Afterword, etc. Otherwise, list the work under the name of the book's author. Words such as *Preface, Introduction, Afterword,* and *Conclusion* are capitalized in the entry but are neither enclosed within quotation marks nor underlined.

A book review:

Auteur, Robin. Rev. of <u>Literature and Culture</u>. Ed. Chang Lee. <u>Critical</u>

    <u>Studies</u> 104 (1991): 1-48.

This is a citation for a review of a book entitled *Literature and Culture.* The review, which does not have a title, was published in a journal entitled *Critical Studies.*

Auteur, Robin. "One Writer's View." Rev. of <u>Literature and Culture</u>. Ed.

    Chang Lee. <u>Critical Studies</u> 104 (1991): 1-48.

This is a citation for a review which has a title.

"One Writer's View." Rev. of <u>Literature and Culture</u>. Ed. Chang Lee.

    <u>Critical Studies</u> 104 (1991): 1-48.

This is an anonymous review of *Literature and Culture.* Place it on your "Works Cited" page under the first word of the review's title; if the review lacks a title, begin your entry with "Rev. of" and then alphabetize it under the title of the work being reviewed.

An encyclopedia:

Auteur, Robin. "Literature and Culture." <u>Encyclopaedia Britannica</u>. 1984

    ed.

This is how you cite a signed article; note that the article is from the 1984 edition of the *Encyclopaedia.*

"Literature and Culture." <u>Encyclopaedia Britannica</u>. 1984 ed.

This is how you would cite the same article if it were unsigned.

An article in a scholarly journal that numbers its pages consecutively from one issue to the other through the year:

Auteur, Robin. "Literature and Culture." <u>Critical Studies</u> 33 (1992): 231-

59.

Auteur's article appeared in the journal, *Critical Studies*, in 1992; the volume number was 33 and it appeared on pages 231 through 259. Even though each of the four issues of *Critical Studies* published in 1992 has a separate number, you do not need to indicate the issue number since the pages are numbered continuously throughout the year.

An article in a scholarly journal that begins each issue during the year with page one:

Auteur, Robin. "Literature and Culture." <u>Critical Studies</u> 12.2 (1993): 9-

21.

Note that you now must provide the volume number followed by a period and then the issue number, with no spaces in between.

An article in a weekly, biweekly, or monthly publication:

Auteur, Robin. "Literature and Culture." <u>Critical Studies</u> 30 Mar. 1945: 1-

12.

If you are citing from a very well known weekly, such as *Newsweek* or *The New Yorker*, you can omit the volume and issue numbers.

An article in a newspaper:

Auteur, Robin. "Literature and Culture." <u>Critical Studies Times</u> 17 Mar.

1947, sec. 6: 9+.

Because newspapers often have a number of sections, you should include a section number before the page number so that your reader can find the article easily. Auteur's article begins on page 9 of section 6 and continues on to a later page.

A personal interview:

Lee, Chang. Personal interview. 26 Apr. 1974.

Auteur, Robin. Telephone interview. 14 Feb. 1983.

Note that the interviews are *with* Chang Lee and Robin Auteur, not *by* Chang Lee or Robin Auteur.

A lecture:

Lee, Chang. "Literature and Culture." University of Wisconsin-Milwaukee.

31 Oct. 1995.

A television or radio program:

Literature and Culture. Public Television, Charlotte, N.C. 3 Feb. 1996.

A film or videotape:

Literature and Culture. Dir. Chang Lee. MGM, 1948.

A recording:

Auteur, Robin. "Literature and Culture." Chang Lee Reads Personal

Favorites from Around the World. Harmony, HAR 4853C, 1988.

A performance:

Literature. By Chang Lee. Dir. Robin Auteur. Urban Theatre of the Arts,

Urban, Wisconsin. 4 July 1912.

A file from the World Wide Web:

Auteur, Robin. "Literature and Culture." Critical Studies.

http://www.litcult.wor .vvv.ecp.tlc/text/rmudts/ittip.html (18 May

1995).

Note that the citation includes the author's name (if available), the name of the article, the name (underlined) of the entire text from which the article was taken (if available), the URL (Uniform Resource Locator), followed immediately by the date that you visited the site.

At this point, you may have decided that you have had enough of citations. If the particular form you are looking for does not appear in this list, consult the *MLA Handbook for Writers of Research Papers* or some other more extensive reference book. The basic principle of citation is that you should be absolutely clear about essential research information in the most concise format possible.

FINAL WORDS

Much more could be said about writing essays about literature and culture, but perhaps the most important goal for such essays is that they provide a sense of satisfaction to both the writer and the reader. Writing an essay invites analysis, research,

CREDITS

Gould, Lois. "X" by Lois Gould. Copyright © 1980 by Lois Gould. Reprinted by permission of Charlotte Sheedy Literary Agency.

Harjo, Joy. "The Woman Hanging from the Thirteenth Floor Window" from *She Had Some Horses* by Joy Harjo. Copyright © 1983 by Thunder's Mouth Press. Reprinted by permission of the publisher, Thunder's Mouth Press.

Harper, Michael. "Nightmare Begins Responsibility" from *Images of Kin* by Michael Harper. Copyright © 1977 by Michael S. Harper. Reprinted by permission of University of Illinois Press and the author.

Hemingway, Ernest. "The Sea Change" from *Winner Take Nothing* by Ernest Hemingway. Copyright © 1933 Charles Scribner's Sons. Copyright renewed © 1961 by May Hemingway. Reprinted by permission of Scribner, a division of Simon & Schuster.

Hughes, Langston. "Dream Deferred" from *The Panther and the Lash* by Langston Hughes. Copyright © 1951 by Langston Hughes. Reprinted by permission of Alfred A. Knopf Inc.

Hurston, Zora Neale. "The Gilded Six-Bits" as taken from *The Complete Stories* by Zora Neale Hurston. Introduction copyright © 1995 by Henry Louis Gates, Jr. and Sieglinde Lemke. Compilation copyright © 1995 by Vivien Bowden, Lois J. Hurston Gaston, Clifford Hurston, Lucy Ann Hurston, Winifred Hurston Clark, Zora Mack Goins, Edgar Hurston, Sr., and Barbara Hurston Lewis. Afterword and Bibliography copyright © 1995 by Henry Louis Gates. "The Gilded Six-Bits" was originally published in *Story*, August 1993. Reprinted by permission of HarperCollins Publishers, Inc.

Jen, Gish. "In the American Society" by Gish Jen. Copyright © 1996 by Gish Jen. First published in *Southern Review*. Reprinted by permission of the author.

Johnson, Charles. "Moving Pictures" from *The Sorcerer's Apprentice* by Charles Johnson. Copyright © 1985, 1986 by Charles Johnson. First appeared in *North American Review*, September 1985. Reprinted by permission of Scribner, a division of Simon & Schuster.

Kaneko, Lonny. "The Shoyu Kid" by Lonny Kaneko. Reprinted by permission of the author.

Kincaid, Jamaica. "Girl" from *At the Bottom of the River* by Jamaica Kincaid. Copyright © 1983 Jamaica Kincaid. Reprinted by permission of Farrar, Straus & Giroux, Inc.

Komunyakaa, Yusef. "More Girl Than Boy" from *Neon Vernacular* by Yusef Komunyakaa. Copyright © 1993 by Yusef Komunyakaa. Reprinted by permission of University Press of New England.

Lassell, Michael. "How to watch your brother die" by Michael Lassell from *Decade Dance*, 1990. Reprinted by permission of Alyson Publications, Inc.

Lee, Li-Young. "Persimmons" from *Rose* by Li-Young Lee. Copyright © 1986 by Li-Young Lee. Reprinted by permission of BOA Editions, Ltd., 260 East Ave., Rochester, NY 14604.

Le Guin, Ursula K. "Sur" from *The Compass Rose* by Ursula K. Le Guin. Copyright © 1982 by Ursula K. Le Guin. First appeared in *The New Yorker*. Reprinted by permission of the author and the author's agent, Virginia Kidd.

Levine, Philip. "Making Soda Pop" from *Unselected Poems* by Philip Levine. Copyright © 1997 by Philip Levine. Published by The Green House Review Press. Reprinted by permission of the author.

GLOSSARY OF KEY WORDS

This glossary provides definitions of the critical terms used throughout this text to talk about literary and gender studies. Some of the terms are familiar literary ones which draw our attention to the formal features of a text, such as couplet, metaphor, and plot. Other terms hope to aid you in developing a critical vocabulary for talking about the way that gender functions in both literature and society.

authorship: The status accorded to the conscious creator(s) of a text. Who is in position to be considered an author has shifted in the course of history depending on the availability of education, access to publishing, and other social and economic forces.

bisexuality: Sexual attraction for either sex.

canon: A collection of key texts generally deemed to represent the best and most important aspects of a particular field. The literary canon, for instance, refers to the list of texts considered to be the most important ever written. All canons, including the canon of American literature, are produced under specific cultural circumstances and gain acceptance in part because they are thought to represent the specific values and beliefs of a given society.

capitalism: Refers to an economic system based on (1) private (rather than public or collective) ownership of the means of production, (2) the market exchange of goods and services, and (3) wage labor.

class: A term used to distinguish among groups of people in a given society based on the distribution of wealth, resources, and opportunities. In classic Marxist theory, there are two social classes—the bourgeoisie (owner class) and the proletariat (worker class). Contemporary cultural critics tend to expand the definition of class to five groups: the ruling class, the professional/managerial class, small-business owners, the working class, and the poor.

commodity: Any object or service that can be bought and sold in the marketplace.

connotation: Refers to definitions of words or phrases derived from linguistic and textual association. Connotation is more multiple and fluid than **denotation**.

convention: The customary rules of a particular literary form, for example, a **couplet** at the conclusion of a **sonnet**; or, the formal characteristics of a **genre**, for example, the happy ending in the fairy tale.

couplet: A pair of (usually) rhymed lines that may or may not comprise a stanza in a poem. Gwendolyn Brooks's poem "the mother" opens with this rhymed couplet: "Abortions will not let you forget / You remember the children that you got that you did not get".

critical reader: A person who reads carefully, questioning the assumptions and expectations she brings to a text.

critical thinking: A mode of inquiry that challenges cultural biases, inherited assumptions, and uninterrogated ways of viewing the world.

denotation: The "dictionary" meaning of a word or phrase; definition removed from linguistic or social context. See **connotation**.

essentialism: The word used to refer to theories and assumptions about cultural differences that render them natural phenomenon. For instance, the idea that women are biologically weak, maternal, emotional, etc. is called "essentialism" since it ascribes a psychological and corporeal essence to the traits conferred upon women by patriarchal cultures.

ethnicity: Refers to the cultural background claimed by a person; distinguished from race which tends to emphasize an essentialist biological difference between human beings.

femininity: The actions, behaviors, and characteristics which are in culture associated with, but not limited to, persons of female biological sex. Femininity is neither a stable nor a universal category; it has changed through history and it applies in various degrees and modes to different groups of women and to men.

feminism: Refers to both a social movement that argues for women's equality *and* to an analysis of the arrangements of power between women and men. Historically, in the United States, feminism was linked to women's involvement in the anti-slavery movement. A century later, during the movement to garner for women the vote, feminism as a term for the struggle for female equality gained wide public visibility. Its second wave of the twentieth century, the period of the 1960s to 1980s, featured a proliferation of activity in as well as outside of the academy. The 1990s have been dubbed feminism's third wave.

gender: Refers to the roles (not the anatomy or biology) of individuals by differentiating between two opposed sets of characteristics, social positions, and personality traits: masculine and feminine. Just which characteristics belong to which gender can vary tremendously over time and between cultures, and between different social groups within cultures. See also **sex, essentialism,** and **social construction.**

genre: A term originally used by literary and art critics to refer to categories of works marked by distinctive styles, form, or content. In literary studies, genre is used to group together texts that share a set of formal characteristics: the same kinds of plot, the same strategies of characterization, the same visual form, the same use of language. Poems, short stories, novels, and plays are the most well-known genres in literary study.

heterosexuality: Opposite-sex sexual attraction; those institutional forms and practices (romance, the family) based upon and reproducing the naturalness and normality of such an attraction. The term did not come into general usage until the late nineteenth century.

hierarchy: Any system of social organization that creates relations of power and disempowerment, with governance being held by those holding most power. In the United States, we speak of **gender, race,** and **class** as social hierarchies.

homosexuality: Same-sex sexual attraction; grammatically analogous to **heterosexuality,** yet in material terms homosexuality lacks the institutional stability and status of heterosexuality. The term as a sexual identity did not come into general usage until the late nineteenth century, yet it predates the term *heterosexuality.*

identification: This term is related to identity but emphasizes the social constructedness of identity formation by suggesting human agency, or how individuals choose identifications despite that in many cases, as in that of skin pigmentation in the United States, identity can be chosen for us.

identity/identities: Most simply, identity is who you think you are. The circumstances of one's birth, family surroundings, and national belonging may all contribute to a sense of identity. Identity formation takes place within institutions and will shift depending on factors both within and without the control of the individual.

ideology: A concept that refers to the shared assumptions of a culture that often go unnoticed and unquestioned. The term was developed by Karl Marx to describe the systems of belief that functioned to make capitalism acceptable even to workers who were not profiting economically from it. In general usage, ideology refers to the wider range of cultural assumptions that help to perpetuate current systems of power and domination.

masculinity: The actions, behaviors, and characteristics which are in culture associated with, but not limited to, persons of male biological sex. Masculinity is neither a stable nor a universal category; it has changed through history and it applies in various degrees and modes to different groups of men and to women.

metaphor: A comparison of one thing to another without the use of *like* or *as,* for example, "knowledge is power." Metaphors are often effective because they forge analogies that are not obvious. In the unusual juxtaposition of ideas, metaphors create new avenues of meaning.

multiculturalism: Refers to a movement affecting curricula, teaching methods, and scholarship in a variety of disciplines within universities and colleges in the United States. Multiculturalism seeks a renewed awareness—both in scholarship and in institutional formations—of the multiplicity of nations, ethnicities, races, and cultures that have historically contributed to what is now contained within the rubric of U.S. national identity.

narration: The act of telling events and the events so organized themselves.

narrative: An account—written, oral, or filmic—of events, often told in chronological order.

parody: A mocking and humorous imitation of a literary work, character, cultural institution, or concept.

patriarchy: Literally refers to "rule by the father" and to family and clan systems in which one older man has supreme power over all members of the group, including women. As used in analyses of gender and society today, it refers to the social organization that simultaneously privileges men and masculinity while denigrating women and femininity. Patriarchy often justifies women's subordination (in the family and elsewhere) by emphasizing women's seemingly "natural" biological differences. Patriarchy structurally relies on a **sexual division of labor** in which women are assigned to the private realm of the familial and domestic, while men are assigned to the public and economic. To say that patriarchal relations are structural is to suggest that they exist in institutions and social practices and hence cannot be explained by the individual intentions, good or bad, of women or men, but must be seen as more broadly constituting social organization.

plot: The pattern of events or action in a narrative. Conventional plots are structured with a beginning, a middle, and an end.

point of view: The perspective from which a narrator, character, or authorial voice observes and speaks. The reader is usually limited to the point of view provided in a particular text, though some texts employ multiple points of view. The variety of points of view range from "first-person" in which the main character, or "I" of the story, narrates events, to "third-person" or "omniscient" narration in which a narrator, presumably the author, narrates events with a full knowledge of all characters, to "third-person limited omniscient" in which the author narrows what the narrator can know to the perspective of one speaker.

prose poem: A poem written without conventional line or stanza breaks to resemble a prose paragraph. Jamaica Kincaid's "Girl" might be considered either a prose poem or a poetic form of prose.

race: Many people tend to think of race as a fixed entity linked to biological realities. However, many scientists as well as critical thinkers resist the idea of race as having an **essential** origin, finding that it is more accurately a **social construction**. This does not mean that there are no differences among human beings in terms of color, region, or cultural specificity, but that the idea of race as defining distinct and transhistorical categories of human beings is both socially and scientifically invalid. Race functions as both an **ideology** and an organizing strategy for U.S. society.

rhyme: The matching of final vowel or consonant sounds in two or more words. So-called "masculine" rhymes end with a stressed syllable, while so-called "feminine" rhymes end with an unstressed syllable. "Eye" rhymes match syllables on the page but not to the ear. Approximate or imperfect rhymes are called "slant" or "off" rhymes.

setting: The location, time, and era in which a narrative or drama is placed.

sex: The biological division of humans into classification according to reproductive capacity. See **gender**.

sexual division of labor: A social arrangement in which the reproductive, child-rearing, and domestic labor almost always associated with women is unpaid while men labor for wages in the public sphere.

simile: A comparison using *like* or *as.* For example, "she swore like a truck driver."

social construction: A concept for talking about subjectivity in which the individual becomes a social being, a subject, through cultural processes, most specifically language. Construction refuses the notion of an essence, or of the subject as preordained, or as existing prior to culture. The act of constructing also points to the way we take up positions of knowing in relationship to **ideology**, or how ideology places us within cultural discourses.

sonnet: A poetic form consisting of fourteen end-rhymed lines ending with a **rhymed** couplet.

symbolism: The mechanism of transference in which one thing stands for another or many other things. Symbols can be visible objects, words, persons, or actions.

tone: Often defined as the author's or narrator's attitude towards a subject, tone can be interpreted by analyzing the associative **connotation** of the language, not merely the word's **denotative** meaning.

INDEX OF AUTHORS AND TITLES